GERALD BRENAN: THE INTERIOR CASTLE

By the same author

The Rise and Fall of the British Nanny
The Public School Phenomenon
Love, Sex, Marriage and Divorce
Doctors

*

One Foot in the Clouds
Chameleon
The Office
The Centre of the Universe is 18 Baedeker Strasse
- and other stories
The City Beneath The Skin

GERALD BRENAN: THE INTERIOR CASTLE

A Biography

Jonathan Gathorne-Hardy

W·W·NORTON & COMPANY

NEW YORK · LONDON

W. W. Norton & Company, Inc., 500 Fifth Avenue,
New York, N.Y. 10110
W. W. Norton & Company Ltd., 10 Coptic Street,
London WC1A 1PU

1 2 3 4 5 6 7 8 9 0

CONTENTS

Acknowledgements

My first thanks are due to Frances Partridge who not only read and carefully and astutely commented on the manuscript in its first enormous length, but let me read and quote from the very large correspondence between Gerald Brenan, her husband Ralph and herself; let me see and publish extracts from her unpublished diaries and photograph albums; and gave me many hours of stimulating discussion. My debt to her is enormous. I owe almost as much to Lynda and Lars Pranger who allowed me to question them, while putting me up, for several weeks over five years and who gave me full access to the large Brenan archive held at Mecina-Fondales. Indeed all those connected with Gerald Brenan – and it is a measure of the affection with which he is remembered – gave me complete co-operation and generous help. His son-in-law Dr Xavier Corre, his grandchildren Stéphane and Marina Corre, his nieces Lady Cary and Lydia Piper, Joanna Mason (née Carrington), and Richard Garnett all receive my grateful thanks. I would like to thank Jaime and Janetta de Parladé for much useful material and talk and unstinting help, especially in Spain. And in this respect, as well as many others, I would especially like to thank Professor Juan Antonio Díaz López. I am extremely grateful to my editor Julian Evans for his skilful and tactful dealing with my manuscript, and to Professors Paul Preston and Nigel Glendinning for their shrewd comments on it and for their invaluable help throughout the writing. This took far longer, and was also, so far flung was the research, far more expensive than I had bargained for. Despite the generosity of Christopher Sinclair-Stevenson, far beyond the call of my advance, I ran out of money halfway through. I would like very gratefully to acknowledge the help of the following institutions and one generous individual: the Vicente Cañada Blanch Fellowships, the British Academy, the Society of Authors (the Author's Foundation), Hélène Heroys Literary Foundation, E.M. Behrens Charitable Trust, and Dolf Mootham. With the obvious exception of Dolf Mootham, these represent only the warm, melting tip of an otherwise frozen iceberg of foundations, institutions, funds and trusts to which I applied. All these required often lengthy references and I am very grateful to Professor Paul Preston, Dr Theodore Redpath, Sir Raymond Carr, Lord Thomas of Swynnerton, Michael Holroyd and Victoria Glendinning for the work they so kindly did on my behalf. I would also like to thank the two last for professional advice on various aspects of biography. The completeness of the select bibliography as regards the writings of Gerald Brenan owes a great deal to Jack Wells. I am as usual grateful to Sandra den Hertog for deciphering both my many notes and the manuscript and for expertly typing them. Tom Staley and Cathy Henderson made my research at the Harry Ransome Humanities Research Center, at the University of Texas at Austin, much easier, more valuable and more pleasant than it otherwise would have been. I also gratefully acknowledge the University of Sussex Library (MSS section) for letting me see and use their Woolf-Brenan correspondence; the University of Liverpool Library; the University of Bristol Library; the University of Reading Library; and McMaster University, Ontario. Finally, I would like to thank the following, who have all contributed in various ways to the vast collection of information from which this biography was eventually written: Dr Igor and Mrs Annabelle Anrep, Prof. Dean Baldwin, Julio Caro Baroja, Mrs M. Bass, Dr Ian Battye, Susan Bell, Michael Black, Mrs H. P. Blosse-Lynch, Michael Bott, Ronald Brown, Sally Brown, Loïs Bucher (née Morgan), William S. Burroughs, Ethel de Croisset, Angela and Mark Culme-Seymour, Lord Dacre, D. W. Davies, Bunny Dexter, Rosemary Dineage, David Donnance, Margaret Drabble, Rose-Marie Duncan, Anthony Edkins, Mr Emberlin, Frank and Constance Ellis, Sir Angus Fraser, Gillian Furst, Prof. Juan Pablo Fusi, Eduardo Garrigues, Gretchen Holbrook Gerzina, Ian Gibson, Mr and Mrs Jean Gimpel, Sir Lawrence Gowing, Helen Grant, Richard Percival Graves, Prof. Peter Green, Angel Gutiérrez, Margaret Osborne de Gutiérrez, Margaret Hanbury, Mrs Charles Hamilton, Desmond Hawkins, Dr Tóke van Helmond, Lady Anne Hill, Prof. Michael Hitchcock, May Holder, Anna Horsburgh-Porter, Gerald Howson, Robert Kee, Mary Kennedy, Barbara Kei-Seymour, Mark Le Fanu, Dr Arthur Lehning, Lord N. Gordon Lennox, Gay Litchfield, David Machin, Ann L. Mackenzie, Hetty MacLise, Ronald Mansbridge, Antonio Martin, Carmen Lopez Martin, Maria Lopez Martin, Prof. Jeffrey Meyers, A. E. Money, Col. Morkill, Christopher Moorsom, Johnny Morris, Lady Diana Mosley, Rafael Martinez Nadal, Bayard and Pilar Osborn, Dorothy Ormiston, Mrs L. Ormsby, Mrs Palmer, Sir Richard Parsons, Henrietta Partridge, Mr Perkin, Prof. Julian Pitt-Rivers, Mme Poppet Pol (née John), Sir Victor and Lady Dorothy Pritchett, Vernon Richards, Ian Robertson, Anthony Rota, Prof. Barbara Ozieblo Raykowska, Prof. P. E. Russell, Mr Rust, Peter Ryan, Mrs Savoury, Christopher Scarles, Baroness Marjorie von Schlippenbach, Clare and Sydney Sheppard, Dr Kenneth Sinclair-Loutit, Robert Silvers, Charles Sinnickson, Mr and Mrs B. E. Smythies, Edward and Susan Southby, Prof. Frederic Spotts, Mrs Stevens, Peggy Strachey, Rosemary Strachey, Kevin Taylor, Karen Usborne, Lord Weidenfeld, Brian Welsh, Vivien White (née John), John Whitworth, Mr Wilkins, Michael Wishart, James Woodall, Giles Wordsworth, Mrs Sheila Wilson-Wright, Francis Wyndham, and various inhabitants of Yegen.

The author gratefully acknowledges permission to reproduce photographs as follows:

© *Francis Partridge*, for numbers: 9, 10, 11, 13, 14, 16, 17, 19, 20, 21, 22, 24, 28, 32, 36, 40, 44, 45, 50.

© *Lynda Pranger and the Mecina Fondales Archive*, for numbers: 1, 2, 3, 4, 5, 6, 7, 8, 12, 15, 18, 23, 25, 26, 27, 29, 30, 31, 33, 34, 35, 37, 39, 41, 42, 43, 46, 47, 48, 49, 51, 52, 53, 54.

© *Methuen and Co.*, *London*, for number 42.

© *JC Powys Estate*, for number 38.

'The detailed biography . . . is one of the best aids to the understanding of human nature and is especially revealing in the case of writers because we already possess in their work a more or less intimate revelation of their inner selves; by contrasting this with the outer features and circumstances of their lives, we are able to get the most complete picture possible of what a human being is like.'

From *The Literature of the Spanish People* by Gerald Brenan

'To display in its full totality all the shifting, complicated trends of behaviour one calls a man . . .'

From a passage dealing with the task of a biography in a letter from Gerald Brenan to V.S. Pritchett, 27 August 1941

'I thought of the Soul as resembling a Castle . . . containing many rooms, just as in heaven there are many mansions . . . However large, magnificent and spacious you imagine this castle to be, you cannot exaggerate it . . . Besides, it is not everyone who, like itself, possesses all he needs within his own dwelling.'

From *The Interior Castle* by St Teresa of Avila

Introduction

Before I began this biography I foresaw two problems with considerable anxiety: the fact that Gerald Brenan had written his own life, the first volume of which, at least, was superlatively good; and the question of his letters.

For the first twenty-five years, the main source material is in Gerald's *A Life of One's Own*. While I have used this, I have done my best not to *plunder* it. A reader of that book will certainly find a familiar outline here; but anyone who has not and wishes to explore Brenan further will find a great deal that is new – and delightful.

With Gerald's second volume, *Personal Record*, in which he takes his story fairly fully up to 1953 and then in a purfunctory way to 1972, it proved useful only to follow the self-told tale closely in a few key incidents: his love affair with Dora Carrington, Lytton Strachey's companion, for example, or his adventures in the Spanish Civil War.

The other difficulty, that of the letters, was simple – quantity. At a rough estimate, three to four million words of letters survive, many from relatively early on. But though the biographer may groan, it is perhaps not legitimate to talk of difficulty, since the second problem now began to solve the first.

Gerald, in an arresting but simple image in the *Preface* to the first volume of his autobiography, compared his life to a train journey. 'There is the scenery that rolls by outside,' he wrote, explaining how he planned to proceed, 'and there are the incidents that take place in the carriage. I saw at once that I must confine myself to the carriage. That is to say, I must write upon the things that had closely concerned myself and say little of the rest, which in any case I did not remember so clearly.'

And this he did. But what about the figure sitting in the carriage? What desires drove him and inhibitions hindered, what conflicts tore or fantasies sustained? How did he strike other people, his wife, his friends, the women he pursued? What was he *like*?

As I read the letters a Gerald began to emerge very different to the balanced, determined figure who is more and more in command as the autobiographies proceed. And some of the things the second Gerald had done or failed to do or felt clearly had fundamental roots. They flung their influence back, allowing, indeed necessitating, a completely different interpretation of the events of his childhood. And this interpretation was reinforced in vital areas by family papers, in particular his mother's journal of his first twelve years (a journal which, typically and significantly, Gerald dismissed as 'totally without interest', according to Lynda Pranger who lived with him for sixteen years at the end of his very long life).

My fears, therefore, proved groundless. As my fascination grew, I ceased to groan at the towering boxes. And my first anxiety – that I would simply be repeating, but in my own much inferior words, a portrait he had already done himself – was equally unnecessary. The portraits were quite different.

Before embarking on my exploration of that very long, packed life, there remained one last minor problem: myself. I first met Gerald when I was twenty-two and knew him, therefore, for over thirty years, during which time I became very fond of him. But there is always a danger for a biographer, not of identifying – that is to an extent essential – but of transference. Any biography is to a degree an autobiography. And, despite the fact that two of our greatest biographies do feature their authors (Boswell and Mrs Gaskell), there is a convention that the biographer should not intrude himself or herself. This is perfectly sensible. A biography must attempt to be objective – and it is much easier to be this, and to avoid authorial transference, as the writer, if absent. So although I may surface a few times briefly in the footnotes, I made the decision that I should not appear in the book until its distant end, an end at which I played a small but necessary part.

JONATHAN GATHORNE-HARDY
Binham, Fakenham, Norfolk
February 1992

PART I

Towards
a Life of His Own
1894–1919

ONE

Birth and Before

1

Gerald Brenan, when he came to write his life, virtually ignored his ancestors. He plunged straight into the extraordinary circumstances of his almost mythical beginning.

There were good reasons for this. The Brenans had a long tradition of bitter family feuds. These were often accompanied by a furious ripping-up of family papers, making later research difficult or impossible.[1] There were aspects of his ancestors of which he was slightly ashamed and which he despised. And, of course, in autobiography as in biography, the first five or ten pages of ancestry are usually the most boring.

Yet important clues lie there. The two overriding themes were the army, and money. On his father's side, there were three generations of professional soldiers. And behind these, stretching back into the eighteenth century, were Simpsons, Eccles, Hobsons, Hawkslys – northern industrialists in cotton and shipbuilding. More money came from his father's grandmother, Rose Green; again from shipbuilders, and from her father who was a wine merchant in Sloane Square. Still more flowed from his mother's family. His mother's father, Ogilvie Graham, was descended, via small eighteenth-century landed gentry in County Down, from ancestors who came to Ireland from Scotland. He did well out of cotton, and then did even better in Irish linen, setting up mills in Belfast. He became one of the richest men in Ireland and was finally knighted.

From these torrents of money, tiny streams eventually trickled by devious routes and one by one down to Gerald – much diminished, it is true, but without which he could not possibly have lived the life, nor written the books, he did. (In later years, he sometimes felt rather guilty about these *rentier* resources and in his autobiography reduced them still further. In letters and conversation they could sometimes reach vanishing point.)

More puzzling to him, since he felt less useful, was how he could have sprung from such a background. 'Few writers,' he wrote, '. . . have had poured into their blood so much of what Gertrude Stein calls "stupid being".' He felt a sort of sport. Reading his great-uncle Simpson's diary he castigates the boring record: 'Every day the menu of his luncheon and dinners and the number of times he had to take a blue pill.'[2] Yet what did he expect – Virginia Woolf? More germane as to genes is that John Simpson was recommended for a VC and rose to become a general* – showing, if nothing else, courage, toughness and will-power. These are useful qualities for writers too, as Gerald was amply to demonstrate.

Nor were these military figures without dash. Gerald's great-grandfather, Colonel Edward Fitzgerald Brenan, served in Spain with General de Lacy in 1835–6. In 1840 Edward met the Simpson family who were touring Europe, fell in love with Emily and eloped with her. Her sister Margaret, a livelier diarist than her general brother, wrote, 'Naughty Emily runs off with Colonel Brenan. Papa pursues them in a carriage.' (He didn't catch them and they were married in Paris that October.)

In love a lifelong and often tortured romantic, Gerald himself also had a distinctly military side. V. S. Pritchett, when he first met Gerald in 1937, thought he was, with his quick bustling manner, one of those military men gone Bohemian ('not uncommon in England'). In his autobiography he describes him as a 'piquant mixture of the military man, the poet, scholar and traveller'.[3] Gerald did not see it like this. When Pritchett referred to his 'military qualities' once in a letter, he replied that he had no military qualities – 'You mean my independence.'[4]

But it was more than independence. Gerald acquitted himself well in the First World War and, with the obvious proviso that he could not bear the slaughter, enjoyed it;[5] his enjoyment of the Home Guard during the Second World War sometimes verged on the comic.

---

* It gave me a curious feeling to find that a letter informing Simpson in 1874 that he had been awarded £100 p.a. for military services was signed 'Gathorne Hardy' – by my great-great-grandfather.

When he became over-excited, this buried military man was apt to leap barking forth in commands and precipitate action.

Gerald denied and repressed this side of himself because it reminded him of his hated father (no doubt one reason it burst out so explosively). But other traits of which he was well aware descended in this military Brenan blood – 'A thin, rapid and decidedly bitter rivulet'. Great grandfather, grandfather and father all had wives they dominated and who gave way to them. In a letter to Carrington in 1923 Gerald admitted he was the same and begged her to marry him so that her independence should help fight this 'ghost' of his father he felt stirring in him.[6] All these earlier Brenans were cruel-tongued and sarcastic, and alienated their sons thereby. Gerald was not cruel – he was an exceptionally kind and gentle man – but he could be surprisingly spiteful and sarcastic when angered.

Yet sarcasm is often just a gift for words and wit twisted and gone sour. Just as soldierly elements can be useful to a writer, so can those of the successful businessman – drive, energy, ambition, intelligence. That is why, in England, it is so often the ancestry to our art and scholarship. Certainly, Gerald was unique in his family for his dreaminess, his sensibility, his passion for knowledge, his love of literature – but his more robust qualities, like the money that finally allowed them to function, were rooted deep in his military and mercantile background. And even that poetic side can be derived. In many ways it was not Gerald who was a sport, but his mother Helen.

2

The Graham family was almost classically *nouveau riche* – boisterous, boastful, extravagant, energetic, keen on sport and social advancement, 'dog-orientated and house-orientated'. None of them, Gerald also noted, ever read a book; none of them liked being alone.

The dynamo of all this, the linen and cotton millionaire Ogilvie Graham, did not attempt the usual leavening of aristocracy – instead he added America. He crossed the Atlantic fifty-six times – fifty-five of them by sail [7] – and on an early trip he met and married an American woman, Louisa Lanfear. For her he bought in the 1850s (or possibly built), a large house outside Belfast: Larchfield, where Gerald was to spend a considerable part of his childhood.

Helen, born in 1862, loved her family: three brothers and a sister and the almost continuous presence of innumerable cousins, aunts and uncles (one entire wing of Larchfield – Long Wing – was reserved for those needing temporary homes).[8] She lived with them till she was thirty. Yet, though she had all their garrulous, warm-hearted love of life, in crucial respects she was not like them.

Socially gauche, she had a clumsy, almost buffoon side, which her son inherited. Her niece remembers how she preferred to sit on the ground with her legs out, even into her seventies. She was always forgetting to take her hat off. Conventional social life often bored her. She was hopeless at the games and sports obligatory in a big Victorian household. As a result, she sought solace in solitude. She was imaginative and loved reading; and discovering, during her rather meagre governess education, a gift for languages, became a fluent reader of French and German. The daughters of the family always went on the Grand Tour. When she was twenty-four Helen, accompanied by a maid and a cousin, went to Italy and picked up that lovely language too. They returned via the Rhine and Paris, sightseeing every moment of the way. Thereafter, she had a longing to travel.

All this was totally at variance with her conventional Graham background. Gerald wrote in *A Life of One's Own* that her mind was too ramshackle and muddled for any deep knowledge or culture. That only means it was untrained. Her behaviour with both her sons bears all the marks of someone determined to satisfy through her children desires frustrated in her own childhood and youth. This may even have included the desire to write. In later years, when they all lived at Edgeworth, she used to write one-act plays for the village children. One of them remembers how 'She used to sit watching the plays and laugh till the tears ran down her cheeks.'[9]

Helen Graham also had, like Gerald, a passionate nature given to love (and sudden, unreasoning jealousies). In the early 1890s, most likely in 1892, she fell in love with the Grahams' local clergyman, a poor Protestant. Appalled, the family packed her off to tour Italy again, followed by the Middle East. The clergyman was replaced by one much older.

In Cairo, Helen met young Hugh Brenan, probably on leave from his regiment in Malta. Met, fell in love, asked to Larchfield – and shortly afterwards married.

Much less is known about her husband at this period, thanks to various Brenan rip-ups (a spectacular one in 1941, when Hugh even destroyed the photograph albums).

One or two significant facts remain. Hugh's father, another Gerald, was adventurous, bad-tempered and bad with money – he deserted his regiment and fled to China in 1861 to avoid debts. He died when Hugh, born in 1870, was six, and Hugh's mother Rose (Green) married again – a Captain Matthias.

Hugh Brenan was therefore brought up with a stepfather. He was at Haileybury College from 1884 to 1886; left to join the South Down Militia (a recognised route into the regular army) and in 1893 was posted to the 2nd Battalion, the Royal Irish Rifles.[10]

Family memory recalls early money anxieties,[1] and the most likely explanation of his rapid entry into the army and short stay at Haileybury, from the ages of fourteen to sixteen, is financial. (He was not expelled.) If so, it would help explain, if not excuse, much of his later behaviour over money to Gerald and Gerald's brother Blair.

It also explains, Helen herself said in later years, his marriage. He came to Larchfield, saw warmth, glamour, gaiety – and wealth.

Helen had fallen in love. Yet she, too, as she also admitted, was under intense, mundane pressure to marry. When they married, on 1 June 1893, she was over thirty. A Victorian spinsterhood loomed.[11]

What was Hugh Brenan like? He had a kind and gentle side, though it seems only to have come out when people were ill (Gamel Brenan once said she'd rather have him as a nurse than anyone). When he exerted himself, he was capable of considerable charm. No doubt he exerted himself now. However, he was a touchy man and it is never easy entering a new, large and united family (he himself had just one sister, Maud). He may have felt the eight-year discrepancy in their ages in some way humiliating. In 1893, aged twenty-three, he had only just been gazetted 2nd lieutenant. His antipathy towards the Grahams may have begun at the start. In later years he resented any of Helen's attempts to see her family, as he resented all efforts to escape his control.

In fact, exaggeratedly English despite his name (he was only quarter Irish), it is clear he was already to a considerable degree the fiercely self-centred, rude and autocratic man he was increasingly to become. Gerald tells an anecdote to illustrate this, the significance of which he does not fully appreciate.

During the early days of their honeymoon, his father, who

enjoyed boating, decided they would punt from Lechlade to Richmond. On the second day, the tablecloth at the Tadpole Inn was not very clean. 'Once and for all understand this,' declared Gerald's father. 'In future I expect to see a perfectly clean tablecloth at every meal I sit down. It will be your business to provide one and, if you don't, I shall want to know why.'

This certainly illustrates autocracy. There is also more than a touch of sadism. Gerald's mother disliked boating. And one thing Gerald doesn't mention is that the distance from Lechlade to Richmond by Thames is well over 150 miles. The idea of sitting in a punt for the ten days or so it must have taken is grim, to say the least. At the same time – a feat.

But much the most interesting thing is: who told Gerald? The only person he could have learnt the story from was his mother, and it is not a sympathetic story. It reinforces other evidence that when she gave birth to her eldest son, which she did about ten months after they were married, Helen Brenan set about, no doubt quite unconsciously at first, creating an ally.

The newly married couple rejoined the 2nd Battalion, the Royal Irish Rifles, on Malta and Gerald was born there in Sliema at 12.15 a.m. on 7 April 1894. The address on the birth certificate is given as 10 Gda Ridolfo. Hugh's age is given correctly as twenty-three; but his wife's is tactfully reduced from thirty-two to thirty.[13]

The birth was extremely difficult; after it Helen Brenan was too ill to feed Gerald. Two Maltese she-asses who had recently foaled were obtained and Gerald, like some hero of legend, was fed for the first four or five months of his life on donkey's milk.[13]

His adoring mother noted other details. When born he looked Chinese* – as he did again from the age of sixty onwards. And he had a great thatch of stiff black hair, too thick for his brush. It was still causing astonishment to strangers seven months later and had to be cut once a week.[13] (This prodigious effort on the part of his hair

---

* Gerald was often told this when a small boy, as he was about the donkeys. What we are told about ourselves when young has considerable influence. Many years later he was to invent a Chinaman, Ying Chü, as the half-humorous mouthpiece for the author and only 'character' in *Thoughts in a Dry Season*. Similarly, knowledge of the donkeys may have strengthened the resolute Brenan obstinacy that was so useful to him.

seems to have exhausted it, and it all began to fall out relatively early on.)

Almost as important as his mother, who recovered very slowly, was Annie Crease, his 'Nana'. A large, stout, gentle woman, she was to remain central for many years. Like so many crucial people in his childhood, she was deaf or in some other way soundless, communicating only with a soft, beaming benevolence. (He describes her as 'simple'.)

Gerald fell ill on 10 May, a month after his birth, and, as his mother remained very weak, his father was given permission to take them all back to Ireland. His son was hurriedly christened on 11 May – Edward Fitzgerald – and the party, including one of his tiny Maltese donkey wet-nurses, embarked on the P&O liner *Australia* on 12 May.

It seems to have been a nightmare voyage. Gerald, despite his Nana's devoted nursing, was very sick. So was his mother. The cabin was full of cockroaches. But when they disembarked at Plymouth the whole ship – whose interest in Gerald and his entourage had been great – turned out to cheer them ashore.

Fresh difficulties faced them here. Southern Railway officials refused to allow a donkey into the compartment. A whole carriage had to be reserved, at vast expense.

The family reached Larchfield at the beginning of June. The story of their arrival is still remembered; how the donkey was led clattering up the stairs and down the length of Long Wing into a bedroom prepared with straw; and how Gerald was then installed next door with his Nana, Annie Crease.[14] He was to remain at Larchfield for the next two years.

TWO

The Women on His Side

1

Larchfield was built in early Irish Victorian: stucco, a large park with clumps of oak and rhododendron, a mile or two of stone wall. There was a home farm, stables, an artificial lake. It was grand, but also primitive. There was no hot water on tap, no electricity, no central heating, no bath or bathrooms; much running and scurrying about went on in the huge crowded house, with its peat and log fires, its lamps and candles and endless brass jugs of hot water, its long dark corridors and forbidden places.

In this busy, bustling, noisy maelstrom, Annie Crease sheltered little Gerald like a large, soft, infinitely safe and almost silent mother hen. During the two and a half years Helen Brenan and her son were based in Larchfield, Annie became one of the foundations of his being. Helen was not always there. At one point, early in 1895, she rejoined Hugh in Malta, returning with him on 7 February. In any case, the nanny conventions of the period meant he spent most of the time with his Nana in the remote Long Wing. On her half-days he 'roared all afternoon' and could hardly be quieted. If separated for long periods, he became ill.[1]

Annie Crease became fundamental; she did not replace his mother as the most important figure in Gerald's life. For one thing, they made extensive visits away – to a Mrs Chase's lodgings at Somerdale near Chichester; for one whole summer in 1896 to Southsea. But mainly Helen was never replaced because she more than made up in intensity of attention any lack in time.

One of the main sources for the details of Gerald's childhood (from nought to thirteen) is a journal his mother kept on the twenty large cardboard pages of a photograph album. Here she marks the rapid emergence of his character: at one and a half and thereafter (for the rest of his life in fact) he is 'very excitable'; at two he has a quick temper and is dominating. There are actually two Mrs Chases at Somerdale and Gerald – already 'very like his father' – enjoys imperiously ordering both of them from his nursery. He is obstinate. Mischievous. Charming. 'Very affectionate.'

But it is Helen's extraordinary determination to teach him that is fascinating. In her eagerness, Helen had stumbled on the early and concentrated stimulation advocated (controversially) by certain advanced American educationalists. And her highly intelligent little boy responded delightedly.

At seven months he already had a vocabulary of twenty words; at one he could pick out O, I, A and B on his bricks; at sixteen months he was walking everywhere, loved being read to and could pick out the whole alphabet. By two he was saying the alphabet, could count to ten, and was '*very* fond of [my] reading'. Gerald was later to attribute his almost obsessional pursuit of knowledge to various figures and factors – a Rev Mr Earee; his friend Hope-Johnstone; and being denied a classical and university education by his father. These were important factors, no doubt, but, in behavioural terms, only reinforcements.[2] The real foundations – as of other major traits in his character – are all here, delineated in his mother's bold, black, rapid handwriting.

She also 'poured into' him, in Gerald's evocative phrase, her love of flowers – so that by the time they went to join his father at Aldershot at the end of 1896, he knew the name of every flower in the garden, 'even hard ones like "Cineraria"'. And when they returned for a last visit to Larchfield in February 1897, Gerald's farewell presents (he was not yet three!) were C. A. Wood's *Natural History* and Ann Pratt's *Wild Flowers*.[1]

The reason for the farewell was that his father's regiment (now the 1st Battalion, the Royal Irish Rifles) had been ordered to South Africa. They left to join him at Ladysmith via London and sailed on 25 April.

2

For some reason, Annie Crease could not come on the same ship. This minor earthquake in his solid world clearly shook Gerald. He developed whooping cough. There is talk in Helen's journal of his 'being very difficult to make obedient'. Fortunately, Annie arrived ten days later.

Except for one much worse, and related, catastrophe, the eighteen months Gerald spent in Africa and, to a lesser extent, the seven months later in India, were remembered as a sort of Eden. Africa, in particular, was infused with golden memories, in which his mother and her biblical stories, the strong flavours, the fierce desert wildness and its extraordinary flowers, remained a passionate recollected whole – but a whole in which each separate element was to retain its power for many years.

The flowers – he knew them before they arrived. Annie Crease had given him a *Child's Life of Christ*. Entwined in its big illuminated capitals were the flowers of the Holy Land – many the same as in South Africa. As the train trundled slowly from Cape Town to Wynberg, frequently stopping under the hot May sun, Gerald recognised them. Wherever the train stopped he rushed to pick them. And, as he describes the 'sun-flattened landscape', their hot dry garden near Ladysmith where he gets covered in dust, the waterless gullies and struggling thorn trees across the shimmering veldt, it is interesting that what moves him most is the contrast between the brilliance of the flowers and the dryness and desolation of the landscape. He writes of the excitement, even as a child, of coming suddenly 'among the withered grasses of the veldt, on some bright, gleaming Calyx'. It is precisely the contrast you often get in the hot barrenness of southern Spain. But there is another aspect here.

The past dictates the future, the future returns and invades the past – and both are part of the character, and explain and extend it. Gerald saw his later youth and young manhood, in broad terms, as a desperate struggle to survive and escape from an excessively conventional and hostile background. All his life this drew him to others who had done the same, who were independent. This extended to plants. 'The botany of extreme climates,' he noted in *South From*

Granada, 'has its special fascination. There is a thrill to be got from plants that surmount great natural difficulties, especially when they do so with excess and bravura.' He singled out what he did from his memories of Africa because it was a metaphor of how he saw his life. Indeed, more than a metaphor. It will become significant that at a deep level he made an identity between the landscape and its flowers, and himself.

3

Africa also cemented the love affair between Gerald and his mother.

After tea, as the sun began to cool and before his father returned from camp, he would be released by Annie Crease. Running onto the verandah, he would find his mother waiting in her white piqué dress and leg-of-mutton sleeves. He would climb onto her lap, and lessons would begin.

They were as concentrated as ever. On the boat, he'd gone through the *First Reading Book* for the fourth time. By his fourth birthday, in April 1898, he had finished the *Third Reading Book* and could, to all intents and purposes, read. Number training continued as before; geography was started.[1]

But what he really enjoyed were her stories. She read history to him: Boadicea in her chariot, Alfred burning the cakes, Canute and the waves. She told him the tales of the great explorers: Vasco de Gama, Ibn Battuta. Wonderful stories – and all true. But the stories she invented – she was highly imaginative – were just as exciting.

Gerald's enjoyment was so intense that it became internalised. His mother records now how he told long stories to himself. Since this requires two people, as it were ('Gerald jumped on to the horse and . . .'), this is probably why he talked about himself in the third person for much longer than most children.

The content of these stories was probably often biblical. Of all the stories his mother read, rocking him on her knee, he loved the Bible best. Not the New Testament, which bored him, but the Old: Genesis, Exodus, the burning of the cities of the plain, the crossing of the Red Sea, this was a world he could respond to – exotic, violent, rich in the marvellous and the terrifying.

Moses was a favourite: found romantically floating down the Nile in a basket, leading the flight from Egypt, the dramatic interview with God amongst the clouds of Mount Sinai. Gerald always thought of this later when called in for a talking-to by his father: 'It seemed a model for one-sided confrontations of this sort.'

So real were these characters – Moses, Jacob, David and Jonathan – that they seemed almost contemporary. One day he was heard asking his English grandmother if she'd ever known a pharaoh.

This grandmother – Rose Matthias, his father's mother – was the fourth member of their little party, and another important figure in Gerald's childhood.

Rose Matthias, then fifty-seven, was a Londoner who lived in a flat at 99 Cadogan Gardens, but who spent each summer and Christmas with them, while they usually stayed with her when in London. She too was stone deaf, with a black collapsible ear trumpet on a long flexible tube which gave her the air of a snake charmer.*

Wrapped in her deafness, she glided about the house, her long silk dress rustling. She would sit for hours sewing, occasionally whispering – 'Helen says' – and then repeat something told half an hour before. She was, in Gerald's description, as vegetative as a plant in a pot and took in as little. But this gentle charm made him love her, and whenever she took him on her ample lap he felt soothed.

She had vaguely Buddhist leanings and he describes her later not so much reading, as absorbing knowledge by passing her eyes and hands over large obscure volumes of Eastern thought. He recounts how she remonstrated with his mother for wanting to turn an old rockery, choked with weeds, into an ordered area for Alpine plants.

'But it's a mass of weeds, Grannie.'

'You have all the rest of the garden for your flowers. Weeds have their right to live too.'

This made a deep impression on Gerald. Many years later in Spain he made special provision for weeds, planting, for example, various species of large thistles; the choice, no doubt, in distant deference to the Maltese donkeys.[3]

Of his father, at this time, Gerald speaks and writes little because he saw him little. During the week he returned from camp after bedtime; on Sunday there remained only the gaps between services

---

* Deafness seems to have been an hereditary weakness in the Green family, passed down to Hugh. Her sister Addie – Gerald's great-aunt and later saviour – was also deaf.

(it was a religious family). But it is clear he was not yet the dominating, terrifying figure he later became. This developed as his character deteriorated after 1900 and, later still, in proportion to Gerald's gathering rebellion.

Hugh Brenan was a typical, almost a cartoon soldier. He was particularly keen on smartness, on appearance. He liked riding, playing polo, shooting – and wanted Gerald to like them too. And in fact Gerald already enjoyed riding. He always remembered the excitement of sitting in front of his father at this time and galloping past the river Khip. He was 'very amusing'[1] with his father, admired him, irritated him.

Hugh Brenan, although he liked a joke (particularly a practical joke), was not a sociable man. In the mess, he usually fell asleep after dinner. 'But,' wrote Gerald, 'when he was awake, he was very awake, talking in a clear, matter-of-fact tone that in the family circle could easily become abrupt and cutting, and laughing, when anything amused him, in a whole-hearted, staccato way. He was always very much himself, very concrete and definite, and he was completely lacking in imagination.'

But he was, it seems, jealous of Gerald from the moment he was born. He teased him. He was strict. He hated boasting and took every opportunity to cut Gerald down to size. There are clear indications that Gerald resented all this and, aware also of his father's potentially explosive temperament, was already – half-apprehensive, half-challenged – reacting. He was the most mischievous child the Graham family had ever known. Much of this was directed at Hugh. He once gave the belt of this dress-conscious man's dress uniform to a Kaffir. Another time, on board ship, everything had been packed and carried ashore. They were about to disembark, when suddenly his father could not find his shoes. Gerald had thrown them away.

Helen Brenan noted these stories in her journal. In later years she related them, and many others, proudly and again and again, to her grandchildren, Gerald's nieces.[4] The inference is that, seeming to control Gerald, she also unconsciously encouraged him.

4

The second love that grew during this period was that for Gerald's Nana, Annie Crease. The journal is full of references. '*How* he loves his Annie – "My funny little heavy big fat nanna dumpi".' And, as with all small children, but usually unrecognised, it had all the complexity and intensity of adult love – including jealousy. Annie brought in a tiny baby one day to show Gerald. He was furious. 'I don't know who wants that little beast here. It's no use. If I were its mother I'd smack it.'¹

It is not surprising, therefore, that Gerald's first sexual experience should have been with Annie Crease. Little Gerald had long been fascinated by the Kaffir wives, with their long, swollen breasts swinging naked. But what lay beneath the bead aprons round their black waists? One night, a scorpion frightened him. Annie let him into her bed. After a while, thinking her asleep, Gerald burrowed down. Annie pulled him back. He waited once more till she seemed asleep, then dived again. This time, with calm acceptance, she let him explore the dark secrets of the mushroom-smelling darkness.

Gerald never forgot the experience. In *A Life* . . . he writes that he thinks this 'division I had made of sex into two different compartments' affected him later.

What does he mean by this? Is it a first gentle nudge to prepare the reader for his later sexual pursuit of lower-class women? Annie was lower-class and became associated with sex; did his mother, upper-class, become so with something more idealistic? Or does he mean sex was something hidden, dark, secret – and by extension shameful? He probably meant to suggest both elements, but it is a cryptic remark, like all Gerald's pronouncements on sex.

In fact, because of a curious process of juxtaposition which operated in his autobiographical writing, he may also have been unconsciously revealing something he never clearly recognised, the close association he later formed between the bliss of loving and the agony of being left. Shortly after this – both in *A Life* . . . and in reality – when Gerald was four and three-quarters in December 1898, Annie Crease left to get married.

This was the first major crisis of Gerald's life. The shock can be gauged by the force of his suppression – common in such circumstances. He never mentions her again, either in *A Life . . .* or *Personal Record*. And the magnitude of what had happened can be inferred in other ways. Weakened by the psychological wound, he succumbed to typhoid soon after she had gone. It was almost certainly now that he began to wet his bed again, and continued to do so for at least two years.[5] He began, for the first time, to be shy with strangers.[1] His anxiety about being separated from his mother became acute. His mental development, so astonishingly precocious, now suddenly 'began to slow down and encounter difficulties'.[1]

And the strength of their abruptly ruptured love can be measured in reverse, as it were, by Annie's feelings for him. He was her favourite. They eventually resumed contact in 1921, and never lost it.[6] When she died, in the 1930s, she left all her money to Gerald.[7]

Surrounded as he was from earliest childhood by so many deaf people it is hardly surprising that, in later life, Gerald was monumentally unmoved by music. It bored him and usually sent him to sleep. Except for song. Annie Crease used to sing to him. Even at two he loved to sing a song she had learnt from the soldiers.[1]

> Oh! give my love to Nancy,
> She's the girl that I adore.
> Tell her that I'll never, never
> See her any more.

Perhaps it is significant that this is the one verse he could still remember in old age. But all his life the sound of someone singing could pierce him to the heart and make him weep.

5

The Boer War was about to break out. Annie Crease had chosen December 1898 as her moment to depart because the whole family was about to leave as well. With the consummate timing it was to refine still further in the years ahead, the War Office now sent Gerald's father's regiment, which had mapped the frontiers of Natal, to India, replacing it with one which didn't know the country at all.

On the station, waiting for the train to Durban, Gerald noticed a new plant. For some reason – perhaps the drama of departure – the name, oleander, became deeply imprinted.

They sailed for Colombo in Ceylon (now Sri Lanka) on 5 January. By the time they arrived Gerald was running a temperature of 104.8°.[1]

There was no treatment for typhoid at that time. The mortality rate in general was three out of every ten; for young children, closer to six out of ten. The disease ran its agonising course, with his mother's anxious record: 'high fever', 'very restless', 'high temperature'. Not till March was he well enough for them to join Charlie Graham's family in the hills.

On 7 April, his sixth birthday, they descended to Kandy, to see the Temple of the Tooth – a pilgrimage which signally failed to protect Gerald in later years. Then, on 9 April, his father left for India and Gerald and Helen sailed for England on a Lloyds ship, *The North Deutchan*.

The summer and autumn of 1899 were spent at Larchfield. The journal records steady learning: grammar, history, geography, reading and writing. But now, significantly, religion was stepped up. Soon he knew the Ten Commandments and the Creed, as well as his established base of Bible learning. Gerald himself could only remember how, with the tight nanny regime which pertained, he minded seeing so much less of his mother.

On 15 November they sailed for India again on *The City of Corinth*. A month later, after a brief stop at Malta (the oddness of seeing the place where he'd been born), they arrived at Calcutta.

6

Africa was remembered as an 'Eden'. But a small child, a small *English* child at least, does not, wrote Gerald, enjoy India; rather 'he feels it drift remote and very hot across the mind'. He retained memories of smells and heat, of a huge banyan tree at the entrance to a village. But two other memories were more crucial.

His father took it on himself to teach Gerald mathematics. This made him exceedingly irritable and bad-tempered. Once, in a paroxysm of anger, he kicked Gerald's bearer. Gerald saw this and was horrified.

The second event took place when all three went to some gardens near the river Hoogli, where the men of the East India Company were buried. Thickets of bamboo separated them from the Hoogli, with a narrow tunnel, too narrow and too low for his parents, twisting through it. Gerald pushed along and then suddenly burst out into blinding sunshine. It was – the memory lasted all his life – a considerable shock: the huge expanse of river, the dancing light, a jetty with a boat. Staring transfixed, Gerald felt, above all, it was *important*.

Very soon after this, his father was ordered home to become Adjutant at Berkhampstead. The family sailed for England at the beginning of April 1900.

7

In his autobiography, Gerald notes that this was the last time in his life that he was ever to spend any length of time alone with his mother. He has a Proust-like memory of waiting for her evening after evening to come and kiss him goodnight – lying awake in the darkness and 'listening to the rumbling sound of the ship and the slip-slopping of the waves and longing for her to appear'.

Emotion does not often feature either in *A Life . . .* or *Personal Record*. Agony over Carrington, excitement over girls, once lust; but emotion rarely. Now, as his rather plain mother at last arrives in the cabin, it does: 'I would smell the fragrance of her hair as she stooped over me and feel the smoothness of the fine skin against my lips. In evening dress, with her large, full neck and soft, antelope-like eyes, she was – to her son at least – beautiful.' (The texture of a woman's skin, incidentally was later to be Gerald's invariable yardstick of sexual attractiveness.)

His mother seems, as always, to have been immediately responsive to his anguish – a continuing legacy, like his bedwetting, of Annie Crease's departure. She set herself to build up his confidence, and with intuitive insight chose the way Gerald had found himself – his short, but fairly unusual past. His fantasies at this time, which he whispered to himself for comfort, were of epic trips up rivers, escapes from crocodiles and lions, thirsty treks across deserts. Helen reinforced this. She continually told him he was extraordinary. Not only for himself but – the proof – for what had happened to him. Geography had, as it were, pressed upon him, leaving much of its magic, so that, taking up stamp collecting, he felt as he laboriously pasted in a stamp of Djibouti an answering pressure and received something of the Somali coast.

This special quality, gained from travelling, made Gerald feel unique. More than that: he felt from the age of six onwards that he was to have a unique, logical and remarkable destiny which was laid out for him and which he had to fulfil.

There were two other strands to this. A sense of unfocused destiny is not all that uncommon, though perhaps not always as young as this. But it is usually found among people of uncommon will. That is, it is not really a sense of destiny so much as a sense, usually unconscious, of the will-power to get what one wants.

The second is summed up by a photograph of Gerald in India looking like a tiny pasha. He is on ponyback in a solar topee surrounded by his ayahs and servants and bearers. There is a family story of how he once held up an enormous Viceregal procession for five minutes – ranks of elephants reined in, whole regiments marking time – while Gerald chatted to Lord Curzon, who had misguidedly paused to pat his head.[8] He must have been aware, in the army, of the obvious deference paid to his father, who could kick bearers. The confidence which the middle classes of this period sometimes nearly destroyed in their children, with their vanishing nannies and brutal schools, they also partially gave back with the base from which these customs sprang – money and class.

The element of foreign travel, which Gerald later chose to isolate – and which was certainly important – was by no means over, though there was a short respite. The moment they returned, Hugh was redirected to Africa for the Boer War. Gerald and his mother spent most of 1900 at Larchfield.

A French nursery governess, Julienne, was now engaged, and this language too was added to Gerald's heavy curriculum.[1] But learning, already associated with his adored mother, was now bound to her still more closely. Larchfield was full of boisterous Graham relatives. Once again, a tight mother-separating nanny regime operated. But every morning at seven, Gerald was allowed to jump out of his cot and race down the passages to Helen's room. He got into her bed and for an hour she taught him and read to him. This practice, which he loved, continued till he was thirteen.

Out in Africa, meanwhile, Hugh had caught malaria. He was invalided back to England in November. He was almost totally deaf.

8

Hugh Brenan's deafness was to prove permanent. It brought to an abrupt end a so far scarcely dazzling Army career. There is only one mention of him in the Regimental History and his name is spelt wrong. 'Captain Brennan moved with his Company to Thaba 'Nchu and engaged in anti-guerrilla work.'[9] There also remained a cartoon of him as a hedgehog.

It had already been decided that Gerald was to go into the Army. On their trip from India, his mother had hung a colour lithograph of Sir George White, the hero of Ladysmith, with his big red face, above his bunk. 'You must be like him.' The tragic truncation of his own career no doubt made iron Hugh Brenan's decision on this point.

Deafness also much exacerbated the hedgehog's already very considerable irritability. Gerald seems to have interpreted this in almost ridiculously classic Oedipal terms. It was probably in December 1900 that his parents had him circumcised in an unsuccessful attempt to stop his bed-wetting. When he was fifteen, Gerald thought his father had had him castrated at this time.[10] It may be, therefore, that the sexual difficulties which were so to bedevil his adult life had their origins here – as well as in the incident where Gerald soon, somewhat enigmatically, seems to place them.

But the most immediate effect of the deafness was acute restlessness. In the next year and eight months the family was to live in ten different places.

After Christmas at Larchfield, they spent ten days in London. Then in January 1901, taking Julienne with them, they went to Jersey. Here his father took Gerald sailing, while Julienne continued to teach him French, which was already 'good'.[1] But Hugh was soon sick of Jersey, and in February they moved to Paris. Here he had another bout of malaria, despite which he managed to make Helen pregnant again. By the end of February they had reached Montreux in Switzerland, via Dijon and Lausanne. Wherever they went, Gerald and his mother, both equally indefatigable, looked at museums, art galleries, churches, all of which bored Hugh intensely.

They stayed at Montreux for two months, so that Gerald could go to a private school and improve his French still further. In *A Life . . .* he says he never went to it, taking a dislike to the 'military organisation' and the smell of urine, and ran away to explore the town each day instead. Helen's journal makes no mention of this prolonged truancy, and it seems unlikely he could have remained undetected for two months. But for however long he did, it impressed him as the ideal method of dealing with situations of this sort.

In April they were on the move again, returning jerkily to England via Clarens, Freiburg, Baden-Baden and Rotterdam, to take a house briefly near Harwich – Dover Court.

One object of all this dashing about had been for Hugh to consult European ear specialists. None had held out hope, and now he received a fresh blow. In May, his childless great-aunt Simpson died (sister of 'naughty Emily'). Hugh had been her heir and since she was extremely rich – with a Georgian manor near Petersfield and hundreds of acres – had long indulged in landed-gentry fantasies. Now he learnt to his horror that she had only left him £10,000. He was still very well off. The army kept him on half pay till at least 1924.[11] The £10,000 brought in about £800 p.a. (say £25,000 in 1990 terms*). Helen had been given a handsome dowry. But the incident intensified an already neurotic apprehension about money.

His solution, as with all problems at this time, was to move again. The family took a house called Bassetts near Little Baddow, Chelmsford. Here at last they paused till October.

At Bassetts, during the summer, Helen read Gerald *Robinson Crusoe* – planting a seed which was to have many ramifications. And here, as elsewhere, Gerald remembers the flowers – meadowsweet, loosestrife, great willow herb, cowslip. Until he was eight, he wrote in *A Life . . .* , flowers formed the landmarks of his aesthetic life, corresponding to the discovery of new poets and painters later on. But it was more than this. Flowers served to mark each new territory, limit it, making it possible to know. Botany grew out of his desire to feel secure in the family's peripatetic life.

It was a hot, very dry year and the unusual length of time they

* For comparable values of the £ see Appendix A.

spent at Little Baddow stamped it on his memory so that, sixty years later, it still glowed. 'It was at Bassetts this summer that I first came to know and love England: its aimless zigzagging lanes, its clumps of squat blackberry bushes, its dwarfed oaks and short hedgerows with their rough leaves, the pebbles that came loose on the surface of the road when carriage wheels dug into it, the film of dust. A dull country, without surprises, but stamped with a character of its own and, above all, intimate. When you got to know it you felt you had been let into a secret. In the drought the green tufts in the fields grew whiter and whiter, the oak leaves more blue-grey, and then in September the rain fell and there was a huge crop of mushrooms.'

And twice again, at this point in *A Life . . .* , the reader is pushed towards his later adventures among the working-class girls of London and Spain. The first occurs when on going to church ('the usual boredom') his parents stopped to talk to the village children. This whole group was forbidden to him. Gerald, an only child for long periods alone with adults, watched fascinated.

The second push is more direct. Julienne had left. She was now replaced with Célestine, a dark and lively young Parisienne with sparkling eyes. One afternoon she and Gerald went for a walk by the canal, its coolness and lushness very evident in the drought. There were some water lilies. Gerald asked her to pick them. Célestine tried to reach them, but began to sink above her knickers. She got out, took off the knickers, tucked her skirt round her waist and waded back in again. Having only till then, and only once, felt the mystery women kept hidden under their skirts, Gerald now saw it for a moment full face. And he was allowed a longer look. A little later she took him to her attic room, undressed and covered herself in cheap scent, rubbing it into her body.

She was, notes Gerald, the only woman he knew, in his lonely and sexless youth, with any sexual connotations – and she was lower-class. The memory vanished, to surface when he was sixteen and furnish forth his sexual fantasies.

Célestine vanished too. It seems likely that Gerald was not the only one tempted by her sparkling eyes. Helen was now heavily pregnant, and the new nursery governess hadn't been there six weeks when she was suddenly sent packing. If it was because of Hugh, this was not the only time Helen behaved in this precipitate way.

In early October, they took a furnished flat at 7 Sloane Court for the confinement. Blair Brenan was born on 14 October.

Gerald seemed far more interested in the slums than this event. This is another instance of his mother exciting him about something she wasn't able to experience properly herself. In fact many Victorians were excited by 'the slums' because they represented all the urges they repressed in themselves. Poverty itself was fascinating. And in Gerald's childhood it was all still much closer and rougher. Baedeker warned travellers to avoid 'poor neighbourhoods' after dark.[12]

Gerald could remember Cumberland Market full of hay wagons. The slums themselves extended as close as Clare Market off the Strand to the west; south, they were only kept at bay by the river. His mother poured out her melodramatic imaginings – the more lurid from their vagueness – and on foggy evenings Gerald would gaze out into the thrilling light of the gas lamps, trying to pierce the gloom, her tales sounding in his ears.

In fact, his reactions to his brother's birth were straighforwardly jealous. For the actual birth, he was sent to friends nearby. In protest, Gerald 'invented' charcoal and nearly set the house alight.[7] As far as rivalry went, he must have felt he had enough to cope with in his father. And, since the new baby was ungetatable, it was on his father he focused his feelings.

This restless, deaf figure soon had them on the move again. In January 1902 they went to Dinard near St Malo on the northern French coast.

Gerald had now discovered the solace that was to last his whole life. They caught him 'reading to himself at all hours by gas light'. He could also read French. There had come 'that wonderful moment when at seven or eight one discovered one had a second life because one had a second language'.[13] He could now speak French fluently.

But it is probably now that he wrote his name all over the walls of his room, in one of their lodgings. Hugh had to pay.[14] One night, Gerald said to Blair's nurse, 'Call out to my mother and ask her if I can have some bread.' The nurse did; Helen said no. 'Isn't my mother a most ridiculous woman,' said Gerald, 'just because father's there she said no.' Helen also noted that, 'If he gets into trouble and is scolded, he won't speak to me.'[1]

In March, Hugh Brenan seems to have at last decided it was time to settle down. They returned to Larchfield, dumped Gerald and Blair and the nurse, and set out house-hunting in southern England.

9

Gerald was kept fully occupied at Larchfield. A Miss Walker, calm and plain – 'a model of the sexless species' – had been engaged to teach him. She concentrated on Latin, cunningly starting with the names of flowers and their classifications. Perversely, Gerald reports in *A Life* . . . that this bored him. But writing to Bunny Garnett* years later, he gives it a typically romantic flourish: '*Bellis perennis* I wrote in my big hand and then *Taraxacum Dens Leonis* and they gave me a magic authority over the vegetable world which I have never lost.'[15] In fact quite soon he loved Latin. By the time he was thirteen, he was *en route* for classical scholarship.

His grandfather, Sir Ogilvie Graham, had died in 1897, after some business losses. But there seems to have been no diminution in the lavishness of Larchfield life. The house was as usual crammed with aunts and uncles; there was an abundance of cousins to play with. There were ponies for him to ride. Yet Gerald does not seem to have been entirely happy. His mother received 'gloomy reports' from Miss Walker. The fact was, of course, that he couldn't bear to be separated from her.

He seems to have found some comfort in the servants. Mrs Lapin, as the sister of his Nana, must have been particularly significant. Lively, kindly, in a messy black dress, she was a Dickensian figure, with 'yellowish blousy hair, pins stuck all over her blouse, a face in perpetual movement; in character – a sort of pantomime widow, always in a hurry yet never able to resist a bit of gossip, a prodigious chatterbox, an irrepressible fountain of winks and nods and smiles and finger-to-the-lip gestures.' Needless to say, she was deaf, and spoke in a loud whispery voice that was very penetrating; but her point, as far as Gerald went, was she loved the grandchildren. She waged wars with cooks and butlers on their behalf and stole for them.

And yet, with a sort of ache, he describes how at the same time this rich and vivid life was in fact always just out of reach, cut off by

* The writer, David Garnett, always known as Bunny.

the gulf of class privilege. A tiny dark staircase outside the pantry led like a tunnel down to the servants' quarters in the basement. Standing, listening, Gerald would see them go down and hear laughter, cheerful Irish voices welling from the depths. Here, clearly, were the fun and life in the house – and here he was forbidden to go.

Now, in Gerald's account of this crucial incident, comes a cryptic sentence. 'This feeling was to have a marked effect on me in later life, so much in our characters being determined by the things that we cannot do precisely because a longing to do them inhibits us.'

To what in later life does this refer? Not to life and fun and laughter. He had a great deal of all three. Nor, specifically, to mixing with the lower classes. He did this too, intimately, especially in Spain.

The cryptic note alerts us that he may be referring to sex. If so, he seems to be saying that sex, as the most basic and vigorous manifestation of 'life', was so much longed-for it somehow became impossible. In fact the logical inference should be that this aspect of life, sex, was also intensely longed-for and forbidden – just as he was forbidden to see the servants – and for that reason became inhibited.

This is a penetrating, if somewhat melancholy analysis. But that he should choose to express something of such profound importance in this elliptical and coded way reveals another facet of his autobiographical writing.

Every autobiography is an attempt to find patterns. But behind the figure who emerges through the selection and orchestrating of material is another slightly different one, concealed in the shadows, who is doing all the orchestrating and choosing. It is this figure the biographer often finds more interesting.

Numerous times already Gerald has prepared the ground for sexual adventures among the lower classes. This is not because he thought them reprehensible. On the contrary, he thought them romantic. But he wishes the reader to be ready to believe they took place. Adventures he certainly had but, except in a few instances, the straightforwardly sexual element was minimal. Something replaced it which was almost as intense, more curious, had diverse roots and was in the end perhaps more useful to him. The memories he called up to suggest the first, the sexual element he wants to impose, in fact more strikingly reveal the second, which he wishes to conceal.

Except for his Nana, what impresses one in all the incidents he relates is that his position is not one of participant but of observer:

staring at Célestine's nakedness, watching the village children his parents spoke to, gazing out into London's gloom for hidden wickedness, seeing the servants descend to their quarters, listening to their laughter floating up. The excitement and pleasure in all this were far more precisely the excitement of looking – the pleasure, that is, of a voyeur.

10

By 4 June 1902, Hugh and Helen had found and rented the house that was to be their home for the next fifteen years.* The party from Larchfield – Gerald, Miss Walker, Blair and his nurse – arrived on 31 August.

Miserden was a small isolated village about nine miles from Cirencester. Miserden House itself was eminently suitable for a fantasy country gentleman. Set on the road close to the centre of the village, it was a substantial square house built in 1810 of the prevailing grey Cotswold stone. It had a fine flagged hall, a green painted verandah, servants' hall (their rooms in the attic), rambling kitchens full of cockroaches, stables, a coach house. There were baths and central heating; without electric light, the house retained the romance of lamps and candles. The garden was large. Three terraces led to an old brick wall; then came extensive kitchen gardens and a paddock. There were chestnut trees, two yews, a medlar. To the left, the ground swooped into a valley and the beechwoods of nearby Miserden Park.

At one end of the house was a gabled cottage. Here Gerald had his own little room, with thick walls, a fireplace, lattice-paned windows looking over the garden. The jasmine outside was so thick he climbed in and out by it till stopped.

It is all very much the same now. The verandah has gone; the jasmine and the cottage vanished into a new wing in 1928. The beechwoods of Miserden Park were thinned in the Great War (they were very good for planes). The Brenans are still just remembered:

---

* We know the date so exactly because Gerald's earliest surviving letter expresses his excitement over it. 'My dear mother . . . I'm so pleased about our new house . . . your loving Gerald Brenan.' The hand is not big at all, but already small and neat. He is busy stamp collecting, 'Lappin' is making him a dressing gown, he is '*very*, *very* pleased to hear he is to have a pony'.

Helen was popular and very active in the village, for a while president of the WI; but Hugh has left little trace. All that remains is that he wasn't liked and had 'a whacking great ear trumpet'.[16] The village is still just as isolated, impossible to find in a maze of tiny lanes.

Once installed, Gerald's lessons were resumed with Miss Walker. Now eight and a half, he spent four hours a day on English, Irish and European geography, Latin, maths, Greek history, English dates and history to Henry VIII. He studied the Bible and knew his catechism. He was 'very good' at English.[1]

He resumed, as well, the love affair with his mother. It is remembered, perhaps significantly, as much by its pains as its delights. The winter of 1902 was exceptionally severe. Helen caught pneumonia. Gerald was sent to the Hamilton Mills next door. He retained a strange memory of standing in a large bedroom and people coming in and crying out. It seems, repeating the pyromaniac protest at Blair's birth, he'd lifted coals out of the fire on to the floor – a protest at being removed from his mother when she needed him most.

They played tense and agonising love games together, his mother just as involved as he was. She would ask him, suppose she were to die, would he approve of his father marrying again? Although he longed for her love, Gerald would harden his heart. 'Why not, if it made him happier?' She was so wounded by this she didn't speak to him for several days.

But these were just blips in the long bliss of their now unbroken time together. There were walks and teas and games and talks; and every morning he would race along to her room, get into her bed, and she would tell him stories. According to Gerald, his mother and father, though they shared a bedroom, never made love again after Blair was born,[17] and they had separate beds.[7] It is hardly surprising that his father should feel jealous of the close, intense relationship between mother and son.

But, this aside, the most important thing about Miserden was the countryside. The Cotswolds round Miserden are spectacular. Although confined within a range of 1000 feet or so, they behave like mountains: steeply undulating valleys, flowing with streams, sweep up to broad upland plateaux covered in sheep, stone-walled and marvellous for galloping, then plunge down again in miniature ravines. There are great beech forests, the sound of wind and pigeons in trees. It is rich in wild flowers and wild animals.

Determined to produce a little soldier-gentleman correct in every detail, his father made shooting compulsory. Riding, also compulsory, Gerald loved. In November 1902 he went hunting on Minny, his pony. In March the following year he went again, falling off. By Easter 1903 he was riding all over the place by himself.[1]

For eighteen months idyllic day followed idyllic day, suffused with the beauty and calm of this lush country. Suffused, too, with Miss Walker. As well as their four hours' lessons every day, each afternoon, whatever the weather, they sallied forth together – either up and along, or down into the green depths, under the huge beech trees past 'the moat and knoll of a Norman castle, to a gloomy weed-choked lake. The ghost of a headless lady haunted these trees: the owls had their nests in their trunks and hooted all night.' Sometimes they went as far as the Roman road, Gerald darting ahead, Miss Walker, true to her name, sensibly coming behind. He had begun Roman history now and was amazed by the idea of the legions tramping through these woods, whose weird language he was learning. But Miss Walker left in August 1903. His childhood was coming to an end.

Gerald at nine and a half was flowing, confident, sensitive, full of fantasy, original, mischievous, open – loving and much loved in return. Few children can have been so primed with knowledge, or so enjoyed it. There was no reason, at this point, why his development should not have been fairly straightforward. It was not, of course, a perfect childhood. Few are. Most children sustain wounds, and the important element here is repetition. The significant wounds in Gerald's childhood were the departure of his nurse and his father's temper. He would always, probably, have been over-reactive to authority, and oversensitive to the dualities of love and loss, love and pain. But he would have substantially recovered, had already done so, despite the reinforcement of his mother's absences, the exaggeration caused by his father's deafness.

These, in terms of repetition, were but the light taps of a finger compared to the events about to descend on him. These could more accurately be likened to the violent blows of a sledge-hammer. The first descended in September 1903, when Gerald was sent away to his prep school, Winton House.

THREE

First School, First Love

1

Prep schools are virtually immortal. Winton House was still going strong in 1935. E. F. Johns Esq, MA, was still head-master. 'This is the school,' said the prospectus proudly, 'to the boys of which Charles Kingsley dedicated *The Water Babies*.'[1]

The school was set on high ground close to the Hampshire Downs, just north of Winchester. Gerald rapidly showed his mettle. On his first day he explored a sewer under the road; then he led a party from his dormitory onto the roof. One senses wild excitement; freedom from governesses, younger brothers, parents. But a few days later he walked out one morning and did not return till evening – the solution that had been so efficacious at Montreux.

This brief start was soon crushed. Little boys are totally conform-ist, and demand total conformity. By an appalling mischance, his mother had sent him to school with a pair of boots that fastened by a strap and buttons, instead of the more 'manly' sort which had elastic sides. This was discovered. In a moment, Gerald was surrounded by a hooting mob: 'New boy. New boy. He's got buttons on his shoes. He's got buttons on his shoes.' Gerald's self-confidence, never tested, collapsed at once. And 'by a fatality deriving from a pair of buttoned shoes, I was sent spinning down a slope into the abyss of unpopularity'.

Now his life became frightful. Harried and bullied all day, at night his bed was jumped on, his sheets were stripped or made soaking wet. The swimming baths, in whose cold and smelly waters – Orwell's 'faecal smells' – the Water Babies sported, were nothing but a ducking-pond to Gerald. 'Throw him in the deep end – duck him! Duck him!' A particular torture was to be put in the rackets court and have a football kicked at you. Gerald would rush, mad with terror, like a rat in a trap, while the ball hurtled off the angles with a 'hollow booming' sound, striking him on the rebound or directly. Sometimes he managed to make a friend, or rather strike up an acquaintance, only for his unpopularity to be invoked and for him to be dropped instantly. It was, he said, like being a Jew in Germany in the 1930s.

Nor was it just the boys. 'We call him the Radical Reformer,' said Mr Johns to his parents with sinister playfulness, 'because he has no respect for any of the rules.' Now, and for two and a half years, respect for the rules was thrashed into him.

2

Gerald's days at prep school haunted his dreams well into his fifties. Dreams of racing through classrooms, having lost his Kennedy's *Elementary Latin Primer*; dreams of taunting masters and bullying boys; 'a creature whose gums and teeth seem to break out of his mouth like the seeds from a cracked pomegranate, hissing, "I'll pay you out, I'll pay you out."'

Books, the pleasure initiated by his mother, now became a necessity. He devoured them: adventure stories, especially in faraway lands (and especially Rider Haggard and Ballantine; Stevenson left him cold),[2] adult melodramas like *The Deemster* by Hall Caine and Marie Correlli's *Mighty Atom*, which made him cry.[3] Books became the solution to life, almost preferable to it. He had begun the first twist towards a position where the life of the imagination, the life in the head, could be more important than life outside.

Gerald describes books now as his opium – but this is misleading. They blocked out the bullying, the beating, it is true, but they were not an opiate. They were shots in the arm, feeding his mind, keeping him alive, oxygen beneath the deep suffocating sea of school life.

And on this sea, he came upon a second solution, perhaps harking back to his mother reading aloud *Robinson Crusoe* that idyllic summer at Chelmsford. He became obsessed with islands. Choosing from the map on his classroom wall some tiny dot in the middle of an ocean, he would search the library for references. Then, to make concrete his longing to escape, he would draw it – an inlet, a winding path to the empty interior, his dwelling. But now, carried away by plans, he could not stop: ports appeared, houses, a town, mines, railways. Gerald had to move on.

He says the significance of this was that for many years he believed happiness could be achieved by giving up, not by acquiring things. This may be so, though Gerald in adult life was normally acquisitive, if much more than normally generous in giving up what he had acquired. The significance is surely simpler: happiness could be found by running away to some remote spot.

Fantasies about islands are not uncommon among children. They gripped the little Brontës for instance. But Gerald's were of uncommon strength. Fifty years later, the image he chose to describe Yegen was of a place surrounded, enveloped in a turbulent ocean of air. 'Island' was an habitual image for the house he bought after that in Churriana.*[4]

But the most obvious effect of his treatment was on his work. This highly intelligent little boy, trained since the age of seven months for this moment, now failed completely. 'Dreamy and lack of concentration', Helen copied gloomily from his reports into her journal. 'Very naughty . . . lazy . . .'

Both parents were clearly appalled. It is likely Gerald was too. They sent him to Currough in Ireland with a French governess for practically the whole of the summer holidays in 1904. This, and his own desperate efforts, seemed to pay off. By December of that year he was first in the school for geography, Latin grammar and composition, and maths.[5]

But soon the bullying and beating got him down again. He got measles and 'flu and burnt his foot in a fire (illness and injury as a response to, and escape from, stress were becoming established). By June 1905, his reports were atrocious again.

---

* As well as the Brontës, imaginary worlds and lands of this sort were invented by, among others, Nietzsche, Trollope, Stevenson and Auden. A study has been made of contemporary inventors of imaginary worlds. Sixty-four worlds were analysed. Their inventors, usually starting at the age of seven, often said they had been very lonely as children and created their worlds to compensate and escape into. But a number said they had very stable childhoods, particularly secure in the love of their mothers, and it was this that made them feel able to set out and explore in this daring and imaginative way. Gerald combined both elements. (*The Development of Imagination*, David Cohen, Stephen A. Mackeith, Routledge 1989.)

But now, in this archetypal school career, an archetypal 'good master' came to the rescue.

Mr Clark was 'A young flannel-bagged, Norfolk-jacketed giant . . . He had black curly hair like a negro, a very loud voice and plenty of good nature.' He was the games master. This should have removed Gerald, who was hopeless at games, from his interest totally. But Mr Clark had one secret and rebellious flaw – one that was rare and highly dangerous at that period. He did not think little boys were made and saved by games alone. In very special cases, qualities of daredevilry and recklessness could count. His model was Clive, who had never been any good at cricket, but could climb trees and steeples like a monkey – *and Clive had conquered India.*

It so happened, Gerald's account delightfully continues, that Gerald too liked climbing trees. When he was supposed to be watching cricket, he would climb to the very top of a nearby sycamore, carrying a book. Here, perched on a tiny green island of trembling leaves, the blue sky above, far below but out of sight the cricket, revealed only by distant cries and the familiar thud of ball on bat, he swayed gently to and fro, blissful with his book.

One afternoon Mr Clark was passing underneath. Suddenly, to his astonishment, a book thudded to the ground. Mr Clark looked up and bellowed. Gerald appeared.

From now on, Mr Clark was an ally. Since he was also the most popular master in the school, Gerald's stock rose. When Gerald burnt his foot, Mr Clark had him to live with him and his wife. Partially freed from his tormentors, his natural cleverness began to function again. Carried by academic success and that current at schools which, as he says, inevitably leads to the top, his last two years were as enjoyable as the first had been terrible.

3

So far from being relieved to escape, it is a curious fact that those who have unhappy homes are often those who suffer most at a boarding school. In their absence, they imagine disasters.

During his years of torture Gerald was haunted by the fantasy that his family had lost all their money and been forced to move into the slums of a large town. Then, more significantly, that his father had committed some monstrous crime and was about to be carted off to prison.

Gerald's life at home at Miserden was not unhappy during those years, but it is clear that his father's character deteriorated. Deafness was the main problem, compounding all the others. Throughout his life he experimented with various solutions. At this point – 1903 to 1907 – he had a little silver trumpet shaped like a snail's shell. With brisk, alert, abrupt movements, yellow moustaches bristling, he would swivel rapidly between one person and another, insisting that things were put concisely and briefly: 'through an ear-trumpet a hesitating voice is agony.'

The frustration this caused, his boredom (he had no job, few friends, didn't read), his natural irritability, chronic restlessness, his imprisonment in his immense and overbearing male egoism, the bitterness of his truncated career – all this built up and then erupted in periodic explosions. Gerald describes their life as like that on a volcano. 'Every morning we would look up to see if the sky was clear or whether smoke and lava might be expected to come raining down on us.'

Gerald's account is irresistible, even if one suspects exaggeration. His mother, he said, explained all this by 'the liver'. Really, Hugh was good and kind; but when his liver was attacked he became a monster. Both she and Gerald, but his mother in particular, became adept at judging the state of this delicate but all important organ. There was an infallible test.

His father rose at eight. Dumb–bell exercises were followed by – desperate prophylactic – a tumbler of liver salts and the bathroom. If this was full of Gerald's mother, he'd rattle the door and she'd scurry out. After shaving (frequent cuts), he'd dress, talking loudly to himself.

Finally, at 9.25, he'd descend to the dining room. This room, even now, is dark and full of foreboding. It is not difficult to imagine Captain Brenan's rattling descent, the military rap of his shoes on the flags. Helen would be sitting anxiously, watching, knitting. His father would be at the sideboard pouring his coffee in complete silence. Now there was a hush. This was the moment, this the test. If it tasted all right, he would say 'with beaming face, "The coffee is excellent this morning. Congratulate Frankton."' Then everyone would relax. His mother would make some jolly remark. But if it tasted bad – 'This is *filth*', even yanking the bell – then the inhabitants of the volcano would run for cover. Gerald adds that the odd thing was, the coffee was always exactly the same – disgusting.

In fact, so far from exaggeration, this is an understatement. Ann Cary, one of Hugh's granddaughters, remembers him at Edgeworth throwing the coffee – tray and cream and all – bodily out of the window. Nor does Gerald exaggerate his subsequent behaviour. Because on these mornings, maddened by deafness, his liver raging, his father would cast about for someone on whom to vent his fury. This person would inevitably be Gerald's mother.

Gerald describes the ensuing rows – watched, wide-eyed and trembling, by himself. His father cutting and rude, his mother at first meek. Finally, becoming more and more cruel and sarcastic, his father would insinuate something against the Graham family. At once Helen would flare up and lose control. His father, frightened by what he'd said, would noisily leave the room. These rows would continue in gaping silences. After one of them, in January 1904, his father didn't speak to his mother for an entire term.

This bullying continued throughout their marriage. By 1910, Hugh often treated Helen like one of the servants. She was, says Mrs Blosse-Lynch, by then (she was forty-eight) 'rather red and shrivelled with the habit of rubbing her hands together at times of stress. She did this whenever Hugh came into the room. He would say, "Helen, put more coal on the fire," which she did.' Ann Cary remembers how at Tewkesbury once in the 1930s he wouldn't let her get out of the car to look at the cathedral. 'She will *not* get out of the car.' Helen just sat in the back and cried.[6]

In the row before the term's silence, his father made a furious gesture and his mother fell at his feet. Horrified, Gerald thought she had been struck down. But reflecting on the incident at forty-five years later, he realised it was not that. His father was sadistic; he was not capable of violence. It was, he says, her 'melodramatic masochism' which had misinterpreted the movement. There was, that is, something exciting, almost pleasurable, in that swoon at his feet.

His mother seemed to need such treatment. She enjoyed being dominated. She rebelled, she planned to leave – but always she was drawn back, attracted by his 'tight remote character', fascinated by 'the whip-like phrases' he would use on her.

Something of this dark streak was shared by her son. Later,

Gerald would allow himself to be tormented for six years by Carrington. Torment and frustration were to reappear in his love life. Pain became an important element in his aesthetic. It seems likely that some element of masochism was involved.

These rows and the bullying also complicated Gerald's view of himself. As he became increasingly alienated from his father, he increasingly imitated and identified with his mother. He valued and exaggerated any characteristic they shared. If they did not share it, he pretended they did. Conversely, a number of Gerald's contradictions come from his reacting against the many sides of himself that were like Hugh.

Nevertheless, it is important not to exaggerate the effect of the rows on Gerald's home life. They upset him – but they were few and far between. His holidays were happy.

What strikes one is the freedom and indulgence. He could do more or less what he liked, provided he was in time for meals; and even these he could take as a picnic. Much of his time was spent out of doors. In summer he dammed the streams and caught crayfish; in winter he tobogganed. Nature – to be a decisive element in his life – was unconsciously absorbed in the beautiful Cotswold countryside on long walks and pony rides, even bike rides – his parents having bought him one of these still revolutionary machines in 1906.

His father's behaviour towards his passionately adored mother was eventually to turn Gerald against him, but at this period relations between father and son were quite good. His father occasionally disciplined him: '. . . penetrating memories of my childhood came into my mind,' says the hero of Gerald's best novel. 'My father reproving me for my untidiness and laziness.'[7] But, not wanting the whole household against him, Hugh was usually kind and friendly. He taught Gerald billiards and croquet and badminton, took him hunting and, as cars came in, driving.

Cars, in fact, became something of an obsession. First Hugh bought a five-seater Wolseley. It had no windscreen, solid tyres, and couldn't climb hills. Gradually he bought more and more. He sold his horse and Gerald's pony, hiring animals when they went hunting. At one time the family had three cars. Gerald's father was a natural engineer. He began to spend hours lying flat on his back under the cars, cursing and wrenching, drenched in oil.

Gerald incidentally was the opposite – a natural non-engineer.

The world is divided like this, the non-engineer's function being to break or be unable to mend the things it is the engineer's function to repair.

But the cars give further clues to the marriage. Gradually, Hugh built up a series of hobby occupations. He had a carpentry shop and his skills reached cabinet-making standards.[8] He spent much time manipulating, or contemplating, his shares. As his time filled, the pressure eased. He was always irritable and periodic explosions occurred, but he would feel guilty. He recognised Helen's sweetness, and that she loved him. 'He, after his fashion, was fond of her.' Since this admission comes from Gerald, strongly biased against his father, one can take it that the marriage trundled on in relative peace.

His parents were attentive to his needs to an astonishing degree. Blair was still too young to play with, so cousins were asked to stay. He went to the home of Mackenzie, his best friend at Winton House, and had him back in return. Mackenzie stayed the entire Christmas holidays in 1906. The journal notes dancing lessons *every afternoon*. Had a weakness been detected here? If so, the lessons were doomed.

Neighbours played little part in this respect. Dull and scattered and middle-aged, as far as Gerald was concerned they might have been childless. There were no girls. Only one had a son his age.

But one neighbour was important. The Rev. Robert Earee, then in his thirties, is remembered in Miserden to this day. 'A miraculous man,' said May Holder. 'Very clever. Always walked in the village in his cassock and biretta. Very friendly with King Edward. He could do anything.'

He could also tell you anything. The point of Mr Earee from Gerald's point of view was that he had encyclopaedic knowledge. He was the most fascinating and stimulating person he had ever met. He was, as it were, the book made flesh, or books rather (there was a lot of flesh to Mr Earee); those books his mother had read him, and was now so proud he read so many of. Sitting listening to Mr Earee telling him how to extract opium from poppies, how aspirin came from willow bark, Gerald seems to have decided he wanted to be like that too.

And one other aspect of life at Miserden should be noted. Tramps were still much more common then than now. Flora Thompson, writing about the 1880s in nearby Oxfordshire, spoke in terms of 'hundreds'.[9] These mysterious figures were another part of that dangerous, near criminal, and anarchically free underworld which both horrified and fascinated the English middle class. Gerald would have seen them on the road or coming to the back door. They seem to have made a particular impression on him.

4

The most exciting part of the holidays was that which was spent abroad. Until Gerald's Larchfield grandmother died in 1907, the family spent at least part of each year in Ireland.* After this they went more frequently to France, going to Dinard in Brittany for the Easters of 1908, 1909 and 1912.

But Gerald and his mother had been alone together – 'bliss' – to Paris in 1905. These visits to France cemented the earlier ones; love of France, he wrote later, was 'very close to my childhood and posters like *défense d'afficher* are wrapped round my heart.'[10] They must have reinforced as well the idea that happiness was to be found abroad.

The visit to Paris was Gerald's first clearly remembered experience of the sea. In *A Life* . . . it evokes a short poetic description in which every element is present – light, movement, smell – but strangely absent, and what we expect, is sound. This is a peculiarity of his prose, and no doubt another consequence of being brought up by so many deaf people. Before this, in *A Life* . . . there is not a sound of any consequence between his Nana singing 'Nancy' and the hollow boom of the football in the rackets court. Conversely, when he did notice sounds, he did so with piercing intensity and they were to provoke some of his most poignantly beautiful descriptive writing.

During the Easter holiday at Dinard in 1908 something happened of much greater significance. Gerald was now fourteen. Retiring as usual after their supper one night, he found the full moon 'pouring' into his little room. He stepped on to the balcony and looked down at the 'long glittering path' it made on the sea. The 'glittering path' may have revived a memory of the tunnel through the bamboos in India, with its similar sudden effect of light on water. In any event,

---

* Gerald was ambivalent about the effect his Irish background had on him – usually playing it down. He used to say he was one-eighth Irish. If you count the Northern Irish (who certainly have a great deal of 'Irishness' about them) then the true amount is three-eighths – nearly half. By the time he was eleven Gerald had spent over a quarter of his life in Ireland.

he had an extraordinary experience: '. . . a sense of some enormous force and beauty existing around me, a pressure, a state that promised unspeakable delight and happiness if only I could join myself to it . . . the natural world appeared to have a power and authority that seemed overwhelming.'

Experiences of this sort are not uncommon. What matters is the use made of them. Often, it is religious. But the feeling of an outside power breaking in can be reversed, as it were, with the youth or young man (and it is usually young men) themselves breaking through (hence the significance of the path, the tunnel). Thus it is often, notes Peter Levi in a study exploring the subject, an important ingredient in the make-up of a certain sort of artist. This is the Rimbaudian artist, one who is in touch, or has been in touch, with a greater reality, who has had, that is, transcendental experience. As a result, he feels special.

The experiences usually start at adolescence and Levi suggests they may be connected with awakening sexuality in a particular way – 'the emergence of repressed sexuality without object'.'' And it is true that at the end of this year Gerald was to discover masturbation.

On the next page he describes the first time he fell in love. This, too, might be taken as confirmation of Levi's thesis, but if so it reveals something else as well. Chronologically, the event should come at least nine months later. The placing of it here introduces a second peculiarity of his autobiographical writing, the phenomenon of his subconscious joining up two events which belong together even if they have no apparent connection.

Gerald could be both extraordinarily perceptive and penetrating about himself and others – and extraordinarily obtuse. The contrast was so striking – it astonished Carrington – that it has to be explained; indeed there is an explanation. But by this method of juxtaposition he often reveals truths, about himself or events, which he either doesn't want to give away or of which he is unaware. Thus, in *A Life* . . . , the very early association of love with being left is shown by the way he places his agony at his mother's pneumonia just before he goes to Winton House, though again nine months separate the two events.*

---

* The process is rather like that of psychoanalysis, where the subconscious reveals connections by association. Though this phenomenon of juxtaposition often comes in his letters, it is interesting that we will find Gerald employing, when he comes to write *A Life* . . . , a method very close to analysis.

5

His first love – she thirteen, he fourteen – was called Nancy. It was the main reason he fell in love with her: 'Oh give my love to Nancy', his nurse had sung, 'That's the girl that I adore'. (Years later and years after his affair with the first Carrington, he was to fall in love with a second Carrington partly because of her name alone.) His parents had taken rooms in Cheltenham during the Christmas holidays in order that he should meet girls. He kissed Nancy at a dance, and from then on he went to her house every day. She had brown hair, hazel eyes, a turned-up nose and teeth which stuck out slightly between full lips. The game was hide and seek. Gerald and Nancy would hide in a locked cupboard and kiss passionately. After the boring dinner at their lodgings, Gerald would slip out and bicycle back to her house. The moon would be shining. Not the thunderer of Dinard, but 'the nightingale-voiced orb which arranges the *mise-en-scène* for lovers'. He would gaze up at her window. She would look out and wave. And so, like a *novio* gazing up at his *novia* in Spain, Gerald experienced for the first time the ecstatic delight of romantic love – chaste but passionate, uplifting, frustrating, above all intense – the complex feeling that he was, really, to value above all others all his life.

It soon faded. Childishly written letters arrived at Miserden. He saw her again that Easter, but the spell was broken. He still had their first dance card when he was sixty-five.

6

During the term-time Gerald's parents sometimes went abroad alone. In the autumn of 1904, his mother and grandmother went to Andalusia. They brought him back some of the delicious almond *turrón*, with its consistency of flaky fudge. Gerald never forgot the taste.[12]

One of these journeys, which Helen and Hugh made to the Loire, suggests that the marital friction wasn't all one-sided – and incidentally shows Helen behaving in a way strikingly reminiscent of her son many years later. Her cousin Nellie Graham had come too. She fell in love with Hugh and he was attracted to her. (Hardly surprising since, if Gerald is right, he had not made love to his wife since 1900.) There was a terrible row on the trip. Helen took her meals by herself and referred to Cousin Nellie as 'The Adulteress'. They cut the holiday short at Chartres and came home. Helen did not forgive Hugh for two years.[13]

But his parents were never away when Gerald was at home. The holidays were devoted to him, continuing also the pattern of intense coaching. In the summer of 1907, a Mlle Montagu was engaged to start him on German.[5] And, though the pain of leaving his mother never lessened, school itself was now happy too.

That summer term he was captain of the school. He was first in work, proving especially good at classics, where he'd been first since 1906. He had planned and superintended a rock garden. It was the centrepiece of parents' day.

On this fortuitous peak Helen ends her journal. It was just as well. In September 1908 Gerald left for Radley. Once more the sledgehammer was about to fall with crushing force.

FOUR

Repression, and Liberation

1

Most public schools during the Edwardian age – 'bloated continuation of the Victorian', as Gerald once described it – were, with the exception of their classical sixth forms, usually institutions for teaching games. Beating with birch or some other form of wooden weapon was the normal punishment. They mirrored and then magnified the intense class-snobbishness of the period with their fagging and infinite gradations of privilege and authority, all symbolised in a Byzantine complexity of dress – tassels, ties, collars, waistcoats, caps, boaters, scarves and socks. Terrified of sex, they employed a rigid segregation by age, a move which, designed to suppress romantic love and homosexual desire in a girl-less world, of course violently inflamed both passions.

It had been hoped Gerald would go to Harrow, but the lists were full. He gained exhibitions (minor scholarships) to both Winchester and Radley. Radley's reply came first and was accepted; and Radley, in all the respects just outlined and many more, was among the most extreme.

In 1899 Radley had shown both courage and compassion by taking in Oscar Wilde's son Cyril. Since then it had steadily ossified. Nearly all the masters were games-mad (even today Radley, positioned in undistinguished country near Abingdon and Oxford, is anchored like some great Victorian Gothic ship in a sea of rugger posts). Out of twelve pages in the school magazine of 1909, seven are devoted to games. By 1908 the Social Tutors (house masters) had each been there an average of twenty-four years. Numbers of boys sank from 258 to 196 – a sure sign of decay. The headmaster, Dr Thomas Field, was one of those giants of useless Victorian learning.

Just in passing, as it were, he knew the whole of *In Memoriam*, most of *Paradise Lost*, and vast chunks of Thucydides and Herodotus off by heart. He thought the school was perfect.

Gerald's father probably thought it was perfect as well. He had now clearly decided it was high time he took a grip on his son's – the future soldier's – education. His mother felt Gerald's taste for reading, his aptitude for classics and learning should still be encouraged. (Naturally enough. They were due to her.) He could enter the Army later, via Oxford, as her brothers had done. Gerald's father totally disagreed. An incipient dreaminess he'd noticed must now be stamped out. Maths would do this. There was a dangerous sluggish-ness at games. Besides – the clincher – he couldn't afford Oxford. Gerald was therefore entered for the despised Sandhurst-oriented 'Modern' side. This meant, essentially, abandoning Latin and Greek, which he liked, for mathematics and science, which he loathed. It was to be three years before the significance of this sunk in.

2

Thus Gerald was plunged into a situation which, even in its bare aims, was totally inimical. It rapidly became clear that it was *all* inimical.

Used to freedom at home and the glories of Head Boy liberty at Winton House, his life was now minutely regimented. For instance, all meal places were dictated. Neither position nor companion could be altered.

But this was a minor detail. Gerald's father had deliberately put him in Croome's Social – the leading games house. A. C. M. Croome was a maniacal all-rounder: a golfing writer for the *Daily Telegraph*, fierce football enthusiast, 'when he left', carolled the school history, 'one could not think of the cricket without him'. He was, said the same source, unfortunately for Gerald, 'at the height of his powers',[1] and he very soon noticed the new boy. Gerald could not throw a cricket ball at all. His system at football was to hover at the edges, or rush up and down evading the ball while pretending to pursue it.[2] Soon it was seen that he read books. Once again, he plunged into the abyss. For three years, in that gas-lit school, he 'was liable at any moment to be kicked, hit, mobbed, thrown in the bushes, as well as called by every sort of abusive name. The games prefects took such opportunities as they could find for beating me . . .'

Radley has preserved one of the instruments. It is a fives bat – a light, springy, two-foot-long club, with a flat palm-sized end. The names of the boys beaten stretch down it, like the notches on a gangster's gun. Nor was it just prefects. There were the 'bloods', senior boys who virtually ruled the school[1] – 'detestable young men', calling themselves Cha-rles and RRRupert 'and everything they did is abominable to me'.[3]

Lt-Colonel Morkill, the last person alive who was at Radley with Gerald (whom he did not remember) could still recall the beatings. 'One witness, one beater. Trousers were on, but the elbows tucked in, the backside raised, tight as a drum. Then he'd set about me. It was extremely painful.' Lt-Colonel Morkill (good name for a soldier) remembered the intense and agonising cold in winter. They slept in cubicles down each side of the dormitories. Under every bed was a shallow metal bath filled each night with three or four inches of water. In winter it became icy, even freezing solid. You were meant to immerse yourself. Lt-Colonel Morkill could remember making frenzied splashings to simulate 'bathing'.

Gerald says in his autobiography that throughout his life he often found himself acting either like his mother or his father. At Winton House it had been his mother: submissive, accepting the dotty values of his enemies, accentuating his clownish side – bad at games, abstracted by reading – till people laughed and he became popular. Now he drew on his father: stoic, angry, silent, returning 'hatred for hatred'.

Desperate, terrified, enraged, he pathetically took up boxing – 'but without success, since my shoulder muscles were weak'. This humiliating failure went deep. In 1916 he had a terrible dream: 'I saw a toad which was being attacked by a dog. It lifted its paws in vain for it had no strength with which to defend itself.' This dream filled him 'with intense pity and horror'.[4] Gerald, in fact, had particularly strong arms – thick, muscular, hairy; but all his life he was convinced they were weak.

Failure to subdue his tormentors by force threw him back on the positions prepared long before at Winton. Once again, he retreated into his redoubt.

3

It was a redoubt whose walls were lined with books. And here Radley, surprisingly, was a help.

The Wilson Library, to which as a scholar he was allowed instant access, was extraordinarily well stocked, perhaps due to one of the few cultured masters, Mr Wilson-Green. As well as classics like Hardy, the Brontës and Jane Austen, and adventure and explorers' tales, the biographies of generals, the memoirs of Empire and school that you'd expect, there were, in Gerald's time, also (a selection): Borrow, Wells, Shaw, Belloc, Samuel Butler, books on archaeology, wild flowers and birds, and poetry – Clough, Swinburne, Poe, Shelley.[5]

As if to compensate for his soundless childhood, Gerald fastened avidly on such music as he was given – the music of words. As early as 1897 his mother noted on reading him poetry, 'He has an excellent ear for sound.'[6] No doubt this is one reason he had already become proficient in French and German, and quickly begun to master Latin and Greek. It was also to be a major basis for his critical aesthetic – in a sense of his entire life, because, some time in 1909, he discovered poetry. First Poe, with 'Annabel Lee', then – with the force of revelation – Shelley.

Shelley – rebellious Shelley – is the great poet for adolescents; and, it must have seemed to Gerald, among all adolescents for him. Suddenly, the beauty he had felt so strongly was expressed in magical, musical, intoxicating fashion. More than that, the violence of these experiences was shared, explained, given a goal. Delighting in the poetry, it is indicative of his developing thoroughness that he should seize the only two lives he could find – Salt and Dowden. In the large worthy tomes of Dowden the identity became complete down to the minutest particulars. Shelley had been tormented at prep school and then at Eton, till he seethed in the 'misery of his own extravagant and impotent rages'. Even the nature of one of the instruments – a kicked ball – was the same. Shelley 'lived intensely in his own imaginings'. Shelley had difficulties with his father. Shelley had a brother too young to play with. Shelley didn't like games. It even turned out that Shelley couldn't dance.[7]

'I vowed that I would dedicate my powers to thee and thine: have I not kept the vow?' With Shelley's words to the pursuit of beauty by poetry ringing in his ears, Gerald's future life seemed to fall into place: nature, the inner life, the freedom to explore and express them in poetry. 'After reading Shelley,' he wrote, 'I became something of a prig, but at least I never doubted or looked back.'

His passion for Shelley did not yet produce full-scale rebellion; but it seems clear that either from now on, or a little later, he began to write poetry. The image of Shelley, the romantic idea of himself as a poet, were to be central to him for many years.*

The second thing that lined his inner retreat at Radley was maps. His drawing of islands, his fantasy escapes, continued but now there came a narrowing of focus. He discovered in the Wilson Library the *Universal Geography* of the great Elisée Reclus – probably the Hachette edition of 1895 in seventeen volumes. This is a marvellous work. Its detailed accounts of the geography, peoples, history and customs of remote regions are enhanced by hundreds of maps and thrilling gravure illustrations, some actually '*d'après nature*'. Gerald began to work out an epic journey: down through Europe, the Balkans and Greece to the Near East, then on through Arabia, Persia and Afghanistan, and then on and on, ever eastwards, over the Pamir Mountains until he reached the vast deserts beyond, the desert of Sinkiang, the Altai Gobi desert in Mongolia, and on still further until, like Marco Polo, he reached China.

* Like many writers, though for his own reasons, Gerald concealed the intensity of his desire to write, both early and late. In particular he concealed the part poetry played in this desire. He hardly referred to his poetry (which he invariably called 'verse') in his autobiographies till he reached his thirties. It is perfectly clear that he wrote a great deal of poetry long before 1920. Notes on the back of a 1917 diary (MSS, MF (Here and elsewhere MF refers to the Brenan archive held at Mecina-Fondales.)) refer to ten parcels of early literary work left at home. There was enough pre-1914 poetry (and possibly some prose) to fill two volumes. These have been destroyed, but judging by those that remain they were substantial – certainly requiring contributions from Radley days. And in fact, a letter to Carrington dated 14 January 1921 says quite clearly that he began to write after reading Shelley. The tenacity of his idea of himself as a poet is the easier explained the earlier it began.

4

In the August of that same 1909, Gerald's mother told him excitedly
that a new neighbour had rented Waterlane Cottage from their friends
the MacMeekens.* He was brilliantly clever, a brilliant talker, and a
great reader of books. True, he dressed oddly – that is, like an artist,
peculiarly. But all was saved by his background, which was impeccable: cousin to the Duchess of Buckingham, another cousin a Master
of Foxhounds. By a coincidence, he had gone to Winton House. She
had told him her son read poetry. He wished to meet Gerald. He had
suggested tea.

John Hope-Johnstone – Hope – was one of those delinquent
upper-class Bohemians who leaven the English class system. His
father had run through a fortune, then retired to a flat in Brighton to
take morphia. His mother had inherited a second fortune, which she
spent on roulette and cards. These fortunes lasted long enough to
take Hope from Winton House, Bradfield and Harrow. They ran out
while he was at Trinity College, Cambridge, forcing him to leave.

Lack of money – or rather not having any money at all when he'd
expected a great deal – was decisive in Hope's life. Forced to live on his
wits (he would not contemplate a profession), his time was spent sponging and plotting one scheme after another. In the end, as each failed
and he aged, he became embittered; finally, to Gerald, impossible.

But now, aged twenty-six, he was still romantic, even glamour-
ous. He had devised, partly to save money, a system of tremendous
journeys. He had recently completed one across Asia. But it was not
only poverty that drove him to travel. Hope had a passion for
exploration. And, although intensely desirous of money, he also
despised it and those who had it (a common combination). But it
meant he was a genuine ascetic, who could go for months – and
hundreds of miles, for he was strong – on virtually nothing. He had

---

* Gerald sets this momentous meeting a year later, in the summer of 1910,
when he was sixteen. But the list of significant dates (MSS, MF) which he had by
him when he wrote *A Life* . . . , and which he elsewhere adhered to, clearly shows
1909. One can only speculate why he should have changed it. He may have
amalgamated two meetings in the interests of impact – an artistic adjustment to
biographical truth he would have regarded as perfectly justified.

an intense love of learning and of poetry, for which he had a subtle ear. All this added a powerful element of idealism to his wanderings. When he arrived as the new tutor for Augustus John's children he was pushing a pram, which he'd already shoved across Turkey, full of grammars, poetry and books on metaphysics.

Hope seems to have taken Waterlane Cottage to store his books and to give himself and the Johns a respite from each other. As a tutor, he was stimulating and eccentric. The children learnt the theory of relativity or how to write gothic script in black ink with a calligraphic pen, or the Bible. Hope's aim was less to teach than to draw out. All the Johns remembered his greed. When the cream arrived at his place, it invariably all spilled 'accidentally' over his plate – perhaps a reaction to subsisting for months on stolen roots and bruised fruit.[8]

It was towards this figure that Gerald set out that August 1909. He had to struggle through beechwoods. He felt extremely nervous. He didn't, he wrote in *A Life . . .* , think anyone else in the world read poetry except him. He reached the cottage, hesitated, pushed open the door and saw – a miracle.

'I saw a slim, dark-haired man, dressed in a pale buff corduroy suit. He had sandals on his bare feet and a brightly coloured silk handkerchief round his neck and he was sitting at a kitchen table playing a tune on a penny whistle.'

Gerald could not, in retrospect, remember many details exactly; rather a series of shocks. Hope in his loud, definite, totally clear voice, asked him if he'd read from Yeats' *The Wind Among The Reeds* and then did so himself in 'a strange chanting resonant tone which seemed much to enhance its beauty'. He pulled out a copy of Blake's *Jerusalem* with drawings by Aubrey Beardsley. Soon he was showing Gerald round: one tiny whitewashed room, with steep stairs to the single tiny bedroom. The walls were covered in books; more books on the floor and window sill. The bed was unmade, dishes unwashed. Hope talked about Augustus John – a genius, possibly greater as a man than as an artist. So to gypsies, Borrow (probably about *Lavengro* and *Romany Rye*) whom he admired,[9] and from there to the difficulties of Arabic. Here was something Gerald knew about – the East. At last he was able to burst into voluble and excited talk.

The afternoon ended with Hope discoursing on mathematical logic – not Gerald's strongest subject – and saying how he wanted to see something of all the world except Australia. Gerald was to be with him alone only twice more in the next three years. But he had found his saviour.

5

Gerald certainly read Borrow at Radley,[10] and it is likely that, fired by Hope, he read him now. The Wilson Library did not have *Lavengro* or *The Romany Rye*. He would have read *The Bible in Spain* and *Wild Wales*.

There was a peculiarity about Gerald's reading. If something affected him, or he thought it important, he would read the book again and again – and this for the rest of his life. Thus he was still re-reading Borrow in the late 1940s, when he made some curious discoveries about him. There was a reason for this habit, apart from sheer enjoyment, but it meant he not only got to know these books very well, they became part of the architecture of his mind. Borrow influenced *South From Granada*, but is detectable long before that.

Detectable also is Richard Jefferies, another writer he first read now. Jefferies' pieces are, in effect, pantheistic poems in prose to the trees, the fields, the wheat, the winds, the clouds, the woods, the animals of his native Wiltshire. For all the elements of whimsy and idealisation (the insides of his cottages always exquisitely clean), his writing at its best equals D. H. Lawrence, who may well have copied Jefferies' use of repetition – repetition for emphasis, to get his descriptions exact, to mirror, in the prose, the repetition of nature. He can achieve an extraordinarily sustained exaltation and identification, a sense of the self-sufficiency of such feelings. He loved the presence of history in the countryside, as Gerald was to do, and became learned in it for that reason. He loved solitude, which is necessary for all these emotions.

It is easy to see how this must have worked on Gerald, reinforcing Shelley and his own bent. He kept up his botany at Radley.* He

---

* In a passage cut from *A Life . . .* , Gerald describes how powerfully the scents of flowers moved him at this time. Escaping from the madness of Radley – one has an image of Ferdinand the Bull – he would drink in 'their drenching, penetrating perfumes'. He planned to organise smells like colours and bought a book by Piesse, a French scent manufacturer.

also found he could escape games by joining the Natural History Society (a 'moribund institution', according to Gerald). By 1910, with him as secretary, the school magazine says it is 'flourishing'. This entailed huge expeditions, Gerald on his three-speed Rudge-Whitworth, often as far as the Berkshire downs, where there was a pub that sold delicious cream teas. He was often accompanied by the one master who'd befriended him – quiet, precise, 'natty' Mr Wilson-Green. He was too wet to be a powerful influence ('Garden City Socialism'), but he took English literature and French, at both of which Gerald was very good, and admired and encouraged him.

Virtually the only other congenial figure he mentions is Gerard Thornton (he calls him Morton).* He was a scientist, and together they went looking for snails and fossils.

But it was on his long, already very long, walks – in the solitude that Jefferies told him was essential – that he now had more and more frequently the nature experiences that sustained him.

He describes one that took place one summer at school camp, just after the school had broken up. It is probably significant that it occurred after a long, hot and painful route march, which had ended at Silbury Hill. Gerald, leaving the other boys sprawled about the canteen, climbed to the top. The sun was setting over Salisbury Plain: 'Its long horizontal rays, a little blurred by the dust and heat, fell lazily and with a striking accent upon the great expanse of turf that stretched below and seemed to turn it into a lake.' This tranquil scene struck Gerald into a state of the most violent turbulence. He wanted to hurl himself into nature, to force his way out to become the earth, the plain. At the same time, he felt himself invaded, possessed. It was not an oceanic emotion, but a Dionysiac one, and plunging down that precipitous slope he 'ran shouting and gesticulating across the turf'.

6

Once again, associated synapses seem to fire in the autobiographer's brain. Gerald's next topic, another of dionysiac turbulence, is masturbation.

* Sir Gerard Thornton, FRS. Quiet and modest, he discovered the species of Plesiosaur named after him and was knighted in 1968 for work among soil microbes.

This was fraught with terrible difficulties. For one thing, Gerald at fifteen and sixteen was extremely prudish. Like Dowden's Shelley, he shrank from any 'coarse and awkward jest'. Public schools, then as now, were deafening with coarse and awkward jests.

But principally the difficulty was the Edwardian attitude to this pleasant and harmless activity. The obsession with masturbation throughout this period seems, today, fantastic. Sermons were devoted to it, boys and masters prayed earnestly to be free from it, boys were taken aside and compelled to confess to it. And the battle began early with frightful warnings from prep school masters. Cyril Connolly describes in *Enemies of Promise* how he was told (about 1916) the world was full of appalling temptation, particularly for Etonians. He was to report anyone who tried to get into bed with him, and urged to avoid anyone older: 'Above all, not to "play with ourselves". There was an old boy from St Wulfric's who became so self-intoxicated that when he got to Oxford he had put, in a fit of remorse, his head under a train. That miserable youth, I afterwards learnt, had attended all the private schools in England.' The point was that, carried to extremes, masturbation was fatal: '. . . self-indulgence', wrote Dr Acton, 'long pursued, tends ultimately . . . to early death or self-destruction'.[11] So terrified were doctors that there were cases in America (England was not alone in this madness) where they resorted to 'heroic' surgery, and persistent masturbators were castrated.[12]

The intense anxiety, often terror, induced in whole generations of public-schoolboys by such pressures hardly needs pointing up. There were, however, solutions. Doctors agreed it was possible to sublimate sex. Games could take the place of sex. So could art. But this had a corollary. If art and games could, as it were, shunt sexual energies into 'higher' channels, then sex could drain those energies away. There is absolutely no evidence that any of this redirecting can take place. In fact, all the evidence is that it can't and doesn't.[12] But in this context, particularly that of art, it doesn't really matter what the truth is but what you think. If you think sexual activity will weaken your ability to paint or write or act then the likelihood is it will do that. And this idea was very common during this period. Henry James always believed passion threatened his art. So did Cyril Connolly.*

* Barbara Skelton told one of her lovers, Mark Culme-Seymour, that Connolly would often only make love to her once a month in order to improve his artistic output (Mark Culme-Seymour, in conversation with the author).

Radley was in the mainstream of Edwardian sexual lunacy. Lectures were given on the perils of masturbation. The school circulated a pamphlet, purportedly written by a doctor, promising insanity and, with deliberate and menacing vagueness, 'disease'. It would be odd if Gerald had not been affected by all this. In fact, he was affected profoundly. We have already seen one instance both of his anxiety and his (entirely typical) ignorance: his belief at fifteen that his father had had him castrated when he was six. In the spring of 1910 he had to go to the sanatorium with 'flu. To his horror, his urine turned red. Excessive masturbation! The pamphlet was right – syphilis!* Soon, predictably, he found that masturbation seemed to dull his reaction to nature and to poetry; striking, that is, at his nascent emergence as a poet. This, and his guilt and fear, led to frantic efforts at control. When he was sixty-seven he told Loïs Morgan, a young girl he was attracted to, that guilt about masturbation had made him unable 'to lay hands on himself'. All his life he had had to use pillows and other objects. [13]

A well-attested reaction to the conflict generated when something is both intensely desired and pleasurable, and also forbidden and made a source of guilt, is for it to become an obsession. [14] This quality was sometimes pronounced in Gerald's attitude to sex in later life and its roots almost certainly lie here.

The same sort of thing took place over homosexuality. Passionate but chaste romantic homosexual love was universal at public schools; there were also, much more rare, various forms of active homosexuality. Radley, in the guarded words of its historian, had at this time a low 'moral tone'. This means homosexuality was – another favourite word – 'rife', a fact borne out by the old Radleian Lt-Colonel Morkill. Gerald doesn't mention it once. Yet it seems unlikely that someone like Gerald – so susceptible to physical beauty, so romantic – did not fall in love, however secretly and chastely. That he did, and was then torn by more guilt, is suggested by the quite excessive reaction he had afterwards to the mildest hint of homosexual advance. When he was thirty-two he black-balled someone from Bunny Garnett's dining club simply because he was 'an old pet' – i.e. homosexual. [15] Not until

* In fact this was almost certainly acute glomerulonephritis, an inflammation of the kidneys caused by a streptococcal infection deriving from a sore throat. It had nothing to do with masturbation.

his late sixties could he bring himself to ask what exactly it was homosexuals did together.[16]

In fact, it seems more likely that not just his later adult obsessions, but all Gerald's sexual inhibitions and difficulties, which were to distort his character and whose effects were to ramify out into his life and his writing, should be located here, among the confusions inculcated by Radley; rather than, as Gerald would have it, in the contrasts observed by the bright-eyed little boy, fascinated observer, looking and listening at the servants' quarters in Larchfield.

7

'I dreamed of tall blocks of flats or skyscrapers in which the floors were rented according to the intellectual energy of the occupants, the most intelligent being on the top. I myself lived in the lift.'

Thoughts in a Dry Season

Virtually nothing remains of Gerald amidst the thick dust of Radley's archives: only an announcement of his promotion to lance-corporal in the Corps. But patchy scholastic records do exist. By the end of his first year – summer 1909 – he had won the form prize, the Divinity Prize, come second in science and maths, first in English and French. He was at once moved into the top form on the army side. There were several boys of eighteen; the average age was 17.2; Gerald was about to be sixteen. By Easter 1911 he was second in English and fourth in French. He won the Scott Essay prize every single year, the Divinity Prize again in 1912, and also shared the Old Radleian French Prize. Geography and history were both very well taught, according to the school inspectors in 1911 (as was French); he would have done well there too.[17]

His considerable academic achievements at Radley were almost ignored by Gerald. When, in *A Life . . .* , he reluctantly details his academic success at Winton House, he adds hastily that of course any idea that he was intelligent is quite wrong. 'I was moderately bright sometimes and dull at others. Such intelligence as I possess has always been of an intuitive kind, short-winded, easily confused, hampered by a bad memory and in no way to be relied on.'

Throughout his life, in his books, letters and conversation, Gerald insisted, despite a great deal of clear, indeed overwhelming evidence to the contrary, that his mind was really muddled. He was almost stupid. A familiar image was the Malaga telephone exchange – girls gossiping and smoking, forgetting to plug in connections or plugging them in wrong. Partly, of course, this was straightforward imitation of his adored mother. He saw her as muddled and forgetful; therefore he was too. (And here is one explanation of why he felt he had to continually re-read important works.)

It was also modesty. His father regarded modesty as extremely important. His method of instilling it was frequently to remind Gerald that he was worth nothing.[18] Mother-induced consciousness of his powers was to alternate with father-induced worthlessness all his life. But extreme modesty is a middle-class English virtue. You do not often find it in Americans, for example, or Spaniards or Italians. This is because in the close-meshed, enclosed, over-crowded world of the public school, boasting is intolerable. It is therefore crushed. Radley exaggerated Gerald's modesty until, while in personal terms one of his most charming qualities, it can seem, constantly reiterated in print, not just baffling but irritating.

It was made more complicated by a further mother-father split in his view of himself. He was, in fact, not just highly intelligent, but was eventually to develop the application, the care, the appetite for knowledge of a scholar, and one furnished with the fruits of enormous reading held in a powerful memory. Yet – and here lay his distinction – this side was often illuminated by shafts of brilliance, sudden flashes of original perception. Gerald always admired the things that came to him intuitively – the similes, the rush of extraordinary ideas, the poetry. He associated that side of himself, not only with his mother, but also with his Nana and his silent grandmother, and he saw his cleverness and memory deriving from his father. He therefore came not only secretly to despise the scholar side but also – perhaps in echo of his parent's rows – to feel it was in some way inimical to his poetic intuitive side.

But Gerald also ignored his scholarly achievement because in fact to do well, even very well, on the Army side was not considered particularly distinguished. The consciousness that he was being wasted must, by the time he was seventeen, have been considerably augmented every time he saw Hope.

8

From a letter almost certainly dated July 1911 one can deduce Gerald's eagerness to see Hope and their growing intimacy. 'Dear Brenan', wrote Hope, a form of address which at that time was itself a move to informality. He asked him to tea, but added, 'It probably wouldn't do to come back the very day you return.'[19]

Hope's regular visits to Waterlane caused a tremendous stir in the neighbourhood. He was entertaining, in the rather mannered, anecdotal style fashionable at the time. Compton Mackenzie thought he was, along with Norman Douglas, the most enjoyable conversationalist he had ever met.[20] When excited by an audience of two or three, he would quote Oscar Wilde: 'As Oscar said . . .' Wilde was still simply not mentionable in polite society. As a result, many men thought Hope was homosexual. He was not, or not entirely, though he was susceptible to strong romantic attachments to young men under twenty. According to Gerald, he really liked young girls. But he was impotent. In later years he would put his hands timidly on the thighs of girls of thirteen. Then their mothers would hear of it and he would be banned from the house.[9]

But his basic quality was his passion for self-education. He seemed to know everything – literature, history, science, painting, geology, botany; he was Mr Earee multiplied by a thousand. In particular, he loved odd, out-of-the-way bits of information. Augustus John said he was a walking encyclopaedia. And he was a born teacher, expounding his huge and fascinating knowledge to the exhilarated seventeen-year-old calmly, lucidly, without any assumption of superiority. Not just to Gerald. He describes his mother listening with furrowed brow to Hope discoursing on fourth-dimensional geometry. But it was Gerald who caught fire. Hope's fanatic self-education, his retention of peculiar, esoteric detail, was his most important legacy to Gerald.

There were others. The décor at Miserden was a jam-packed mixture of Edwardian clutter and chintz and the Far East – Benares trays, brass frogs and lizards, hollow elephant's feet.[21] During the last few years a new 'Cotswold' movement had come to the area, an anti-Victorian, Ruskin/Morris inspired cult of craftsmanship and simplicity. A key figure was Edward Gimson the architect, whom Gerald had met, through the MacMeekans. Gimson, as far as Gerald went, held a revolutionary doctrine: death to the drawing room – bare stone walls, plain tables, an oak cupboard, a silk hanging. Gerald thought it absolutely beautiful. Now he saw the same with Hope; simplicity, bareness, a few but, despite his extreme poverty, perfect objects – a polychrome Delft bowl with a blue peacock on it, white and gold Worcestershire teacups.

Even then, Gerald noticed flaws, demonstrating a percipience about people at eighteen which showed him Hope's lack of it. He had a glossy impermeability, some inner blindness or deadness which made it difficult for him to understand people. He preferred ideas.

And Hope was totally subversive – Gide-like. Despising money, needing to exploit the rich, he was the enemy of the family; work, marriage, politics were all quite ridiculous. All that mattered was knowledge, to travel, and to study 'the arts and sciences and to cultivate one's higher faculties'.

Gerald's rebellion had begun some time before. During the masturbation crisis, panic had led him to prayer. Miraculously, you might think, his urine had lost its lurid tinge and his 'flu cleared up. But a boy in the next room had died of meningitis. Gerald took this as a condemnation of prayer and, he says, never prayed again. This was sealed a year later, in the summer of 1911. Under the influence of his reading, Gerald used to take his books at Radley and lie beside a pond. One day, after, as it were, a slug of Shelley, he suddenly stood up and said loudly, 'I do not believe in God.' He awaited a cataclysm, but nothing happened. Still he waited. Still nothing. He had destroyed the baleful Victorian 'God who has made so many atheists, the crude and repressive Father Deity who had cast over the world the image of his frown'.

Yet Gerald never became an atheist himself. He retained a feeling for religion all his life, sometimes seeming to flirt closer than the edges. But he was, now, in effect, creating from his reading, from Hope, from himself, his own religion.

To the young, all books are manuals. He had been reading William Morris and H. G. Wells; but the book that had prompted his outburst – and also presumably the pond – was Henry Thoreau's *Walden*, ironically enough a copy belonging to his mother.

The whole of *Walden* is a sustained attack on the materialistic world, and a fierce argument to escape into self-sufficiency and self-exploration. A man had to respond to his inner nature, not get stuck in the 'deep ruts of tradition and conformity'. The vast majority of people were quite simply fast asleep all the time – they did not *feel*, did not 'inwardly explore . . . [their] own higher latitudes'. Only one thing he could not respond to – the book is Thoreau's account of two years beside Walden Pond in Concord, Massachusetts – there was no travelling. Gerald was not yet ready to sit beside a pond.

For the rest, he felt he might have written the last pages of it himself. It had as great an influence on him as Shelley, and this down to the minutest particulars. Thoreau, a transcendentalist, stressed the importance of dreams. Throughout his life, Gerald had the most extraordinary dreams, which he sometimes wrote down. They are both delightful and witty. There can be few people who dream publishable dreams, as Gerald did.

But principally he looked with Thoreau's eyes along the clogged length of his parents' deep ruts of conformity – and was appalled. So far from self-sufficiency, the place swarmed with servants: gardener/ chauffeur and a handyman outside; cook, housemaid, parlour-maid inside. The house was too hot (central heating was still quite new then); the food was over-plentiful and largely, somehow obtrusively, for carnivorous appetites. The meat, for instance, was often high.[22] Glowering in the dark dining room, eating high beef or chunks of pig (the Miserden butcher did all his own slaughtering), the words of *Walden* must have rung in his ears: 'I eat at a table where were rich food and wine in abundance, and obsequious attendance, but sincerity and truth were not.'

Gerald's life now became, over the years of seventeen and eighteen, more and more ascetic. He gave up lunch, then reduced breakfast to a snack. He forced himself from bed at five o'clock and went for long walks. This was not a simple reaction against gorging. His parents were asleep, dead. Gerald wanted life, to live every day, every hour as intensely as possible. Food clogged the mind, impeding and coarsening exploration, vision.

To this end, drawing on Culpeper's *Herbal* and his reading about the East, and actively advised and assisted by Hope, he began to experiment with drugs and other exotic substances. Hope gave him the name of a chemist in London, Lowe. Gerald sent for, and obtained, a startling list: 'storax, olibanium, galbanum, laudanum, frankincense, liquid amber, benzoin, acorus calamus, Balsam of Tola,

Balsam of Copaiba, Balm of Gilead, ginseng, galingale, ylang-ylang, ambergris, attar of roses'. He wrote for 'some gambir, the produce of the *Nanchia* or *Unicaria gambir* from the East Indies: it is taken by the Malays to chew . . .' Mr Lowe, apparently shrinking from this (Gerald kept the letter), sent instead a 'big, blackish-green lump of Cannabis *indica*, or hashish, and a bottle of *Anhalonium Lewinii*, the active principal of mescal'.

Gerald's room, too, was now transformed. The large cupboard next to the fire was cleared of his collection of fossils and flowers and birds' eggs (the very stuff of a solitary boy) and replaced by hashish, ylang-ylang and the rest. Then: 'Fresh herbs were strewn on the floor in place of a carpet and bundles of roots and dried herbs hung from the walls. The letters *Om Mani Padine Hom* were written in charcoal over the bed and on the opposite wall was a piece of cardboard inscribed *Aum Shivaya Vashi*. From the ceiling hung a revolving incense burner of my own invention that sent out three different sorts of incense smoke at the same time, while the window recess contained a colour plate of Buddha sitting under a Bo tree, which I regarded as a good subject for contemplation.'

Gerald now adds drily an observation that has for some time been gathering in the reader's mind. 'Not exactly,' he writes, 'the sort of room, my parents must have felt, for a youth who would shortly be applying for a commission in His Majesty's Forces.'

Clearly, Gerald's parents had lost control. His mother, somewhat in advance of her time, had a neurotic fear of drugs. This was so great she would not even have aspirin in the house. Her son had now openly installed such a cache as would, today, get him either instantly clapped into gaol or given a large fine. Her reaction was to pretend that nothing was happening, though she did begin to tease Gerald, which maddened him. And, fearful that her own youthful eccentricities had returned much magnified, she redoubled her support for the Army. Gerald, according to his niece Ann Cary, never forgave his mother for supporting his father in such matters. One might think he could hardly have expected anything else. Yet psychologically he was right, for she had prepared the ground.

All this was to become much more difficult when Gerald's rebellion became open. But he was still too frightened. To the outside world, his father was a fussy, insignificant little man, made irritable by deafness, who bullied his wife. To Gerald he was terrifying – and remained so for many years (in imagination perhaps for ever – he was still having nightmares about him in his mid-seventies).[23] The cunning thing about his behaviour in 1912 was that it was within family bounds – just. There was a tradition that he could do what he liked in his room, and that he could miss meals provided he gave notice. His father had a fetish about dress (they changed for dinner every night, for instance – though this was still fairly common). Gerald grew his hair as long as he dared, as Dowden told him Shelley had done. But he was very careful sartorially, never taking off his collar and tie until out of sight of the house. His father had no idea of the explosion that was building; and a sign of this – and also of a certain sensitivity on Hugh Brenan's part – is that Gerald was allowed to give up shooting about now, something he had always disliked.[23] His father, since Radley had clearly failed, also put his trust in the Army. When Wilson-Green wrote saying he didn't think Gerald was really suitable for it, Hugh Brenan wrote a furious letter back. How *dare* he suggest such a thing!

But in private, his parents were extremely worried. His mother asked Hope if he thought Gerald was 'quite mad'. One night he overheard them talking about him. He heard the words 'mad', 'cracked'; even, he thought, asylum and reformatory. They were clearly considering having him shut up.

When the tides of rebellion have passed, the rocks of childhood and youth are found to remain. Gerald was later to feel he'd half-loved the stagnation, the conventionality, the deep dead sleep of English upper-class country life. It gave him a special sense for the great boredom of Spain – the infinite boredom of a *pueblo* at midday beneath the hammer of the summer sun, its timeless quality, when not even the flies can move. In a flight, he even imagined it under-pinned his ambition to write the timeless sentence, to prefer artists who arrest the flow – Cézanne to Rubens, Flaubert before Balzac, Gogol to Dostoevsky.[2] Above all, he might have added, Proust.

But now his contempt and disgust spread out to encompass all their friends, 'elderly, wooden and philistine', with their bridge, their hunting and shooting. Mrs Chrissie James, with 'a profusion of reddish-purplish veins that spread like the map of a river system over her cheeks', or Mrs Hewitt with Chippendale chairs too precious to sit on. Harmless figures, if dull, to whom they went for tea and invited back, about whom his mother gossiped, but who now, in the heat of Gerald's reading, were like people seen through the quivering air above a bonfire, distorted and loathsome.

His ideas coalesced like this, in a series of jumps and discoveries, from observations made in rage, from books, from his own experiences. By 1911 he had joined his disgust at material possessions and his hatred of Radley to the old fantasies of travel. A paper preserved from this time set it out. Happiness came from freedom, no one could be free with material possessions, therefore: the nomadic life.[24] The great problem was – how to organise it?

The nomadic life could also be expected to provide something else: privation, discomfort and pain. Gerald had noticed that starvation, the arduous walks at dawn, had produced the intensity of feeling that he sought. In 1911 or 1912 he had a revelation about this. It took place at the dentist. There were no local anaesthetics then and visits were often painful. He went dutifully to Mr Peake twice a year. One visit, he noticed that 'some clouds were scudding by and as I watched them, so far away, so remote from the scene of my pain, I became aware of their peculiar beauty . . . like a paradise I was forbidden to enter . . .'

His nature experiences had often had this element of a path leading somewhere – the passage through the reeds in India, the moon on the sea. Suddenly, he had found the gate – pain. And these exalted, intense experiences were necessary for poetry. Shelley had said this – but Shelley had said ecstasy came haphazardly. Gerald did not agree. You could induce it. The more he induced it, the better his poetry (which was very bad) would become.

And there was another side, which we have touched on; one he did not explore, was perhaps not even aware of. Sexual pleasure is also one of the most intense experiences. Gerald was at his potential height at this time, but also violently repressing himself. These exalted experiences had, hovering over them, an invisible sexual element. That this was painful was due to that masochistic streak he had noticed in his mother and which he shared.

At the beginning of 1912, the nomadic problem was partly solved. While he was browsing in a Stroud bookshop (for years he'd spent all his pocket money on books),* the young girl assistant suggested he

---

* For some years Gerald augmented his pocket money by stealing from his mother. He justified this by the nobility of his aims compared to hers .

read W. H. Davies' *The Autobiography of a Super-Tramp*. She might, says Gerald, as well have handed him a bomb. But the bomb was already in place – it was a lit fuse.

It only, however, moved the problem further on. The nomadic life could be lived as a tramp – but how would he support himself? He cannot have felt he was really cut out for any of the occupations Davies suggested: artificial flower maker, hymn-singer, street musician. And it was now becoming urgent. He took his exam to Sandhurst in July. As he ended his time at school, Gerald quailed with horror at the prospect ahead.

9

It is difficult to exaggerate the effects that Radley and Winton House together had on Gerald's character. In the first place, he was given the grounding of a good secondary education. Gerald often writes as if he were virtually self-educated, which was true as regards anything more than this. But Radley had taught him a full range of subjects up to the equivalent of today's A-levels.

As far as more profound effects go, Gerald himself cites only two: extreme diffidence and shyness, and a dread of aggression. A certain diffidence, with strangers, was lifelong; with a corollary that the relief of it vanishing, as it instantly did with anyone congenial, often led to over-excitement. His horror of aggression lasted many years. Frances Partridge can remember how in his late thirties he would still rush from the room at Ham Spray if any fierce, logical argument developed. 'There is nothing under different circumstances I might not be capable of except cruelty, my horror of which is the deepest thing in me.'[25]

Like Shelley, what he had suffered led him to identify with all suffering; his compassion expanded to cover humanity. His feeling for the poor derived from this; as did his extraordinary sweetness all his life to those in trouble.

His experience of group life – the mob in the swimming pool, the swaggering 'bloods' – expanded likewise into a deep distrust of all groups and cliques. This was behind his criticism of Bloomsbury. If there was any danger of his being incorporated, he would walk away – onto the streets, out to Spain. Loving company, he now almost equally loved solitude – source of bliss, but also of sadness. Walking away gives a sense of power and of despair. He made a note on a dream he had in 1970 while writing *Personal Record*. 'That's me all over. Wanting to escape and hide. Wanting to be left out. Put that in your autobiography for that's the essence of you. Not all those stupid things you're writing down.'[24]

He was never at ease with dominant men, yet the closest male friendship of his life was with someone, himself complex, in whom dominance was certainly one characteristic. Gerald's relationship with Ralph Partridge was constantly stirred by, among much else, his feeling that he had to face this challenge.

Another reaction to his father and the schools was that he seemed to have decided at some buried level that he would never again do what was expected – or what other people expected. Gerald's perversity was often extreme. He would disagree automatically. Perfectly good, badly needed offers would arrive from publishers or universities – 'Naturally, I refused immediately.'

'Naturally.' Here we begin to approach the heart of what seems to have happened to him.

To do the opposite of what people expect, or to advance views opposite to what you think, is partly a form of disguise, of hiding what you actually think or wish to do. The frank little boy had now totally changed. 'I grew up in a bitterly hostile world – my school and to a certain extent my home – and I learnt to protect myself. There were . . . incidents of misplaced frankness and deep humiliation and they cured me of ever wanting to tell the truth to other people.'[26] 'What does it matter how many people are taken in,' he once wrote to Bunny Garnett, 'if one does not take in oneself?'*[27]

The rows between his parents, their opposing temperaments, might have set up conflicts in his own character. Gerald resolved this rather neatly. He simply allowed them to sink in unchanged, and let each operate as the occasion dictated. Frequently throughout his life, he noted when he wrote it, he could explain his behaviour by one or other of them surfacing in this way.

But now, under the onslaughts of Radley and Winton House, a much more general burying had taken place. The boarding-school

---

* 'If' is the key word here. His vulnerability to self-deception never struck Gerald, and he was often taking himself in. This attitude to the truth persisted and can make his letters tricky to evaluate.

experience is a long, endlessly repeated lesson in loss. The constant returns to home, to mother, only to be ripped away each term, starting at the age of eight or nine, don't mitigate this pain; they reinforce it. In Gerald's case they came as a double reinforcement to the devastating loss of his beloved Nana. And prep and public schools then did not tolerate the expression of strong personal feelings; they therefore became buried.

Many prep and public schoolboys of Gerald's generation, not allowed to show or admit to feelings, eventually ceased to have them. This did not happen to Gerald; on the contrary. But he was to have difficulty with emotions and feelings all his life. His sudden reserve, the way he sometimes seemed able to control his feelings, to become detached, could shock people.

He was, of course, aware of this – to an extent. 'But I do have a heart,' he once wrote to Frances Partridge, 'though it only comes out in emergencies. I have often envied the loyalty of your nature. It is your finest quality. I am disloyal in tongue and sometimes in feeling. I need crises to bring out the best in me, to tell me where I stand and what I really feel. All the rest is a stream of surface impressions, for I have the most mobile and disorientated mind in the world.'[25]

If you bury feelings, a great many other things get sucked down too. Not just emotion, but whole processes of thought, ideas, creativity. Once it is understood that something of this sort had happened to Gerald, much that might seem contradictory or odd in his life ahead becomes clearer. It was noticeable quite early. As a youth and young man he could be extraordinarily vague and absent-minded. His friends were genuinely worried that he might step in front of buses or walk over a cliff.

By the 1930s, when V. S. Pritchett met him, there was a sense, sometimes, of something impersonal about him, 'as if he came from another world'.[28] It was an inner world, intense, active, full of contradictions, often quite bizarre; Gerald used various metaphors to try and describe it and its genesis.

'I was brought up to think that people more often dislike me than like me, and though experience shows me that this is not always true, still every time I experience coldness or enmity where I did not expect it, I return into myself – to the island which I alone inhabit and whose protection I feel I ought never to have left.'[29] Potent as the island image was for him, he hit on a more telling one on the single occasion when he made an extraordinary descent into that hidden territory and returned to write, in one feverish week, an equally extraordinary account which he called *The Lord of the Castle*.

The idea of an interior castle contains both a sense of defence, and of a place from which to launch an attack. And castles can have hundreds of rooms – libraries, bedchambers, kitchens, towers from which to survey the surrounding countryside, dungeons for criminals or the mad; and the people in one set of rooms might be astounded or deeply shocked if they knew about some of the things going on in another.

The schools also intensified a final facet of Gerald's character that was about to make its first explosive appearance. Solitary, already living much of his time in books, in poetry, and the rest in his imagination, it was probably inevitable that he would have been a romantic. But prep and public schools involve separation from family and parents, who are therefore missed and nostalgically and romantically dreamt of. The same is true of sex. Girls are fantasised about and glorified. Fantasy and unreality in such fundamental areas twist the whole personality; romanticism becomes inherent.

Gerald went to considerable lengths both to reveal (almost boast about) the romantic cast to his life, and to deny any trace of it. In the same way, in his letters and conversation truth was one of the things he was most concerned about – and the least. The contradictions and complexities arising from the distortions of his character consequent on Radley and Winton House, their evolution, his efforts to escape them or come to terms with them, were to occupy him for his remaining seventy-five years. They may not have made him a writer, but they made him the sort of writer he became. The contest fascinated him, sometimes obsessed him; it was often difficult. 'I was like a man engaged in a motorcycle race whose engine gave him so much trouble that he was compelled to give more attention to it than to the course.'[30]

10

It is probably to understate the urgency and seriousness of Gerald's dilemma in the spring and summer of 1912 to call his reaction merely an explosion of the romantic temperament.

His father had never yet been openly defied with any determination by anyone in the household. He had a strong will. He was adamant that Gerald should go into the Army. Gerald was planning to fail the entrance exam into Sandhurst. But even if he did that, he now believed his parents would send him to a reformatory.

A glimmer of a solution came during the spring holidays of 1912. The family went to Dinard, and Gerald was allowed to go on a two-week bicycling holiday alone into the interior of Brittany. As he rode inland, the air filled with the scent of hawthorns, the blazing gorse, he felt as if he was returning to the seventeenth century. The peasants, astonishingly, still wore traditional costume: the women in a woven and starched *coif*, the men in a short jacket or blouse and broad-brimmed hat, with two ribbons down the shoulders. Stepping off the ferry at Bénodet, Gerald noticed an old man under a tree with a beard and a donkey pulling a curious vehicle like a barrel organ. He was an itinerant knife-grinder. He had travelled all over Europe, to Russia, the Balkans, Turkey, even, Gerald thought – was he dreaming? – to the Caucasus and Anatolia. There were knives everywhere. 'And the further East one went, the more knives there were and the sharper they had to be.'

So the last piece of puzzle fell into place. If the time ever came when he needed to be a tramp, this was how he'd support himself.

On his return to Radley that summer, his mind concentrated by the approaching exams, he realised the time had come already. Flight was the only solution. And, lying in the sanatorium with bronchitis, he saw other advantages. Dependent on his skills as a knife-grinder, he would of necessity be poor – itself an aim. Poverty would produce pain and suffering which in turn would lead to those states of exultation that, good in themselves, would also improve his poetry.

No sooner had he decided, than he became intensely nervous. It might be easier, and more pleasant, to have a companion. Who better than his mentor Hope? He wrote a letter from his bed. He was setting off in August, plus a knife-grinding machine, for Asia. He'd probably settle east of the Pamirs, among the tents of the Kirghizi. Why didn't Hope join him?

Gerald waited three agonising weeks and them came the reply: Yes.

Writing years later, he says he found the reply, in retrospect, astonishing. Here was a man nearly thirty, agreeing to set out on a crackpot, near impossible journey with an over-intense, over-talkative eighteen-year-old he hardly knew. This is true, but Hope was in difficulties too. Augustus John was bored of him. He kept on finding his drawings and books disappearing and suspected Hope (rightly) of stealing them. Without his job, Hope was penniless – and his solution on these occasions was to take to the road. Besides, as their instigator, he approved of Gerald's aims.

The Sandhurst exam was in June. Gerald passed. It was virtually impossible then, if you were upper class and from a public school, to be too stupid to hold a commission in the Army.

Thus the die was cast. Gerald returned to Miserden seething with suppressed excitement. The next seven months were to produce events both of heroism and high farce, a combination not infrequent in Gerald's life from now on.

FIVE

The Walk

'I dreamed that I was a white hare leaping through a dark forest. Following a narrow path I came to the edge of the trees and saw the stars showing through a rift in the clouds. I saw one particular constellation, then raced back under the trees.

'This was a very moving dream (1916) and has always been very important to me because it showed that the hare was my totem animal. I too lived by flight and escape.'

Thoughts in a Dry Season

1

The 1912 summer term at Radley ended on 30 July. Almost as soon as he reached Miserden, Gerald hurried over to Hope's cottage. They seem to have decided, in the interests of secrecy, that they should only have one meeting. The discussion, therefore, was intense.

Hope, in any case on the verge of the sack, now seems to have caught fire from his highly excited friend. He said that in his view the ultimate goal must be China. Gerald said there could be no question of his going beyond the borders of Takla Makan. Here he would stop and join for life some possessionless, nomadic tribe. There were other disagreements. Hope vetoed knife-grinding. A grinder was an impossible vehicle for their kit. He suggested a donkey and cart. His experience of cut-price travel suggested their joint capital – £32 (say £1300) – would be ample.

Gerald, desperate to escape, his father already giving advice about Sandhurst, agreed to everything. He even allowed Hope to re-direct his own swift route to Yugoslavia via the St Bernard Pass and northern Italy, to a more meandering one via Provence, Florence and Venice: more beautiful, Hope said, more interesting galleries and architecture. But anxiety over money made Gerald insist on one thing – they must go prepared to sell quack medicines. To this end they would take galingale, extract of an Asian root used by quacks because of its medicinal smell. They argued over books. Finally, they agreed to meet in Paris on 27 August.

Now Gerald laid his own plans. What should he take? Hope had suggested as many grammars as possible; Gerald, his anxiety switching to food, wanted cookery books; Culpeper's *Herbal* for the quack medicines; laudanum, incense and hashish for exaltation; plus essential reading – Shelley, Blake, Yeats and William Morris. All this was packed up and despatched secretly to Hope. Only *Walden*, and the drugs, were kept out.

Next, disguise. A Radley friend, Douglas-Jones, had agreed to pretend Gerald was staying with him, and delay pursuit. But pursuit there would certainly be, even extradition. Disguise, therefore, was essential. Gerald sent to London for black hair dye, a false moustache and a long cloak with stars (this to facilitate the medical sales). The cloak proved too expensive, but the other two items arrived. To evade pursuit he had decided to travel – in a first acting-out of H. G. Wells – as a gas fitter. He went to Cheltenham and bought a shiny black bag, a high butterfly collar, a purple bow tie, and a tall bowler hat. Then, his imagination now at white heat, he went into a newsagent and bought *The Gas World*. He also obtained brochures for trips to America.

Into this euphoric dottiness struck shafts of common sense. It would be cold in Yugoslavia and Turkey during the winter. Amongst the boxes in the attic he found an old uniform coat. Tight-waisted, and also an extremely tight fit, billowing into 'ample skirts', it was faded now, smelling of moth balls – but warm.

Money was the preparation that gave most anxiety, as well as being the most important. Gerald was cheated over his valuable stamp collection, being paid mostly in useless second-hand books. Then the post office in Cirencester refused to cash his savings and Gerald had to go to London. But on this occasion he did not steal from his mother. The journey had already taken on religious significance – a religion in which the way, the journey itself, was also the goal; he would not sully his ideals by theft.

And all this had to take place while ordinary life went on. His at times barely controllable excitement had to be stifled for tea with the MacMeekans or tennis at the Mills'. He had to listen, seething, while his father gave him advice on officer cadetship and his mother lightly teased him.

On his last night, he could not sleep at all. He put the American travel brochures on the top of his waste paper basket. He slipped out and took some of his father's spanners to pass as gas-fitter's tools. Then he packed his escape clothes and equipment, including a trowel, into his going-away suitcase. Most of the rest of the night he spent writing a long letter to his mother in which he at last expressed the rage that had been gathering in him for the past three years: his anger at his father, his loathing of their conventional life and their hypocrisy, his antipathy to the Army. He underlined most of the last paragraphs of *Walden* and directed his mother to them, then slipped out and posted the letter to Douglas-Jones. He told him to give it to his mother when his flight was discovered.

The next day, 26 August 1912, after deceitfully casual goodbyes, he set out for Paris.

2

The route was at first highly devious. Their chauffeur drove him to Cirencester, his bicycle on the roof of the car to use during his visit away. But once left at the station, Gerald started to put the various cogs of his plan smoothly into motion. Concealing himself in the gents' toilet at the station, he emptied his case of gas-fitter's garb and equipment and drugs, and unfolded his military coat. Having left the suitcase behind, he tied those to his bicycle. Thus encumbered, he set off for Southampton.

But now things began to go wrong. There was a strong head wind, and it soon began to rain. By Swindon, he realised he would miss the ferry. A change of plan was necessary. He would sell the bicycle in Marlborough and take the train to Southampton. It was time to don his disguise. Slipping behind a haystack, he put on his collar and tie and gas fitter's suit, poured the dye over his hair, and got into the overcoat. He baulked only at the moustache, which was enormous. Then he buried his suit with the trowel (every detail had been covered) and set off again.

By Marlborough, the rain was driving, and the dye was running down the gas-fitter's neck. To his astonishment, no one would buy the bike, even though it was almost new, even when he reduced the price to a pound. Shop after shop refused. But time was pressing. He was standing on the station platform waiting for a train, planning to sell the bike later, when a policeman came up. In Gerald's account, he is a figure out of musical comedy. 'I hunderstand . . .' etc. Could Gerald *prove* the bicycle was his?

Appalled, already fearing pursuit, Gerald realised his danger. He could be detained while the police checked his story with his parents. He was forced to use the one advantage he most despised, the one, indeed, that was half the cause of the entire venture – class. But it was an advantage, at that time, formidable indeed. His accent alone was 'a weapon that, among the gentry, had replaced the sword'. He produced a card of his father's. He was on his way to a friend, and had dressed up for a lark. With a confident smile Gerald produced the huge moustache as proof.

It worked just long enough to bewilder the policeman. At that moment the train came in. Gerald thrust the bicycle at him and told him he could keep it. He leapt aboard and the train pulled out.

This unforeseen event nearly proved fatal. In fact, Gerald was saved not by the various deceptions designed to this end, but by the humble gas-fitter's tools. Using his father's card, the police at Marlborough telephoned Cirencester. Soon, the constable at Miserden was at the house asking the cook if 'the young master' had left the house that morning with his bicycle; and a little later cook was telling Gerald's father that the police had the bicycle in safe custody. Hugh Brenan, assuming a theft, and having nothing better to do, decided on an officious visit to Cirencester. Maddeningly, the car wouldn't start. When he looked for his spanners, he couldn't find them. By the time a man had come and put things right, it was too late. Hugh Brenan put his visit off.

Next day the terrible truth came tumbling out: Gerald's flight, his letter, the brochures, the lot. Opening *Walden* as directed, his mother must have read with sinking heart that if someone 'advances confidently in the direction of his dreams, and endeavours to lead the life he has imagined, he will meet with success unexpected in common hours'. If Gerald was not like other people 'perhaps it is because he hears a different drummer'.

In fact, had it not been for the spanners, it is conceivable he would have been caught. Barking commands down the telephone, his father not only alerted the police, he engaged a private detective. Gerald was not, to put it mildly, an inconspicuous figure. He was rapidly traced from the Marlborough train to Southampton, and then to the Le Havre ferry. But by this time it was too late. Gerald was already in Paris. He and his parents were not to meet for another six months.

3

The first thing Gerald discovered in Paris was that the *rendezvous* hotel Hope had suggested did not exist. His panic subsided a little when he remembered Hope had also said 'by the Botticelli fresco in the Louvre'. They met on Gerald's way there, on the Pont Neuf.

One look at the gas-fitter, and Hope suggested new clothes. The bowler and suit were sold, the military coat kept. They bought French workmen's clothes: two blue cotton jackets, trousers (Hope's blue velveteen, fashionably wide at the hips; Gerald's straight black corduroy); a Breton beret pulled over one ear.

Next, they had to resolve their luggage. Hope was a man who could not move, like a snail with its house, without his shell of books. Fifty volumes were strewn about his little hotel bedroom, some large. Light reading was whittled ruthlessly, leaving relatively few: Shelley and Blake and Yeats of course, also Angela de Foligno's *Visions* and Aleister Crowley's *The Bhagavadgita Book 777*. Gerald protested, on the grounds of weight, at a six-volume edition of Gibbon. In fact, it was the only one he read completely – the first of many readings. Hope, who had never been enthusiastic about quack medicines, had forgotten Gerald's Culpeper's *Herbal*, probably on purpose. Gerald was also dismayed to see no cookery book.

Since the journey was the point, grammars were essential. One for every country they might pass through, and where Hope had none (Mongolia, Tosk, Kirghizi) Bible Society booklets. Maps do not seem to have been an item. Family legend – the journey is dimly remembered to this day – has it that they had only a school atlas and drew a rough map in chalk on the bottom of their cart.[1]

The plan was that they should take a train to Valence, about fifty miles below Lyons, where they would buy a donkey and cart. Gerald, still terrified of police pursuit, wanted to start as soon as possible. But all these activities – getting a sack and cord for the books (Hope's suitcase had disintegrated), but mainly Hope's need to see the Louvre properly – meant that it wasn't until Friday 30 August that they climbed into a third-class carriage – another first time – for one of those interminable, crowded, smelly, noisy, hot, wooden-seated, smut-filled journeys south, so evocative, so uncomfortable, but for Gerald, at long last, so real.

It was dark when they arrived in Valence, and they took rooms in the café-restaurant Joubert near the square. The next day they bought a small cart for 100 francs, but it proved impossible to find a donkey. The remainder of the journey's purchases were quickly made. Gerald, still anxious about food and no doubt with the kitchen at Miserden vaguely in mind, suggested various pots, a grill pan, kettle, tea, cookery books . . . Hope, who was in fact rather a good cook in the French style,[2] swept it all aside. The point was simplicity. Most of their food would be stolen or begged. A simple iron cooking pot, a rod to suspend it, earthenware bowls and some cutlery would be ample. As for tea and coffee, they were drugs and would cloud the mind. Hashish, with its vision-inducing power, was the only drug they'd be allowed. Gerald was thrilled. They also bought a tarpaulin to cover everything and to use as a tent.

Valence is less than 200 kilometres north of Marseilles and it was now mid-summer. Gerald bought a light woollen shirt which came to his knees. This he wore the whole time, day and night, occasionally washing it. (Neither then, nor ever, was Gerald over-addicted to middle-class cleanliness.) His other shirt he threw away, since it came from Radley.

Thus equipped, they set off down the Rhône valley at 2.30 in the afternoon of 2 September, Gerald pulling, Hope, in a desultory way, pushing. (The times and places, up to 29 December, with short comments, were meticulously transcribed into a 1917 diary.)[3]

Something had occurred earlier, and did so quite soon now, which suggests that there was, as far as Gerald was concerned, an important unspoken aim to the journey. To the English, France at that period meant sexual freedom. At supper in Paris on the 28th, two tarts had come up to their table, soliciting. At once Gerald had thought, for just 10 francs, he could 'achieve that enormous, that almost inconceivable thing – going to bed with a girl'. A few days down the Rhône, covered in dust from the cement factories and very hot, they stopped one afternoon for wine. A blousy young girl dressed in nothing but a cotton frock, got on to Hope's knee and, shoving her hand inside his trousers, said, 'Come into the back room. It'll only cost you five francs. I'll make it worth your while.' Hope, while expressing approval – 'Just a proposal and a price. That's how it should be' – was in fact intensely embarrassed.

But Gerald was at once, again, very excited. Her youth, her over-ripe sexual appearance, her nakedness under her dress (to become for him a potent image, perhaps because it aroused echoes of Célestine), all set him on fire. He longed to return. Typically, in *A Life* . . . , he partly conceals the simple desire to lose his virginity, the straight-forward and clearly powerful sexual impulse, by also making it part of the scouring-off process the walk symbolised: 'I hankered for sordidness – sordidness of situation, sordidness of act – because I thought that that would help me wash away my sheltered upbringing and to plant me more firmly in reality.' It was to be quite a number of years – precisely when, it is impossible to determine – before he managed to achieve that 'sordidness of act'.

On 7 September, they bought a donkey for 100 francs at Bourg St Andéol, a tiny Guedir which they renamed Mr Bird. Mr Bird had an excellent character and had been trained as a circus donkey. He could do various small tricks and occasionally danced.[4]

And, with Mr Bird dancing in the pages, we can follow them in the brief entries of Gerald's diary as they travelled, very, very slowly, through some of the most beautiful scenery in the world: 'Mon 8th – Orange. 10th – Avignon, slept under the trees. 12th – Arles – slept near gypsies.' They rose at dawn and were on the road before the stars had gone. Breakfast – bread, milk, honey – came after two hours. We can follow their course today: to Avignon on the N7, Les Baux (D571 and D5), then Salon ('Stole quinces') on the N113. But the roads then were virtually empty, the traffic still mostly horse-drawn. As they walked through the clear cool mornings they read: Gibbon for Gerald, grammars for Hope, getting his grounding in Persian and Arabic. Hope, extremely good-looking, slim in his sky-

blue velveteen trousers and broad-brimmed black hat, clearly conscious of the romantic figure he cut, would take out his pipe and play
the 'Old Jamaica Air' or, more lovely still, the setting of Mistral's *O
Magali*. Then the grey olives, the vines, the whole sun-drenched
landscape would seem 'to sway and dance to the tune . . . At such
moments there was no romantic part into which I could not fit him.
Bedouin by the desert thorn-scrub fire, Alastor on the lone Chorasur-
ian shore, long-sleeved, flute-fingering magician, playing the air that
brought the puppet world to life. Whenever I saw him at such times
he diffused strangeness and mystery.'

And so they slowly continued till the sun reached its height. By
this time Mr Bird had done anything between ten and twenty miles,
and travelling was over for the day. They pitched the tarpaulin tent
and had lunch – bread, cream cheese, grapes. Then came the endless
hot afternoon when they longed for the evening. They'd sleep or
read. Gerald would go for a walk in the heat, steal vegetables or fruit
for supper. The high aim of their pilgrimage, their poverty, made
such petty pilfering highly meritorious. Finally, the sun would sink,
the cicadas seem to grow louder. As it became dark, they'd light a
fire of olive wood, hang the pot and toss in potatoes, carrots, green
vegetables and a Maggi soup tablet, along with thyme and other wild
herbs. It was so delicious that it constituted their sole meal during
the entire time on the cart. After this, throwing an occasional branch
onto the fire, they talked – especially did Hope talk, telling Gerald
about his life, reading him poetry, dispensing from his enormous
store of endlessly interesting knowledge. Eventually, they would
settle for the night, sleeping under the stars, Mr Bird tethered
nearby. Sometimes the little circus donkey would become lonely and
Gerald would feel his soft nose and hot breath on his cheek.

A year later Hope was to write, 'You are one of those people who
get helped.'[5] This was acute. Gerald, as time would show, was more
than capable of looking after himself. Yet he retained all his life, and
it was very appealing, a certain innocence and helplessness, an air of
vulnerabilty in the face of the world. Though he never thought
he was good-looking ('When I look in the mirror I see my father'),[6]
photographs at this time, and Carrington's portrait later, show a face
capable of extraordinary intensity; and then youth! – with its
idealism, its vitality, its strength, and an enthusiasm which may have
sometimes bored Hope but must also have flattered him. It is clear

from later letters that he fell romantically in love with Gerald and remained so for two or three years.[7]

And what of Gerald's feelings for this pipe-playing magician seen through clouds of 'hashish' in the light of the fire? It is noticeable that throughout his life Gerald's close male friends were strikingly good-looking. And Hope, with his fine-cut features and dark hair had, significant addition, an ivory skin, very clear and pure. 'I knew no one more sympathetic, more understanding, more charming.'[8] Or more intelligent. It was this last that both fascinated him and which dictated the level of emotional balance and – for both were aware of the slight tension – which made it possible. It was warm, friendly, with moments of great intellectual intimacy and also completely impersonal, off-hand and emotionally distant. They had no name for each other; surnames, Gerald noted, would have been too distant, Christian names too close. So they said 'Hello' and 'I say', with special emphasis – and this lasted *thirty years*!

'19th – St Maximin, camped in Dingle' (interesting entry – 'Dingle' is one of Borrow's favourite words). '21st – passed Sillom, where Mr Bird danced. 22nd – Draguignan . . . 25th – passed Grasse, slept in garden. 26th – Cagnes. 27th – passed Nice – slept quarry on Corniche Road.'

Between Grasse and Nice Gerald wrote his first recorded poem.

> I stand before the open door
> Of my new life, and yet I long
> To be that happy child once more
> And leave these hours of grief and wrong.[9]

A little later he recorded his mother's birthday in the diary. It was probably now he sent, to Hope's irritation, a long letter of self-justification to his parents, attempting to allay his own anxiety and pangs of guilt.

On 29 September they crossed the border into Italy. The weather began to break. It rained. Hope (an ominous weakness) insisted on two nights in a hotel at Ventimiglia. They bought umbrellas and continued slowly across Italy. More rain. The diary reflects increasing anxiety about where to sleep at night – the tramp's perennial nightmare: stable at Genoa (7 October), shed, Rista (8th); old rail tunnels, barns; '12th – camped in misty valley among chestnuts, stole vegetables.' On the 13th at Lerici, Gerald walked off alone to look at Shelley's house.[10]

Once they'd crossed the Apennines, the weather cleared but grew much colder. There were frosts at night. By Florence (22 October) Hope was beginning to crack. He discovered you could get a large *café au lait* for 15 centesimi, and insisted he had one every morning. They were now beginning to look distinctly odd and were at first refused entry into the Uffizi. They should at least have bought Italian workers' clothes but, as Gerald notes, their French ones had taken on the sanctity of a monk's habit. The aesthetic quality of their life, its purity and poverty had given it, to Gerald especially, a totally religious note. They even had their own language made up of ironic quotations from the Bible, scraps of Shelley, etc.

His parents were now – and one can hardly blame them – in a state of extreme anxiety about their son pressing on determinedly, and alone, for the mountains of Pamir. Family legend says 'it broke his mother's health'.[11] Aunts, uncles and cousins were roped in. At the *poste restante* Gerald found a huge bundle 'of moral and theological dissertations'. But at least they promised to send his usual £2 for Christmas – which he must use to come back. In any case, he at last felt safe from them – and the further east he and Hope went, the safer.

But the further east the colder and the more difficult to get food. At Ravenna (3–7 November), he remembered years later how he stared ravenously at the pastry in the shops.[12] He was deep in Gibbon and, in the wintry sun, imagined the invasion of the Ostrogoths and the collapse of Italy.

In Ravenna, too, they got into conversation with Reynolds Ball, a shabbily dressed young Englishman. He turned out to be a painter, with plans to become a blacksmith, at present tutoring in Venice. A 'vague, woolly-minded man,' wrote Gerald, 'sexless, confused on all issues, but with a benevolence that shone out in everything he did.' At first Gerald wanted to preserve inviolate their little order, but soon melted. Ball was to be one of his best friends for several years.

They agreed Reynolds Ball would come with them to Cavarzere, where he could catch the boat to Venice. But, struggling towards the Po marshes in a thick mist, Hope suddenly announced – further evidence of deterioration – that he wanted to go to Venice too. Gerald, desperate to press on, aware of dwindling money, was forced to acquiesce. He had one compensation. They overslept at Cavarzere and, leaving Mr Bird and the cart, had to race fourteen miles down the towpath to catch another boat at Chioggia. Still before dawn, having had no food or drink, soon exhausted, it was proper privation at last. Gerald's resulting exaltation fully bore out his theories about pain. What Hope thought or felt he doesn't record. One can gain an inkling from the fact he insisted they stay nine days in Venice, with large meals and beds with sheets. At Venice they saw Ball's paintings (lousy) and met his employers, the Wilsons – vegetarians and theosophists, and makers of art jewellery.

On 22 November, they returned to Cavarzere, and Gerald's account begins to read like some eighteenth-century picaresque novel. Their appearance was now so bizarre – children pointing in the streets and following them – that they were arrested on a charge of murder and spent the night in gaol. The following day the 'mistake' was admitted, and they were let out. After a frosty day in Padua, Gerald lying for most of it 'in the manger of a trattoria, covered in hay, reading the immortal Gibbon and the no less divine Shelley and chewing dry bread',[12] they set out on the last lap for the Balkans.

They crossed the Austrian border at Cerviguano, and, leaving Mr Bird at Aquieleja, made a detour into Sagrado on 2 December. Here, again, their appearance caused uproar. The police, irritated, arrested them as spies. They were put on a train to Monfalcone on the gulf of Trieste and once more thrown into gaol.

They were there for five days, a prey to boredom and hunger, hunger they partly dispelled by paying for one meal a day – wine, spaghetti, rolls. As for boredom, the prisoners had cut a hole in the cell shutter and could see across to the bedroom window of the gaoler's daughter: 'Whenever she appeared, which she did frequently, a burst of song would greet her. She would then kiss her hand, pretend she was going to undress' – and close her own shutters. By some quirk of association – perhaps Célestine again – the longing that this image evoked was to remain with Gerald for decades.

After further adventures out of eighteenth-century picaresque or even nineteenth-century *Boy's Own* fiction (at one point they were about to saw themselves free with a file), they were released, regained Mr Bird on payment of a huge bill, and on 7 December set off for Trieste.

Before this, an embarrassing disclosure had to be dealt with. The

Daily Telegraph, which Gerald's parents read, had a long report, giving names, of 'two undergraduates' arrested for espionage. Gerald wrote a quick letter explaining that he'd met Hope in Venice and then, getting carried away and safely out of their reach, an amusing account of gaol and how they'd nearly escaped by file and gutter. Would they send all letters and money to Rijeka?*

It was a long journey to Trieste, and dark long before they got there. They trudged for two hours through the freezing night, the lights twinkling ahead. They stayed an extra day in the city, to rest Mr Bird. Also, their papers were not in order to travel into what is now Yugoslavia, then Bosnia.† The consul, a kindly man, gave them a letter for the consul at Rijeka, who would give them (indeed *had* to give them) proper papers – *Reisekarten*.

Even more serious was money, which had now nearly all gone. Hope was expecting some from his elder brother. There was Gerald's Christmas money. With these two sums they now decided to cut out Bosnia (to avoid the Balkan War) and take a boat to Athens. The aim was Constantinople by the end of the winter. Quack medicines, too, seem to have been abandoned as too time-consuming. Gerald was now desperate to reach the Pamirs and settle down.

But at Rijeka – disaster. Never underestimate the reach of the English middle classes. One of Gerald's uncles knew the consul. When they went to collect their papers, this man – 'a sort of dwarf', Gerald angrily describes him – kicked them out. Then, after four days, another huge bundle of letters from home. Gerald's announcement of Hope may have allayed one anxiety – of him alone – only to replace it with one far more terrible (one, as we've seen, in fact, not totally wide of the mark). With horror, they recalled Hope's 'As Oscar used to say . . .' And Gerald's insouciance had maddened his father. What did Gerald mean, he asked furiously and inaccurately, by enjoying a walking tour at his expense? His mother said her hair was turning grey. Only his grandmother wrote a kind letter. She couldn't send her usual £2 for Christmas because Hugh wouldn't let her. His father and mother of course gave nothing.

They now had 30 lire left. They should have stayed cheaply in

---

* Gerald's account gives the names in Italian. I have given them as they are today, with the various border adjustments between Italy, Austria and Yugoslavia, though even as I write some of these may once again become out of date.

† And, again, as I write, probably Bosnia again.

Rijeka, but Hope insisted on a three-day expedition into the Balkans to see the Byzantine frescoes. Art was more important than food. The clear winter skies, the cleansing cold, the strong sense now of the east, the exaltation of starvation (they ate nothing at all the final day) – Gerald had to agree.

On 23 December Rijeka delivered its final blow. Hope's money arrived, and was – or so he said – far less than he'd expected.

It seems likely that Hope had decided some time before to winter in Venice. This he now announced. The austerities had become intolerable. It was madness to go on.

Gerald now had no money at all. He would have to continue on his share of selling Mr Bird and the cart. But no one would buy them. In the end they had to give them to the Rijeka innkeeper to pay for their stay. He gave for everything else – tarpaulin, pot, plates, etc. – the equivalent of 30 shillings. Hope handed it all to Gerald, adding 10 shillings. 'Generously,' says Gerald, with considerable generosity himself, considering he'd just been ditched.

On the dark afternoon of 23 December, Gerald set out alone, wearing the long, tight-waisted overcoat. On his back were a roll of two blankets, the blue Italian umbrella bought three months before, Blake, a Bible, and a cake of soap. He had £2 to get him over the last 3000-odd miles to the Pamirs.

4

That night he slept supperless in an empty shed. The next day brought the first calamity. His shoes had been long disintegrating. Now one sole fell off. The cobbler in Zenj said they were irreparable. Fortunately, he had a pair of high-heeled elastic-sided shoes for 25 shillings.

Still as obstinately determined as ever within, Gerald's surface nerve had gone now he was alone. He was gripped by shyness and timidity. People stared. He should have shopped around, but he had the heels cut off and bought the shoes. Three-quarters of his money had gone at a stroke.

The road from Zenj left the sea and headed up into the mountains. It was morning. That evening, Christmas Eve, Gerald was given shelter in a farm. In the small, hot, crowded, animated kitchen one man spoke English. They were astonished at his story. A collection was made for him. They gave him lots of beer and curdled milk and cabbage soup. A girl sat on his lap and, to cheers, said she'd go to bed with him. For a while Gerald imagined the 'inconceivable thing' might be about to happen. But that night, in the hayloft, he slept alone except for a very old man.

His account now becomes almost dreamlike. He was no longer able to fill in his diary, and an account he wrote for Hope in 1916, and on which he relied when writing *A Life* . . . , stopped at Rijeka. But it must indeed have seemed like a dream – or a nightmare.

Using a page torn from their cheap atlas, which showed neither roads nor villages, he kept south and east (but more south. The coast, since nearer Europe, meant safety); on and on, on unpaved, dirt roads, rutted and pitted, through stony valleys, mountains, forests, past rushing rivers and occasional isolated farms. It grew very cold, snowing frequently.

The great anxiety was where to sleep. Farms were free; but too early, they wouldn't let him in; too late, he risked being savaged by their half-wild guard dogs. Inns cost money. The worst fear was that he'd find nothing.

Finally, this happened. Late afternoon, then evening came without a house or shed in sight. In the growing darkness the road climbed into a forest, the snow drifting deep. Some way in, he heard wolves in the distance. Pouring with sweat through fear and exertion, he hurried on. After two hours, the road descended and at last cleared the trees. But Gerald now saw that an animal had left the forest too and was following him. Dog? Fox? Wolf? He ran at it with his blue umbrella and it loped off. Terrified again, he ran down the road. It was snowing again as he ran on and on, exhausted, at last almost in a trance: 'I was alone and in that aloneness found a sort of melancholy exhilaration.'

At length he came to a farm and was given shelter in a barn. Next day, as usual, he asked for work. They didn't even have enough for themselves. He should go inland towards Sarajevo. The farms were bigger and richer.

Gerald had been struggling on for about two weeks. He now turned due east into the same snow-covered landscape of mountain and plain, mountain and plain, into the Dinaric Alps. It was icy cold.

At each step he felt the safety and warmth of the coast dragging at his back. This, he knew, was the ultimate test.

It was too much. 'One dark evening, in a snow storm, on a Bosnian mountain, I turned back.'[13] In *A Life* . . . he says he turned and raced for the coast road below Spoleto (now Split). But the 1911 Baedeker,[14] on which it is possible to trace his likely route, shows he probably struck it somewhere near Ragusa (now Dubrovnik). Towards the end of January 1913, after further vicissitudes, he was back in Venice.

The relief was enormous. It was not wholly shared by his friends. Hope, comfortably installed in Ball's place as the Wilson tutor, was fairly appalled to see him. Wilson himself had a reputation for parsimony (like many vegetarians, his frugality of diet spreading out) but felt obliged to house him. Desperate to get Gerald a job and money, he even risked lending his dinner jacket for a promised position as a waiter, but one look at the surly adolescent with his long, unkempt hair and the restaurant owner changed his mind.

Pressure on him to return therefore began from all directions. Gerald wrote long, 'hopeless, unavailing letters, bargaining and arguing for my liberty'.[15] At last a brilliant compromise occurred to him. He would go, provided his father would let him learn a trade that would eventually finance (the aim of course not mentioned) the next assault on the Pamirs. He'd decided to copy Ball and be a blacksmith, only adding, as snobbish inducement, 'Art'. He wrote to Mr Mills, a neighbour he liked. Would his father allow him to train as an art blacksmith? Mr Mills wrote back saying he was sure Hugh Brenan would discuss anything.

On this slender undertaking, Gerald agreed to return. During the last few days, high on hashish, he wrote poetry. One verse survives:

> The moon and stars are up above
> Though you cannot see them shining.
> Nightingale sings songs of love –
> You would deem it for love pining.
> But you know it married is,
> Enjoying sweet felicities.[16]

For many years Gerald was to comfort himself that Shelley's early verse was also very bad; but the vaguely amatory theme may have been prompted by the fact that he now kissed his first girl.

Finally, the money arrived. He composed a telegram – 'Prodigal son arriving lunch Thursday. Prepare fatted calf' – wisely decided not to send it, and set off home.

5

In *A Life . . .* , Gerald represents his reaction to the Walk at this time (and for a long while afterwards) as a sense of bitter failure and shame. At one level this is another example of his excessive, almost ridiculous modesty. He had accomplished on foot a journey of approximately 2510 kilometres or 1560 miles,* more than a quarter of the way to his goal, the last part of it for three weeks alone, penniless, through some of the wildest and most inhospitable country in Europe in the depths of winter. Yet – always remembering that to deprecate real achievement is in England often a form of boasting – he does genuinely seem to have felt he failed. It was for this reason that he could not bring himself to describe the last three weeks in his 1916 account for Hope.

Hope himself, already literary mentor and substitute father, was to remain the most important person in his life for many years. He may have been unwelcoming in Venice and had ditched Gerald in Bosnia – but he had let Gerald choose. That is, he had treated him as an equal, as a grown-up.

Gerald had also grown up literally. At school, he had been small, squashed. He returned tall. 'It was as though I had discovered for the first time that there was air above me.'

It is clear that at a deeper level Gerald was completely aware of the significance and magnitude of what he'd done. As well as the diary, he kept the document of his release from Monfalcone prison on 8 December 1912.[17] It was the start of a lifelong habit of keeping such things. Despite numerous bonfires like past Brenans, an amazing amount of his life is preserved – locks of hair, faded flowers, pocket diaries, tickets, lists of dates, letters, letters, letters . . .

But to keep such stuff argues the importance of the life. In fact, to achieve so much and call it failure is really of course an admission

* As near as I can calculate. But this is probably an under-estimate, due to the winding of the route and the obscurity of the last 200 or so miles.

of extraordinary confidence. He had actually expected to reach the Pamirs – such was his estimate of his strength and courage. He had been prepared to sacrifice everything (and one might note here the emergence of an obsessive quality). 'Anyone who sets before himself as a way of life the ideal of Everything or Nothing is following, whether he knows it or not, a path that lies parallel to that set by the saints.'

The religious nature of the Walk finally confirmed his sense of destiny, long prepared by his mother and his nature experiences. Once again, but now with proof, he felt he was greater than other people, set apart – 'In a way I could never reveal to anyone else.'[18]

But it confirmed his destiny in the particular as well. A life of poverty, of hardship, of intensity was possible. And exaltation followed – if the resulting poetry as yet left something to be desired. He was determined to set out again for the Pamirs – or at least somewhere – as soon as he could. To this end he kept the notebook he had made of the costs and quality of the wines and food on their route.[18]

He was indeed to set out again, and several times, if under different circumstances. But he had now, in the late February of 1913, a certain amount of rather unpleasant music to face.

SIX

The Consolations of the Rebel

1

A Cook's agent met Gerald at Southampton with money and clean clothes; he organised a bath and – to Gerald's deep regret – a haircut, then saw him on to the train to Cirencester.

His mother and father were at the station. It must have been a tense moment. His father had clearly laid down 'the exact degree of affection tempered by silent reprobation' by which he was to be met. But his mother could not control her delight.

The next morning Gerald was summoned to the study. The tone was curt. His father – a product of his deafness – could now, as often before, be heard rehearsing both this, and various phrases, while dressing: 'I've taken a good deal of trouble Gerald to think about your future . . .'

The irascible little ex-captain was clearly, in fact, in a state of barely controlled fury. His absolute and dictatorial rule had, until this incident, hardly been defied. Now there had come defiance so enormous it almost beggared description. Almost – but not quite. Gerald's father, having said they would not refer to what had happened again, did at once refer to it, and quickly found himself more than equal to the task. Out poured a long, furious diatribe: wasted education, open disobedience, mother's health, money, ruined prospects – the lot. Gerald listened in silence. Finally, 'I've taken a good deal of trouble to look into your future because I want to give you the widest possible choice . . . You yourself have ruled out the Army. You are too old for the Navy. I think you will agree that you are not suited to the Church.' His father ranged the many possibilities, rejecting each in turn. At last there remained only two – the Indian police or the Egyptian police.

The hero, says Freud, is a man who first defies his father, then defeats him. But Gerald was still exhausted. In the face of this controlled flow of bitter anger he found that the words, 'Father, I want to be an art blacksmith', froze on his lips. Since it would need more languages, he chose the Indian police.

His father, no doubt secretly pleased Gerald had chosen the more distant field of operation, pressed home his advantage. He knew the real cause of the trouble – and of course he was quite right – poetry. Gerald must promise to give up reading poetry until after his exams. Gerald promised.

Then there was Hope. On top of anxiety about homosexuality, Hope's total perfidy had now been revealed. A postcard survives which he'd sent on 7 August 1912 solely to throw them off the scent.[1] 'My God – how they must detest me,' Hope wrote, and it is clear from this letter that Gerald had been forbidden to see or correspond with him.[2]

In fact, of course, he had no intention of keeping this or any of the other prohibitions. Quite the reverse. And his rebellion began at once. Like so many of his generation, one of the most important freedoms Gerald was determined to wrest back from the grip of convention and his parents was sexual freedom. According to his own account, soon after the return from Venice, he had 'a small adventure' and lost his virginity.

2

'Since copulation is the most important act in the lives of living creatures because it perpetuates the species, it seems odd that Nature should not have arranged for it to happen more simply.'

Thoughts in a Dry Season

His parents had taken on a housemaid called Minnie, 'a fair-haired buxom girl who was engaged to the first footman at the Park'. Gerald made advances, was accepted, and had his 'first sexual experience . . . the affair . . . continued at intervals for several years'. It disgusted Gerald; thanks to Radley, for a long time anything even remotely connected with sex was likely to cause what he called 'reactions', that is guilt and self-disgust.

Does Gerald mean what he seems to be saying? In the ordinary way, one would suppose he does. And Mr Rusk of Edgeworth (the next village), very old but very bright, remembered hearing that Gerald had 'carried on' with one of the servants at Miserden.

Unfortunately, the ordinary way is rather seldom the required route with Gerald. As far as sex goes, what he says is usually a mass of contradictions, or contradicted by other more reliable evidence. Thus, shortly after this, in 1916, he wrote a poem strongly suggesting that he was still a virgin. He was about to go to the front: 'Yes, I may die tonight/All things undone/And one thing unattempted . . .'[3] The first time he actually uses the words 'to make love' to someone is not till 1919 with a girl he called 'La Égyptienne'. Yet he says categorically a number of years later that when he first met Carrington he hadn't 'properly' made love to anyone.[4] He describes in *Personal Record* how much later on in their love affair he used to compel Carrington to let him make love to her as proof of her affection, but manuscript evidence at Texas makes clear she wouldn't allow him to make love 'properly'. During the late Twenties, he had 'affairs' with girls he picked up, and his suggestion in *Personal Record* is that most were sexual affairs; but Gerald freely admitted at the time that they were usually chaste.* (He is apt to use the word 'affair' in its Edwardian sense of flirtation.)

It is, that is to say, more confusing than it seems – and the confusion is deliberate. Sex is one of the few important areas where Gerald – for not just understandable but totally sympathetic reasons – could not bring himself, in his published autobiographies, to tell the truth.

Yet the general picture is clear. By the time he first tried to sleep with Carrington in 1921 he had already had experience of being impotent. And it was impotence that was to bedevil his sex life and his love life. Though Gerald referred to it from time to time it was not till he was quite old that he could bring himself to reveal the full extent of the problem, and even then it could still upset him. One trouble was contraception. He used a French letter and this put him off 'so much it often made me impotent'.[5] Then he learnt to withdraw,

---

* See under Chapter Eleven.

but it made little difference. He was nearly always impotent the first time he tried to make love. This is so common as to be almost universal. Most men press on and – in an hour, next morning, next day, in a week – everything is all right. But Gerald seems to have found the humiliation so piercing, so painful, he couldn't bear to press on. More and more, as time passed, he couldn't even bear to start out.

He himself sometimes thought it was because he had an unusually low sex drive. It is possible. Despite Kinsey and Masters and Johnson, this is a tricky calculation. But there is more abundant evidence that his libido was at the very least average. He was always extremely susceptible to good-looking women, frequently attracted to them, often falling in love. On the whole, probably because of his early closeness to his mother, he was more interested in women than men. He had one or two very close male friends, but women marked the chapters of his life. As far as libido goes, the one major sexual affair of his life suggests it was potentially higher than normal.

Yet it is important to be clear about the effect that impotence – the fear of impotence – had on him. It meant he had far fewer physical affairs than he made out, and eventually none at all. The steady diverting of this powerful drive slowly altered his character, marking his behaviour and conversation and ultimately – though by no means necessarily to its detriment – his writing.

And so what of him and Minnie? To most men the first girl they make love to is not 'a small adventure'. Certainly not to Gerald who had twice, on his great walk, longed for that impossible, 'inconceivable' thing to happen. But small is probably the accurate description. He later wrote to V. S. Pritchett that when young he didn't particularly want sex but 'preferred cuddles with housemaids'.[6]

3

It was soon after this, in May 1913, that Gerald went as planned to stay with his great uncle Vincent's family in Bristol to study for the Indian police exam.

. They lived in a suburban house on the far side of Durdham Downs. Vincent Brenan, who at sixty-five had recently retired from a senior position in the Chinese Customs, was a vague, amiable man with a prominent Adam's apple and baggy trousers. With him and his younger wife, Gerald led a suburban life of tennis, tea parties, and repartee with cousins – two girls and a boy still at school. Gerald, now nineteen, must have been the focus of considerable interest. His escapade had convulsed the Brenan clan. But the girl cousins were not Minnie. Gerald sometimes 'almost wept' with frustration because he had no girl.[7]

However, his real life still centred on the Walk and its ideals. Whenever he could he escaped to explore the poor quarters and doss-houses of Bristol – a slumscape he was to use in his first novel *Jack Robinson*. Especially did he roam the docks, fantasising that he would work his passage to Canada, South America or the Middle East.

In July he took the Indian police exam. For some odd reason, German was considered essential for India and Gerald had done badly at it. His father decided he should go to a crammer at Baden.

He had a brief respite before setting off. He had resumed contact with Reynolds Ball on his return from Venice and in August he asked him to Miserden. This gentle man charmed Gerald's mother and grandmother and reassured his father (that Ball's father was the Canon of Peterborough no doubt helped). As a result, Gerald was allowed to go and stay with him in London.

Ball had taken two rooms in Cumberland Market. Gerald slept on a mattress. He was introduced to Ball's friends, among them Francis Birrell and Hubert and Arthur Waley. Hubert was to give his name to a character in Gerald's most successful novel; Francis and Arthur to become his friends; especially Arthur, just twenty-five, haughty and with 'a thin, high, cutting voice and the profile of an Arab sheikh.' But now, leaving the ascetic Arthur behind, the other four teamed up. They sat for hours drinking Green Chartreuse in the Café Royal, then wandered back arm in arm to continue talking till dawn.

He also met Wyndham Lewis and others in what Hope later disparagingly, and probably jealously, called 'the arty crowd'.[8] Some time after this he met the painter Bomberg. Gerald says that, encouraged by Ball, he suddenly saw the possibilities of a London literary life but that this 'faded rapidly'. It depends what you mean by rapidly. He was still discussing it with Hope in February 1914,[9] and he took up with this group quite soon again on leaves during the war. Lewis came close to printing one of his poems (a parody of Pound). A London literary life probably remained at the back of

Gerald's mind right up to the point when he tried for a while to live it in the 1920s.

The significance of this brief London visit is talk. Gerald was by nature, as he had been as a child, naturally gregarious, rapidly stimulated by conversation. With Birrell and Ball, the diffidence and solitariness compelled by Radley melted into easy intimacy and friendship. Gerald says that Hope's lessons on not 'lowering the drawbridge' soon caused him to withdraw again.* Hope may have praised solitude, but in reality it was Hope who had first brought Gerald out. The withdrawal that took place now was due to circumstances – the visit to Germany.

4

Gerald arrived in September at the Adams household at Freiburg-im-Breisgau near Baden, just below the Black Forest, to continue cramming for the Indian police.

In appearance at this time, a photograph taken in 1913 shows a tall, conventional, rather solid figure, with a plain face and a determined, even obstinate expression. But it is possible to detect a humorous slant to the mouth and the small, widely spaced eyes are clearly fixed on distant horizons.

The Adams' four or five pupils seem to have bored him. One had been to Winton House (no particular commendation). Another, livelier, later became Lord Melchett. (A curious detail for Gerald to include, but not alone. Despite his dislike of the English class system, he often evinced a sort of Edwardian housemaid's innocent excitement at a title.)

---

* *A Life* . . . reveals a fascinating and subtle example of Gerald's juxtaposition operating here. He had difficulties and inhibitions about his feelings, as we have seen and will see and for reasons we have explored, but they were at a very deep level. They did not, except at this profound level, affect his ability to form intimate friendships or talk intimately. On the contrary, they probably caused him to seek greater satisfaction and get greater pleasure from these exchanges. Nevertheless, his very brief, glancing reference to Hope and his own withdrawing into solitariness again, sets off those deeper associations. In the very next paragraph he feels compelled to describe what happened with Minnie, out of context, nine months late, and seemingly totally irrelevantly – though in fact, of course, it was not irrelevant at all.

The two resident masters were slightly more interesting. Herr Sartig – 'very tall, immensely thin, with arms that hung down like wires, cropped hair, high starched collar and duelling scars' – was a great walker. Together they explored the Rhine Valley. Herr Sartig was also interested in the fine arts – the old German masters, Rodin, Hödler. Gerald was keen enough to take up drawing.[10] His interest in painting was another of those mother-introduced subjects Hope had enormously developed, particularly in the galleries and churches along their walk. As a result, Gerald's taste inclined to Cézanne, Seurat, Picasso and the Italian Futurists. Amiable argument with Herr Sartig took place.

Mr Halsey, the second master, came straight from some farce about crammers. A dour, silent Yorkshireman, looking like a 'dull twin brother of Napoleon', he was in love with his collie dog, called Old Girl. When Gerald joined him on his walks, he found Mr Halsey could talk only about her.

At Christmas, instead of going home, he moved on to the Tilly's phonetic institute in Berlin. With the Tilly family, the farce became edged in black. The whole family gave lessons, from the nine-year-old youngest son's beginner's classes, to Herr Tilly's lectures on art. It was a large family – six daughters and two sons – but being rather rapidly whittled away by a proneness to suicide: 'three of the sons had killed themselves already, the last to do so having jumped off the roof the week before I arrived'.

Apart from a brief visit to Miserden in April, Gerald remained in Berlin until June 1914. Throughout his ten months in Germany, the most important events continued to be interior ones. Once again, Hope was both instigator and guide.

After wintering in Venice, Hope had set off east to Syria, with a commission to buy things for Roger Fry's Omega Workshops. In November he wrote to Gerald asking to see his drawings. Fry might take them. But the letter was really to express his excitement at a new poet he had discovered – Rimbaud. It was absolutely vital Gerald read him. 'You have much in common with him and might understand him better than I do.' He told Gerald to read Berichon's *Life*, and also Laforgue; meanwhile praising some poems Gerald had sent.[10] By December, fifteen- and twenty-page letters were pouring from Hope, with Rimbaud as a major theme. One of thirty-six pages on 27 December from Damascus compared them both to Verlaine and

Rimbaud, entreated Gerald to read *Les Illuminations* and added, 'I think you have a future as a poet.'[11]

The effect on Gerald was extreme (and seems to have been virtually instantaneous). Rimbaud was a revelation equal to or greater than Shelley. And as with Shelley, it started with more or less total identification.

Indeed, having bought and devoured the volumes as directed, he hardly needed Hope to point the obvious resemblances: the adolescent passions for poetry, reading, nature, for magic, drugs and the East; his repugnance for the conventionality of his bourgeois family (Rimbaud's father, too, was in the Army, but in fact it was Mme Rimbaud who equalled Hugh Brenan), which seethes and boils in his early poetry and against which he reacts identically – flight into 'reality' as a vagabond and tramp.*

And there were resemblances Hope knew nothing about. Meeting a girl in May 1871, Rimbaud described remaining as dumb and frightened as 'seventy-six thousand newborn puppies'. Nearly all his love poems express doubt and uncertainty, and his suffering came from his inhibition in front of women. Rimbaud too wished to break the egotistic and conventional shell in order to penetrate to 'reality'. His method was debauchery – but only because it was the way to torture and pain. Why not go straight to the torture itself? Gerald must have felt he had found a far swifter and surer way.

In *A Life . . .* he says that as a result of Rimbaud-intoxication he wrote a great deal of poetry, realised it was very bad, and thought 'I had better give up the idea of being a poet.' This is almost the exact reverse of the truth. His determination to be a poet, and the ceaseless writing of poetry, continued for twelve years or more. And though it finally sank into some deep recess of the castle, it never died, but was transferred to his prose, and continued in a longing, a regret, and in sporadic but quite frequent bouts of poetry all his life. His last but one (privately) printed work was a selection from his poetry.[12]

---

* In 1945 Gerald wrote a penetrating and unpublished essay on Rimbaud, including an account, now in the MF archive, of why and how he identified with him. The similarity of their rebellions is indeed at first sight striking. Yet what other form could they take, given they had to be the opposite to comparably conventional backgrounds? The children of Rimbauds and Shelleys rebel too – becoming solicitors and naval officers, but they don't, naturally, write books or poetry, much as their parents long for them to do so.

The 'mass of poetry', as Gerald describes it,[13] has been destroyed. No doubt it was pure Rimbaud. He spent a year after this writing a long prose-poem which he actually called *Illumination*.[14] All young writers learn by imitation and pastiche. With Gerald the process was quite astonishingly prolonged. For twenty years writers could enter the castle, pass through and emerge onto his pages more or less unscathed. It was partly a product of the intensity of his immersion and later, in his book on Spanish Literature, making a virtue out of necessity, he was to make this initial absorption one of the central – and most valuable – tenets of his critical aesthetic.

And of course it affected his life. Underlying all the varied (and often disguised) expressions of Gerald's romanticism was, as we have seen, the most basic of all – the same as that of Don Quixote: life according to books. Winter that year in Berlin, always very cold, was fearsome: temperatures 16–20°C below zero, heavy snow, howling winds. Gerald, short of money and often very hungry (his parents, rightly fearful of further flight, kept him on five shillings a week), embarked on a series of huge torture walks. In mid-December he nearly got to Armenia; he planned one back to Bosnia.[15] In this savage cold, he found he could walk barefoot. He did so. He spent an entire weekend, sleeping out, walking thus through the Black Forest. The hero of *Jack Robinson* finds that, 'So long as I kept moving I did not feel the cold.' Gerald's food on this occasion was a few bars of chocolate. From pain came poems.

It is possible something else took place at this time. Returning from *Romeo and Juliet* one night, he describes how a sudden and overwhelming desire to write came over him. Taking out the notebook he habitually carried, he found words pouring from him as if dictated. Lurching in the dark from lamp-post to lamp-post he wrote without stopping; indeed unable to stop. He filled the notebook, and also masses of scraps of paper – and at last the fit passed.

These moments were to recur every few years throughout his life. Sometimes they lasted five days and complete works resulted. One was published. Gerald felt he was inspired. Nothing written then should be altered at all.[16] Furthermore, he felt that if only he had somehow organised his life to harness these moments of power 'which open up all those chambers of the mind that are usually sealed'[17] he would have written something 'of value'. It is possible, though the works produced – often interesting for other reasons – don't really bear this out. In any case, he produced much of value by more prosaic means.

The more certain significance of these extraordinary explosions is personal. They were not just literary; they were explosions of energy. Something would trigger adrenalin and *manic* energy would surge through him – having to escape in forty- or fifty-mile walks, forty- or fifty-page letters, almost unstoppable talk. This energy is another explanation of that obsessive, compulsive side to his character. All at once this prodigious flow became locked on to one goal. It was his alcohol, and perhaps a reason he never needed drink. It came to be something he valued highly, making up for his lack of looks and not being able to dance. And this energy, without which, though it guarantees nothing, nothing considerable in art can be achieved, as John Carey once observed in one of his *Sunday Times* reviews, was not the draining variety, not vampirish. On the contrary, it was catching and invigorating.

Writers are not born but made – and made by the sort of complex interactions we have been tracing. Rimbaud meant that the first of Gerald's energy explosions – which seems to have been a development from his earlier nature-induced experiences – should have literary expression. This in turn finally completed the long process of his decision to write – to be a poet.

If indeed it was Rimbaud. It seems reasonable to assume so. Gerald himself says that these events were usually sparked off by something he'd read. He was now following Rimbaud closely. (Even the walks have an element of this. Rimbaud, in later years, was given to wild excesses of physical exertion. 'His long legs,' says one of his biographers graphically, 'covered the ground in enormous strides, like a horse.')[18] And Rimbaud is, above all, the poet of inspiration.

But Gerald places *Romeo and Juliet* at Freiburg. This does not entirely remove Rimbaud, but makes it less likely.* Here we run into a difficulty. It is clear that Gerald, writing years later, wanted in some degree to lessen the role of Hope in his development. He makes Rimbaud his own discovery, whereas their correspondence shows this was not so. And this echoes the earlier time at Radley, when

---

* Hope wrote from Damascus telling him to read Rimbaud on 16 November; Gerald did not go to Berlin till the end of December. Time, but not a great deal.

Gerald postpones his first meeting with Hope by a year; that is, until after he says he discovered Shelley.

It is a minor point. Gerald fully acknowledges his debt to Hope in general; he had no need to do so in the particular. And writers who influence us strongly when young become possessions, part of ourselves. Gerald's omissions may well have been unconscious.

Hope's letters have another side. He sent Gerald great inflaming litanies of distant cities: 'How about Balkh and Ghazin and Tashkent and Bokhana and Kashgar and Khotam . . .'[19] And when Gerald responded with his own wild plans, Hope answered perfectly seriously. 'As for [your chances of] landing at Alexandretta with a fiver I hardly know more than you at present, but I don't fancy them.'[20]

Once again, Hope's aim was China. His letters took on the exalted ring of their private gospel – indeed he compared one of them to the letter St Paul sent to the Corinthians. He kept alive the spirit of the Walk, and Gerald's own great treks were not only in order to experience pain. He was, just as much, hardening himself for the next stage.

Nor was he alone. Several times Hope mentioned a young man, Taylor, who shared their ideals and 'will do anything'. Gerald must see him. He had £50 per annum from a wealthy, estranged father.* Two letters survive from Taylor to Hope. Like Gerald, he sent Hope his dreams. He longed for advice about where to travel. 'My desire for wandering [is] a physical pain.'[21] He asked advice about Picasso, Blake, Dostoevsky, Nietzsche – Nietzsche who, with his concept of an heroic ideal is, like Shelley, so exhilarating to the young.

The sense is of the forming of a tiny, dedicated band, and this reflects a last aspect, one which Gerald, reacting to his later distaste, ignored. Hope's huge letters – fifteen, twenty-six, thirty pages, one of forty pages, all in tiny spidery writing – are those of an intensely

---

* Money is a relatively minor theme of all these early letters, nor, judging by their number and date, has Hope removed any of them, as Gerald surmises. Hope was liable, when penniless, to panic in these obscure and distant places. He clearly hoped these sons of rich men would contribute, when they could, to the pilgrimage – at present sustained by him alone. They agreed. Poverty was honourable. Both sent small sums of money. But gradually Hope's sponging increased, in the end souring relationships somewhat. Gerald, writing *A Life* . . . in 1950–60 after years of exasperation, retrospectively expressed some of it now, when that situation hadn't begun.

lonely man longing for affection. Gradually, that personal intimacy he shrank from face-to-face became manifest in his writing. There are long passages of revealing introspection. As well as their private language from the Walk (Serbian – Drugi for comrade, Otač for Gerald's father) he ends and begins 'Caro Mio'. He wishes he was with Gerald. He says he'll send a handkerchief, a diklas. 'Wear it and think of me.' There are several outbursts of jealous anger against Ball.[22] It would be an exaggeration to call them love-letters; but they are letters where love is present.

5

When Gerald returned to Miserden on 10 April 1914, just after his twentieth birthday, for a two-week holiday, he had been away eight months. Yet he seems to have spent part of it in London, since this is when he mentions meeting Bomberg.[23] Then on his return for good in June, he quite soon went to stay at Bristol. This, and the ten-month 'agreed' absence itself, all suggest things were still tense between his father and himself.

It must have hurt his mother. Gerald hardly noticed. His mind was now seething with wild plans for flight (wild – except that he'd proved himself perfectly capable of such things). As he left Germany, he wrote to Hope. He would fail the Indian Police exam, then become a tramp and explore the Levant, or possibly become a trapper, or go to West Africa . . . Meanwhile, travelling vicariously, he sent Hope, as well as stories and poems, £2.10: 'It is most important you should not have to turn back at Baghdad for want of a pound or two.'[24] On the journey back Gerald listened eagerly while the ship's purser said that for £2 he could get him on a ship to the East Indies (Rimbaud had gone to Java).

He wrote to Hope again from Bristol on 6 July. The aim had now switched to Spain, where he would travel with a donkey. He would learn Spanish in any case, since this would open up South America. (In fact, they had several times discussed Spain as a possibility before.) He had been trying to see Taylor.[25]

This he finally accomplished around 20 July after a brief return to Miserden. He took a steamer to Bristol and was met at Hayle by a tall, good-looking young man of twenty-five, with an austere, determined face.

Ernest Taylor came from a rich brewing family who, on his refusal to join the family firm, had turned him out. With his £50 per annum he rented a cottage at St Ives and lived on honeycomb from his bees, milk and ships' biscuits which arrived in barrels from London and cost less than bread. At long last Gerald met a contemporary equal to his lively mind and ever-growing love of talk.

'How quickly one makes friends when one is young! The week [in fact nine days] I spent at Penbeagle, Taylor's cottage on the Zennor road, was one of the high points of my youth. It passed in an orgy of talking, reading poetry, discussing Blake and Nietzsche* and drinking the green tea I had brought with me till the dawn began to show in the sky. Fogs came and lifted, suns rose and set, the fuchsias and the hydrangeas flowered, while time stood still for two young men who felt they could never say all they had to say to one another.'

They talked about Hope, now supposedly *en route* to Samarkand. Gerald told him every detail of the Walk, and about his future plans of escape. But on 28 July his visit was over and they had to go to Falmouth to look up steamers for Gerald's return. They walked all night to get there.

There is no doubt at all that within a few months Gerald would have embarked on one of his new schemes. In a letter to Hope he said he was expecting either £70 or £30 from 'his people'.[25] All he needed was money.

The news at Falmouth that Austria had declared war on Serbia meant nothing to them – they spent the night on the beach. But once back at Miserden it rapidly became clear that momentous things were about to happen. Gerald reacted as he would now so often react (he did just the same in 1939) – precipitately, idiosyncratically, romanti-

---

* Nietzsche's appeal to Gerald requires explanation since the essence of his thought – hatred of pity and sympathy and an aristocratic domination of the weak by the powerful – should have been fundamentally antithetical to him. But Nietzsche also posits a stern and ascetic way of life with a spartan need to endure pain; he is virulently anti-Christian like Shelley – a position Gerald later repudiated but now found sympathetic. And Nietzsche elevates the will and energy into supreme forces embodied in his artist-supermen. This must always attract youth – and perhaps at this point especially Gerald – who feel full of power and energy and often want to be artists.

cally. He wrote to the Montenegran consul, situated, oddly, in Harrogate, offering his services in their army. Turned down, 'there seemed nothing left that I could do' but try and join the Foreign Legion. But before a reply could come, he was forestalled by his father, who set off importantly one afternoon to try and get a commission for himself in the Territorials.

It was an afternoon when Gerald and his mother had been to the Mills'. Writing elegiacally, as everyone did looking back at that last August of nineteenth-century civilisation about to end – and how else could they have written? – Gerald described the warm misty sunshine on the cornfields, the corn waiting to be cut, the knowledge of young men already dying.

They got home to find his father. He had been turned down because of deafness. But there were some vacancies, a chance of something for a son (and with what delight he must have grabbed it!) if he had one from a good public school. Hugh was waiting with Gerald's commission in his pocket.

Gerald went up to London next day to be measured for his uniform at Hawkes' of Savile Row. He was about to play his part, as he realised quite clearly then, in one of the great events of his time.

SEVEN

War

1

Gerald joined his regiment, the 5th Gloucesters, at Chelmsford and at once proceeded to make himself impossible. The other officers – heavy drinking ex-businessmen, gentlemen farmers, ex-public-schoolboys – simply seemed barely grown-up versions of the Radley bloods. He therefore ignored them. He moved out of the mess into lodgings, subsisting on cake, bread and Rimbaud. In October Frankie Birrell and Reynolds Ball came down and they all walked on the Essex coast; Ernest Taylor also visited him: young men whose dreams had all been shattered.

Shattered – but also temporarily replaced. War is, after all, in bouts extremely exciting. The three generations of military Brenans – whose qualities had seen him through the Walk – now asserted themselves again. On the whole, Gerald, as he quite often said himself, enjoyed the war[1] – as did many young men, until they were killed. He was a brave, successful, conscientious and enthusiastic officer. He particularly liked the opportunity for excessive, testing-to-the-limit exercise. In November 1914 he took part in a three-day training exercise. There was a gentleman's agreement they should let each other sleep. Gerald roused his company, force-marched them through the night and captured the 'enemy' forces. The enemy forces were naturally very annoyed.

He spent the two days of Christmas at Miserden, receiving presents of money, four khaki silk handkerchiefs and a collapsible aluminium cup. He then returned to the nearly intolerable company of the 5th Gloucesters. The only thing that cheered him up was hiring a horse at Chelmsford on 27 December and going 'for a long, exhilarating ride'.*

However, you don't, in the British Army, read Rimbaud, break gentleman's agreements and ignore your officers' mess with impunity. On 26 December Gerald had been officially seconded to a new unit, the 48th Divisional Cyclists' Company. The idea of the bicycle as a miraculous modern invention, strong in the 1890s, had lingered on in the Army. The Cyclists' Company seems to have been envisaged skimming the battlefield with messages or rushing *en masse* in support – an adjunct of the cavalry. But it was essentially a gang of competent misfits, and Gerald at once felt at home.

Indeed, more than at home. He joined the Cyclists in January 1915 in the village of Great Totham. On his first evening, he noticed that instead of the popular dailies the other subalterns read, if they read anything, one of them was hidden behind *The Times*. Suddenly, in the silent mess, he dropped it with a roar of laughter.

'I saw a good-looking man of powerful build with the brightest blue eyes I had ever beheld in my life.'

Ralph Partridge was eventually to become, and remain for forty-five years, Gerald's closest and most intimate friend. He was, in fact, a character almost as complex as Gerald himself, but at this early stage what stood out were his good looks, and the sense of power and confidence he radiated. Gerald could not understand why someone so clearly a leader should have been seconded. Then he realised that was why: 'He did not submit easily to authority he regarded as stupid or incompetent' – and there was no dearth of that. He combined immense vitality and energy with an almost equal capacity for doing nothing. He was an athlete (a rowing blue at Oxford) but had refused to play games at his public school. He was extremely observant and

---

* The quotation comes from Gerald's war journal (MSS, Texas). Though he did keep regular daily or weekly journals from time to time, they were usually of very limited duration. His normal practice was to write them up, often several years later, from letters and entries in pocket diaries. They are really fragments of autobiography, but in roughly journal form – though even this is sometimes abandoned. This War Journal, for instance, was written up in 1923 almost entirely from his letters to Hope, and is quite short. These journals were always shown around and are not overly intimate. Though on the whole accurate and truthful, they are not by any means always so. The 1914–18 journal was partly written to be read by Carrington and is not, therefore, to be entirely trusted, for instance, about Ralph Partridge, whose character he wished to coarsen in her eyes; or about anyone he slept with, since he was trying to make her jealous.

intensely curious about his fellow human beings and this combined with a sharp and delightful sense of fun. Gerald's sense of humour was still latent under considerable layers of priggishness. Now, in Ralph's company, it began to stir.

We shall have to deal with Gerald's portrait of Ralph in due course, but its chief plank (not too clumping a word) was that Ralph at this period was not cultured, though he later became so. It rather depends what you mean by cultured. The son of an Indian civil servant, he had been a central figure at Westminster, where he had been head boy and gained a classics scholarship to Oxford in 1913. He was a brilliant and witty debater in the Cardinal Club. He didn't work; he had no need to. He had very intense powers of concentration and would read and retain the necessary information in the few weeks before the exams. Noel Carrington, at Oxford with him, said, 'He could gut a book in half the time anyone else could.'[2] A study of the comments in his Oxford notebooks shows he had read widely and intelligently.[3] True, he did not read much during the war; certainly not as much as Gerald. But probably no one on the Western front read as much as Gerald.

There was also a sexual element to their friendship. Ralph's easy sexual confidence (he'd had shopgirls at Oxford), his abundant appetite abundantly satisfied, attracted Gerald – and provided vicariously the success he still signally failed to find. This is one side of Ralph Gerald played up in *A Life . . .* , while his own efforts – so sympathetic, so poignantly understandable in the circumstances, and clear from letters and his poems – he played down.

Two incidents took place now, however, which he did briefly include. In November Gerald had been turned out of his rooms at Chelmsford for making a pass at the daughter of the house. Unfortunately, the family were Methodists.

Then, after two months of hectic training – Gerald, typically, took his platoon on two colossal bicycle runs to London and back – the Cyclists' Company embarked for France. Here, a few days after he had landed, he 'had been to bed with a girl', a peasant, at Merris, not far from the front at Armentières. For a moment, the heart leaps. But the account is shrouded in the usual Geraldian ambiguity. Taylor, writing to Hope about it, said, 'Brenan tells me [about] a woman in his billet who languished after him and when all else failed assured him with passion that she was *absolument vierge*.'[4] (Many accounts of Gerald seducing turn out to be Gerald seduced, or rather failing to be seduced.) But Gerald's laconic reference – 'I had been left wondering why I had done it' – does not come till two years later in 1917, when it is juxtaposed with a description of a waitress getting into his bed at St Omer with all her clothes on. Also, there is a suggestion in his verses celebrating the girl of Merris ('I had the *étoiles* of your eyes') that it was not a total success – 'Such poor endings/To such evident beginnings'.[5]

Whatever happened, it was soon swept away by the adrenalin of war. On 7 April, his twenty-first birthday and eight months after the war had begun, Gerald at last went up to the front.

2

This was not an active visit – though Gerald did his best to make it so. He was invited up by Taylor (they had been regularly corresponding since they met), who by chance was in charge of a machine-gun post – one of the most dangerous positions. Gerald was thrilled. Someone was shot next to him 'like a rabbit'. He rushed an open space under shellfire – 'it was marvellous we escaped' – adding insouciantly that shell fire was 'very amusing – it looks very beautiful, toy-like: you cannot think it dangerous'.[6] Taylor said he'd be killed in a few days if he went on like that, adding, with unknowing irony, that he'd sober up in a week or two.[7] It took a month.

The two young men were together for six days. It was perfect spring weather. They walked under the elms, picked the flowers, and had a picnic by a fire, with coffee and cream, bread with farm butter and honey. Gerald noticed how it all chimed with their reading – Rimbaud, Laforgue and now Baudelaire; the terrifying contrast of beauty and sordidity, squalor and exaltation, how reality was stood on its head; that lush green grass 'sprinkled with cuckoo-pint and cowslips' was also scattered picturesquely with cows. But the cows were all dead. At night, shells burst over a monastery, by day planes passed 'like large slow birds'.

Above all they talked. About their reading (Taylor only had Blake, so Gerald lent him his Laforgue), about the Walk and how they would continue its spirit after the war, a great deal about Hope.

When last heard of, Hope was supposed to be *en route* for

Samarkand ('This is the absolute dream of dreams come true,' Gerald had written ecstatically to Taylor).[8] In fact, he'd caught typhoid in Baghdad as Gerald joined up and was stopped in his tracks. He was forced to return slowly to England.

Gerald and Hope corresponded throughout the war. Hope's fifteen- to twenty-page letters are a curious mixture. At first, still affected by typhoid, lonely and depressed, they were intense, even hysterical. He was terrified his boys would be killed. Then exalted memories of the Walk – 'I too look back with passionate regret on the days in Provence and Italy'[9] – combined with literary lectures, crafty schemes for his own safety, requests for money, and encouragement: 'You are capable of great heights.'[10] Thus encouraged, the poet/tramp Brenan more than balanced the military Brenan. Balanced – and shielded. Gerald was to pass unscathed through some of the most frightful scenes of the war, insulated, as at Radley, by books and his writing (he wrote, mostly poetry, in bursts all the time), and now by his ideals, Hope- and Rimbaud-inspired, which together he called the Great Venture. In his letters to Hope he affected to despise anything else.

But Gerald and Taylor had more mundane Hope matters to discuss. Hope had returned virtually penniless. Both young men sent him money. Then they agreed to pay regular amounts into an account, the residue to go to the survivors if any of the band were killed. For the same reason, Gerald and Taylor made their wills in Hope's favour. Later, the regular payments grew into a fund to be used after the war on the Great Venture. Gerald's pay as a subaltern was £254 per annum, more as a captain; on this he saved about £100 a year, all sent to Hope.[11] But Hope could be tricky. Not because he spent the money. That was allowed, if absolutely necessary. But because he invested. Gerald was outraged. 'To enter anything in order solely to make money is profoundly wrong.'[12] It was a sin.* Hope was contrite. But he was to try again later, with disastrous consequences.

In May, while Taylor, to Gerald's intense anxiety, moved to the Ypres front, the Cyclists' Company moved to a moated farmhouse

---

* Gerald and Hope's letters are much concerned with moral issues, but the terms are Rimbaudian. 'Virtue' was to see the world intensely, as it really was. Anything that clogged or distracted this vision was a sin. Money of any kind was dangerously distracting; speculating certainly was.

called Château d'Oosthove. They trained and, at night, dug trenches. After digging all night, Gerald would often sit reading (Flaubert, Laforgue) or writing poetry. At dawn, he would hear the cocks crowing from far away across the lines.[13]

Ralph had seduced a fair-haired, blue-eyed buxom farm girl. Gerald, whose timid advances in this direction had collapsed, held a ladder as Ralph climbed into her little bedroom. After the last parade they would both bicycle into Armentières. Ralph knew a good hotel with loose waitresses. After pâté, omelettes, and champagne he would disappear while Gerald sat with his book. Once, on their way back, coming into the courtyard where an acetylene lamp was flaring, 'I saw one of [the] waitresses lying on a heap of straw with her skirts pulled up to her waist.' Soldiers were queueing for their turn.

Gerald soon became impatient with the chores they were doing and now volunteered for the dangerous job of capturing German prisoners from behind the lines.[13] But the war suddenly struck on an unexpected quarter. His cousin Byron Brenan, Vincent's son, was killed at Ypres. Gerald, who all his life was extremely conscientious about family matters, at once set out to find the grave so that he could tell Byron's mother.

The news was moderately upsetting to Gerald – to Hope it was devastating. Seeing that a 'Lt Brenan' had been reported killed, he leapt to the conclusion it was Gerald. He walked about in an agony on Hampstead Heath[14] and then sent a frantic letter to Taylor. The letter has been destroyed, but in it Hope expressed something of his feelings for Gerald. Taylor was evidently considerably surprised by their force. 'I shall not tell Brenan of all this until I hear again from you.'[15]

Gerald, accompanied by his batman Dartnell, found the battlefield with difficulty: 'Shell craters, mounds, rotting sandbags, coils of wire, latrines, graves in jumbled proximity, with rats, flies and the faint inescapable smell of putrefaction mingling with that of chlorate of lime.' He found the tiny cemetery where his cousin was buried and then he and his batman struggled back.

He returned on 20 May to truly terrible news. Taylor himself had been killed.

At first Gerald could hardly take it in. Taylor had been his first really close friend. He wrote in anguish to Hope – 'Until I see his grave with his name on it I shall not fully believe' – told Hope how much he longed to see him, and immediately set off for Ypres again, now also feeling certain that he too would soon be killed.[16]

During the trip (which was, of course, totally unauthorised) and afterwards, he painfully worked out how to deal with this death. As well as numerous poems about him, he spent a good deal of time writing Taylor's biography, partly in the form of a tone poem by Laforgue.

Gerald did not find the grave, since it had already been overrun by Germans. But he found a man who had been with Taylor when he was killed. Taylor had been firing a machine-gun at retreating Germans when he had been hit in the leg. This had been bandaged and he was sitting up firing again when a sniper shot him through the ear. Taylor's last letters had been full of premonitions about his death.*

Gerald and Dartnell came back through Ypres itself. It was totally deserted, except for three military policemen. 'Whole streets were burning and packs of dogs roamed about, feeding on the corpses which one could smell everywhere . . . in the cafés and *estaminets* half-filled glasses still stood on the tables, for with the first rumour of gas, the whole population had fled in panic.'

At the beginning of June Hope's feelings, intolerably upset by these events, finally burst forth in a letter which Gerald must have thrown away. Gerald was clearly considerably embarrassed, but quite sharply put him in his place. 'I always understood your covert feelings for me – this last year I mean, but one does not talk of one's feelings.' They had 'discovered the exact path . . . we had a special way by which we always understood each other and yet avoided all sentimentalism . . . You remember how we never walked arm in arm

* Gerald's account of Taylor and these events in *A Life* . . . is slightly different. He says his life of Taylor was short. But of his two volumes of war writing, it is recorded (MSS, MF) as filling most of the second volume. He says, after reading all their letters later, it was clear, at nearly thirty (in fact twenty-seven), that Taylor 'regarded me as a child: most of them began, with affectionate irony, "Dear Arabia" because I talked so much of that country'. This is not the impression the letters make on me. All three wrote to each other using nicknames: Hope was Drugi or Mr Bird, Gerald Drugi or Arabia, Taylor Penbeagle after his cottage. They were affectionate letters, but not ironic. Taylor was both deadly serious and excited in discussion of the Great Venture, just as full of plans and ideas. It was for this, despite premonitions of death, that he longed intensely to live. I think Gerald's remarks are examples of how his reticence about his early writing and his appealing but often unnecessary self-deprecation could lead him into subtle distortion.

or shook hands.' To make sure there was no ambiguity he explained that by sentimentalism he meant 'that sort of feeling which certain people – and women have – and which is impossible for us'.[17]

Hope did not reply till July: 'I'm afraid I encouraged instead of discouraged a certain desperate feeling – I know at one time I was entirely obsessed by it and some form of saying so seemed a necessity.' But he could not hide his true self from Gerald. Was it all that serious? He had been ill and suffering 'a great deal of loneliness'. But the incident has shown him 'the wickedness of what I myself always knew was wicked'. He would prevent such lapses in the future.[18]

They both needed each other too much, and were too fond of each other still, for there to be a breach – though one can detect a certain wariness for a while. But the exchange makes clear that the emotional remoteness between them which Gerald attributes to Hope was as much, or more, due to him.

3

At the end of June the Cyclists' Company moved south in Picardy to a village at Hébuterne, a mile behind the front line the British were holding from below Arras to the Somme. Skimming with the cavalry was now recognised to be a fantasy. The Cyclists were really a fatigue company. They were set to digging trenches eight hours a day.

In August, Gerald's teeth gave trouble. Gerald sometimes welcomed toothache, harking back to his first curious discoveries about pain. This time it was too severe and he had to go to a field hospital. 'Agony,' he told Hope.[19]

The long monotonous summer declined into a beautiful autumn. In September they moved again to the village of Bus-les-Artois, five miles behind Hébuterne, and Gerald had a pretty house in the middle of the village which no one else wanted because it had a huge unexploded shell in the fireplace. It had vegetables in its garden. Here they remained all winter, digging communications trenches and mending roads.

He grew closer to Ralph. 'The only man out here I like.'[20] Yet all male friendships have elements of competition and rivalry. 'I looked up to him as a hero, supremely good at many things that I should have liked to be good at.'[21]

More and more Gerald admired Ralph as a soldier. He was Roman, not Greek – Mark Antony: 'There was the same reserve of mental and physical energy, the same formidable presence when aroused and also the same tendency to indolence and sensuality.' But Gerald, if he did not quite have the leadership panache Ralph was soon to exhibit, was an extremely competent and resourceful soldier – much admired for this reason by Ralph. Nor could Ralph rival him in vitality or zest for life. Among the attributes Gerald endowed Ralph with in *A Life* . . . that leaves Ralph ahead of him only in success with girls.

Throughout the autumn and winter the two made frequent trips into Amiens together so that Ralph could make love to someone. While he did so, Gerald 'would go to the cathedral where I would sit entranced by the splendour of the thirteenth-century glass, till it was time to start for home.'[21] Ralph used to tease and laugh at him for these aesthetic substitutes. Gerald would hardly have been human had he not felt some elements of jealousy and resentment, feelings which, for the moment, he managed to suppress.

And of course activity continued on the Hope front. To demonstrate Hope's skill in teaching Gerald would take over-lengthy quotation. He was like the best sort of university tutor: tactful, concise, clear, perceptive and illuminating – even elegant. For instance, he'd obviously noticed (as Helen Brenan had long ago) Gerald's sensitivity to the music of poetry – he had a 'musical' ear in the sense of reckoning quantities, rhythms, stress, the cadence of words. Hope therefore suggested that perhaps the best way into Rimbaud might be through the sound of his verse – and so it proved.

Then – how apt his pupil was! The feeling was that Gerald was a genius. Hope had only to point the way. And it is true he did show extraordinary literary maturity for twenty-one. All this time Hope had been sending him *Blast*. Gerald got the point of Eliot at once (as he did of all the modernists, especially Joyce and, in different vein, Proust).

'T. S. Eliot seems to me a good and interesting poet.' He was obviously trying to change things. Suddenly, as he wrote to Hope, he realised how the *same* poetry has been for years. Now '"And female smells in shuttered rooms" seems to me as full of romance as

Keats' "Charmed Casements" etc., full of quite new romance, perhaps the beginning of a change of values in poetry.

'I don't know why I talk of art and literary stuff now. Five men were killed and seven wounded by one shrapnel [burst] not an hour ago and only a hundred yards from here. I saw them picking up the bodies.'[22] Which was of course why, precisely, he wrote at once of such 'stuff'.

He also continued to write his own poetry, his life of Taylor, and to read ferociously – his usual poets, Stendhal, Tolstoy (*War and Peace* and *Sebastopol*); the letter about Eliot also asked for Chesterton, Max Beerbohm and still more French poetry. In October Gerald read for eleven hours at a stretch.[23] Not easy. He was already developing his formidable concentration.

4

Gerald's first leave came on 25 October. It was only a week and he spent it all with Hope in the tiny cottage Hope had rented at Boveridge Hill near Cranbourne in Dorset. He did not tell 'his people', leaving a false letter which unfortunately wasn't posted. 'They suspect nothing,' he wrote afterwards, adding with youthful melodrama, 'I have to do some pretty cruel things in my life.' If he died, Hope was not to tell. 'Leave them to their poor illusions.'[24]

Hope quite often embarked on the hopeless pursuit of some girl or other in order to convince himself and anyone else that his tastes were perfectly normal. He may have felt this was more than usually necessary with Gerald at this point. At any rate, he now talked at some length about a girl he had met at the Slade.

She was a girl with startling blue eyes and corn-coloured hair, he said, whose name was Dora Carrington. Everybody called her Carrington.

Gerald's imagination was fired. She sounded exactly the sort of 'modern' girl he longed to meet. And 'modern' in this context meant not just unconventional, bohemian, emancipated, but also that she might, perhaps, let him make love to her. He spent the war years dreaming about her.[25]

(The news of Gerald's sudden fever, passion growing at a crazy distance, is contained in the manuscript of *A Life* . . . . Gerald cut it out of the final version. One wonders why. It is a significant omission, since it makes much more explicable his later behaviour with Carrington and Ralph. The most reasonable explanation seems to be that Gerald didn't really want his behaviour too accurately explained.)

5

Gerald returned from leave on 4 November, longing to be in just *one* attack. But by the 13th he'd moved into his first Observation Post (OP).²⁶ Observing was to be his main task, with quite long and often dramatic interludes, for the rest of the war. An inspired choice by the Army – and strangely prophetic; to choose someone who during his life was to observe both nature and people with so much pleasure and so perceptively, and eventually make such brilliant use of what he'd seen.

First it rained, then snowed. The trenches were neck-deep in water and collapsing. Gerald (now learning Serb) was reminded of the Walk, the countryside beyond Trieste. Would Hope send more Rimbaud, Hall's *Ancient East*, some Strindberg and the second volume of *Arabia Deserta*?²⁶

He also had another amorous adventure. Going to collect the bread from the baker's cottage on the 15 November he was suddenly doused with water as he came to the door. Going in, he found the fifteen-year-old daughter blushing in extreme embarrassment. She was a shy, exquisite creature, white with flour, dressed only in a short thin smock which showed every detail of her small breasts and slim figure. Gerald fell in love on the spot. He wrote poems to her and told Hope she was very beautiful. He took to visiting but, despite coarse encouragement from the mother, the lovely fifteen-year-old was too shy even to look at him.

He seems to have thrown this delicate incident into the lists against Ralph's full-blooded pleasures. His friend was delighted. 'Dear Heart . . . Glad to hear you've secured a real Basrah – does she respond?'*²⁷ But the necessary ambiguity of Gerald's replies (seeing that they upset the young girl, he had, with typical sensitivity,

---

* Gerald's war letters to Ralph have been lost, but this one-sided exchange and others suggest that they were more mundane and more human than the often rather exalted ones he wrote to his master, Hope.

quickly given up his visits) soon confused Ralph, and he gave up asking about her.

Hope's military career, meanwhile, was stagnating. His acute short sight was the problem, but he talked vaguely of getting into the infantry and dying. In fact, he was angling for a cushy job on the French railways, through his cousin the Duchess of Buckingham.[28]

6

In February 1916 Gerald had his second leave. He spent it with his parents who were living in London. The war drew him closer to his father, who had a job guarding the docks. Gerald particularly admired the commonsense firmness with which he resisted the distasteful and hysterical war-fever, refusing to believe, for example, the atrocity stories.

He was now, thanks to Hope, Frankie Birrell and Reynolds Ball, going to parties with artists and writers. He saw Wyndham Lewis again and met Nina Hamnett. With Hope, he also met Ezra Pound (Gerald introduced as a poet), whom he disliked intensely, owing to Pound's dogmatism and various prejudices, though he'd read and admired his poetry. As a result he wrote a number of Pound parodies later in the year.

He would have found London, thanks to the tango and the foxtrot, on the point of going dance-mad – something it did completely, to Gerald's horror, after the war. Dance was to remain the major medium of seduction until very recently, when it seems to have become unnecessary. Gerald learnt the steps, he thought he could feel the rhythm – but at the first note he became paralysed. He saw it as a major handicap.

However, he had one slightly qualified success. On his last night but one he went to a party at the Johns' in Chelsea, and met Alick Shepeler, who had been a great beauty at nineteen 'in that her teeth stuck out'. (Gerald's first love, Nancy, when he was fourteen, had had sticking-out teeth.) Alick worked at the *Illustrated London News* and was half-Russian and half-Irish with a rich Russian accent with 'gurgles like air blown through water', and 'flattering inflexions when she liked one'.[29] She more than liked Gerald. After several gins they kissed passionately for the whole evening. In *A Life . . .* , Gerald says next day he saw she was older and his love vanished (she was thirty-three). But his journal contradicts this. He remained in love several months, writing passionate love poems to her from France. The journal also shows that 'next day' was on their entwined walk back at dawn, probably to her flat.[30] In fact, it is possible he tried to make love to her. She had had affairs with various men, including Augustus John* and Wyndham Lewis, and lived, says Gerald, for passion: 'Love – and she was very passionate and melting in that – was her escape from destiny . . . Then remember there weren't such a lot of beddable girls in those days.'[29] He describes her squalid bedroom in some detail – the filthy, unmade bed, tufts of hair in brush and comb.[29] If he did try, it doesn't seem to have been a success. One of the poems runs, 'You've nothing to forgive me for?/(For that I'm hardly glad)' (a note to this adds 'it ended in nothing')[21] and the disparaging way he describes her thereafter, in *A Life* . . . and various other references, is typical of the way he dealt with women with whom he'd failed or who had rejected him.†

7

In the spring, the Cyclists' Company was broken up and merged with VIII Corps' Cyclists' Battalion. Ralph, however, whose extraordinary potential as a soldier had now been recognised, was sent back to the infantry – to the 6th Warwicks.

Gerald felt, and did increasingly till his own 'show' in 1918, that he had been relegated to the sidelines while Ralph was in the thick of

---

* John did a portrait of her. It was burnt by mistake at Alderney, but Michael Holroyd has a version. It reveals someone pliant and attractive.

† Gerald believed this expression of failed love to be so universal that he made it the basis for one of his *pensées* in *Thoughts in a Dry Season*: men who failed to satisfy women sexually 'often end by bearing a resentment against them. It is their male pride which has suffered, for men have more pride about their sexual prowess than they have about their charm or good looks, and so they pay off on their partners their shame at their failure'. I'm not sure it is so common. But it demonstrates something in him which was so to a particular degree. Gerald had a sort of moral sturdiness and self-confidence in sexual matters which contrasted with his sensitivity and timidity. He seldom or never felt guilty or ashamed about his behaviour in love or sex. He thought everyone was the same as him, and if he behaved oddly, as we shall see, neither made any effort to conceal his behaviour nor showed any sign he thought it was odd.

it. This feeling alternated with another, equally strong: fear. Not fear of danger or death, but fear of failure. That when it came to the 'real thing' – attacking a machine-gun, the need to kill someone, a really dangerous patrol – he would funk it. (It was now he had his pathetic, Radley-echoing dream about the toad that could not lift its arms.)

As a result, he volunteered, somewhat eccentrically, to conduct one-man reconnaissances behind enemy lines. When this offer was turned down he tried to join the Flying Corps. He wrote restlessly to Hope wishing that he could be taken prisoner so that he could try his hand at escaping. He planned a cottage for them in the south of France.[31]

Hope however was now totally obsessed with himself (though he managed a catty reference to Alick Shepeler – a platitudinous woman who, in any case, never *mentioned* Gerald). Hope was about to join up and was terrified. The writing of his last letter physically stumbles into silence: 'I go into the army tomorrow – I hope to die – can't write any – ' as if he were, at that second, actually expiring.[32]

Gerald's restlessness was compounded – and then assuaged – by the Somme offensive which built steadily all spring and into the summer. His OP was in a position of importance, opposite the hamlet of Serre where the left hinge of the crucial advance was located. He was to watch this closely and send back reports on its success. (His usefulness here, and the importance given to the task, is shown by the fact that, though gazetted captain in June, he was kept on in the same job.)*

During the last days of June he watched the increasingly frenzied activity along the front before him. Then, just after sunrise on 1 July 1916, the huge attack began which was to sweep the Germans aside. Gerald saw the entire battle. To Hope, long afterwards, he sent a laconic and dismissive account, to show how far above such mundane things he was. It 'was singularly unimpressive. A little noise and smoke and quite a few little figures like ants . . . moving aimlessly or falling, or crawling.'[33]

What he felt and described both later and at the time were totally

---

* In *A Life* . . . he says that his battalion was unaware he had been gazetted captain, but since such promotion depends on battalion reports this is in the highest degree unlikely. Once again Gerald's modesty inhibits him from admitting this relatively early recognition – early, since he was in a company and battalion that had not so far, like those at the front, been decimated.

different. It began 'with a bombardment that shook the air with its roar and sent up the earth on the German trenches in gigantic fountains. It seemed as if no human being could live through that.'

Gerald watched through his binoculars while tiny khaki figures crept forwards, with the silver-tin triangles on their back glinting in the hot sun. Then long bursts of machine-gun fire swept out from the enemy lines. More and more of the triangles, which were to identify the troops to British artillery, faltered, fell and lay still. Alas, the Germans had not only survived the bombardment; they had survived unscathed.

When it became fairly clear, even through the din and swirling smoke, that the advance had been checked, Gerald scribbled off a report and then, unable to contain himself any longer, plunged down into the battle to see what was happening. The noise was terrific, shells still crashing down into the smoke and sending up plumes of earth. At last, out of the smoke, staggered a man, his 'face and uniform were smeared with blood . . . his features distorted with terror and [he was] crying out something I could not in that infernal din understand'. It was probably a gas warning, because when Gerald finally regained his OP – realising he could find out nothing – gas shells were falling nearby.*

Nothing, not an inch, was gained in front of him. No British Army corps has ever suffered such terrible losses in a single day. And Gerald had first-hand experience of the consequences of this appalling defeat as well. About ten days after it, he was sent with his platoon to Colincamps a mile or so from Hébuterne, on a burial party. Hundreds of bodies came up every night in a trench railway from the front: 'Legs had broken off from trunks, heads came off at a touch and rolled away, and horrible liquids oozed out of cavities. A sickening stench filled the air . . .' For three days Gerald endured in this nightmare place. He took a shovel and worked himself. By the end, his nerve had gone. He felt he couldn't have 'gone over the top'

---

* It may be here that Gerald caught a whiff of gas himself. In a BBC broadcast to Spain in 1945 called 'An English Writer Discovers Malaga' he says his lungs are weak because he was gassed in the war. Gamel Brenan refers to this once or twice. But it cannot have been serious, since he mentions it nowhere else. Nor do his subsequent astonishing feats of walking in the Alpujarra mountains of southern Spain furnish much evidence of weak lungs.

even if ordered. 'The stench had brought the fear of death to my very bones.'

Nevertheless, even after this, and quite soon (probably 16 July), he set out with Dartnell to find Ralph. To take him some pâté – appropriate comment on what was going on – and, no doubt, once again to test himself. He gives, in a narrative of sustained descriptive power and brilliance, another marvellous account of the Bosch-Paul Nash landscape through which he and his batman passed – a landscape which once more plunged into nightmare, at Mametz wood.

Here, apparently very rare, actual hand-to-hand fighting had taken place between large numbers. 'What seemed extraordinary was that all the dead bodies there lay just as they had fallen in their original places, as though they were being kept as an exhibit for a war museum. Germans in their field-grey, British in their khaki lying side by side, their faces and their hands a pale waxy green, the colour of rare marble. Heads covered with flat mushroom helmets next to heads in domed steel helmets that came down behind the ears. Some of these figures still sat with their backs against a tree and two of them – this had to be seen to be believed – stood locked together by their bayonets which had pierced one another's bodies and sustained in that position by the tree trunk against which they had fallen. I felt I was visiting a room in Madame Tussaud's Chamber of Horrors, for I could not imagine any of these bodies ever having been alive. Yet the effect in its morbid way was beautiful.'

He failed to find Ralph, but learnt on his return, after a difficult time dodging heavy shelling, that the 6th Warwicks were at Ovillers, on the extreme left. He and Dartnell set out again at once, Gerald presumably still clutching the pâté.

Ralph had been in the full fury of the battle, already, not yet twenty-two, in command of a company (he was soon to command a battalion), calm, brave – and loving it. Gerald, when he found him, saw he was 'in his element'. Ralph described the battle laconically, and they had a lunch of Hungarian goulash and champagne together. At the far end of the trench was a German machine-gun emplacement.

A mild, sad envy can be detected in the letter Gerald sent to his father ('My dear Daddy') after the battle. Partridge wants the war to go on for ever. It must be 'very exciting to be in one of these shows'.

Some men are terrified, but Gerald found 'the excitement always keeps me up'. Shell-shock 'generally means lying on one's bunk and screaming and trembling. Most shell shock cases are funk.'³⁴

The tone is very different from the dismissive or exalted one kept up with Hope. Gerald seems to have sent letters to his parents regularly through the war. All but two have vanished in various Brenan bonfires but, if these were typical, then they were long (twenty or thirty pages) factual accounts, often revealing of his state of mind. He always included lists of requests – decent soap, new boots, etc. He must have sent long lists of books. He sent them souvenirs. His parents responded with regular parcels, often containing food. These Gerald would share out among the men under him in the OPs.

8

The tone of Gerald's letters to Hope was different because they had, of course, a different purpose. Now, after the Somme, he had need of that insulation and escape.

After hanging about at Vox Vrie Farm near Ypres, Gerald moved in November into his new OP – a mill on the left-hand side of the Ypres salient. He also had a large dugout all to himself – a cave of black circular steel covered in earth and bricks and 'proof against everything but a direct hit by a 5.9'. It had a bed, two tables, shelves for books, a washstand, and a cupboard plated with tin to keep mice out. Two cats served the same purpose.* Snug, alone, his job now and for the next eight months was to observe the huge featureless plain, pocked with water-filled craters, and report back what he saw.

For long stretches of time he saw nothing. Or the mist and fog hung so thick they would have obscured anything that might happen. He went for long walks through the deserted countryside, and these little imitations revived the great Walk, which once more filled his letters to Hope. He ate what his men ate – plus a Maggi soup tablet in

---

* This is the first mention of pets in Gerald's life. As far as I can ascertain there were none at Miserden or Edgeworth, though his father once gave him pleasure by saying, revealing a rather grim daydream, that he would have liked to keep a dog 'to serve his purposes'. People either like dogs or cats, and from now on Gerald was a cat lover.

water with vegetables and Lapsang tea. He read Gibbon again, also Tolstoy's late novels and tracts.[35] It was probably now that, as well as poetry, he wrote and sent Hope his long account of the Walk.

Hope replied in kind, but from Corfu. His imminent death had been averted when the Army had discovered how short-sighted he was. According to Compton Mackenzie he had been 'caught saluting a drum which he'd mistaken for the Regimental Sergeant-Major'.[36] (Someone he shouldn't have saluted anyway.) He was seconded to Intelligence and spent the war, under Compton Mackenzie, comfortably in the Middle East. He, too, was writing poetry. One of his lines Gerald thought of the greatest beauty: 'Birds, why do you sing like that?'

Every now and again, the war would suddenly invade Gerald's peaceful life. The moment a bombardment began he would rush down a communication trench to the front line with one of his men. Now, until the bombardment was over, all was chaos. It must have been terrifying – the heaviest ever experienced, in that war or the next. The whole ground shuddered, no matter how deep the dugout. The noise was deafening. If it was daylight, the shells would be visible, passing 'like ghostly pencils overhead'. But usually it would be in the dark. When the din, the shaking, the blinding flashes were over, Gerald and his soldier would creep forward with a feeling they were approaching the site of 'a just committed crime'. They would hear the groans of the wounded. Once, he stumbled over a head completely severed from its body.

But those trips – made because he was intensely conscientious, to prove himself, so that he could at least partly undergo what Ralph was undergoing – were quite useless. He couldn't report anything the battalion wasn't perfectly well able to report itself. He often irritated them by his presence.

9

Gerald's next leave was on 9 January 1917. His father had just sold the Miserden house to the Wills tobacco family, who were in the process of buying up everything there, and bought another in the little village of Edgeworth, a few miles along the same plateau.

This house was burnt down in the 1930s but a replica was built so one can still get an idea of what it was like. Set in seven acres, with steep gables like a Charles Addams cartoon, the rooms were lower and darker than now. There are several large barns, an inspection pit in one; Gerald's father did his carpentry in another. There is the sound of rooks and the wind in trees.

Like Miserden, Edgeworth is enmeshed in tiny lanes. A hideout, where Hugh and Helen retreated, 'retiring', as Gerald wrote in his first novel, 'like badgers and marmots to their holes and burrows, hiding behind parlour maids, shuffling themselves under indispositions and previous engagements, shutting off behind double doors the world of laughter and geniality'.[37]

Yet it was in, as it is now, a beautiful place, deep in the same beautiful, miniature mountain Cotswold countryside of thickly wooded valleys falling to streams, water-meadows and still more woods. The house overlooked one of these precipitous gulfs and a steep, tortuous, then still unmetalled lane – death to cars – twisted up into a tricky right-hand turn and a gate at the top.

During this leave he met for the first time the niece of their neighbour Mrs MacMeeken. Ann-Marie Van Dummreicher was half-Italian, half-German and extremely pretty, with a cat face and delicious well-shaped body. When war broke out she had become a land girl working for the local baker, so as well as her other charms she was covered in flour, now something of a leitmotif in Gerald's girls. She was attracted to him and at some point he seems to have made love to her (as usual precisely when is not at all clear). On this leave a later letter from Ralph suggests that she pursued and Gerald retreated.[38] Her father had been in the Egyptian civil service so he called her La Égyptienne.

Gerald also went to London and showed Wyndham Lewis his parodies of Pound:

> A white box of cosmetic on the table
> Oh that she were here
> To smear my heart with it![39]

Lewis was delighted. 'His eyes lit up with any attack on his friends.'[40] He was going to publish the poems in *Blast*, but then he was called up and the magazine folded.

10

The winter seemed to last for ever, as Gerald now felt the war would. The water froze in the shell-holes, the blasted landscape – no trees, just stumps, no hedges or discernible fields, just the cratered frozen mud – lay under snow. Gerald avoided the other officers, he told Hope, so that he wouldn't have to hear talk of girls, and sat like an anchorite in his dugout reading for hours at a time – the Brontës, more Tolstoy, the Bible, 'huge' histories on top of Gibbon. He wondered if he should desert to Spain (they must learn Spanish) and lead the life of a tramp. Or the Pamirs again, Yarkand, China.[41] At the same time, he longed to be still more deeply involved in the war, to command a company and fight like Ralph.

Despite his prodigious reading, he couldn't summon the intense energy he had brought to reading poetry. Gerald's deepest horror, revived by this long stagnation, was that he should become dead like his parents. Against this, he summoned the ultimate reality: 'I have only one real desire – the desire to suffer.' And the sign of deadness was, precisely, that lack of poetry. 'Only a few days ago it [the fire] was alive, and all day I was able to read the gospels and Tolstoy with eagerness . . . Worst sign – I have ceased to be able to read poetry.' The longing for war, that is, had a deeper layer – the longing for pain.[41]

Spain is mentioned several times in his letters, but usually as a jumping-off point, possibly for Turkestan. To this end, in March he began to read Sven Hedin.

He was still reading the great Swedish explorer late at night in bed, on the two-day pre-battle leave at St Omer in March, when the waitress he'd flirted with earlier came into his room and, without taking off her clothes or even her shoes, got into his bed. Gerald's account in *A Life* . . . is amused and touched, and almost certainly accurate. He often lets the reader infer he has made love when he hasn't, but (unless this is one) no example exists of the opposite. But he made full use of the incident at the time. His account to Ralph was of necessity so confusing (Gerald did not very often straight-forwardly, in so many words, lie) that his friend wrote in perplexity, 'I don't understand what you mean by nights – you can't mean, oh no not for an instant, impossible.'[42] Some time later Gerald hinted he could have got VD. Ralph was suitably impressed and wrote offering 'pills of every hue'.[43] When Gerald wrote it up in 1923 he went into lyrical overdrive – '. . . the taste of early fruit, pulled from wet trees before the sun is up, cold as green figs eaten at daybreak – her long thin body'.[44] But he was engaged then in one of many protracted campaigns to capture Carrington and was continually inventing affairs and amorous incidents.

The battle for which this leave was to prepare him was the Ypres summer offensive – the second great convulsion by which the Germans would finally be dislodged. On his return from St Omer at the end of March he was given a new OP two miles from Ypres itself. His sector was extremely important, since it was the centre of the main attack. Gerald's position was therefore crucial. He was (at just twenty-three) the only observer for the entire corps – and as such provided, among other things, with a telescope instead of binoculars. There were fewer than a dozen like him along the Western front. He also had a general reconnaissance brief and during that spring and summer, day and night, often during shelling, had to traverse the lines. He also had to act as guide to generals and other senior staff officers. He knew the intricate, tangled maze of trenches and tunnels backwards.[45]

His role now demonstrates another aspect of Gerald at war. His new OP was thirty feet up in two tall elms. Here Gerald had built a cunningly camouflaged nest. When Ralph came to see him, Gerald flapped laughing towards it like some huge khaki bird. What Ralph admired about Gerald, among much else, was his *technique* in the war – the ability not just to do it well but with his vitality and humour to make it bearable.[46]

Sometimes nothing could keep the brutality at bay, not all the resources of the castle, not humour, not courage. Late in June, Gerald was eating breakfast in his dugout. Dartnell was on leave. A new batman was approaching with the coffee. They were being shelled and, hearing a close one, Gerald instinctively pushed back his chair into the dugout. At that moment, another shell exploded above them. Gerald was hurled into his cave, but the batman was blown to pieces. Gerald helped gather what he could and they took the remains to the cemetery. The padre was there, the grave ready. By the time he returned, a second breakfast was waiting. 'A man whom I did not know very well had been killed within a few feet of me. That was something that had happened to me several times before. One learned to shut one's mind to such things for, if one didn't, one would not be able to carry on. But the rapidity of this proceeding shocked me. While a second breakfast was being made for me, this man, still warm, had been buried and prayed for and had a cross put over him.'

But everything was now swept aside in the excitement of the Ypres offensive. This was due to start on 31 July. At long last, Gerald was to go over the top. He would go with the second wave, sending back reports by runner. The weather was fine and tanks – that cross between a car and a suit of armour – would be used. Best of all, Ralph (who now wrote to him as 'Argos of the tree tops') would be there with him. Since Gerald had last seen him, Ralph had won an MC and been buried alive by a shell. He was only saved by his batman digging him out.

On the morning of 29 July Gerald was standing outside his dugout when a shell landed some distance away. He heard the whine of shrapnel coming towards him. The next moment he was struck a violent blow and knocked flat. His sleeve and jacket were ripped and rapidly soaked in blood (as was the *Little Review*, where Eliot's poems were appearing, which was in his pocket).[47]

To his horror, he was taken to the base hospital. He expostulated furiously, but he was to be robbed of his battle. Two days later he was in London, in the military hospital at Camberwell.

11

The wound was clearly a great deal more serious than Gerald, in his typically offhand way, lets on. He was in hospital for three months and not allowed back for seven.

Ralph, too, was wounded in August, getting a bar to his MC. He returned to England, but they don't seem to have been able to meet, though they corresponded about things like Gerald's possible VD.[43]

Gerald's behaviour in hospital suggests that he must have been brooding about Carrington ever since Hope had described her in 1915. As soon as he was allowed out, he set off to find her. He took to eating in restaurants where artists went in the hope of seeing her. Once he thought he saw her, but was too frightened to approach (he saw later he'd been mistaken). 'She had become the symbol of the kind of girl I wanted to know.'[29]

It is probable, therefore, that when he met Hope in August and September, just back from the Aegean, they talked about Carrington as well as literature. Certainly, Hope made an oblique reference to her in a letter of 18 December.[48]

Gerald left hospital in October and was then sent on courses and shunted about various regimental depots – Sevenoaks in October, then Colchester in November. In December he went alone for a blissful five-day walking tour in the Lake District. There was snow on the passes and it was cold and clear. He walked tirelessly, at one point passing, by what was to prove an extraordinary coincidence, a Watendlath Farm near Keswick,[49] and reading Wordsworth. When he got back to Colchester he wrote a long poem called 'Ecstasy' in Wordsworthian blank verse. He also found a letter from Hope asking for £70. He planned to invest their money in French War Loan. Gerald seems foolishly for a time to have stopped vetoing Hope's speculative wheezes.

By February 1918 he was at Tonbridge in Kent. 'Filthy, unspeakable, disgusting, hog-like officers. They seem to eat and drink all day – they make me almost physically sick.' He reacted as usual: solitude, the Walk, reading – Hardy, Shelley and Hogg's *Life of Shelley*. 'Five hundred pages to cover two years! On the same scale a life of Wordsworth would cover ten thousand pages.'[50] In March he was posted back to France.

12

The battle of Ypres, which had raged for nearly six months with terrible casualties, had carried the line exactly six miles forward, to the village of Passchendaele: 'that place with a beautiful name' as Gerald called it.

He rejoined his regiment at Poperinghe on 12 March, his OP sited in a house that was slowly sinking into the ground. Between now and May he observed, did fatigues and led patrols into no-man's-land at Bailleul, which necessitated a four-mile trudge at night on narrow pathways above thigh-deep mud.

As the end of the long and terrible war approached (Gerald

guessed – accurately – the autumn) he became furiously impatient. He wrote a long letter to Hope on 3 May. He had been reconnoitring the line. Two of his men had been killed. 'When I shut my eyes I can see the piles of bodies waiting to be buried. Blue uniforms of French soldiers on the bright green grass; the blue sky, daisies and dande- lions, the ground drenched, absolutely drenched with blood, so brilliant and red – the faces of the corpses like finest marble . . .'[51]

He had been reading: *Adolphe*, *Don Quixote*, Laforgue again, Maupassant. Also, 'I read the first instalment of Joyce's new book in the *Little Review*. It is incontestably a work of genius.'

It is a letter, from a young man of twenty-four, whose desire not to be killed is almost unbearably poignant. 'And the spring moves on like a procession, there is such a sweetness over all the fields, new birds arrive and begin to sing and one of the few springs of my own short life is wasting away. And I feel in me a strength to live and to love all this and be part of it. O cottage in Spain and the life on the roads and books and liberty!'[51]

In fact, the Cyclists' Battalion was at that moment being readied for death. On the same day, something which probably prompted the letter to Hope, Gerald was given command of his first company – B Company. On 15 May they were moved far to the south, to Châlons-sur-Marne in champagne country.

The plan was that they should support the French, who were engaging the enemy forty miles to the north. The period at Châlons was to train them as rapidly as possible in the use of French weapons. Gerald, as the only man in the battalion who could speak French, spent most of it interpreting.

He had time only to dash off a last letter to Hope (begging him to stop speculating with their money. Hope was switching wildly about and had now plumped for Italian War Loan)[52] when their call came. The Germans had broken through near Chemin-des-Dames. The new mounted infantry – 'Our value at once apparent,' Gerald wrote proudly – were rushed north. The order, dated 31 May 1918, has a certain ring to it: 'Fighting kit only will be taken.'[53] At last the moment had come for which he had so passionately and so anxiously longed. Gerald was about to face the supreme test.

13

On 1 June Gerald's company took up their positions in gently undulating farmland across the Vendières-Verneuil road. The French were on their right, the Germans about three miles in front. That very night, at 4 am, the Germans attacked, but were repulsed. The following night, after a day of feverish preparation, Gerald's company advanced at 4.30 am and took a ridge 200 yards further forward. On the third night, the night of 3 June, he sent out a dawn patrol – a lance-corporal and four men. While he waited anxiously for their return, they crawled through the long wet grass to a farmhouse midway between the lines. Here they surprised nine Germans having breakfast and brought them back as prisoners. They were members of a *corps d'élite*, the 39th Prussian regiment.*

The French and English divisional headquarters were overjoyed, but Gerald clearly felt that he should have led the patrol himself. Although he'd had virtually no sleep for the last three nights, he none the less suggested he lead an attack on a mill about 1½ miles away to the right. The French were delighted and agreed to give machine-gun support from their nearest company and lay down an artillery barrage.

Gerald's initiative, made on impulse, left little time to prepare. And just as they were setting off, a French officer arrived with a detailed map. The moment he saw it, Gerald realised he'd made a terrible mistake. The mill was in fact much closer than he'd realised to the village of Verneuil. This was a key point on the German left flank and therefore strongly held. But the mill was crucial to the village and would itself also be strongly defended. Two platoons would almost certainly be far too few. In a panic he rushed to get this, his first major attack, cancelled. The CO was in conference. With sinking heart, Gerald set off.

Half a mile from the mill he stopped the column and explained the attack. Two parties, led by NCOs, would rush the two entrances.

---

* On the whole I follow very closely Gerald's account of these events. But where he differs from the Official War Diary, made on the spot by his CO Major Baldwin and which he did not have by him when writing *A Life . . .* , then I follow the diary – as in these details (Public Record Office – WO 95, 816).

Gerald would follow with 'support' and mop up. This was the accepted method for such attacks and the accepted role for the officer. But from the back of the column he heard – everybody heard – a voice say, 'I thought an orficer was supposed to lead.'

Gerald was, naturally enough, stung. Should he? But they were already an hour late. There was no time to work it out. As they crept forward he was more and more certain it would be a disaster whoever led, but hadn't the courage to cancel it.

Then, all at once, he realised the significance of that hour's delay: *they hadn't heard a sound*. No machine-gun, no artillery. At last a reasonable excuse. He called the sergeant – 'Those bloody French' – and led his platoon back. Major Baldwin was sitting up and completely exonerated him.

But Gerald felt very guilty. He knew he was brave, he could take shelling and lead patrols (he had in fact already been put in unsuccessfully for an MC for his patrols at Bailleul six weeks before).[54] But now he'd narrowed the test to a simple point. Could he engage in personal hand-to-hand combat? Could he kill someone? Also – 'I thought an orficer was meant to lead.'

Now, after the first proper night's sleep in five days, Gerald began to lead patrol after patrol with reckless courage.

On 6 June the French took over Vendières. The Cyclists' Battalion moved back, but were told they could go out and raid as appropriate. Gerald decided to go that very night.

They set off at 3 am, Gerald, a lance-corporal and two men. Across a stubbled field on their stomachs and then, reaching an orchard, at last able to stand up. Gerald remembered the feeling of freedom. He found himself thinking of the time long ago when he'd explored his nurse's bed. In the pale moonlight, he could see across the valley. They were close to the village of Trotte.

With hammering hearts, they crept to within twenty yards of it. They located guards and machine-gun posts. They saw it could be taken and that it commanded the valley. Light was coming up. They crawled back to the orchard, back across the stubble on their stomachs, and reached their positions at dawn. And at once, and all day, Gerald was engaged on his duties – mostly translating.

But Trotte was still not reconnoitred sufficiently for a successful attack. Gerald set out again the next night, with a sergeant and two men. Once more they reached the hamlet, muffled in the pale moonlight.* They crept slowly about it, in the very deep shadows of the buildings and carts. No dogs. Two more guard posts.

Gerald was determined to do this thoroughly. He needed to see further along the road to the furthermost guard positions. They had done this and were returning, bent double to make use of the shadow of a wall, when a German came from a building and walked towards them. Gerald prayed he would turn off, but he kept on. In a moment he would see them. Gerald took out his revolver. The German stopped, suddenly alert, five yards away. Gerald put up his revolver and said '*Hände hoch*' – '. . . but he paid no attention. Slowly and deliberately he unslung his rifle from his shoulder and raised it to aim at me. I saw his blue saucer eyes just under the helmet, saw the Lombardy poplar behind him waving its tips against the sky, and I did not want to pull the trigger.'

So – it had come. The confrontation. And now a very odd thing happened. It was as if his complex character was stripped into its most simple, opposite elements. This extreme situation, his male Brenan side in full command, suddenly called up the mother in him, the poet – perhaps heralded by the earlier flash-memory of his nurse. And the poet won. He could see the pale undersides of the poplar leaves with great intensity. In a trance, he heard the soldiers call, 'Shoot, sir, shoot.' But it was the German who shot. Two men leapt forward and either shot or bayonetted him. He suppressed the image. 'Probably bayonetted.'

Gerald appeared unhurt, the bullet passing between arm and side. The patrol rushed back towards their lines, just managing to fling themselves down in the stubble behind a dead cow as the machine-gun opened up. Rats poured out of the belly of the cow and scuttled over their backs and away. They lay for a long time as bullets passed over them 'their notes suddenly altering when they swished through the carcass'. At last it stopped and they wriggled back on their stomachs, reaching their lines at dawn.

There was no need for a company commander to lead patrols. Gerald had already led three, and it seems that he had in fact been

---

* It is a fascinating indication of the extraordinarily high pitch to which his senses became strung that when he returned to the scene of these patrols on his honeymoon in 1931 he remembered them taking place under a full moon. When he checked with his pocket diary of the time he discovered it had been a new moon (MSS, Texas).

slightly wounded by the German's bullet. Nevertheless, he now led two more patrols, and was setting out on a sixth when he was stopped at the last minute by the French, who didn't want anyone else out in front because they were sending out a working party. Without sleep for nights, strung up to breaking point, Gerald 'with unspeakable relief' returned, went to bed and slept till the following afternoon.

On 12 June the battalion was relieved; on the 15th they were on a train for Long; by the 18th they were at La Catalet, Abbeville, far behind the lines.[55]

It will come as no surprise to learn that Gerald, in his later accounts, regarded what he'd done, as with the Walk, as a total failure. The authorities felt differently. As the battalion entrained for Long, he learnt that he'd been awarded the MC and the Croix de Guerre. Gerald decided the Croix de Guerre was for interpreting. He wrote and told Hope. 'I feel too ashamed for words about it.'[56] The whole eleven days at the front are not even mentioned in his journal.

14

The effort had clearly tested Gerald to the limit and he now collapsed with Spanish 'flu. This was not a light matter. It was killing thousands at this time. The wound was not so small (it was described as 'a bit serious' in a letter to his mother from 18th Corps HQ).[57] He was sent to a hospital in Paris on 24 June, to Croxteth Hospital outside Liverpool on 16 July and spent most of August in a convalescent home at Moffat, just across the Scottish border.

Here he went for long walks across the moors, one lasting four days. He also wrote to Hope describing the people. 'The men look like butlers who have gone out for the day in their master's shooting clothes and the women are of several sorts: some are of the elderly class which imitates china knick-knacks, others are like ants, earwigs and certain species of beetle – one would like to enquire their Latin names.'

Though the fighting did not end until 11 November 1918 and Gerald was not officially demobilised till May 1919, his war, despite a good deal of shunting about, was effectively over. It is interesting to try and analyse how it affected him.

One might start with those knick-knacks and earwigs. Exalted and often rather unreal at first, by the end his letters had begun to develop a fresh, vivid, descriptive prose – you may remember the 'blue uniforms of French soldiers on the bright green grass; the blue sky, daisies and dandelions, the ground drenched, absolutely drenched with blood, so brilliant and red' – a vividness that was enlivened by Gerald's idiosyncratic humour. He was, in fact, learning how to write. He makes much in *Personal Record* of his long and painful apprenticeship in English prose. In fact, he wrote well quite early – and learnt to do so through his letters. Gerald's problem was not how to write, but what. And he wrote something like the equivalent of two average novels in letters during these four years. It is now that letter-writing became established as a necessary habit.

But this is somewhat on the periphery. The war itself seems to have affected him remarkably little. He never dreamt about it, though he continued to have nightmares about Radley and Winton House into his fifties. He hardly mentioned it again – referring to the events which won him his medals only once in his life. He says in *A Life* . . . that, deprived of the excitement of war, he felt flat and dispirited for about a year. There was no evidence of this at the time in either his behaviour or letters, quite the contrary, but it may have been so.

In a more general way, both Gerald and Ralph were prone thereafter to see potential disaster in every international flare-up. Both emerged (Gerald had entered) with a hatred of violence; but this was not quite straightforward. Ralph had an aggressive side and this sometimes found expression in argument. 'He *loved* arguing,' said Frances Partridge. 'He got very red and excited and his eyes flashed. It stimulated him.' Gerald, on the contrary, hated it. But Ralph had experienced weeks of horror in the trenches, not days; weeks of the stench, the discomfort, the not washing, the terrible bombardments, the death, the terror. His hatred of violence was more fundamental than Gerald's and after the war he was early, easily and permanently converted to pacifism. Gerald's loathing of personal confrontation (the German sentry can be seen as the ultimate expression of Radley) was lessening by the 1930s. It never extended in the way it did with Ralph, and though he hated the violence of the Spanish Civil War and the Second World War, he was always quite clear that in 1939 the British should fight.

This difference in experience may explain another difference.

Ralph came out of the war feeling he had done his bit. He no longer wanted to compete. He was quite without ambition. Gerald was not particularly competitive but there was a lot he wanted to achieve.

On the other hand, one cannot exactly say that Gerald had had it easy. There is another reason for this difference in reaction. We have seen how the ideals of the Walk, his retreat into reading and writing, insulated him. But they did so in a peculiar way. Gerald put it succinctly in *A Life* . . .: 'Before the war my dull, sheltered childhood and my romantic disposition had made me think that the medicine I needed was reality. This had taken the form of poverty, hunger, doss-houses, deserts and mountains. I imagined I could only maintain and hold on to my visions by such means. I could only burn up the impurities in my nature and become a real and authentic person if I sought them. Now, in the middle of the war, a life in the infantry offered me much the same opportunities.'

His vision, that is, allowed him to a certain extent to incorporate the war. It became part of the process. That is why, whenever he did refer to it afterwards, it was with pleasure.*

It also meant that his ideals – of 'reality', to feel intensely, to be poor, to suffer, to write, to read, to be free – emerged not just intact but stronger than ever. It was these that, not without a good deal of trepidation, he had now in August 1918 to set about implementing.

---

* For example, in a letter to Chatto and Windus, 21 November 1952: 'I enjoyed much of the war, though I was in two or three of the worst battles.' Or to Frances Partridge, May 1983, he said that, if no one had been killed (rather a large proviso) he'd say he 'enjoyed it and I remember it with great vividness'.

EIGHT

Finding Carrington

1

As often during Gerald's life, but acutely, even desperately, over the next ten years the vital element was money.

The plan in June 1918 was that Gerald and Hope should take a cottage in Provence. Gerald vaguely wondered if his Croix de Guerre might help here.[1] But between then and October an incomplete series of letters gradually revealed the full catastrophe of Hope's dealings with their money.[2] They (especially Gerald) had been saving for four years. They should have had about £400 (say £8500). Hope had lost the lot.

Gerald seems neither to have blamed Hope nor felt any resentment. Hope was still by far his closest friend. And earlier letters must have prepared him (the news, for instance, that Hope, in pursuit of their money, was suing the Italian government). Also for some time Hope's letters had had a distinctly unidealistic ring. He needed comforts, if simple ones. He could not possibly live in a garret. 'I am older and wickeder.' (He was nearly thirty-six.) He needed 'a certain luxe'. Gerald appears to have accepted Hope's explanations (whatever these were. Hope guiltily culled much of the correspondence later on) and resolved that in the future he would have to rely on himself. Nevertheless, his forbearance was extraordinary.

It was this financial disaster which now inclined Gerald much more definitely towards Spain again. Spain was known to be cheaper.

None of this, nor any of his other plans, had Gerald yet dared communicate to his father. Hugh Brenan had told him on his return from France that he would support him provided he did something of which he approved.[2] Gerald probably guessed this would not include France or Spain, whether in the form of straight tramping or with cottage and books.

He returned to Edgeworth in September still silent on his future. No doubt he wanted to enjoy for a while the hero's welcome. And there was his mother. The most agonising side of the rows with his father was her pain. To please her he went to communion with her that month – as he did occasionally till she died. To please her – and yet, one feels, to please himself. Religion moved depths in him – not religious depths, at least not Christian, but profound none the less. This time he had sat up reading *Macbeth* all night. When he went out early into the fresh September morning the sky 'was blue and kind, the clouds white and cosy were sailing past . . .' When the priest said, 'Lift up your hearts,' and the response came, 'They are lifted up,' Gerald was suddenly pierced with such a poignant sense of the sweetness of life that he nearly cried out.[3]

Ralph came to stay. On his return from Italy, where he had gone as a major, he had resumed his undergraduate life at Oxford. He had written to Gerald in July 1918 with the extraordinary and perhaps not totally welcome news that he'd met, through Hope, the girl Gerald had been thinking about, actually searching for, since 1915 – Carrington.[4] Galling, even maddening. At the same time there were ameliorations. She had heard of Gerald from Hope – no doubt favourably and romantically.*[5] Now at least he could meet her. And Ralph was fickle. He talked just as much of his Italian conquests.

Around 14 October Gerald at last wrote, from Cambridge where he'd gone on military matters, and told his father his plans.[6] What he said precisely we don't know. Later, he said he went to Spain to educate himself, but there is no mention of this at the time. The idea of educating himself seems to have evolved naturally: to emulate Hope, because he enjoyed it, no doubt gaining impetus from Ralph's

---

* In *A Life* . . . Gerald says Ralph met Carrington through her brother Noel (Michael Holroyd follows him). But Ralph's letter of 7 July is quite clear and there seems no reason he would make it up. This may be another instance of Gerald in retrospect and unconsciously wishing to diminish Hope's astonishing influence on his life, because this was a momentous introduction. Hope had re-met Carrington in 1917 and pursued one of his pointless flirtations. She didn't terribly like him, telling Gerald he accumulated knowledge so that he could show off and that he was incapable of real feeling. Gerald says they quarrelled over this, but it can't have been serious since it left no other trace. The criticisms were telling since in the end Gerald came to make them himself.

being at Oxford. In July, he had bought Frazer's *The Golden Bough*, the first of the great classics in every field of knowledge that he purchased, helped by his captain's pay, throughout 1918 and 1919.

But whether he mentioned education or not, his father was instantly furious. As far as he was concerned he'd spent considerable sums giving Gerald a perfectly good education already. He felt he had to insist – a position in the Indian police was 'too good to be neglected'. Gerald was still nervous of his father. He was no longer frightened of him. He replied refusing point-blank, adding that, even if he had joined the Indian police in 1914, he would have left as soon as he'd saved enough to get out.

Gerald seems to have behaved as provocatively as he possibly could in other ways. He said he would vote Labour in the forthcoming election. As soon as he got back from Cambridge, he took to the roads, returning at intervals to Edgeworth. There was a pause only for the Armistice on 11 November. (Gerald was so excited he danced with a policeman in the streets – simple steps, one imagines.) The village was riveted. 'He had socialist principles,' said Mr Rust, aged about sixteen at the time. 'Used to walk about in ragged clothes, in rags, in tramp get-up. He used to sleep out. It was the talk of the village. His old man would turn him out. Said he was a disgrace. He never came back often.'

It could not go on. The volcano was now in constant eruption, its liver at white heat, its single terrified female inhabitant cowering. On 29 November Gerald left for Northern Ireland.

He stayed there five months; partly at Larchfield, partly at his Uncle Ogilvie's house in County Down, partly at a regimental depot near Oranmore. Soldiers, or at least officers, seem to have been allowed to choose where they waited for demobilisation. No military activity took place, but occasional attendance was expected.

Gerald suffered. The colonel reminded him of Judge Jefferies. He loathed Gerald on sight and talked, with sure instinct, 'of killing, hanging bloody Germans and Irishmen and Conscientious Objectors'. The colonel, as well as *The Golden Bough*, may have inspired Gerald's comment on the allied peace plan, which also horrified him. 'It is like the Adonis ceremony of eating the holy bull. We have eaten the Germans in solemn and public manner – and become Germans.'[7]

Also, the nightmare dance-mania now sweeping England, especially London, had reached Ireland. Gerald went to one ball.

The desire to dance was torture. All he could do was stand at the bar. Suddenly, he rushed out in agony and walked over the bog till dawn.[8]

In February 1919, there was a reconciliation. His father, through his mother's mediation, became extremely reasonable.* He felt he would eventually 'come round' to Gerald's plans and might then help him financially. But he hoped Gerald would one day earn something, however small. For the rest, he mustn't stay too long at Edgeworth (using it to save money), mustn't have long hair there or wear 'curious clothes' (i.e. dress as a tramp).[9]

Gerald told Hope he at once agreed to these conditions. The long-term goal remained Central Asia in 1920 (from this and other indications it would seem his mother had told him she thought his father would take about a year to 'come round'). For the present, Gerald would get a cottage in Spain. Hope would join him. He was already learning Spanish.[9]

Official demobilisation did not take place till May, but Gerald was allowed to go two days before his twenty-fifth birthday on 5 April. He spent the next three weeks in full-dress rehearsal for Spain. Sleeping rough, he made a great sweep across the mountains of the north of Ireland, from Drogheda to Galway, up the coast to Achill island and back round to Galway. As he walked in the mists up the bleak valleys, fantasy took over and he was already in Central Asia. How wonderful to spend a lifetime like this. 'Now and then letters from me would reach Europe. They would read like the letters from a dead man, so toneless would they be.'[10]

By 28 April he was back at Edgeworth. There now occurred what Gerald describes as 'a stupid and pointless episode'. He seems to have lost his virginity. 'Seems,' because the account is distinctly odd in the Gerald manner about sex – dismissive, callous, disgusted, irritated. But for once, on the central point it is not ambiguous. He says, for the first time in so many words, that he has made love to a girl. Or succumbed to her, since it was La Égyptienne.

One evening, when he was seeing her home, they had kissed

---

* Far more reasonable than Gerald lets on in *A Life . . .* It was loss of money that terrified Hugh Brenan, as much as a desire to control Gerald. A neurotic reaction, since he was very well off. This never occurred to Gerald. But his outburst at this point in his autobiography was a reaction to what he saw as a lifetime of financial injustices.

under the trees and then made love. During the spring and summer of 1919 they continued to meet and make love. La Égyptienne, with her lovely body and cat face, would arrive in the woods in a mackintosh and nothing else. She would throw it off and dance naked in 'Oriental fashion'. She maddened Gerald by her sentimentality, she maddened him by comparing him to Baudelaire, he was appalled when she fell in love with him. He really only did it 'from want of something better to do'.

The tone may be because he wanted to conceal that it was the first time,* and to hide his relief, or due to his 'reactions'; probably both. It was as significant as that milestone is to young men; it was not nearly as important as what took place in May. It was then that he met Carrington for the first time.

2

At the beginning of May 1919 Gerald spent three days at an inn near Oxford with Reynolds Ball. On the last day, Ralph and Carrington appeared unexpectedly.[11]

They only stayed half an hour, but Gerald would have been struck – everyone was – by the intense cornflower-blue eyes under bobbed, page-boy hair. The hair itself was light brown and very fine, but as she turned – or as you turn it in your hands now, for a thick lock survives† – it caught the sun and turned gold. He would have noticed most of all her smooth, milk-white skin; as soft, said Maria his servant in Spain later, as the material they used there for petticoats.[12] And there was something little-girlish about her, inno-cent, vulnerable, with her turned-in toes and nervous arm move-ments. Men were always moved by this and Gerald's capacity for

---

* We are still left, of course, with his statement to Frances Partridge that he hadn't made love properly to a girl before Carrington. But it must now be abundantly clear that one cannot take *au pied de la lettre* anything Gerald says on this subject. Perhaps by 'properly' he meant Christopher Fry's 'as near a virgin as makes no difference' in *The Lady's Not for Burning*.

† Given to Gerald in 1921 (Gerald to Joanna Carrington, 7 July 1971). Now in the MF archive in Spain, along with a second lock which he cut off after her death (much darker) and various flowers she gave him in 1932 – an iris, clover leaves, some grass.

pity and protectiveness, still latent, were to prove almost his strongest emotions.

The next day the three had a picnic and shortly afterwards went on a two-day walking tour of the Cotswolds. Now Gerald got to know her better. Restless, almost as energetic as he was, Carrington's chief quality was the way she focused on the companion of the moment, provided she liked them. Her sympathy was concentrated, intuitive, delightful. She instantly, as Julia Strachey noted, got someone's 'point'. And there was an exciting feeling of impulse; you could say, 'Come to Spain' – and she'd set off, on the spot. She was lively, humorous, inquisitive, stimulating, flirtatious, and also not to be taken in – that innocence was deceptive.

It seems possible that, at an unconscious level, Gerald fell at least half in love on the spot. That was his way (particularly when, as now, he'd been readying himself for years). Bunny Garnett was certainly told he was in love with her.[13] And Carrington – what did she see and feel?

Gerald at this time was an extremely romantic figure. A poet – the only time he went to Garsington, Lytton Strachey introduced him to Ottoline Morrell as 'the new Shelley', and that was how Carrington saw him for years[14] – he had all the romantic poet's attractive, distracted vagueness. Hopeless as to times and distances, she noted later. This, and his diffidence, gave him in his turn a vulnerability to which she too responded – Carrington had a maternal side. At the same time, in complete contradiction, she must have known something of Gerald's war. He casually let slip mention of La Égyptienne, but said she bored him. He was quite tall (about six foot), hair just not thinning, with the body, especially the legs, of an athlete, and a moustache. His arms concealed their strength in an extraordinary, touching clumsiness. The sullen, obstinate adolescent expression had long vanished, and he was full of eagerness and nervous energy, pressing forward impatiently; he walked 'at a tilt' as one of the old inhabitants of Miserden remembered[15] (Richard Jefferies says this is a characteristic of those who walk a lot). He talked, dark eyes intent, face ardent, a great deal, mostly obsessively and self-centredly about his plans. Yet, she noted acutely in a letter to Strachey, he was curiously remote and detached, and too obstinate to be influenced.[16] She was baffled – and intrigued. He reminded her, she told Bunny Garnett, of Trelawny – a bold and almost too romantic adventurer. Yet the fact that he was about to set out on a long and distant journey was perhaps, really, the most exciting and attractive thing about him.

To understand this fully, and the much more tangled depths into which Gerald was gradually to be drawn, until for seven or eight years Carrington completely obsessed him, it is necessary to learn a little of her history, and something of those around her. It can be brief. Carrington and her circle have been considerably written over.

She was born in March 1893 (so she was a year older than Gerald), one of five children of a fifty-six-year-old retired Anglo-Indian railway engineer. He had married the governess of his sister's children who, when she had children, was quite unable to stop governessing. She harried and disciplined and pried and punished her children till Carrington, at least, came to hate her. This was compounded by her nurses, who regularly beat her, treatment that left its legacy in a lifetime of nightmares. She fastened all her love on to her father, and also on to one of her brothers, Edmund – Teddy.

In this simple configuration lie all the clues to an exceedingly complicated character. Her mother's disciplines enjoined a need for secrecy, but secrecy was not just necessary – it gradually became a deep pleasure, containing the delicious, remembered excitement of defying authority. It also meant endless tiny lies. By the time she joined the Slade in 1911, she told Gertler, 'I couldn't speak the truth if I wanted to.'[1] As she got to know the various figures in Bloomsbury, she was horrified by their frankness until she learnt that in personal matters it was really a technique, a sort of game, which in fact hid deep reserve. Yet the odd thing about this most private, most devious of creatures was that she was capable of ruthless introspection quite beyond most of those close to her. All the most penetrating insights about Carrington come from Carrington herself.

She was totally uneducated, despite two years at Bedford High School. But she won all the art prizes. At the Slade, she blossomed – if that's the word to describe the cropping of her hair, the wearing of trousers and the dropping of the feminine Dora to become the more boylike Carrington. These changes had profound roots. Her hatred of her mother led her to reject, indeed loathe, her femaleness. 'How I hate being a girl!' she told Gertler – a refrain repeated. She was deeply ashamed of menstruation – calling it the fiend.

There was another way of dealing with this problem – and it was a problem, since in character she was deeply feminine. The solution was not to let the woman in her physically grow up, to remain for ever the little girl in love with her father. And this conception of herself is revealed in the self-portraits which sprinkle her letters; even when she is thirty-six, they are still of someone of about fourteen. So strong was this, so necessary, that the moment her father died in 1915 she instantly chose and fell in love with another one: Lytton Strachey.

It was, on the face of it, an odd choice and an odd combination – and at first a precarious one. Even odd physically: Carrington rather dumpy and eventually almost plump, restless, her voice usually a slightly rushed patter; Lytton somewhat languid, with, in Max Beerbohm's words, his 'emaciated face of ivory whiteness', his long spade beard and very long, bony, stooping, folding, bending, deck-chair-like body and his astonishing voice – now piping and fluting, now swooping to a *basso profundo*. More germane, he was a thirty-five-year-old homosexual who had never, hitherto, been remotely physically attracted to a woman. He was both bored and flattered. He continued to lead his own life while she remained in tow, indeed unshake-offable. But Carrington had a secret weapon. She could write, or rather spontaneously dash off, the most extraordinary and enchanting letters. She seduced men with her letters; we shall see something of their quality emerging as Gerald falls under their spell. And she was intelligent, even if often choked by the intensity of her feelings and the confusion of swirling and conflicting moods.

Lytton became more and more interested, even, in a vague way, attracted. All homosexuals feel there may be a heterosexual buried somewhere inside them, and an attempt was made to disinter the one in Lytton when he and Carrington shared a bed on holiday in Wales in 1916. Fortunately it failed – the last thing Carrington wanted Lytton to be was a lover.

The decisive step came when Lytton and she moved together into a mill-house at Tidmarsh, a village near Pangbourne. It was shortly after this that she met Ralph.

Ralph's attraction to Carrington had not been the evanescent flare of lust that Gerald must have hoped. Instead, he fell in love with her. Carrington's initial reaction had been ecstatic: his good looks, his humour, at times wit, the almost reckless feeling of life and pleasure he gave to everything, above all the ease of talk. 'It is so good to find someone,' she wrote to Lytton, 'you can rush on and on with,

quickly.'[17] Then, as Ralph's presence more and more suited Lytton*
– itself the most important single criterion – other factors came into
play. She was quite often alone at Tidmarsh when Lytton went
visiting and could have been lonely. Besides, becoming involved with
Ralph showed she was not dependent on Lytton. Her great horror
(the greater since at a profound level it was true) was that he might
think this. When she learnt via Virginia Woolf that it was also one of
Lytton's fears, that she might become too clinging and clogging and
suffocating – 'a permanent limpet' in Carrington's words – the effect,
says Holroyd, was like an electric shock. All her love affairs were
embarked on with this as an important factor – significantly nothing
to do with the supposedly 'loved' one.

Then Carrington, despite a complicated attitude to sex, was not
unsusceptible to male charms. When early in 1919 she painted Ralph
naked she found she could hardly concentrate on the brushstrokes.
Shortly after that, in March, she and Ralph (who spoke Spanish, as

---

* Ralph's first visit to Tidmarsh in 1918 was not a success. All his life he held
his views passionately and, enjoying the confrontations, expressed them as
forcefully as he could. On this occasion he suddenly exploded about pacifists – they
should be shot. Not the most tactful utterance in the house of a conscientious
objector and his pacifist companion; yet perhaps an understandable one from
someone a few months out of the most frightful war in history, who had personally
seen hundreds slaughtered and narrowly escaped himself.

But no newcomer into a closed circle is liked at first. Lytton soon discovered, to
his surprise, that this handsome man was not just extremely intelligent, but quick
and clever, with a potential feeling for literature and art. Lytton liked nothing better
than an apt pupil – especially if he was male, young and good-looking. Soon they
were all three reading Elizabethan and metaphysical poets together. Ralph picked it
all up with his usual rapidity and by 1919 was bicycling over from Oxford
continually, to talk about literature, painting and Einstein – and to see Carrington.
He was soon arguing in Bloomsbury fashion to such effect that Carrington asked
Lytton to give her lessons in arguing.

The orientation of a lifetime – and Ralph became, among other things, a
cultivated man of letters, a *New Statesman* reviewer for over twenty years, an author
– is not suddenly 'created' at the age of twenty-five, as Holroyd, following Gerald,
tends to suggest. No more did Hope 'create' Gerald. Rather, in each case the
impression is of something latent being encouraged and led out.

We shall deal with Gerald's attitude to Ralph in this respect in due course, but it
is almost the only time that Holroyd gets his emphasis wrong, and he does so
because he followed Gerald. Holroyd's book is still incomparably the best – I think
a masterpiece and a delightful one – on the period and the group he follows through
it. The recent biography of Carrington, for instance, has not replaced his portrait.
On the contrary. (See *Lytton Strachey* by Michael Holroyd, Penguin 1971; *A Life of
Dora Carrington*, by Gretchen Gerzina, London 1978).

well as French and German), her brother Noel and his sister Dorothy, all went on a walking tour, mostly to southern Spain: from Malaga to Ronda (passing by chance, in the little *pueblo* of Churriana, the house Gerald was to live in for some eighteen and a half years), then from Cordoba to Seville.

Gerald, incidentally, nowhere says why he chose the south of Spain to live in. No doubt he didn't think it necessary. Since the Treaty of Utrecht in 1716, which ended the War of the Spanish Succession, England had had a doorway into Andalusia. Then, from 1832 on, after Estébanez Calderón published *Esceñas Andaluzas* (*Sketches of Andalusian Life*), the province was discovered and taken up by foreigners: Borrow and Ford, Gautier and Mérimée. As a result, during the nineteenth century, Andalusia *was* Spain – with its orange trees and palms, its flamenco and *sevillanos*, its sherry, its gypsies. It still is, to a considerable extent. The Andalusian aristocrats are still Anglophiles, with English wives and English toothpaste in the bathroom. To a romantic like Gerald – especially one who packed Borrow and Ford to take, as he did – Andalusia was almost inevitable. But no doubt Carrington and Ralph's trip cemented his resolve and may even have directed him to the deep south. It also marked the next stage of Ralph and Carrington's relationship.

They returned lovers, with Ralph determined to marry her. Gerald said a year later that whenever he and Carrington had been alone together, he'd felt Ralph at his shoulder. Anything he might have felt had to be concealed, from himself, perhaps, even more than from others.

Besides which, Gerald was busy preparing for his great journey. This necessitated frequent trips to Hope, who was at a brief crest editing the *Burlington Magazine* in London. Partly this was for reassurance. He was excited, but also very apprehensive about going alone, without Hope. But mainly it was for advice about which books to take (a list remains, no doubt one of many, in Hope's scribble: Pope, Bunyan, Pepys, Evelyn, Defoe, Congreve, Prior, Addison). [18] Some time late in the summer they were boxed up and sent by sea to Almería. (See Appendix B for details.)

And he saw Carrington. She asked him to stay at Tidmarsh on 2 July, meeting him at the door with her 'sweet honeyed smile', long cotton skirt and intense blue eyes whose long-sighted focus seemed, to Gerald, to see deep inside him (Julia Strachey saw them as *too* open, reflecting, blocking off, 'screening her feelings'[19] – not necessarily a contradiction). It seemed to Gerald an idyllic country existence; farm butter, honeycomb, home-made cakes for tea, outside the orchard and meadow in the sun. Ralph was happy, Carrington gay and teasing to Gerald; only Lytton slightly marred it for him. Gerald found him aloof. He was never really able to get on with Lytton.

Carrington suggested they meet in London and they had two days alone there in the middle of August. Gerald 'rattled on' non-stop and felt they were both 'charming and innocent and amiable'. He felt they were embarked on an 'enduring friendship'.[20] She asked him to meet her and Ralph in Cirencester on the 27th and he did.

Early in September Gerald took his seventeen-year-old brother Blair on a two-day hike down through Wiltshire. Blair adored him, not least for standing up to their father; but Gerald was also a kind and conscientious brother – when not totally preoccupied with himself and his concerns, which was usually. They reached Snap, a deserted village near Aldbourne, another place Gerald was to live in (it was a year for coincidences). And then, invited by Carrington, they called in at Tidmarsh on the way back.

Always Carrington. This time she asked Gerald to come and stay once more before going to Spain and it was almost the last thing he did – spending the night at Tidmarsh on the way to London and Hope. It was now that she suggested they corresponded while he was away.

On 25 September Gerald sailed from Dover on the *Hollandia* bound for La Coruña and Spain.[21] It was to be a conjunction that would have, in the long term, as momentous an effect on his life as anything hitherto.

PART II

Two Great Loves

1919–1930

'What most delights the traveller from Northern Europe as he makes his way through Spain is its emptiness. Bare mountains, bone-coloured rocks and hills, flat heaths and páramos, hardly a house. And then suddenly a pool of greenery and a white village. In such a country one can breathe.'

Thoughts in a Dry Season

'I was as proud of my affair with her as I was of having been in the line at Passchendaele. The tears I shed for her were, I thought, my true medals.'

Gerald writing to V. S. Pritchett, 4 April 1979,
about his love for Dora Carrington

NINE

Yegen

1

Gerald landed at La Coruña on 28 September 1919. After some false starts into Galicia, sleeping rough, he was finally on a train to Madrid by 4 October.*

There were few modern roads in Spain seventy-three years ago, and a great many of the rest were still unmetalled (in Andalusia none were metalled). In compensation, the country was covered by a loose net of iron roads – *ferrocarriles* – by which little trains very very slowly made their way, carrying goods and passengers. Even the mainline trains were so slow – 8–10 mph on average – that it was more like bicycling. As the train trundled south Gerald devoured every detail of that huge hot 'yellow oxhide land',¹ wondering, at each cluster of huts, at some distant *pueblo*, what 'strange mode of life went on there'.² The train kept on stopping. Sometimes for hours in the sun for, it seemed, no reason at all; at others for the third-class carriage (where Gerald invariably sat), wooden-seated, hot, smelly and crowded, to empty and be reinvaded by peasants, with bundles of vegetables, with 'terrified fowls', as Orwell described the same sort of journey, 'carried head downwards, with sacks which looped and writhed all over the floor and were discovered to be full of live rabbits', and finally by a flock of sheep driven in and wedged into every empty space.³

After two days in Madrid (sleeping one night on a bench of Venta

---

* Where there are discrepancies here with *South From Granada* and *Personal Record* it is because I have usually followed Gerald's letters and detailed notes written at the time, rather than his published accounts which sometimes altered things for (quite) legitimate artistic reasons (thus, for example, he says he explored thirty Alpujarran villages when he looked at seventeen).

de Baños railway station some way north of the captial) he reached
Granada on 10 October. It was raining. It is the measure of Gerald's
delight – free at last! Alone! – and impatience, that he set out almost
at once south-west towards Malaga in two punishing thirty-five mile
stages. First to Ventas de Huelma, in pouring rain; then, up at dawn,
he climbed all day in hot sun, reaching the 7000-foot top of the Sierra
de Tejada as night fell. Without stopping, he plunged down in pitch
darkness, sliding and slipping, soaked in sweat, at last reaching
Sedella and a straw palliasse, alive with fleas* and bedbugs, in a
posada, cheapest and most primitive of local inns.

Gerald now set out for the coast road and then east towards
Almería and his arriving books. At Motril he suddenly struck north
to explore the Alpujarra, the foothills of the Sierra Nevada. Given
the remoteness and cut-offness of the region, a surprising decision.
Or perhaps this was itself a reason. Perhaps someone told him the
cheapest houses would be there. Gerald himself says it was instinct.

Spain (leaving aside Switzerland) is the most mountainous country
in Europe. The Sierra Nevada is the range running about 100
kilometres west-east from below Granada to above Almería. It rises
to nearly 11,600 feet, and is rising still as the tectonic plate carrying
Africa grinds up into Europe. At this height, rain turns to snow.
There are considerable regions of perpetual snow, even glaciers. The
Alpujarra is wrongly described as a region of foothills – foot-
mountains would be more accurate. Themselves rising to 6000 feet,
slashed with precipitous and savage ravines, they would be, aside
from a few rushing torrents fringed with green, as wild and empty as
the Sierra above – but for one thing. The mountain Berbers, who
colonised the Alpujarra during the Middle Ages, noticed that the
slowly melting snows and ice of the Sierra Nevada furnished an
endless supply of water. Instead of letting it rush wastefully to the
coast, they tapped it. Starting right up in the Sierra itself, at 8000
feet, and extending work probably begun in Roman times, they built
channels – '*acequias*', a foot deep and three feet wide – which led out
horizontally from the descending rivers. *Acequias* were built out at
descending and appropriate levels – every 1000 feet or so – and then
continued for fifteen or twenty miles winding round the Alpujarra

---

* So common were fleas that they invaded the language. The Spanish for bad-
tempered is *tener malas pulgas* – 'to have bad fleas'.

mountains. From these, in turn, the rushing ice-cold waters could be released for irrigation as terraces were constructed. This continued over the centuries. Huge trees grew up, villages; long before Gerald arrived almost no slope, unless actually vertical, remained uncultivated.

It is, at first glance, much the same today. The bulging slopes descend in a series of little steps, small flat terraces, conforming in shape to the mountainside. Wheat or barley on some, maize, beans, vines, olives, fruit trees on others, so that they descend in a patchwork of gentle colours: yellow and gold for the corn, bright green for the maize, lighter for beans, grey-green for the olives, deeper green for the vines, and different greens again for mulberry, fig, apple, cherry and almond. And this intricate tapestry flashes with water from the streams and springs and irrigation channels whose rushing, running and trickling sound continually in your ears.

It is clear from Gerald's account and others that there were far more trees then – even more giant chestnuts, more poplars waving along the water courses. Carrington writes of the walk from Órgiva to Yegen passing through 'the most marvellous cork forests. Huge twisted trees . . .';[4] Gerald of the ilex wood up the Mecina Valley. All gone. Look closer, and you see that the lower terraces have often been abandoned, as have the outer fringes. You see whole slopes running wild with broom and cistus, bramble and barrenness.

Yet, looking up or across a valley, you can still discern the curve of the terraces, rising one upon another like a pile of stacked plates. And it is this aspect, with the intense cultivation, the flashing waters, which often makes the Alpujarra seem like Malaysia. Bruce Chatwin, when he went there in 1987, said it reminded him of Afghanistan.[5] And in fact that is an analogy. To appreciate what Gerald was doing one must imagine that, just before the recent war there, some young Englishman had decided to go and settle in a remote village in Afghanistan with 2000 books.

'I knew,' wrote Gerald as the Alpujarra struck him, 'that I had never seen a more beautiful country than this Spain.'[6] Its beauty confirmed his instinct. But it was more than this; it was also its opposite that confirmed him – the poverty, the sordidness, the pain. In one of the *posadas* 'the sheets are very dirty and covered with bloodstains where people have scratched their bites'. And this was right and proper, after sheltering so long at Edgeworth. 'This little room full of breathing, moving,scratching, sighing workmen seemed to me to represent something holy and beautiful.' He must – everyone must – rub themselves in this, in humanity: 'Vile and stupid and cowardly as it is, the crowd is our family . . . a part of ourselves from which we can never escape.'[7]

But Spain stirred still more profound depths than his need for pain and reality – profound though these were.

The beauty of Spain, of the Alpujarra, burst on Gerald in the way of his earliest visions – the sparkling river in India, the moon-path at Dinard. He now had once again the recurring dream that symbolised this, of himself as a hare racing down 'a dark pathway' through a forest to spring out and see ahead the 'constellation of stars'.

This, and the earlier memories, may even have stirred the earliest memory of all – the birth memory – if such memories are possible. If so, it would explain why in the note describing this, he then goes on to say that the route has to be sordid, through the bloodstained sheets of the *posada*, 'the acrid smells of the yard and of the chamber pot lie at the entrance gate of that imposing country'.[8] That something of this sort was going on in his subconscious is confirmed from another angle. Walking down a dried watercourse at this time he suddenly came on a tall plant with delicate, tissue-papery pale pink petals. He could not remember ever having seen it yet to his surprise its name leapt into his head – oleander. In fact he had seen it before. He was four and they were leaving the paradise of Africa. His mother pointed it out beside the station.[9]

And once again his dreams confirmed this. In November, badly bitten by fleas and bedbugs, exhausted by walking and lack of food and illness – and therefore exalted – he reached what, from his description, must have been Trevélez. There, in another cheap *posada*, he had one of those dreams which 'come to one only every few years and cast their shadow and sweetness over the whole of the following week. I dreamed that I moved in a familiar country which I have not visited since childhood among people wonderfully kind and gentle whom I had known far better than my parents and somehow forgotten. In the house or garden was it? where we were they were playing some music, and then I awoke and heard music indeed, flutes and voices just outside in the street.'

He got up and looked out. It was a procession. 'Young men with lanterns slung on boughs. As they passed singing their piercing song – how high and piercing you can scarcely imagine, the dawn was making the houses paler and the trees greener – the stars to vanish . . . it seemed a continuation of my dream . . .'[10]

There was a sense, that is to say, at some deep level, that he had come home.

2

Following, in the rough notes that remain, Gerald's search for a house, to and fro across the Alpujarra during October and November one has a feeling of frenzy: '19 October – Órgiva; 20th – Nigüelas; 21st – Pinas de Rey; 23rd – Torriecón, Castaras; 24th – Busquístar; 25th – Trevélez, Bérchules; 26th – Ugíjar; 27th – Válor; 28th – Mairena, Laroles, Picena, Ugíjar; 29th – Yegen . . .' and so on for two pages.[11] Years later, he told Ralph he was driven by terror. He would fail, be forced to return to England and have to submit to his father and some nightmare job.[12]

There were no roads, only a fine network of mule tracks. His Spanish was already more than adequate to the task, but it was made much harder by illness. Thinking himself in Arcadia, he drank freely from puddles, irrigation channels, springs.[13] As a result he caught dysentery. Gerald thought it was the oily food and, increasingly dehydrated by diarrhoea, continued to drink indiscriminately. The dysentery got worse.

Yegen had offered a possible house. But he still had four on offer in Ugíjar. He continued, diarrhoea now permanent, to criss-cross the Alpujarra, with one break at Granada to try and regain strength and have a corduroy suit made (this was to look respectable for landlords, but made *posadas* charge more). He finally clinched the Yegen house on 1 December, though the owner Don Fernando Moreno could not move out till January. Gerald calculated he had walked 630 miles in two months, and this often weighed down by books.

Even now he did not stop, but hurried down to Almería (fifty miles) to order furniture. He was so weak that when he finally retreated to Malaga he was forced to take the train from Nerja.

He stayed at Malaga till 5 January 1920. His first months in Spain were a nightmare of money not arriving. Frantic letters went to Hope and Ralph, who wired what he asked; especially Ralph, clearly worried about him. Gerald repaid – when he could. Now, in Malaga, he had no money at all (he had just lost £7 and been robbed of still more). He had to subsist on the *desayuno* (breakfast) his landlady gave him – coffee and bread. Starvation is the best cure for dysentery and he slowly recovered.

All day long he lay in his black Cordoba hat and new corduroy suit on the Malaga beach with its gritty, dirty grey sand. He had, of course, continued his reading these last strenuous months – mostly the Old Testament, with commentaries, also Flaubert. But he had already discovered early Spanish poetry. He was struggling through Garcilaso when suddenly, in the *Elegía Segunda* to Boscán, he read lines which, with their marvellous mimicry, so exactly expressed the melancholy of the waves breaking on a long beach that he almost wept:

> Tú, que en la patria entre quien bien te quiere
> La deleitosa playa estas mirando,
> y oyendo el son del mar que en ella muere.*

'How extraordinary,' wrote Gerald about this years later (and it is not only extraordinary but moving as well), 'when one comes to think of it, that the words written down by a Spanish poet 400 years ago should so completely fill and take possession of the mind of a young Englishman, who knew scarcely any Spanish, that they seemed to him the natural expression of his own soul! Such is the magic power of poetry.'[14]

He had one fearful shock in Malaga before he left. He read in a newspaper that Reynolds Ball had died of typhus in Poland, working to help the Ukrainian refugees from the Russian Revolution. He kept the cutting all his life.[15]

Money at last arrived, and after a detour into Granada (the dentist) and some shopping trips to villages, Gerald moved into Yegen on 13 January. It was to be his home, with long absences due to loneliness or love, till 1924 – and a base for visits till 1934.

---

* 'You, who are in your home town with those who love you well, are looking at the sea-shore and listening to the sound of the sea dying upon it.'

Yegen was a Berber village like those of North Africa. So are many in the Alpujarra: a series of interconnected, drab grey boxes as if made, Gerald noted, by insects. Whitewashing the outside was too expensive. Built on the hillside, there were no metalled streets, only steep cobbled paths, some covered at intervals against the sun, down which goats poured with pattering feet and donkeys and mules clattered with loads of hay or grapes. This, and the fact that the animals were stabled beneath the houses, gave the village a fresh, solid, farmyard smell. It also meant millions of flies and fleas. None of the houses had running water and there was no electricity – it was very silent after dark. There were no lavatories; just the fields and the stables.

The most notable features in Yegen were – and are – the air and the view. Suspended, at 4000 feet, high above the turbulence nearer the coast, the air was nearly always totally still. Sound carried for miles: the running streams, the men in the fields singing *cante jondo*, even dogs barking in Ugíjar six kilometres away in the valley. But occasionally there would be tremendous storms of wind, the air would turn icy, the houses shake, the floors bulge, the chimneys roar. There was, wrote Gerald, 'a feeling of air surrounding one, of fields of air washing over one that I have never come across anywhere else'. Clouds, like whales or huge motionless boats, hung high above the village, 'held there by waves of moist sea air rising to surmount the great Sierra'. It suggested two of his most powerful private archetypal images. 'This is my desert island,' he wrote to Blair.[16] Later, he became Crusoe (or Robinson) to Carrington's Friday; his first novel was called *Jack Robinson*. The second image – though Gerald was not to become aware of its personal significance for many years – was of a castle.

The view was 'perhaps the most beautiful in the world. At one's feet in the "plain" or rather basin of Ugíjar, are row upon row of desert hills, rounded, carved and shaped by wind and water, covered with little bushes or else with almond trees. Beyond is the coast range, through a broad gap in which one sees the sea – some forty miles away. The sun rises out of it every morning. The mountains are completely bare, but are not steep or jagged. They are wonderfully modelled by a network of gullies or ravines – and on the left is one mountain, square in shape, of enormous size and weight which, if I could draw, I would like to draw all day.'[17]

Yegen, like many mountain *pueblos,** was divided in half: the *barrio de arriba* (upper), and *barrio de abajo* (lower); rivalry equalled that between *pueblos*. Gerald's house was in the top half. It was the largest in the *barrio*, with a hall and staircase, five large rooms and four small, with low ceilings of plaster and beams, on the second floor two large usable attics, which led 'by way of an arcade' onto the flat roof. (The three flats into which it has been divided today are still sizeable.) There was a dovecote and garden. There was even a lavatory. A hole in a plank down onto the chicken run.[18] This was fine in summer but chilly in winter. Don Fernando's goats, pig and cow on the ground floor provided flies.

The rent was less than £12 a year, but this must be seen in Gerald terms. Not only did money not arrive; he had very little anyway. He had started either with £250 (letter to Hope in April 1921) or £160 (*Personal Record*) from his gratuity, to which he added £12 at Christmas and £8 on his birthday (his letters to Hope are full of detailed sums). He planned to live on £100 a year, selling out the while. But he had appalling expenses: '6 months' rent – £5.10, furniture – £15, suit – £3 . . .'[19] 'I shut my eyes and spend – like a child taking nasty medicine.'[20] By May his capital had shrunk to £90.[21]

But his money, in turn, must be seen in the context of Spanish poverty. Figures are sparse, but out of 1,026,416 small landowners and tenants in Spain, 847,548 earned less than one peseta a day. To this should be added two pesetas to cover consumption of their own produce.[22] The peseta was then worth about ten pence.† Landless labourers earned even less, and often went unemployed several months of the year. There was no form of state, church or village aid and they would have starved had shops not given credit. The very poor – and Yegen was one of the poorest *pueblos* in the Alpujarra – often had no furniture except a cooking pot, and ate like animals on the ground. Conditions in parts of Spain were almost incredible – unique in Europe. They had not altered or improved since 1780.

* *Pueblo* is not properly translated by village. It could contain anything from several hundred people – as did most of those in the Alpujarra at this time – to 15,000. Nor does village convey the intense local patriotism and love felt by the Spaniard for his *pueblo*. His loyalties were to *pueblo*, region then, distantly, country. A better comparison for the *pueblo* would be the *polis*, the Greek city-state.

† The figure of ten pence is Gerald's, presumably from the rates he obtained, in a letter to Hope of 5 November 1919. It agrees with the figure for 1919 in *Historia Económica de España en el Siglo XX* by Ramón Tamames, 17th ed., Madrid 1986.

Of course, Gerald took advantage of this. It was the foundation of his island. But he took it in and many years later wrote with controlled fury of the vast agrarian problems, whose injustice and inhumanity he pinpointed as the greatest single cause of the Civil War.

He went, that is, not just to Afghanistan, but to an Afghanistan in many respects still in the eighteenth century. Yegen, though poor, does not seem to have touched the extremes of Spanish poverty. Though the countryside was supporting to its limit, it was very fertile. Nevertheless, Gerald must have appeared quite rich. For one thing, he had actual money – coins. A great deal of barter still went on. The lack of specie was fascinatingly demonstrated when he found they were still using coins minted at the time of the Roman Republic, part of a hoard re-introduced, though quite when he didn't discover.*

The moment he moved in, Gerald whitewashed the outside of his house – another sign of wealth. María, his servant, stood underneath to wash off the drips. In *South From Granada* he says he planned to look after himself; if so it was a resolution that sensibly crumbled at once. In a very poor country it was one practical way of helping. Besides, he was used to servants. It was cheap (he paid María a peseta a day) and the village would have been shocked if he had not employed anyone; even by whitewashing he became 'a tourist centre and caused the greatest merriment'.²³ The villagers were horrified when he fetched water. Nearly all his life in Spain Gerald had servants, often several.

In February it snowed – 'Magic.' He thought of getting skis. Gerald didn't let up, indeed the speed with which he got his house ready was almost frantic. While it was being plastered and shelved he hurried round the villages, buying up their best pots and pans. He laid in provisions: an *arroba* (thirty pounds) of honey, three hams, almonds, raisins, eighty pounds of figs. Twice he made the exhausting journey to Almería for furniture. The first time, broke from the usual non-arrival of money, he wired for a £20 loan to his father, who had told him to ask in emergencies. His father refused. Gerald told Hope it was as though he had stuck a stick with a glove into the cage of a strange beast. 'The beast bit off the glove.'²⁴ He therefore had to

* As he describes in *South From Granada*, he bought these, and about twenty others which he traced, for a peseta each. In 1940 he presented them to the Ashmolean Museum. There were coins from six or seven Iberian and Punic cities in Andalusia, with several from Adra.

return on foot empty-handed, catching 'flu on the way. He told the bank to cash £35 of his gratuity and Hope to send £10 or £15 *at once*.

There was a reason for all this haste. Gerald says several times that he was not depressed, bored or lonely at Yegen during the first two years. This picture of superhuman cheerfulness is nonsense. He was frequently all three. He had now been in Spain for six months. He was lonely, continuing to grieve over Ball,* desperate for the company of friends.[25] 'I am gloomy myself and so is everything about me . . . all day hail storms have been sweeping past, the sky grey, the air cold – a peculiar contraption on the roof – a large board tied to the chimney . . . to prevent the fire from smoking; but in the wind the heavy board rattles with a melancholy sound . . .'[26]

Fortunately, relief was close – and was the reason he hurried. He had known since 20 January that Ralph, Carrington and Lytton were all coming to stay. He owed this largely to Carrington.

3

Carrington began writing to Gerald in November 1919 as soon as he had a settled *poste restante* (at Ugíjar). They are charming letters, in her best dashed-off vein; humorous, vivid, interested, concerned – even the spelling has charm. 'It's no good sending you skees.'†[27]

Ralph and she were continually anxious about him – 'attempting to cross that range of mountains quite vaguely'. He mustn't be reckless. He aroused the mother in her. She sent cooking instructions to avoid oil, with cooking diagrams. At Christmas she sent him a plum pudding – 'I made it myself.' (It vanished into the Spanish post.) She asks for 'Some very long letters please'; Gerald responded

---

* Gerald and Ball had corresponded during October and November. Gerald sent him poems and stories he had written. It is indicative of his volatility, and of how the driving force was escaping his father, that as late as November 1919 he applied to join Ball in Poland, but must have been turned down. Rather as with Taylor, Gerald spent January writing a long account of Ball (MSS, MF).

† Though in fact this was something they shared. Oddly, for a man who read and wrote so much, Gerald's spelling was prone to eccentricity all his life. E.g.: 'cheep' for cheap, run 'amuck', 'plummer' for plumber. Oddest was his spelling of Rex – 'Wrecks'. Perhaps a subconscious condemnation-cum-description of Rex Hunter, Gamel Brenan's first husband. His Spanish spelling, too, was erratic – and I have left some examples in quotation intact.

with thirty-six pages in November, twenty-six in January, two of sixteen pages in February. Partly no doubt because he knew Lytton read them, he took trouble. Drafts and notes remain. He was repaid. She loved them. They were literature. Only Lytton wrote better letters.

These charming letters of Carrington's, alive and various, automatically attract. But the element one notices is of conscious, or at least half-conscious, enticement. She at once schemes to get the holiday plans for Italy changed to Spain. If successful, she might 'drift down' and see him – alone. 'You are rather like me you know . . .' Ralph? 'I certainly will never love him but am extremely fond of him.' To this balm, she adds she could be *very fond* of two or three people. By 12 January, 'Lytton likes you very much and so do I . . . Oh Brenan I wish I could be out with you and make things better.' The p.s. (her favourite vehicle) announces she soon will be – she has just noticed Lytton studying a Spanish grammar. By 12 February, she has announced that they'll sail on 19 March: 'Are you a little excited?' By 6 March it's 'My love your Carrington.'[27]

The possible effect of all this on the lonely, highly susceptible young man can be imagined – but whatever it was, Gerald repressed it. She might only be 'extremely fond' – she was still Ralph's. Besides, he was now totally distracted by the desperate need to get his house ready.

The moment money arrived, he extravagantly took the bus from Ugíjar to Almería. He returned with the furniture (and also half his books) but once again penniless. Ralph and Lytton were already waiting for him at Granada, planning to set out for Yegen in two days. Gerald borrowed five pesetas from María and set off at once to walk the forty-odd miles to Lanjarón. He passed a few hours being bitten in a *posada* there, and was up at dawn for Granada. Even Gerald's iron constitution was faltering and, having walked to Granada, he fainted on a tram. When he arrived at their hotel, he found they had already left to catch the bus to Lanjarón. Sprinting through Granada, he caught up with them boarding it.

Gerald had blithely instructed them in February to take the train to Guadix, then cross the Sierra Nevada by its highest pass – the Puerto del Lobo. 'At the summit of the pass, abandon all paths and follow the bed of the river . . . one good day's walk.'[28] Now, in the unbelievable luxury of the hotel – with cane chairs, cognac, bath, friends – he began to get the measure of the problem. Lytton sat gloomily silent – tall, gaunt, bearded, fearful.

It was decided to take a carriage to Órgiva, then go by mule to Yegen. They set out, picked up the mules, and then, on the advice of the muleteers, took a short cut across the river by the ford. But as they approached it – a torrent! The water rose steadily up the sides of the mules. Lytton shrank in terror. There was nothing for it but to picnic and return to the hotel.

It was a difficult evening. Lytton hadn't wanted to come to Yegen, but Ralph's loyalty to Gerald had compelled him. Staying alone in Granada with Carrington had seemed even worse. Now, his stomach was beginning to go from Spanish oil. The journey was exceeding his worst nightmares. Carrington and Ralph were quarrelling. Suddenly, they all rounded on Gerald. The muleteers had already made one fearful mistake; were the mules really all right . . . ? And if the *hotel* was like this, what of his house? Warm? Comfortable? Food? The wine?

Once again they set off early. For a while it was quite jolly. The carriage bowled along. They took the long route over the river by the bridge. But then came the mules. Now it was found that Lytton's piles made it too painful for him to ride. He had to walk, except when crossing the river. Each time they did this, which they did frequently, he clambered up and perched precariously on his agonisingly painful bottom – that same bottom, Gerald must have by now been apprehensively thinking, that was about to be lashed by the winter winds. The sun was setting when they reached Cádiar below Yegen. Lytton was exhausted and could go no further. But one glance at the best bed in the *posada* and he again shrank in horror. He would have to go on.

Darkness was falling and they could not risk the easy but longer route. It was decided they would simply have to go straight up the mountainside and join the track 2500 feet above. The ascent was, and is, dramatic, frightening – with ravines and precipices plunging at the side – even, for Lytton clinging side-saddle as his disability forced him to, painful. Up and up they went. The light faded and it was night. The stars glittered in the thinning air. Stones fell and, after a long pause, echoed from the depths of the abysses. Even when they reached the top there were still six miles to go. Gerald and Carrington hurried ahead.

The rest of the five-day holiday was not a great success, and

Gerald seems to have blotted it out. Lytton took some time recovering and was bitten by bedbugs; he only left the house once. Gerald painted an extraordinary picture of him side-saddle on a mule: bearded, spectacled, long and thin, with his large 'coarse red nose', holding an open sunshade above his head – like some figure in a limerick by Lear. Gerald was preoccupied with finding food fit for Lytton's delicate digestion, really impossible from the scrawny chickens, salt dry cod, unrefined oil, beans. The coffee sold was in fact toasted barley. The Yegen wine was harsh and sour.* Gerald had bought special wine from Cádiar, but it ran out. Ralph and Carrington, however, loved their visit. On one picnic Ralph displayed his splendid limbs naked in a tree. Carrington thought the country beautiful – 'some of the best visionary days I have ever spent'.[29]

The last night, with escape imminent, Lytton was at his most delightful and amusing. But his trials were not quite over. They managed to get on a bus to Almería – one of those Spanish buses, crowded, jolting, roaring, disintegrating, stinking of petrol fumes and passengers, that proceed in a series of explosions and clouds of exhaust. On the train, he had to lie on the floor of a compartment inches deep in orange peel. At last, like an errant rocket returning after going badly off course to some terrible planet, they reached Madrid.

When asked what the visit had been like Lytton replied, 'Death'; yet in the end he was glad he'd gone. He looked back with pride on his adventure.

And Gerald? 'My house seemed so large and empty, silent. María's voice so discordant, I could not bear it: all the debris of your departure there so tragic.'[30] He was alone again.

---

* According to Gerald, but Gerald's memory for drink is liable to be faulty since he did not require it and wasn't interested in it. There seems no particular reason why it should be different now from then. It is made from the same grapes in the same way. After the picking, the *gazpacho* mats through which the juice has been pressed still hang drying in the sun, stained red and strong-smelling. The Yegen wine is pale, rather good and very strong – 17°.

4

'An old peasant said to me: "They say it's the same sun you see all the world over, but I shouldn't be surprised if there were two."'

Thoughts in a Dry Season

The moment they left Gerald had 'flu again. It is fascinating to chart the resurgence of earlier patterns in response to his subconscious feeling of a 'return'. As well as illness in reaction to stress, toothache returned to intensify beauty.[31] There will be other cases.

Gerald's loneliness was short-lived. When he'd arrived, his neighbours Maximiliano and Rosario had given him supper every night. When he'd got back late and tired from Almería they'd lit his fire and put on the kettle. In his absence they'd started up his garden. 'This kindness,' he told Carrington, 'is the more touching in that I have done nothing to deserve it – I am so shy and reserved, I violate many of their customs, and till I came back this time from Almería (when I bought the children some presents) I had given them nothing.' Another man gave him a full load of wood free. 'Five hours chopping.' His kettle was mended for nothing.

He found a natural kindliness among the Spaniards, as did (and do) many people. 'They have,' wrote Orwell, 'there is no doubt, a generosity, a species of nobility, that do not usually belong to the twentieth century.'[32] And though, of course, intensely curious about him (all his neighbours watched him unpack), they were not in the least surprised Gerald had chosen to settle in Yegen. An obvious, indeed (given the competition) inevitable choice. The stranger had special status, as in ancient Greece where Zeus protected him. The reputation of the *pueblo* was at stake, and he was treated, particularly if of some wealth, with great courtesy and hospitality. The position is strongest for two years; the stranger is then assimilated into the community.* (Gerald was always reviving his special position by going away for long periods.)

---

* Becoming a legal member of the community with the *empadronamiento* – the act of being inscribed in the parish register. This, and other anthropological information and insight in this section, come from Julian Pitt-Rivers' classic and marvellous study of an Andalusian *pueblo*: *The People of the Sierra*; and from discussions I had with the author.

Gerald's standing was emphasised physically: the poorly fed men of Yegen, compared to Gerald's English hugeness, were tiny. Don Horacio, the priest, when Gerald came to church (invited, and instructed to conceal his Protestantism), always conducted him to the bishop's throne beside the altar, and from this embarrassing elevation he had to watch – and be watched. He was, since educated and in the house of a wealthy man, rapidly addressed as Don instead of Señor – Don Geraldo (he corrected Blair on this 'small' – meaning important – matter in a letter of December 1920). But it would be a great mistake to think all this distanced Gerald in any human sense. Even in the seventeenth century foreign visitors were astounded at the familiarity with which grandees were treated by retainers and inferiors. The Spaniards, but particularly the Andalusians – an aspect of the egalitarian spirit which permeated its *pueblos* – judged people for themselves, not by rank. Neither María, nor anyone he employed later, were 'servants' as the English, as Helen and Hugh Brenan understood the word. It was the warmth, the spontaneity, the genuineness of feeling, undistorted by class or acute inhibition, that Gerald loved most in his village.

Like him, they considered the rich (*los ricos*), as a class, wicked. As in many poor communities, generosity was highly regarded. To generosity Gerald added his own particular charm and kindness. He understood – who better than an Edwardian public schoolboy? – the importance of form. He took trouble over their customs. He was, all his life, a man of impeccable upper-class English good manners to strangers. Then the openness and closeness of *pueblo* life almost dictated politeness, even charm. But closeness leads to strong, sometimes violent feelings. These found expression in gossip; charm face to face, behind the back-betrayal. Gerald discovered he loved gossip and (verbal) betrayal. Some of the most delicious pages of *South From Granada* are on the scandals and dramas of village life – and their perpetrators.

Don Horacio fell in love with the colossally fat wife of the doctor, and had to leave. 'Cecilio . . . hawk-beaked like an Armenian or a Kurd, with crafty, feverish eyes . . . was a sort of malign Micawber, restlessly optimistic and engrossed in perpetual plots and plans for making money . . . How many illustrious Yegenese governments he had toppled down in the past twenty years I cannot say, but no one trusted him.'

This figure, incidentally, had a son Paco – pleasant, humorous and, according to Mark Culme-Seymour who met him in 1933, without any morals at all. He dropped in every day and Gerald and he went shooting partridges together (adolescent scruples seemingly overcome). He was to play a part in Gerald's love-life later on.

All his childhood and youth teased and excited by allusions to, and glimpses of, lower-class life, Irish servants, tramps, the slums; then held back, shielded – Gerald was now immersed to the eyebrows. He observed always, took part from time to time; when he couldn't he lived vicariously. In late August and September he helped with the harvest. All day under the hot sun the mules went round the paved threshing circles scattered over the hillsides. Winnowing waited till night for the wind, 'the mountainside dotted with lights, voices, talking, singing, guitars. From all the threshing floors, shouts, music. In the night wind, the beaten corn is thrown into the air. The grain rattles down like pebbles, the chaff, a cloud of golden dust, is carried away.' Gerald took his turn with the fork, pouring with sweat. The wind dropped, the fires blazed up. 'Drinks, talk, the women with naked feet crouching on the ground like herded animals their eyes shining in the flame, their voices piercing, their bodies motionless.' They made love during the night, often twice. 'A race of Hercules,' thought Gerald, watching with burning eyes. He alone had no companion.[33]

5

'Those who have some means think that the most important thing in the world is love. The poor know that it is money.'
Thoughts in a Dry Season

His parents, especially his father, continued to write to Gerald urging him to get a job. One can have some sympathy – most fathers expect their sons of twenty-six will have jobs.

The more they corresponded, the more determined Gerald became never to have a job. Suddenly, hope came from an unexpected quarter. His father's Aunt Adeline was the widow of a Prussian, Colonel Baron von Roeder. As a result, she was ultra-patriotic during the war; and especially fond of Gerald after it. She would introduce him proudly: 'This is my nephew Gerald, who has given his life for his country.' She seems to have got wind of Hugh's treatment of his brave Military Cross-winning son and thought it wrong. She was in any case sympathetic to him. She had written two novels herself and at one time had been a publisher's reader. At some point she told Gerald he could rely on her in any emergencies.[34] As it became clearer and clearer that he was not going to get an allowance out of his father, a glorious plan seems to have occurred to him – Tiz (as he called her – Serbo-Croat for aunt) could give him one instead. At once he enlisted an ally well-versed in such machinations.

Hope once gave Bunny Garnett several useful tips on how to extract free meals from hostesses. He told him that he regarded sponging as an upper-class version of being a tramp.[35] Gerald did not see it like that, since you had to kow-tow to their values. In fact he was now thoroughly disillusioned with Hope's ideals. He spent all his time, he wrote caustically, in plans 'for black-mailing your uncle or swindling someone or other, for setting up a hairdressing salon and making three thousand in two years . . .'[36] However, when Gerald's own vital interests were at stake, he did not hesitate to use Hope's sponging skills.

His first surviving instruction comes, significantly, just after his father had refused to lend him money in Almería. Hope must go and see Madam von Roeder *at once*. Unless he did, 'it is all up with my chances. And my chances are real ones.'[37] Hope passed on information about Gerald's straits, no doubt not minimising them. These accounts so infuriated Tiz that, still full of energy at eighty-two, she embarked on an angry correspondence with Hugh – and both were renowned for their vituperative letters. But it seems likely that Hope now made the quantum leap of a professional sponger. Tiz had no children. Why an allowance just while Gerald was at Yegen? Why shouldn't the young genius have a permanent allowance; why indeed shouldn't he become her heir?

A cryptic postcard of July suggests that Tiz was increasingly angry with Hugh. Once again, Gerald urged Hope to continue pressing his suit. Possibly as a result of this news he now dropped a hint to Ralph about a scheme, 'extremely likely to succeed', that would make him independent of his parents forever.[38] And in September he was at last able to tell Blair ('but don't tell father or mother') that Tiz would not only give him £50 p.a., plus 'large Christmas presents', but had made him her heir.[34]

Fifty pounds a year – say £80, when everyone's Christmas presents were thrown in – was very nearly enough to scrape by on at Yegen. He now began to plan various harebrained schemes to augment his income. But he was safe. If he continued to play his cards right with Tiz – and Gerald played them assiduously even when half-mad with boredom for seven years – safe for life.

What precisely was Hope's part in all this? In *Personal Record*, and in a letter to Carrington, Gerald says Tiz thought of it herself, but Hope encouraged her. This was not how Hope saw the matter at all. He thought it entirely due to him. At one time he even suggested they should share the inheritance. Neither does it satisfactorily explain Gerald's subsequent behaviour. He was a generous man, but not foolishly so. He often said that curbing some of his initial impulses saved him about £300 a year. Yet when Hope was old, Gerald settled him in a quarter of his house. When Ralph wrote and remonstrated, saying he should shove Hope out since his presence was making it impossible to sell the house, Gerald replied in lofty tone: 'I regard friendship as a thing once given can never be taken back.'[39]

But other letters tell a completely different story. Writing to Ralph about his will on 16 February 1951, Gerald said he owed Hope an immense debt for persuading Tiz to make him (Gerald) her heir. 'I feel a deep regret that I have not done more for him.' And, again, when he wrote to Miranda a year later (4 December 1952) on the same subject, he was clear and unequivocal. She was to look after Hope in the event of Gerald's death because 'I owe it to him for Aunt Addie's £5000 – which you will inherit'. Whether Hope actually suggested Gerald might be her heir, or so fed and orchestrated Tiz's indignation that she found she'd thought of it herself, Gerald knew that Hope's intercession had been essential.*

* Gerald's own account in *Personal Record* does not square with any of the facts in his letters at the time, or those written later. I have chosen to follow the letters, which also explain his behaviour.

6

So the time passed. Gerald got a kitten, which he called Anastasia – an exile's name. In June, after a frightful murder in the village, a ghost terrified everyone, including Gerald[40] – a ghost that was to materialise again twenty-three years later in *The Spanish Labyrinth*. Just before the harvest, he helped María make jam: pouring honey and sugar onto fifty pounds of peaches. The postman gaped – 'The Englishman's food!' He also bought 250 pounds of grapes for raisins, figs, apples. He added a sofa and two armchairs covered in patchwork. In winter it snowed again and Gerald went for an enormous walk. In fact, thirty- and forty-mile walks and expeditions punctured his time – five days on the Sierra de Trevélez in June, for instance, a ten-day stay with Don Fernando and his wife near Granada in January 1921. But two deep imaginative currents carried him through Yegen, both just as important as the events of real life. The first was noticed by the *pueblo*: 'we used to see him reading and writing and thought he did it because he had nothing else to do.'[41] True, in a way.

While Gerald was making jam, 500 more books arrived at Almería. To Blair, he explained his plan; to study folklore, science, comparative religion and psychology and then see how these abstract forces and ideas expressed themselves in action through philosophy, works of the imagination and history.[42] But in fact this rather fuzzy scheme – which really meant reading everything ever written – imposed no order: in May he was reading Dostoevsky, in September science and metaphysics (especially spiritualism), Swift, Góngora and Calderón, in December Tolstoy, Gorky, *Don Quixote* and Plato. And this reveals his method – copied from Hope – of keeping his interest at white heat. As well as following any vein or subject that caught his fancy, he read dozens of books at once. Sometimes he could be reading as many as fifty, all on a special shelf with pieces of paper sticking up to mark his place.[43] Two methods impressed the material: as before, repetition (he read Gibbon's *Decline and Fall* . . . for the third time in 1920) and copious notes. Often these spilled over into his letters – a habit which continued all his life. For instance on 20 May he wrote to Carrington about *The Brothers Karamazov*, about Dostoevsky's astonishing sense of architecture, seeming to lead 'one along the paths of some terrible subterranean labyrinth . . . after-wards one retains the suspicion that this labyrinth is somehow the type, the macrocosm of the human mind.' An illusion? That does not matter. The letter continues with a long and fascinating comparison of Flaubert with the great Russians.

Reading for Gerald was not a passive occupation. The text had to be explored far beyond what was obviously there. It was a process of discovery, almost of creation and with him required something of that Rimbaudian inspiration he still deemed essential for writing. There were times, therefore, when he couldn't read. But when he did, his energy and concentration were formidable. He would read for nine, ten, eleven hours at a stretch. He loved the process of reading and learning, as he gloried in the strength of his long legs striding for hours across the Sierra. Nor was there order here. For quite long periods he would read all night – 'my energy for reading', he wrote to Carrington on one of these occasions, 'seems inexhaust-ible'.[43] At dawn he would stand up, stretch and walk to Mecina Bombarón while the sun rose from the sea, and swim in a pool under the chestnuts.

His writing, too, had begun soon after his arrival. By May he was busy making notes for a book about Yegen, some of which survive:[44] botanical notes, customs, *coplas*, descriptions of the villagers, 'and onto that . . . I keep grafting more personal matters'.[45] This, of course, is a rough description of *South From Granada*. Gerald used to say he'd written all his books by accident, almost by mistake, 'drifting' into them. So it may have seemed, but in fact we shall find that most of them had gestation periods of many years – thirty in this case.

He began a story about spiritualism; then a more serious project which lasted three years – a bestiary, an account of his friends as animals, owing much to Swift and Góngora. Gerald was aware how much of his early writing was pastiche, explaining it as the usual learning through copying of most juvenilia. It was more fundamental than that. For one thing it was a vein he followed till he was nearly forty, so hardly juvenilia. Apart from pleasure in using his knowledge of archaic forms, one has the feeling that such enormous quantities of information have been absorbed that some has to be regurgitated. Then Gerald said on various occasions that he always preferred to be in disguise – an expression of that general process of concealment and burying we looked at earlier. To live in a foreign country, to speak a foreign language is, in a sense, to be in disguise. One view of his progress as a writer is that not till he found the 'disguise' of writing about Spain, through which and from which he finally wrote about himself, were his gifts released.

Another example, with different implications, occurred in October. Ralph had just joined the Hogarth Press. Had Gerald anything they could publish? McSwinney, the Irish hunger-striker, had recently died. Gerald was angry – 'I see the Irish point of view when I try to imagine that I am Ireland, my father is England'[46] – and sat down after tea to write to Carrington. He had a solution to the Irish problem, a modest proposal *à la* Swift (too *à la*, as it turned out) – all the Irish should be exterminated. Not shot (they might shoot back), but starved. Suddenly, as he wrote, Gerald was seized by one of his manic fits of energy and inspiration. Grabbing more paper, he wrote till 2 p.m., broke off to continue his letter to Carrington, started another to Ralph, then continued his 'proposal' till he finished it at dawn. He had a brief walk, and found he was still too excited – 'my hand aches but I cannot stop' – and now launched into a sustained, comprehensive and brilliant critique of Gibbon, as stylist, historian and man.[47] He then finished his letters to Carrington and Ralph and wrote one to Lytton. He'd written for nearly twenty hours with scarcely a break, the eighty pages virtually unblotted, his small hand-writing concentrated to the microscopic.

Demonstration of stamina aside, it was well aimed. Gibbon was Strachey's idol – and he was impressed. (Gerald told Frances Partridge later that he felt a sense of rivalry with Lytton and the only way he could get at him was by attacking Gibbon.[48]) Virginia and Leonard Woolf approved of the 'Proposal', but didn't publish it (though they later used some of the 'Bestiary'). Allen and Unwin also turned it down. But by such letters Gerald began to be thought talented, to have promise. He was also able, using Ralph, to try things out for publication without seeming to do so.

His poetry – still his main ambition – didn't seem to improve, struggle and pour it out as he did. There is a peculiar aspect to this. Modernism involved, as literary movements often do, a rebellion against 'poetic', conventional diction and a return, in prose and poetry, to the vernacular. But it was also a move to what one might call the vernacular of behaving and feeling. Characters could defecate, swear, menstruate. Gerald, as we've seen, was a modernist by intellect and temperament – he was now eagerly awaiting *Ulysses* – but not aesthetically or artistically. It never touched his work. His poetry, sonnets on death and love and pain, is often sentimental and abounds in archaisms, in thous and thines, in 'th'ephemeral beauties' or, on lust, 'the thirsting for the scabbard of the sword'.[49] He was obsessed with rhyme, which he couldn't manage. (Carrington had had to bring him out a rhyming dictionary, something as fatal to a writer as a thesaurus.)

In the smell of dung, the villagers copulating at harvest, his poverty, the blood-stained sheets of the *posadas*, Gerald lived the return to reality. Perhaps that is why he felt no need to express it – or perhaps that makes his reaction odder still.

7

Apart from Hope, the only person Gerald showed his poetry to was Carrington. With Carrington we enter the second great imaginative current which gathered speed through 1920, 1921, and 1923, and which eventually swept him away out of control.

Carrington's beguiling, enticing letters began as soon as she got back. On 5 May she wrote: 'May I tell you how fond I am of you and how much I think of you with great emotion.' She sent this 'with the purely masculine side of me', a code Gerald would only later appreciate. Again and again she dreamt of flying out with her paintbox and settling in Yegen. The more Ralph's pressure on her to marry increased, the more she seemed to cling to Gerald. On 18 October: 'The married state is *not* a good one. And I WON'T *ever* get married so there . . . I will be and always shall be, your Carrington.'

Her mother had trapped her, and she'd escaped; when her men tried (and only Lytton didn't), she struggled to escape – and then tried to come back in case they were hurt. But there were more fundamental difficulties. Detesting the female side of herself, trying to remain a little girl, she didn't need or particularly enjoy making love – at least not with men. It usually left her with feelings of shame and disgust – very like Gerald's 'reactions'. Gertler wooed her passionately for three years – and was allowed to sleep with her once.

She enjoyed kissing, but what Carrington really wanted from her love affairs was intimacy and excitement. She loved discovering a new person, the confidences, the talk, the quick interchanges with someone sympathetic and close. She loved the secret letters and meetings. And she loved all this as much in the head, in daydreams and letters, as face to face. Friendship carried to extremes, the intensities and intimacies of love – with very little sex and absolutely no possessiveness. Surely that was possible?

Gerald, of course, was the last person to be put off by her sexual scruples. On the contrary. If he knew about them. It is likely he did. Her treatment of Gertler had become an open scandal at the time. There is a subtle pinprick at Ralph demanding 'only the solidest satisfaction' in one of Gerald's letters.[50]

But everything she did was enchanting. Nearly twenty-seven, he had never had a girlfriend before. She praised his work and his letters, and passed on Lytton's praise. She worried about his 'flu. He loved her sensibility. Nature, her surroundings, seemed to stream into her ears and eyes and nose and out at the ends of her fingers. That autumn, on a walk, she found two adders hung on a roller by a keeper. 'They were the most lovely creatures. I had never held an adder in my hands before. The feeling was amazing, the soft pliant bodies with the cold smooth scales. All mottled black and ivory. I opened their dead mouths and saw their black fangs . . . Then crossing the fields near the Mill we saw a cow give birth to a calf in a field, and almost the minute afterwards she rose up and walked across a little river ditch, with the absurd little white calf, with its knees knocking together, and its natal cord dribbling in the sun, stumbling after her, like some clumsy big dog.'[51]

The beauty she described left her exhausted – 'rent me inside' – as Gerald himself was often rent. Her letters are ungrammatical, badly spelt, but 'they contain such suprising images, so vivid, so sensitive, that I am always being delighted by them':[52] he said he would pinch them. Gerald, even then, had no need to pinch anyone's images, but from now on the poetry he somehow couldn't organise into his poems found increasing outlet in his letters. He raised his game with Carrington.

Her letters sustained him at Yegen; they also made it harder and harder to stay. 'There is a person here I'm tired of,' he wrote to her in October. 'That person is myself.' In February 1921 he went restlessly on an expedition to Almería and Cartagena. He had toothache, which as usual 'seemed to sharpen my senses,' and wrote, as a proper poet should, feverishly at café tables – with spidernibs and *'encre noire fixe'*.

A waiter told him there was mixed bathing in the summer, 'often nude!' At once Gerald was 'hopelessly inflamed . . . on fire'.[53] Everyone has patterns of energy and libido, but with Gerald, all his life, this periodicity was marked. In sex, particularly so. Partly, fear of impotence (as much or more than actual incidents of it) deeply inhibited him, leading to irregular eruptions. But his suppression was also deliberate. It was either copulation or art, as he explained to Carrington.[54] In between studying the history and architecture of Cartagena, he gazed with agonised longing at the Spanish women in the *paseo* 'with their air of bloodhorses'.[53]

He returned nearly broke, and nearly overwhelmed by loneliness, the desire for a mistress, the desire to come home (which was not due for a year). He went back to Almería, no doubt to gaze on the nude bathing, in early May. On the 8th, back in the village, he wrote a desperate letter.

He loved them all at Yegen, but 'I am as much alone with them as I am with the hills and the trees'. He confessed he always ran away from girls. 'You are one of the few, almost the only, young lady (I have met few!) whom I might have fallen in love with.' Now she was Ralph's. Adultery he couldn't understand, at least by someone who knew the husband. But 'Why, confound you, did you ever meet Ralph? Platonic affection is mostly nonsense . . .' The whole long letter (and it is twenty pages of tiny handwriting) is a passionate cry – don't marry him. Be for me.

It was too late. On the very same day – Gerald had clairvoyant moments like this – Carrington wrote to Lytton, herself in torment. She loved Lytton, he could never love her. 'I had one of the most self-abasing loves that a person can have. You can throw me into transports of happiness and dash me into deluges of tears and despair, all by a few words . . . So in the café in that vile city of Reading, I said I'd marry him.'

She was marying to preserve the *ménage*, so as not to be a limpet, to stop tormenting Ralph: '. . . so now I shall never tell *you* I do care again. It goes after today somewhere deep down inside me and I'll not resurrect it to hurt either you or Ralph. Never again. He knows

I'm not in love with him. But he feels my affections are great enough to make him happy . . .'[55]

Gerald learnt of their marriage by the next letter she sent him. He at once got 'flu. But having closed the trap herself, Carrington now felt the urge to escape imperative and leapt to hold him. The marriage meant nothing to her, she wrote on the day it took place. 'To you, I shall ever be Carrington, and to myself . . . I couldn't have married anyone else, unless perhaps – but you shall never know this perhaps. Perhaps? Or perhaps not!'[56] She wrote him four letters on her honeymoon, one of sixteen pages. If Gerald wants to send her a particularly passionate letter he must put the stamp upside down so 'the faithless wife can read it before he reads it'.[57]

This was enough for Gerald. He never lets on in *Personal Record* the extent of his concern about his parents. The letters to Blair and Ralph often express his anxiety: what is his mother feeling? Has his father forgiven him? Will they have him back?[58] When his father, no doubt worked on by his mother, said he would pay Gerald's fare back now, provided he spent four out of five weeks at Edgeworth, Gerald accepted instantly. But the most important reason he returned was to see Carrington.

He felt he was returning after an eternity. How long is indicated by his saying in *South From Granada* that it was 'after years'. In *Personal Record*, where he tried to be accurate, he said two and a half years. In fact, it was nineteen and a half months.

TEN

The Impossible Business of Love

> *'When we find that we are giving several different explanations of our conduct, we know that we are deceiving ourselves.'*
> *Thoughts in a Dry Season*

1

Gerald arrived back in England on 21 June 1921 and at once – the new order of priorities – went to stay with Tiz. On the 27th he went to Edgeworth, and on 2 July to Tidmarsh, where he arrived bearing presents of hams. Three days later, Carrington set up a secret meeting for 7 July – 'Ralph goes away all day'; they must rendezvous at a pub near the Uffington White Horse on the Downs.[1] Gerald wired acceptance.

Indifference often excited Carrington. It was a reaction beyond what one might call the normal Proust/Stendhal reaction and which may have derived from her childhood passion for her brother, who always ignored her. But there was a related aspect. Dr Igor Anrep remembers how, in the late twenties, when he was sixteen, Carrington suggested they share a taxi after a Bloomsbury party. 'I was *very* young and innocent – I hardly knew her.' Suddenly she seized him in her arms and began to kiss him. When he started to respond, she thrust him away and withdrew outraged into her corner.

Her biographer recounts other instances where innocence excited Carrington in this way. She calls it teasing.[2] Behind the tease hides the bully; it often seems more like a straightforward enjoyment in the exercise of power. Julia Strachey detected this – something malicious and cruel, witchlike, first 'getting hold of the wax images, then sticking them with pins'. She thought Carrington was half-aware of this propensity and, frightened of hurting people, 'eeled' away out of guilt.[3]

Gerald was to get hurt, again and again. But initially he was the beneficiary. As they sat by the Uffington White Horse, Carrington suddenly began to kiss him passionately. When he responded, she did not withdraw. Returning to Edgeworth, he says in *Personal Record* that he resolved out of guilt over Ralph not to kiss her again. This is hardly borne out by an immediate, delighted flirtatious exchange of letters as to who had enjoyed it most (Carrington won: '. . . you didn't feel a shepherd's toothbrush burning and bristling into *your* face.')[4] She also chided him about a model he'd picked up on the boat.[5] She'd done the same earlier over La Égyptienne.[6] Gerald took this in.

He was asked to Tidmarsh again on 22 July for two nights. He remembered nothing, except 'One immense thing stands out. I was sitting in the sitting room when Carrington passed across the window and all at once something overturned inside me and I felt that I was deeply, irretrievably in love.'

They met again for two days in London, Gerald using some dusty mews rooms off Fitzroy Street which Hope had lent him. They had supper with Blair, went to a Shaw play, and gave themselves up to 'an orgy' of kissing. At one moment, coming into the room and seeing Carrington lighting the gas and putting out the teacups, Gerald's life at Yegen suddenly 'rose before me in all its barbarity, its loneliness and its dullness, and the only conceivable way of living seemed to be with a girl who in the evening should put the kettle on the fire and pour one's cup . . .'[7]

They parted on 4 August, Carrington on the way to a long-planned holiday at Watendlath farm, near Keswick in Cumberland, with Ralph and Lytton. Gerald gloomily prepared to return to Spain. At every turn, experiencing an entirely new form of pain, he heard her voice and saw her vividly before him (an effect he carefully noted).[8]

He and Hope had at last fixed on their money-spinner: photography. Much cumbersome equipment had to be crated up and shipped to Almería – crated single-handedly by Gerald, since Hope, recently sacked by Roger Fry for lax attendance, had fled London to avoid creditors.

But the bulk of Gerald's attention was devoted to Tiz, with whom he stayed at Ashley Place (near Victoria). Tiz was over eighty-three, midget-sized, only wore Victorian clothes and had been – one almost adds 'of course' given her family closeness – stone deaf since childhood, a defect which didn't prevent her talking incessantly. Destined to become a major comic figure on Thurber lines, relayed to his friends (and later in *Personal Record*), she became someone Gerald was fond of – and maddened by. This time she nearly killed him. He woke in the middle of the night with a terrible headache, hardly able to breathe; he only just made the window. Tiz had left the gas on, unlit, at one of the mantles (she regarded electricity as dangerous). 'All,' he wrote furiously to Carrington, 'because I've sold my soul to the Devil for a little money.'9 But it was not a little – £5000 then was the equivalent of £95,500 in 1990. He invented toothache, then dentists, for temporary relief. But Tiz had him on a string – and kept tweaking it. 'If I treated my aunt one shade less considerately than I do,' he told Ralph nervously, 'goodbye to my only means of support and almost only hope for the future.'10

But Carrington was missing Gerald too. As was Ralph. It was not just fondness. The extreme divergence in the newlyweds' sexual needs meant, as Gerald put it, that rows were continually being 'hatched in the bedroom'. Ralph liked having things out, confrontations; Carrington emphatically did not. As so often with young couples, a third person eased things. Would he be able to join them? Gerald, about to depart, thought not. 'But if you sent a wire – to the *Mews* – who knows – I might . . .'10

The wire arrived (plus £5 sent secretly by Carrington). At once Gerald dropped everything and left. On 18 August he arrived in Cumberland.*

Watendlath was (and is) a squat white farmhouse set high up a mountain valley. There is a smell of freshness and sheep, the sound of running water and the wind in pines. Alix and James Strachey were there, just back from a visit to Freud. It rapidly became cold and often wet. Alix, James and Lytton (suffering from blisters after a single foray) stayed in, reading and writing. Carrington did a lot of painting, watched by Gerald.

But their chief occupation was kissing. Every day Ralph set out fishing, accompanied by Gerald and Carrington, with a boring egg

* As it then was. Now Cumbria.

picnic. The moment he was busy, they went behind a bank and gave themselves up – Gerald repeats the phrase – to an 'orgy of kissing'. Once, still more exciting, they went into a barn full of dried bracken and lay writhing in each other's arms all afternoon – only pausing to look out for Ralph, then resuming.

This went on for twelve days. Yet Gerald's feelings were not, he wrote, remotely sexual. As day after intense day passed, he was raised to a state of such exalted ecstasy that he hardly ate or slept. He never forgot Watendlath. Like the Walk, he referred to it again and again. It symbolised the peak of their love. He kept the green dress she wore for forty years; the lock of hair she gave him then[11] he kept for ever. And what made it the more intense and terrifying was that no one noticed, even when their intrigue continued in the house (she would stuff notes under his door – 'You must not go till Monday' etc.). Alix and James translated French. In the evenings Lytton read aloud – 'Hyperion', among other things. Ralph took Carrington to bed each night; each morning at eight, Gerald went and sat on their bed to chat, feeling, not surprisingly, 'in a strange state of mind'.[12]

So vehement, especially in later notes[13] and letters and in *Personal Record*, is Gerald's denial of any sexual feeling that his different explanations repay examination:

1 He had been seduced.
2 His innocence was extreme, even in those more innocent days.
3 He only associated sex with lower-class girls.
4 Carrington's figure was flat and boyish,* only in love could you find her attractive.
5 Guilt over Ralph made sexual feeling impossible.

The fact that, by letter and by action, Carrington seduced Gerald, which she did, does not, of course, destroy sexual feelings. With Gerald, rather the contrary. He was certainly innocent in one respect (which was one reason it took him such an extraordinarily long time to recognise his state) – the note of all his utterances at this time is a delighted one – so *this* is love! But, even if not all that successful, he was not particularly innocent sexually (in bed with four women, by his own admission). He took pains, as we saw, to emphasise his attraction to lower-class girls, and it is true that it was to be one of these with whom he had the most intense and prolonged physical

---

* In fact, as already noted, dumpy and almost plump.

affair of his life. But he was to be strongly attracted to as many, or more, middle-class girls. His strictures on Carrington's figure are all very well – but he has just spent three pages in *Personal Record* describing that he was, precisely, irretrievably in love with her.

In fact, Gerald's sexual desire for her became so strong he had to leave: 'It was getting more than I could stand. I was no longer satisfied at being with you, not even kissing you – I did the only possible thing in coming away.'*[12]

He felt desire; at the same time he was able to repress the knowledge and, later, forget it. Partly, he knew perfectly well that Carrington wanted passionate friendship without possessiveness, and that for her sex always seemed to lead to possessiveness. He was always having to pretend not to feel things he did feel. But he was not just being disingenuous. We shall often find Gerald revealing things in his letters – usually about matters of love, as he had been doing this last year with Carrington – long before he became aware of them himself. The most likely explanation is that it is another operation of that psychological mechanism which we explored and which gave rise to the title of this book. It allowed him to conceal things from himself to an unusual degree.

With his guilt, it worked as it were in reverse. Of course, on the surface he felt considerable guilt. Carrington had only been married to his best friend for two and a half months. And guilt always increases in proportion to the likelihood of discovery. Ralph's imminent arrival – at one point he actually appeared over a mound, just

---

* Carrington's desire was much less strong, but it all gave her great pleasure – 'You can't guess how much pleasure you gave me,' she wrote years later (10 November 1930). Soon after Watendlath she sent him a nineteen-line poem:

> His sunburnt face all wet with rain
> Was laid upon the bracken brown
> (Yet why was our love all tinged with pain?)
> He said he loved my grass green gown
> Yet it was grey, I still persist.
> We peered out from the open door
> And watched for one in rain and mist,
> Then threw back on our bracken floor
> Hugging and tossing as before.

Clearly, hiding it from Ralph, on whom she was probably still unconsciously revenging herself, was one of the pleasures for her. But one also gets a sense of how it fascinated her to raise in men that excitement she didn't strongly feel herself.

missing their spring apart – his good humour and sweetness, all
stung Gerald keenly. At the same time, an engine of love seemed to
have been started in him. The more he loved Carrington, the more
he found himself loving Ralph.[12] But Gerald's behaviour is only
properly understood when one realises that at a deeper level he had
no guilt at all. He would hardly have been human had he not felt, as
he kissed her, some fleeting sense of revenge for Ralph's scornful
laughter at Amiens. But at bottom he really felt that Carrington
should have been his. He'd heard of her first, dreamt of her, looked
for her. And when he'd found her, how well they got on, how suited
they were! Their sensibility, their devotion to their art (Gerald, like
Ralph and Lytton, always took her painting seriously), their vagueness and clumsiness (Ralph said they even peeled apples in the same
way), their feelings about life and parents, even sex – all were the
same. Compared to him, Ralph was, as far as Carrington went, a
philistine – a word which became for Gerald a codeword for Ralph's
unsuitability for her.

And Ralph himself? Gerald said he suspected nothing because he
thought Gerald too feeble sexually to be a rival. There may be truth
in this – though it also obliquely reveals the element of Gerald's
revenge; but in fact Ralph had noticed enough to insist that from now
on he see all their letters.[14] The future was to be fraught with danger.

2

Poverty drove Gerald back to Spain (otherwise, he told Ralph, he'd
spend half his time in London),[10] and he left with Hope on 8
September. They split in Paris – Hope for Madrid, Gerald to spend
nine days (at Carrington's surprisingly urgent insistence) with the
Dobrées, at their home in Larrau high in the Basses-Pyrenees.

Here, in the small mountain village, hardly altered today, of tall,
box-like white or grey houses, in a much magnified Lake District –
deep valleys thick with grass and bracken, rushing, trout-teeming
rivers – lived an intriguingly assorted couple. Valentine, the wife,
with jet-black hair, was moody, short, voluptuous, creamy-skinned,
and restlessly energetic – a dedicated painter, excellent cook, and a
singer. Extremely highly sexed, she had got into the habit of infidelity
during the war and – condoned by her husband – was making no

effort to get out of it. Bonamy Dobrée was quite different: a dry, clever, precise academic (Gerald noticed he dug their cabbage patch at the same time each day). Frustrated in her mountain fastness, Valentine, it is clear from subsequent events, desired Gerald (Carrington had warned him she liked seducing young men). On long walks alone together, when they bathed naked, or while (that intimate exercise) she painted his portrait, she told him about her lovers – Janko Varda, Mark Gertler, John Rodker. Gerald was able to note that she would certainly, as he told him, attract Ralph,[15] but as for himself he could only talk obsessionally about Carrington, whose letters arrived by every post.

After the Prado, Hope and Gerald had a nightmare journey to Guadix; then, driven by Gerald's desire for Carrington's next letter, started at dawn on the thirty-mile walk over the Sierra Nevada he'd planned for Lytton – 6000 feet to the Puerto del Lobo. Hope, soft from months of sponging, arrived a wreck.

To Ralph Gerald now wrote that, long-term, he was planning to go to Greenland, then to Alaska to pan for gold – 'some girl one would pay to sleep with'.[16] Throughout Yegen – indeed all his life – the hare in him would occasionally leap up with exciting suggestions. But – like so much with Gerald – only in his head. In fact, he plunged at once into the rhythm of Yegen life. Little Angela flung herself into his arms. Gerald began to reorganise the dusters.

He also had to organise Hope. Vast quantities of books and photographic equipment were fetched from Almería. Also thousands of small cardboard squares, box after box, each a slightly different colour, bought in pursuance of some complex colour theory in Germany for £5 (a bargain apparently).

But Hope, disliking what he called 'the adhesiveness' of human beings, his physical attraction to Gerald long past, provided the ideal intellectual companionship. They read in different rooms, sometimes continuing through meals. Then talked for hours. Once again, Gerald learnt from this hugely capacious, crystal-clear mind.

And Hope brought discipline back to reading. Again, Gerald read for ten-hour stretches: early Greek philosophy, Latin, astronomy, physics, botany, science.[17] And one might note here another Hope-induced trait which had acted on his naturally intense curiosity and was already well established; Gerald's feeling that he had to read everything on a subject, no matter how obscure. For instance, after

Tolstoy, Pushkin, Dostoevsky, etc. he read little-known Russians like Andreiff, Sologub and Arbyebashoff. Indeed, on a subject that interested him – that is, most subjects – he got anything he could lay his hands on, the more recondite the better.

As often, reading dictated writing. Stendhal (and no doubt memories of Carrington) contributed *The Psychology of Happiness*; Marlowe (not Pope) a long narrative poem in heroic couplets; and in a verse opera his fascination with the lower middle-classes, inspired by Wells, went slightly over the top with a cast of forty commercial travellers. He began a 150-page autobiographical narrative, and in addition a mass of poetry poured back to Carrington, with Watend-lath still haunting and entrancing him: 'No lonely valleys but bare rivers by/To wind over their bodies and their faces/And chain them better in their gay embraces.'[18]

Unfortunately, none of this work made any money – though some of it was meant to. He was to send Ralph an article on Victorian literature, which never got written.[19] In February 1922 he finally finished the 'Bestiary', and sent it to Carrington. The work, he said airily, of a few evenings (actually one and a half years of frequent and concentrated effort). But money remained very tight. Tiz sent some – but Gerald was too nervous to ask in all the frequent emergencies. His father would not help. As usual, Ralph supplied – £4 in November, for example, £10 in March 1922 (his generosity the more admirable since, until his father died, he had only his £130 p.a. from the Woolfs). At one point they had to pawn Gerald's binoculars. 'Only photography can be relied on for support,' he wrote to Ralph, seemingly hypnotised by Hope. Unsurprisingly, not a peseta was earned – and vast sums were disbursed on Customs dues (£23) and darkroom construction.[20]

And all the time Gerald had the music of Carrington's letters. For her – probably for both – their affair should always have been letters. She wrote every week, sometimes twice, 180 pages in seven months, light, vivid, humorous descriptions of her life, the lines of love tossed in. Drawings, endless promises to come out, compliments, gossip, confessions. A Slade friend Phyllis was to marry a M. de Janzé. Carrington was jealous. At the Slade she was beautiful, clever, original, completely immoral and 'I longed to possess her in some vague way'.[21] Not so much confession, perhaps, as veiled warning.

From November to January a massive *obra* – Spanish for work –

went on. Not just Hope's darkroom, but whitewashing (Gerald again), new shelves, glass in the windows, curtains, and a long, completely new room out of one of the granaries – the *granero* – with new windows and which could be closed off, near a huge, hooded open fire, with thick red curtains to make it cosy. (Today, it is a granary again.)

The *obra* was briefly interrupted by Christmas. Astonishingly, it seemed that the Christmas pudding sent out in 1919 had reappeared. Carrington was thrilled: 'I can hardly believe after nearly three years that plum pudding could have risen out of its grave and shrieked at the postmen of Malaga.'[22] Food standards rose briefly in response to Hope's greed – Christmas Eve was fried fish, sweet potatoes, zabaglione, grapes – then slumped back to the usual range of lentil pottage, salt cod and vegetable stews, omelettes, bread, unrefined oil, cheap wine and delicious water. From 1 to 8 January 1922 Hope and Gerald went on an expedition to the coast to escape the *obra*. They took a donkey, Hope played his flute and for moments they were on the Walk again.

Gerald employed one of the masons, Frascillo, as his gardener because, he said he enjoyed his talk (the man was a hopeless gardener). But he gives no examples of their discourse, and he may really have been more interested in Frascillo's daughter. Paquita was tall and beautiful, but was struck by sudden fits of madness. Then she would become a nymphomaniac, leaving the house at night to sleep with the harvesters up from the coast. Frascillo had slept with her himself because he had heard it cured insanity. It didn't, and she had a child which eventually went completely mad and had to be shut up.

The note of sexual frustration increased into 1922. 'Have I to spend the prime of my life like a monk in a cell?' he cried to Ralph. It made it impossible to concentrate. 'My God, what joy to be as regular, slow, respectable a thing as a cabbage, a stomach, a kitchen clock.'[23] He must get a mistress, within eighteen months.[24] (He did.)

His longing invaded the dances he arranged. These were a prominent feature of Gerald's Yegen life, still remembered today: 'He couldn't afford strong drink. He never danced. He liked people to dance and drink. Sometimes they lasted till three.'[25] The dances took place every month or so, depending on funds. Gerald would supply wine, *aguardiente* (a strong steel-tasting spirit), tobacco. Thirty or forty people and the 'band' (two guitars, say, and a lute) would gather in the *granero*, the table and chairs pushed back. They danced country dances, one, for example, over crossed straps on the floor. A little later on, the younger ones would do the Foxtrot. Gerald wrote to Carrington after a dance that he and Hope gave in February 1922: 'The smell of sweat, the heat, the high, piercing erotic scents of the women. The singing, dancing, stamping, laughing, shouting and the faces of every age gleaming in the oil lights. And then, when it is all over, they will go home to their houses and lying in heaps on their dirty beds, full of fleas and sodden with sweat, will sleep together.' One of the two village tarts was there, with beautiful ears and throat. If only, if only she wasn't meant to have syphilis.[26]

In late January Gerald went to Órgiva to meet the Dobrées. Waiting for them in a *posada* he had what seems to have been a familiar dream: '. . . a lace curtain fluttered in the windows of the house facing me and reminded me of a hope I have always had, yet never realised – that if I looked often enough into upper-storey windows, I should end by seeing some girl in the act of undressing.'[27] Inexorably, the years of acute sexual frustration (he was now nearly twenty-eight) forced him into different forms of expression, whether fantasy or not.

Perhaps it was the imminent arrival of Valentine which sparked the dream. The visit went well – full of gaiety and laughter, Gerald told Carrington. While Hope entertained Bonamy, Gerald and Val went for long walks, but naturally he 'couldn't fall in love'.[28] Slightly more than this went on. Gerald had been planning for Ralph and Carrington to come to Yegen. Valentine now told him that she very badly wanted Ralph to come to Larrau. If Gerald agreed to urge this and came himself, she would distract Ralph (and with Valentine 'distract' only meant one thing) so that Gerald could spend a lot of time alone with Carrington. She sang her siren seventeenth- and eighteenth-century songs in English, French and Italian, something she'd refused to do for him at Larrau. Gerald capitulated. Valentine then tried to seduce him, climbing into his bed early one morning. Gerald infuriated her by immediately leaping out.[29] His feelings about her were clearly ambivalent. A poem he wrote about her in 1923 still mingles fascinated sexual attraction and acute disgust: 'fat breasts . . . blood flower lips . . . more dog than sun in her perpetual heat.' But her singing was beautiful. The Pope-like stanzas end, 'All this and yet diseased, malicious, mad. /Balance this sum – add Beauty to the bad.'[30]

In *Personal Record* Gerald says he panicked when the Dobrées had gone and tried to get Carrington to change back to Yegen. There is no evidence of this in either of their letters. Gerald is just 'mad with joy'; Carrington equally so, sending £20 for his fare, and promising more to get him to England afterwards.[31]

Hope would look after Yegen. He had Augustus John's seventeen-year-old, extremely good-looking son Robin for company, who had arrived in March to recover from discovering his father had been sleeping with his pretty Chelsea girlfriend. Gerald bought a huge quantity of rugs and plates for presents and on 5 April, two days before his birthday, left for Almería and Larrau.

3

Gerald arrived, penniless again, at Pamplona on 9 April. In addition to sleeping bag and tent, the bundle of presents he was carrying was so heavy Carrington couldn't lift it when it eventually reached Tidmarsh. But he was now on fire to see her. He walked the thirty miles to near the border and spent the night at an inn in the forest of Iretz. He was told the Pyrenees were impassable. The pass would still be blocked by snow. Also there were bears in the great beechwoods.[32]

Gerald left his luggage at the inn to cover the bill and set off on the steep seventeen-mile climb at dawn. As he cleared the tree-line at 4500 feet, then as now (but on a track, not a road), he would have come out onto a huge bare mountain, desolate and forbidding, its colossal views probably hidden by cloud. Then down again, through the tall, lichen-covered beech trees, cowbells sounding, a feeling of freshness, the sound of water, running and bounding in his eagerness.

Frances Partridge remembered such appearances: 'he was *extremely* romantic, extremely adventurous. We all thought so. And so full of eccentric life and laughter – he never said what one expected. I can see him now, as they say, leaping down the hillside in his wild way, an amazing figure appearing out of the mists – it was very thrilling.'

However, the romantic figure, as indeed he was, and no doubt enthusiastically welcomed at first, was arriving into rather a fraught scene. Valentine's father had appeared, a retired general from a Twenties farce who told endless tales of the campaigns. Bonamy Dobrée kept reading from his boring biography of Thomas Dekker. Ralph – a classic response – had taken violently against Valentine and was very rude and aggressive. While Carrington, after streams of loving letters, was inexplicably cold to Gerald.

In fact, she was distracted with desire for Valentine. And here yet another skein has to be twisted into the tangle of Carrington's emotional responses. She was sexually far more lesbian than anything else. Not for three years could she bring herself, agonising over the revelation, to tell Gerald straight out – though she had already hinted at it with typical obliqueness. Over Phyllis de Janzé, and also with Valentine – 'You know my feelings for her are far from ordinary.'³³

Gradually things improved. Carrington painted Gerald's portrait – his ardour, in the painting, both patent and touching. They kissed. It seemed as if it was going to be Watendlath all over again.

Lytton decided he'd like to see Pau. Gerald and Carrington agreed. Valentine said she'd drive them, whereupon Ralph refused to go. On the way back, the car broke down and they had to walk to a nearby hotel.

In *Personal Record* Gerald says he had now abandoned all conscious scruples over Ralph. It was a perfect place for the two lovers. Gerald's room was directly above Carrington's, both looking out onto the river, which was in full, deafening flood. After dinner, he went up and stood at the window, waiting. Before long, he heard above the roar the call of a cuckoo – their agreed signal, and suddenly he knew he'd be impotent. This made it impossible to go down. Gripped by a terrible shame, sleepless, longing for her yet certain and terrified of impotence, Gerald sat or paced in agony, listening to the river, sometimes hearing Carrington call, once even reaching her door; so passed 'the most terrible night of my life'.

He went down at dawn, confessed; they kissed. She comforted him and chided him; surely he could have guessed she'd have been perfectly happy just lying beside him. They were chatting, Gerald sitting on the bed, when Valentine came in, longing to know how it had gone. Seeing Gerald apparently just leaving after his night of love, she hurried tactfully out again.

Back at Larrau, Ralph suffered a comparable ordeal by boredom – chapters of Dekker plus a complete campaign in Kashmir with photographs. But now – in an equally classic reversal – his hostility to Valentine turned to violent attraction. While Carrington painted, watched and kissed by Gerald, Ralph and Valentine shut themselves up in her studio all day, presumably making love. As a result, Ralph, Carrington and Lytton left abruptly for England four days later.

Gerald, at once missing Carrington, desperately wanted to follow immediately. (He made an interesting comment on his feelings to Hope. Missing her was torture, '. . . but then, very soon, as always happens with me, the pain began to find some outlet in my imagination and was changed into purest pleasure.')³⁴ But Valentine begged him to stay, promising to drive him to fetch his luggage. It seems highly probable that she made another pass at him. At least, that is the most likely explanation of why she suddenly 'took against me'. When she did drive him, she abruptly stopped the car after six miles and made him walk the rest of the way – seventy miles, since the direct passes were now blocked. No doubt Gerald, totally absorbed in his concerns and the prospect of seeing Carrington in England, didn't even notice, but in view of what was soon to happen, it was a fatal second rejection.

4

Events now moved, at first with delightful, finally with horrifying speed.

They began quietly enough at Edgeworth. Pelman in the evening (Gerald won); his father gave him a cheque and they went riding together. He went to Communion with his mother. 'The wonderful beauty of the language recited in a half-whisper, the smell of mould and wet masonry, the mysterious titles of God, repeated in the Gloria and above all the sweet taste of the wine, taken fasting.' Exalted and sharpened, Gerald went to morning service after breakfast, enjoying the domesticity of it. 'All the time one is getting up and kneeling down and opening and shutting books.'³⁵

Gerald's thoughts ran incessantly on Carrington. Ralph was now conducting a flagrantly open and passionately sexual affair with Valentine. It is clear from a p.s. (all their secret communications were now like this to avoid Ralph) that Gerald and Carrington had already decided to make love.³⁵ Passionate, non-passive friendship allowed occasional acts of love, especially with someone soon to be 2000 miles away. Letters shot between them, Gerald's none too subtle – 'Who are you thinking of – Valentine?'[36] But more fundamental reactions had begun. Gerald was showing the violent mood-swings – elation, despair, anger, jealousy – that love always induced in him. And already, at Larrau, he could not bear to be apart from Carrington. He could be seized with such terrible agitation that he had to find company.[37] One is suddenly reminded of the distress he'd shown as a child when his mother or Nana Crease went away. Carrington was beginning to stir deep waters.

On 11 May he went to Tidmarsh. In the past three years, he had spent only four days alone with Carrington. Now, in spite of frequent visitors and trips to London to see Tiz, they were together for three weeks. Ralph commuted to London for his work at the Hogarth Press and to conduct his affair. Lytton had his social visits. As soon as Gerald and Carrington were alone they made love – or did according to Gerald's diary abstract, where a simple code – 'X' for kiss, '*' for copulation – punctuates the minute record of these two months.[38] *Personal Record* is far vaguer. According to the abstract, they first made love on 15 June, again on the 25th ('in a wood' – it was bluebell time and a beautiful spring). On the 27th Morgan Forster and the Woolfs came to tea. (It is evidence of Gerald's growing reputation – as a result of his letters and talk more than his writings – that Forster came especially to meet him.)[39] Gerald, who thought Forster's novels sentimental, found he liked him; he also took to the Woolfs, whom he'd been longing to meet. They asked him to stay. The next day Ralph went to London, and Gerald and Carrington made love twice more, after which Gerald returned to Edgeworth.

If the abstract is accurate, this was considerably above Carrington's usual ration. She at once began to retreat. 'I shall manoeuvre the 〰〰〰* all right,' she wrote, but warned that he must not mind if she were difficult. 'I have lost something which seems to prevent me ever giving myself away completely ever again.'[40] Gerald quickly wrote a cold letter. He wanted nothing; just 'a few perfect days a year'. Carrington answered, 'I want to shout I LOVE GERALD

* The symbol Ralph, Carrington and Gerald all used to denote making love. Gerald denied in a letter to Bunny Garnett on his edition of Carrington's letters that it invariably meant this. I have never found an example of it meaning anything else.

VERY MUCH.' First minuscule movements of that yo-yo whose alterna-
tions were nearly to break him.

On 6 June came the bombshell. In bed with Ralph in Marlborough, Valentine, still smarting from Gerald's rejection, shopped
them.*

Ralph had a nature as furiously jealous as it was passionate in
love. He told Barbara Bagenal (one of Carrington's great friends at
the Slade) that he would have to kill Gerald. He drank half a bottle
of whisky and drove to Tidmarsh in the car Lytton had just given
him, where he had a frightful row with Carrington, and then sent a
wire to Gerald ordering him to meet him in London at the Hogarth
Press. A horrified Gerald also received a second, secret, telegram
from Carrington begging him not to tell.

The scene in London was extremely unpleasant. Throughout
their long friendship Ralph and Gerald had quite often provoked each
other, and one element in play with Gerald was that of standing up
to his father. Now he could only hope to placate and, having decided
to protect Carrington, deceive. Honest and extremely loyal himself,
what most infuriated Ralph was the idea that Gerald had hatched an
adulterous plot. Gerald denied this, then and thereafter. It was not a
'plot', just a vague arrangement for Valentine to distract Ralph so that
he could see Carrington alone. No doubt this was technically true,
but it is rather *faux-naïf*. He knew perfectly well what 'see alone'
meant to Valentine and how far adultery was from his mind is shown
by his own admission that the only reason he didn't sleep with
Carrington was because he was terrified he'd be impotent. Ralph
questioned him point by point, leaving the room each time to
corroborate everything with Valentine, who in fact wasn't there. By
concentrating his mind entirely on what had happened at Larrau,
admitting only kisses, denying all love-making at any time, Gerald
got through, and then returned to Edgeworth.

The next day he had a brief lunch with Lytton and Carrington at

* That this was the reason – and that Gerald realised it – is shown by *The
History of Poor Robinson*, the barely fictional account he wrote of the whole
Carrington imbroglio in 1927 (MSS, MF and Texas). In this, Robinson (Gerald) and
Flutterby (Carrington) become lovers and are betrayed by Buzzabelle (Valentine) to
Perrywag (Ralph) because Robinson refused to be seduced by Buzzabelle. Valentine
was still seething in 1926 and warned Janko Varda that Gerald was over-
sophisticated, dangerous, perfidious and untrustworthy (Gerald to Joanna
Carrington, 24 February 1966).

Tidmarsh (trembling so much he could hardly hold his knife and fork). He returned to Edgeworth, the enormity of what had happened beginning to overwhelm him. His friendship with Ralph ended. Never to see Tidmarsh or Carrington again. He took to his bed with 'flu and sent her a suicide letter. 'Do not blame yourself or me . . .' The writing is heavily smudged with tears (or drops of water).[42] He may have sent another to Blair. His parents were extremely kind; relieved, Gerald thought perversely, to have proof he wasn't homosexual.

He spent 12 and 13 June in London, sending wires to Tidmarsh and waiting hours at various places for Carrington to come. She never came. He left for Spain on the 14th, saw Augustus briefly in Madrid, and was back at Yegen on 21 June, his life apparently in ruins.

5

Superficially Gerald carried on as usual. María had had another baby and the house was in chaos. He, Hope and Robin John (an adolescent more reminiscent of the 1990s, who spent all day on his bed with a guitar) decamped to El Horcajo (Big Fork), a bulging mountain high in the Sierra above Trevélez.

But at first he also wrote via Hope and Barbara Bagenal (with whom he'd flirted) desperate letters to Carrington. She, too, was desperate at first – she lost a stone in July and couldn't stop crying; and she soon found she missed him far more, she told Lytton, than she'd expected.[43] She missed the life of letters, the excitement of it. Ralph was too robust for her, Lytton so easily bored; only with Gerald was she totally at ease. Perhaps, she wondered – as always astute about herself – it *was* herself she was loving in him.[44]

Both knew Ralph was the clue. Very soon Gerald began – it was to be a major theme of his life till 1927 – his campaign to get her back. He told Ralph his feelings for her were virtually platonic. Besides, Ralph knew that Gerald really preferred love-in-the-imagination. Beneath his rage, Ralph's affection was staunch; the moment Gerald had left he'd written to say he'd always send money.[45] (Gerald's response had been to send *him* a cheque.) By October, Ralph seems to have decided that Gerald had really done what he had out of vagueness (that is, become too attracted to Carrington). By

27 November, he and Carrington could resume (closely scrutinised) letters. By 22 December, Ralph and Gerald were friends again.

In September, Ralph ended his affair with Valentine, but from now on Carrington encouraged him to sleep with other women. His relationship with her was never the same, which at a profound level is what she wanted. She had never wished to get married. He came to love her deeply again, but protectively not, eventually, possessively, and less and less sexually.

To Carrington Gerald's line was that, like Shelley, he thought sharing love actually increased it. As for possessiveness and jealousy, wrote this man soon to make scenes to rival Othello, he hadn't the faintest idea what they were.[46]

But for Ralph the most convincing evidence that he had changed – and this might also make Carrington jealous – would be other girls. In January 1923 Gerald suddenly announced that for two months he'd had a regular affair with a married woman in Yegen – 'M'. Her husband was both impotent and a sodomite. Gerald enjoyed entering her life, though he often got bored and left before dawn. In July, he had another, shorter affair 'with a neighbour'. This one told him indecent stories and made him laugh a lot; 'This eating, drinking and fucking has a kind of cheerfulness about it . . .'[47]

Did these affairs take place? It would certainly be a great relief to think so. But there are strange features. Gerald's reason for breaking them off was fear of syphilis.[48] It is not impossible that the housewives of Yegen had syphilis but it is unlikely. Then why did he not mention these affairs in his autobiographies? In *Personal Record* he was far from reticent about his affairs; nor was it out of consideration for the people of Yegen. He didn't think anyone in Yegen would read *South From Granada* and mentioned things they minded far more, as we shall see. He was perfectly open about the one indisputable affair he did have there, and the letters which describe that are also different – excited, fascinated, naive. The letters about 'M' and her companion are highly literary and also have a world-weary, nonchalant tone: the lechery 'really means little to me . . . only a slight disgust'. They much more resemble letters describing a similar incident at Toulon in 1926, which Gerald later admitted he'd made up.

With perhaps only apparent irrelevance, Gerald's next sentence goes on to discuss his imagination – 'All activity in the area labelled imagination is better than anything outside it.'[49] It seems equally possible that he visited the two Yegen prostitutes and invented these affairs both to reveal and disguise this. (Later on, out of a slight shame, he often pretended the prostitutes he met in London were not really prostitutes). One of the Yegen prostitutes, we know already, attracted him and was thought to have syphilis. She lived next door and his account of her technique – 'Professional, a quick, on-the-spot air, as of a hospital nurse who is conscious of her own proficiency' – suggests familiarity. Oddly enough, both of the Yegen prostitutes' names ingeniously fit the initial 'M' in his letters. One was called Maxima; the other nicknamed La Prisca – a sort of peach. The usual Spanish word for peach is *melocotón*.*

If this is so, it would help explain what happened some months later. Gerald did not immediately succeed in making Carrington anything more than mildly interested. He was more successful at Christmas, when he spent six weeks in Granada. He met, flirted with and fell slightly in love with an American girl he called 'E'. He wrote and told Leonard Woolf he was going to marry her, knowing Leonard would tell Virginia and Virginia Carrington, which she did.⁵⁰ The results were gratifying. Carrington was extremely piqued,⁵¹ even though Virginia thought it might be a joke. Gerald, delighted, wrote denying he'd written to Leonard and saying it was a malicious invention of Virginia's, a denial he repeated forty years later to Bunny. The letter to Leonard, however, is there still, in the Chatto and Windus archives in Bristol.⁵²

Then in September 1923 he escaped for a three-month trip to Almería, Cordoba, Seville and finally Morocco. Hours of reading (again, often all night) and chronic short sight necessitated new spectacles, which he failed to find in Almería. But, an old fantasy now finding expression, while peering through a hole in a bathing hut he saw a beautiful girl 'with exquisitely grained skin' undressing.⁵³ However, Antonia Fuentes, daughter of a bullfighter, would only talk to him swimming and Gerald gave up his pursuit.†

He was much more successful in Seville. Señor Serylowski, an optician of Polish extraction, seems to have gone rather over the top

---

* The Peach charged a peseta a go, two for the night; Maxima charged two eggs.

† He would have been at a serious disadvantage in the water. Some peculiar density of composition, Frances Partridge noticed at Toulon in 1926, meant that unless he thrashed with great energy he instantly sank.

with Gerald's eyes: two pairs of new spectacles, a monocle, and blue goggles to wear in the sun.[54] Seville, much smaller then, tourist-free, delicately Moorish, charming, carefree, fragrant with scented orange blossom, enchanted Gerald. He was seized by one of his fits of inspiration and a huge quantity of poetry (some to Antonia Fuentes) poured out; especially in the Kursaal, largest of the *demi-mondaine* cafés, its girls with 'those large brilliant eyes with their clear whites which can throw a signal as far as one can throw a tennis ball':[55] signals returned with interest, no doubt, via the monocle. And, with Larrion, a dissolute Englishman for whom 'even actresses were too respectable', Gerald immersed himself for three weeks in Seville's underworld. Brothels, with their expectation of performance, terrified him sexually;[53] but he was fascinated and often moved by the brothel world, the world of tarts and whores, love and drink, beggars with running sores, 'old hags dropping their excrement under the railway arch . . .'[56] Wherever he went he explored them (Gerald's superficial diffidence often vanished under the disguise of Spanish; he even became a mimic).[57]

One night he picked up Pepita – tiny, seventeen (in *Personal Record*), incredibly lovely in an embroidered chemise. He bought her a box of chocolates. She sat wriggling on his lap till five in the morning, by which time (very unusually) Gerald was too drunk even to try and make love. The next night – a strawberry ice which Pepita ate 'chattering volubly . . . she seemed to live in a permanent state of fidgety vivacity'; then all night carousing, a restaurant, getting drunk – a terrible moment when she wanted to dance – a carriage, as dawn broke, coffee at the Torre del Oro by the river. Gerald 'looked at the cold sleeping water and the solemn line of houses' and felt he was seeing Seville as it ought to be seen. The third evening he finally got the delicious creature into bed, 'And I never knew till that night the richness of pleasure that can be extracted from copulation.' All that he minded was that, being a prostitute, her pleasure might be simulated.[56]

He'd found, in all probability with the Yegen prostitutes, that paying, the position of dominance, would make him confident. Also, prostitutes don't mind, indeed are often relieved, if clients just chat. This was an important discovery, though he didn't fully exploit it until he returned to London. In fact, little Pepita isn't really an example, since he found her in a brothel. But the attraction he felt for very young girls almost certainly has this as one element of its root. It does not matter so much if you fail with someone very young. Pepita was actually fifteen not seventeen.[58]

All these adventures and many more went back in a series of long, vivid, entirely delightful letters – later to form the basis of Gerald's fascinating account in *Personal Record* – to Carrington and Ralph who, as far as the campaign went, were interchangeable.

The campaign was completely successsful. Once more, as Carrington says, she was able to daydream about him; her presents (books, the *Nation*, *New Statesman*, Eliot's *Criterion*) and her letters streamed out, increasing noticeably if Gerald was at all cool or slow to reply. She had fun with Valentine, 'the seasoned adventuress',[59] and was delighted to discover her real name was Gladys. And, in typically swift inserts, she revealed herself: she used to tease him and 'behave badly . . . simply because I loved making you care for me'.[60] She countered 'E' with her own American, Henrietta Bingham, the beautiful, bisexual daughter of Judge Bingham. Henrietta nearly took Tidmarsh, which they were trying to get rid of, and excited Carrington greatly because while being shown round she took 'as much interest in me as if I'd been the housekeeper!'[61] None the less, from Gerald's point of view, this was to be a fateful meeting.

6

Carrington's letters kept Gerald going during the long last lap of Yegen. Hope, sick of the primitive life, had returned to England in September 1922, to join his old wartime comrade Compton Mackenzie on *Gramophone*, a magazine he'd started. Robin John followed soon after.

The only surviving fragment of a diary gives a clear picture of the way many months must have passed at Yegen.

Diary[62]   *February 1923*   *Yegen*

Monday 19th
Strong wind all night, slept badly. Got up after 9. Breakfast. Reread some Virgil and Horace. One chapter Dowden's life of Shelley. Shelley's translation of the Homeric, Hymn to

Mercury and some lyrics. Copied out 2 double sheets foolscap, and wrote 400 words on Theme of Bestiary. Walked up and down for ½ an hour to think out a dialogue. Went out from 2 till 4 – walked up mountain: wind, cloud, hail. Improvised and wrote down a few lines of Poem on Dawn: this is now fully prepared, I think. Tea. Read Spanish Poetry – then Tacitus. Head tired – composition hopeless. After dinner 2 hours construing Virgil, and some Tacitus in English. Bed 11.15// More poetry than usual; Latin poetry costs me very hard work at present. Quiet night. Stars.

Tuesday
A bad day. Read nothing. Copied Bestiary, corrected and made additions. Wrote 2 long letters. Copied out in evening and wrote for 2 hours. Late to bed.

Wednesday
Virgil. Read La Bruyère. Felt very gay all day: danced The Sevillana: walked out in rain, wind and mist: got very wet. Spent about 6 hours writing letters, mostly tedious ones. Otherwise wrote nothing, read nothing.

Thursday
Virgil and Horace till 11.0. Walked till 12.30. Letter from E [his American]. After lunch read 50 pages of Proust. Went for a walk after tea. Restless, unable to write. In evening finished Dowden's Shelley and read part of Trelawney and Peacock's Recollections. Find I have caught bloody cold. Rain. Wind. A bad day.

Friday
Got up at midday, with a cold. Read Tacitus morning and evening. Also Taylor's Epicurus. Copied a few pages and wrote a letter to R [Ralph]. Execrable day.

Saturday
Read Plutarch's Aristides and Cato. Went out at 11.30, walked to farm in mountains, returned 3.30. Exhausted by cold in head and lack of food – went to sleep. After a meal read Laforgue's Hamlet and notebooks also some Mallarmé and Corbière.

Sunday
Still had cold. Read Tacitus most of day; Began Mungo
Park's Franck. Read 2 reviews sent by D. C [Carrington].
Some Virgil.

Monday
Tacitus. Hume's Morals. Letter from D. C. and E.

Tuesday
Finished Tacitus Annales. Long walk. Extreme depression.
Evening read all 'Lonely Nietzsche' and wrote long letter to
D. C. Late to bed.

Wednesday
Tired because slept little. Otherwise well. Began
'Précursenes de Nietzsche' and read Bartholomew Fair.

One might note that cold. So frequent were his colds and more
especially 'flu that he came to resemble a one-man epidemic. The clue
is in a letter to Bunny Garnett in 1929: 'How do you tell when you
have a temperature? I put my hand or arm in my mouth and I know
I have one if it tastes sour.'[63] Refreshing doses of ''flu', as he described
them, no doubt contributed to Gerald's longevity.

But there were other diversions during those twenty-one months,
apart from his long trip in the autumn. His Christmas stay in the
lovely city of Granada (the name means pomegranate) introduced
Gerald to the long-established English-speaking colony, whose endless, gossipy, theatre visits, tea and dinner parties and dances he
attended. A senior member was the American Mrs Wood, with
whom he stayed, once a famous beauty, then aged eighty-three who,
heavily made up, like Tiz in Edwardian clothes, waged a relentless
battle against age (successfully – she lived, unimpaired, to be ninety-
five). 'Conversation tired her more than most things, possibly for the
reason that she felt obliged to do most of the talking herself. This was
not because she had much to say, but because listening tired her even
more.' But she was kind and when Gerald became for a while the
official *novio* of a Spanish girl she slipped him some money to help
spruce up.[64] From the end of her garden he would have looked upon
a central site in his penultimate book – the foundations of Los

Mártires, where St John of the Cross wrote *The Dark Night of the Soul*, which were still visible in the 1920s.

He also briefly met Federico García Lorca, then just beginning to become well known as a poet and playwright. Gerald, the sole of one shoe about to fall off, noticed Lorca's beautiful clothes – also his good taste and manners. He seemed 'rich beyond dreams', but they got on well. Had Lorca not gone to Madrid, 'it might have meant a new friendship'.[64]

On 3 April the Woolfs came for ten days via another doyen of Granada, Lindsay Temple, who had been Lieutenant Governor of Nigeria and wished to talk colonies with Leonard.

They talked literature, according to both Virginia[65] and Gerald, twelve hours a day, Virginia drawing Gerald out, in Bloomsbury fashion, by endless questions – but, again typical of Bloomsbury, totally unpatronising. There was, he wrote, something warming about this distinguished writer, 'approaching the height of her powers', listening to Gerald who, starved of company, was extremely voluble ('chatterbox' was her description), without putting him down or 'betraying boredom'. There is no evidence either were bored. He was also very conscious that they wanted to see if he'd make a writer for them.

But it was not all literature. Gerald describes Virginia in the *granero* in the evening, with her long face, with its large grey, greyish-blue eyes lighting up when animated. She would stretch her hands to the fire, bending, and then 'her face revealed her as a poet'. And Leonard, steady, masculine, pipe-smoking; both of them scrambling up a hillside, Leonard looking almost boyish; Virginia excited as a schoolgirl, lost in the beauty of this remote spot. And they spoke, at least Leonard did, very freely. On a walk with Gerald he said that on his honeymoon he had tried to make love to Virginia but she got into such a state of excitement he had to stop, 'Knowing such states were a prelude to her madness.' Since then, he had given up all ideas of sexual satisfaction 'because she was a genius'. He never flirted with a woman, 'only expecting, in return, that she would not either with a man'.[66]

And even now Gerald did not forget his campaign. Either then or possibly later, he seems to have sensed or known how, with Virginia's aversion to lust, overstrong male sexuality frightened and irritated her, and, half-sharing it, he said things to Ralph's detriment that he hoped would get back to Carrington. 'You are evidently right,' Virginia wrote when they'd left, 'he [Ralph] suspects all brain workers, who don't rampage about the purlieus of Soho chasing after pretty powdered girls.'[67]

The visit was a success. According to Quentin Bell, Virginia had 'liked him very much'.[65] Leonard read the 'Bestiary' and said he'd publish an extract in the *Nation* (author to be 'B. Buffon'). Tiz was so excited when she heard about the publication that she instantly took out a life subscription.[68] Virginia was sure Gerald would 'write something very very wonderful one of these days'.[69] He wrote several letters and sent her poems. A little later, Leonard asked him to review a book of Spanish plays, though Gerald refused.[70]

But Gerald's letters to Virginia, almost uniquely in his vast surviving correspondence, have a strained, almost sycophantic quality. Hers to him, if kindly, do not, after the first few, reveal any great interest. He saw them both from time to time over the years but, though amiable enough, they never became close. So well had they got on at Yegen, that Gerald was apparently disappointed[71] to find no record when Virginia's *Journals* came out (she never kept her journal when travelling). The only entries, made later when she'd decided he wasn't after all a talented writer, are usually fairly waspish.

Shortly after the Woolfs left his parents arrived. Gerald put on a brass tie-pin and shaved with unusual care.[72] This visit too was a success. The tidiness of his house, the evidence of 'seriousness', the Englishness of his Granada 'set', and no doubt Gerald's recent guests (it had been arranged that B. Buffon's latest work would arrive at Edgeworth),[69] all impressed his father. When the Brenan parents left by mule a month later Hugh had promised Gerald an extra £100 a year provided he bought some new clothes and came back once a year.

Poverty was over – in Yegen at least. £150 p.a. was still not enough to survive on in London. But by June Gerald had decided he would come back for good in the spring of 1924.[73] This was typical. Gerald once said, looking very serious, to Constance Ellis (a friend in the 1970s), who had suggested they plan some trip: 'Constance – I have never planned anything in my life.' Constance Ellis was deeply impressed.[74] In fact, nothing could be further from the truth. From the age of about twenty-five, all major and many minor moves in the apparently spontaneous, haphazard life of the poet were actually founded, with military precision, on a rigid grid of careful pre-planning.

Relief from Yegen life also came with his huge walks into the Sierra Nevada, when for hours at a time – writing in his head, poetry, letters to Carrington – he would stride tireless, immersed in that vast ocean of air. He found he could walk twelve hours without stopping or tiring. Once, in October 1921, he walked in one go from Granada to Yegen via the Lomas de Bacares (9000 feet), leaving at three in the morning and arriving twenty-two hours later – a distance he variously estimated at fifty-two, sixty-two and seventy-two miles. This is a feat, apparently, at the very limit of a professional mountaineer's capacity.*

The Sierra Nevada, isolated by the last ice age, and where there were still wolves until the late forties, has evolved some twenty species of flora that are unique. Gerald's childhood interest in botany now revived, and extended to the village itself. He was delighted – baby memories stirring – that the country people were greatly given to eating thistles: the young stems of the golden *Scolymus hispanicus*, in Spanish *tagornina*, which made some people come out in spots; also the head and roots of the thistle *Silybum marianum*.

If he returned from his enormous walks by daylight – seeing below him first the thin plumes of wood smoke – he would almost invariably hear song. Chance had thrown Gerald into a region whose main, almost sole, mode of expression was both poetic and musical – and musical in the one way he could appreciate. A *copla* is a three- or four-line verse meant for singing. It can cover – and there were (are) hundreds of thousands of them, continually added to by improvisation – everything: the village, chickens, children, war, death, cooking

---

* But it is possible. In the interests of biographical veracity, I did most of this walk with some companions in July 1988. We left out the fifteen or so miles by road from Granada to the foot of the Sierra Nevada, and the last twelve miles by road from Bérchules to Yegen. I was thirty years older than Gerald had been and had done something agonising to my right toe (it turned out to be a gout episode). Juan Antonio Díaz López had recently broken his ankle. Only Rupam Maxwell and Paco and Candy Muñoz were intact; furthermore, to complete my excuses, July is considerably hotter than October. Thus hobbling, it took us a day and a half, but it was clear that someone unencumbered by packs, as we were not, and also young, fit and very strong could just have done it in twenty-two hours. You can't estimate the distance accurately because of the endlessly zigzagging, twisting mule tracks (now much obliterated – another source of delay). I'd say we did nearly forty miles, so Gerald walked about sixty.

– but especially love. They cannot be danced to, but can compress into their tiny space an astonishing beauty and poignancy.

> Arrímate a mi querer
> Como las salamanquesas
> Se arríman a la pared.

('Draw close to my love, as the little lizards draw close to the wall.')

And all day at Yegen, from the fields, from the flat roofs, carried by repetition, you would suddenly hear these little songs arching through the still air. Not only did the human voice move Gerald, but the form of these minute poems echoed his own gift for condensing and distilling the essence of something into a memorable phrase: a gift already becoming evident in his letters, which marked his conversation, and which he demonstrated in *A Holiday by the Sea* and, particularly, *Thoughts in a Dry Season*. Also – again, something that suited Gerald – they were not exactly personal. Gay, sad, sensual, spiritual, it was idiosyncrasy of situation, something objective, they caught.

> ¡Olé que olé, graciosa!
> Parece tu cuerpecito
> Una botella de gaseosa.

'*Olé*, my lovely. Your body dances like a bottle of soda water.')[75]

No doubt all violent exercise has in it an element of masochism; Gerald talks of nature 'beating' its way into his system, his back wet with sweat, returning to a cold wash, his supper in front of the fire, the *Criterion*, exalted like a mystic from mortifying his flesh in these heroic expeditions. In pain, he lived more intensely. And there is an interesting parallel in the language with which he describes the initial and most important aspect of his reading;[75] it is the feminine language of submission, of giving himself totally to new modes of feeling.

It would be possible in fact, though tedious, to detail the prodigious range and extent of his reading these last two years. But two books were particularly important. He first read James Joyce's *Ulysses* in June 1922. 'He is an undoubted genius. A large part dull and stupid, but the rest magnificent . . . building richness, variety and, somehow, beauty of modern life . . . He is a great and extremely original artist.'[76] He read it again in August 1923: '*Voilà quelque chose d'énorme.*'[77] *Ulysses* was the subject of one of his principal literary arguments with Virginia, who said no great work of art should be so boring (although the Hogarth Press would have published *Ulysses* had it found a printer who dared print it).

Then in February 1923 Gerald began to read Proust. Except for occasional beautiful or interesting passages, he told Carrington casually, he often found him boring.[78] Gerald not infrequently reveals something very important to him by saying the opposite. Writers who succumb to the Proust drug sometimes never recover; Gerald escaped the most virulent Scott-Moncrieff type; nevertheless, another view of his very slow evolution as writer is that not till he'd worked Proust out of his system over some thirty years, first by simple regurgitation in *Jack Robinson*, later by writing history and literary criticism, could he at last emerge himself. And one of the reasons Proust affected him so strongly gives an essential clue to an observation made earlier; why he was not remotely influenced by the modernists he was so quick to recognise (Proust's psychological penetration is essentially and traditionally French, not modernist). His feeling for beauty, for nature, was so strong, so intimately bound up with his idea of himself as a writer, that, as he was well aware, it was to him the most important element in anything he wrote.[79] (At a tangent to this, those almost violent moments of nature possession ceased the moment he fell in love with Carrington; a fascinating corroboration of Peter Levi's speculation about these states.)

It took time for the drug Proust to get a grip. Meanwhile, often in bouts of uncontrollable excitement, manic fits of energy, dozens of projects got started and abandoned: an autobiography, a thousand-line poem in heroic couplets, an essay on architecture; the academic-facetious mode persisted into further rewrites of the 'Bestiary'; a new disguise (long-lasting) appeared – George Beaton.[80]

But far more significant were the exile's lifeline – his letters: 215,000 words to Carrington (who herself sent some 95,000 words), another 60,000 to Ralph. Say four novels. Hope had established the habit, now it was vastly extended – letters as diary for recording, as confessional, for introspection, for comfort, for furthering love-plots and deceiving, for working out ideas, for feeding (perhaps originating) his later addiction to love-in-the-head. He might, one feels, have made a considerable journal keeper.* But he needed an audience. There was a strong element, if as usual disguised, of the performer in Gerald; as maker of the dramatic gesture (the Walk, Yegen itself); particularly, in later years, as talker. And Gerald learnt to write in his letters; in Carrington's case, from letters he received too. Not artless, quite, but artful at such high speed you don't notice, her pell-mell, Molly Bloom flow taught him humour, quick observation, gossip, how to condense, to allude. She had an extraordinary skill at what one might call the anthropomorphising of objects or events. In Vienna '. . . the food is horrible. Everything has an overcoat of batter, the meat often wears two waistcoats to conceal its identity. The very cakes wear masks. The butter is ashly pale and tasteless. I had a chicken last night that tasted of fried mongoose . . .'[81] Gerald made this a distinctive feature of his prose, as witness, for example, his virtuoso performance with the sea in *A Holiday by the Sea* or with Yegen's 'oceans of air' in *South From Granada*.

And through his letters he established himself, in the society he was about to enter, as a writer of promise. Even Lytton was impressed. 'I hope you will go on writing . . . to my mind there is a streak of inspiration in it [Gerald's writing], which is very rare and very precious indeed.'[82]

Gerald was to go through years and endless gyrations trying to acquire what he thought was required to write good English. And yet: 'Some rumours from the village,' he wrote to Ralph on 11 January 1924.

> Felipe found the keeper lying on the floor on top of his wife. In his own house, too, among his own vermin – think of that! The keeper had unslung his gun and laid it down beside him. Felipe, the lost innocent of idiots, snatches it up in a fine pretence of rage and fires at him. Misses. His ten infants rush out and overpower him. Victoriana gets up and wipes her

---

* To a biographer, letters, as opposed to journals, can have the drawback of discretion or of being tailored in various ways to their recipient. But discretion was rarely one of Gerald's faults; and, especially later on, the pressure of his feelings quite often made him seem to forget whom he was writing to or, indeed, that he was writing to anyone at all. Furthermore, letters have the great advantage that they cannot be read by wives; and they are far harder to destroy than journals. And as confessionals they are, for the writer, perhaps more efficacious. They leave the house. The events are no longer, as it were, on the premises.

thighs with her skirt. 'You bloody idiot,' she says, 'you fucking old egg, always interfering!' Felipe abandons his home. The wife of the keeper, young, beautiful and vigorous, comes in with the crowd. 'Aren't you ashamed of yourself, demeaning yourself with this syphilitic old bag?' And Victoriana is, it is quite true, the most hideous, dirty, stinking old reptile you could imagine – mother of ten starving brats. But she has, so the villagers say, this fatal body that makes her to men what valerian is to cats.

Note that 'wipes her thighs with her skirt'. By the end of his time at Yegen Gerald was, already, in possession of a prose which, if not yet capable of sustained poetry, was as full of life, as clear and direct, as observant and humorous, as when he returned there, in literary terms, thirty years later in *South From Granada*.

7

At the beginning of December Gerald returned to Yegen from Morocco after his three-month round trip.

It was only two years since the savage tribes of the Rif Valley had virtually destroyed a Spanish army at Annual. Only kept in check now by a policy of bribery, a bold traveller like Gerald who penetrated deep still risked death or castration. He went from Ceuta, Tetuan and Xauen to Zoco al-Arbaa. In Tetuan, after a lot of drink and kif he was nearly seduced by an elderly, wealthy Arab, al-Hadj. Gerald was revolted and appalled. He felt it would have been worse than murder, though the lascivious al-Hadj seems only to have managed to plant a few lecherous kisses on Gerald's fingers before, on being asked to take off his trousers, Gerald fled.[83]

He returned for something far more exciting, to him, than adventures in remote places. He'd learnt in September that Ralph and Carrington were to come for Christmas. One of the principal agents in this long schemed-for visit – Carrington had been working to reassure Lytton all August[84] – was Frances Marshall.

Aged twenty-three, dark, sparklingly pretty, high-spirited with a delightful laugh, Frances worked in the bookshop started by Francis

Birrell and Bunny Garnett, then in Taviton Street. Here she had caught the eye and soon the heart of the handsome traveller from the Hogarth Press. By the time Ralph and Carrington left for Yegen, Ralph and Frances had lunched and dined and danced together* and when they didn't meet he wrote her daily letters in 'a long, high-powered and concentrated courtship such as I'd never been subjected to before'.[85] He told her everything.

Ralph soon found deeper qualities: a convinced pacifist since the age of twelve, a love of nature and music, great sensitivity, maturity, an ability to soothe, combined with an excellent brain trained in the Moral Science course at Cambridge (philosophy, psychology and logic – she completed the two-year course in one year). Against her adroit calm Ralph's moods of furious argumentativeness would break and then be gradually dispersed. Although she was also being courted by Philip Nichols, it was Frances who suggested Ralph and Carrington should cement their reconciliation with Gerald by a visit. Both must have realised that if Gerald resumed with Carrington, Ralph could devote himself more easily to Frances.

The Christmas visit – three weeks – was often extremely fraught, due to the intensity of Gerald's feelings. He kept detailed, almost hourly notes.[86] They had, Carrington wrote to Lytton, 'hectic . . . fascinating conversations';[87] Gerald gave a dance; just before they left, in Granada, Ralph came and without thinking, sat between Gerald and Carrington. Gerald was so upset he went to bed. It was Ralph who came and comforted him. He also, with great cordiality, said Carrington and Gerald could have the same 'rights' as he and Frances – to go around together and kiss.

There were hiccups. Almost at once, in Paris, Ralph, who never ceased to love Carrington despite eventually much stronger feelings for Frances, became jealous again.[88] (A bulging envelope arrived from Gerald for Carrington. One page was the letter, for Ralph's eyes too; the rest a passionate eight-page p.s.). Carrington herself (unknown to Gerald) was again terrified she'd lose Lytton – Ralph would go off with Frances, whom they met in Paris, and the *ménage* would collapse. But, though ostensibly returning to be near Tiz (who paid his fare),

* Both of them danced very well indeed and once won a tango prize together. Frances herself came second in the Ballroom Dancing Championship of England in 1920/21, where the competitors had to dance on the huge stage of the Queen's Hall in Regent Street.

in fact the real object of Gerald's return, for both him and Carrington, was to renew their friendship, which Carrington allowed would include secret lovemaking.

Before that, Bunny Garnett came to stay briefly on his honeymoon with Ray Marshall, Frances's sister. Just over thirty, well-built, fair, Garnett's blue eyes had an extraordinary hypnotic power over women; subjected to their searching, swivelling gaze, few could resist him. Amiable, astute, with a slow, gentle voice, he later became a close and loyal friend, but the visit might have been difficult since Bunny had recently made his name with *Lady Into Fox*, which had won the Hawthornden Prize and James Tait Black Memorial Prize in 1923. Gerald, like most writers, felt threatened by the success of contemporaries and had spent the past year furiously and extravagantly attacking the book; however he managed to get round this by praising its Defoe-like aspects and its fine punctuation[89] – compliments which must have required some dexterity in the paying since neither quality is remotely detectable in the book itself.

And so his long first sojourn in Spain drew to an end. Long at the time – as the years passed it grew longer and longer. In *South From Granada* Gerald speaks of 'years' in such a way that all reviewers thought there were a great many of them; Cyril Connolly said ten years. By 1948, Arthur Lehning, who helped him with *The Spanish Labyrinth*, thought it was sixteen years.[90] This elongation was of service to Gerald when he came to write about Spain since there is a tradition that the *pueblo* is the repository of national wisdom. And it continued until, quite recently, discussing him as an historian, Paul Preston, Professor of Spanish at London University, revealed he thought Gerald had been at Yegen well over twenty years.

In fact it was three and a quarter years. What effects did it have? Gerald himself said it made him an egotist. An egotist? Certainly there were numerous times when he talked obsessively about himself. Yet he was not remotely a selfish man. He was also fascinated by other people and their lives, to the extent, often, of living vicariously. An egotist without an ego, as he once described himself to Ralph.

But, apart from aspects already touched on, the most important effect of Yegen was the most obvious – it embedded Spain in him. We will try and see later why this in many ways quintessentially upper middle-class Englishman, who never had any close Spanish friends, who quite often said he preferred France (whose language he spoke far better; his Spanish, if fluent, remained Andalusian kitchen Spanish), and who, quite rightly, never regarded himself narrowly as a Hispanist but always as a writer, why he should none the less have been, among much else, the greatest writer on Spain, England, or arguably any other country, has produced. But the clues – perhaps more curious than Gerald realised – lie in these last three and a quarter years.

On 20 March 1924, three weeks before his thirtieth birthday, Gerald left for England. He somehow carried four chairs, a brocade bodice, chintzes and a mass of plates – presents for Carrington.[91] Also his notebooks. In one of these was a *copla* the mule boy had been singing when Bunny and Ray had left and which Gerald had quickly copied down. It became a favourite and was included in *Thoughts in a Dry Season*, but could also serve as a prophetic epigraph for the next six years of his life:

> En la orillita del mar
> Suspiraba una ballena
> Y en sus súpiros decía,
> 'En amor hay siempre pena'.

('On the edge of the sea a whale lay sighing. And among its sighs, it said – "In love there is always pain."')

ELEVEN

Leaving Carrington

1

Gerald was met at Victoria Station by Carrington on the evening of 2 April 1924. They went, talking excitedly, at once to the Belgrave Hotel and spent the night together. It was a success. 'I simply can't tell you how happy you made me,' she wrote the next day.[1] It would take care, cunning, but bliss seemed to stretch ahead.

First there were more urgent matters: where to live, in that London of trams and street criers and prostitutes and coal smoke; above all, what to live on. Awaiting his arrival was a terse, rude, autocratic letter from his father – more or less saying, do something I approve of, or I stop paying. One can have every sympathy over Gerald's irritation with his father (he quotes the maddening letter in full) but he leaves things out. His father was deeply neurotic about money. In July 1925 Gerald found this wealthy man in such a panic that he was ruined that he was 'very moved' and offered to give up his allowance.[2] More germane was that once (quite easily) mollified, Hugh not only paid, by July he had doubled the allowance to £100 p.a.[3] He paid bills: the oculist, plus spectacles in May;[4] by January 1925 he was paying Gerald's rent.[5] No doubt there were others.

Yet the anxiety and humiliation were acute. Long after Radley, the War, even Carrington had evaporated from his subconscious, he was still, at seventy-five, dreaming of this period – how to justify himself, how to placate his father. He solved both problems now more or less simultaneously. He said he would write a life of St Teresa. He had just finished reading a life of her and been fascinated (and fascinated almost as much by St John of the Cross). There was a mass of published material. A religious subject would please his mother. Besides, quite profound elements in his character responded to those early church histories and lives of the saints (of which he'd read many). His feeling for religion, his interest (via Mr Earee and Hope) in peculiar facts and people; perhaps even the severities they practised found an echo. But the real reason seems, at first, rather odd. This austere sixteenth-century Spanish saint reminded him of Carrington:[6] her 'impassioned tortured life', her complexity, her self-doubt, her charm and her skill at using it, the way she loved, then didn't love. The more he read – and he worked on St Teresa for over thirty years – the more resemblances he found. In the Thirties, for instance, he told VSP* to read her letters in *Spanish* 'to get an idea of her running, garrulous but vivid and natural style. The latest discovery about her is that she had lesbian inclinations when at her convent.'[7]

The other source of money was Tiz, to whom he went, immediately after the Belgrave Hotel, in 28 Ashley Place, the same cluttered gas-lit flat near Victoria where she'd once nearly killed him. This tiny (4′ 4″), fidgety, restless, curiously dressed, increasingly eccentric figure, communicating deafly and impatiently via pads of paper and now eighty-six, was, as well as maddening Gerald, to be one of the main comic weapons in his social armoury. Frances Partridge remembers him giggling and describing how, because she couldn't be bothered to dye her white hair, she shoved her hairbrush up the chimney and brushed soot into it – one of many stories he used to make the delightful portrait in *Personal Record*. Tiz gave him £50 p.a., but frequently added little cheques and disgusting meals, and met his bills. Once she gave him £100 – 'to keep not spend'.[8] It went in two months.

Gerald himself, given that he was determined to write and study and not get a job, did what he could. He often cooked rudimentary meals for himself. He nearly translated Calderón for the Cambridge Dramatic Society, but in the end they gave it to J. B. Trend; unknown to him then, later a staunch ally. He did a few pieces for Leonard Woolf – about five during five years. He tried to give Spanish lessons, at six shillings an hour. Over a year he got Bunny

---

* Sir Victor Pritchett. Always known as VSP.

and Ray, Logan Pearsall-Smith and Lady Colefax's son Michael* (both through Hope), finally Sebastian Sprott.[9] None was a stayer. As usual, Ralph saved him in emergencies. Until Tiz died, Gerald had under £200 p.a., was always anxious about money, could often not repay hospitality, sometimes not afford food or rent (yet, an indication of how low wages were, he always had someone who 'did' for him, if only for an hour a day).

First he rented a room in Taviton Street, then a month at another in 10 Millman Street. In June he took Roger Fry's studio at 18 Fitzroy Street, which he had till 1927. One big room, small bedroom, gas ring, shared lavatory on the landing below; Nina Hamnett's previous residence was betrayed in grease stains and many wine rings. Laid across the rafters, Fry's paintings of ugly women, in his usual depressing colours, stared gloomily down at him. London in the early Twenties had changed little from Victorian times. From his window he could see tailoring sweat-shops; street cries floated up – the muffin man, a small group of ex-soldiers playing. This was not all he saw. The one huge advantage of Fitzroy Street, according to Gerald, was that opposite was a girl's bedroom. With any luck he'd see her undressing.[10] Three guineas a week. It has now vanished into 18–24 Fitzroy Street, a vast concrete-brick-and-glass fronted hall of residence for the LSE. As one goes in – the click of snooker balls.

* A minute biographer's point. Nigel Nicolson, in a footnote to the edition of Virginia Woolf's letters, says that gossip Gerald was teaching Michael Colefax was false. Presumably he'd asked Gerald. But Gerald's memory was at fault. His July 4 1924 letter to Carrington makes clear he did.

2

'Some people take a pride in being unhappily in love because they consider that the strength of their feelings ennobles them and raises them above the common herd. Thus Hazlitt in his book Liber Amoris *wrote an account of his violent but unrequited passion for his landlord's commonplace daughter. Its key phrase is: "I am in some sense proud that I can feel this dreadful passion – it gives me a kind of rank in the kingdom of love." He showed his pride by publishing his book during his lifetime.'*

Thoughts in a Dry Season

Things began to go wrong with Carrington almost at once. Within ten days he complained that their relations were 'dim', she really only wanted him in Spain. Escalation was rapid. She wrote in July that she was coming to London with Ralph but couldn't see Gerald. This man who 'did not understand the possessive instinct' exploded: 'You have hardly any of the feelings or sensibilities of human beings . . . If I could make you unhappy I would.'[11]

It would be possible, from their letters, to chart in minute detail practically every moment of the affair. It would not be boring; but it would be very long (by 1928 he'd sent her a further 256 letters, about 286,000 words. She sent 248 letters). The outline is simple: Carrington could only love where she did not possess and was not pursued or pressed, as was the case with Lytton; at the same time she couldn't resist wanting discreetly to resume her 'intense friendship' with Gerald. With many letters, a few meetings, and allowing occasional lovemaking, Gerald pretended he wanted this too. In fact he wanted far more. As he pressed to get it, Carrington, feeling trapped – as her mother, Gertler, Ralph had all tried to trap her – retreated. Gerald became furious, desperate, then contrite. But this clear picture was distorted, made tortured, complicated, endlessly drawn out, in both trivial and fundamental ways, by their different situations and complex characters.

For one thing, Carrington was very busy. On 1 July the Tidmarsh *ménage* moved to Ham Spray, the pleasant, secluded George III/Victorian house she had found for them in Wiltshire, just under the enormous green wave of the Berkshire Downs. Here their busy social life at once resumed. Once apart from Gerald, she often forgot him almost entirely. Gerald had nothing. All day he struggled alone with St Teresa. He tramped out to distant swimming pools, envying the couples. At night, he lay listening to the dogs bark, children's voices, a barrel organ, 'and the unhappiness of life seems to mount up like water in a glass until it overflows'. How could he write when so poor? Tiz must die. No one wanted Spanish lessons. When would she come?[12] This element faded as Gerald built a social life, but there was another. Loving in her letters, Carrington was often distant in public, or even ignored him in the most humiliating way. Then there was Ralph. Terrified he would go off with Frances, Carrington would make up to him, driving Gerald frantic with jealousy. At the end of 1925, Ralph ceased to sleep with her and he and Frances became lovers. The *ménage*, despite strains, survived (largely owing to the generosity and good sense of Frances). Slowly, Carrington relaxed.

Feeling trapped, anxious to keep Ralph, she would cancel appointments at the last moment, not send the letters for which Gerald rushed to every post, turn up late and then – at one of their frequent breaks – suddenly become anxious about losing him. She dreaded being disliked and her guilt came into play, that 'envelope of guilt which . . . surrounded her like a cloud of mosquitoes wherever she went . . .',[13] as Julia noted. Guilt made her behave as she did, both in order to have a reason for the feeling and to obtain the release of punishment. 'When you are severe I always feel very gay,' she told Gerald.[14] But then she felt guilty over what she was compelled to do, at hurting him. All these forces made her go into reverse and – excited now by her witch-sense of power – try and seduce him again.

And how seductive she could be, how intense his pleasure when, for a week, a month, it went well! And, once again, how enchanting her letters. 'I feel I may paint all the better for this interval. A ghostly cat wails in the garden. Please eat enough. I wish I could send you fried carrots in my letter.'[15] They would eat together in front of his fire, she cooking and ordering ingredients in advance: 'A Dover sole, 1 lemon, a grapefruit, and 4 ounzes of Mr Crusoe.'[16] For a few hours he could imagine they were married.

There was a further complication. In the summer of 1924, often ironically borrowing Gerald's room (generosity he came bitterly to regret), Carrington was seduced by Henrietta Bingham, with her oval face, straight dark hair parted in the middle, long eyelashes and caressing Southern voice. Carrington was astonished to find she could experience intense physical pleasure without guilt or disgust. She felt she'd been 'a blasted fool in the past to stifle so many lusts I had in my youth, for various females'.[17] It only lasted a few months, but Henrietta, who carried the yo-yo system of attraction to lengths unthought of even by Carrington, was still obsessing her, 'tormenting my dreams', in 1927. Yet the experience also frightened her[18] and the lusts remained stifled in her head, where perhaps she preferred them. She never seems to have slept with any other 'females', though they constantly attracted her.

Gerald had several clairvoyant dreams at this time warning him of the threat to *his* Carrington. In one, someone he loves is dead, in another he saw Carrington's blood-stained head in a tree.[19] He was right. *Personal Record* describes how as time passed he insisted they make love when they met, to prove to him she wanted him. As usual with Gerald, there is some doubt as to what they did in bed. Elsewhere he says their lovemaking in London was 'kept, by her wish, to an elementary and imperfect form'.[20] But whatever they did, it frequently went wrong and the reason was, as she haltingly explained in an agonisingly honest and (given her intense secrecy) courageous letter, due to the fact that she was half 'saphic'. Yet here again she would suddenly reverse; a number of times – once when he was ill, or when he himself was reluctant, she would leap into bed and seduce him.

Cruelty alternating with kindness – classic brainwashing technique. By the end of 1924 and intermittently through 1925 Gerald's behaviour became highly neurotic.

He would spend all day in bed, often weeping, in an agony of misery and despair, or nervously, rapidly pace the room under acute tension, waiting, expecting, listening – but for what? He used to put his head in a cushion and shriek. Once again he was terrified of being alone at night, and awaited its approach in mounting panic. He would lie awake with beating heart unable to sleep till dawn. He'd ring up at odd hours, raging, suspicious, crying, furious, pleading – till Carrington dreaded his calls. His letters became epistolary tantrums – berating, breaking off and begging forgiveness all in ten pages. He'd write angrily refusing to come to Ham Spray before he'd been asked. Frances remembers him there, an agitated figure, often on the verge of tears. He had day-long headaches, indigestion, diarrhoea, bad eyes, bad teeth. He worried incessantly about his health, and worried his friends. Sometimes he felt he was going mad.

Carrington sent him to Dr Ellie Rendel, the daughter of Lytton's elder sister, to whom they 'all' went. A lesbian with a deep voice, she was a profound pessimist, rather gloomy as a comforter. She first prescribed veronal; later, as symptoms intensified, submitted him to a minute examination. 'I am to eat mercury every three days and after meals strychnine and hydrochloric acid. The mere prospect of eating her violent foods does something to cure me.'[21]

But Gerald himself considerably complicated and exacerbated their difficult affair. Carrington's intense secrecy was only matched by his indiscretion. Partly a reaction against the timid and conventional discretion of his family, where much was unmentionable, it was also the necessary indiscretion the lover of gossip needs if he is to attract and repay confidences (Ralph, scarcely more discreet than Gerald, for similar reasons called secrets 'a theft on the community'). Carrington's letters are full of furious protests.

Then his relations with Ralph were complex. Still swept, increasingly without cause as Ralph ceased to sleep with her,* by raging suspicions, at the same time he needed Ralph. Ralph was one of his chief *confidants*. They discussed Carrington and Gerald for hours – again to her intense irritation. She felt trapped with inveterate 'discussers of relations'.[22] But Ralph was astute, comforting, very sympathetic, and knew it all. The sharing of Carrington cemented their friendship; but it also reinforced that deep element of jealousy.

It will also be clear by now that Gerald had considerable will-power. So far he'd done everything he wanted: the Walk, a house in Spain, no job, an allowance. But he couldn't get Carrington. That he was half-aware of this aspect is revealed, during a letter to Helen Anrep, in a sudden outburst: 'Inside me I feel this something alive and violent and untouchable that shrieks and cries and *will* have its way and *must* have its way . . .'[24] Baulked, determined not to give up, another side emerged. 'My terms are – your visits to London must belong to your life with me – not a continuation of your life with Ralph . . . You must make a special effort when I tell you I am unhappy.'[25] 'You little realise,' Carrington would reply to these commands, 'how much you resemble your father when you write as you do . . .'[26]

At the same time, Gerald often saw the hopelessness of their relation absolutely clearly. He could not bear it. He had fantasies of fleeing to distant places – the hare dream again – and becoming a dustman.[27] He fought and struggled to break free, but he was like a bull with a *banderilla*; however violently he tried, the dart had gone too deep.

Yet – to what extent did he really want to escape? There was, at this time, a fascinating, and perhaps significant, return to a seminal incident in his childhood. He went to the dentist in Hampstead. It

---

* In later years Gerald justified sleeping with his best friend's wife on the grounds that Ralph was sleeping with other women. Ralph's view, set out with his usual clarity, in a letter of 21 January 1924, was that Carrington had a minute sexual appetite, he had a strong one. He had to find satisfaction elsewhere. Why should he share Carrington's minute appetite, still loving her, with Gerald?

was very painful. 'As he drilled I looked out of the window and saw in the blue sky a white cloud floating past. And out there, where the cloud was, it appeared to me there lay happiness.'[28] Her power to hurt fascinated him; the pain itself, he confided to his journal, made him 'feel a superiority that is different from vanity to all who have not got it'.[29] Indeed, he revealed his pride by showing his journal, from which these descriptions of his sufferings are a distilled drop, to everybody (Frances cried when she read it) and, like Hazlitt with *Liber Amoris*, by trying to get it published in his lifetime.

3

> '*Do you have the feeling I have about the sea, that it is a god, a great god Pan who is not only outside you but inside you – as your unconscious, your id, the book of feelings out of which one's thoughts arise?*'
>
> Letter to VSP, September 1943

Gerald's second close *confidante* over the years of Carrington was Helen Anrep, whose husband, Boris, was then Europe's leading mosaicist. By birth Californian, she was French and English by upbringing. Small, light-haired, with rapidly blinking blue eyes, she was sexy, attractive (she'd had numerous affairs, including one with Henry Lamb) and a good cook; she was also immensely sympathetic, one of those people who like to be of importance in others' lives, to advise, to help, to manage – especially, in Helen's case, young men's lives.

She had two young children who needed teaching and in August 1924 she asked Gerald to stay at Warren End, a cottage on the Romney Marsh in Kent. It was right against the sea – 'The sea . . . oily and unctuous like a drop hanging from a cabman's nose',[30] practised Gerald, writing to Carrington. In the next letter 'the sea has crept up once again to the door like a lame crocodile, has raised its flat expressionless eye to the level of my bedroom window'.[31] Prophetic arabesques.

He seems to have talked about Carrington, in the intervals of teaching, nonstop for the six weeks. Helen, as well as sympathy and wisdom, had an ironic, humorous way of discussing love's difficulties, which distanced them. So easily prone to over-excitement, finding himself swamped by emotion, irony was a note he was always to respond to. Nor were their talks one-sided. Helen was falling in love with Roger Fry (it was she who'd got Gerald the studio), a love considerably encouraged by Boris's insistence, as befitted a Russian aristocrat, on installing an eighteen-year-old distant relative Maroussa in their house as his mistress. Fry, thirty years older than Gerald, had eccentric elements – extreme gullibility, a belief that Shakespeare's sonnets were better in French, and an inclination to parsimony (too mean to buy a new one, his chess set had lumps of coal for knights and draught pieces for castles) – but he was an intellectual of restless mental activity, ready at any moment for a frivolous or serious discussion. In these respects exactly like Gerald, who became very fond of him. Helen struggled with the problems of her breaking marriage throughout 1924/25, Gerald, to his delight, becoming deeply involved.

We can get a picture of Gerald at this time. Little Igor was eleven and had word difficulties. (Frances remembers him spelling sausage 'soig' in a game at Ham Spray.) At the end Gerald felt he had made 'great strides'; Igor thinks not. Gerald's system was simply to give him dictation from Bertrand Russell's *ABC of Atoms*. But Igor remembers someone very thin in a pair of skimpy, skinny, tight blue cotton trousers, a shirt, and seeming very, very young. He'd had wonderful adventures, like rolling a huge cheese right across Spain. His fine hair was already thinning and his long upper lip (a marked feature) was still moustached. Helen could recall the romantic young figure twenty-five-years later, his pockets full of books, quoting Dryden and other 'obscure' poets from memory. She confessed she'd fallen slightly in love with him.[32] (Gerald didn't notice but Boris did and thought they were having an affair. He refused to see Gerald again when he later sided with Roger Fry.)

The moment he went away, Carrington, though they'd decided not to meet for a while because of rows, naturally felt she had to see him – 'Please . . . please . . . please'[33] – and naturally, succumbing at once to his fever, Gerald invited her down to Warren End. She came for five days. According to Gerald they made love 'again and again'. Igor, lying down, could just see the tiny bed in their tiny bedroom through the crack under the door. He remembers them locked in each other's arms on the bed for hours on end. He also remembers

Carrington being very nasty to Gerald. This, judging by ecstatic letters after she left, he surmounted; but then he saw her thank-you letter to Helen on the kitchen table, tore it open and read her comment: 'that ridiculous Brenan'. Once again – pain, rage, despair.

She was like a fever, a disease; yet it was a disease with remissions. A Brenan expert, if such there be, would have been alerted to one of the things that filled these remissions by the sea similes – for it was at Warren End Gerald first thought of *Mr Fisher*.

4

In *Personal Record* Gerald describes how at some time during 1924/25 he gave Arthur Waley his poetry to read. It was no good, he knew, but did it show promise? The reply, made abrupt through embarrassment, must have been fairly shattering: 'No, none that I can see.'

Gerald says he never read poetry again, and gave up writing it entirely except for a brief, intoxicating fountaining in the mid-Fifties. This Rimbaud-like renunciation is so far from the literal truth that it was actually to Waley he was sending his poetry in 1939 and the early Forties.[34] He wrote poetry throughout the Twenties and was still calling himself 'a poet' in 1928.[35] In fact, he continued to write poetry at various times all his life (it is an infallible sign he is in love) and the second last book he published was a selection from his poems.

Nevertheless, there is metaphorical truth in the statement. He abandoned his long and passionately held ambition to be a poet. His 'poetry', his intense response to nature, would from now on have to find expression in novels.

Up till July 1927, when he showed the manuscript to Bunny Garnett, Gerald did about seventeen months hard, if intermittent, work on St Teresa. Unless distracted by Carrington crises, he read eight hours a day with his usual energy in the British Museum or London Library – he estimated something approaching 500 volumes. In the evenings he sorted notes in front of the fire. There were many incidental felicities on the way, like St Francis Borgia, hugely fat with a nine-foot circumference, who suddenly became ascetic, his skin falling in folds so he could roll himself up in it three times like a carpet.[36] Struggling to form an appropriate style – he wanted something both pleasing and spontaneous, but capable of brevity and tautness (all qualities abundant in his letters) – he read Tacitus and St Simon. This combination of Latin and French produced something which – reading the 150 big blue sheets of foolscap covered in Gerald's condensed house-maid's hand – Bunny not surprising described as 'not English'. (Another style, or series of styles, he toyed with for St Teresa, at least in a letter to Carrington, was Joyce's in *Ulysses*.[37] An arresting idea.)

The Yegen pattern of reading and writing several things concurrently was now set. He started a second story about a commercial traveller – only one this time, because presumably his story with forty-nine of them had proved difficult to manage. Then, in March 1925 he abruptly abandoned St Teresa for two months and started *Mr Fisher*.

Gerald's account of this is dramatic. Riding on top of a bus to Tiz in September 1925, he suddenly found he was thinking the thoughts of someone else. He leapt off, bought a notebook, and at dictation speed began to write a novel – continuing for several hours.

No doubt one of these fits of inspiration did take place at some point, but not without a good deal of groundwork. In a note at Texas to the original manuscript he says he had the idea at Warren End in 1924. A little later, he wrote in his diary: 'I shall create for myself another self, the opposite of my true self, in which I can live and act and jeer and laugh and so escape from the insoluble conflicts and unimagineable, unintelligible torments.' It was, that is, in providing distance and irony, a sort of literary equivalent to Helen Anrep. An antidote – but also a lure. The heroine, Tom Fisher's sister, was Carrington (even called Dora). Gerald sent sketches and descriptions, which she corrected.[38] Tom Fisher embodied what Gerald felt Carrington was doing to him – withering him into cynicism and egotism (for this reason Tom Fisher spoke like Hope). The early draft is autobiographically revealing in other ways. The incest theme has Tom able to have an affair with Dora because she does not frighten him. Dora: 'Childhood – told lies in preference to truth . . . anxiety to please and obsequiousness in private, but critical and ironical of Tom in public. Always took sides against him.'[39] She leaves him for Hubert (Ralph), whom Tom dreams of murdering. The sea similes and metaphors were another early feature – the book may even have started from them. And their form, which he developed from Carrington's letters, served to echo or counterpoint the interior action.

It was these that impressed Arthur Waley, to whom Gerald read *Mr Fisher*. Waley, whose opinion was of value, expressed it at the Cranium Club.*[40] Ralph and Frances were also impressed. Eddy Sackville-West had heard that both it and its author were '*very remarkable*'.[41] Virginia begged to be allowed to see it. 'Ralph said he had read enough of your novel to perceive a masterpiece.'[42] *Mr Fisher* boosted Gerald's confidence and seemed to provide solid proof of literary promise. By 1927 he'd written nine chapters and thereafter, though it languished, for thirty years kept notebooks of Tom Fisher sayings.

His reading, on top of St Teresa, continued its Yegen patterns. He was now taking Proust in ever larger doses – reading him twice, possibly three times in this period, even though the final volume did not come out till November 1927 (the first draft of *Mr Fisher* has the most enormous and elaborate sentences). His habit of rereading meant his literary judgements altered throughout his life, and what made Gerald so stimulating to talk literature with was the awareness that he was working out his ideas afresh each time. But there was a bias. The effect of his childhood and youth – his father, Radley – continued to work like a yeast and one result was a marked, and suddenly surfacing prejudice against English writers. Reading Racine now, he notes how far better he is than Pope or Dryden. As for English prose, 'I doubt if there is any perfectly adequate and sustained writer but Hume.'[43] Jane Austen really only had the viewpoint of a governess. The English novel was 'Obsessed by social conduct and lacks understanding in depth – *Wuthering Heights* and parts of D. H. Lawrence being the only exceptions . . . Our moral preoccupation with conduct has killed most of the rest.'[44] Jane Austen, George Eliot (attacked by implication) and others were usually rehabilitated – but with a wrench. This bias increased his thrust into foreign literatures.

His reviews in the *Nation* are totally different from his other writing at this time – concise, authoritative, clearly distilled from much reading, in a clear strong prose; no doubt this was the reason

* Started in October 1924 by Tommy Tomlin and Bunny Garnett in order to see their London friends once a month at dinner. Gerald became a member, as did Lytton, Bertrand Russell, the writer Goldsworthy Lowes Dickinson and others. Named after Mr Cranium in Peacock's *Headlong Hall*.

Lytton admired them (praise invariably passed on by Carrington)⁴⁵. He was already fascinated by St John of the Cross. 'He was very small – her "half-friar" she [St Teresa] calls him . . . at night the monks shuddered to the sound of his lashings.'* It is interesting, in view of what came later, that Gerald already dislikes verse translations and prefers the Spanish with an exact prose rendering.⁴⁶

And these reviews show another characteristic. He is reviewing the first volume of Allison Peers' *Studies of the Spanish Mystics* and writing in general of the sudden growth of mysticism in the sixteenth century, when Spain 'which for eleven centuries had occupied itself with the external world, opened its eyes at last upon the changing weather of the soul'. And then, in the course of this restrained and scholarly review, having set the scene in that remote age, he suddenly takes off, as he was often to do later, into one of those imaginative flights, so illuminating, so invigorating and so evocative. Putting aside the excesses and looking 'into the minds of educated men, we shall see a strange shifting and exacerbation of the field of consciousness. The chatter of society has died away, and we are transported to a region where solitude is unbroken, where tears and self-torments are the only solace, and where the soul, its senses refined by stillness, shivers to every breeze that blows upon it. The instincts, pressing out like naked roots towards the soil and not finding it, take new directions. This is the region of "mystical experience".'⁴⁷

It is not, evidently, a region to which Mr Peers is capable of carrying us. Gerald deals with him swiftly. A few words of faint praise – 'Interesting material arranged into order' – then, 'vitiated by bias, suppression, and misconception'. He hasn't read vital texts; all very long it is true, like Baruzi's 790 pages or Mrs Cunninghame Graham's 'long volumes'. In fact, the book is really little better than hagiography.⁴⁷ Allison Peers was not to forget.

---

* Review in the *Nation* 31 January 1925 of Jean Baruzi's *St Jean de la Croix et le Problème de l'Expérience Mystique*, and his *Aphorismes de St Jean de La Croix*. Unsigned, but certainly Gerald's, both stylistically and because he refers to the subject later.

5

'A dream about Bloomsbury. It was like a sky packed with ice-blue clouds. There was something cold and glittering about it. A lot of frozen conversation drifted down.'

Thoughts in a Dry Season

In October 1925 Gerald sent Carrington a bulletin: Tchekov with Miss Baker, lunch with Tiz and 'Col Prickit (yes)', a Mrs Kapp, an American millionairess whose clergyman husband had just run off with their housemaid, Hope, Arthur Waley arriving with a chicken and a mass of gossip. 'I have climbed on so many buses, seen so many people, talked so incessantly that I now feel as though I'm going to have pneumonia.'[48] He hastened to add he was not happy, but of course unhappiness is a potent goad to the social life.

Needing solitude and naturally gregarious in about equal measure, Gerald rapidly built up an active, even frenetic social life. People dropped in a lot, Frances Partridge remembered. The Birrell and Garnett bookshop where she worked, and which had moved to Gerrard Street, was a centre – always full of gossip and laughter. Here came familiar figures: 'Woolves, Bells, Garnetts, Duncan Grant, Keynes, MacCarthys, Saxon [Sydney Turner], Anreps.'[49] There was the Cranium Club – an evening in 1926 sitting between Bunny and Leo Myers 'who opened out like a rose and told me what trouble he had with his digestion';[50] another when they all came back to Gerald's rooms. Tea was an important meal at this period, which suited Gerald whom too much drink made mad and sick, and who didn't in any case need it; perhaps people drank less than today.

Except at parties. There were a lot. Bottle parties, where there was no particular host or hostess, just someone's rooms. Parties in Duncan's vast, mysterious and shadowy studio in Charlotte Street; at Francis and Vera Meynell's. People got drunk, and some got very drunk indeed. Bunny describes a party where they drank absolute alcohol.[51] As well as youth, sex, drink, high spirits, there were parties with a point – a play by Virginia, someone buying a whole sturgeon.[49] And Gerald gave parties – not many, always bottle parties. He was a good host and, because people liked him, everyone always came. He gave one on 5 December 1925, which cost him £5 (and to which he asked Valentine and Bonamy Dobrée).[52]

To cope with all this, Gerald learnt to smoke Russian cigarettes.[53] He never inhaled. This fact, and the lateness of the habit, gave an amateurish puffing quality to his smoking, with the two cigarette fingers held rigidly straight and his arm moving abruptly in and out in an odd mechanical gesture like a toy.

But at these parties 'above all there was continuous passionate dancing' – dancing for pleasure, to seduce and be seduced: tango, blues, Charleston, Black Bottom. Before this point, Gerald often slunk away unable to bear it, as he did from a Colefax party in March 1925 – to a pub with Boris Anrep, though in fact by then Boris was already, quite rightly, suspicious that Gerald was an ally of Roger Fry's. Roger's plan was to get Boris shut up as insane – according to Gerald. And Gerald – both ferrying and writing letters, giving advice and generally in bliss, reported every move to Carrington: Boris guarding the telephone; Boris calling Helen Mrs Anrep; Boris, finally, warning her that Roger was raving mad.[54] The Anreps separated in June.

Hope turned up irregularly, usually needing support. Gerald woke each morning to the sound of kissing – the noise Hope's patent new rubber shaving brush made when used.

And every two months or so the dutiful son went to Edgeworth, usually for the weekend, sometimes for a week or two. His mother, 'Tremulous with happiness', was always delighted. They went to church. 'Gerald is a great friend of Mr Lytton Strachey.' His father was more tricky. Gerald reined himself in; his father jogged, swung Indian clubs, did carpentry, letters, bills, sniped at his mother. The meals were huge (once a cow's tooth was found in a cake). Gerald 'had a limp feeling in the knee joints as though one's veins contained not blood but bath water and a sensation in one's head as though one were digesting one's lunch with it.' Yet he loved it too – the peace after London, the greenery; in winter snow, icicles; in May he'd sleep on the lawn. At Christmas and other times he and his father went riding. They visited neighbours. Gerald was attracted to Susie Simon, the sexy-looking, kitten-faced twenty-four-year-old daughter of the nearby Drummonds, whose husband had run off with her jewellery.[55]

He saw a lot of Bunny and his friends, Tommy and Garrow

1 Helen Brenan, Gerald's mother, taken in the 1930s.

2 Hugh Brenan, Gerald's father. 'When I look in the mirror I see my father.'

3 It was a childhood with the full panoply of Edwardian servants – here in 1900 with Gerald aged six at Fort William, Calcutta.

4 Gerald with his ayah, Hatton, who
nursed him through typhoid. March
1899, Ceylon.

5 Gerald at Winton House aged about ten

6 Gerald in 1913 just after the Walk with
Hope-Johnstone.

7 Hope at Yegen in 1923.

8 Gerald in November 1915 with the moustache he kept until 1929.

9 Ralph Partridge in about 1918, taken in Rome.

10 Carrington (L) with Phyllis de Janzé, (R) an ex-Slade friend, and one of many women to whom she was attracted.

11 The view from Gerald's
window in Yegen, taken in
1933.

12 Photograph by Hope of
Gerald reading in Yegen in
1922.

13 Gerald and Ralph at Watendlath
in August 1921, taken by
Carrington. Gerald's expression
repays examination.

14 Frances Partridge in August 1930
after swimming at the Ham Spray
bathing place, a backwater of the
River Kennet.

15 Winny Stafford, probably taken by
Gerald when he took her to
Bognor Regis in June 1928.

16 Valentine Dobrée, Hope and Bonamy Dobrée at Yegen in 1922.

17 Ralph and Lytton Strachey walking in France early in their friendship.

18 Baroness Von Roeder in 1928, Gerald's great Aunt Addie – 'Tiz'.

20 Arthur Waley in about 1929.

19 Bunny Garnett talking to Ralph at Hilton, the Garnett house near Cambridge. 1930s.

21 Roger Fry and Helen Anrep in the garden of her Suffolk house. Early 1930s.

22 (*From L to R*). Unknown Cuban, Gerald, Ralph, Juliana in a *merendero* on the beach at Adra. Summer 1929.

23 Gerald, with his athlete's legs, at East Lulworth in 1931.

24 Ralph and Frances on a visit to Suffolk in the 1930s.

Tomlin, the Penrose brothers, Frankie Birrell. Yet the feeling with these – with any group – is of Gerald outside: liked, welcome because of his animation, his humour, his originality, but holding back. This is still more true of Bloomsbury.

Gerald made inroads into Bloomsbury. He was known, considered an interesting and original figure, a promising writer, went to some parties (but not, for instance, to the 'hub' parties given by Maynard and Lydia Keynes). This was about the extent of it. Yet there is no doubt he could have penetrated much further had he wanted to. The tight Cambridge/Apostles group – Keynes, the Woolfs and Bells, Lytton, Duncan Grant, Roger Fry, Forster, etc. – now allowed, as it were, associates from literary London. Forster regarded Gerald sufficiently to ask his opinion of *A Passage to India*. Not only had the Woolfs made the fearsome journey to Yegen, Leonard now asked Gerald to go to Spain with him.

And Gerald and Bloomsbury were suited in many ways. It suited him as it were physically.* Ham Spray was so devastatingly cold that Lytton and Carrington often had to go to bed to get warm. They would hardly have survived without chamber pots. Rodwell, Helen's house in Suffolk, was freezing, filthy – and beautiful. Gerald agreed with Bloomsbury's belief that common sense, reason and honesty should govern behaviour and human relations, and agreed most where he was least able to practise – in 'no rights to jealousy'. He agreed that the young should freely address and criticise the old (and when he was old himself allowed it), with the importance they attached to women, and the overwhelming importance of talk. The freshness of their curiosity, the total, if sometimes self-conscious frankness enjoined, the great range of conversation from flippant to profound and sometimes flippant about the profound, the fact that literature was central: all this was ideal for Gerald. He once described Lytton lying back in a green armchair, very long and black, looking 'like a bird just landed from some foreign country where culture has reached heights not approached in England'. In a celebrated passage years later he compared the set pieces, after dinner at Virginia and Vanessa's, to the performance of an orchestra, where continual practice among close friends on the same themes – the differences

---

* Bloomsbury too, like Gerald, had a tendency towards sex-in-the-head. Lytton once said that if one saw an attractive boy in a train and then tossed off you could claim 'in some senses to have been to bed with him' (Frances Partridge to author).

between the generations, for instance, or between writers and painters – and the ability to stimulate each other and to allow solos, Virginia with 'a cascade of words like a great pianist improvising',[56] all produced talk of a brilliance never heard in England before.

Yet much later VSP was to say he considered Gerald to be one of the best talkers in England.[57] He was, even then, quite capable of producing cascades himself. And Gerald's description of Blomsbury, perceptive and flattering though it is, artfully conceals a criticism. It suggests something 'frozen', something static and sterile.

When Forster brought him *A Passage to India*, Gerald did not like it (a view he later revised). He said why. Forster (somewhat contrary to Bloomsbury principles, one might think) never spoke to him again. Gerald learnt much from Bloomsbury and admired them. 'It was the most civilised society England has ever seen,' he told Leonard Woolf. 'I feel a deep gratitude for being allowed to know most members of the group.'[58] But he developed strong reservations about them. He felt they were too smug, too exclusive, too snobbish, too close to a class and way of life that was dying, far too financially secure to be in touch with poverty and therefore what was, for the mass of people, reality. They were as bigoted about religion, though in reverse, as the Victorians they despised. Nor were they of importance creatively.

How much of this did Gerald feel or express at the time? Certainly not his objections about their money. Gerald was doing his best to join them. It wasn't until later that it became fashionable for the middle and upper classes to feel guilty about money. Frances Partridge thought he felt very little of it. 'Besides, that world was *intensely* critical of itself.' Perhaps – but not precisely in Gerald's terms. He saw at the time that they had no Pound, Proust, Eliot, Joyce, Lawrence; the writers carrying literature into new fields. As for Virginia Woolf, he already felt – a view not as common then as now – that her essays were her greatest work, making her novels appear, as he told her, 'a trifle laborious and pedantic'.[59] In *The History of Poor Robinson*, which he wrote in 1927, the Superior Order of Cambodians (Bloomsbury) is not allowed to doubt 'that they belonged to the most refined, the most distinguished and most intelligent body of men in the world'.[60]

In the end, perhaps the most powerful objection was, as suggested much earlier, emotional. Bloomsbury was a group and, ever since Radley, Gerald couldn't stand groups. 'I could have never settled down in Bloomsbury,' he wrote years later, 'because I react violently if I feel myself imprisoned in any set.'[61] This was why he held back, and this was probably one of many reasons – vastly extended by then – why he eventually chose to live abroad. But even now he had to escape – and his principal escape was into a world of girls.

6

'He sometimes regretted that he was not living in an age when running away from women was regarded as a mark of Christian virtue.'

Thoughts in a Dry Season

The whole of Gerald's period in London, in *Personal Record*, his letters, in his reported conversation, is suffused with sex; or not only sex, but young women – their faces and bodies, their chatter, woes and jokes, their lives. In *Personal Record* he lays the emphasis on working-class girls. Bunny Garnett describes him as always in pursuit of someone he'd fallen in love with on sight. He had 'An insatiable interest in women and though full of illusions, a great understanding of them.'[62] (All his life Gerald was drawn to womanisers in order to talk about women to them.)

But how to get these women? He knew in Spain, he told Carrington, but not London. In one respect Fitzroy Street had fulfilled its promise. Gerald could see a young woman undressing opposite. He was surprised when, seeing him watching, she drew the blinds. He began to have a fantasy of watching her undress, not minding, in his rooms – to *live* the voyeur scene.[63]

Then, on 18 March 1925, there was a fire at Madame Tussaud's. Gerald managed to pick up a girl in the crowd of spectators who attracted him. The reason, he said was – chaste scholar's lust – because she had the same name as John Donne's wife, Anne Moore. Long-limbed, long-haired, brought up in an orphanage, she had a music-hall Cockney voice, a rich lover who didn't sleep with her and a poor boy of eighteen in her lodgings who did. She worked in a shop in Oxford Street and reminded him of Pepita. 'I see I was really made to live in the servants' hall or the wings of a theatre.'[64]

He picked up his girls in Lyon's Corner Houses, prostitutes' cafés, pubs, the street. No doubt there were many he didn't record, but they flit in and out of his journal, and he often tells Carrington – to interest her, to show he didn't need her, probably hoping to make her jealous. Now she never was. He kisses a young country girl, Olive Earle, with a beautiful skin and, so he tells Carrington (they were not seeing each other), 'that sleepy expression which goes soon after childhood'.[65] 'I can imagine nothing more enjoyable,' Carrington replies silkily, 'than kissing an exquisite olive in a Hansom cab.'

Gerald virtually never slept with these girls, though that is not the impression one gets from *Personal Record*. But he was totally honest, even indiscreet, about himself to Ralph and other friends (he gained much more kudos from these encounters than he did from his difficult passion for Carrington). He could even joke about what he came to call his 'old trouble'. Impotent with a girl, he took Damaroids, a popular remedy. He was still impotent, he told Bunny and Ralph, until she left, whereupon he was struck with the most enormous erection which nothing, not even cold water, would curb.[66]

Ralph thought it very strange he had these girls in his room at all (they sometimes stayed several days). 'But he was lonely,' said Frances. 'He hoped perhaps he *would* suddenly be able to make love to them. It was not really so strange.'

Loneliness, of course, was a major reason; a desperately urgent one during his night panics. Perched, as at Yegen, above a fascinating new world (all his rooms were on top floors) he loved to descend and explore it – showing, as always, a sure eye for the extraordinary. Bunny remembered him picking up a tough old tart for company who earned her living putting her head in a lion's mouth.[67] And then – to use a typical Gerald gear-change signifying a change-up in emotion – and then these girls moved him deeply. In *Jack Robinson* two prostitutes have to share one dress, the other waiting wrapped in sacks. He was poor, but they were much poorer, and Gerald, who told Gamel Brenan that pity was his strongest emotion, gave them five shillings, ten shillings, and shared his meals, his room, his bed with them. It was a 'shabby, run-down' world,[68] but it was, especially compared to Bloomsbury, real.

In fact, almost the only girls he made love to during these years were middle-class. There was Susie Simon, who turned out to be as passionate as she looked ('her heart trembles in a bath of glandy secretions').[69] He told her about the girls he watched undress, and they made love in a Strand Hotel and his rooms, but her Catholic conscience caused her to break it off (no doubt pricked by the sudden, brief reappearance of her husband).[70] There was Lettice Kirkpatrick, daughter of Sir Cyril Kirkpatrick who built the largest dockyard on the Thames. Gerald met her in December 1925 and was trying to seduce her two years later. He was unsuccessful, but he made a revealing comment about himself in an apparently muddled journal entry about her. He told people he wanted to marry Lettice, but pretended it was in order to force himself out of bed to write. Of this rather childish joke, he noted how he longed to tell everyone everything about himself but did so by giving 'false motives'.[71] The point here is that that powerful burying process that we have studied produced in reaction an equally powerful, almost obsessive desire to reveal himself – hence that reckless self-indiscretion, which later, on occasion, became marked. This contradiction sometimes resulted, too, in extraordinary statements about himself which startled people and which, as Gerald noted elsewhere, only he could decode.

The 'truth' in this instance – that he wanted to marry Lettice – was true of nearly all the girls he met, middle-class or working-class. Indeed, the one working-class girl he did make love to – a Jewish cinema usherette who 'didn't mind if I was an effective lover' (upon which, according to his letters to Frances and *Personal Record*, Gerald became perfectly effective) – was one he said he very nearly did marry.*[72]

Practically the only girl he didn't want to marry was the one who was his most constant companion. Winifred Baker – Freda (or Squinks) – was a beautiful, educated, ex-ballet dancer, who taught music and made the mistake of falling seriously in love with Hope. A depressive, she was intelligent, and Gerald enjoyed talking to her and, drawn by mutual loneliness, they went to plays and concerts together. (Carrington took him to concerts, too. It was the only musical interlude in his life. He even bought 'one of the new wind-up gramophones'.) Freda came for weekends in June and July 1925,

---

* Yet, to show how difficult it is to pin Gerald down, even these categorical statements may be untrue. In *Personal Record* he says he met Rose Ditton, undressed and made love. In his journal and to Frances it is Rose Simmons (correspondence over libel in the Jonathan Cape archives makes it clear both Roses are the same). But in the journal, she had 'had little experience of love' and all they did was 'sit in my rooms rather vaguely till midnight'.

when he took a cottage at Shalbourne to be near Carrington – a recurrent fantasy of them both, which was a disaster. It was followed by (for Gerald) another – his performance in Lytton's play *A Son of Heaven*. He had, as palace guard, few lines, but was so nervous that, though reduced to 'Yes, your majesty', on the night the palace guard stepped forward and said, 'No, your majesty.'[73] Just as well it wasn't a ballet, the original conception. The play was followed by another agonising scene with Carrington and they again split up.

After that Gerald and Freda slept together regularly once a month for six months, meetings always marked in his journal by 'reactions' – regret, disgust, guilt. He was still seeing her in 1927. Then she fell in love with the composer Philip Heseltine, who was supposed to be impotent. However, he gave Freda a child and she vanished from Gerald's life.

She was the most soothing of his women, if rather soporific; the most exhausting – Carrington aside – was Tiz.

7

At the beginning of 1926 Tiz, now eighty-eight, became ill. Gerald had to see her every day, mostly so that they could discuss and look at her urine together. 'It's gone back to that dreadful orange.' She recovered, but somehow the daily visits continued through March. She talked incessantly about her will, and had many unnecessary meetings with Mr Taylor, the family lawyer. These always exhilarated her, and after supper she and Gerald drank crème de menthe out of Baron von Roeder's old eye-baths. 'I do it in memory of my dear husband. He died, without a single complaint, of influenza. The executioner arranged the most beautiful flowers on his grave.'[74] She exhausted Gerald, maddened him, bored him, but he was moved by her. By her loneliness, her gathering infirmities and perhaps above all because she longed to see him far more than he could bear, yet had to accept his endless excuses and evasions. 'For she was in love with me, with the hopeless love of the old for the young' – a love whose impossible yearnings Gerald knew as he was writing – aged seventy-five – only too well.

Servants had suddenly become a major problem. A trusted figure called Emma had retired and, to Tiz's irritation, died (old people

dying always made her cross). Gerald was put in charge of replace-
ments, something which rapidly proved impossible. He got an agency
to send a stream of elderly spinsters and widows, but few wished to
get stuck with an eccentric, deaf old lady for a minuscule wage and
less food. If they did, Tiz instantly found objections. Or would
pronounce them a jewel, then 'Not a jewel but a charlatan! A
disreputable woman! A cat burglar!'[74] Gradually it emerged that
Tiz's real plan was that she and Gerald should live together. It would
be an excellent preparation for marriage. Work would be trifling.
Gerald could cook – eggs and tins – she would dust. For a nightmare
two weeks this harebrained scheme was put into practice. Then
Gerald rebelled and forced onto his great-aunt a fifty-year-old, surly-
faced, squat figure called Bessie (Eliza in *Personal Record*). Bessie later
revealed a pent-up emotional side and was obsessed by the mandolin.
She had been seeking a deaf employer.

In October 1925, having been separated from Carrington for three
months, Gerald had told her he was thinking of going to Toulon. He
now decided to implement this plan (he had to ask permission both of
Tiz and his father). St Teresa and *Mr Fisher*, who were languishing,
might revive there. Bessie might easily be sacked. But probably a
major reason was to excite Carrington – and in this it was successful.
They met on 20 April, after a letter-filled gap of nearly nine months.
Gerald left for Paris on 22 May 1926.

8

One senses an almost violent feeling of release and relief – a scouring
off of Bloomsbury cocktail parties and chat, Carrington, the gossip of
the Cranium Club – as Gerald plunged south for sixteen hours in the
stench, noise and hideous discomfort of his wooden-seated, shut-
windowed, third-class compartment. It was packed full of Armenian
refugees being sick. But at last, he told Ralph, he felt again the
'greater reality' of his life. And it was an equal relief to be alone
again.[75]

He had just spent a blissful week in Paris. He'd picked up a tart,
not to make love to but to hear her life story. He'd gone to a voyeur
establishment which ended by disgusting him, though not so much
that he couldn't write a long, vividly detailed and humorous descrip-

tion to Ralph. And he'd seduced Elaine, a twenty-four-year-old English girl engaged to a Czech tennis champion. They made love and Elaine 'broke into a kind of ecstasy. She . . . had never thought such pleasure was possible.'*76

Gerald remained in France for six months. First at the Hôtel de la Réserve in Mourillon, at that time just outside Toulon – a Toulon still largely a port, with horses and trams and narrow streets hung across with washing. In September he moved inside the town, into a room at 9 rue Courbet. He made two brief visits to Cassis to visit the artistic community led by Colonel Teed and Roland Penrose, where he also got to know Janko Varda, a slim, fawnlike Adonis and one of the womanisers Gerald was always drawn to. (Varda had arrived gloomily in England before the First War, warned by his father of the puritanical and virginal English women. He had been agreeably surprised by the first one he met: Valentine Dobrée.) Apart from this, and a brief journey up behind Nice to Colmars to escape the August heat, he stayed in Toulon.

As usual, he read voraciously: Proust, Swift, St Simon, Don Quixote, Mérimée. But the main business was writing. At first he laboured doggedly on at St Teresa, *Mr Fisher* (now partly in verse) and the commercial-traveller story. Then, in early October, he was suddenly struck by a prolonged burst of manic energy. It was sparked by Ralph, who had arrived with Frances on 15 September. They had read what he'd been writing and Ralph thought the commercial-traveller story boring (perhaps this was because Gerald was writing it in sonata form). Why didn't Gerald write an 'almanac'?77

Gerald had been reading Swift's spoof prophecy of the death of the astrologer and almanac-compiler, Dr John Partridge, and possibly a satirical piece on almanacs by Quevedo which had inspired Swift. In a flash it all coalesced – aptness of name, past fantasies about Ralph, the old need to expel his reading, the facetious side of his humour. In two days and nights he wrote all but seven pages of *Dr Partridge's Almanack*, to be his second published work: twenty pages

---

* A tart he'd picked up earlier had told Gerald she really preferred women – and what women liked was for her to *faire la minette*. This is slang for cunnilingus and Gerald told Frances Partridge years later (letter of 1 June 1981) that in his experience it was better to stick to oral practices 'which are simple and natural' rather than 'risk' penetration. This may be the explanation of what was then a rather rare reaction to Gerald's lovemaking – and also to veiled references on many other occasions.

describing Partridge's life in the grave, 300 separate prophecies, then twelve pages of fantasy – 'the psychoanalysis of vegetables'.

In November he had what must have seemed another brilliant idea. His first ambition – his hare side – had been to be a tramp. He had, indeed, *been* a tramp. He would write a fictional autobiography of a tramp, disguising the author as George Beaton, revealing him to those who knew (Carrington) by the title – *Jack Robinson*. In two furious weeks of writing, Mr Crusoe finished the first two chapters of what was to be his first published work.

The visit of Ralph and Frances was a success. Gerald thought Ralph had 'never been so charming'. Frances had vivid memories of Gerald there. He wore a light coat, pressed white trousers and cord shoes. (It is worth noting that, when he could afford it, Gerald was something of a dandy. He was noted for his trousers in London – they had special raised seams designed by Gerald and were cut to cling elegantly to his slender legs.) He was now smoking fifteen cigarettes a day and his teeth had begun their steady exodus: two fell out at Toulon.

Gerald's room was large, shabby, dark, with a big black bed. It contained his gramophone and neat piles of books. He wrote all day with his spidery pen at café tables, usually in the Brasserie du Coq Hardi. But the three would meet at Cap Brun for lunch and to swim and for Gerald to describe his adventures of the night before – 'his girl life'.

This was extensive and, in *Personal Record*, often funny. He was taken to another voyeur's brothel by a girl he'd picked up (not a tart, says Gerald automatically) where, through a tiny window, he watched a whore have a queue of sailors – one every five minutes. The memory Gerald retained years later was of the whore stretching out an arm from time to time to take a bite from her apple.[78] Yet it is a significant memory. Gerald's intense interest in these matters often seemed less an interest in sex *per se* than an interest in the oddities human nature manifested there. His letter to Ralph on the Paris establishment is neither disgusted nor prurient but just fascinated. He'd found that almost the whole thing was in fact mechanical – a series of life-sized, elaborately erotic, whirring clockwork toys.[76]

His Paris success was not repeated until his last two weeks, when, on the advice of a lieutenant in the submarines he'd met, he invited into his bed the girl who cleaned the rooms – Marie, a big, solid, silent peasant from an orphanage. Her body was hard and 'smelt of wet earth like a garden after rain'.

But success continued inside his head. Walking in a cemetery soon after his arrival he found a beautiful young widow putting flowers on her two-month-dead husband's grave. They talked. Reluctantly, yet not reluctantly, she agreed to let him come and see her after dark, and then he seduced her with almost too great ease – 'She herself could scarcely restrain her lust.' The letter reminds one strongly of his long letter about the two women in Yegen. There is the same literary, weary, man-of-the-world note – 'my mind remained aloof and melancholy'; the same vivid observation – 'a smell of olive oil and a hot stuffy air'. It is convincing, but Gerald told Frances he'd made it up in a letter to Ralph because he'd been reading *The Milesian Tales*.[79]

In fact, it was in a letter to Carrington,[80] and was a drop in a great torrent of letters he sent back to upbraid her (among much else, he'd learnt of her affair with Tommy Tomlin), dragoon her, finally woo and recapture her. In this he thought he was successful. When he left for England on 14 November 1926, forced by Tiz and his father turning the financial screws, he had concluded from her letters (lost for this period) that she'd agreed, at last, that they would be 'definite lovers'[81] – a conclusion fortified when she suggested they meet in Paris.

They met and spent the night together. But Carrington had also come as much, or more, to see her beautiful, immoral friend Phyllis de Janzé. She vented her irritation by making Gerald travel back separately in case people thought they were, indeed, definite lovers.

9

Gerald's last three years in London followed the same sort of pattern as the first three.

He'd no sooner returned than Tiz, losing a pound, sacked Bessie on the spot, not for stealing but because of her irritating, overemotional reaction when accused. The pound was found, Bessie reinstated and at once – she was lucky not to be sacked again – seized one of Tiz's pads, tears pouring down her cheeks, and scribbled, 'If only you *knew* madam how much I loved you.' Gerald, summoned by telegrams, was so stimulated by this scene that on leaving he walked into a ladder and nearly knocked himself out.[82]

But shortly after this, in February 1927, Tiz had a series of strokes and began cracking up. She had an illusion she lived in two flats both numbered 23 Ashley Place. Every morning she'd go to the taxi rank and ask for 23 Ashley Place, arriving in seconds at the flat she'd just left. The result was confusion and Gerald would have to come and help puzzle out which 23 Ashley Place she was in. Just before this, already anticipating the end, he'd asked Carrington to come and choose some furniture.[83]

For about eight months, despite only seeing each other once or twice a month and periodic storms, they managed to get on. In January 1927 Gerald got a new top floor flat, near Garrow Tomlin, at 14 Great James Street: a fine, panelled, elegantly proportioned front room with three sash windows, a back bedroom looking on to a tree, small kitchen and bathroom.* Two guineas a week (Tiz had to double his allowance). He took it, he said at the time, entirely to attract Carrington, who was to share it. She'd frequently complained of the cat's-mess squalor of Fitzroy Street and hinted that nice rooms would tempt her.[84] Besides, he'd been struck by her passion for Ham Spray. The flat didn't do this especially, but it fixed in Gerald's mind the idea that, though he might not attract himself, he could do so by where he lived.

Preparations took a month, while he borrowed Freda's flat and then took rooms above Viani's in Charlotte Street. Helen lent him furniture and, despite a furious row in February, Carrington and he had great fun painting the flat in March. Carrington had been much impressed by Yegen – with its simple, almost austere appearance, and the strong peasant furniture and fine things he'd bought in the junk shops of Granada (Spanish faïence, and Manises plates – cheap then, extremely valuable now). Gerald had distinctive and instinctive good taste – honed by Hope – and Carrington said she would trust it 'a hundred times more than Roger's'.[85] They painted the flat apple green and vermilion, Gerald fussing about every detail.[86]

But the first person on whom he tested its attraction was a beautiful young prostitute, Lily Holder, he found standing with her

---

* Compulsorily 'residential', the flat, at the top of a pleasing eighteenth-century terrace house of mostly offices, is still much the same. The bedroom has gone to enlarge the kitchen, and the tree gone altogether.

back to a wall between Greek Street and Piccadilly.[87] They slept chastely together – Gerald fascinated by her extraordinary pale, translucent skin, blue eyes and languid movements (she was on cocaine), and moved by her melancholy – then Lily Holder vanished. She continued to haunt him. He searched the streets. In May he stood fruitlessly for several days and evenings running outside an address she'd given him near Regent's Park.

And from the flat he leapt with alacrity back into his social life, now much facilitated by a bicycle. He made friends with Desmond and Molly MacCarthy, especially Molly. A plump, affectionate, distracted but highly original figure, she was a mimic with a genius for fantasy and humour – taking flight in sudden, erratic rushes until her soft voice broke in helpless tears of laughter. She loved outings to Brighton, giggling, putting pennies in slot machines. Her deafness, agonising to her, with a box whose batteries ran out, was of course no impediment to Gerald. It was with the MacCarthys that Gerald first met Cyril Connolly, then Desmond's secretary. Lily Holder also sailed under the name Connolly, and Gerald excited Cyril about her and later introduced them. Hope returned – rich! Gerald told Carrington, buying suits, giving him £50, and about to get even richer by selling paintings to Americans (Hope knew, then or later, Derain, Modigliani, Soutine and Chagall), and, Gerald added revealingly, still making him feel like a pupil – tongue-tied, inept, deferential.[89] Alick Shepeler, his brief love of 1916, still at the *Illustrated London News* and now 'a ruin', reappeared and insisted on expensive restaurant meals every three months, though she recipro-cated.[89] Ralph of course he saw continually (except when Gerald was being swept by jealous storms). He met Bertrand Russell, saw more of Leonard Woolf and still more of Arthur Waley.

In some respects Waley and Gerald were very different. 'Uncon-trollably silent',[90] hermetically discreet about his private life, Waley was above all an intellectual, a scholar, who hid his intense shyness under monologues in his high, sensitive voice on such subjects as Li Po and Chinese poetry. This bored Bloomsbury; it often bored Gerald, but none the less it irritated him that Bloomsbury should feel bored. He soon found that Waley was an acute and penetrating critic, and became aware of the kindness and sweetness beneath the shy exterior. Both became experts on alien countries, both had leanings to hypochondria. Waley also loved gossip. The friendship, renewed after their brief meetings earlier, was among the most long-lasting from this period, along with that of Frances, Helen and Roger.

Waley was attached in some loose, ill-defined but permanent way to Beryl de Zoëte, though he was supposed to be impotent (something else which no doubt drew Gerald to him). Beryl was quite a number. Hyperactive, adventurous, even wild, often silly, she became hysterical if she didn't get her way. She grabbed Waley from his mother in 1918 and seemed to develop some hold over him. Once beautiful, she had had numerous lovers, usually on her incessant trips abroad. Yet she was highly intelligent and loved literature; she did the masterly translation of Svevo's masterpiece, *The Confessions of Zeno*. No one ever knew her age, though it was believed to be immense.*

10

In July Tiz recovered sufficiently to sack Bessie. The new servant was huge and not very patient. She picked Tiz up and shook her violently in the air. Gerald, as he wrote to Carrington, hurried over in response to the telegram.[91]

It was almost the last of such lighthearted missives. For months Gerald had been getting more and more unreasonable. The row before painting his flat had been because he was furiously jealous at Carrington's staying in Ralph's flat in London, not Gerald's, when she'd hurt her back riding. It was not just Ralph; he was wildly jealous 'if there is a young man visible even miles on the horizon!'[92] In May Gerald went to Ham Spray for the first time in two years (Lytton had banned him as too upsetting). He stormed out not, as in *Personal Record*, because Carrington sided against him in an argument, but because she humiliated him in front of Ralph and Frances by not coming to his room.[93]

The feeling is of Gerald trying to wrench her out of him, while she conciliated, apologised, finally wearied. Her last reported dream of Gerald was of him suffocating her.

* John Morris, Controller of the BBC Third Programme, described how he told Beryl that he wanted to show some visitors over London Bridge. *Beryl*: Why? *Morris*: Because it's the oldest bridge in London. *Beryl*: Nonsense, I can remember it being built. John Morris thought of Rider-Haggard's *She* and felt the hairs rise on the back of his neck. (Honor Tracy to author.)

In July there were vague plans to meet on the Uffington White Horse where they had first kissed. On 29 July Gerald delivered an ultimatum – she *must* come. But on the same day, Carrington wrote saying she had to go to Munich. Gerald let his ultimatum stand.[94]

She returned and wrote a sad letter suggesting they part. She blamed herself. Her nature made her incapable of intimate relations; it was (he had told her everything) 'No pleasure finding oneself impotent. Which is what it amounts to.'[95] Gerald, on his way to Warren End, sent a curt, two-line note, followed later by all the possessions she had left at Great James Street to soothe neurotic Mr Crusoe. He at once got 'flu, but at last he really seemed to be free.

11

Just before the break, Gerald, who was reading forty books on beggars and tramps,[96] spent a week at Coombe Bissett in Dorset working on *Jack Robinson* and a new work, *The History of Poor Robinson*. In October and November he went to Lyme Regis to continue his *Robinsons* and inject more sea into *Mr Fisher*. Released from Carrington, his spirits leapt, his energy was boundless, particularly compared to the feebleness of Lyme, where the only active thing was the magnificent ladies' lavatory. This travelled, he told Ralph, 'every year a foot or two towards the sea. What the ladies will do when they have to dive to reach it, I cannot say.'[97]

He did two travel talks for the BBC on Spain in April 1928 (probably through Blair, who now worked there) and wrote a good deal of poetry – mostly to girls. But his main work was *Jack Robinson*, which he worked hard at until July 1929, reporting progress regularly to Bunny Garnett. Bunny had become his literary mentor and an influential one. He had already extravagantly praised *Dr Partridge's Almanack* – parts of it showed Gerald 'was the greatest writer of the age'.[98] He excited the Woolfs who, inflamed with publishers' envy, attacked Gerald for not giving it to them and begged for his novel.[99] By August 1928, Bunny had got the Nonesuch Press, where he had been a partner since February, to offer Gerald £100 if he finished it.

Finishing, it was clear, was now the problem. While Bunny poured out a steady stream of books, Gerald had so far finished nothing, 'except a great many letters'[100] as Carrington noted caustically. 'Do you think Gerald will ever finish anything?' Arthur Waley said to her at a party in May 1928. 'I ask because one would like to read his books, as he is by far the most interesting writer I know.'[101]

In fact, he did now finish his first substantial prose work. *The History of Poor Robinson* is a 25,000-word acount of the love affair written, according to Gerald, in the style of *Candide* or *Diatribe du Docteur Akakia*.[102] But in fact, not Voltaire but anger forced his own strong, clear prose from Gerald for the first time outside his letters and a few reviews. Only one 'satirical' detour is marred by his usual facetiousness, archaisms and imitation.

Gerald told Ralph, deviously, that he was the hero, but the animus against Ralph (Perrywag), who reads pornography and complains when Robinson, whom he pities and despises for his 'incapacity' with women,* fails to supply him with pig trotters and high-class tarts; and also to a lesser extent, Lytton (Dr Artichoke), whose disciples are taught to admire his original use of clichés – to read him is 'like walking on the finest linoleum carpet' – is far more vicious than against Carrington (Flutterby).[103] Fuelled by this, Gerald finished it in a few months.

12

Having left Carrington, Gerald made one last superhuman effort to obtain the skeleton key to women – dancing. He took lessons, made progress, 'but no sooner did I attempt to put what I had learned into practice than an invincible paralysis came over me. It was quite useless for my partner to take hold of me: roots seemed to grow down from my heels into the floor so that I could not even walk. All the inhibitions I had suffered from all my life, all my early attacks of shyness came together in an absolute command – that I must not move my legs to music.'[104] He gave up in despair. The last account of him attempting to dance is when he imitated the dance of the

---

* Apart from Gerald's account of Ralph laughing at him during the war, when they were both very young, there is no evidence at all that he pitied or despised Gerald on this account. For one thing, he didn't know the extent of the 'incapacity'. No one did. But the fact that Ralph's pity was all in Gerald's head didn't make it less painful or humiliating.

termites as described in Maeterlinck's *Vie des Termites*.[105] Fortunately, Gerald had other keys.

Vera Birch, aged twenty-eight, nearly fainted with admiration and excitement when he read her *Dr Partridge*, and begged him to write about her. (He didn't, but he wrote semi-erotic poems *to* her, which he copied from *Pills to Purge Melancholy*, published in 1707.) She was the sister of Lord Gage and her husband Frank, who produced plays in Cambridge, wouldn't or couldn't sleep with her. Small, beautiful, delicately complexioned and flirtatious, she filled Gerald with fantasies of marriage (which he seems to have seen in terms of a giant tranquilliser), and he was in love with her from November 1927, through a lonely Christmas at Great James Street, till February 1928 when, as she cooled and he at once became agitated, the affair came to an end.

In April, he had a tantalising brush with Lily Holder. Now, instead of melancholy, she was gay, even manic, wanting to get drunk, her conversation like that of a character in Dostoevsky – fantastic, brilliant, profound, ironic, witty and maudlin. After a few meetings, eating at Gennaro's, and in pubs, she vanished.

But just before this, in March, he met Winny Stafford.

Winny was to be his constant companion for ten months. She was nineteen, equable, sturdy, healthy, confident, and had large brown eyes with very clear whites. She was the eldest daughter of a slum family in Bermondsey; her father drank and beat his wife. Winny ran away after a quarrel with her Jewish boyfriend and had been on the streets for a year.

In April 1928, Gerald set her up in a room in Lamb's Conduit Street, just off Great James Street, where Roger Fry stored canvases, and got her to take a job as a 'Nippy' in Lyon's Corner House. They saw each other all the time, for supper every other day (Winny cooking), weekends, expeditions. Gerald went again to Coombe Bissett in May, then took Winny to Bognor Regis in June, and possibly to a cottage near Rochester in July. But there were still the terrible nights; quite often he would pick someone up. 'We talked, embraced, they went away and I felt that their brief presence made my bed less hostile.'[106] By March, he'd also got a telescope. Frances remembers him telephoning them urgently to come and see a beautiful girl having a bath (Ralph and she were living in a flat next door). When they arrived the window under observation was totally steamed over. 'But what can you see?' 'Enough', said Gerald, in a state of high excitement. Gradually, the steam cleared and there emereged a rather fat middle-aged man drying himself.[107]

Gerald's voyeurism was a long-evolving product of childhood influences considerably reinforced by his intense natural curiosity, sexual frustration due to timidity and inhibition, and a cast of mind and character which on the whole preferred imaginative and intellectual pleasures to physical ones. It was at times to grow quite marked – and quite odd – until, during his fifties and sixties, it seemed to diffuse out into a more generalised and vicarious fascination with other people's lives – especially the lives of young women. But it should be emphasised that it was never anything remotely like a thorough-going perversion. Perhaps even the word 'voyeur' is too strong. At its most extreme it was just an intensification of something that most people have felt observing unobserved.

But now tarts and telescopes were not enough – besides which tarts, even just hugged, cost money. In August, Winny gave up being a 'Nippy' and came to live with him. They rose late, had breakfast; Winny bought lunch, then at four o'clock went and picked up young men at the Astoria or Carlton Dance Club.[108] Regular as clockwork, she was back at twelve. Each night Gerald had 'a delicious sense of safety and peace'.[109] Frances remembers Winny at this period. She was very cheerful, 'very *wholesome*'. She liked Gerald, but often made fun of him. She thought he put on his middle-class accent. 'Drop it and talk natural.' She would imitate his walk, clicking her fingers and singing tunelessly 'tra-la-la-la'. Gerald would listen, pause, then suddenly explode (a marked characteristic) in shrill laughter.

He never made love to her, he told Ralph, but now at last he could watch in his room the 'perpetual dressing and changing and powdering and [all] the pretty girlish movements these things occasion'[110] – and she didn't care twopence. He also indulged his H. G. Wells/commercial-traveller fantasies, putting on a bowler hat after Winny's Sunday lunch and, imagining he was a small trader just married, setting out with her to see her friends: a girl who lived with a burglar in Bethnal Green, another who'd married a fence. He also introduced her to his own friends (only Bunny didn't find her interesting). He was thirty-four and had never lived with a woman before – unless you count Tiz – and he was in bliss.

Tiz, in fact, finally collapsed in October. Gerald had been alerted when she'd suddenly turned up in a taxi at three in the morning when he was in bed with Winny. She'd come to ask what day of the week it was. Shorty after this she began to cash cheques all the time, leaving large sums lying about in taxis and elsewhere. At once Gerald leapt to the defence of his inheritance and he and his father had her certified. Gerald searched until he found a suitable mental home run by Catholic nuns in Denmark Hill. He took her there, and then quietly crept away. Three days later he went back. Tiz was sitting in the hall in her fur cape and plumed hat. She had sat like that all day for three days, from breakfast till bed, waiting for her nephew to come and take her away. Her reproaches were dignified and Gerald's guilt was intense. Gradually she retreated into the distant past and a fantasy world where she was in a hotel with his parents on the top floor. A difficult inmate because of her restlessness, she spent her time 'visiting' them, and soon hardly recognised Gerald when he called.

But no sooner was this settled, than he had to face the final incident in his long relation with Carrington.

13

In February 1928, six months after they had parted, Carrington couldn't resist leaving some flowers at Great James Street. They met a few times during the summer, normally in company. Each time, under surface detachment, Gerald's emotions flared again and he trembled on the brink of begging for a resumption or of provoking a row so tremendous it could never be repaired. This finally occurred in November.

Carrington was in the habit of giving away Lytton's old clothes. She now asked Gerald if he'd like one of Lytton's 'practically new' suits and a tie. What followed is subtly different to the account in *Personal Record*, and shows that Gerald was determined to break free. He refused the suit and said he'd noticed she was giving away his presents (he'd seen Frances wearing a scarf left behind in Ralph's and Frances's flat). Carrington ignored this, but sent two ties 'to tie our love'.[111]

At once Gerald exploded. 'What would she have done,' he said furiously to Frances, 'if I'd sent her a bunch of Winny's old knickers?'[112] And one of the ties was frightful, a disgusting, shiny, wood-silk.[113] Gerald the dandy had just bought some charming Madras cotton ties at Roses's in the Burlington Arcade. He made an enormous parcel of all the presents* she had ever given him and left it with an angry note (for which he had needed a rough draft)[114] at Gordon Square. That night he got extremely drunk at a party of Alec Penrose's and then went to Edgeworth for a week. But the *banderilla* which had been in him so deep and so long had indeed at last been wrenched out.

So long: they had met in 1919, but Carrington had been in Gerald's thoughts and fantasies since 1915. She was, after his Nana, his mother and father and his two schools, the last great formative influence on his character.

But as well as pursuing Carrington with every wile and trick he could command, Gerald had also been desperately trying to break free. The disruptive and destructive effects consequent on the break-up of marriages or long-term affairs have been charted, and a proportion of Gerald's erratic behaviour with tarts and his middle-class girls was probably due to this. He certainly thought so: 'If I ruin my life,' he told Ralph, 'I shall blame Carrington.'[115] For months he remained very bitter about her – a bitterness from which he also got a certain melodramatic pleasure. Was he, he wondered to Frances, perhaps *permanently* embittered?

In the long term, Carrington had cemented his relations with Ralph, but did so with an underlying tension composed partly of Gerald's repressed jealousy. Ralph's position in the friendship was in this respect easier. He was easily irritated by Gerald, but he wasn't jealous of him – he had nothing to be jealous about.

In other respects, too, Carrington set up patterns which lasted many years. From now on, 'love' for Gerald was inseparable from pain, jealousy and intense agitation. Indeed, as far as he was

---

* Their presents to each other were one of the most delicate and delightful features of their affair. For Christmas 1921 Gerald gave her a vellum-bound book of poetry so expensive Lytton had shrunk from buying it. Once, completely broke, he gave her a collection of wafer-thin, highly coloured glass Christmas decorations; another time a picture of *Mimosa pudica*, the sensitive plant, as well as innumerable objects, books, shawls and scarves and stuffs. She gave him books too, clothes, her ingenious glass pictures and paintings.

concerned, it wasn't love without these elements. He also seems to have decided, at an unconscious level, that in future he would have to be the one in control.

Gerald's own view was that Carrington did him a service by breaking down the selfish, egotistical shell he'd formed while solitary at Yegen. But, as we have seen, he'd dug his defensive position much deeper and much earlier. And it is true that probably only a woman who, by continually leaving or forcing him to leave, and then returning or enticing him back, mimicked the departures and returns of his nurse and the recurrent pain at losing and then regaining his mother each term at Winton House; only some pattern of this sort could have succeeded in getting deep enough to reawaken that emotional side he'd buried then. And much later Gerald came to feel this too. 'She caused me such agony and misery,' he told Frances, 'that something was awakened in me.'[116] But she awoke only to maim. Apart from some brief flare-ups, Gerald did not dare allow himself to 'love' again, in his sense, until he was over sixty.

Gradually, he forgot the pain Carrington had caused him, but she continued to haunt him for twenty years, eventually only returning in the form of powerful dreams, from which Gerald would awake and lie in the darkness, swept again by the sweetness and sadness of their remembered love.

14

For the last five years Gerald had partly paid for Yegen by letting it from time to time to various friends and acquaintances. He told Frances in December that he was returning to write there, because only writing could assuage his pain. No doubt this was an element, but in fact he'd decided in October when Tiz went mad. That is, the major reason, as usual, was money.[117]

Gerald seems to have met Tiz's no doubt considerable hospital expenses, partly paid by her annuity, by selling the lease of the flat. But this didn't solve his own perpetually rocky finances. During her decline, Gerald had got into the habit of borrowing from her and not paying back. He'd accepted endless little extra cheques. Two can't live as cheaply as one, and Winny's expenses had had to be defrayed by pawning a valuable ring Tiz had given him to keep safely.[117]

Now this had all ended; once again, Yegen was essential. In fact, Winny was ending too. She'd decided to marry her old Jewish boyfriend. She came and cooked odd meals – Christmas breakfast for instance – but, except for a brief return in March, their amiable life together was really over. Gerald gave her a good deal of Tiz's furniture, including a 'Mahogany cabinet inlaid with blue faïence and decorated gilt scrolls' from the Great Exhibition of 1851. He gave Blair other pieces. He kept very little for himself.

But presumably he wasn't out of pocket from this partial winding-up. However, if he'd saved anything for Spain it now immediately went again, because as he was about to set off Lily Holder/Connolly, the beautiful prostitute he'd intermittently pursued over several years, suddenly reappeared, and this time she needed Gerald.

He had heard in January 1929 that she was in the Paddington Infirmary on the danger list and in great pain. Gerald visited her every day. On 25 January she had her ovaries out and slowly began to recover. Gerald's visits were curtailed. He saw Molly and Frances and other friends, went to Edgeworth and the dentist. Bunny read what he'd written of *Jack Robinson*, praising and criticising, but mostly praising. But for six weeks his life centred on Lily, who now craved tinned salmon and cheese.

On 2 April she came out. Gerald had hired a boat at Richmond. 'For three months she had not been out of doors. The sky was blue, a pale sun shone, the first buds of the poplars and hawthorns were coming out. She lay back on the cushions, the curl of her brown hair that had come loose dangling against her neck, her eyes glittering and dancing with happiness. For once she had entirely forgotten herself and was given up to ecstasy.'

For two wonderful weeks she lived with him. She slept till two or three, Gerald working at *Jack Robinson*. They set out together at six, often to the cinema. Supper at Queen's off Leicester Square, then into the low life of tarts and ponces which fascinated him. For about the only time in his life he drank a lot, wine and brandy, then Bass in his flat till three. Prone to despair and boredom, Lily was lifted by drink into flights of fantasy, where 'wit, bawdy and a tragic feeling about life' mixed together and moved him deeply. She lived for these moments of intensity, of what she called 'merriment'.

After two weeks, she found a flat and moved out. Gerald paid the first month's rent and bought her the essential 'good' dress for ten guineas. There is a moving description in *Personal Record* of her panic before starting work. She lingered, then thought a man at the corner was a 'bogie' (policeman). He bought her another drink, she hesitated – 'like a schooner before the wind catches its sails' – then he took her to Regent Street and left her to the tide. As she vanished, he felt with sinking heart familiar pangs – pain, jealousy, agitation.*

Love was to be avoided at all costs; but once caught it could not be resisted. Gerald began to haunt the prostitutes' bars and cafes and then stand for hours outside her flat. She made dates and broke them. On 20 March she made a particularly solemn promise – 'On the grave of my mother, Gerald' – and broke that too. Gerald had supper with Blair and Rhoda,† who both urged him to give up. The next morning he got up very early, walked through the streets as dawn was breaking and set off once more for Spain.

---

* Cyril Connolly took up with Lily (whom he called Lily French) and in his only published journal gives two examples of her spirited conversation – or, rather, monologue (see pp. 188, 189 of *Cyril Connolly – Journal and Memoir* by David Pryce-Jones, London 1983). The same book also has a full and vivid description of Winny and Gerald living together (pp. 177).

† Rhoda Gwynn, an interesting, strong-willed girl, whom Blair had married in June 1926.

TWELVE

Juliana

'*There are women whose bodies are so sensuously developed that one knows at first sight that all their thoughts and perceptions must filter through them.*'

Thoughts in a Dry Season

1

Gerald went first to Avila, city of St Teresa. But his heart was still in London, and it was Lily he thought about. There was a brief respite in Madrid, where he picked up a girl at a cabaret show. Spanish, as usual, freed him from inhibition and loosed a flood of eloquence on her beauty. But they got too drunk. Gerald was violently sick and Marrija had to be taken home. (Skipping down the Madrid streets next morning, Gerald, struck by hangover brilliance, invented a new dance and decided to become a professional dancer.)[1]

From 29 April to 8 May he stayed at Almería. Now, writing fifty pages in ten days,[2] he poured Lily unaltered into *Jack Robinson*. He said later his love for her was just a Carrington flare-up in a Baudelairean setting, but these pages, some of the best in the book, belie that.

This delayed return to the remoteness of Yegen (he arrived on 9 May) suggests reluctance – and it was justified. At first all seemed well. 'The beauty of the green trees and running water and starlit mountains astounded me.' The house was freshly whitewashed, 'as clean and fresh as this paper'.[2] But it soon became clear that his servant María (soon to be dubbed Black María) had got completely out of hand. Inside, the house was chaos. Her hens, goats, sheep, rabbits, a cow and a donkey seemed everywhere – creating smell, fleas, flies. She was waging a lawsuit with the *ayuntamiento* (the *pueblo* council) over a Will. She paced the chaos, alternately whining and raging. Also, because Don Fernando had died, Black María had decided she was Gerald's landlord. Gerald had barely arrived before he decided, with his usual forward planning, that he would go to Seville in October to work.[3]

In fact, his landlord was the widow Doña Clara. But here rose further complications. Doña Clara had lost her own children and had often thought, although frightened of her, of adopting Black María's illegitimate daughter by Don Fernando. Doña Clara was fond of Gerald and now, clearly having planned this for years, she delicately suggested that if he married Angela, whom he'd always liked, perhaps even loved, she would immediately make over to them all her valuable Yegen property, some 2000 acres. And when she was dead, all her equally valuable property in Granada.

Gerald's desire to get married was now intense, even desperate (only equalled – familiar dichotomy – by intermittent terror at losing his freedom). Though in the end he refused, he does not let on in *Personal Record* the extent to which he was tempted by Angela, now a beautiful seventeen-year-old.[4]

So, once again he was immersed in Yegen life. He read a lot, mostly for St Teresa, but also, with great excitement, Italo Svevo. He went for huge walks, one at the end of June, which knocked him out for two days, of forty-five miles to 12,000 feet, 'to see the streams rushing out of caves of snow onto green meadows'.[5] He worked at *Jack Robinson*, following Bunny's detailed criticisms and, buoyed by his praise, now certain it would make money. He missed England and was fed, to his surprise, by two long letters from Winny, and of course gossip from Ralph, who wrote, 'I know of no particular infidelities, which are always more stirring than virgin passions – unless Beryl's prolonged performances to the Foreign Legion in Morocco can be so classed.'[6] He and Frances planned to come to Yegen in the autumn.

But if the main concern was marriage, how first to find a girl? He described to Bunny how in May he'd heard about a bachelor in Ugíjar who had engaged a country girl as a servant and slept with her – and a terrible pang of longing went through him.[8] Shortly after this, he saw Juliana.

Juliana Martín Pelegrina came from the poorest family in the village, living in the last and poorest house, the Casa de Narciso (still last, still poorest – with a marvellous view out towards Ugíjar). With a dumpy figure and frizzy hair, she had large, firm breasts, high Slavonic cheekbones, a delicious mouth, slanting eyes, now sleepy, now seductively large and bright with clear whites; she also had two features irresistible to Gerald – a very fine skin, exquisitely soft, clear and luminous, and she was just fifteen.[9]

Gerald's campaign to get Juliana – first buying her, wooing her, finally seducing her – was seen by Ralph and Frances as machiavellian. The whole thing was a good deal more frantic than as described in *Personal Record*, and also required a very great deal of adroitness and perceptiveness, but the machinations were less those of a prince than of the peasants whose life he now, at last, fully lived.

A peasant – but a rich peasant. Inflation in Spain was greater than in England, so the peseta was only worth eight pence – even less than in 1919.[10] Gerald engaged Juliana as a maid and at the same time paid her mother, Isabel Pelegrina Tellez, to keep her in the village (that is, in his house).[11] Given, naturally enough, to adolescent moods, she turned out to be lazy, impulsive, good-natured to the point of being what Spaniards call *blanda* (easily put upon), quick-witted, loving amusement and dancing, at which she excelled, food and drink, she was also extremely sensual and, as Gerald eventually discovered, very highly sexed.

It took two and a half months. On Ralph's advice (not Stendhal's, as Gerald wrote),[12] he flirted with other girls in the village to make her jealous. Not till late August did she take the first decisive step of letting him kiss her. One great obstacle was Black María, who was furiously jealous. Twice she sacked Juliana. Finally, he bribed her.* On 10 September, María moved Angela out of Juliana's bed. Gerald oiled the locks. Various further obstacles – his own scruples (or first-night impotence), María's tardiness at leaving the house (he had to threaten to shoot her) – delayed the final seduction until 14 September.[13]

But Gerald then began an eight-month, completely successful,

---

* With an immense sum, according to ancient gossip still retold in the *peublo*. Not censoriously. Gerald's behaviour was totally condoned – 'That's what men are'; the behaviour of Juliana, her mother and María was condoned because of their grinding, terrible poverty.

passionately physical love affair such as he hadn't dreamt was possible. As far as sex went he had, up till then, he realised, just tinkered. He was *astonished*, he told Bunny – and how different his letters on this episode are from those in the past – to find she wanted sex every night. Equally astonished 'to find I practically never fail in this marital duty though I rather shirk the extra *corvée* of two or three times she would like . . . is this marriage, tell me? This *daily* act? Having always thought myself, with reason, nearer impotency than potency . . .' he finds he can make love for hours.[14] Gerald's seduction had been helped because Andalusian folklore had it that Englishmen made marvellous lovers. Folklore was right. Soon the extra *corvées* were being included too.

At the end of the month Ralph and Frances came to stay. Gerald was already talking about giving Juliana a child. While they were there he made love to her in her mother's house. He would arrive at breakfast, sighing, yawning and scratching his flea bites. He had acquired 'an extraordinary little cardboard bellows filled with Keatings Powder, called a *bufador*, which he puffed frantically'.[15] All four made shopping expeditions into the villages for plates and jugs, and went to the sea, where Frances shared Juliana's bathing hut and also got covered with her fleas. 'She was completely natural with him and Gerald relaxed,' Frances remembered. 'And, yes of course, he clearly enjoyed having such a resplendent sex life to show off to Ralph.'

This continued unabated when they'd gone, naturally making work quite impossible. Also, despite bribery, Black María was still explosively jealous. At one point she irritated Gerald so much that, like his father, he hurled a tortilla and plate out of the window.[15] He therefore embarked on manoeuvres of Byzantine complexity and expense and finally managed to replace her with a new María, María Martín – or White María. After that, on 16 October, he left as planned for Seville and work.

2

While in Seville, Gerald was sent a cutting from the *Evening Standard*. Under the headline 'WAR HERO REMEMBERED' it said that 'for his self-sacrifice on our behalf' Marianne von Roeder had left her nephew £7700. In fact, Ralph had told him in July that Tiz had died, though there would be no money until February 1930 (Gerald at once decided to return to England in May). Hugh Brenan, however, stopped his allowance on the spot. Fortunately, Ralph, as usual managing all his practical affairs, obtained advances from the bank.[16]

Gerald ignored the Seville World Exhibition, then in full swing, and spent his days at the Café Central trying fruitlessly to finish *Jack Robinson*. To Bunny and Ralph he reported endless prostitutes and possible VD, but now guilty over Juliana whom he missed, seems only to have slept with one – and this partly because he was irritated by disapproving letters from Helen.[17] But his own letters are almost entirely filled with his need to marry, now becoming obsessional. Juliana? Lily? Or some working-class girl in Seville? In November he went to Granada and, apparently quite seriously, employed a *terciarista* (slang for intermediary) at 500 pesetas to find a wife. He had given himself two years to get one and to finish *Jack Robinson*. Since *Jack Robinson* had thirty pages to go, the priority was emphatic.[18] By 11 December he was back with Juliana.

The picture of them at Yegen in the mild Spanish winter is charming. They rose late, had breakfast, then Gerald read medieval poetry on the roof while Juliana sang and worked downstairs. Sometimes he taught her to read; they quarrelled and made up, scrambled up the mountainside in the warm sun 'where 100 yards away one hears the buzzing of a bee'. In the evening they played *monte*, ate melon dipped in honey, followed by green chartreuse, played his gramophone. 'I am a little in love,' wrote Gerald. He found the indolence and peace extraordinary. Then Juliana would leave him, and Gerald read Pastor's *History of the Popes* for an hour. 'Later on I creep into the big bed in the sala beside Juliana – soft limbs, warm kisses, scent, sweat, whispers – and that is even stranger still.'[19]

Gerald also gave his dances, and at these the young men clustered hungrily around Juliana who, now sexually rampant, flirted openly and provocatively. Spanish boys and girls expect a lot of mutual jealousy and are outraged if it isn't there. Gerald was extremely jealous, nevertheless he shot off in March 1930 to explore Morocco, leaving his friend Paco to guard Juliana, although he knew she attracted him. He travelled to Melilla, Tlemcen, Ben Ousif de Figuig in the Sahara (under water), then back by Melilla and Almería: a month.

On his return, Paco said that as his friend he'd felt it incumbent on him to test Juliana's fidelity. He'd lost no time but had done so the first night. She'd succumbed instantly. Thereafter he'd made love to her every night to keep her from the village boys. In his letters, Gerald said he'd instructed Paco to do this.*[20] Either way (and the first seems more likely) Gerald was angry. On Paco's advice, he pretended he'd consulted a *niño dormido* about her fidelity. This is a child put into a trance by a wise woman which then answers questions (it was still taking place during the *feria* at Ugíjar in 1987). Juliana was astounded, guilty, contrite; Gerald's authority was restored. At the same time he began restlessly to think of London and they started to quarrel. 'I long to be free from . . . the enormous stupidity of love.'[21]

Juliana had often pressed him to give her a child, knowing no doubt that he would support her even if he didn't marry her. Now she pressed again and, on an impulse, after wine at lunch, Gerald suddenly decided to give way – on condition he took the child.

Or thus in *Personal Record*. Yet, as we saw, Gerald had considered this from the start, long before Juliana had thought of it. And her requests, as relayed in his letters, have a distinct air of trying it on. There are other, more cogent, more interesting reasons to suppose the move was really decisively Gerald's. During the war, Ralph had tried to get a girl with child at her request.†[22] Able, at last, to compete with Ralph sexually, Gerald would emulate this too. Also, Gerald was losing more teeth, and his hair was thinning rapidly; but this only increased his jealousy of the *pueblo* young men. On the way back from Morocco he'd shaved off his moustache to look younger.[23] Frances felt at the time that he'd made Juliana pregnant to spite Paco and show he'd won.[22] But, perhaps most fundamental to this deeply romantic man, and at once the least and most tangible reason, was his love of Spain. 'I felt,' he told VSP many years later, 'I was sleeping with all the village girls in Spain, uniting myself to the old agricultural life of the Mediterranean.'[24] But if he did this at all, it had to be done to the fullest. 'The poetry lay in the fucking and I

---

* There is a story in *Don Quixote*, sometimes published separately as *El Curioso Impertinente*, where a man who is jealous of his wife asks a friend to try and seduce her. The friend succeeds. Gerald had certainly read this, but Paco, a semi-educated man, could well have done so too.

† Later he and Frances went and looked, but failed to find it.

gave her a child deliberately because that seemed a more complete and thorough way of fucking her.'[25]

Juliana had a period soon after he got back and, released now from all restraint (their method of contraception had been withdrawal), Gerald flung himself into lovemaking with total abandon. 'Not only did her body excite me enormously,' he told Ralph immediately afterwards, in a letter equally devoid of restraint, 'but her completely shameless character and the violence of her lusts. Physical love is certainly a sort of madness: the satisfaction of one's body soon becomes trifling owing to exhaustion: it is then a kind of rage comes over one's mind and compels one to the most fantastic acts . . . I try to think if there was not something we forgot to do and remember with regret that I never, as she suggested, gave her a beating.'[26]

On 25 April Juliana still not having missed a period,[26] Gerald packed her off to Motril with Paco. He gave her his gramophone and 700 pesetas (two years' wages for María).* Then, on 30 April, he left for Granada and England.

3

Gerald was never to have an experience like Juliana again. Many men, probably most, never have it at all. It is hardly surprising that for the rest of his life whenever he dreamt of returning to his 'youth', it was usually to the age of thirty-six. He was still referring to her when he was ninety-three, as he was dying.[27]

Yet what effect did she have? It would be pleasant to record that having had indisputable proof of his sexual competence and energy, his problems here were at an end. Certainly for a while he was more confident, but deep inhibitions of Gerald's sort are not a few twigs to be swept aside by the first swift flow of the life force; rather do they have the strength of instinct. Gerald's fear of impotence, the event itself, returned – and caused him frustration and pain. But was it all loss? The diverted stream may turn aside into strange and fascinating country which the coarse rushing river completely misses. He himself

---

* Apart from his native generosity, Gerald gave money to Juliana because he was terrified she or her mother would gain a hold over him (or his child) by threatening to reveal he had made love to a minor. Money gave him a measure of control.

would not, could not, forgo the intensities he experienced there. Then, the Nippies in Lyon's Corner Houses, the prostitutes of Regent Street, Soho and Seville were drawn to Gerald precisely because they sensed he didn't want to use them. For the same reason he was able to enjoy numerous 'flirtations' with girls who realised it was not sexually serious, but were none the less stimulated and flattered. And they, like the prostitutes, felt able to confide. His gossip/voyeur/vicarious-living side, whose other roots we have explored, gained tremendous impetus from this suppression, and in valuable ways – he was more amused and amusing, sharper and more observant about people, endlessly speculative and inventive. And this was why he was so interested in the phenomenon of love, why he *fell* in love, and why he was so fascinating about it.*

In many respects Juliana was fundamentally less important than his inheritance, into which he sailed immediately on his arrival in London on 7 May 1930. He discovered that after all the usual deductions he would get £6570 (£178,966)† – together with other sources, £350 (£9534) a year.[28]

Acute poverty was over, but this and his father's neurotic anxiety about money throughout Gerald's childhood had left scars. His generosity remained exceptional. Nor could he ever bother about investments or financial 'management'. But all his life Gerald had to be careful and was frequently over-anxious about money. His archives are full of scraps of paper from all periods covered in sums – the figures touchingly minute. Periodically, there would be a major panic. Ruin! Then, usually, some forgotten source or sum would

---

* From believing that having sex made it impossible for him personally to write, by 1946 in a long essay, 'Falling in Love', Gerald seems to have moved to the position that it was impossible for anyone to write about love or, really, feel it without sexual suppression. For 140 years the poets of love have been those who sublimated or were forced to: 'Shelley, the poet of ejaculatio praecox; Keats – thwarted by illness and rejection; Baudelaire – syphilitic and impotent; Leopardi, a hunchback; Hölderlin, mad; Nerval, impotent; Stendhal, severe sexual problems; Proust, a voyeur and an invalid.' (No doubt the list was a comfort to him.) He also noted that romantic love, depending as it does on difficulty, grew up in Southern Europe where the sexes were strictly segregated – especially so with the spread of Mohammedanism. By the late 1950s and 1960s, Gerald would say of the generation whose freedom so excited him that they seldom experienced intense love. (MSS, MF).

† Figures in brackets, here and elsewhere, represent approximate values at 1990 prices.

surface. But his anxiety in acute crises of any sort was apt to manifest itself financially. When the crisis was death this could shock people.

But he was safe. More substantial legacies were to come. Gerald, of course, recognised that he could never have written the books he did without them but, having never experienced it (though he often pretended he had), he perhaps did not fully appreciate the luxury of never having to write a book he didn't want to, and never having to bother about time or advances or where the next book would come from.

Now, sexual confidence and money confidence, even if temporary, manifested themselves almost at once. He'd no sooner arrived at Edgeworth on 4 June than he began to make advances to a young woman hotelier in Gloucester. Since he could now think of nothing else, he suggested marriage, as he described in a letter to Ralph. '"Is that an offer of your heart, sir?" "No Madam, but of a far more reliable and faithful organ!" "If you prove your case, *accepted*."'[29] There is no evidence the suddenly reliable organ got the chance.

Gerald had arrived at Edgeworth in a brand-new car, bought four days after arriving in England. It was a twenty-four h.p., two-seater Ford convertible with a yellow hood and a dicky. The garage man 'explained the levers' and he set off. Fortunately, his father had taught him the rudiments years before, but it is a measure of the emptiness of 1930s roads that he arrived intact. He even negotiated the steep hill and tricky right-hand turn at Edgeworth, but once in he drove, to Ralph's delight, straight into the corner of the house, removing a large chunk, bending the axle and destroying what he called the buffers.[30] His relations with his father over cars remained fraught. Neither drove well. Gerald had very bad sight, while his father had a malfunctioning eye which eventually would have to be removed. Family history recalls them both returning furious to Edgeworth having booked a reckless driver to discover they'd taken each other's numbers.[31]

In fact, this visit went well. The last time Gerald had been there, after he'd finally left Carrington, Hugh had just refused to let Helen have her brother Ogilvie to stay. Three days later Ogilvie Graham died. Hugh was struck by remorse and thereafter made Herculean and partially successful efforts to be kinder (though his great niece can remember him whistling for Helen if he wanted her).[32] But to Gerald, of whose intelligence he was secretly frightened, he was 'extraordinarily nice and friendly' (though the sight of the convertible caused a wave of panic that Gerald might soon blow his entire inheritance).[33] He was delighted to get his £100 p.a. back. Also he had a new deaf-aid and could hear a little.*

Gerald stayed three weeks, careering about in his car, seeing neighbours (Susie Simon, who was embarrassed when Gerald 'veers towards sex', and tried to convert him to Catholicism)[34] and returned to Radley for the only time in his life – I 'strutted about the place'.[35] He even played tennis.

He spent a weekend with the Johns, where he had a somewhat accident-prone outing with Poppet, Augustus's attractive and amorous daughter. 'His *tiny* car boiled over twice in Savernake Forest, giving me the giggles and irritating Gerald. Then, in a punt on the canal, his pole got stuck and he fell in.' It was the end of what, to the extremely flirtatious sixteen-year-old, had been 'quite a serious flirtation'.[36]

One of the Tomlins† had told him he should visit the writer Theodore Powys at East Chaldon near Weymouth and Lulworth and had given him a letter of introduction. Before that, Gerald spent a week trying to finish *Jack Robinson* in a cottage at Rodcot Bridge on the Thames near Oxford, and then drove down to Dorset and, though he did not know it, his future wife.

---

* Ralph and Frances met Gerald's parents for the only time shortly after this. Frances remembers Helen as 'comfortable, a pleasant, friendly, upper-middle-class woman, with slight red threads in her cheeks. She wore a hat in the house. Hugh Brenan was jerky and jumpy, like Gerald. I remember some electric contraption, and a great many wires sticking out of his ears and rising above his head like a pixie in a pantomime.'

† Tommy in *Personal Record*, Garrow in Gerald's journal. In fact, Bunny was his closest contact with Theodore Powys.

PART III

A Writer at Last

1930–1953

*'John Brenan of Malaga, in the Province of Andalusia,
in the Kingdom of Spain . . . married to Margeret
Gemell, a French lady'*

Extract from a statement dated 6 February 1789,
made by an Irish Justice James Horan, who
received it on oath from one Joseph Brenan of
Crutt, Co Kilkenny. The statement is preserved
among the Brenan Family Papers.

THIRTEEN

Gamel

1

Gerald's desire to get married had received additional and alarmingly practical impetus on 3 June. He learnt then that he had indeed made Juliana pregnant. His agitation made him rush out and pick up a black prostitute, or so he told Frances.[1] He began at once to pay Juliana five times what he'd paid White María, that is 150 pesetas a month;[2] but it also meant that within a year or so, if he kept to his other conditions, he'd be looking after a newly weaned little baby single-handed.

With this no doubt prominent in his mind, he arrived at East Chaldon on 6 July and took rooms with Mrs Way.[3] The hamlet, set in the swelling downland Dorset Hills, is much the same today as then – isolated, tiny, a feeling of remoteness though only ten minutes by car from East Lulworth. Mrs Way's cottage is still there, one of three little flint cottages opposite a farm.

Two days after he arrived Gerald set off for a walk up a steep lane between high hedges. Suddenly, standing 'mysteriously'[3] beside a haystack he saw a beautiful young woman, looking at the ground (for flints, he discovered later). With thick, dark, 'blue black'[4] hair, a white, almost translucent skin, she walked off very slowly – a curious flat-footed walk bent as though pulled over by her noticeably large breasts. Something dreamy and peaceful about her reminded him of his grandmother, the grandmother sympathetic to weeds. Gerald at once wondered if she'd marry him.

2

The young woman, whom Gerald thought must be the Miss Powys he'd heard was in the neighbourhood, was in fact Gamel Woolsey. Her early history is full of gaps.[5] Her father, William Walton Woolsey, had come down to South Carolina from New York after the Civil War, with a wife and three children. (One of these, Gamel's half-brother John Woolsey, became the federal judge who gave the famous decision in 1933 that Joyce's *Ulysses* was not obscene. Gamel was also proud of her aunt Sarah Woolsey, who as Susan Coolidge wrote the bestseller *What Katy Did*.)

In 1871 Woolsey bought a plantation, Breeze Hill, near Aiken. Here his first wife died in 1888, but in 1892 he married a girl of great beauty still in her teens (he was now forty-nine), Elizabeth Gammell. In 1893 his eldest daughter Marie was born and fairly soon after this a second daughter, Elizabeth – later to call herself Gamel.*

It was, according to Gamel, an idyllic Southern childhood. A nanny she adored (black, according to Gerald, white in a 1934 letter), thrilling her with a sixpenny novelette of ruined castles, secrets, a lovely lady Imogen;[6] riding with her passionately adored half-brother Conran (Con). Dreamy, vague, poetical, beautiful, she was also extremely clever and very precocious. She read Frazer's *The Golden Bough* before she was ten. When she first met Christianity, she told Gerald, she 'took it to be just another mythological cult of the Attic-Adonis sort'. She was reading French and Latin fluently by sixteen, and reading a great deal generally – poetry, novels, mythology, fairy stories.

Was it all so perfect? The other half-brothers describe a strange girl they didn't understand and felt wasn't happy with them. Gamel was even more reticent about her past, more intensely secretive about

---

* Gerald's description of his marriage in *Personal Record* is courageous, subtle, and as honest as such accounts can, probably, ever be. But he notes that 'Gamel' is Norse for 'old'. This is a significant tilt away from accuracy. It does mean old, but old also in the sense of ancient lineage – and this was the reason Gamel chose it. The Gammells were an old and distinguished Charleston family, though ruined in the Civil War (and so somehow the more distinguished). Gamel, though not remotely snobbish, the reverse in fact, was proud of them. She herself always had, to people who noticed such things, an air of almost aristocratic distinction.

her inner self, than Carrington. Yet from her childhood or youth came a deep vein of melancholy, compounded by a pervasive guilt. At various times she describes feeling she really deserved to be a slave. Even more profound (and melodramatic) was her identification with the little boy in *The Snow Queen* – a sliver of ice had entered his heart, killing love.

It is impossible to locate the cause of these reactions, though one feels they must have been far back. The nanny, or nannies, no doubt left. There is a suggestion, in some of the poems (the only real clue to Gamel's secret feelings) of guilt about her love for Con. Or if not guilt, then a sense that her deepest emotions had somehow become trapped there. If so, it was another odd correspondence with Carrington. Gerald dated her melancholy much later, from her adolescence, which was certainly difficult.

Her father died when she was fifteen, and her mother returned to Charleston with her two daughters (who disliked each other). Here, when she was twenty, Gamel contracted tuberculosis – she spent a year in a sanatorium and had half a lung removed. Her tuberculosis, which returned, no doubt gave her skin that translucency Gerald had noticed. Gamel herself felt that her melancholy and guilt began before that, when she was seventeen,[7] She fell in love with Edward Jennings, a childhood friend. Shortly afterwards, discovering he was homosexual, he shot himself. And about now her mother began to drink heavily, so horrifying Gamel that when Gerald met her she still wouldn't drink anything at all.

Around 1921, she ran away to New York to become an actress. Here she met a New Zealand journalist, Rex Hunter. A drinker, a bad poet, he was a good-looking, charming and successful womaniser. He seduced Gamel and in 1923 married her. Gamel was pregnant, but soon afterwards had an abortion – or possibly a miscarriage. They lived a poor but bohemian life, first in Patchin Place, later in other apartments in New York, met various writers (among them e. e. cummings, Theodore Dreiser, John Cowper Powys, possibly W. B. Yeats and John Masefield), and Gamel published poetry in little magazines.

She told Gerald much later that Rex Hunter only really wanted or thought about sex. Certainly, the heroine in her entirely autobiographical first novel is often exhausted by her husband's insatiable passion – but not only exhausted. This book, and more particularly her early poems, reveal a delight in physical love which is both strong, warmly and sensuously described – and at the same time curiously detached:

> Feeling this passion in the flesh
> Is beautiful beyond the dust,
> And men have toiled long lives apart
> For things not half so fair as lust . . .[8]

But Gamel did not love Rex, and by 1926 they had drifted apart.* She returned to 5 Patchin Place, that cul-de-sac famous in literary history, and took the apartment below John Cowper Powys. Here, in 1927, she met his brother Llewelyn, who was at Patchin Place while he did a spell as visiting critic for the *New York Herald Tribune*, and Llewelyn's wife, Alyse.

Alyse Gregory, beautiful, highly intelligent, an early and strong believer in feminine independence, indeed in personal independence generally, was then forty-three. She had met Llewelyn while she was managing editress of *The Dial*, the foremost literary magazine of the period; met him, published his work, fell in love and, despite her principles, in 1924 married him. Her principles were to some extent salvaged by the fact that Llewelyn was having an affair and trying to have a baby with a Betty Marsh, and this, for Alyse agonising three-part affair, continued till the end of 1926.

Llewelyn Powys, also forty-three, was the youngest of that extraordinary clan, Welsh only in name and in fact rooted in the West Country, whose joint lives now get far more attention than their books. With his ravaged good looks, great mane of greying hair, almost euphoric high spirits and energy (apparently a common symptom of late tuberculosis), his passion for literature and life and his brilliant theatricality with a magnificent theme – his defiance of death – he was both thrilling and warming to the lonely, lovely 'little poetess' as his brother John called Gamel. They also shared consumption – the poet's disease. Alyse could not have children and, though of course total sexual freedom was allowed, extra to it was Llewelyn's right to have a child. Betty Marsh was about to be repeated.

By the end of 1927 Gamel and Llewelyn, with Alyse's slightly irritated encouragement, were lovers. Quite soon Alyse realised

---

* In 1934 Gamel wrote, 'I can remember books I have read and plays I have watched far better than four years of married life' (Gamel to Llewelyn Powys, undated but probably April 1934).

uneasily it was not to be a casual affair. Gamel's poetry – with its sensuousness, its romantic themes and images, its nostalgia and sensitivity – not only impressed Llewelyn, it moved him. Despite her seeming pliancy, he found she was essentially ungraspable. 'You twist and shape me to your will,' she wrote in a poem, 'Immutable':

> I bend to all the moods that pass;
> But I am proud and secret still,
> And but more truly what I was.

She fascinated him, and when he and Alyse left for Europe and Palestine in April 1928 he was more than half in love with her.

Alyse was nervous, but her feelings were complicated because she was almost as attracted to Gamel as Llewelyn was. In the autobiographical novel she was writing at the time – *King Log and Lady Lea* – the heroine, after suggesting her husband has an affair, deserts him and lives with the other woman in a covert lesbian relationship.*

Soon after Llewelyn and Alyse had reached Holland, Llewelyn heard that Gamel was pregnant. He was thrilled – but didn't dare tell Alyse for a month, when she was devastated. Worse was to follow. In October, they learnt from John Powys that, after an accident in a taxi and because of her tubercular history, doctors had insisted on an abortion. But, moved by Gamel's desperate unhappiness, John begged Llewelyn to 'give, O great master, the wench *another chance*'. Alyse's journal shows her pain – torn between fear of losing Llewelyn, her determination to leave him free, and her pity for this 'generous, sensitive, deep-natured girl . . . so passionately in love with him'.[4] But she agreed.

In May 1929 they all three arrived more or less simultaneously at East Chaldon. (Powyses had been gradually colonising East Chaldon since 1904. It was Powys *territory*.) Alyse and Llewelyn went into their old coastguard cottage White Nothe (sometimes written 'Nose'), one of a little line of cottages on a cliff above the sea; Gamel into lodgings twelve minutes away. A difficult situation, but at first made possible by the generosity of both women.

They visited each other every day. Gamel devoted herself to Llewelyn; collecting worked flints for his collection, mending his

---

* I am indebted for this observation, and others in this section, to *The Brothers Powys*, the excellent family biography by Richard Percival Graves, London 1983.

clothes, listening to him read poetry. Both women worried about his health. Llewelyn would have attacks, then recover – and set out on huge dramatic walks, from which he might return with the blood bubbling in his lungs or splashed bright red on his handkerchief. But for Gamel, if fraught, it was an enchanted summer of happiness. They made love in her lodgings, they made love on the Downs. One midsummer night, on some sacks under a cedar tree, he reminded her later, 'You told me you would love me for ever until you died.'⁹

By July, Gamel was pregnant again. Yet still they managed to co-exist, still Alyse remained content. 'I thought of his spirit not dying, that eager spirit that I loved, so I accepted her with tenderness too; this brave and beautiful girl, who accepted *me* with such generosity.'⁴ Above all, she felt that Llewelyn loved her no less. About mid-August, the blow fell. They were having supper with Gamel when she told them she had been having temperatures and sweating at night. A doctor had diagnosed signs of consumption and, she said, with tears streaming down her face, had ordered an abortion.

They travelled up to London and stayed with Bertie Powys. John joined them and Gamel, now really an honorary Powys, went miserably into hospital – looking, thought Alyses, in her pathos, with her transparent skin, almost magically beautiful. Llewelyn was distraught; in an agony over Gamel, desperate that he was to lose his second child. He was beyond comfort. 'We are sundered,'⁴ wrote Alyse, plunging towards despair.

On their return Llewelyn was more tender towards Gamel, more passionate, than ever. He saw her continually, taking her out to meals, on expeditions. It was a winter of wild storms and gales. They made love in potting sheds and barns; in one, sheltering from the icy hail, 'It was like making love in a cathedral.'⁹ Alyse was now bitterly unhappy. Desperately fighting her furious jealousy, loathing herself for it, seeing her husband and his mistress draw closer and closer, she increasingly thought of suicide. 'Only my death can free us – all three.'⁴

In fact, unknown to her, Gamel's feelings were steadily undergoing a profound change. One factor was mundane, but not insignificant. All those concerned in this drama refer to Gamel as a girl. This gives an inaccurate impression. She told Gerald she was twenty-nine. Her and Rex's passport of 1924 says that she was born in 1897. In fact, the real date (which she never told Gerald) was almost certainly

1895.* She was still young-looking and beautiful, but she was thirty-five – her attempts to have a child were probably at first as much on her own behalf as Llewelyn's. But for fifteen years she had led a life of turbulence and poverty (she had a minute income of £125 a year). She now longed for peace as much or more than Gerald and it must have been abundantly clear she was not going to find it at East Chaldon.

Then, beyond this, Gamel had an extremely tender heart. She was acutely conscious of Alyse's sufferings, and appalled by her part in them. Llewelyn thought of nothing else but his own child; Gamel, after a miscarriage and two traumatic abortions, all shortly spaced, now dreaded and seems to have prevented yet another pregnancy. But without that, their love had no *raison d'être*. There was no longer any justification for taking the husband of someone she now loved almost as much as she did him.

By April 1930, Llewelyn was aware that her love was waning. In June, she left her lodgings near White Nothe and took rooms a good half an hour away in East Chaldon. Alyse saw this 'as a device to lure him into spending longer hours with her'.[4] In reality, it was the reverse – a decisive step in distancing herself.

Gerald, unaware of the recent move, saw her full suitcase and thought she hadn't unpacked for a year. He took it as evidence she didn't want to stay, and psychologically he was right. Gamel was not strong enough to extricate herself from a situation that had become impossible, painful and destructive; or, more precisely, she was strong enough, but to initiate wasn't her method. It seems clear, from the speed with which events moved, that when Gerald saw her slowly looking for flints on that 9 July, she was desperate to find someone who would help her escape.

---

* This according to various papers left by Kenneth Hopkins e.g. 'Bertrand Russell and Gamel Woolsey' (privately printed), Warren House Press 1985. He died before he could finish the research for his biography of Gamel, but where I can check his facts they are accurate. I therefore follow him here and usually elsewhere in this section. Gerald himself always thought Gamel was born in 1897, as an undated letter to Hopkins makes clear: 'the poet Garcia Lorca was also born in 1897 though he always gave . . . [the date] as 1900. Poets are obsessed by time.'

3

Gerald met Gamel at Theodore Powys' on 10 July. He then had to go to London for three days, but on 14, 15, 16, 17 and 18 July he had her to tea and they talked into the evening (fortunately their rooms were in adjoining cottages).

It seems likely that Gerald now decided in earnest to try and marry her. After that very first tea, on the 14th, he wrote to Carrington for the first time in two years. Perhaps now, he suggested, they could meet again. He didn't mention Gamel, but Carrington guessed at once what was up.[10] Such swiftness meant a certain fragility of decision and on 18 July he asked Hope down to buttress it. To his immense relief (and a mark of how much, still, Gerald valued the opinion of his old mentor) Hope approved.[11]

Confirmation came with her work: *Middle Earth*, a manuscript collection of her poetry, recently sent to Simon and Schuster with Llewelyn's backing, and an unfinished novel *Mariana* (later *One Way of Love*). Gamel's skill as a poet came too close to Gerald's most precious ambition and not until she was dead could he see (or admit) that she had a genuine talent. But the novel was different.* Here

---

* The nineteenth century moves in Gamel's verse – Tennyson, Shelley, even, in her sonnets, Keats – but it has been fully absorbed. Quite often she reminds one of the de la Mare of *The Traveller*, when at his evocative, echoing, plangent best. But she had a true voice of her own, a private and peculiar view,and at her own best, as in *Love that Moves the Stars*, could hold her joy in the beauty of life and love, and her painful awareness of mortality and transience in perfect balance. Her extraordinary technical skill alone means that the worst of her poems are better than the best of Gerald's. For a fuller account see Glen Cavaliero's introduction to the *Collected Poems* (privately printed), Warren House Press 1984.

One Way of Love is the story of Mariana Clare (a doubly poetic name) and largely about her affair with Alan, which more or less exactly duplicates Gamel's marriage to Rex. One notices – and Gerald would have done so particularly – the dreamy sensuousness of the writing about love-making and lust (a favourite word); the sensitivity to nature and sympathy for the poor; the narcissistic, physically self-aware, romantic, melancholy, little-girl heroine tending to self-pity; and the strong sense of place and time, time holding her like a vessel, time passing and having passed. Her writing is fluent and easy and not unlike that of Willa Cather, the Cather of *My Mortal Enemy*: the same innocent eye, the selection, above all the cadences and economy of the prose. At the end, it is the humorous, almost light-hearted acceptance of the heroine that lifts the book. Her dilemma is to be loved, to

were clarity, beauty of image, penetration, proof of a creature of 'exquisite sensitivity' but with 'a mind sufficiently cold and exact to record it'. Gerald was bowled over, carried by the magic carpet of words, 'into the hidden and most essential part of Gamel's mind'.[11] He was also, quite simply, excited by the (for the period) frank descriptions of love-making, of which these were many. He also thought these among the best written passages.[11]

The writer's key to a woman's heart (or bed) is not dancing but the promise to get her novel or poems published. Gerald at once wrote to Bunny to say, among many other superlatives, that he'd discovered an extraordinary and 'important work of art'. He promised to bring both novel and poetry as soon as he could.

Gerald's discovery of Gamel's writing convinced him he wasn't making a mistake. He at once decided, as he had with Carrington and 14 Great James Street, that the best way to win her was to get the perfect house. The one they found (Ivy Cottage Farm, Langdon Herring) was let, but it was by the 'melancholy waters' of the Fleet below this substantial square building that Gerald kissed her for the first time and that evening, 30 July, she said she would live with him.

Gerald now sent two short, ebullient letters announcing his engagement to Ralph and Carrington (and so to the whole of London); but upon Gamel there descended a deluge – poems, notes, letters: 'O my darling, my sweetheart, all my life and health and my heart are yours . . .'[12] She spent the night with Alyse and Llewelyn, and Gerald walked over to gaze at the lighted cottages and 'remembered Wordsworth's poem to Lucy and thought "if only that light was Gamel's!"' He scribbled a Lucy poem of his own by the moonlight.*

But it was that night that Llewelyn, who had been watching with growing horror the events unfolding so rapidly before him, told Gamel she must tell Gerald about him. The following night, as she and Gerald drove back from an expedition to Stonehenge and Avebury, she did so.

---

be made love to, yet not to be able to love in return. Will it always be so? Well – so be it. It is one way, at least. She and her new lover go up to bed on an undefined note of hope, 'a feeling of secret happiness in the air, of adventure about to begin'.

* 'Is that her window? That her light?
  And is she breathing, sleeping there?
  The flowers that day-long scent the air
  How much more rich their scent by night! (MSS, MF)

Gerald had guessed, he says in *Personal Record*, something of the situation, but hadn't supposed a battered wreck like Llewelyn capable of attracting anyone. Now he learnt that he was wrong. While they sped through the darkness, Gamel told him the full story – of her love affair, the pregnancy and abortion, her collapse and, since then, increasing despair and loneliness. Yet it was not quite the full story – she concealed the earlier part of the love affair in New York, nor did she tell him she'd come over specifically to have Llewelyn's child.[13]

Gerald was deeply moved. He stopped the car and kissed her, but then, struck by a terrible suspicion, asked her if she was coming to him simply to escape. With tears pouring down her cheeks, Gamel said no – she was attached to Llewelyn, worried about his health, but everything was over between them. It was clear that she would marry Gerald.

He spent the next three days – 7 to 9 August – in London. He delivered Gamel's manuscript to Bunny (Bunny's comments on the novel were favourable, though he thought Gerald's disparagement of the poetry 'very unjust'. But he was really far more concerned with what he considered Gerald's own 'masterpiece', *Jack Robinson*, a few more pages of which were also delivered).[14] Gerald bought scent, soap, tea, food for Gamel and also talked about her incessantly at various lunches, teas and suppers with Ralph and Frances, and Helen.

Meanwhile, Llewelyn, in a torment about 'Mr Brenan', went to see Gamel. Alyse had promised she would let him go, but Gamel said she had 'practically' decided to marry Gerald. She also almost certainly said (it is the theme of all her subsequent letters to him) that it would make no difference to 'their love'. An ambiguous promise, but one which Llewelyn would probably have taken to mean that they could continue to sleep together (as Betty Marsh had done after her marriage). Few men, however, who pretend total sexual freedom seem able in practice to tolerate it for anyone but themselves. Llewelyn had so far acted towards both his women with gentle, considerate but none the less total selfishness and now, 'in desperate passion', he said, at the climax of a very painful scene, that he would have to leave for America immediately. He and Alyse had gone before Gerald got back.

Under intense stress, Gamel sent Gerald a 'reserved' letter, upon receipt of which all his old agitation returned and he panicked. In a frantic, passionate reply he begged her to leave Llewelyn, to send a telegram, no – *telephone* at once; 'I love you more than anything.'[15] Then he rushed down to East Chaldon. But Gamel had begun to collapse. Her temperature rose, she spat blood, and haemorrhaged, she thought from the abortion a year before. It was as if Llewelyn was at work in her. Gertrude Powys, the handsome masculine sister Gerald had confused with Gamel, took her into Chydyock, the remote farmhouse half an hour above the village.

Gerald himself raced back to London and returned that evening with Dr Ellie Rendell and a Fortnum's hamper (it seemed to him the Powyses fed Gamel entirely on lettuce). Ellie Rendell advised rest, then specialist treatment in a sanatorium – and in fact a sanatorium was quickly found in Norfolk by Gertler, via Carrington.[16] They waited a week, then Gerald hired a Daimler to carry Gamel to London. It was the start of a nine-month honeymoon (originally planned for Ireland), the first six weeks of which were to be extremely fraught.

4

While he was in London Gerald bought Gamel some clothes. This was a far more significant move than might appear.

One of the things that had begun to delight him was to discover in her an ironic, pessimistic wit, a clear intelligence, totally at odds with the murky, pseudo-religious, mumbo-jumbo world of archaicism, neo-platonism and magic he supposed surrounded the Powyses. Now this world returned in virulent form. Gertrude Powys had patiently explained to him at Chydyock – something he clearly hadn't gathered – that Gamel was considered almost sacred to the Powyses – their muse, their holy woman. Her love with Llewelyn was also sacred. Vows had been made to the moon. Now Gerald would help her recover, and she could continue with her holy love. Once again he was in a Carrington situation. Though managing temporarily to suppress what he felt, Gerald was appalled.

At the same time all Gamel's nascent humour and lightness vanished. Sick, still shattered and intensely guilty after her scene with Llewelyn, she relapsed into apathy and silence. It became more important than ever to Gerald that she should win the approval of his friends, who were all no doubt gossiping furiously over what must have seemed Gerald's typically extreme and precipitate moves. By October, Carrington had heard 'Ten different accounts' of Gamel – and the feeling is, not all favourable.[17] Her clothes! Frances remembers a bright purple skirt covered in big woollen flowers, 'as 'twere a mead', said Gamel whimsically (she loved Chaucer). Frances said they got much better once Gerald started buying them* – something he said irritably he never did.[18]

Certainly he didn't now, because when they arrived at Rodwell, on the way to Norfolk, for a disastrous test weekend with Helen, Roger and Molly MacCarthy, he noticed at once, and again, how wrong her clothes were. She hardly spoke, or when she did, got it wrong with further whimsicalities: 'puts one in mind of old folk tales', in a Southern accent still so broad it reduced Molly to hysterics.[19] He himself didn't help by complaining loudly if privately to Helen how self-centred and selfish Gamel was.[20] (Gerald all his life never seemed to regard verbal disloyalty as in the slightest degree significant – sometimes the pressure of his feelings compelled expression; sometimes, no doubt, he knew he still *felt* loyal; and also, the act of disloyalty, as a form of indiscretion, often seemed to excite him. Gerald liked to shock.) When they left, taking her cue but no doubt injecting a certain malice, Helen said that if Gerald found Gamel 'rather boring' he must remember it was only the tuberculosis.[21]

Boring – the greatest, indeed the only Bloomsbury sin. On the instant, Gerald found his love draining away. Furious with Gamel for existing, with himself for getting into this situation, guilty, he tried without success to get rid of his feelings in a raging exchange of letters with Helen. It was a heatwave August, and for days he felt like Byron on his honeymoon[21] – except that, when they stayed at the Crown and Anchor Hotel at Trimmingham, he now discovered with familiar pain that he was totally impotent with Gamel. They arrived at the nearby Mundesley Sanatorium on 1 September.† It

---

* All newcomers go through such tests, of course, and for women clothes are often the litmus. When Frances came into Bloomsbury, Carrington wished she would dress more to her taste (Carrington to Gerald, 10 February 1924).

† Both are still there. The big, wooden sanatorium at Mundesley, embedded in a golf course, has been added to and is now Mundesley Hospital. The Crown and Anchor stands derelict on its cliff, roof fallen in, the North Sea winds blowing through its broken windows.

immediately started to rain, and did so for the rest of the month. At the same time, huge letters began to arrive for Gamel from America. Miserably aware of Gerald's feelings, still weak, she retired deeper and deeper into herself – thinking, Gerald gloomily imagined, entirely about Llewelyn. To comfort himself, he picked up an attractive, twenty-six-year-old Chilean visiting an older 'protector' at the sanatorium. They kissed, but she wouldn't go to bed with him.

And yet, even at this height of their crisis, his determination to marry Gamel 'would not and could not alter'.[21] Why? They had in fact only been living together for about ten days. This determination needs exploring – since forty years of married life were based on it. One of Gamel's most striking characteristics was the way she agreed with what anyone said. It became a standing joke among their friends. Yet this amiable response was not simple. Partly, she had copied the reaction from John Powys (who combined it, unlike Gamel, with flattery). There was a degree of pride in it, even arrogance – why bother? Also, she hated her own opinions being disagreed with, regarding it as a form of personal criticism, and so hid them. But it was linked to another side of her complex character, one she was fully aware of, and this was a deep vein of passivity, an inability or reluctance to act or decide herself. Undue dependence on others is another classic symptom of TB. But there was a psychological element as well, connected with guilt. Like her heroine Mariana, she let events, with her 'fatal passivity', carry her – and the implication was, if they carried her to disaster she deserved it.

Gerald's strong desire to protect had first been aroused by the girls and prostitutes he'd helped in London. Now, his enormous energy, his capacity for pity, responded eagerly to all this (as did other people. Frances often noticed the effortless way Gamel got people to do things for her).[22] But he must also have sensed his will would not be frustrated with Gamel as it had been with Carrington.

But it was not just that he knew he'd get his own way with Gamel. In *Personal Record* he said he stayed because he couldn't leave someone so ill and so helpless. To which temporary imperative, he added his deep desire to settle down. To see this in a different perspective it is necessary to look at the recent events through Gamel's eyes. Gerald felt Gamel had been like Tennyson's Mariana, waiting to be rescued by a white knight. He was the knight. (Actually,

Tennyson's Mariana knows she has nothing to wait for but death.)
This is not the whole picture; nor was it Gamel's.

So gentle and sensitive had she found Gerald that at first she
thought he was homosexual.[23] To her he was a poet who came and
stood outside her window in the moonlight – and she was upset by
the, no doubt understandable, frostiness of his reception by the East
Chaldon Powyses. 'It must have been difficult for a proud and shy
creature to be treated as we have all treated him,' she wrote to
Llewelyn.[24] That tender, excitable, vulnerable, emotional self, hidden
years before, which Carrington had stung into life and then crushed
by her attraction/rejection system, Gamel called up by the calmness
and peacefulness Gerald had sensed instinctively the moment he'd
seen her. And it was this very deep need she responded to. Llewelyn
had often noticed, and enjoyed, her strong maternal side.[25] Bom-
barded throughout the honeymoon by desperate letters, and equally
desperate ones from Alyse begging her to take Llewelyn – Gamel
wrote explaining why she could not leave Gerald: 'All his grown life
he has been lonely. After dusk he cannot bear me out of his sight. If
I go onto the balcony and am out of the room for five minutes, Gerald
will follow me. It is not love though he loves me very much; it is
necessity.'[26] Despite all his later irritation and impatience, he was still
displaying this need thirty years later.*

Gamel's own feelings are more opaque. Her need to agree and
please was not superficial. To Alyse, she insisted that she would
never, and had never wished to, take Llewelyn. His passionate
letters, often recalling their love-making – 'Your large lovely breasts
with the exquisite hazelnut nipples I know so well'[27] – clearly tore
her. For a while – Gerald was quite right – she seems to be running
two love affairs. But it was, in a sense, for both Gerald and Gamel,
an arranged marriage where what each was having to arrange were
their own emotions – and perhaps this is not so uncommon. Gradually, her letters to Llewelyn become cooler: their love was eternal,

---

* Not till 1949 and another major crisis in their marriage did Gerald start
saying Gamel had become his mother. But he was aware even at the start there was
a much stronger than usual maternal element in his attraction to her (one notes, in
this context, that both Gamel and his own mother were unusually and noticeably
submissive to their husbands). In an early draft of *Personal Record* he called his
relations with Gamel 'Oedipal' but, along with several other extremely self-
revelatory passages, he later decided to cut it out (MSS, Texas).

unique – but spiritual, secret; she explained her continuing and intense guilt over hurting Alyse; letters which first began 'My darling' and ended 'I love you I love you', came by infinite and skilful gradations to 'My dearest Lulu . . . with love from Gamel.'

As for helplessness – so far from helpless was she that when they left Mundesley and came to Wells-next-the-Sea on 2 October she had decided to leave Gerald, feeling that he did not want her. Only his despair, his now reiterated love, won her round. She promised she did not love Llewelyn, and at once Gerald's own love rushed back. He found he could make love to her. At last they could begin their honeymoon.

5

Gerald and Gamel were based at Wells-next-the-Sea, that little Norfolk port as charming now as it was then, for two months. Smug, 'shamelessly married' letters to Ralph described their life. They worked in the mornings – Gamel at her novel and the proofs of *Middle Earth* (she'd heard of its acceptance on arriving at Mundesley); Gerald, after eighteen months' turbulence, at last concentrating on *Jack Robinson* again; in the afternoons they walked; in the evenings read or corrected the morning's work – setting a lifetime's pattern. People came to stay: Bunny and Ray, Gertrude Powys, Bertie Powys.

Fat letters arrived from America, but now Gerald brought them in with a smile. (Somewhat forced. But though he still complained about this correspondence, he himself was conducting a much larger, secret and often flirtatious one with Carrington at the same time. He wrote three times as many letters to her as Gamel did to Llewelyn.)

Gerald, fizzing with energy, continually shot up to London: to see Ralph and Frances, see Carrington, go to the oculist (he had a slightly unusual astigmatism), and to arrange Gamel's divorce.*

In November they toured the Yorkshire Dales (and Haworth and the Lake District, including Watendlath. In a sudden agony of sadness he wrote to Carrington – do you remember? do you remember . . .?)

---

* This would have necessitated a visit to America, judged too expensive. In the end, they pretended it had taken place, putting, on Rex Hunter's advice, an advertisement to this effect in some American papers. Their own marriage, which took place years after they had lost touch with Rex, was in fact bigamous.

One letter was so indiscreet she burnt it.[28] 'Your beauty and charm filled my whole mind then: now nothing will ever *fill* that ramshackle place again.'[29] Odd, and perhaps significant, that he did not say 'heart'. At Watendlath he made another marvellous discovery about Gamel. She had extraordinary stamina. She could walk eighteen to twenty miles a day with him, like him drinking from the streams.[34]

From here, too, he wrote and told his father about Gamel. 'The news appears to stun him.'[31] Gerald told Gamel he'd kill his parents if they didn't like her, but he needn't have worried. Their week's visit to Edgeworth on 6 December was a triumph. His mother felt a kinship. Her own mother had been an American from the South. But in any case she soon came to love Gamel, as did Hugh. Gamel brought out his gentle side and, several times ill at Edgeworth, she used to say, as we noted earlier, that she'd rather have Hugh as a nurse than anyone.[32] But from the first he had 'a presentiment' that the marriage would make for everyone's happiness (even Gamel's mother, an alcoholic for years, had apparently had some sort of hazy vaguely favourable dream).[33] But above all Hugh Brenan detected *class*: 'Centuries of breeding,' he intoned in an ecstasy, 'have gone to make her mouth and chin.' He showered money on them: £100 on the marriage; 'And when my book comes out (malicious man) an allowance.' He even offered Gerald a horse.[34]

The moment they separated (Gamel had to go to East Chaldon to get ready for Italy) Gerald longed for her. 'Every day I get more impatient, every day I miss you more . . . And look forward to . . . ing you very very very very very much indeed, my dearest sweetheart your Gerald.'[35]

And suddenly, at last, Gamel began to feel for him. 'I am sitting by the fire in my bedroom, and by the candle's light writing these words to tell you that I love you. My love for you is beginning (more every day) to break its restraints and press towards you. Suddenly, like the tide at Wells, it passed some barrier and is flooding all the country. I love you. It is not like any feeling I have ever had before. It is a strange new thing.'[36]

In eight days she sent him four letters from East Chaldon (one begins 'My dearest child . . .'); she dreams about him, longs for him, and reassures him, perhaps not a hundred percent accurately, that 'It is curious, Gerald, that I do not seem to think of the past here particularly'. Each letter has more xxxxxxs. The last has twenty. 'Mine are multiplication marks too.'[37]

On 23 December, pretending to 'his people' that Gertrude was coming as chaperone, they sailed for France and Gerald drove them south for Christmas at Chartres.

6

On the whole of their five-and-a-half-month trip together, there was only one major scene and that took place at Aix, soon after Chartres.

Gerald went into their hotel room and found a letter Gamel had written to Llewelyn lying open. It was a love letter. 'I could put up with that,' he wrote untruthfully in *Personal Record*, but she had also said she was very unhappy and hating her journey. In fact she'd been in continuous high spirits, particularly enjoying Gerald's medical treatment – expensive food and wine in celebrated restaurants. There was a confrontation. Gamel said he'd no right to read her letters. In any case, if Llewelyn knew she was happy he'd be so upset he could have a haemorrhage. Gerald did not yet appreciate the extent of her need to please people and agree with them – nor how she hated anyone to disagree with her. But, he says, he never again 'had a serious quarrel with her. When annoyed, I merely withdrew into myself and she did the same.' But this aspect of their marriage – the inability to have rows – was also partly of Gerald's making and probably derived from his hatred of his parent's marital fighting. It meant he had to express the irritations of married life in another way: his method was in comments to friends.

He was now still bitterly hurt, however, and also furious. Turning, as he did in such circumstances, into his father, he refused to speak to her. He didn't speak for a whole day, from Aix to Nice to pick up letters, then to Portofino. And he was still so upset when they arrived at Amalfi that he went to bed with 'flu, also now worrying about his growing baldness.[38] Gamel herself worried about him. He was tired, feverish and much thinner – all, she realised, because of jealousy.[39]

He very soon recovered. The only thing that excited Gerald as much as love was travel. Travel excited his passion for learning, which he could now satisfy in a direct and immediate way. And to his delight, Gamel shared his passion. Together, they *studied* the country – its art and literature, its history, archaeology and language. They read, not just *Guides Bleues* and Baedekers, but numerous books on Etruscan and Roman civilisations, and the debts to Greece. Each afternoon in the Hotel Minerva on the Capo di Sorrento, to which they'd moved on 3 February, they learnt Italian and then read Dante and Thucydides. They spent three days at Pompeii, and hours in every gallery. Gerald was even interested in the politics. Apparently Mussolini was 'very good . . . but we have no opportunities of discovering what is really going on'.[40]

Gamel shared another of Gerald's passions. 'I am one of those absurd people,' he said to Frances once, 'who can get a thrill from saying – here the Sibyl sat, here Virgil had his villa, this is the site of Anermas!'[41] Is it so absurd? Surely that imaginative leap, that empathy essential for profound historical writing, however much it is later informed or altered by scholarship, begins somewhere here. In 1968 Hugh Trevor-Roper wrote and told Gerald he looked on him 'as my ideal historian – you *see* the past in the present, and the present in the past, imaginatively . . .'[42]

Walking, studying and reading in the afternoons, the mornings were devoted to writing. Gerald struggled with *Jack Robinson*; Gamel finished off her novel with, to him, astonishing rapidity. *Middle Earth* had come out and the mildly erotic nature of some of Gamel's verse had elicited a passionately erotic, almost pornographic response from 'Imogen', who seemed to live in Oxford.[43] Imogen's letters were to weave a slightly batty thread through the next twenty years.*

It was a fertile interlude in other ways. On 25 January Gerald heard that Juliana had had a daughter on 7 January. She looked like him and was to be called Elena after his mother. Then soon after this

---

* Gamel was unable to answer these letters, especially as they became more and more strongly pornographic. Gerald did so, at first with some excitement. But Imogen was indefatigable. Ralph was called in, and Frances remembers him red in the face composing answers. Then friends had to help. Finally Burgo, the Partridge's son, took over. Janetta Parladé can remember the stir at Ham Spray when a matchbox full of Imogen's pubic hairs arrived. They were red. But in the mid-Fifties Imogen nearly slipped up. A letter arrived with the address imperfectly snipped off. Heywood Hill, who was staying, was able to deduce that it came from the house of Lady Cynthia Asquith – but whether from a resident or a guest discreet enquiry then (and since) was unable to discover. A little later, a letter came from 'Genevieve', 'I am Imogen's sister. She has been unwell.' The letters stopped.

Gamel told him that she was pregnant. This made marriage essential in order not to shock Hugh and Helen (quite apart from the £100). For his parents' consumption, Gerald told Blair they were going to marry in two months.[40]

On 22 March they set off south, and now Gerald discovered yet another thing in common – Gamel shared (or seemed to share) his pleasure in the ample opportunities travel offered, especially in cheap and squalid accommodation, for acute discomfort. They had, in fact, moved to the Hotel Minerva for its stinking 'feet' lavoratories, which meant it was much cheaper and empty of tourists. Now she passed a sterner test. The south of Italy was still very primitive. There was no road to Taranto and Metaponto, the site of Pythagoras' last days, and the car was put on a rail truck. The only house on the bare plain was the station-master's. Their room had no door, was inhabited by bugs, rats and chickens, and was so filthy they didn't dare undress. For supper – beans. 'This,' wrote Gerald wittily, 'in a place where the founder of mathematics had said that a man who could eat beans was capable of devouring his grandmother.'

In fact, it seems to have been Gamel who insisted they saw the old Greek city sites, including Sybaris, about which Gerald was eventually to write. Freed from the enormous strain of being with Llewelyn and Alyse, of poverty, of decision, Gerald's letters resound with astonishment at Gamel's energy and gaiety. Returning to Naples on 1 April, they made another trip to Paestum and got to grips with the past in the most literal way possible. Among those deserted temples still set in marshland as in eighteenth-century illustrations, they found Roman and Greek coins, an amber bead, Roman glass and 'a beautiful silver ring with a cameo in it'. Gamel was 'out of her mind with excitement'. Not surprisingly, added Gerald drily, after an archaeological diet consisting solely of 'uninteresting flints'.[44]

By 11 April they'd reached Rome on the slow journey home. They were getting increasingly worried about getting married. It had so far proved impossible. Now they decided on a bold step – they would marry themselves. They chose the Church of Santa Maria d'Aracoeli on the Capitoline Hill, once a temple of Juno. Climbing the fifteen steps, they held hands before the altar and Gerald put a ring on her finger: 'With this ring I marry you for better, for worse, in sickness and health, till death do us part.' Gamel did the same.

And that, Gerald ends lightly, was the only ceremony he and

Gamel ever underwent – except that later Gamel changed her name by deed poll. 'For true marriage, as I understand it, is made in the heart.' Moving, romantic, convention-defying – but not entirely true. Gerald and Gamel in fact got married in Hampstead Registry Office on 15 August 1947, in circumstances we will examine then.

Unfortunately, the main reason for the marriage in Rome also vanished there. Gamel had another miscarriage. It must have been bitterly disappointing for her. The repeated efforts to have children make it clear she wanted them. (Her heroine Mariana did too, 'even many children'.) No doubt Gerald was very worried for her, but his letters, apart from general gloom and now money worries, do not say what he felt on his own behalf – probably a good deal of relief.

On 19 May they left Rome for Assisi, where they met Roger and Helen. The quarrel had been made up and Helen put forth all her charm, 'captivating' Gamel.[45] But Gerald was never again to sit on her bed talking till 2.30 in the morning about his love affairs.

As they travelled back, Gerald and Gamel shopped for their new home, wherever that might be: cloth, pottery, rugs and furniture.* In June they crossed France, visiting all the places where Gerald had fought in the war. He found that he could remember very little, except his terror that he might prove a coward.

The long journey had brought out the best in them and Gerald and Gamel were always happiest when travelling together. They arrived back in England on 7 June 1931 to begin married life in earnest – a start where Gerald, at least, was once again to be racked for a while by agonising uncertainties.

---

* Jaime Parladé, who later sold things for Gerald, remembers in particular an eighteenth-century baroque Venetian desk, decorated in coral (clearly, from its small size, a present for Gamel); from Lombardy a fine late seventeenth- or early eighteenth-century chest of drawers inlaid in ivory, and a lovely eighteenth-century folding screen, bought, as Gerald told him, quite cheaply. He had shown extraordinary skill and taste, since they are all now collectors' pieces.

FOURTEEN

Marriage

1

Gerald and Gamel reached East Chaldon, to which Llewelyn and Alyse had also fairly recently returned, on 11 June.[1] Ralph and Frances noted that he was already 'obsessed' with house-hunting. He also showed them photographs of Gamel naked 'in various postures' in an Italian hotel bedroom.[2]

The respectable newly-weds then spent a week at Edgeworth, to which from now on they were invited frequently. (Hugh was not just attracted to Gamel, he loved her agreeing side. Rhoda, Blair's wife, had a strong will and always disagreed.) Soon after this they went to Ham Spray. The visit was not a success. Gerald was extremely anxious that it should be, Gamel was nervous, and Carrington, to put it mildly, was not helpful. There was a paper game and she suddenly said, 'What's this? I don't recognise it? Is it a camel?' It was taken as a reference to Gamel and produced silence, then nervous giggling.[3] Nor was her wedding present, actually begun four years before, the height of tact – a patchwork double-bed quilt made out of all the dresses she'd worn over the past ten years.*[4]

In early August, Gerald and Gamel found a cottage minutes from White Nothe. They rejected it because it was close to woods, and it

---

* Carrington and Lytton decided Gamel was a bore. Earlier (10 August 1930) Carrington had sent Lytton a poem on the couple ('Camel' was in fact one of her pet names for Gerald).

> When a Camel
> Weds a Gamel
> What sort of mammal
> Will appear?

She was not, it seems, entirely above jealousy.

seemed Gerald had a horror of woods, based on Edgeworth.[5] This is the first and last we hear of this particular phobia.

The fact is, he was extremely jealous of Llewelyn – and with reason. Soon after they'd arrived back Llewelyn had taken Gerald for a walk and, in his 'deep, rich, weak voice',[6] with tears starting in his sunken eyes and trickling down his ravaged face, begged to be allowed to see Gamel alone sometimes. Gerald, moved, remembering his agonies over Carrington, agreed.

Gamel and Llewelyn's first meeting, according to Alyse's journal, seems to have been on 3 August.[7] The question that has to be answered is: was she unfaithful with him?

2

In a letter to Frances of 10 October 1967 Gerald states cetegorically that Gamel saw Llewelyn alone every Sunday at this period and that he forced her to make love to him by saying he would haemorrhage if she refused. Gerald guessed this at the time, and proved it later by finding a book of erotic poems Llewelyn had given her with underlinings and dates.

Certainly, Llewelyn longed for this. And Gamel's letters just before they met are less calming than earlier – 'Oh Lulu think of meeting again'; and 'I shall meet you coming over the hill.'[8] It is impossible to say she didn't, and it is just possible she did, once or twice, succumb to his no doubt very passionate pleading.

Yet the balance of probabilities is that she did not succumb. If she did, she almost immediately stopped. Only a week later, she realised Llewelyn must be unhappy and apologised for being so difficult. 'My whole personality recoils from difficulties with other people now.'[9] She cancelled a visit, because it upset Gerald. Very soon, Alyse noted how cold she was to Llewelyn.[10] Nor was it in character. Her loyalty towards (and guilt over) Gerald and Alyse was now very strong. Gamel agreed with people; she did not violate her deepest feelings.

And Gerald's evidence is suspect. Frances accused him, in 1967, of being a voyeur. Stung, he agreed he had become 'obsessed' at the time with spying on sunbathing girls and couples with telescope and binoculars, but it was simply because of Llewelyn and Gamel, and because . . . because . . . and the letter careers away over eighty pages covering, among much else, his entire sexual history, and in the process of denying the charge, confirms it.[11]*

But there is no doubt Gerald was made upset and, despite his insistence to the contrary, made jealous by Gamel and Llewelyn, and no doubt he consoled (or distracted) himself in this way. He also often said later that the discovery of Gamel's continuing love for Llewelyn killed something deep and imaginative in his love for Gamel, and prevented intimacy at a profound level. Gamel agreed (but it was in a letter to Llewelyn).[12] There is certainly truth in this – yet it is not quite so simple. For Gerald, jealousy was an integral part of love. It is equally clear that the pain and agitation attendant on Llewelyn, so far from destroying his love, at first intensified it. Also, for Gerald, like his father, love and marriage were mixed up with ownership – he wanted to control and possess. Or at least, he wanted to be *able* to control and possess. He could control their joint life together; he could not possess Gamel.

She preferred to live in an inner world of dreams and myths and fantasy, the private world she called 'middle earth', where poetry played a central role. This profound centre, which included all intimate personal feelings and the deep experiences of her past, she guarded from everyone. It is noticeable later how little Gamel's intimate friends – and she had some very close and intimate friends – knew about her. They 'divined things', 'one sensed it' – Gamel had said nothing. Llewelyn himself said she was 'unpossessable'. It is difficult to have a very deep marriage with such a person.

But depths are not everything. One can have too much of them. With Gamel enjoying and requiring Gerald's energy, his need of her, 'his very unusual intelligence and sensitivity,'[13] and Gerald at last calm, himself needed, equally fascinated by her mind and her beauty, they were for several years happy together, sometimes very happy.

---

* 'Obsessed' is also his word in a long and extremely revealing passage in the manuscript of *Personal Record*, which he later decided to excise, about his voyeur experiences on the couple-filled cliffs of Lulworth. Llewelyn, incidentally, wrote erotically to women at other times, principally to Rosamund Rose. But it was then precisely because he could not make love to her. It was fantasy (Richard Percival Graves to author, 22 February 1989).

3

Over August and September Gerald and Gamel finally moved with their new furniture and hundreds of books, into tiny, thatched Weld Arms Cottage, in East Lulworth, rented (eight shillings a week) from the Bonhams who then ran the pub attached to it. Lit by oil lamps, it had three small dark rooms downstairs (including the kitchen and bathroom) and three upstairs. The twisted strata of the Lulworth cliffs, Rings Hill and the castle woods provided huge walks for Gerald.

They lived here, with long visits away, till September 1935. Life was frugal – Gamel had brought her £120 p.a., but the slump was now biting. Gerald gave up the car, bought oil stoves and a load of peat for economical heating and worried Ralph about his investments. Maude Champ came in from 8 a.m. till 3 p.m. for ten shillings a week to do housework, and make lunch (or they went to the pub); Gamel cooked suppers – her fish chowders and curries – 'with wonderful skill' according to Gerald, in one of the few letters he wrote to Rex Hunter.[14] They went to London, but Gerald gave up the Cranium Club and they had people to stay: Ralph and Frances, Arthur and Beryl de Zoëte, Molly MacCarthy; Augustus and Dorelia, among other Johns.* They also got a cat, first of an enormous line.

Gerald and Gamel looked for somewhere permanent to live and shopped, with Gerald's usual skill, in local antique shops. And they worked. Gerald, as always, read several hours a day, but as writers Gamel was the more successful. *Middle Earth* was now well out, and in October Gollancz accepted *One Way of Love*. Gerald, still unpublished, struggled to revise and finish *Jack Robinson*. But it bored him so much that by July 1932 he'd taken up *St Teresa* again.

They saw Powyses, Theodore and Violet for occasional teas,

---

* It is all still the same – the thatch on Weld Arms Cottage thick with green moss, the pub serving prawns and crabs, still one village shop. But the pilgrims' ears are liable to be shattered from time to time by terrible explosions from the Gunnery School, established in 1943. The Brenans are still just remembered. Bill Bonham, then a small boy, remembers Gerald as 'a tall, absent-minded professor sort of chap'. He even remembers someone coming called John, and his wife shouting at him, 'Go to the shop and get some tomatoes.'

Llewelyn and Alyse more and more often as a couple (they had moved into Chydyock – a four-mile walk away, or by bus half an hour). In November, Alyse noted Gamel 'is happy, there can be no doubt of it'.[15] Tortured, Llewelyn now only saw his rival in her – her clothes, her scent, her every act and gesture *serving* Gerald as once she'd served him. When Gamel wrote in December, they hadn't seen each other for a month.

On 14 December, Gerald met Ralph on the way back from Garrow Tomlin's funeral in London (he'd been killed flying his plane). Ralph told him Lytton was ill.

Christmas was usually at Edgeworth, but they decided to spend the first week of 1932 there instead. It was still warm in a year destined for terrible cold, and on Christmas Day they had a picnic (of caviar, in fact, bought for everyone at Ham Spray). 'I read aloud some songs of Campion,' wrote Gerald to Ralph. 'The sky was covered with soft thick clouds like the breast feathers of pigeons and in places a little blue showed through.'[16] Then they walked together to Burdon Abbey and hired a car to take them home.

4

So often has the drama of Lytton's death and what followed at Ham Spray over the next two and a half months been described that it sometimes seems more a part of literature than life. The events march in the mind with the inevitability of classical tragedy.

They are familiar and can be truncated; that does not make them any the less harrowing. To the attrition of a long terminal illness, the house crowded with physicians, anxious friends arriving and leaving, Lytton's continual diarrhoea, his temperature soaring to 104°, then sinking back; to the cruel alternation of hope and despair which steadily exhausted all but the night nurse (a woman of striking stupidity) was added growing anxiety over Carrington who was, as her worst fears became realised, in the grip of a nightmare. And there was no let-up in the relentless cold. The winter sun, golden on the deep frost, imparted an icy beauty impossible not to contrast with Lytton's dying.

Gerald was at his best when friends were in trouble. An almost daily stream of anxious and loving letters poured from him, with presents, offers of help, and good advice. As Lytton worsened, he and Gamel moved to London to be at hand if needed, and on 19 January Ralph asked him to come down.

Gerald's chief task seemed to be to support his friend, upon whom the greatest burden was falling. As they ate a picnic on the Downs above Hungerford, Ralph described how anxiety over Carrington had suddenly become acute. A note had been found in which she expressed her intention of killing herself if Lytton died. Ralph said when that happened he would call in Tommy Tomlin, whose neurotic instability he believed would deter Carrington acting while Tommy was actually present.

This moment seemed about to occur when they got to the house. Lytton was sinking. Gerald met Carrington very briefly, then had to go and collect Tommy from the station. That night they both stayed at the Bear Hotel, Hungerford, talking late; then Tommy asked if he could share Gerald's room. To Gerald's embarrassment, instead of taking the spare single bed, Tommy (who was notoriously bisexual) clambered into Gerald's narrow bed, where he at once burst into tears.*

On 20 January Gerald went back to London, but Lytton died that night and, at Frances' request, he returned next day to Ham Spray.

Carrington was in bed, and Gerald learnt from Ralph that an hour before Lytton died, the very afternoon he had left for London, she had been found unconscious by the belching exhaust pipe of the car. When, on this second day, she asked to see him (a meeting Gerald had been dreading) she asked questions about him and Gamel but was, he felt, completely remote.

On 25 January, Gerald left to join Gamel for a week's rest at Edgeworth. But there was no rest for those at Ham Spray now engaged in the struggle to keep Carrington alive. In *Personal Record* Gerald describes himself as 'detached'; his letters at the time are not detached. Nor could he relax. He found it impossible to work.

Carrington's last letter to Gerald is dated 6 March 1932. He had

* With appropriate juxtaposition, Gerald places this incident in his journal immediately after the only other bright moment to occur in the whole agonising saga. As he lay dying, Lytton's long buried early ambition to be a poet fluttered briefly to life. One night he began composing a poem under his breath. 'Don't tire yourself Mr Strachey,' said the night nurse after a while. '*I'll* write all the poetry that has to be written.'

sent her some smoked salmon from Fortnum and Mason's. 'Only Gerald, the poorest of our friends, thinks of such things,' said Ralph. She wrote thanking him, ending as so often in the past, 'Your fondest amiga.' On the back of the envelope, Gerald wrote, 'How can I think of anything but you?'

Five days later Carrington killed herself. Gerald was informed by telegram and at once hired a car and drove to Ham Spray. He arrived at nightfall to find Ralph scarcely coherent. There he learnt the details of what had happened: her procuring the shotgun, the bungled execution, the terrible wound, her slow and agonising death. Gerald stayed for three days and then, after the inquest, Ralph and Frances came back with him to Weld Arms, from where they set out for France. Ralph thought it might distract him to tour his old First World War battlefields, as Gerald had done.*

5

Gerald told Ralph he thought that he'd got over Carrington years before. Now he realised she was far too 'deeply embedded in my mind and life'. He at once got 'flu, which apparently made his private parts swell alarmingly (a typical Gerald 'flu symptom). He recorded several nightmares about Carrington's death.[17]

But in fact the swelling private parts marked, as far as his letters went, his fairly rapid return to buoyancy. Blair and Hugh Brenan were having a terrible row, probably over money. Blair said his father must come to London to discuss it; Hugh that Blair must come to Edgeworth. Gerald suggested they met halfway, 'On a raft on the Thames, say at Runnymede.'[18]

Improving weather brought the consolations of the spyglass. Frances remembers Gerald hurrying over the cliffs in the same excited way he used to rush about London after girls. The chase was the point. 'He was easily satisfied. He'd see a couple and they seemed to be making love. Then he'd get his binoculars to his eyes and see they were eating a sandwich.'† The oddest thing, she said, was how

---

* Frances remembers they left at once. A letter of Ralph's to Gerald on 28 March suggests they didn't go until 1 April.

† Igor Anrep also remembers binoculars. Mark Culme-Seymour, who was conducted over the cliffs in 1934, recalled a telescope.

Gerald saw nothing odd in his behaviour at all. Igor Anrep, his old pupil, also noticed this aspect when taken on to the cliffs this year. 'But it upset Gamel. She was ashamed of it and frightened Gerald would get caught.' How very different in some respects her new husband was from Llewelyn must sometimes have struck her forcibly – Llewelyn, who wrote hymns to her beauty or with whom she used to sit for hours watching the movements of a butterfly.

But in fact it was Gamel's troubles, calling forth all Gerald's powers to comfort and sustain, that helped him most of all to recover from Carrington's suicide. In January, her only close English friend, Nan Wilkinson, died. (She was the wife of Louis Wilkinson, Llewelyn's best friend.)

In February Gollancz, who had already printed 1500 copies of *One Way of Love*, suddenly panicked and decided not to publish. Despite numerous efforts, it proved impossible to get anyone else to take the novel. Gerald and Gamel bound two of the proof copies, giving one to the British Museum. This disappointment, coming at the height of the Carrington drama, was therefore somewhat overwhelmed by events.*

In July, Llewelyn had a severe TB crisis, vomiting blood and haemorrhaging internally. He was too ill to visit, but Gerald and Gamel carried ice, fruit and flowers to Chydyock. Gerald noticed how calm Gamel was in the emergency.

She was soon involved in one on her own behalf. A lump in her breast, which she'd discovered at the beginning of July, was now judged potentially dangerous and on 21 August they went to London. Gerald's anxiety forced immediate expression in a stream of letters to Ralph, some written in the nursing home itself. He described the tricky hour-and-a-half operation, and how 'a lot of little knots and

---

* 1928 had seen the furore over *Lady Chatterley's Lover* and *The Well of Loneliness*. But publishers remained jumpy – with reason. In 1934, James Hanley's *Boy*, with scenes of sadism and sex, was withdrawn as a result of police prosecution. Gollancz themselves had been involved in a court case with *Children Be Happy*. Gerald, Bunny and Ralph all tried to get *One Way of Love* published with Leonard Woolf, Faber and Faber, and later with other publishers. ('The indecent novel by Mrs Gerald Brenan has come our way,' Virginia wrote to Clive Bell on 29 February 1932.) Gollancz reconsidered it in 1934, but again refused. Hamish Hamilton turned it down (on the grounds that it would not pay) in 1965 (Hamilton to Gerald, 17 August 1965, Texas archive). It was finally published in the Virago Modern Classics series in 1987, nineteen years after Gamel died. The *Irish Times* compared her to Jean Rhys and the book sold 10,000 copies here and in America.

lumps' were removed. It was not malignant but Gamel may have been treated with X-rays.[19]

To help Gamel recover from all this, Gerald decided they should go to Yegen. (There is no mention, oddly, of his daughter as a reason for going.) He made a Will, from now on an invariable procedure when he went abroad, and one he clearly enjoyed. He gave a copy of *Jack Robinson*, which Bunny was already busy 'selling on to Chatto and Windus',[20] to Theodore Powys. The car seems to have been resuscitated for the trip and on 3 October they set off together for Spain.

6

'A fire of olive wood, the light blaze of an aromatic plant, red curtains, canarias cigarettes, a voice singing a Malagueña in the far-off kitchen – how often have I written letters in just these circumstances!'

Gerald to Ralph Partridge, 16 October 1932

They arrived at Yegen on 11 October and stayed nearly eight months. The house was newly whitewashed, María (White María) attractive and efficient. She now introduced Gerald to her twenty-seven-year-old sister Rosario, a cheerful, pretty, plump, shrewd young woman of forceful character, who had been cook at the *posada* in Cadiar and was to cook for them.

The fact that five days after they got there Gerald felt compelled to tell Ralph 'I hardly ever see Juliana' may well mean the opposite. She was still clearly on the sexual rampage, with a new boyfriend Amador, pregnant again, no one knew by whom, sleeping with everyone, and 'more than ever a remarkably seductive young woman'.[21] Gerald may not have seen her, but she made every effort to see him. It was rumoured she was buying love philtres to win him back, rumours soon confirmed 'By a neighbour of Juliana's who listens to everything that goes on in her house by means of a long hollow cane'.[22] María and Paco begged him to touch nothing sent by her. One guesses that if Gamel had not been there, no love philtres would have been needed.

If Juliana was conspicuous by her early presence, his daughter was noticeable by her absence. Even Ralph was slightly shocked. The reason may be that on their arrival half the village had told him she wasn't his.[21] He did see her eventually, and when they left had decied she was exquisite, 'with a distinct resemblance to early photographs of me'.[23] But it is likely, from his reaction at the time,[24] that not till she began to develop his own unusual eye defect did Gerald feel absolutely sure she was his, and this helps explain certain aspects of his relations with her later on.*

Having so far failed to find a house in England, another reason for coming to Spain was to see whether or not to live there. At first enchanted, they planned to buy the Yegen house and an extensive *obra* was put in hand. A huge fireplace was built in 'the handkerchief room' (still so called), and fly-screens fitted to the windows. They bought more furniture (Gerald had already bought an 1830 *chaise longue* at Bordeaux on the way out).[25] But by December, when it was pouring with rain, they were both suffering from the isolation and very depressed. They spent Christmas in Granada (seeing Mrs Wood, now ninety-eight) and wondered whether to buy a house in the *vega* (the lush valley to the west of the city). Then Gerald thought of France – 'which I should prefer'[26] – except it was too expensive.†

Gamel however loved Spain and steadily got over her gloom. She wrote chatty letters to Alyse and Llewelyn, kept a diary, planning a book, rapidly learnt rudimentary Spanish, and got a cat – Misika.[27] It became, in memory, an idyllic interlude:

> In a huge chimney, on a dais
> (When we were young and still for hire)

---

* Some people in Yegen still believe Miranda was Paco's daughter, as did Honor Tracy. Apart from the distinctive and unusual eye trouble she inherited, and the fact that, like Gerald, she was tall, no one who has seen her son, Gerald's grandson, can have the slightest doubt who her father was.

† Gerald had no interest in Spain at this time except as somewhere cheap, beautiful and sympathetic to live. There is no evidence that he read a newspaper, or had the faintest idea what was going on politically, except that he had noticed with pleasure that the Republic had resulted in a mass of erotic and pornographic writing (he gives all the prices). Not that he was politically insensitive. On the contrary, his views were already clear and remarkably prescient. He saw that the Nazis were quite capable of provoking a war and guessed that the Polish corridor might be the cause of it. The British government, he told Bunny (18 April 1933), must be firm and stand up to them. He thought war was not likely for three or four years.

We sat on sheepskins by the fire;
Our household much what Homer's was.[28]

Gerald struggled with *Jack Robinson*, thinking longingly of a new novel. But his main task was to exorcise Carrington. His method was not biography, as with Taylor and Reynolds Ball, but to write a 'journal' of the years 1925 to her death, using pocket diaries.* Gamel typed it, as she was from now on to type all his books. (Alyse typed Llewelyn's books.)

He completed this in January 1933 and returned with a groan to *Jack Robinson*. Then in February and March they had a succession of guests. Helen and Roger came for two weeks and, after a few days at Yegen, they toured the south together – Almería, Alicante, Cartagena, Malaga, Cadiz and Murcia. (When he and Helen got back, Roger, appalled at the poverty in Yegen, sent Gerald money to distribute. Gerald sent him a list of the people he'd helped.)[29] On 9 March, Ralph and Frances came for three weeks, met at Almuñecar and taken in a vast loop via Ronda up to Yegen.

On 27 March, Gerald finally finished *Jack Robinson*, after nearly five and a half years. 'It has cost unbelievable efforts,' he told Bunny.[30] Nearly half of it was quite new. While Gamel typed he collapsed into bed with 'flu, meanwhile starting to read for *St Teresa* again.

Their visit was nearly at an end. They had now decided they would come back in a year and adopt his daughter Elena. Only one thing remained: the Russells.

Gerald had met Bertrand Russell once or twice, but in fact he was a friend of Blair, who had suggested Russell and his new girlfriend, twenty-one-year-old Peter Spence, should go to Yegen.[31] Gerald later had reservations about Russell but, as nearly always with new people, meeting him was 'the most exciting thing to happen to me for years'.[32]

* This is the largest of Gerald's journals – 248 single-spaced typed pages. Like most of them it is not a real journal but autobiography in the form of a journal. As a result, it falls between the two. Except for the final passages, where events were still vivid to him, and which he incorporated virtually unchanged into *Personal Record*, it is not as well written as his autobiographies. At the same time it lacks the essential distinguishing element of a journal – life on the wing. For this reason, though he tried several times, Gerald was never able to get it published. Bunny, who was besotted with Gerald's writing long before such a condition was warranted, wrote after reading the journal that he felt 'profound respect . . . breathless . . .' (Bunny to Gerald, undated, Texas archive).

They showed the sixty-year-old 'jaunty Mr Punch' the ropes and then left him to various misfortunes. Russell barely survived food poisoning and, when he got back, Trumpers found lice in his hair.[33]

Gerald and Gamel returned very slowly. Two days swimming at Almería (Gamel loved swimming – Gerald no doubt wanted to check on the nude bathing), then back via Avila and Castile, visiting all the convents St Teresa had had anything to do with.* They were in England by the end of June.

7

In September that year Gerald put an advertisement in the *Weekend Review*: 'SPAIN – House to let in Southern Spain. 3000 feet altitude facing sea, mild, dry climate. 5 bedrooms, 3 sitting rooms, library of 3000 books . . . servants . . . Beautiful country. Living cheap . . . Rent £2.10s. od a month. G. Brenan. East Lulworth, Wareham.'[34]

For the next six months Weld Arms life went on as before. They continued to look for houses until November, when they finally made up their minds to live in Spain; among others, Hope came to stay; they visited Ham Spray, Edgeworth and London – where Gamel met the Woolfs for the first time, impressing Leonard. Gerald helped Bunny raise money for Theodore Powys and slogged at *St Teresa*. But the most important event was the publication of *Jack Robinson*.

When Chatto and Windus brought it out, under the name George Beaton, on 12 October 1933, Gerald was thirty-nine. Although he had been writing for fourteen years, it was his first published work. It was also, incidentally, the first money he'd earned, apart from the war and a few odd sums, in his life.

Reviews were rather sparse, but not bad, though one must remember the kindly English tradition of being lenient to first novels. Cyril Connolly reviewed it favourably,† so did Desmond Hawkins in the *Weekend Review* (better than Priestley, comparable to Defoe),[35]

---

* They also visited many of the places associated with St John of the Cross: Fontiveros, Arévalo, Medina del Campo, Beas del Segura, Almodóvar del Río, Baeza and the little Trinitarian monastery near the village of Iznatoraf.

† According to Frances Partridge in her obituary of Gerald in *The Spectator* of 31 January 1987, she said Connolly called it a work 'of genius'. I cannot trace the review.

J. C. Squire's *London Mercury* devoted two pages to it, a Miss Sylvia Lloyd, seemingly unaware of the kindly tradition, said Gerald 'turned everything he touched to prettiness'.[36] Bunny, in effect the book's sponsor, was now literary editor of the *New Statesman*. In the 'Books in General' column of 14 October, he launched into a paean of considered hyperbole – 'By far the most exciting literary event of the year, perhaps of many years.' Prompting Virginia Woolf to write in her journal, 'Gerald Brenan's book is unmitigated trash – a sickly slab of plum cake iced with fly-brown paper, in spite of Bunny.'[37]

It is possible her waspishness concealed the recognition of a poetic talent, an eye and power of descriptive prose, to rival her own. Certainly Roger Fry felt that. 'I can't think of any English landscape and still-life in prose that equals the best passages . . . It would be tempting to compare your landscapes with Virginia's – e.g. your skies with the skies in *Mrs Dalloway* – because you are so much nearer the artist's vision.'[38] And it is the quality of much of the writing one notices today.

Jack Robinson is a picaresque novel in which a fifteen-year-old boy, whose mother is a second-hand bookseller, becomes hypnotised by books of adventure, rather as Don Quixote, another possible influence, became enthralled by the romances of chivalry. As a result, Gerald's hero runs away to have a series of unrelated adventures, most of them as an apprentice tramp to various master tramps (the book is dedicated to Hope); he meets a lovely, lively Cockney girl called Lily (the real Lily), has a (possibly chaste) affair with her, falls in love, Lily dies, and Jack, after wandering about London, returns to his mother, though he plans to set out again.

The novel derived some of its force from Gerald's intense desire to escape his claustrophic upper-middle-class upbringing, and in this, and in the picaresque form which was not common then, it can perhaps be seen as in advance of its time. Writing of J. D. Salinger's *The Catcher in the Rye*, the critic David Lodge wrote, 'It showed many of the characteristics of the sort of picaresque novels that abounded in the Fifties. They were about people who ran away from an environment which was seen as socially stifling – John Wain's *Hurry on Down*, Kingsley Amis's *Lucky Jim* and Alan Sillitoe's *The Loneliness of the Long Distance Runner* were examples in England. There wasn't very much political content in these books; but there certainly was a rebellion against what were seen as false social values.'

But even more important to Gerald was that upon his vague structure (in the end virtually abandoned) he had been able to pour years of pent-up poetic lyricism – and do so successfully throughout the book in passage after passage of acute if romantic observation: hens 'standing like china teapots in exquisite but absurd clusters or running here and there in their snowy plumage over the pale green field'; a man's beard grows 'thick and furry and as it were hungrily upon his throat'; London (as indeed it was then) 'a vast low-storeyed city spread like a negro mud-village over seventy square miles'; and above all the English seasons, the English countryside, where 'In the silence could be heard, like an expression of the far-off, the pipit's songs, undulating softly across the empty valley like the flight of their bodies.' In fact, in the end the reader is swamped by similes and metaphors. The lyricism is undisciplined. And Gerald's fascination, intoxication even, with language leads him into absurdities, and words like vaticination, immundicity and asseveration start to clog the sentences.

There are other criticisms, but only two relate to later work. He told Ralph that the easiest parts of writing novels were plot and character – and these were also the least interesting and least important. What mattered was the creation of moments of intensity, which equalled reality. If you are solely concerned with 'moments of intensity' you are really pursuing one of the concerns of poetry – as Gerald acknowledges.[39] As a result of Gerald's boredom with character his fifteen-year-old semi-working-class hero hooked on adventure stories soon ceases to exist and becomes thirty-nine-year-old Gerald, reading and commenting on, among much else, Joyce, Eliot, Rimbaud and Rabelais. This means that the story, without narrative or plot very dependent on an arresting and consistent hero, soon becomes boring.* Indeed, for the last sixty pages, where Proust takes over completely, even picaresque incident is abandoned and

---

* It was for this reason that the Spaniards, who invented the form in the sixteenth century (in reading through which century Gerald had been much struck by it), usually had lower-class, often criminal heroes. *Picaro* means rogue. The form arose out of particular economic conditions – 'the ruin of the middle classes by inflation, the need so many people had of living by their wits, the hardships of the writer's life which threw him into low company' (*The Literature of the Spanish People*). Or, if not a rogue, the tension is supplied by the hero being young and innocent (or just innocent, as with Don Quixote), and making his way by streetwise wit or luck through a wicked world from which he is finally saved by faith. In *Jack Robinson* the hero's salvation (i.e. Gerald's) is art.

Jack expounds a complex aesthetic in which Proust's involuntary memory is replaced by moments of intensity/reality.

Gerald was a penetrating critic, not least of his own writing, and he soon became aware of all these faults and others. He was already worrying when he read the proofs and this no doubt reinforced his early decision to be George Beaton. When he met Virginia Woolf in 1935 he apologised for it – 'It is fatal to try and excuse one's work,' she noted scornfully[40] – and in the end he almost loathed it. Yet, having read it, what one remembers are passages of extraordinary skill and beauty. Bunny wrote to him in 1974 'that the book you dislike most is the supreme expresion of your poetical gift written in a prose which you never surpassed . . . is a strange index to your psychology.'[41] Not really. Gerald hated, to the end of his life, to be reminded of poetic gifts he felt he had never realised. He had wanted to be a poet. It was not enough to be 'a poet in prose'.

8

'A good marriage has a pull like the earth's gravity. A passing
moon can raise a tide, but it quickly subsides again.'

Personal Record

In September there had been talk of selling the car. This never took place and it is possible his father now gave Gerald an allowance, as he had promised. At any rate, in November he 'set aside' £500 to buy a house in Spain.

Then, on 17 October, they had a young brother and sister to stay who'd answered the advertisement, Mark and Angela Culme-Seymour. Mark was twenty-two and writing a novel, poems, and planning a life of Alfred de Musset; Angela, twenty, was also writing a novel. Gerald, as he told Ralph, immediately fell in love with them[42] – especially with Angela, who was extremely pretty and, Gerald guessed, easy as to morals. Indeed, quite rapidly they both seemed very easy as to morals. 'They sleep together, I haven't the slightest doubt incestuously, and what will María and Rosario make of that?'*[43] He also reduced the rent to nothing, Mark thought in

* Gerald talked so much about this and so excitedly, that it became generally believed. I questioned both Mark and Angela and they denied it.

retrospect because he was so attracted to Angela. And certainly when Gerald and Gamel, after Christmas at Edgeworth, set off for Yegen again on 15 January 1934, Gerald's behaviour increasingly became that of someone conducting a pursuit.

They took the boat (plus car) to Lisbon and then, although he was already getting a cold, Gerald immediately did the enormous drive to Praia da Rocha in the Algarve, then a charming little seaside town, since ruined. 'And when he arrived,' wrote Gamel, passively resigned, 'with his usual terrific energy, he insisted on completely unpacking and putting everything away at once.'[44]

The cold became a spectacular 'flu, then pneumonia. The Portuguese doctor strapped Gerald into a sort of straitjacket of thermogenic cotton so that he became boiling hot, gave him Piramidon and injected him with silver.*[45] But he could have injected cyanide, for all Gerald would have objected. It is noticeable how all his life doctors brought out a submissive, feminine side of his character – he almost seemed to want them to cause him pain like dentists. He'd let them do anything. For six days his temperature wavered between 101° and 104° and Gamel became seriously worried, begging Ralph and Frances to come out as quickly as they could. This had been planned for 20 February, but in response to impatient letters from Gerald, now recovering, they hurried out early. 'Gerald's behaviour was astonishing,' Frances remembers. 'The moment we arrived he was *frantic* to go – and did so almost at once.'

The reason was made clear *en route* to Yegen. Angela had paid a quick visit to London and was due back shortly – but only for a week.[46] Driving furiously, Gerald managed to get there before she left. (In fact, she stayed a month.)

In *Personal Record* Gerald describes being attracted to Angela but, fearful of hurting Gamel and sick of promiscuity, he 'drew back'. To Ralph he said Angela pursued him. 'I have stood a severe siege and come out triumphant.'[47] In fact, any besieging was conducted by Gerald. He read Angela's novel, found it absolutely 'brilliant'[48] and promised to get it published. He took her for long walks, told her she

---

* Piramidon, according to Dr Ian Battye, my advisor on these matters, was abandoned in 1950 because of its side effects (liver damage). He could find nothing on silver and pneumonia, but it is possible: 'Portuguese doctors were rather *avant garde* in their medical treatment at that time.' Gerald swore by Portuguese doctors from then on.

reminded him of Carrington, and made her put her left hand in his right-hand trouser pocket. She found him fascinating and attractive and they used to lie kissing hidden by the beans. One night he crept into her bed but after a while suddenly sprang out again 'before anything had happened'[49] – much later telling Frances that he'd been afraid he would be impotent.[11]

In fact, there may have been a double reason for his impatience to reach Yegen. Gerald fell in love with young girls, sometimes passionately, all his life – observed by an on the whole tolerant if sometimes exasperated Gamel. But it is as difficult to find out if he ever made love to them as it was to discover when he first did this or what he did with the prostitutes he picked up in London. In a suppressed portion of *Personal Record*, he seems to suggest that fear of impotence kept him totally faithful.* In the book itself he talks vaguely of 'flirtations', adding 'young bodies have a special charm', a delicacy which is meant to leave the reader assuming that to resist these charms was sometimes well nigh impossible, and in one case, with the charms of Joanna Carrington, the inference is stronger. The same confessional letter[11] to Frances says he was unfaithful twice – with a Bedales girl and with that same Joanna Carrington, who seduced him. The sad thing is – and it is sad, because the suggestive fog Gerald spreads over all this is clear evidence, as it was before, of how much he minded – that both these incidents, like so many of his 'affairs' before, evaporate when examined closely. It is odd that he didn't mention to Frances the almost certain infidelity that did take place now – the only certain one – in thirty-nine years of married life. Perhaps its very ease led him to forget it.

Mark and Angela met Juliana on this visit. 'She still has a lovely face,' Mark told his mother, though he noted that because her young fiancé was away on military service, her mother guarded her fiercely.[50] But Gerald, as before, could easily bribe the mother; besides he, or another child of his, would be a far better catch. One day, he later told V. S. Pritchett, he made an assignation with Juliana, slipped down and made love to her twice in the tiny, squalid, windowless back bedroom on an old maize-straw mattress, watched

---

* 'And if throughout my life first times were apt to be an ordeal which my fear of failure shrank from, I ought not to regret that because it helped to keep me faithful to my wife in spite of the flirtations I was several times drawn into, just as during my promiscuous period it saved me from catching venereal disease.'

by their wide-eyed little daughter.* 'A deep happiness welled up inside me. I felt I would like to live with [them] in this little shack for the rest of my life. I felt I loved her.'[51]

It was only a brief episode. Angela left, Gerald calmed down. He felt closer than ever to Gamel because she'd been so understanding 'in sometimes rather difficult circumstances'.[47] Just before they came out, Gerald had polished up *Dr Partridge's Almanack* and sent it to Chatto. He resumed a new novel and told Mark his greatest ambition was to write a life of St Teresa.

But the main task was to find a house. For two months Gamel and he crisscrossed Andalusia and patrolled its coast – an empty coast, particularly empty of English people, except for a few near Malaga, and whose humble little fishing villages – Torremolinos, Fuengirola, Marbella – were still just that. They nearly bought two houses in Pelayo at Algeciras, one near Granada, another at Berja; a journey down the Coin valley attracted them to the *cortijos*† there. At the bottom of this valley, two miles or so from the sea, lies the little *pueblo* of Churriana, right against what is now an international airport. Here at last they found the large house that was to be their home. It belonged to Don Carlos Crooke Larios and for two weeks Gerald bargained, eventually getting it for £1120 (around £34,000).[52] Gamel paid half. There remained only the problem of Gerald's daughter.

It is important, in this context, to remember how very different attitudes to and ideas about child-upbringing were in the 1930s. There was a long tradition among the upper and middle classes that the heaviest burdens of childcare should be carried by others – nannies after a child was born, prep and public schools from the age of eight. There was little knowledge among most people of the harm done to little children if loved figures vanished or were changed – and vanish and change they did. As a result, middle-class society was not child-oriented to anything like the extent it is now. Least child-

---

* '. . . a child of 2½': if so, this puts the incident on their previous visit, in 1933; as does a reference to Gamel having been ill. But the letter, an extremely vivid one, ends with their taking his daughter back to England. It is quite possible Gerald made love to Juliana on both visits. He certainly wanted to.

† Farmhouse. In Andalusia the word also often refers to the stone sheds, now increasingly converted and built up into houses, used for hay, animals and by herdsmen at various times of the year.

oriented of all was Bloomsbury, by whom Gerald was strongly influenced in matters of this sort. Thus, when Gerald told Ralph, 'We are going to farm [her] out for about a year as soon as we get back, so you will not see her,'[53] it occasioned no particular surprise. Ralph didn't even comment.

In fact, this was probably a stratagem to bolster their resolve, since it was never carried out. Both Gerald and Gamel were clearly fairly appalled by what they'd undertaken. Elena, now three and a half, was not pot-trained, her nose ran all the time, and her accent was so thick even Gerald couldn't understand it. 'I can't conceive how children are trained,' Gamel wrote gloomily to Llewelyn. Gerald also hadn't the faintest idea. They only knew that it would be 'boring, irritating, an interference with our writing and an expense that we can not afford'.[54] They took his daughter to Churriana, partly because they thought they could give her a better life,* but really because he'd said he would.

As to their feelings, Gamel's strong maternal instinct was awoken, and she talked of having 'a whole crêche of children' herself.[55] They renamed the little girl Miranda Woolsey Brenan, following the Spanish custom of incorporating the wife's name, and Gamel and Miranda eventually became very close. Gerald told Ralph, '*My affections are certain for anyone dependent on myself.*'[56] He underlined it, and this was something he showed in various circumstances throughout his life; but his 'affections' for Miranda received an immense boost from the reactions of his parents. They were horrified. So, would Gamel have no children? Far more important – what would people think? Furious letters passed, and financial reprisals were threatened. Gerald agreed to keep his fatherhood secret. About Gamel and children, 'She herself has no definite leanings either way,' but it was too dangerous to her health for Gerald to allow.[57]

This frank contradiction of what Gamel was in fact saying is partly explained by Gerald being in contact with his father. Nevertheless, it is a significant statement. From now on an almost inevitable refrain in Gerald's letters over any matter remotely contentious is 'and Gamel of course agrees with me'. She would have liked children and, with care, could have had them. At the same time – could she be bothered to have them? She would have liked Gerald to press her into it – but Gerald didn't want any more children. Had Gamel

* See notes on pp. 266, 286 and 288.

insisted he would no doubt have allowed it. (Indeed they did once rather half-heartedly, too late, try.) She acquiesced, but her acquiescence was not simple. She drifted; she also minded – and the minding was at the same time a sort of punishment which she thought she deserved. It was one of several equally profound frustrations (many nothing to do with Gerald) which slowly distilled a bitterness which eventually undermined her.

But this was a process taking decades. Now Gamel embarked on Miranda with great kindness, conscientiousness, considerable interest and apprehension. Gerald paid Juliana* a large sum (1000 pesetas)[58] and they spent three days with Miranda in Almería 'to practise'. On 23 June the new little family set sail for England.

9

Gerald seems to have felt too poor (and the cottage was too small) to get a nanny. The harassed couple were soon engulfed in the complexities of childcare. 'We are bringing up Miranda, tell Rhoda,' he wrote anxiously to Blair, 'on Cow and Gate food and boiled milk, and halibut oil every alternate week. Is that a good regime? Mother pooh-poohed these new-fangled views on milk . . .'[59]

* Until he legally adopted Miranda, which was complicated, Gerald was nervous that Juliana's love for her daughter would prove too strong and she would claim her back, which she certainly could have done. He therefore continued to pay her 250 pesetas a year to give him some leverage (Gerald to Ralph, October 1935). But this fear somewhat contradicts his statement in *Personal Record* that Juliana 'neglected' Miranda. In fact, all the evidence from her other children, her sisters and the village is that she was an excellent mother. Mark Culme-Seymour said Miranda was the cleanest child in the village. She gave up Miranda chiefly because she was desperately poor, and had said she would. Gerald's letters speak of her weeping, and her son Angel says she never forgot her. Once, in her late forties, she pursued an English couple through Granada, thinking mistakenly she'd seen Miranda. As far as I can discover, Gerald never saw Juliana again. Yegen still says he bought her a house there, but Angel denies this – though 1000 pesetas (£50) would have been enough then. Her first husband, whom she married shortly after this, was killed in the Civil War. She then had a long affair with a civil guard, through whom she met and married an ex-civil guard, Francisco Muñoz Moreno. He dealt in property in Granada. Thus bettering herself, she died, according to an anonymous informant, 'laden with jewels'. She had four sons by various fathers and her end, if jewel-covered, was sad. She was blind for the last seven years, and died coincidentally a few months after her only daughter.

They clearly did their best, but not even angels could have done much to mitigate the cataclysm that had exploded little Miranda's world – she didn't speak for a month,[51] and was still wetting her bed three years later.

Llewelyn was very ill again, and Gerald and Gamel once more traipsed up to Chydyock with ice and fruit. Chatto had accepted *Dr Partridge's Almanack*, almost certainly on Bunny's advice, and proofs arrived in July, interrupting the easily interruptible *St Teresa*. They went to Edgeworth in September and Gerald noted with irritation how he was still tongue-tied in front of his father.[60] (Another old pattern revived. Gerald made a pass at one of the parlourmaids.)* The Culme-Seymours were back. Gerald had been corresponding with Angela, just married to Johnny Churchill, Winston's nephew. He now wrote glowing letters to Bunny, urging him to get the work of this 'born writer' published.[61]

In September Roger Fry suddenly died, after breaking a bone slipping on the bathroom floor. Gerald was devastated. Roger was the most intellectually stimulating of his close friends and the one he most admired (as Roger admired him. He told Gerald he was one of the people whose opinions he most valued and wanted: 'I believe so strongly in your penetration').[62] Roger was also very fond of Gamel and was always planning to paint her. But above all, as Gerald still poignantly remembered forty-six years later, 'I really loved him.'[63]

Dr Partridge's Almanack came out on 12 October, as had George Beaton's last work. This elaborately written firework display,† dense with archaisms and flights of 'fantasmagoria', ingenious and high-spirited facetiousness, amused Brenan fans like Ralph and Frances. And indeed it is sometimes amusing. 'Fourth February. The moon among the fishes denotes great inconvenience to the fishes.' But a little of this goes a long way and Gerald put in 300 prophecies. (Frances said it was *designed* to sag.) It seems only to have received one review – a rave from Bunny – and by Christmas had sold thirty copies.

October was spent buying more furniture, in particular an enormous and extraordinary glass table-top from Peter Jones – frosted

---

* My informant, a sweet shy woman in her seventies, wished to remain anonymous. 'Was Gerald persistent?' Apparently he was. I noticed that, even then, she strongly resembled Gamel.

† Already described on pp. 220–21.

green glass like a slab of frozen sea – destined to be a prominent feature in Churriana life. They also bought a gramophone for £15. Gamel, unlike Gerald, was fond of music.[64] These, along with other pieces of furniture, curtains, books and pictures were crated up and shipped for Malaga. And, in November, Gerald, Gamel and Miranda* (who had now begun to talk) embarked themselves.

The English papers reported, with some foreboding, ripples on the Spanish political scene. Gerald dismissed them. 'I don't take a very dark view of these disturbances, as far as we are concerned.'[65] He was far too excited at setting out towards their new life.

* A book came out in Spain in 1990 containing interviews with relatives and people who had known Juliana (*Ciega en Granada*: *Murio buscando a su hija la hija de Brenan*, Antonio Espejo Ramos, Granada 1990). This contains the suggestion that Juliana subsequently tried to see Miranda and Gerald prevented it. I can find no evidence of this, though it is just possible. In numerous letters to Ralph after he had first taken her he expressed anxiety that Juliana might try to recover Miranda, and this is why he continued paying her for so long. Had Juliana asked to see Miranda, he would certainly have reported this to Ralph in the context of his anxiety. In later years (1950s and 1960s) he several times asked Miranda if she would like to see her mother, and had the same offer conveyed to Juliana. Neither took him up. It should also be remembered that Juliana may have felt some guilt at what looked like selling her child, and wished to obscure this.

FIFTEEN

Churriana

1

There was now a road to Yegen, and after a brief visit to Churriana to dump Miranda on a Mrs Bush in Torremolinos, Gerald and Gamel set off by bus, via Granada, to collect their furniture.

The summer in southern Spain, even in the Alpujarra, can be searing, almost terrible in its heat. Autumn, beautiful all over the world, falls here with an extra accent, healing and calming. Round Yegen, the chestnuts in the trees, bristling and big as tennis balls, land with a soft thud. Everything suddenly becomes soothing and gentle the pale yellow fire of the poplars, the mist of the olives, and the vapours which come floating up the deep valley from Órgiva, filling it with a quiet, frothy, aerial sea.

Gerald left all this beauty, which had given him so much intense pleasure, without a qualm. He always preferred to look to the future. Besides, age (he was nearly forty-one) had brought a change of perspective: 'It is cold in winter, no sea in summer, supplies very scarce, boring after a week or so, the house is falling down, the flies and fleas are everywhere, expensive to live in because we are always having to leave it.'[1]

They loaded everything into two lorries (Hope's stuff taking a maddeningly large amount of space). The last day, 23 December, they got up at 4.30. Gerald and Gamel went round saying goodbye; Rosario and her husband Antonio and María climbed aboard – the team that was, with the addition of children, to see him through till 1972; and then the two swaying, laden lorries, like prairie wagons, set off westwards towards Malaga.

He'd been coming and going for fifteen years and the villagers had been quite certain he'd never leave.[2] 'Now I don't suppose I shall ever stay more than a day or two at Yegen again.'[3] Nor did he.

2

During the eighteenth century Gibraltar had become, not just an English but a foreign gateway into Andalusia. Some French, but in particular as many Germans as English had come to Malaga, and then often married into Spanish families. They came for trade – particularly wine. The whole of the fertile Malaga *vega* was then planted with vines. By 1900 Malaga was one of the most prosperous and sophisticated cities in Spain. Then the phylloxera of 1914 wiped out the vines. Malaga was ruined. And this was compounded by the 1914–18 war and its aftermath, when her numerous German trading contacts collapsed.

Many of the great families suffered, including the Larios family, one of the most powerful in Andalusia. (By the end of the nineteenth century this family controlled Algeciras and acquired, through marriage, the dukedom of Lerma.) Don Carlos Crooke Larios of a cadet branch was eking out his living with a poultry farm in 1934, which was why he sold Gerald his house. This, La Casa de Los Heredias, had in fact been built by a Don Manuel Larios in about 1840.

The first on the left as you entered the *pueblo* under a line of huge eucalyptus, the house initially – despite its tall windows, the lower ones with their trellises of wrought iron, and single balcony – presented a long, blank-seeming front to the narrow street.* But behind the double street doors to the left, the ones normally used, and the short, wide but dark passage beyond, could be glimpsed what first caught Gerald's eye, a flash of lightness and green – curious echo of his childhood pathways and tunnels leading to paradise.

Except, as you stepped through the passage – there *was* paradise!

---

* It was still the first you passed when I last went in 1989. The eucalyptus had all been blown down. There was a plaque to Gerald on the wall: 'Aquí Vivio/ Gerald Brenan/ 1935–1970/ El Excmo./ Ayuntamiento de Malaga/ En Homenaje a su Memoria/ Noviembre 1983.' Eucalyptus, incidentally, is not indigenous to Europe and was first introduced from Australia during the nineteenth century. The huge, now vanished Churriana trees were probably planted about the same time Gerald's house was being built.

Suddenly, there were towering trees – a giant pecan, an equally giant avocado, palm trees, fifty-foot bamboos – oranges, lemons, shrubs and flowers and vines, the ordered riot of an enormous southern garden – its two acres seeming almost a tiny estate – all surrounded by a fifteen-foot- (five-metre-) high wall. The house itself was large, an 'L' with a truncated base into the garden, inturned and elegantly of its charming period. It had five rooms downstairs, plus kitchen, pantry, bathroom and coachhouse; with upstairs five or six bedrooms, second pantry, bathroom, and a *mirador*, or tower. In front, a sweeping view of the Mediterranean two miles or so away, with its fleets of little fishing boats; behind, the *vega* and the Sierra de Churriana.

In fact, house and garden were so dilapidated it all at once reminded Gamel, to her delight, of South Carolina and romantic, ruined plantations.[4] The house leaked and swarmed with rats and chickens. An army of masons descended and tore the place to bits. 'Then they began to repair the damage they had done – like socialists rebuilding their country after a revolution . . .' Supposed to last two months, the gigantic *obra* lasted six. It included the garden. Three little cottages were knocked down and replaced by one for Rosario, Antonio and María. Pipes were laid from the little *alberca* – the rectangular irrigation tank alongside the house – to carry the water out into the garden, where it would be variously directed by novice gardener Antonio's mattock.

Pesetas poured from Gerald's pocket (£500-worth by the end), but his letters crackle with pleasure and energy. He cut bamboos as thick as Ralph's thigh, made a ridiculous fuss over his scratched hands, tried, as all expatriates do with their friends, to get Ralph and Frances to join him. Did they not realise the eggs were so fresh they were stamped with the name of the hen who had laid them?[5] Once again – a sign of coming home – he felt like Robinson Crusoe.

Winter was exceptionally cold that year. Snow fell, and Gerald and Gamel sat inside the large fireplace. But by May Gamel was swimming in the *alberca* (four strokes each way) and soon, sucked up by the sun with astonishing speed from the rich black earth, flowers that were two feet in England grew to five and 'One is vaguely reminded, as one walks about, of gardens one knew as a child.'[6]

Miranda came back at the end of March, and spent all her time with the servants. Gerald paid them 120 pesetas a year, but everything else was free and Antonio, a gentle man of great sweetness and simplicity, could sell off the surplus from the garden. The change from the Alpujarra, where they had known real hunger, was dramatic.

Nor, as Gamel noted, were they servants. Helpers was her word. Over thirty years, at any time of the day, Rosario and María would come to talk, gossip, complain or ask advice. Gerald and Gamel followed their lives in detail. And as they made friends in the village, that gossip flowed in too.

In one central respect, it often seems that Gerald and Gamel barely lived in Spain at all. Their friends, with in Gerald's case two not very significant exceptions, were drawn partly from the expatriate community and, to a far greater extent, came from England to stay with them. But, in his close involvement with Rosario, Antonio and María and later their children, Gerald preserved a taproot, and a thick one, into Spanish and *pueblo* life.*

No close friends came at this period. Bertie Powys, the architect, came with his wife for two weeks – 'Mrs Powys like a stale ham sandwich'.[7] In February, Gerald found a house for Vivien and Edwin John and four friends (one, Caitlin, later to marry Dylan Thomas). Vivien remembers Gerald's quiet, beguiling voice, his obsession with irrigation, and his affection for Gamel, which brought him hurrying down to ask them up to hear Gamel's amazing and marvellous dreams. Gamel's dreams were extraordinary, but when they arrived it would be Gerald who recounted them.

The English expatriate community still wore solar topees. Many were the caricatures of his childhood against whom he'd rebelled – brick-red ex-colonels and their wives, ordering biscuits from Fortnum's. Gerald was in fact an uncensoriously gregarious man (unless bored) and here they just amused him. In England they would have appalled him, just as it would have appalled him to live in a seventeen-roomed house with three servants. In many more ways than he noticed, Spain allowed him to be himself. At the same time, the

* Gerald once told me that he'd made love a single time with both Rosario and María, and that this romantic echo of the *droit de seigneur* was what held them all together. You can't ever be absolutely certain with Gerald, but I think it is in the highest degree unlikely (so unlikely that when talking to Rosario's daughters, I didn't even dare raise it). But it shows that – fascinated, extremely astute and acute observer as he was – he saw his relationship with them as essentially paternalistic.

Churriana house was not in any way luxurious. There were no flushing lavatories, no form of heating except the big fire in the *sala* and, later, oil stoves, no running water except in the bath, which itself required an incredible palaver to activate. Such things hardly signify in balmy Andalusia except in winter (and there is no cold like a damp, penetrating 50°F in the south). At such times, Churriana was, no doubt to Gerald's unconscious satisfaction, austerely uncomfortable.

Like most expatriates Gerald missed England ('badly') and had to justify not living there.* He solved the dilemma now, in his reading at least, rather neatly, by returning via a series of nineteenth-century novelists and then making some sharp criticisms: 'But there is a fundamental, irremediable sentimentality in all Victorian novelists, it seems to me. They call into play too many of our lower feelings, just as the films do. One hopes the bad characters will reform, one hopes the good characters may be spared, whereas in the greatest novels one watches, surely, without hoping at all.'⁸

As the *obra* ended in mid-May ('You never saw such . . . [an] unconcentration camp as this has been')⁹ Gerald and Gamel returned to work. Gamel was finishing a novel about Dorset and planning a detective novel.¹⁰ She also did a certain amount of cooking – the *cuisine* of the Cádiar *posada* not thought suitable for some guests. Gerald embarked on a new novel.

He wrestled obstinately with novel after novel, as he had with poetry, for years at a time until he was nearly seventy. Yet suddenly, as now, it would strike him that 'I am not a novelist and I find the effort of sustained imagination very great . . . my own life is the only thing I am interested in to write freely about'.¹¹ Then he would forget, or subjugate this knowledge, or suspicion, to his will.

Since 1933 he had been writing a crib of Bunny's despised *Lady Into Fox* – *Lady* (Helen Anrep) *Into Bird*. By July 1934 he'd written

* Gerald ostensibly moved to Spain because it was cheaper, so that Gamel would not have to cook and do housework, and because of her TB. There are deeper reasons we'll come to, but someone told me that Jung once wrote that all expatriates hated their fathers. I cannot locate the observation, but a one-man survey has found it borne out surprisingly often. Similarly, an American survey has found that religious mixed marriage and exogamy (marrying out of one's group) is found far more frequently among those who have parental conflicts. By changing race or religion or country it is hoped to avoid them (see J. S. Heiss *American Sociological Review* 25(1). 1960)

10,000 words and it had become a five-act play in comic verse. The new novel was to be like Svevo, and was only finally swept away by political events in Spain.*[12]

These events do now appear to make an impression on him – he comments on the talk and likelihood of a military dictatorship (which would only make Spain 'easier to live in'). His viewpoint seems still to be from England. Hitler *must* be stood up to, but he expects a war in 1939.† Ralph and Frances should come to Spain at once. Far safer.[13]

In fact he was taking things more seriously than he let on to Ralph. That strange, intuitive instinct he had, which had woken in brief flashes, often in dreams, a number of times at crises with Carrington – suddenly operated now. 'I have myself a foreboding,' he wrote to Bertrand Russell on 20 May 1935, – 'how much founded it is I cannot say – that something tragic and terrible is going to happen to this country.'

On 17 June 1935 Gerald and Gamel sailed for England on a last brief packing and furniture-collecting journey.

3

In July, after Lulworth and Ham Spray, where Frances was about to give birth to Burgo Partridge, Gerald and Gamel went to Edgeworth, from where Gamel made the first of many visits to Wales. J. C. Powys and Phyllis Playter now lived there.

Gerald found England exquisitely lovely. 'After Spain, everything seems half-asleep. England is the most poetical of countries and certainly there's a close connection between poetry and sleep.'[14]

He also enjoyed Edgeworth. 'It is my root in the earth.'[15] He wanted to see his mother, he wrote his novel; he also had items of business. He planned to ask his father to give him £50 p.a. to make up for the inroads made by Churriana. Gerald's difficulties with his

---

* He later burnt all the manuscripts of these early novels. Frances remembers the *Lady Into Bird* novel being fairly sharp about Helen.

† This is percipient and Gerald was on the whole consistent in this view; but he also quite often wavered. In anything he said on this subject to Ralph there was always an element of coat-trailing. If Ralph had been a rabid re-armer instead of a pacifist the balance of Gerald's pronouncements would certainly have changed.

father were either over Hugh's bullying Helen or money. More usually money. His father was well off and Gerald saw no reason why he should not help them. Hugh Brenan did see reasons. One can sympathise with both. On this occasion, Hugh delayed his decision on the £50, but was 'very nice'. He gave Gerald a cheque for £12 and also took Miranda for two weeks.[16]

This was the second reason for going to Edgeworth. Miranda now features considerably in Gerald's letters, quite often with some exasperation. But it is clear he was extremely conscientious. In August, he wrote her a book of 'Canterbury Tales'. He left her at Edgeworth because he wanted her to get to know Blair's two daughters, Ann and Lydia.[17]

A less reliable way of boosting his income was introduced by Bertrand Russell. The great philosopher and mathematician persuaded Gerald to join a chain letter for ten-shilling notes. By 17 July, Gerald told Bunny, ten shillings had already arrived – which is odd because B. Russell and G. Brenan were still bottom of the list.[18] Gerald may have pretended, because Bunny had been very scornful. If ten shillings had arrived, the anomaly no doubt formed part of the animated discussions when Gerald and Gamel spent a week at the end of August with the Russells at Telegraph House.

Throughout his life Gerald felt he had to rise to the challenge offered by men of dominant personality, probably because they raised echoes of his father. This was true of Russell, Augustus John, Cyril Connolly, Hemingway and others – it was also a considerable part of his complex relation with Ralph. ('I associate you with defence and aggression,' he told Ralph at this time.)[19] He was flattered by Russell's friendship, but one has the feeling of Gerald very much forced into continuous top gear. He took voluminous notes in their bedroom (very useful when he wrote *Personal Record*), and kept his end up by steering the conversation into literature.

It is also interesting, in view of his later row with Ralph, that while there he wrote: 'I am a *complete* pacifist where there is a question of war in NW Europe.' He'd now decided it was essential to make terms with Hitler.[20]

September was spent at Lulworth, saying goodbye and packing. '510 books, 100 records, two tables, mattresses . . .' There is a quick, vivid picture of what their life must often have been like in the little Weld Arms Cottage. 'Gamel is calling me to our supper of bacon and mushrooms. No, she says it will not be ready for one minute.' Gerald is reading. The peat fire is smoking slightly.[21]

A rather nervous traveller now, at forty-one, he made a new Will (everything to Gamel and making provision to keep Juliana quiet if she tried to get Miranda. Miranda herself to be taken over by Blair).[21]

It was the time 'of mists, fogs, first frosts, brown leaves, lamplight',[21] and he left with a wrench. On the last morning, 22 September, he scribbled to Bunny, begging him to come to Spain. 'I'm sad to go. I looked at a little field this morning lying under a brown autumnal wood and heard the voices of children rising with the smoke in the valley below and felt things I have not felt for several years. How mysterious English landscape is under its skin of commonplace.'[22]

4

The letters from these early years at Churriana are full of contentment. When they woke, Gamel wrote, hearing the cries of the fish-sellers, the sun 'fell in stripes from the slatted shutters on the red and white diamonded tiles . . . the pattering feet of the milk goats sounded like raindrops . . .'[23] They worked, then walked together each afternoon. Every night, before bed, they went out into the mild November air to one of their orange trees and ate an orange. There is a charming picture of them both in bed together, both with 'flu – 'An agreeable languorous illness and we enjoyed it.'[24] Gerald read Hakluyt's *Voyages*, Gamel investigated the origins of Christianity, 'lying surrounded by bibles and books in French and German on the Jesus problems'.[25] (This had nothing to do with nascent religion. Gamel was never remotely religious. '*I do not like religion*,'[26] she once emphasised to Llewelyn. Her researches were stimulated by a discussion they had had while with Bertrand Russell.)

Improvements were made: an enormous and expensive boiler was installed, under which a fire had to be lit. They built a little fountain and the garden, with this and the endlessly filling, regularly emptying *alberca*, was filled with the sound of running splashing water.

By January 1936 Gerald was writing 'furiously' at his new novel. Various letters at this time reveal aspects that were to be permanent in his writing life. He spent far more time writing notes, planning and preparing to write than actually writing. This was done quite quickly (in this instance, 100 large pages in a month – a good deal, given his small hand). He then laboriously cut seventy percent, and then rewrote, re-cut, and endlessly corrected the remainder. He expected to spend at least five years on a book. Time was his great weapon (and perhaps enemy).* A more certain enemy of work was sex since 'They are mysteriously related', and the letter to Bunny reiterating this familiar connection leaves no doubt as to where the axe had to fall. 'Writing is my religion.'[27]

There is also a brief and tantalising reference, in a letter he sent Helen Anrep in February, to an account of Yegen he was writing for 'an American paper', in which he hoped to include sketches of 'the eminent visitors'. There is no further mention of this, but it shows that the idea of writing on this subject was still very much alive and active in him.[28]

Gerald missed the social life of England – yet the missing was a relief. His dislike of 'group' feelings, his reactive, sensitive, excitable temperament had made it impossibly distracting to his work. In Spain he found by chance just the right combination of monotonous calm to let him write, with sufficient social junketing to keep him stimulated. (He found the same combination in England during the war, then in many respects oddly peaceful.)

A social life necessary for stimulation was not negligible. Clare Sheppard, Molly MacCarthy's niece, and her husband Sydney were living next door and became lifelong friends. They were very poor and remembered Gerald's generosity; Clare also remembered Gerald's despising the local cocktail parties – but always dashing off to them. Angela (Culme-Seymour) appeared with her husband Johnny Churchill. She introduced Gerald and Gamel to her mother Jan Woolley, staying at Torremolinos, and her half-sister, fourteen-year-old Janetta, who was also extremely attractive and 'who has set my heart on fire',[29] Gerald told Ralph.

---

* One often has the impression with Gerald that he knew unconsciously and instinctively that he would live a very long time. He did not really complete a book satisfactorily until he was nearly fifty, was sowing wild oats at sixty, still complaining of adolescence at seventy and wrote books as dense, as brilliant and as well written as any before that in his eighties. But this sense of time ahead allowed him to spend many years on books which, had he had any feeling of urgency, he might have abandoned earlier.

In some respects, Gerald and Gamel's social life reverted to the eighteenth and early nineteenth centuries before the railway brought the weekend. Guests stayed weeks, sometimes months. When the Russells arrived on 3 February they stayed six weeks. Expeditions led by Gerald were to become a feature of Churriana life: on 11 February he hired a lorry, filled it with armchairs and took them all – Sheppards, the Churchills and guest,* and the Russells – to the beach. It was such a success that two days later the lorry load of armchairs went wobbling up to Antequera.[30]

Nevertheless, as time passed, he began to tire. Bertie's wife, Peter Russell, made scenes. Gerald longed to read in the evenings but had to bear up 'like Atlas, one end of the conversation'.[31]

When the Russells left Gamel wrote to Llewelyn, 'I get so tired of always talking. I wish human beings were more silent creatures.'[32] She added that though she admired Russell, she could never like him. His guiding forces were vanity and love of power. This may reflect her irritation at the obvious way in which Russell showed he was attracted to her (which may also explain Peter's scenes). His passes later led to a long breach with Gamel.

On 7 August, after Duncan Grant had been for two days, Ralph and Frances came for two weeks. Once again they went to Antequera. 'Gerald was brilliant on these occasions,' said Frances, still remembering the trip they made at this time. The Partridges went on to Barcelona, but Gerald and Gamel stayed on to explore the Torcal, a region behind Antequera of fantastic rock formations. One thinks of huge garden gnomes and toadstools, but this extraordinary place is saved from cosmic ludicrousness by its savage wildness. If Ralph ever wanted to kill himself, Gerald noted, he could hurl himself through the three-yard opening 3000 feet down into the Cisma de la Mujer, the Woman's Chasm – 'A poetical ending.'[33]

Immediately after Ralph and Frances left, Hugh and Helen Brenan arrived. Hugh was selling Edgeworth and the visit was to comfort Helen. (Hugh therefore veered between wanting to comfort her and cancelling the trip, and Gerald had found himself in the unusual position of pleading with his father to come out.)[34] Once again, money was high on the agenda, and this time his father was in the giving vein. As well as £30 for his birthday, he agreed to give

* Anne Gathorne-Hardy (later Hill), the author's aunt.

Gerald £50 p.a. for three years. Ralph had been advising on shares and they now had over £300 (£9000) a year and 'would never have to think of money'.[35] 'One could live on *nothing*,' Clare Sheppard remembered.

His parents left on 12 May 1936. Amidst these preoccupations – guests, *obra*, sponging off his father, expeditions, huge meals (for ten or twelve, Gamel – a true wife to Mr Beaton – cooking) – one thinks for an instant of the *Titanic*. In fact, in March Gerald's letters had started to fill with politics – not of Europe, but of Spain.

To understand what was about to engulf him and Gamel, it is necessary to know a little about what was going on.

5

Many historians have perished endeavouring to thread the labyrinthine complexities of the Spanish body politic during the years up to the Civil War. Even to grasp a superficial idea of what was going on in and around Malaga, which is all we really need to know at the moment, is not easy.

Except in Granada, the working classes were mostly on the land and were anarcho-syndicalists, belonging to a union called the Confederación Nacional de Trabajo or CNT. They were controlled by a pre-anarchist organisation called the Federación Anarquista Iberca, or FAI (or rather only partly controlled, which led to power battles). Working in small, individual groups (or even as individuals), they favoured reform by revolution and violence. The rival big union was the Unión General de Trabajadores or UGT. (Spanish politics had succumbed at this time, as Orwell noted, to a complicating disease of initials.) The aims of the UGT were socialist solutions by peaceful political means. The Left in Spain was thus fundamentally split; and split also, as are all left-wing movements, by the strain of the bourgeoisie trying to ally itself with the workers.

In Malaga and Andalusia the UGT was not strong. The anarcho-syndicalists were split between varying degrees of violent revolution, and were also against the communists, not yet very powerful. They disapproved of bourgeois politics and didn't vote. At the same time, they did vote in a crisis, like the election of February 1936, when paradoxically they voted in a communist, Dr Bolívar, because they liked him.

The excitement in Malaga and Andalusia must be seen in context. Seemingly a democracy, many, even most elections were still, as they had been for years, manipulated and controlled by the *caciques*, or local bosses, especially in the country districts. In towns there was sometimes straight rigging. The vast majority of workers were on the land – yet possessed none of it. The huge estates, the *latifundios*,* had successfully resisted nearly all attempts to redistribute some of their land. The slump in Spain was aggravated because the Right, as it did elsewhere, thought one of the main troubles was high wages. As a result, agricultural wages, in places already near starvation level in a land without any welfare benefits, halved in 1935.

It was against this, and similar measures that the right-wing government had taken, that in the February 1936 elections the initials of the Left temporarily united in a Popular Front and swept into power. They had also been horrified and enraged in 1934 by the savagery with which the Right had repressed a sudden rising near Oviedo in Asturias. Here ferocious units of Moorish soldiers had been employed for the first time, also the Tercio. This, the finest fighting force in the Spanish Army, was a copy of the Foreign Legion. A Major Franco, prominent in its formation during the Twenties, had designed its uniform and wrote its history. Four thousand people, mostly workmen, were slaughtered; 30,000 were imprisoned, many tortured.

Against such events, such conditions, you might wonder who was on the Right. Bastions of established order one would expect: followers of the official Catholic church, the rich, most landowners, the army – which since the nineteenth century was far more politically involved than in England, perhaps more comparable in perceived role to Cromwell's New Model Army – and also Monarchists. The King, Alfonso XIII, had fled in 1931, in the face of left-wing successes and opposition.

But, just as today the failures of Soviet communism have

---

* Estates of 625 acres or over. Figures are very difficult here, but estimates suggest about 10,000 families owned over half the land in Spain, excluding the north and north-east. In this section I follow *The Spanish Labyrinth* by Gerald Brenan, Cambridge 1986; Paul Preston's *The Coming of the Spanish Civil War*, London 1978; Raymond Carr's *Spain 1808–1975*, Oxford 1982.

destroyed socialism in the East and weakened it in Western Europe, so in the 1930s its success gave socialists something to emulate, a possibly ally, and gave the Right, in turn, something about which they could panic. The Right in Spain did panic. It drew all those fearful of disorder or violent change who felt that those vague but powerful things called 'old values' were in danger. They were a very substantial number. As in England now, the seats won in elections gave a totally wrong impression. By the votes cast, the two sides were much closer – 4,838,449 to 3,990,931.

The moment the Popular Front won in February, the generals (including the now-promoted Major Franco) began to plan their revolt. They seemed to have good reasons. Not only the anarcho-syndicalists argued for violent revolution. Largo Caballero, one of the most powerful and respected socialist leaders, had become disillusioned with slow, political, bourgeois action. He was also frustrated by President Azaña, and the finance minister Prieto, a personal enemy. If the Right rebelled, the government would have to give arms to the people, who could then swiftly achieve by force their just reforms. Consciously or unconsciously, this was what Largo Caballero sought; his speeches became increasingly fiery. During April, May and June 1936, with lightning strikes, sporadic shootings and more and more frequent clashes between all the various opponents and groupings, rumours of rebellion and counter-rebellion, Spain seemed to be coming to the boil.

6

In March, soon after the victory of the Popular Front, Gerald wrote to Ralph, 'It is certainly odd Granada which is fanatically socialist should return only Right candidates.'[36] From now on his tension rose rapidly in time with events. By May he felt they were living on a volcano. He had contingency plans to send out a lorryload of books and furniture and was thinking of emigrating to Jamaica. It is possible that he met Largo Caballero now – a letter refers to a meeting as imminent. It would have been through a new friend, Jay Allen, a correspondent of the *Chicago Tribune* and close confidant of the socialist leader. (Allen dashed everywhere and deeply impressed

Gerald, who referred to him frequently and excitedly as 'a crack reporter'.)[37]

On 12 July came 'the servants' strike'. Rosario and Antonio were against the Popular Front. They saw Gerald, Gamel and themselves as an island of sane Granadines in a sea of mad Malaguenians. But Gerald made them take part in the procession and they then continued working as usual. The day before, a communist patrol from Malaga had tried to burn down the Anarchist Centre in Churriana. Anarchists and Civil Guard fought side by side. 'Unheard of! We beat them off.'[38]

The Sheppards reported that Gerald was obsessed. Spanish politics had displaced everything in his conversation, even sex and gossip. He devoured Spanish papers. The moment anything happened he dashed out and questioned everyone. Gamel told Llewelyn that he had already decided to write a book about it all. He had even begun his preliminary reading: 'Communist writings' and Chamberlain's *History of the Russian Revolution*.[38]

On 18 July Gerald went into Malaga to collect his trousers from the cleaner's. As usual, he bought a newspaper – *El Popular*. The moment he read the headlines – 'Military rebellion in Morocco. Ceuta and Melilla seized by the factions' – he knew that once again he was about to be involved in one of the great events of his time.*

* Gerald and Gamel were in the thick of the Civil War for three months, and at first his projected book was to be an eyewitness account. He kept full diary notes and his account in *Personal Record*, written from them, as he told VSP in letters of 27 November 1967 and 8 November 1971 (Texas archive) is exciting. Yet his letters at the time (mostly to Ralph), hurriedly written, often scarcely legible, convey far more vividly their tension, their wildly fluctuating hopes and fears as to who would win, the sense, almost, of being in the firing line. Ralph treated them as bulletins from the front and had them typed out and distributed to their friends (Gerald to Bunny, 15 August 1936). What is also striking, and opposed to *Personal Record*, is Gerald's fury against the generals from the start (see for example Gerald to Ralph, 22 and 28 July 1936). He also saw it as a struggle between liberty and tyranny and not, as it was seen in England, between communism and fascism. For this reason he felt it imperative he help the Left at once, and immediately began to send unsolicited articles to the *Manchester Guardian*, at the same time writing urgently to Bertrand Russell asking him to recommend him to the paper (Gerald to Russell, 24 July and 3, 5, 8 August 1936).

Gamel was also keeping full notes at the time, which she used when she wrote her finest book, *Death's Other Kingdom*. As well as their letters, I have used this in my account, as indeed did Gerald in *Personal Record*.

SIXTEEN

Civil War

Malaga was normal that very hot July afternoon of 1936, except that people seemed unusually nervous. Then, from the Calle Larios, Gerald heard a military band and saw a troop of soldiers marching down the Alameda, the enormously broad main street with its huge trees. They were apparently going to the municipal buildings to proclaim military law 'by order of the government'. Ominously, workmen were massing in the side streets. Gerald decided to get out.

But then – his trousers! He hurried to the cleaner's to find they were not yet ready. He could now hear sporadic firing. Refusing to be panicked like everyone else into a run, he walked 'fast' (Gerald's walking fast was as fast as most people running) towards the bus station. As he arrived the Churriana bus was disappearing – seven minutes early, according to the Churriana plumber who was with him.

Gerald began to feel thoroughly alarmed. The firing already sounded, to the ears of an ex-soldier, like a full-scale infantry battle. Bullets were ricocheting along the Alameda. Everyone was running about, some people with arms. But the plumber and he crossed the dried-up river lower down and managed to hitch a lift in a lorry. The Churriana house was buzzing with excitement and that night, from the *mirador*, they looked out and watched isolated patches of fire leap and flare and spread. Malaga was burning.

Next morning, the city lay under a pall of smoke, which drifted slowly out to sea. The attempt to seize the municipal buildings had been resisted by the Civil Guard and a furious fight ensued, with hundreds of thousands of rounds expended. One soldier had been killed. No one else. 'Such are the battles of the Andalusians.' However, the rest of the soldiers had deserted their officers, and during the night the poor quarter had swarmed into the town, firing the houses of the rich and of noted right-wingers.

Gerald left early for Torremolinos, to see if Jan Woolley would take Miranda to England. Alone with the servants, Gamel listened to the lorries, their sides scrawled with UGT, CNT and FAI in chalk, and full of deliriously excited young men roaring through Churriana. The men shouted the anarchist '¡*Salud!*', raised their clenched left fists and fired dangerously ancient weapons into the air. Suddenly, she was surprised by loud knocking. Going to the door (the servants seemed to have fled – in fact to hide the silver), she found an anarchist patrol come to search the house for weapons. But after opening a drawer of her underclothes and another full of Miranda's headless dolls, they retired in embarrassment. After this, Rosario hung a large Union Jack over the balcony onto the street. But, at what must have been a frightening moment (the anarchist band numbered twenty men), one notes Gamel's coolness and observant humour – the young leader, as well as his gun, had been wearing, 'to my intense delight', a child's gilt toy sword.[1]

On 21 July, still anxious about Miranda's escape, Gerald and Gamel went into Malaga. The city was strange and melancholy, many buildings still smoking and charred, the Calle Larios scattered with broken furniture and glass. They obtained details of the departure of British destroyers for Gibraltar from Mr Clissold, the Consul, and left – full of disgust for what Gerald called 'hysterical Britishers', who were already inventing atrocity stories about the Left, soon to be taken up by the *Daily Mail*, and making colossal scenes about nothing. 'I suppose it seems worse,' Gamel wrote, 'for British subjects to lose their luggage than lesser races their lives.'[1]

They took Miranda down on a donkey to Jan and Janetta Woolley in Torremolinos on 24 July, and waited with the little group till evening,* when a destroyer left with practically all the English community. A crowd of Torremolinos villagers cheered Gerald and Gamel and old women patted them. 'These ones aren't afraid to stay with us.'[1]

They had got Miranda out in the nick of time. Bombs began to fall that night. Malaga was now cut off from the rest of Republican

---

* '7.30 p.m.: We are waiting for Miranda's lorry from the Consulate. By orders from the radio all workmen are standing to. Why? Probably a false alarm, but we are in a state of War' (Gerald to Ralph, 23/4 July 1936).

Spain, except for the easily captured coast road east to Motril. And now – so near the surface of every Spaniard lies his history, so strong is the love of *pueblo* and loyalty to region – Malaga reverted to the days of the Arab *taifa* or kingdom. Buses and trains kept to the ancient boundaries. Malaguenian 'troops' advanced gloriously towards Cordoba or Granada. 'We read,' wrote Gerald, 'of Moorish castles and watch towers beseiged . . . it was a local war we were fighting . . . What happened in the rest of Spain did not concern us.'

Everyone was extremely nervy. There were continual rumours that the Moors were coming, and one night almost the whole of Churriana fled into the mountains, leaving Gerald and Gamel in a deserted and silent village. María's *novio* – a poor, tall, ineffective young man, his aged rifle always standing in the corner of the kitchen 'like an umbrella'[1] – was accidentally shot dead by a friend.

But the bombs were the real danger. They discovered much later that the Nationalists (as the rebel generals called themselves) had incorrect information of a huge ammunition dump in Churriana.[1] Bombs rained down. 'I admire your guts in staying on,' wrote Jay Allen, snatching a moment in Gib between fronts. He begged Gerald to get out if he 'heard the black boys advancing'.[2] Everyone was frightened of the Moors. The villagers were terrified. Irrationally supposing they'd be safe with Gerald, they sheltered in his house. Each night there were forty or fifty of them crouched and shivering in the storeroom. Both Gerald and Gamel commented on the sweet fetid smell fear produces. Partly for this reason they themselves sheltered in the glass-windowed dining room; also 'we had an irrational feeling,' said Gamel, 'that the bombs would come to the front door instead of the back.' In retaliation, the Malaga air force – four tiny droning passenger planes – took off and threw their little bombs out by hand over Granada.

Gamel, a woman of great physical courage, also, like many people of indolent vitality and indecisive nature, thrived on danger and emergencies. She was fascinated by the feeling 'of heightened life, of having some faculty that generally sleeps'.[5] She planned to stay as long as the Civil War lasted, turning the house into a hospital. When, at the end of July, a huge bomb fell, as they thought, on the Crooke Larios family, she hurried out at 4 a.m., bombs still falling, with Dettol and bandages. Don Carlos was unhurt, but the Brenans suggested that the family come and stay with them, which they later did.

But it was not just courage. As a result, one must suppose, of childhood events Gamel, even more than Gerald, had buried deep feelings and the ability to respond at that level. Now, wrung to those depths by the suffering and terror of the poor Churriana peasants, she describes in *Death's Other Kingdom* how she felt the pain of this 'melt the thin icicle in my heart'. Her book moves one in a way that Gerald's account, intensely vivid and dramatic as it is, does not.

War brought all Gamel's faculties into play – she should perhaps have married a guerrilla leader. Indeed, this was in some respects what Gerald now resembled. Bertie Russell had got him confirmed as the *Manchester Guardian* columnist and the moment anything happened he leapt onto his bicycle and 'with his enormous energy'[1] pedalled in the 90° heat the eight and a half miles into Malaga to investigate. Gamel describes how frightened she was a little later when she suddenly saw him striding down the street 'with his peculiar light springy walk'[1] intent on rescuing Juan Navaja, the baker and a right-wing friend, from a lorryload of anarchists from Malaga. In fact, they had come for someone else, but Gerald was so angry and strung up he made his speech anyway to the assembled villagers. 'For God's sake, stop Don Geraldo,' Antonio begged Gamel. 'He's going to get us all shot.'*

This was no idle plea. All revolutions move to a phase of extremism and violence. There had already been killings, but the bombings enraged the Malaguenians. Their anger – which Gerald both understood and shared[3] – was intensified by Nationalist broadcasts, especially those of General Queipo de Llano from Seville.† They

---

* Gamel was frightened for Gerald, but also proud of him. What has to be gleaned from her account of this incident in *Death's Other Kingdom* is that she met Gerald coming back, that is, she'd set out to join him. If he was in danger, she would be at his side.

† Gamel wrote a brilliant and also amusing description of this real-life monster from a fairy story in *Death's Other Kingdom*, which Gerald lifted (unacknowledged) for *Personal Record*. These blood-thirsty speeches were made in full dress uniform with his staff at attention behind him. His occasional astonishing mistakes were corrected without blinking. '"These villainous *Fascistas*," and an agonised voice can be heard correcting him, "No, no, Sir General, *Marxistas*." "What difference does it make?" – says the general and sweeps grandly on – "Yes, you *canalla*, you anarchists of Malaga, you wait until I get there in ten days' time! You just wait! I'll be sitting in a café in the Calle Larios sipping my beer, and for every sip I take ten of you will

now exacted reprisals after each raid – dragging right-wing internees out of the prison and shooting them. Soon terrorist groups of young men from the FAI – the Juventudes de la FAI – roared about the countryside out for blood. Before, except for priests and monks and the very rich, the murders had mostly been local revenge killings – unpopular *carabineri*, exorbitant lenders, local bullies, etc. Now, the slaughter became for a few weeks uncontrollable. People were even dragged out of hotels and shot or clubbed to death. Three lorryloads of Juventudes, the worst of the 'uncontrollables', arrived in Ronda and forced the *comité* to hand over all prisoners, as well as others on various 'lists'. They then threw the lot into that frightful abyss which cuts the outskirts of the town – 512 of them, including some women. There were similar terrible massacres, each side as bad as the other.

In *Personal Record*, Gerald was able to take refuge in the calming perspectives of history. 'They were in the grip,' he wrote of this blood-lust, 'of what the Flemings in the reign of Philip II had called the "Spanish Fury". So humane on ordinary occasions, Spaniards are prone at times of excitement to an hysterical passion for killing and destruction.' But at the time this sudden revelation about the country he loved appalled him. His hatred of violence extended as we saw deep into his past and his character and it was his horror at these events which in particular impelled him later to find out *why*.

Immediately, the violence made it imperative that Don Carlos take up Gerald's offer of sanctuary. Although he was personally poor and popular, everyone with the name Larios was now being shot. One night in August after darkness had fallen, Rosario appeared dramatically. '"They have come," she declared, in low intense tones, like an old-fashioned Lady Macbeth.'¹ There were five of them, plus some chickens.

Don Carlos was a man of great personal charm. He was also, Gerald rapidly discovered, a Falangist,* and one of an extreme,

---

fall. I shall shoot ten of you for every one of ours!' [He bellows] "If I have to drag them out of their graves to shoot them!"'¹ What made these diatribes horrifying was that Queipo de Llano was overseeing mass murder in Seville.

   * The Falange was founded in 1932 by José Antonio, the son of Primo de Rivera, and a man of humane ideals, humour, charm and imagination. He wanted to involve the workers, the poor and the students in a patriotic crusade of national regeneration – but an enlightened one. As well as the usual right-wing goals like support for the church and Empire (that is, Morocco, Portugal and South America),

violent and sadistic sort. He listened gloatingly to Queipo de Llano with the programme, which was illegal, turned up full. Though his presence was meant to be secret (those harbouring fascists were shot – three already in Churriana) he couldn't resist appearing in the *mirador* to yell his applause as the bombs fell on Malaga. Gerald had several furious rows with him.

By mid-August, 'It is a strain being here – we listen on the radio to the tale of towns and cities destroyed, to the threats of the loathsome General Queipo de Llano, the news of shootings and appalling reprisals in store for everyone.'[4] Gerald begged Ralph to write to him more often (in fact letters could get out, but very rarely in). They found it hard to sleep, listening to the lorries pass in the night and watching their lights swing across the ceiling. Once one did stop very close. They heard shouts, loud knockings, cries, protests, screams. Then the lorry drove away.[1]

Yet half the time everything seemed normal. They were – except for Don Carlos' antics – personally fairly safe. Everyone knew the English were not involved, Gerald and Gamel were very popular, and British destroyers steamed to and fro in full view. They had breakfast each morning outside, to the sound of trickling, running water, on the old round green table with its marble top – strong black coffee, goats' milk, marmalade made by Gamel from their own oranges, toast of the delicious Spanish bread. The *alberca* emptied and filled for the irrigation, Antonio gardened. Before going to bed at night Gerald and Gamel went round the garden together smelling the flowers.

By 19 August, the Committee of Public Safety in Malaga – that name of grim association – were killing forty people a night.[5] Then, on 21 August, Gerald and Gamel were woken by a tremendous explosion. Rushing up to the *mirador*, they saw thick black columns of smoke streaming up from the port. They also found Don Carlos leaping with joy. Furious, Gerald sent him down. He then took his bicycle and raced into Malaga. On the way, he passed a charming

---

he was for socialising the banks and the railways, and advocated radical land reform. He admired and emulated the frugality and fervour of the anarchists. It was this idealism, unique among right-wing groups, which led Franco to take up the Falange as spearhead of his intellectually empty movement – thereby, of course, perverting and degrading José Antonio's genuinely visionary aims.

sight: a band of *gitanos*, gypsies, having breakfast – mules, children, young and old busy round their fires. At the port, he found an inferno. The oil and petrol dumps had received a direct hit and huge fires were raging, and were to do so for three days. Workmen in pants were shovelling tons of wet sand in the fierce heat, swirling smoke and flames. It was 'like a scene out of hell'. But what he discovered on his way back was somehow even worse. A bomb had exploded directly on the gypsy camp. Bodies, blood, pots and pans, limbs 'were scattered all over the place'.[6] Trembling with horror, exhausted and tense, Gerald arrived back to hear the broadcasts of Radio Seville blaring out into the street from his house.

After the row that ensued with Don Carlos, Gerald decided they would have to get rid of him. For eight days, every day, often twice a day, Gerald bicycled into Malaga and back in the searing August heat, in danger from bombs, and struggled to get the right papers for him to leave. Don Francisco, a liberal delegate on the Committee of Public Safety (and all liberal men, the governor included, were appalled at the violence of the 'uncontrollables'), helped him – though Gerald did not dare approach the Committee itself. Don Carlos had once farmed for a number of years in Chile, and two of his children had been born there. The Argentinian consul in Malaga, acting for Chile, was able to produce an impressive, formal-looking document, covered in seals and stamps. On 26 August a British destroyer was sailing from Malaga to Gibraltar. But now another problem arose – how were they to get the family out? Don Carlos was a wanted man. All lorries and taxis entering Malaga were regularly searched. In this situation out of the French Revolution Gerald acted like the Scarlet Pimpernel. He simply led the family, all carrying their luggage, straight down the Churriana streets and onto the little train. There were sidelong looks, but they were not stopped.

The ordeal was still not over. A quick coffee at the British Club was followed by a long agonising wait in the hot shed where papers were looked at. At last it was Don Carlos' turn. After prolonged scrutiny the papers were rejected. There was no stamp from the Committee of Public Safety. Gerald bundled them all into a taxi, drove to the Argentinian Consul, drove to Don Francisco, and finally faced the Committee. Both he and the Consul harangued them. At last, 'The tired men sitting round the table' – and how telling is the simple adjective – 'gave way and made out the pass.' Two hours later the whole family had gone.

When Gerald returned exhausted to Churriana he found that just after he had left three armed anarchists arrived to get Don Carlos. Rosario had met them and said in her severe voice, 'You are too late. He has already left the country on his way to Argentina.' It is likely, as Gamel noted, that in a country with many remnants of a matriarchal society, this decisive statement saved his life. There was still plenty of time to catch Don Carlos but the search was not pursued.*[1]

On 29 August the Nationalist planes attacked little Churriana in force. María, Rosario's eldest daughter, can remember being told how they all crouched under the stairs and how Gerald held a big iron dustbin lid over Gamel's head. Seventy bombs fell within 300 yards of the house and Gerald can be forgiven for supposing that someone had told Queipo de Llano about his *Manchester Guardian* articles and that the evil general was out to get him personally.

Nevertheless, his paranoia was a sign of the continuing strain. And every day the danger increased. On 1 September they were both trapped in Malaga. A huge 200-kilo bomb landed close to their hotel. There was a rending crash and terrible cries; 'and the cries,' wrote Gamel, 'seemed to me to be dragged down by the roaring crash of the bomb and carried down with it through the earth.'[1] Next day Humphrey Slater, a young, very good-looking reporter for the *Daily Worker*, took Gerald to the front near the Torcal, where he'd been picnicking only a few months before. They explored the line on horseback and it was rapidly clear to Gerald that the Nationalists could take Malaga whenever they wished. He and Gamel were,

---

* This attempt to get Don Carlos was in one way of considerable comfort to Gerald. Juan Navaja, the honorable, upright but right-wing Churriana baker he'd sought to protect earlier, begged to be allowed to shelter in the house. Gerald by that time had Don Carlos with him and, since Juan Navaja was being actively looked for, did not want to endanger the entire family. Juan Navaja said the British flag would protect them all, but Gerald disagreed. However, he left the door to the garden unlocked and told the baker he could creep in and hide in emergencies. But Navaja hid in a cave, was betrayed and subsequently shot. After the Civil War, his brother accused Gerald of being responsible for his death, and judging by the space he devotes to it in *Personal Record* another twenty years on, this continued to upset him. But the arrival of the anarchists for Don Carlos was clear proof that, had he not escaped an hour before, he would have been arrested. The Union Jack would have been no more of a protection for the unfortunate Juan Navaja.

moreover, rapidly running out of money. On 7 September, having given as much as they could to Rosario and Antonio, they finally embarked on a destroyer to Gibraltar. Apart from Sir Peter Chalmers Mitchell (an anarchist who stayed till February 1937)[7] Gerald and Gamel were the last English residents to leave Malaga.*

In Gibraltar Gerald resigned his position with the *Manchester Guardian*. But Jay Allen was there briefly, *en route* to Madrid and Toledo, and asked Gerald to take over from him on the *News Chronicle*. With Gerald's determination to emulate the ace reporter, an element of farce began to appear. Gerald and Gamel hurried to Tangier, then under the nominal control of the French. It was seething with Nationalists, fleeing Republicans, Italian fascists, and journalists. 'We lead,' wrote Gerald, highly stimulated, 'an Edgar Wallace life. Spies? There are more spies than people to spy on.'[8]

Allen rushed everywhere; so would Gerald. On 10 September they flew to Lisbon to investigate rumours of a mutiny and to see if the Portuguese were supplying the generals. On the 13th they were back in Tangier and a brief meeting with Allen. 'He is a super-crack journalist . . . has secret connections everywhere . . . I could do nothing without him . . . flies to Madrid tonight.'[9] The significance of Tangier was the possibility that the Moroccan tribes might rise against Spain. Gerald, in fact, hadn't the faintest idea how to find this out until, to his great relief, he found an informant. Splenhil was a one-eyed Moor whose work, so he said, took him into Spanish Morocco. He also sold information to the French legation.

Meanwhile, Gerald continued to rush – to such a degree he didn't even have time to visit the notorious Chat Noir – to Gibraltar on 16 September, then back to see his Moor on the 18th. He planned to fly to Granada and Cordoba, to Fez, and perhaps to Malaga. On the 21st he and Gamel shot over to Gibraltar, but immediately returned on rumours of some impending 'incident'. Gerald now managed to squeeze in a flying visit to the Chat Noir to watch a couple copulating – 'charming'[10] – but all the rushing was taking its toll. The writing of

---

* One or two stayed throughout the war. One of these was Walter Grice-Hutchinson. He was a Franco supporter, but none the less rescued people in his yacht. When food was very short, he used this to bring food from Gibraltar to the people of Churriana. As a result, after the war they named a street after him. See *Malaga Farm*, London, 1956, by his daughter, Marjorie von Schlippenbach – a close friend of Gerald's and Gamel's both before and after the Civil War.

the crack journalist, usually so clear, is frequently illegible. He heard that Franco was dead, and immediately their hotel was filled with the smell of chloroform. Sniffing, he tried to follow this important clue, but was told they cleaned the lavatories with chloroform. 'I visited all the lavatories – they were the only part of the hotel that did not smell.'[10] Finally, early in October – a scoop: the Beni Uriaguel had revolted – so had the Gomara. Tribe after tribe was rising. Gerald describes in *Personal Record* how he flew to the telegraph. There were headlines in the *News Chronicle*.

Alas, it was a complete hoax. Nothing happened. The one-eyed Moor had vanished.*

With considerable relief, one senses, Gerald resigned. He and Gamel must have needed, certainly deserved, a holiday. They set out on 3 October for a wandering tour of Morocco – Fez, Marrakesh and on to the great cedar forests south of the Atlas. Gerald was invited to shoot panther and wild ostrich.[11] By 18 October they were back in Tangier by way of Rabat† and the next day sailed for England. They arrived at Plymouth on 22 October, penniless and wearing *djellabas*, and went straight to Ham Spray.

---

* In fact, a study of the *News Chronicle* does not reveal the headlines Gerald refers to. The paper must have got wind of the fiasco from elsewhere just in time.

† From where, on 17 October, after an astonishing four months revealing him as generous, self-sacrificing and full of pity to a quixotic degree, brave and resourceful, emotional, excitable, impetuous and farcical, after all this he wrote to Ralph with typical insouciance – 'I am very bored with the east' – as if nothing had happened at all.

SEVENTEEN

England – and the Start of the Labyrinth

'His spirit knew no pause when an object was to be obtained. His mind, like a lens, concentrated its power into one piercing ray.'
The Adventures of a Younger Son, Edward John Trelawney

1

Gerald and Gamel were not properly settled until they moved into Bell Court in Aldbourne, Wiltshire, in November 1938. Because Llewelyn was very ill again and about to go to Switzerland they first rented a tiny cottage at East Chaldon. The sitting room was seven foot square, according to Gerald.[1]

In December they took what Gamel called 'a degraded villa'[2] in Rouledge, Farnham. Miranda was at nearby Frensham Junior School, living with Jan Woolley. Janetta (now sixteen, one of Gerald's favourite ages), was at the senior school in Down House (she accordingly christened the Brenans' degraded villa Up House). She remembers Miranda wetting her bed and Jan curing her with the present of a torch.

Gerald also bought a second-hand Morris with a sliding roof, for £25. 'A rather smart saloon,' he described it to Helen. But the letter ends with an agonised cry: Franco's men had taken Marbella and shot '300 civilians in cold blood. I cannot bear to go on thinking about these things, yet cannot get them out of my mind.'[3]

2

The Spanish Civil War did not, in general, involve a large proportion of the population in England. But those it did involve it obsessed. It became, to use one of Rupert Christiansen's flashing phrases, like the French Revolution and the freedom of Greece in the 1820s before it, the symbol of 'everything young and brave and golden'.[4]

Almost the moment he had arrived back, Gerald began to devour Spanish history.[5] He also, on 4 November, hurried up to London on 'cosas de la España – I cannot settle down while Madrid hangs in the balance'. He watched Jay Allen buy twenty Austrian Army tanks, thousand-pound notes fluttering about 'like postage stamps'.[6] Allen then drove him to Edgeworth via Gloucester where the dentist, as though sensing Gerald's desire to identify with the Republican cause, massacred his teeth. (Frances, seeing him without his expensive false ones, noticed that every alternate tooth had gone, so that his mouth resembled a medieval turret top. Gerald compared it to Avebury.)[7]

He addressed meetings, including a packed Albert Hall on 9 November, helped Sylvia Townsend-Warner and the Association of Writers for the Defence of Culture, and helped raise money for Sir George Young (just back frm Cordoba) and his ambulances. Janetta remembers Bell Court later on humming with Civil War activity. One of the people Gerald met on these occasions was Professor J. B. Trend, the Cambridge Hispanist. Infuriated that the British press, especially the *Daily Mail*, were concentrating on Republican acts of violence, Gerald wrote angry letters to the papers. But even here, even now, he was scrupulously fair. When Sir Peter Chalmers-Mitchell and others wrote to *The Times* stating that the Republicans were not commiting atrocities in Malaga, he refused to sign.*

He released his feelings in part by having a furious row with Bertie Russell over pacifism† and sending provocative letters to

---

* According to Baroness Marjorie von Schlippenbach. This was also, she said, the reason why Gerald was allowed to return to Spain in 1952.

† Russell was not upset, and on 22 June 1937 wrote from America and asked if Gerald and Gamel would adopt his son Conrad if he and Peter were ever killed. 'We

Ralph on the same subject. He felt a good deal of guilt about not going out to help in Spain. When, in February 1937, he was 'asked, implored even, to go to Madrid to help evacuate women and children', he gave Gamel, as he was to do countless times throughout his life, as his excuse.[8] Gamel, of course, would have gone with him like a shot, and been extremely useful. The real reason was his book about the Civil War.

'Gerald's latest act,' Gamel wrote irritably to Llewelyn in 1937, 'is to read the entire history of ceramics because he had to write half a page about Spanish pottery.'[9] His compulsive need to explore any subject in its totality made it next to inevitable that he would rapidly move on from the mere eyewitness account he promised Chatto soon after he got back. In *Personal Record*, with typical over-modesty, he gracefully gives Franz Borkenau the credit for the transition. Borkenau certainly encouraged him and was extremely helpful, but his first mention of Borkenau is in July 1937. In fact, a suppressed portion of *Personal Record* makes it plain that he'd begun long before he met or read Borkenau[10] – probably, from his letters, in December 1936.[11] On 15 March 1937 he told Chatto he wanted to write two books, one much 'more extensive and serious'.[12]

So far, apart from one short squib and one novel finished with agonising slowness after five years, Gerald's twenty years of writing life were littered with six or seven unfinished novels, fourteen years on St Teresa, and innumerable half-written stories, novellas, plays and verse narratives. His income from writing in 1935, for instance, had been three shillings.[13] 'He starts so many books,' mused Gamel gloomily.[14] She doubted he'd finish this one. Yet by December he was already reading and writing ten or eleven hours a day – and this fury of work is revealing. Gerald's pleasure and excitement in learning had one root in combat. It had begun as an act of defiance against his father. His book could thus easily become his method of fighting for the Republicans, which was why he initially planned to write the book fast enough for it to come out during the Civil War. It is possible that Gerald's relations with his father reinforced this aspect at a subconscious level in another way. Franco and the generals,

---

do not know anyone else whose atmosphere and way of life and general outlook is so completely what we like.' Gerald's answer has vanished.

military men like his father and representatives of the conventional and the rich, were attempting to impose their will on the left, the poor and the radical – the Geralds of Spain. And the violence of his working reflects his horror at the violence in Spain – to explain was to exorcise. With such feelings, one might suppose he would find it difficult to be fair. This was not entirely so. There were cells for the emotions in the interior castle. They could be locked up. And though, when freed (or when they burst out), his feelings were for the Republicans, these feelings did not have the same left-wing ideology – romantic, proletarian-worshipping and often fuelled by class guilt – as those of so many of his contemporaries in the 1930s. Gerald's radical, idealistic side was personal and idiosyncratic, deriving, via dislike of his father, from his ideas of Rimbaudian intensity, and reality through pain and poverty. This, too, made for political detachment. If he called himself to Bunny 'a socialist at long range', he added that he was conservative at short range.[15] His politics were always strongly balanced by common sense and pragmatism. He told Bunny he didn't support the Popular Front, for instance.[15] Also, for some time, he backed non-intervention. His reading rapidly showed him that the Civil War was a Peninsular problem, not an extension of European conflicts; and the violence he so minded 'in the country I loved' would simply be exacerbated if other nations poured in arms and munitions. Not till later, when it was clear other nations were continuing to do this, that it was becoming decisive, and that Russia and Mexico could not, or would not match Germany and Italy, did he become enraged by the British government's weakness and indecision. (Recent research has shown that this 'non-intervention' was a deliberate strategy by influential sections of the government to support Franco.)[16]

3

Just before Christmas, and before his book had taken over from most other Civil War activity, Gerald paid one of several visits to the Spanish Embassy. Although it seems to have been largely right-wing (one of the attachés, for instance, was a nephew of Queipo de Llano), it was probably at one of these visits that he met Luis Araquistain, who was of particular service to his book.* V. S. Pritchett was at the same Christmas party as Gerald and, both of them immediately stimulated, Gerald could still remember the meeting forty-two years later. They at once talked about writing and VSP asked him to lunch at his club.[17]

Gerald had hoped to spend Christmas at Ham Spray, but it was full of Woolleys, so they slumped back onto Edgeworth. 'Cold house, hard cakes, ear trumpets, grey skies, clergymen, conversations on Miranda's shoes – oh oh онононо!' he groaned to Frances, also envying her 'the lovely Janetta'.[18] Hugh was selling the house and it was to be vacated when this happened. Soon 'over the stones of Edgewaggers, the ostrich and the satyr will be dancing and the owl hooting in the desolate places where once the merry laughter of the B family was heard.'[19] There was an enormous and ferocious horse in the stable, rendered almost uncontrollable by his father's authoritarian regime, but Gerald took it hunting twice through the beautiful and frosty countryside – 'Old man's beard streaming from the trees.'[18]

Malaga fell in February, and in April the bombing of Guernica showed the terrible effectiveness of German intervention. During May the Nationalists began to starve Bilbao into submission. None the less, Gerald still thought the Republicans would win.[20]

That same month they took Ley Park, a house at Welcombe, a village right against the sea on the Cornwall/Devon northern border. It was then, as now, set in a patchwork land of little fields and lanes, high banks, thick hedges with, in spring, a mass of primroses and cowslips. In fact, Welcombe is less a village than a group of isolated ugly houses waiting for summer visitors. Lytton and Carrington and Ralph used to go there before the 1920s, and it was Gerald and Gamel's summer place for the next fourteen years. Ley Park (whose name, Gerald thought, got a Civil War letter of his published in *The Times*; in fact 'park' simply means 'paddock' in Cornwall) was a small, square, stucco box, unfenced in a field, with two bedrooms, no electricity, no bathroom or running water (a well). It was 100 yards

* Luis Araquistain, an anti-communist Marxist and a shy but brilliant journalist, started and edited *Claridad* and became, for a while, a confidant of Largo Caballero. He was then ambassador in Paris before fleeing to England. He gave Gerald valuable and detailed information about communist methods of infiltration, quite unknown in 1936. He also read *The Spanish Labyrinth* in typescript. After 1939, his life became tragic, when his wife died and his daughter committed suicide.

or so from the cliff, the air soft and full of the sound of the sea which, when rough, throws up armfulls of spume that sits in foaming, detergent-looking lumps on the grass. Cows graze and, Gerald wrote to VSP, 'At night when the lamps are lit they come and peer curiously in at the windows and their horns stand up against the sea.'[21] There are marvellous sunsets and walks in all directions, especially along the sun-bathing cliffs.

Almost at once, Gerald asked Janetta down for Whitsun. She remembers running over the rocks with him and thinking how surely she would be quicker than this old man (he was now forty-four) – but she wasn't.

Janetta also remembers Gamel passing her driving test. She was proceeding down one of the narrow lanes when suddenly a lot of elephants came round the corner. Gamel giggled and said, 'On what side should you pass an elephant?' The examiner also laughed and Gamel, who was an erratic driver, was sure that was why she passed.

Both Gerald and Gamel worked continuously at their books (Gamel, in fact, had almost finished *Death's Other Kingdom*) and in July Franz Borkenau came to stay. This eccentric Austro-Hungarian sociologist, whose brilliant *The Spanish Cockpit* had just come out, was not easy. Uncouth, abrupt, oddly moustached, he was so nervous he could not sit or walk without constantly turning to see if he was followed. But his fiancée came – a gentle, beautiful Jewish-Arab dancer from the Berlin Opera – so 'the difficult man is softened'.[22] Anyhow, Gerald could always get on with people whose enthusiasms he shared. And Gamel, with her system of floating and agreeing, was fairly all right – except 'I grow confused and tired with the difficulty of cooking and housekeeping in too small cold dark dirty cottages'.[23]

Gerald consulted Borkenau continuously over his book, and Borkenau's letters to him have the ring of teacher to pupil. But Gerald said an interesting thing about Borkenau. 'In conversation his judgements were often wild and it was only when he sat down to write that his intelligence and his sense for reality came out.'[24] This was not totally true of Gerald, but it was certainly sometimes true. It contains elements of Gerald. And it is perhaps not a bad way to proceed – the wildness allows free and original speculations to be flung about, it generates outrageous and daring ideas. The selective, analytic, critical intelligence can come later.

At the end of August, Gamel went to Clavadel in Switzerland

for ten days to see Llewelyn. The visit was a great success. Gamel was 'in childish high spirits'.[25] Alyse wrote in her journal, 'I thought I had never looked on so beautiful a face . . . We are bound together in some incommunicable way.'[26]

Gerald, as often when Gamel went, immediately missed her. Ralph supposed he was out looking for girls on the cliffs. But he wasn't. He was lonely.[27] Ronnie Duncan, the poet, and his wife lived at Welcombe. They became close friends. Rose-Marie Duncan: 'One could see at once how dependent he was on her.' Gamel wrote him charming letters – 'My darling child . . .'[28]

In September Miranda, now eight and a half, was sent to a boarding school in Devon near South Molton. 'We feel both sad and extremely relieved,' Gamel told Llewelyn. 'The peace and silence I must admit are delightful.' She and Miranda now 'lie on the couch together under Gerald's Burnous and read *The Snow Queen*'.[28]

Thus released, Gerald and Gamel went house-hunting and some time in October they found a very small house, Bell Court, in Aldbourne, a village about seven miles from Hungerford and ten from Ham Spray. Considerable *obra* was required, so on 17 November they rented yet another too small cold dark dirty cottage – Half Moon Cottage, just round the corner from Bell Court.

The extraordinary speed and concentration with which Gerald was working is shown by the fact that by this month he had already completed 70,000 words of his book,[29] though Chatto were still expecting he would also write them his eyewitness account.[30] Aldbourne was useful for all this, too, since Borkenau lived close by.

But work was about to be seriously disrupted. Early in December they learnt that Helen Brenan had incurable cancer of the spine.

4

Although it had often been necessary, for his spiritual and personal salvation, to do things that hurt his mother, Gerald loved her and paid full tribute to what he owed her in *A Life of One's Own*. But his description of her death in *Personal Record* is detached and extremely laconic.

His accounts at the time were neither. By Christmas, events at Edgeworth were very distressing. His mother was in great pain and the morphia only made her sick. 'It is terribly painful,' Gerald told Ralph, and made more difficult because his father was exhausted, tense and irritable from sitting up all night.

On 30 December, Gerald and Gamel went back to Half Moon, but Gerald drove up to Edgeworth every day, writing long letters to relieve his feelings when he returned late at night. He was present when she died, and the day before, on 6 January, wrote another long letter to Frances.

His father was trying to keep people away, but Gerald was sure that was wrong, and stayed as long as he could. 'The solitude of dying is the worst thing and I see how they feel it. One must accompany them, holding their hand, to the very edge of the river.

'I did not like leaving. I had a feeling of closeness, of enlinkedness to this despairing figure on the bed that seemed to me very primitive. They all said 'she is delirious, she feels nothing', merely because they had blocked up with their morphia the only organs by which she could communicate with them. I thought differently. She was conscious of her terrible solitude, of new processes beginning in her body, of something frightening ahead. She was anxious and afraid, but she was also suggestible and did what one told her to until, a moment later, she had forgotten what it was. As she knew me and could often understand what I said, I felt I must stay.'[31]

Yet still, almost automatically, he observed, still absorbed and recorded significant, out-of-the-way information. The nurse told him that as one approached the end one began to learn a new way of breathing. 'She tells me it is called the Cheyne Stokes breathing, though why a Victorian doctor should give his name to respiration by which men have died for the last million years, I cannot say.'[31] This observation, made while his mother died, he used in *Personal Record* at the death of his father to show with telling effect how distant he felt from that event.

The funeral was followed immediately by the reading of the Will. Gerald's account of this in *Personal Record* was neither laconic, nor detached – nor entirely accurate. He says that, as a result of Churriana spending, his fixed income had fallen to £130 p.a. His mother had said 'repeatedly' how he and Blair would be better off when she died. Since his mother had left £12,000 (say £330,000), everyone was naturally awaiting the reading of the Will with pleasurable anticipation.

'My father produced the Will. After coughing once or twice in his dry way [Gerald once described coughing as 'the artillery of the home'],[32] "I know already what is in it," he said, "because I dictated it to your mother myself." Then as he read it aloud we learned that she had left everything to him for life, to come to us only after his death.' Fairly devastating – and Gerald adds that not until the Second War did his father allow them any of the income.

Gerald was not at all rich, and it must have been maddening not getting money when he'd expected it. But it was not quite as bad as he makes out. His father was giving him an allowance and with Gamel's money he still, as he had admitted to VSP in July, had £320 (say £8800) a year.[33] His father was also paying some of Miranda's school fees.[34] His father handed the interest over to the two brothers at once (£250 p.a. each) though it is true wrangles about details of this continued till 1940.[36] Gerald was still able to live and write his book without working, and he was also allowed to use the capital for education and to buy houses – and in April 1938 he bought Bell Court.*

Gerald's attitude to money, already complicated by his years of privation and Hugh Brenan's neurotically dominating anxiety about it, received a further twist through his friendship with VSP. Extraordinary as it seems – and it is a comment on English cultural and social life in the 1930s – Gerald never seems to have met, didn't even realise there existed, writers without private incomes. And not just writers, 'Nearly everyone I know has *some* unearned income,' he says in the letter to VSP, one of the first he wrote him, mentioned above. He also says it was the Spanish Civil War, enabling him to compare his plenty with starving villagers, that gave him a social conscience. Gerald had been able to compare himself to starving villagers since 1919. It was the sight of VSP struggling to earn enough to keep a wife and two children by books and literary journalism which for the first time made him feel guilty about his small but sufficient private income. His letters to VSP are full of nervous references to it. He occasionally invents a past of earning his living – a favourite fantasy being that he had to give up poetry in order to do this. His guilt over VSP's lack of money compared to his own possession of it (twice thumpingly augmented) eventually grew until it could only be

---

* The house cost £800 – half paid from his mother's capital; half from a mortgage of £450, which cost him about £20 p.a.

alleviated by an eruption of generosity so enormous that Gerald, after a stunned pause, spent the next twenty years intermittently tortured by regrets and longings for the vanished sum until at last a personal crisis allowed him to ask, as had always been agreed between them, for the money back.

5

By the end of January 1938, with the Nationalists forcing their way through Aragon and Castellón, it seemed only months before Franco would win. In April, Gerald and Gamel had three refugees from Spain crammed with them into tiny Half Moon Cottage, one an underclothes salesman, 'A minute little man with long arms which he waves about like signals.'³⁷ (*Obra* continued at Bell Court till September.) Letters arrived from Antonio and Rosario, but they were always empty. Gerald's letters back didn't get through at all. His servants thought he'd never written. But in February something far more agonising had occurred in his Civil War struggle. He finished the first draft of *The Spanish Labyrinth*,* read it carefully, and came to the conclusion it was no good. For a while he seriously thought of giving up entirely and was going to burn the manuscript. Then, gritting his teeth, he set out to rewrite the entire book.³⁸

Spring and summer were spent partly at Ley Park, partly at Crantock near Newquay, where Blair and Rhoda brought their children to stay at Rose Cottage. In July, on one of many visits to London and the British Museum, Borkenau introduced him to Arthur Lehning, an anarchist and the librarian at the International Institute for Social History in Amsterdam. He and his pretty wife came to stay at Aldbourne in November and he supplied Gerald with books and papers on the agrarian problem and anarcho-syndicalism he couldn't get elsewhere. He later read the manuscript of *The Spanish Labyrinth* for him.†

---

* At this point the book was called *The Reason of Unreason: A History of the Struggle in Spain, Past, Present and Future*. It was Gamel's title. They thought, as she wrote to Alyse some time in 1938, '*La Razón de la Sinrazón*' was a quotation from *Don Quixote*. (It was – from Chapter 1, Part 1. But the phrase is a common one in Spanish medieval love poetry.)

† Other people who helped Gerald, all fully and generously acknowledged,

This visit was also made to consult a doctor as to whether Gamel could or should have children. The doctor, Frances remembered, saw no reason against it *at all*, at which Ralph remarked, 'I think Gerald will find his own sort of birth control.' At the end of August, Gerald announced, in a letter that made clear he hoped to God she wasn't, that Gamel thought she was pregnant[39] – but it must have been a false alarm as there is no further mention of it.

Perhaps Ralph was right – though Gamel's real age was now forty-three – but his typically shrewd comment reveals a facet of their relationship, and a fortunate one as far as Gerald was concerned. Ralph was pessimistic about human nature as well as (or because) astute about it; but his pessimism brought him considerable enjoyment. It always gave him pleasure when people behaved both badly and in character – and Gerald frequently behaved in character. But this is partly why, despite some heated exchanges, Ralph hadn't reacted nearly as strongly as might have been expected to Gerald's extremely sharp and provocative letters about pacificism. Gerald was now clear that Hitler should be resisted by force; he was also bitterly angry at the defeat that seemed certain for the Republicans. He needed to release these feelings, and chose to do so on Ralph. (It is noticeable how his most provocative letters came after some event had stirred him up. 'Heaven help me from raging pacifists,' he wrote immediately after addressing the Albert Hall.)[40] That the rows between them were really emotional not ideological is shown by the number of pacifists Gerald had as close friends during the war. 'He really thought intellectuals *ought* to be pacifists,' said Lawrence Gowing, who was both. Ronnie Duncan, on the other hand, worshipped Hitler and was so right-wing several people thought he was a fascist.

But it is for this reason that the substance of Gerald and Ralph's first major row, which took place on 27 September at Ham Spray (so often the scene, and so a reminder of, their old rivalry), is hardly material. It started as a heated discussion about Munich (not an argument about the settlement – at this point, Gerald seems to have

---

were Arturo Barea, author of the magnificent three-part autobiography *The Forging of a Rebel*. For several years he was the planned translator of *The Spanish Labyrinth*. Gerald also visited Oxford to talk to Don Alberto Jiménez, director of the cultural branch of the Institución Libre de Enseñanza, and his wife Doña Natalia de Cossio.

supported Munich, though not for pacific reasons), moved to a joke (Ralph comparing Gerald to Hitler) and then rapidly degenerated into a violent verbal fight. Janetta, who was there, was terrified. Ralph was blue in the face and 'simply filled with rage'.

'You are *longing* for a war,' he shouted at Gerald. 'You will never be happy till there are two or three million dead. You *loved* the last war, and you are *longing* for another.'⁴¹ Gerald was coldly furious, insulting, goading, cruel and spiteful. At each new dart flung in, Janetta expected Ralph to explode and kill Gerald. She was amazed he dared face such anger – but it was of course precisely because he could get so angry that Ralph was able to stand in for Hugh Brenan, the whole of Nazi Germany and Franco's Spain rolled into one.

Gerald and Gamel were turned out of Ham Spray, laden with Spanish plates and jugs and a trunk all stored there, and drove trembling back to Aldbourne, where Gerald immediately wrote a long account to Bunny and another to Helen.⁴²

The row tore them both. Gerald was ashamed of what he'd said and miserable at losing Ralph. On this occasion they were able to make it up – 'Now we have become two touchy old colonels who cannot meet. An absurd situation!'⁴³ – but there was wariness for some time.

In November they at last moved into Bell Court, and in December Gerald was given a more legitimate outlet for his strong and, indeed, perfectly understandable feelings, when he was asked by the Duchess of Atholl to help her fight a by-election in West Perthshire.

The Duchess was a right-wing Tory and saw clearly, like Gerald, the need to re-arm. When Gerald had first returned from Spain she'd got him, as one who had first-hand experience of German and Italian armed might, to address a group of Tory MPs in a committee room of the House of Commons. Gerald had been extremely nervous but the speech had been a success. After Munich the Duchess had resigned her constituency of West Perthshire as a protest against Chamberlain's not re-arming fast enough nor creating a Ministry of Supply. She wanted to test the issue by vote and, remembering Gerald's clarity and force of expression, asked him to speak for her. Gerald, once more very nervous, said he would canvass but not speak. Arriving at Dunkeld after his long journey on 7 December – 'Steam hissed round the wheels of the Flying Scotsman as I rode north' – he was appalled to see, as he was driven from the station, the walls and hoardings plastered with posters blazoning his name and army rank.

He kept full notes of the three weeks and his account in *Personal Record* is both interesting and very amusing – as were his letters to Ralph. With the Duchess, a small woman of huge energy in her sixties, acquisitive, charming, a near-professional pianist, he got on well. The Duke was at first tricky, especially when Gerald appeared in an elegant, almost effete, pair of red Moroccan slippers recently acquired in the Burlington Arcade; but then it emerged that Gerald's uncle, Charlie Graham, had been in the 4th Hussars, of which the Duke had been colonel. The whisky, hitherto sparse, now flowed.

The election was lost, and Gerald returned in a freezing train through blizzards for Christmas at his father's new house in Cheltenham. Ralph and Frances gave the dandy a pale moon-coloured tie and Miranda a tea-set. The little family returned as soon as they could to Aldbourne and Bell Court.

6

Aldbourne lies where seven roads, ancient sheep tracks, converge in a hollow at the end of several gentle Wiltshire valleys. It is dominated by a fine, large church rising at one end, below which is an extensive green with a pump, some houses and then a second green with a pond. Five pubs served a population, in 1938, of 1024 – though this included the outlying farms and dwellings.*44

Bell Court was built as an adjunct to the big bell foundry in the early seventeenth century and used for making little bells – hand bells and bells for town criers. It was a long, low, narrow building, at right angles to the little cobbled street running down to the central pond. Attached by a small arched court was a damp, two-storey, two-roomed doll's-house-like annexe, which Gerald eventually gave to Hope. A strip of grass ran up left of the house, widening at the end into a small garden. Gerald, with his usual flair, set up a Venus,

---

* It is much the same today. Humphreys is still the butcher, Barnes still supplies the coal, the Palmers' store has moved and became a Spar. Because of television, three pubs now suffice a much larger population, the pond has contracted and been hideously concreted, and the narrow street outside Bell Court is no longer cobbled.

an urn, a marble-topped table and a small, pillared porch taken from a church.

Inside, the cottage was humble and primitive in the way Gerald preferred, and in any case could only afford. The rooms were small (all about eight feet by ten feet), with small windows and low ceilings, but more numerous than you'd expect. Three downstairs – kitchen, little dining room, sitting room with a nice iron fireplace; four upstairs – three little bedrooms and, presumably because the cottage had been once two cottages, two bathrooms, one bath on the landing. There was no telephone at first, and the lavatory was a chemical one – an outside Elsan. An iron range heated the water and Gamel cooked on it, though she mostly used a two-plated oil-burner. Gerald was advanced for men of his class and day in respect of housework, doing some washing-up and laying of the table. But his acquaintanceship with other branches of Bell Court domestic work was hazy. He once threw the vital oil-burner away as scrap; it was rescued just in time.[45]

Two of the Palmer family lived nearby. Mr Palmer was a hurdle-maker then and they were very poor. Mrs Palmer, aged thirty-two, 'did' for Gerald and Gamel all the time they were at Aldbourne. 'They'd sit up very late and then get up late. I'd arrive at 8 or 8.30, they'd not be up.' She came in just long enough 'to get them organised'. She'd wash up, clear out the range and light it, tidy up downstairs, get Miranda off to school. 'Mrs Brenan wasn't a great lover of cooking.' Lunch was usually in The Crown, just down the road. Gamel – 'the sweetest person you ever saw' – worked upstairs; Gerald – 'very quick, but abstracted, thinking on his work, not with it' – in the sitting room. He preferred to use a butler's tray on his knee to a table.[46]

Aldbourne and Bell Court were to be their home till they left England at the end of 1952.

7

> *'I have never had but two pleasures outside literature – travel and having absurd flirtations with girls.'*
>
> Gerald to VSP, 17 July 1951

Couples often come to like least in each other the very things which first made them fall in love. In February 1939, despite their anxiety over the coming war, Gamel went to Clavadel again for a week to see Llewelyn. She and Gerald had now been together nearly nine years and it is hardly surprising if there were some strains.

Rose-Marie Duncan noticed how aggravated Gerald became by Gamel's contant agreeing – though this in fact made a considerable contribution to their harmony. That passive, dreamy, drifting, poetic quality could also suddenly exasperate him and he had recently given her 'a violent lecture' for reading a children's book. He expected, Gamel complained bitterly to Llewelyn, that all reading should be history or information.[47] Her invalidism, too, which had aroused his strong protective side, meant 'As it is, all Gamel's income goes on medicines.'[39]

It might have been better had Gerald been the invalid – as he once remarked to Helen.[48] His huge energy, which also carried her, to a certain extent robbed her of a function. And his endless talking about the subjects that obsessed him, exhausted her. The great thing about marriage, Gerald felt, was 'You can be alone without being lonely.'[49] Gamel would have agreed. She was grateful to Gerald for her privacy, for not probing. Yet too little probing can have drawbacks. 'Gerald has never got in touch with most of my mind at all, or ever wanted to, or would be interested if he did. I'm sure,' she went on to Llewelyn in a letter which, typical of the honesty he showed discussing his marriage, Gerald quoted some of in *Personal Record*, 'large tracts of his mind are equally sealed to me. Malice forces me to add particularly those parts inhabited by the characters in the Thirty Years War, the Spanish 17th century and the minor mystical writers.'[47]

But when she arrived in Switzerland Alyse noticed she 'looked older, very thin and very pale . . .'. Gamel told her (the only person she ever told such things to) that 'she had long periods of extreme melancholy and thought frequently of suicide.'[50] She was racked by obscure but precisely remembered guilts – cats not fed at Patchin Place, not being kind enough to an old Spanish woman in 1936.[51] She wrote and told Alyse years later that she already felt she'd wasted her life by 1938.*[52]

---

* In another letter to Alyse, undated but either 1944 or 1945, Gamel wrote that she had endured 'things I *should not* have endured – for the sake of my pride as an individual living creature – And that by enduring such things I did wrong to my nature from which it will never recover – and wrong to all women too.' To what

This letter also says these feelings began when she was seventeen, the time when the young homosexual she was in love with killed himself. No doubt advancing age, her failure to become pregnant, even seeing Llewelyn, increased them; but such dark and deep upswellings are not to be explained by the inevitable gratings of married life.

Nor is it likely she cared – if she ever knew – of Gerald's flirtation, which began when she'd gone. Laura Rae, at Swindon Art School, was a pretty, sexy, nineteen-year-old daughter of a neighbour, Captain Rae. She showed Gerald a drawing she'd done of the gym instructor and Gerald was riveted to see the gym instructor's penis clearly visible under his pants.[53] Johnny Morris remembers her. 'Very attractive and very available. A dish.' How available to Gerald it is impossible to say. He wrote poems to her.[54] By May, he was intoxicated with Madame de Lieven. 'I daresay my next stage will be to fall in love with historical characters.'[55] By July he was admitting to Ralph he was, perhaps, in love with someone: 'Tra la la la.'[54]

These flirtations, occurring often with startling abruptness at intervals throughout his life, were only once, and then momentarily, of any threat to his marriage. But they had a peculiar significance for Gerald, over and above what such things usually provide; and this was shown by the way that several months later his subconscious would seem to summon him down to remind him of the more fundamental engines of his character. In October he finished the second draft of *The Spanish Labyrinth*. He at once resumed his 'dreary sisyphean labours'[56] – revising, adding, rewriting* – but stopped briefly on 3 December to write a short story. The plot had come to

---

does she refer? Nothing in her marriage to Gerald, by then or at any time, could possibly elicit such a cry. The obvious answer would be the abortions she was compelled to have, but it cannot be those. Apart from TB, they were at least partly, if indirectly, due to Llewelyn or her own guilt over Alyse and by 1944, or indeed before, she would not have referred to them with Alyse like this. Today, the fashionable explanation would be abuse by father, stepfather or brother, but there is absolutely no evidence of this – at least that I have found. It remains a mystery. All one can say is that, though future events added to it, Gamel's life-long melancholy was very deep-seated.

    * The book, though he continued to work on it until June 1941, was at an advanced stage. He showed it to Araquistain at this time who said it was the best historical work ever written on Spain (Gerald to VSP, October or November 1938).

him like magic, during the delirium and dreams of a bout of 'flu.[57] *The Clergyman and the Mouse* was about a clergyman who had a crisis of faith; the springs of love had died, but he was saved, just before he died of cancer of the liver, by falling in love with a mouse. The message was Tolstoyan – love is so important it counts even to fall in love with a mouse.[58] Every so often Gerald had to return to those sources of Shelleyan/Rimbaudian intensity, integral to his character and self-respect, which had set the course of his life. These irregular eruptions of love were one of his chief means of doing this.

But 1939 was the year when, like everyone else, Gerald and Gamel were engulfed by world events – just as the WRAF was about to swallow dishy Laura Rae. Franco's victory in March horrified Gerald. He wrote to various people, including J. B. Trend, suggesting a letter to *The Times* urging Chamberlain to try and negotiate free and safe passage for those Republicans who wished to leave Spain. He also had two more refugees for six weeks.

Soon after this, in April, he volunteered as an air-raid warden, and was told he'd be sent to one of the large towns in the event of bombs.[59]

They spent most of the summer at Ley Park, returning via Ham Spray to Bell Court on 2 September. Blair and his family were there on 3 September and Ann, Gerald's niece, can remember the two brothers furiously and incompetently twiddling the knobs of Gerald's old wireless and then all of them standing and listening, through the crackles, to the declaration of war.

EIGHTEEN

War Again

1

Three days after war was declared, Gerald and Gamel hurried to Blair's flat at 101a Gloucester Road, and Gerald flung himself into the task of finding war work. He was soon offered the slightly Waugh-like job of press attaché in Nicaragua and at once began to read South American poetry as preparation in the empty British Museum reading room.

As government offices vanished behind sandbags and anti-aircraft emplacements were dug in Hyde Park, London was emptying too, the few faces on the Tube glum. Not Gerald's. Thrilled by the prospects of his new job ('People delightful . . . large salary . . . totally independent') he found the peace marvellous. And 'at night the streets are dark as country lanes and the stars shine overhead in millions'.[1]

Partly on the strength of Nicaragua, and partly because everyone was terrified that all empty property would be requisitioned, Gerald offered Bell Court to Carrington's publisher brother Noel and his whole family. They accepted immediately.

But in October, the Nicaraguan job collapsed. Gerald searched frantically for something else. He may also, as he certainly did later,[2] have tried to enlist. In the end he was forced to return to Bell Court, now full of Carringtons, with no outlet for his feverish desire to do something except seethe inwardly at Ralph and join the forerunners of the Home Guard, the Local Defence Volunteers. 'Gerald of course is terribly over-excited,' Gamel wrote to Alyse, 'maddened . . . by inability to do anything.'[3]

2

Gamel, meanwhile, suffered two severe blows.

She had finished her own book on the Civil War soon after July 1937, taking the title from a poet she revered, Eliot's *The Hollow Men*: 'Is it the same in Death's other kingdom?' The book, she told Llewelyn, 'is the story of my heart as well as a story of the Civil War – it is the only thing I ever much wanted published.' Chatto and Cape turned it down but, through Llewelyn, Longmans took it and after dithering about for six months, published in October. It is the best book Gamel wrote and one of the best to come out of the Civil War. Everyone who read it praised it, and VSP gave it an excellent review. But, just as the disappointment over *One Way of Love* had been eclipsed by the horror of Carrington's suicide, so this fine and moving book on a little war was engulfed by a larger.*

Then, on 2 December, Llewelyn died of a stomach ulcer. Gamel, by coincidence, was staying with John Cowper Powys and Phyllis Playter in Wales. In *Personal Record*, where a number of old jealousies revived and discoloured his account, Gerald says she had long expected this death and did not mind unduly. This is quite untrue. She minded a great deal, and Gerald was irritated at the time. She was still grieving bitterly, unable to speak either of Alyse or Llewelyn, when Ralph and Frances saw them in January. They went for a walk – Aldbourne full of soldiers leaving for France, their girlfriends,

---

* I quoted enough, I hope, from *Death's Other Kingdom* in Chapter Sixteen for something of the delicacy and sharpness of Gamel's observation and perception, her humour and the grace of her writing all to be evident. There was a lot of trouble over an introduction. Sassoon? Blunden? In the end John Cowper Powys wrote an absolutely ridiculous one. Gamel, 'an impulsive and romantic girl' (she was now forty-four) married to a reckless 'British officer', had produced what was 'really a tender and wistful threnody over "Old Spain" written by a daughter of the "Old South"'.

Except for one inspired phrase, where she called the false atrocity stories in the *Daily Mail* and elsewhere 'the pornography of violence', the book seemed to vanish. Gerald sent it to Hamish Hamilton in 1957, but Jamie Hamilton turned it down. ('The pornography of violence' has often been used since without attribution. Frederick Benson, for example, lifted it for his *Writers in Arms* in 1969 as a chapter title.) Finally Virago, prompted by Kenneth Hopkins, brought it out in July 1988. The *Irish Times* described it then as a small classic, and this it is.

lorries – and as usual Gerald and Ralph 'forged ahead' (Frances was often slightly irritated at being invariably left with Gamel). Gerald grumbled: 'I can't bear Gamel's Powys mood.'⁴

Gamel did not begin to idealise her love for Llewelyn until the 1950s, but Phyllis Playter and Alyse, especially Alyse, remained her closest friends. Alyse came and stayed three or four times a year and Gamel, with a sense of returning to a magical past, went to stay with her or Phyllis.

3

Gerald sold the car and they bought bicycles, somewhat to Gamel's trepidation; and indeed, when she and Gerald bicycled to Ham Spray a little later, on the empty roads of wartime England, she had crashed off into a hawthorn hedge and badly scratched her arms. Winter was the coldest for eighty-three years. Hitler's mighty modern war machine had to wait, just as the little armies of the past used to do. The snow kept on falling and falling and Baydon, the village two miles away up a steep hill, got its mail by sledge. Gamel gave blood. Pouffles, their kitten, went out just before Christmas and was killed by a dog. 'The house seems empty,' Gerald told VSP.⁵

Empty, however, Bell Court was not. Into its small rooms, on top of the Brenans and a new instantly bought kitten, Miffles, were crammed Noel and Catharine Carrington, their three children and their cook-nurse Winny. By March Gerald, who had to write in the dining room, was becoming extremely tense; very irritable with Gamel, difficult, wild, 'strange,' she told Alyse.⁶ In letters he complained about all the children⁷ and in particular Winny – 'a hulking girl of eighteen'⁷ hurtling in with plates and coal.

No doubt this was true, but Gerald's tense state had other elements. Catharine Carrington was young, sexy and attractive, Noel was away all day. She and Gerald were rapidly drawn strongly to each other, though they restrained themselves for Noel's sake.⁸ The tension this generated was considerably exacerbated by Winny – who was not hulking at all, but lively, buxom and pretty. As for hurtling, what Gerald really wanted was that she should hurtle into his bed, and he told her so. Winny told Catharine, who was both jealous and upset.

During March, Gerald developed trench mouth.* He had a high fever and could hardly eat. Gamel had to sleep on the landing. In April she took him to Brighton to recuperate. Delightful Tom Fisher sea-similes flowed back (and no doubt into the Fisher notebook): 'To see the sea,' he told VSP, from his vantage point on the pier, rug over knees, 'one must look down – but what a sea! Pale green, with the colours and animation of a third-class public bath, slipping and slopping up and down, shuffling and shoffling about like some thyroidless creature . . .'⁹ He also wrote to Ralph asking him somehow to explain to the Carringtons they must go. Ralph managed to do so diplomatically and, after the entire family had run through measles, they tactfully withdrew. On the way home Gerald and Gamel heard some Mosley supporters at Hyde Park Corner. Gerald heckled angrily and then wrote an incensed letter to the *Daily Telegraph* saying they should all be imprisoned. 'This letter was to cost me dear.'

Trench mouth wreaked havoc in the medieval turret-top – seven teeth lost from the bottom row – but Gerald was out patrolling with the Home Guard the moment he got back. Gamel sewed on his medal ribbons. Bombs fell on Swindon, the road to which was to be defended by Gerald, she giggled to Alyse, 'to the death'.¹⁰ The war suited Gamel. As in Spain, the danger exhilarated her. She told Alyse she longed to do 'nothing at all', but her letters to her friend are sharp, amused, busy with feeding the hens, cooking, getting Miranda off to school and Gerald to the Home Guard.

For a considerable time Gerald was obsessed by the Home Guard – he even managed to find Biblical parallels.¹¹ There were parades every Saturday and far more frequently in times of panic.† Gerald was extremely conscientious and went on several week-long camps and courses. VSP and his wife Dorothy remember turning up one evening to find his face covered in blacking conducting a lesson in camouflage. They went into the house and watched Gerald bury himself deep in

---

* Trench mouth or Vincent's infection: characterised by shallow ulcers and bleeding round gums, white spots on tonsils. The Borrelia germ (a name Gerald would have appreciated) is often picked up when the sufferer is very run down and tired but always as a result of habitually poor dental hygene. Gerald could have caught it, as he thought, from a communal drinking mug on Paddington station.

† Many people, including the Brenans and the Partridges, had 'suicide pills'. 'It was a common topic of conversation,' said Frances. 'One saved up sleeping pills, looked at them years later and they had melted and were useless.'

a lilac bush. 'Can you see me?' he shouted. 'Well Mr Brenan,' said a slow Wiltshire voice, 'we can see the light on your glasses.'

Gerald and Gamel didn't mix much in the village. Some people thought Gerald a bit standoffish as he walked rapidly about, short-sightedly not recognising them, often distracted by his writing. But the Home Guard brought him into intimate contact with them for two years, and he is still remembered vividly with a mixture of admiration, affection and amusement. *Dad's Army* has made us laugh at the Home Guard, and certainly some of the stories about Gerald – of which there are several – are entertaining. But the danger in 1940 was real. Hitler was planning an invasion. Had it come, these middle-aged men would have fought and many would have been killed.

Not surprisingly, between June and September there was intense spy-fever. Numerous warnings were broadcast. To his astonishment and indignation, Gerald found he was a prime suspect. When Helen Anrep stayed in August, her blackout curtain flapped and Gerald was accused of 'signalling to the enemy'. This was a serious charge and it was repeated when he flashed a torch on Home Guard duty. On 24 September he was summoned to Marlborough and he describes in *Personal Record* how he then discovered the police had found, near Mosley's British Union HQ at Southend, a piece of paper incriminat-ing him – 'Gerald Brenan, German Embassy, Dublin'. Gerald was able to explain the Mosleyite hostility by his letter to the *Telegraph* and the matter was dropped.*

In August, Hitler decided against invasion. He determined to bomb England into submission.[12] On 18 October Gerald was sum-moned to London to join the ARP. He was there nearly a month, staying with Blair and Rhoda in their new house at 42 Addison Road.

Gerald enjoyed the Blitz. English reserve, its rigid class struc-tures, melted in the heat of battle – as the bombs exploded there was

---

* Gerald's account is at variance with Frances Partridge's in *A Pacifist's War* on several points. His memory was at fault, stretching these events over two years. Her journal makes it clear they were over four months. Then, in fact, Scotland Yard came down. Ralph, calling by chance at Bell Court while Gerald was in Marlborough, found them searching the house. He was able partly to reassure them about Gerald, and then moved swiftly to get Major Cory Bell, an influential local magistrate, to go and vouch for Gerald. Had this not happened, Ralph was told, 'We would have had him behind bars for the duration.' No doubt an exaggeration – presumably Ralph's and Cory Bell's testimonies would have got him off afterwards as they did before – but clearly the episode was more serious than Gerald lets on.

camaraderie, mutual help, often gaiety. There was also sometimes considerable danger. When the sirens sounded at night, Gerald had to patrol the darkened streets, bombs falling round him. Once he climbed into a shattered house and found someone with all their clothes sucked off by the blast. He would return covered in dust. Typically, his letters discount it all: the danger to life was no more than 'flu; 'the danger to property is impressive and, on the whole, gratifying'.[13]

Gerald also managed to squeeze in some vague flirtations. He picked up a baroness and they got very drunk, but when she came back she took a separate bed. In one air-raid, Angela Culme-Seymour found herself by chance in a bunk below him. Gerald leant over in the gloom of the shelter. 'Shall I come down?' 'Yes.' But Gerald didn't. Hours were spent in Blair's smoke-filled basement shelter. Blair made comments he didn't finish. Gerald dozed or looked at 'female vulvae' in Dr Dent's 'vast tomes on sex' while their owner, the other member of the household, smoked and played patience.[14]

Blair, a liberal, gentle man, a good deal less conventional than he seemed, had lived in a *ménage à trois* with his wife and Dr John Dent since 1937. Dr Dent's practice had consisted of elderly neurotics and hypochondriacs, mostly women. Freed, as Gerald put it, by real fears and emergencies from needing imaginary ones, his patients vanished. However, Dr Dent took up alcoholics and drug-addicts and was once more able to earn. He wrote *Anxiety and its Treatment*, a book about alcoholism, and pioneered the use of apormorphine and hypnotism. William Burroughs was later one of his patients.*

In fact, briefly, so was Gamel. She had gone up just before Gerald to be treated for her bicycling. It seemed Gamel had developed a tendency to 'lean into' buses and other passing objects. Dr Dent hypnotised her and put her onto a bicycle in his surgery. VSP, arriving by chance at the house, pitch dark because of black-out and to save money, heard the faint sounds of her practising.

Both Gerald and Gamel returned exhilarated from the Blitz. 'The pleasure of knowing that one is not afraid of these rhinoceroses that

---

* Ann Cary, Gerald's niece, remembers Burroughs coming one August. A nervous man, he kept his raincoat on despite the tremendous heat. I wrote to Mr Burroughs and received a pleasant reply. He remembered John Dent as warm, informal, effective and reasonable as to fees. His knowledge of Gerald was less precise: 'I have read some of his books on animals . . .'

fall from the sky and scatter destruction is one of the most liberating one can know.'[13]

4

Yet what one also notices about Gerald's war is the peace. For weeks at a time, as Gamel told Alyse, they saw no one else to talk to except Mrs Palmer.[15]

They had a lot of time to work. Gerald was now in sight of the end of his huge task. He allowed himself breaks. In June and July he rewrote *The Clergyman and the Mouse*. Laura Rae, Winny and Catharine Carrington raised echoes of his great love and he wrote a long essay *Falling in Love*. Unrequited love leads 'to the worst hell that human nature is capable of suffering . . . Symptoms – sleeplessness, periods of intensely rapid heartbeat, violent alternation of hope, anxiety and despair.'[16] He met Cyril Connolly in London, who asked him to contribute to *Horizon*.[17] And, in a significant conjunction, he told VSP in June that he'd just finished Benito Pérez Galdós' *Fortunata y Jacinta* and also begun 'a leisurely Spanish story' which he hoped to finish 'by Saturday'.[18] In fact, it took five years.

Gamel typed out *The Spanish Labyrinth*, wrote poetry and conversed with Miffles, 'who this afternoon climbed the topmost tip of the plane tree and began to try and sing like a nightingale'.[19]

Cats were always a bond between Gerald and Gamel – at times in the future it sometimes seemed the only bond. And early in 1941 – after Christmas at Bell Court with his father ('Blast Christmas and blast visitors')[20] – they acquired Puffett (a family name in the district) who was with them until they returned to Spain. Julia Strachey, close neighbour and friend, loved the way Gamel was always picking Puffett up and planting huge lipsticky kisses;[21] as indeed, Frances noted when she and Ralph went over to Bell Court in January, she planted them on everybody. Gerald and Gamel were still in their dressing gowns when they arrived, with bowls of steaming coffee on the table. 'It was just like Spain.'[22]

In fact, letters were now getting through from Churriana, letters about starvation, cholera and smallpox. But Spain dominated much of Gerald's imaginative and intellectual life more fundamentally during these Bell Court years. Desmond Hawkins, who came to

Aldbourne at the end of 1943, remembers how often Gerald referred nostalgically to Spain. He had become a double exile – able, almost, only to write books about Spain in England, and books about England when he lived in Spain.* This duality doesn't seem to have imposed any particular stress, and indeed had now led to something extremely exciting. 'The leisurely Spanish story' had developed into an ambitious novel. *Segismundo*, which grew to be gigantic, was about the Civil War and aimed to clothe history – as Galdós had done for that of Spain between 1860 and 1890 – in the flesh and blood of real life and art.

Eager to get on with it, he devoted the first six months of 1941 to one last immense heave at *The Spanish Labyrinth*, writing the last chapter and once again revising it throughout. He finally finished it in June.†

Just before this, in May, Hugh Brenan had unexpectedly remarried, celebrating with a huge bonfire of all the family photograph albums.²³ Gerald was not asked to the wedding and did not meet 'the lucky girl', as he described Mabel Constable Curtis, till the couple came to tea on 23 June. Gerald's new stepmother, about his age (now forty-seven), did not smoke, drink, bicycle or drive a car. She had spent her life looking after a recently dead tyrannical old father and Gerald supposed was seeking a continuation. They moved from Cheltenham and bought a house, a wooden villa, at Budleigh Salterton.

On 27 May Gerald began a diary which he planned to keep all through the war. But letters had been his journal for too long to be

---

* In the fifteen years at Bell Court he wrote *The Spanish Labyrinth*, *Segismundo*, *The Literature of the Spanish People*, the first version of his *Life* of St John of the Cross, and *The Face of Spain*. On returning to Spain he wrote his autobiographies, both centred on England, two novels, his book of aphorisms and his biography of St John of the Cross, which was really only an extension, if a considerable one, of the early version. Nevertheless, this shows that though remarkable, the division is not rigid. *South From Granada* was written after his return and one of the novels was about expatriate life, if one can call that being about Spain; just as the first draft of *A Life of One's Own* was written in England.

† It had taken five years – from the end of 1936 to the middle of 1941, with about six months off for other things. His endless revisions and rewrites were not superficial. As late as January/February 1940 Noel Carrington was astonished to see him reading medieval Spanish history eight or nine hours a day – seeking new threads, or the origins of ones already grasped, to guide him through the labyrinth (NC to author, 18 May/15 June 1987).

changed, and he gave up on 18 July. Friends, weather, 'flu, dreams, Spain, long and perceptive comments on his reading came into it – but chiefly he wrote about the war. The crackling wireless now had seventy-five feet of aerial writhing all over the attic and, like everyone in England, he followed every detail of the war: 'A thread,' he wrote at the sinking of the Bismarck on 29 May, 'connects our bodies to these events in distant lands and seas and we feel better or worse, less ill or less well, feebler or stronger according to what happens to our forces in Egypt, Syria or the Atlantic.'[24]

But what entry after entry reveals is how this thread was also connected directly to Ralph. On 21 June Gerald wrote that when he thought that the war could have been avoided or won in two years, 'I feel a rage I can hardly contain against Chamberlain, Baldwin, appeasers – and, unspoken, Ralph.'

Gerald had just spent ten days at Langdon Davies Home Guard training camp in Devon. He came back thoroughly steamed up, especially as Germany had just invaded Russia and suddenly, out of the blue, he hurled an enormous bomb-letter of his own at Ham Spray. After starting with speculations on the Russian news (something he'd long foreseen) he suddenly exploded: 'Every German woman and child killed is a contribution to the future safety and happiness of Europe, for the worst thing about the Germans is not their character or their aggressiveness but the fact that there are seventy-five million of them. The only satisfactory solution would be the reduction of that figure to forty-five millions . . . I see your pained clergyman's expression. However, I care little for the theological doctrines of pacifism, which it would seem do more to provoke wars than to prevent them . . . Today – death to every German . . .' The letter then veers without pause – no doubt surprising himself as much 'as it did us', Frances noted in her journal – into a violent attack on pacifists – 'Poor creatures.' Gerald signed off, after hoping the letter wasn't annoying Ralph, 'Fondest love Gerald.'[25]

Ham Spray decided the only possible response was a dignified silence. At least, to Gerald. Otherwise, discussion was intense. Julia Strachey, who was inventing a board game, added a move – 'Receive a stinker from Gerald – back ten spaces.' Messages passed via friends, but in September, having returned from the annual Welcombe holiday via (significantly) another Home Guard camp, Gerald sent a measured letter saying that, since he and Ralph had rows about the war whenever they met, they should cease to do so till it ended.[26]

Several efforts were made to effect a reconciliation. On 31 December, an attempt by Gamel failed. Then, in March 1942, Frances suggested she and Gamel have lunch. Gamel *wired* her acceptance and the two wives met in the Three Swans in Hungerford. But they didn't even mention the row. Frances felt she couldn't broach Gamel's 'privateness' – all the same, it is pretty astounding. In May, she noted in her journal, Alec Penrose was at Bell Court. He tried to get Gerald 'to bury the hatchet'. 'The hatchet is none of my making,' said Gerald. 'Oh *isn't* it?' said Gamel. Gerald 'laughed, and sent us his love'.[27] The two men did not meet until the war was over.

Ralph could be just as provocative as Gerald – and not just to Gerald. (At this period, for instance, he accused Raymond Mortimer of enjoying sending young airmen to their deaths.)[28] But this particular row was really almost entirely of Gerald's making. No doubt he should have restrained himself, but among the various elements that caused tension between them – probably more important than the war even if precipitated by it – Ralph's role was the easiest. Ralph was the one who loved the most and probably minded more; Gerald, in any case, was always swiftly absorbed in himself and the future again. But on a superficial level it is a pity they couldn't have followed the war together since they would have enjoyed it.

Gerald's involvement was characterised by those flashes of insight, the sudden original perceptions that illuminated and enlivened his talk, his letters, and his writing. As early as 1940, for example, he'd seen the tide turning 'in about two years' time in a great tank battle . . . near Vladivostock'.[29] He saw beyond the war. Already, in 1941, he saw it might result in socialism, 'because the present times create a longing above everything else for safety'.[30]

Ralph, on the other hand, followed it with a brilliant intensity and huge knowledge. Kenneth Sinclair-Loutit remembers him moving armies on a vast *Times* map of the war with a complete grasp, strategic and tactical, of all theatres – to a degree, Janetta felt, that made his pacifism distinctly odd, especially as he passionately wanted the Allies to win. Ralph explained their position to Frances with some adroitness. 'It's as if all our money had against our wills been put on a certain horse running in the Derby. We may hate horseracing, disapprove of it even – yet we still want the horse to win.'[27]

5

Some time towards the end of 1941, *The Spanish Labyrinth* was accepted by the Cambridge University Press. Nothing survives to indicate why Gerald chose this particular publisher, though it is possible that Professor J. B. Trend recommended them to each other. The earliest letter in the Press archives is dated 18 January 1942 and already concerns the index.

The first half of this year was fully occupied by the Home Guard and *Segismundo*. By March he had written eight chapters. Proofs of *The Labyrinth* arrived in August and Gerald took them to Welcombe. Gamel was delighted when he found that Majorca and Minorca had been called 'The Pythusean Islands', their name in Roman times. 'Only the CUP would have made that mistake.'[31]

At Welcombe, the war temporarily vanished. Mrs Cottle of the Home Farm where they often took rooms* was uninhibited by rationing – rivers of cream flowed over her huge tarts and a table of unlimited butter, new-laid eggs, chickens and rabbit stews. Gerald's sea-metaphors touched everything. 'One's mornings begin with a little surrealist scene,' he told VSP, 'a set of red-gummed teeth in a glass of crystal water. No marine sea pool could be so sylph-like.'[32] He went for huge walks along the rocky shore, where he sometimes had stimulating voyeur adventures, some of which he recounted, and then cut, in the manuscript of *Personal Record*. And at night – such sleeps! 'Everything spoke of sleep. The long low hills looked like bolsters and pillows, the dogs yawned when they tried to bark . . . Only the flowers were awake. They gleamed and sparkled in the clear light like that which one sees rippling under the surface of chalk streams – the light of a sub-aquean world, thick, watery, yet infused with drowsiness.'

Rose-Marie Duncan remembered how, the moment the Brenans arrived, Gerald would come bounding down the cliff to see them. 'The gossip! Tearing everyone to pieces! He was a joy!' The Duncans lived in a dilapidated mill-house nearby. Ronnie, tiny, looking wholly

* The Home Farm, a large solid house, one of the rather few handsome ones at Welcombe, is now lived in by Rose-Marie Duncan. Mrs Cottle's brother was Mr Box, whose wife had been painted years before by Carrington.

Indian, a man of great charm and sympathy, but without small talk, was apt to be scornful and difficult – especially in later years, when the great success of his poetry and verse plays was followed abruptly by total neglect. He admired Gamel's poetry and they became close. Rose-Marie was tall, beautiful, 'bewitching', and capricious. They ran a community farm for pacifists, Ronnie's Hitler-worship making him against the war.

Here Gerald also met George Every, a young monk and school teacher from Newark. He became one of the Anglicans around T. S. Eliot, and wrote for the *Criterion*. An ebullient, outgoing man who, despite a terrible defect which made him speechless until, after violent contortions, words burst out again, he liked to talk all night. Gerald, in his long unbeliever's flirtation with Christianity, wrote him many letters.*

The long weeks Gerald and Gamel spent alone together were punctuated by people, often coming to escape London – as Alick Shepler did soon after they got back this summer and throughout the war. The beautiful girl with a gurgly voice he'd tried to make love to in 1916 was now even more 'a ruin'. She would arrive nervous, overwrought and tired, only able to talk about her cats and the job she'd had since 1910 with the *Illustrated London News*, 'her dyed hair pulled back to show a bald skull and a little hatlet balanced or rather pinned at the back'.³³ Helen Anrep and Arthur Waley and Beryl de Zoëte came to stay. Also, a young, gentle Republican refugee and anarchist, Jaime Gutiérrez, who attracted Gerald with his olive good looks and success with girls. Jaime was later to play a significant role.

Lawrence Gowing was then twenty-two, a conscientious objector whose war work was painting. He lived at nearby Chilton Foliat with Julia Strachey, whom he later married and who was also a pacifist.†

---

* I have found rather few. There is a 1942/3 draft in MF containing an account of the love Gerald really thought supreme – the love of the Troubadours 'which became platonic after 1180'. But the main body of the letter is a fascinatingly dense description of the complexity, difference and excitement of the Middle Ages which shows what a marvellous scholar and teacher Gerald could have been. For an instant there is a feeling of powers – not wasted quite, the books on the Civil War, Spanish literature and St John of the Cross are certainly scholarly – but powers so great in this direction that one wishes there had been more.

† Apart from Ralph and Frances of course, the number of Gerald's friends who were, or had been, pacifists is striking: Frankie Birrell and Bunny in the last war; Johnny Morris, Ronnie and Rose-Marie Duncan, and Lawrence and Julia in this.

They bicycled over every week for tea and Gerald's talk; Julia, eccentrically perceptive with her precise, ironic and idiosyncratic humour. Lawrence, gangling, original, his strong articulate intelligence and exuberant, fantastic humour exploding through his stammer.

Jimmy Bomford in Aldbourne seems to have been a sort of explosion himself. He had made some money turning a tug into a steam boat and selling it to Bryan Guinness. He gambled this into a fortune on the Stock Exchange, then, realising in 1937 there was about to be 'an almighty war',[34] when England would need food, he bought 2000 acres round Aldbourne (£7 an acre). He also bought pictures – Cézannes, Derains, Picasso, Matisse, Degas.* His conversation and behaviour were outrageous, he was a womaniser, coarse, dominant and drank a lot. Jane, his wife, according to Desmond Hawkins, was 'very attractive, very witty, very Chelsea'. She had a glass eye and when she was bored would take it out and roll it about in her hand. Gerald, of course, rose to all this and they got on well, especially as he soon found that Bomford was totally honest about himself, generous and very kind. Most Saturdays the Bomfords, obtaining drink by nefarious means, gave a huge party, with lots of pretty girls and raffish company from London – Dylan Thomas, Tambimuttu, Desmond Morris. Johnny Morris remembers Gerald standing, very polite, smoking in his rapid amateur way, '*talking* while everyone else got pretty smashed all round him.' Once they all careered round the house on bicycles and the pedal of one went through a Utrillo. 'Don't worry,' yelled Bomford. 'We can mend that.'

But the Pritchetts were Gerald and Gamel's closest friends. Maidencourt, which VSP had rented in 1939, was about nine and a half miles away in East Shefford. Both gifted but complementary talkers, sharing a passion for literature, Gerald and he had got on very well from the start. But now VSP took the place of Ralph and Frances as chief correspondent and Gerald wrote some of his best letters to him. Apart from the pleasure he gave, Gerald's deep knowledge of the great classics of literature, fruit of his endless re-reading, was extremely stimulating. The Pritchetts remember him arriving bursting with ideas. At the gatehouse leaping off his bicycle,

---

* After the war he started a second, modern collection. He was one of the first to buy Francis Bacon and Graham Sutherland.

they'd hear him shouting – 'The thing about Stendhal is . . .' VSP had, of course, passed the Svevo test with flying colours, even comparing Gerald to Zeno.* Sometimes Gerald and Gamel would both come, more often Gerald alone, occasionally to stay the night, usually bicycling back after lunch, long rides in those icy winters of the war, arriving as 'the stars shook and sparkled' in the frosty air and when free-wheeling swiftly down steep Baydon hill was 'like being a diamond cutting a pane of glass. The village under a light covering of snow looked like a wedding cake in a shop window with the icing a little worn off.'[35]

6

They spent Christmas at Bell Court again, without his father, who had just had an operation to remove an eye and replace it with a glass one. 1943 began with worries about *Segismundo*, about money, and a sinking of heart about Hope who had suddenly appeared from China.

But one anxiety far exceeded all others, so much so that on 1 March Gerald fled to the safety of his bed with one of his useful attacks of 'flu. Soon after, a month before his fiftieth birthday, Cambridge University Press published *The Spanish Labyrinth*.

* Gerald quite often used *The Confessions of Zeno* as a litmus of a new acquaintance's literary taste. Sending it to VSP he said, in a letter of 3 April 1940, how he himself loved it for its enjoyment of life. 'But then I do not find egotism disgraceful, but on the contrary, natural. Only it requires a certain manner.'

NINETEEN

The Spanish Labyrinth

Every writer whose first book has received a great many favourable reviews awakes to find himself famous – to his friends, to himself, for a while.

As far as the world went, *The Spanish Labyrinth* was Gerald's first book. In the CUP archives three massive, old-fashioned leather-tipped folders are required to hold all the reviews. Academic and Spanish-leaning publications might have been expected to review it, but nearly all the leading national dailies and weeklies made it their main book – the *Manchester Guardian*, for example, giving it thirty column-inches, the *Observer*, whose reviewer was Cyril Connolly, three columns.[1]

In England, paradoxically, the war was one reason for its success. There was a dearth of good books, and a hunger for culture – as sustenance, as escape, as paradigm of what the country was fighting for; shown also by the sales of *Horizon*, the *New Statesman* and the *Listener*, and the queues for Myra Hess' concerts (to which, incidentally, Gamel used to go – a shilling a seat).

But these considerations did not apply to the same extent in America or at all in Mexico, where the reviews were equally large (a full page in the *New York Times* for instance),[2] as numerous and just as full of praise and analysis as the English reviews. But in 1943 the Spanish Civil War was still topical. It was widely regarded as part, a precursor, of the battle then raging. There were also a great many people, not just Spaniards or left-wing radicals crushed by the Republican defeat, who wanted the reason for the war explained. The fairly considerable literature satisfying this interest at the time was almost entirely polemical. Gerald not only showed that the Civil War rose from Peninsular history and was nothing to do with the European struggle, but did so, although he was clearly sympathetic to the Republicans, in terms which were scrupulously fair – apart from anything, a considerable achievement in self-control.

Of course, there were criticisms. Some were motivated by spite or bias. Writers do not forget bad reviews and it is unlikely Allison Peers had forgotten the young reviewer who, in 1927, had dismissed his book on Spanish mystics as hagiography. If he had, Gerald stimulated his memory with further darts: 'It is surprising,' he had written, 'that Professor Allison Peers, in the long account of the Asturian rising which he gives in *The Spanish Tragedy*, should have forgotten to mention either the Moors or the Foreign Legion.' The other book, *Catalonia Infelix*, of this hitherto 'acknowledged expert' on the Catalan question he did not even mention in his bibliography. Peers' attempted counter-attack in the *Spectator* was easily trounced by Gerald's reply two weeks later.[3]

In fact, adverse criticism came almost entirely from Catholic supporters, from right-wing and Franco sympathisers and from fascists. The substance was (as it was with Peers) that Gerald showed left-wing and anti-Catholic bias and, since this was demonstrably untrue, Gerald had little difficulty answering them.* The one substantive criticism in this area – that Gerald failed to account for Franco's considerable popular support – escaped them.

But Gerald had not just achieved a popular, if thoroughly respectable, success. After five years' work, with a single book, he had become one of the foremost historians of Spain then writing.

In fact, of course, it was not five years; Gerald had been studying intensely if intermittently since 1919. And, though ostensibly covering the years 1874 to 1936, he often carried his search forward from the early Middle Ages or even Roman or pre-Roman times. It is this vast scope, always tightly controlled and wholly relevant, embedding his argument not just in its economic and historical roots, but in the geology and rainfall and geography and carried through all the major themes, that makes *The Spanish Labyrinth* so enormously exhilarating. And this sense of moving through the broad expanse of the past is

---

* For examples of these attacks see the *Dublin Review* (June), the *Catholic Herald* (April/May), and the *Bulletin of Spanish Studies* (November 1943, March 1944). The fascist criticism, often virulent, mostly appeared in small Mexican publications. For an example of Gerald's successful self-defence see the *Catholic Herald* (14 May 1943). And see appendix C.

counterbalanced, complemented, by his gift of the short, striking phrase, sometimes almost aphoristic, and by his sudden shafts of intuitive insight.

Gerald's long years of reading do not just explain the maturity and range of his scholarship, they continually invigorate and make arresting his comparisons. When talking of the ruthless flexibility of the Spanish communists he observes that '. . . their going back on so many of their past tenets recalled the feats of those Jesuit missionaries of the nineteenth century who, better to convert the Chinese, suppressed the story of the Crucifixion'.

Gerald was not aiming at great writing – and this at last released him from the clotted imagery of *Jack Robinson*; he was aiming at clarity. Yet the result is undeniably literature. And this too owes something to his reading. Gibbon is detectable: 'Candidates for government service were not troubled with competitive examination.' And like his great predecessor, he had mastered the footnote. Discussing the Spanish Army's propensity to foment revolution, he quotes the biographer of the famous General Weyler proudly pointing out that, of the 600 Army generals, Weyler 'had the noble distinction of never having raised an arm against the government'. 'His biographer spoke too soon,' appends Gerald elegantly. 'In 1925, at the age of eighty-seven, Weyler joined a plot against Primo de Rivera and was heavily fined for it. The punishment was all the harder to bear for his being a notorious miser.'

Another of the pleasures of reading *The Spanish Labyrinth* comes from the swift and satisfying development of logical thought and the building-up of a continual series of clear pictures. And he reminds one here of a second great historian, one who also imposed order on a confused period. Spain, Gerald shows, partly through the decline in the popular influence of religion, partly for other reasons, had become a country in search of an idea to release and canalise its energies. This was the force behind the socialist and anarcho-syndicalist movements, even behind some of the ideas which led to fascism. 'The following chapters,' Gerald ends his analysis, in words which have both the clarity and the ring of de Tocqueville, 'will describe the growth of these ideologies and how by the very fact of their diversity they ended by producing a situation which was insoluble.'

One of these ideologies Gerald unravelled with particular

brilliance – and this was one of many instances where his character and past shaped his history. In fact, the most striking of these is what had happened to him in Yegen. It had often been observed that Spain was a country of intense local patriotisms – the country of the *patria chica*.* Richard Ford had written about it in the 1830s.⁴ But Gerald had *felt* this at Yegen. He made it a central thread to guide the reader out of the labyrinth in a way not really done before.

The dominance of local patriotisms had led Spanish historians into an obsession with 'national character' in an attempt to find a central clue to the diversity.† Gerald was no exception – indeed, it is his astuteness here that delights Spaniards, no doubt partly because many of his insights are flattering. What had drawn him to Yegen was not just its poverty, but that he had found that money was apparently almost despised. A second key thread through the labyrinth was that 'Spaniards live either for pleasure or ideals but never for personal success or money-making'. Orwell and Borkenau had noticed this too, but it was carried much further by Gerald.

Severed by mountain ranges and climate and love of *pueblo* into 'small, mutually hostile or indifferent republics', it followed that the only thing that could unite Spain was an idea or an emotion, upon which the quarrels of tribal life vanished in a 'great upsurge of energy that came, economically speaking, from nowhere'. Thus they had united in moments of furious passion to throw out Napoleon in the nineteenth century, as they had the Moors in the fourteenth and fifteenth – and as both Left and Right did against each other in the Civil War. Spaniards felt 'that to live as they wished, they only needed to get rid of someone'. The realisation that the *idea*, feeling, is all-important was a brilliant one, and is expressed with astonishing concision.

Of course, not *everyone* in Spain was uninterested in money; but four-fifths of the population came from the artisan/peasant class. They were uninterested in money because they could not make any. Denied upward progress, they disdained it. And the ideology Gerald

---

* Untranslatable. *Patria* was first and foremost home or place of origin; the extension to fatherland was secondary. And *chica* means 'small', 'little' – thus a note of tenderness is injected, a feeling of something that has to be protected. Not so much loyalty, but *love* of, first *pueblo*, then region, finally, if at all, country.

† The first thing the Real Academia de la Historia did in the eighteenth century was to institute a study of 'national character'.

traced with particular skill – that of the anarcho-syndicalists – came from this stratum.

Gerald knew these men. Many of the *pueblos* in Andalusia were anarchist; Churriana was entirely so. He bought his antiques from an anarchist in Malaga. More important, they took him back to his youth; like him poor, like him against the rich, they travelled as he had done on foot or mule or the hard seats of third-class railway carriages 'or even like tramps or ambulant bull fighters under the tarpaulins of goods wagons'. Again, Borkenau, Orwell and others had commented on the ascetic, religious fervour of the anarchists (some collectives banned wine, coffee and cigarettes) but Gerald, for a while, had himself turned frugality and asceticism into a religion. He traced their origin from the Middle Ages (it was probably this that Noel Carrington saw him working on) and showed – the past working like a yeast in the present – how these ideas survived in Castile and Leon into the nineteenth century, and were then renewed again in this one. He quotes Bakunin: 'All exercise of authority perverts, and all submission to authority humiliates.' And, as Cyril Connolly wrote in his review, 'we watch the maxim, like vitriol, eating away the face of the government'.

Moved by their 'heroic idealism and charmed by their sincerity and open-mindedness', Gerald loved the Spanish anarchists. But he saw clearly they could not possibly have led to a workable polity – and if they had it would have been a tyranny. And just as one stratum of that divided nation produced anarchism, so others produced other ideologies: Catholic, Carlist, socialist, Falangist and so on. And this sequence of historical analysis – the love of *pueblo*/region combining with aspects of national character to produce competing political and social ideas – went far on its own to explain the Civil War and dictate the coherence of Gerald's book. And there were other threads, also gathered from remote beginnings and brought swiftly to the active present.

A further rather odd circumstance contributed to the success of *The Spanish Labyrinth*. 'Imagine a major European country with no good book about it at *all*!' said Raymond Carr. Yet such was Spain. Before the Civil War, the books mirrored the ideological divisions, mostly clerical or anti-clerical. After Franco, no historians in Spain could tell the truth. Those that escaped were either silent or once again wrote polemical history. As for the very few books in English,

Salvador de Madariaga's *Spain*, in a series edited by H. A. L. Fisher, was pompous and riddled with elements of self-justification. Peers was an immensely industrious Hispanist who for years, in the *Bulletin of Spanish Studies*, almost single-handedly made available huge quantities of information invaluable to fellow Hispanists about contemporary Spain. Nevertheless, despite coining the epithet 'red-brick university', he inclined as a writer and as an historian to be uninspired, rather drab and sometimes inaccurate, and disapproval biased him against the Republicans and the Left. Astonishingly, for years the English historians – Gerald, and after him Carr and Hugh Thomas – had the field to themselves. And Spanish historians suffer from another disadvantage. In England, with Clarendon, Gibbon, Macaulay, Carlyle and more recently Trevor-Roper, A. J. P. Taylor and Steven Runciman, there is a long tradition that it is not shameful to produce well-written history. But, as Paul Preston has noted wittily,[5] Spaniards feel scholarship should have *gravitas*. They enjoy *reading* readable history; they will not stoop to writing it.*

Writing to thank Leonard Woolf for his review in *Political Quarterly*,[6] the first time he'd written to him since he'd sent a careful and moving appreciation of Virginia after her suicide in 1941, Gerald said he had had 'to swim against the tide of my nature' for three years.[7] *The Spanish Labyrinth* was not a novel or a poem and, though he would later admit 'it could hardly have been better as history',[8] he was never particularly proud of it. But at the time, though he only showed this to Gamel, its reception delighted him – especially when

---

* Initially, Gerald had a still odder advantage. I was puzzled why all the reviews kept on referring to him as a farmer. Eventually I managed to find, in Texas, a copy of the jacket blurb to the first edition. 'Mr Brenan, after serving in the British Army . . . settled in Spain and farmed there . . . as a farmer he knows, as no other English author has known, the conditions of life in the widely differing climates and conditions of Spain.' So Gerald was not just a farmer, but a farmer all over Spain. Some American newspapers referred to this 'dirt farmer' who had struggled, presumably for years at a time of acute agricultural depression, in terms almost of wonder. (He 'must be one of the very few Englishmen who emigrated to Spain for the purposes of farming': *Baltimore Sun*.) But since, in that artisan/peasant four-fifths of the population, the agricultural problem was incomparably the most important, it gave Gerald's utterances on the subject a unique force. It is unlike Gerald to allow himself to be put falsely in a position of elevated authority. Publishers usually write blurbs and it is probable CUP did not show their effort to him (there is no correspondence about it). It did not appear in subsequent editions.

the Republican Party in exile unanimously sent him a vote of gratitude and congratulation.[9]

Writing the book had done two things for him. The fighting in Spain 'made me', he told VSP, 'almost ill with anxiety and emotion. I lay awake at nights, had paroxysms of fury, scribbled letters to the press and only cured myself by hard work in the British Museum.'[10] It had, that is, got him through the Civil War. More importantly it had also, for him as for his readers, answered the question why – why it had begun, why the Republicans had lost. 'I saw what I had written was really an indictment of the follies and illusions of the Left, with whose general aims I sympathised.'*

Will *The Spanish Labyrinth* last? History, by its nature, is continually rewritten – to fit new facts, new interpretations, new ideologies, a new *Zeitgeist*. One must suppose the same will happen to Gerald. Certainly, the great British historian of Spain, Raymond Carr, thinks so. 'It is a very intelligent, well-researched book, an intuitive book, but its great success was an accident, due to time. His historical reputation is not permanent.' Yet Carr's own work, though it is decisive in the historiography, has not replaced *The Spanish Labyrinth*. His massive *Spain 1808–1975*[11] in fact covers, owing to the depth of Gerald's scholarship, much the same ground up to 1936, and in extraordinary and fascinating detail. But, despite maintaining an

---

* Gerald had also had fun writing the book. Frances said Ralph asked Gerald where he'd discovered some authority in a footnote. Gerald paused, then burst out, 'I invented him.' I read and reread the footnotes; they are impeccable. But at last I think I found the invention. Dealing with the paradox of Christianity, Gerald wrote, 'An intelligent Chinaman has been more observant. Sun Yat-sen, when he visited Europe, was amazed that a religion which persistently extolled the poor and threatened and condemned the rich should be practised and maintained chiefly by the richest, most selfish and most respectable classes. The political skill and duplicity required for such a feat seemed to him to go far beyond anything that simple orientals could run to.' Now it is possible that Sun Yat-sen, the great Chinese revolutionary (1866–1925), wrote or said something like this. He visited Europe a number of times. He was a baptised Protestant and his religion played a significant role in his thought. 'I do not belong to the Christianity of the Church, but to the Christianity of Jesus who was a revolutionary.' But after a diligent search I can find no record of any utterance remotely like the one Gerald paraphrases. It has a distinct ring of Gerald to me. Of all the authorities cited in the book, or quotations used, only that of Sun Yat-sen is not attributed; nor does the sage appear in either bibliography or index. (See *Sun Yat-sen: Reluctant Revolutionary*, Harold Z. Schiffrin, California 1980; *Sun Yat-sen: His Life and its Meaning*, Lyn Sharman, Stanford 1968.)

astonishing lightness of touch for such an immense book, such is the scale and scope of his knowledge that perhaps it really takes a professional historian fully to appreciate his profound insight.*
More accessible to the general reader and no less scholarly are the works of Paul Preston,[12] but he restricts himself to the years immediately preceding the Civil War. So Gerald remains in print.

The same is true in Spain. There are excellent new books there; students in particular are tempted by Pierre Vilar's *History of Spain* – gnomic, brilliant, above all, perhaps, slim. Yet Gerald is still recommended to students at Alicante, Valencia, Oviedo, Madrid, Barcelona and Seville Universities.†

But *The Spanish Labyrinth* could have a different fate. Some histories survive because of the way they are written and the vigour and sweep of their thought. De Tocqueville's *Ancien Régime* is one of these. Both historians are very much of their countries. De Tocqueville has the clarity which is the genius of the French language, and which derives too from his grand and simple theme. But he has no people! It is the clarity of total abstraction. Gerald is lucid and elegant too, but his book is rich and human. Both men enjoyed making, and had the ability to make, valid large-scale generalisations. De Tocqueville's great theme is that the centralising effect of the *ancien régime* had in fact created equality, but that this had been obscured by privilege. The Revolution, by sweeping away privilege, just revealed what was already there. It is this single and exhilarating idea which gives his book its momentum. The fact that it is no longer accepted, except for details, does not lessen the excitement of reading him – and there are enough attendant insights to make it worthwhile.

Gerald has no single idea; rather it is the masterly marshalling of many threads, the gathering of them into one mighty rope and then

---

* Gerald would certainly have agreed that Carr's estimate of his final staying power was accurate. He himself thought Carr's *Spain* was a masterly book. 'It is impossible,' he wrote when reviewing it, 'to imagine anyone ever writing a better one' (The *New York Review of Books*, 17 November, 1966).

† Professor Paul Preston very kindly did a straw poll of his Spanish collegues for me in May 1989. No doubt Gerald is recommended in other universities as well. As recently as 1983/4 a symposium was organised at La Coruña and entitled 'The Spanish Labyrinth' in homage to Gerald. A series of distinguished historians each took a chapter and read a paper showing how views had changed since Gerald wrote. The changes, observed Juan Pablo Fusi, one of Spain's leading historians, were often considerable.

leading us through the labyrinth and out into the clear air which provides his intellectual excitement. And in his case the main picture is still accepted – if numerous details have been successfully challenged. And he, too, has many insights which still inspire.

The Spanish Labyrinth long ago passed Cyril Connolly's ten-year testing post; it is now halfway to Dr Johnson's benchmark for a good book of a hundred years. Who can say it will not reach it – and then go on beyond?*

* See appendix C for some additional comments.

TWENTY

Life at Aldbourne

'When we pass fifty every gust of wind brings round the bend of
the river the sound of the waterfall that our canoe is approaching.'

Thoughts in a Dry Season

1

In April 1943 Gerald was asked if he would like to command a
boat at D-Day, but he turned it down on the slightly odd
grounds that he knew nothing about boats.

That same month Gamel and Miranda went to London. Living
on potatoes which 'taste like dead men's toes',[1] Gerald was nevertheless blissful. Because 1943 also began with love.

One symptom, common from now on, was that he got younger.
'Why does life,' he wrote to VSP a week after his forty-ninth
birthday, 'get suddenly so delicious when one reaches the age of
forty-seven – tell me that?'[1] The girl in question was twenty-seven-
year-old Mary Salamon, beautiful, 'saturated' in Elizabethan and
modern poetry, but unfortunately (though perhaps to Gerald's relief)
naturally faithful. Gerald wrote some poems[2] but ended, he told
VSP, falling in love with Eustace, the gentle, trusting husband. This
invigorating flirtation introduced another henceforth permanent
Gerald theme – the fight to give up smoking. 'After a long struggle to
keep down the number of cigarettes I was smoking (cigarettes =
girls), I have come back to the coarse, terre-à-terre pipe of the married
man.'*[3]

---

* Svevo's The Confessions of Zeno starts with and partly revolves around Zeno's
titanic battle to achieve 'the last cigarette'.

Another preoccupation was Miranda's education, now that she was twelve. After endless letters and discussions with Bunny and VSP, who knew the school, Gerald fixed on Beltane at Melksham. Cecil Day Lewis had once taught there. One reason for choosing it was its difference from Radley. 'Bloody bedlam,' said Johnny Morris. 'No one learnt anything. Went bust.' Progressive schools can only teach if pupils want to learn. The Garnett and Pritchett children both did well. There are, however, more important things than an education. In the ramshackle, cosy world of Beltane, living in old railway carriages, Miranda was blissful.

Boarding schools can save people. There is no question but that Gerald and Gamel loved Miranda, and she them. Gerald was endlessly conscientious. Nearly 1500 pages of letters from him to her remain: advising, questioning, comforting, conveying his love (as well, sometimes, as less appropriate emotions). According to Frances, Gamel (whom Miranda called 'Mummy'), 'treated children exactly like adults and perhaps hardly knew they weren't. But she gave unconditional love.'

Yet in some ways these two middle-aged writers, often remote in their books, were not really suited to be parents of a young child. Miranda was always very silent when young. The Pritchetts remember her endlessly standing and staring. When she came to Blair and Rhoda, arriving by herself with a luggage label round her neck, her clothes were chaotic. There was an air of neglect. She had her first period with them; Gamel had told her nothing.[4] Beltane from this point of view was an excellent choice, even though Gerald often complained in later years that Miranda wasn't intellectual enough.

2

In June Arturo Barea came to stay, having written to ask if he could translate *The Spanish Labyrinth*.[5] They discovered they had been to the same places in the Rif and got on well at once. Gerald at once agreed he should translate it, but in the end this melancholy-faced and talented novelist was unable to finish it.*

* Barea had done some work by February 1944, and promised the rest in March, then in October 1945, then in September 1947 – by which time he'd done

In July, Gerald and Gamel stayed with his father at Budleigh Salterton. Hugh's false eye seemed totally out of control; now it glanced upwards, 'now shoots with furious beams in an oblique direction'.[6]

Gamel, no doubt as a result of tuberculosis, was always wary about her health. Desmond Hawkins noticed her air of a permanent invalid. Feeling a sudden pain in her stomach, she went at once to Hugh's doctor. He diagnosed cancer.

The strength of his reaction shook Gerald. Devastated, he 'felt like Dostoevsky on the morning of his execution', he told VSP that same day; and added, an observation absolutely fundamental to understanding his character and behaviour, 'I am a person who suffers from a great dissociation between the surface and the centre.'[6] The result could be an extreme surface volatility, an ability to contradict himself, often a seeming disloyalty and analogous swift recovery when people died – all of which would vanish when those feelings, trapped in the depths of their high-pressure artesian well, would suddenly explode out, often to Gerald's astonishment.

Gamel, in this crisis, was completely fatalistic. She slept nine hours both nights they remained at Budleigh Salterton, and soon went into Swindon Hospital. The illness turned out to be only a hernia. Ralph and Frances had heard what was happening from Catharine Carrington and hurried into Swindon. 'She looked thin, and a bunch of flowers lying on her chest trembled with the beating of her heart.'[7]

3

In many ways the war suited Gerald. The frugality suited him, he enjoyed making do.* Nevertheless, on their income of just over

---

half. In the end it was translated, or finished, by José Caro Ruiz for Ruedo Ibérico in 1961, though a pirated Spanish edition came out in Mexico in 1946. Translations were eventually published in Israel (contract signed 1944); Netherlands (1947); France (several – 1963 and 1983); Yugoslavia (1970 – in Serbo-Croat which must have pleased Gerald); Italy (1970); Denmark (1987); the first official Spanish edition was 1984. Penguin first brought it out in 1961.

* When King Zog of Albania became a refugee he ordered a lot of socks, and then couldn't pay for them. Gerald got them cheap. He was delighted, according to his niece Lady Cary, because they were cheap – but just as delighted that they were Zog's.

£400 p.a. (very roughly £8500) frugality would have been enjoined on them in any case. A little red notebook survives with all its pages covered in minute household calculations from 1939 to 1945.[2] The average for the household expenses for each year of the war was £201.5s.11d. An indication of how modestly they lived is that twenty-four bottles of beer (seven pence each) bought in April 1939 lasted till June. For many years Gamel typed all Gerald's books on the back of the typescript of the book before.

It is not surprising, therefore, that one of Gerald's earliest letters to Cambridge University Press concerns money. Does the £50 advance still hold?[8] *The Spanish Labyrinth* made £139.3s.6d in 1943, and £185.9s.2d in 1944 – a significant contribution. Until 1951 it averaged a more modest £24 a year.

But several other ways in which the book could have made him money Gerald turned down flat. In November 1943 Raymond Carr came to Aldbourne and asked him if he would write the volume on Spain for the *Oxford History of Europe* series being edited by Alan Bullock.[10] The interview was sticky. Gerald said he'd practically killed himself doing *The Spanish Labyrinth*. Then he added something that Carr never forgot. 'You can't get at the truth by history; you can only get it through novels.' Driving back to Oxford the chastened young historian suddenly thought: If he won't, why don't I do it? Thus his whole life was changed and with it, in time, the entire course of Spanish historiography in England.*

Then in January 1944 Penguin asked him to do a wide-ranging book on Spain, its plan dictated by him. Gerald agreed, provided they accepted *Segismundo*.[11] This they would not do. And in November 1944 Macmillan suggested he do the history of the Civil War. Gerald refused. He was far too busy writing a novel.[12]

One way he did allow the success of his book to help him make money was broadcasting. In August 1943 he was suddenly asked by a Miss Manton if he'd like to do some schools broadcasts for eleven-year-olds. Gerald became interested, read and researched widely in the London Library and, slightly late, handed in two little dramas on the Armada and the reconquest of Granada. Miss Manton praised

---

* Carr's *Spain* is one of the few histories to list, as Gerald does, novelists in its bibliography.

them, but in an internal memo to 'casting' was forced to conclude that 'though the man writes well . . . somehow he has not got himself geared to the microphone in spite of valiant endeavours'.[13] Gerald was not asked again.

Independently of this, he was also asked to write some talks for *Voz de Londres*, the BBC foreign service to Spain.* The object was to impress Spaniards favourably towards Britain, especially by describing liberal and democratic elements which would appeal to them and also encourage similar developments in Spain, but describing them in such a way as not to antagonise the Franco regime into jamming or banning. The Foreign Office vetted all talks.

Gerald was quite successful at this tricky job; he also enjoyed it. It could count as war work. Exciting telegrams flew to and fro: 'Can you record 3 January?' 'Certainly – 1.45. Thursday. Brenan.' (In fact, after the first two, Gerald's heavy Andalusian accent led to someone else delivering his talks.) There were meetings in the Foreign Office. London was full of exiled Republicans and seethed with plots against Franco – and, of course, against each other.[14] Gerald kept rather lightly in touch with these, though he met Juan Negrín, Araquistain and others from time to time. Over the next two and a half years he wrote twenty three talks of ten minutes or fourteen minutes each, earning 201 guineas (say £4050), plus all his expenses.[15]

In *Personal Record* he describes this work briefly. But he makes clear that it was onerous, ending with a sort of airy stoicism, 'Such is the writer's life, a precarious and harassed one in every age. Everything conspires to preventing him writing what he wants.' That is certainly true of most writers. It wasn't remotely true of Gerald. He had refused several commissioned books because he was determined he would write his major novel. He also turned down the offer of a job at Chatham House (obtained by Ralph)[16] and, possibly, jobs at the Foreign Office and the Ministry of Information,[17] probably for the same reason. But the BBC work, though certainly considerable (and virtually the only hack-work Gerald did in his life), allowed plenty of time for *Segismundo*. During December, as well as two talks, he wrote forty pages of his novel, bringing the total to 350 and finishing Part I. Gamel typed it and, touchingly determined to help over money,

* Other speakers included Salvador de Madariaga, though always in the guise of a South American or to South America; J. B. Trend; Allison Peers; and Sir Henry Thomas, keeper at the British Museum.

translated or wrote from memory some Spanish fairy stories, and also worked on her second novel, *Patterns in the Sand*. She also tried, unsuccessfully, to get some work with the BBC.

4

In April 1944 Gerald was fifty – a classic moment for elegiac sadness. 'I no longer expect the thrill of walking all day across Spanish mountains in an ecstasy of fatigue and solitude,' he told VSP. 'I no longer hope to sit hungry and dirty on a Mediterranean beach listening to the songs of the fishermen. To think that I ever did these things and can never do them again is almost too painful to be borne.' He feels he has only just tasted life, and that is why he wants to write. 'I don't think this is egotism, for it is not a very significant self I wish to perpetuate, but those moments and perceptions that have filled it and which my "I" has merely shared with all human beings, with all living creatures, with the birds and the butterflies and the yellow fungus on the mountain slopes.'[18] He also felt he would never fall in love again.

Gerald's sexual inhibitions and frustrations had been extremely painful; he determined they should not afflict Miranda. It was at this moment – and perhaps not unconnected with it – that he decided to do something about this. But his motives were also connected to a long and deeply held fantasy linking Miranda with her mother.

His method, perfectly sound, was to make men and the whole subject familiar and normal to her. He began by a talk explaining sex, followed immediately (he had discussed and agreed this with Gamel) by a bath together. Miranda, who was thirteen, not surprisingly stared at the object of his recent revelations, and Gerald, suddenly remembering something that had happened years before with Juliana, took her hand and laid it on his penis. 'Make it stand up,' said Miranda. 'I can't,' said Gerald. 'It would only stand up if I were excited and for that you would have to be a grown woman.'[19]

From now on he had baths regularly with Miranda, continuing to instruct her in sexual matters. Desmond Hawkins, a friend of George Every who arrived in Aldbourne now, remembers how Gerald talked about sex in front of Miranda 'for evangelical reasons. He was the only man I'd heard use the word "fuck" in front of his daughter. He felt she should hear it. It was quite startling at the time'.

5

The pattern of their life was now set and continued through 1944 and 1945: BBC talks, writing (in the morning and evening, often a long walk in between), the war, weekend and other guests like VSP and Dorothy, Lawrence and Julia, and Aldbourne social life – 'The Bomfords blew in last night – their usual method of entry – and did not leave till one.'[20]

Segismundo was still making good progress – in June he told VSP he would be the first person to write a thousand-page epic on a butler's tray. Gamel completed her fairy tales. That same month the whole of England tensed itself as the Normandy invasion took place. Mrs Alexander, their next-door neighbour, fainted when it was announced and then took to her bed.

In the summer they went to Cornwall and the sea so worked on Gerald that he took up *Mr Fisher* again. 'And the sea! A flat blue bath edged with bright red cliffs. The fishing boat lying out on it looks like a cake of soap. When the tide goes out, starts going out, one expects to hear the gurgle of a plug.'[21] That the sea might run out became the basis later on of one of his *Thoughts*. Gamel's fairy stories had been accepted (they came out in the autumn), probably helped by Noel Carrington, who worked with Allen Lane and created the Puffin imprint, and she now finished the first draft of her new novel.

Talks followed each other regularly: 'Delegated Legislature' in May, 'Universal Suffrage' in June, 'Hitler and Napoleon' in July, 'Democracy and Demagoguery' in September. A Mr Guyatt wrote and told him he was 'much admired by the Spaniards in the section'.*[22]

Despite what he'd gloomily told VSP, Gerald remained able to

* The most famous of these was Rafael Nadal, who broadcast to Spain under the name of Antonio Torres. But he was a royalist and, as the Foreign Office and more especially the British ambassador in Madrid, Sir Samuel Hoare, became more and more pro-Franco, he ran into trouble. He was finally suspended and eventually resigned just before Gerald came on the scene. Gerald, like another faction in the Foreign Office, thought that the only lasting solution was for Spain to have a constitutional monarchy with a moderate left-wing government. But, with his usual astuteness and clairvoyance he predicted that the Franco regime would last forty years, which it more or less exactly did.

fall in love until nearly twice his present age – and he did so during the last months of 1944 with Ann Alexander, the pretty daughter of their neighbour. She reminded him of Vera Birch and he wrote a long poem to her, 'La Belle Dame sans Merci'. For a while she slept in their spare room, but then she moved to London, her husband came on leave and she decided it was only him she could love. Gerald, after describing all this, told VSP how much he loved Gamel. 'Our marriage is as cloudless, as deeply happy as that of anyone I know'. . .'But I am not "in love",' he went on. 'I am as a rule no more aware of my real feelings than I am aware of being in good health and having two legs.'[23] Gerald, that is, was in the position of most happily married people after fourteen years in that state. Other people concur. Desmond Hawkins felt they lived very agreeably together in an atmosphere of mutual respect. Johnny Morris thought it 'impeccable'. Only Lawrence Gowing detected that it wasn't a very physical marriage.

In a Europe being ravaged as it had been in the Thirty Years War of the seventeenth century, the weather returned there too in a succession of icy and beautiful winters. Gerald loved tobogganing, and Desmond Hawkins and he suddenly decided this winter to go out at one in the morning and toboggan under the full moon. Hawkins remembers how still it was as they walked back in the moonlight, how clear and cold and that Gerald was covered with snow.

6

In February 1945 Gerald suddenly thought he had a bad heart. He gave up smoking in a panic and hurried to the doctor – to find he had the heart 'of a man of thirty-five'. He decided this was because 'it has given up its old touring propensities and music-hall turns and settled down to the solid blood pumping business'.[24] He took up smoking again.

Some time during these last months of the war, or just after, Gamel fell out with Bertrand Russell. The philosopher had returned from America, his marriage going very badly. Gerald and Gamel saw them in London in April. 'It is the story of . . . an old, worn Samson having his conversation cut by a young Delilah. I never saw a man look so sad.'[25] Gamel saw him alone in Oxford just after this. Russell had not only always been attracted to Gamel, he had been moved, as many were, by the poetry and melancholy of her presence.* Gerald thought, and it seems likely, that he made passes at her. In any event, they did not meet again till 1950, and not regularly till Russell was safely married again in the mid-Fifties.

On 8 May the war in Europe finally ended, followed by that in the East on 2 September. Aldbourne lit huge bonfires on the green and everyone, perhaps even Gerald, danced round them. Some old Home Guard men got drunk and threw ammunition into the flames.

In fact, not long after, the Home Guard was disbanded in a huge parade at Marlborough. For the last time in his life, Gerald put on uniform. Johnny Morris remembers his very precise marching. 'There goes Mr Brenan, treading twice on a sixpence.'†

In June they went to Cornwall. Once again Gerald put aside *Segismundo*, now nearly 550 pages into Part II, and took up *Mr Fisher* again, some of it spilling over, or starting off, in letters to VSP: 'The waves saying the same things over and over again like children repeating their lessons.'²⁶ He was also planning to canvas for Labour in the election.

There is no evidence that Gerald saw any particular personal significance in the peace. Not so Ham Spray. After much discussion, Ralph saying Gerald was quite capable of a wounding rejection,²⁷ a letter was sent. On 27 August Ralph and Frances went over to Bell Court without warning the Brenans. It had been over four years since they'd met and, as they pushed open the door, Frances rather looked forward to his surprise. 'Surprised he certainly was. He was sitting by the fire writing and he jumped up with an uncertain expression.'²⁸ There was a good deal of constraint (the row not mentioned), but the next visit a month later was much easier.

---

* 'And so I came to look to you for a companionship I had no longer hoped to find. Your silences said more to me than the words of the most eloquent and explicit. Gradually your beauty invaded my inmost being. I feel it as I feel the night wind in the willows, or the note of distant curlews on a lonely moor. I feel no longer alone, no longer dusty, for your existence sheds enchantment even over this arid world': part of a fragment of a letter from Russell to Gamel, quoted by Kenneth Hopkins. His pamphlet 'Bertrand Russell and Gamel Woolsey' (Warren House Press 1985, edition of 250 copies), gives a sensitive, moderately detailed but rather inconclusive account of the relationship.

† The salute at Marlborough was taken by General Frank Gathorne-Hardy, my great-uncle.

Gerald amused and charmed them 'with his characteristic talk and gestures . . . I said I heard Beryl de Zoëte had become nicer lately. "Oh?" said Gerald, "Well, I met her in London the other day and I wanted to hit her on the head with a hammer. It seems she has been converted to Communism only she will call it 'Democracy'." '[29] Ralph's and Gerald's letters resumed, moving from 'Dear . . .' to 'Dearest . . .' and gradually they took up their old relation, though there always remained potential, and quite often activated, gunpowder elements in their deep friendship.

7

Some time early in 1946 the farmer-owner repossessed Maidencourt, and VSP and Dorothy had to return to London. Gerald's distress was not lessened but it was distracted by the arrival of the Lowinskys about this time.

Ruth Lowinsky and her husband Tommy had been living at Garsington. She was 'a great rumbustous woman, small in size, with a face like a pig, but in great curves and folds and wordy explosiveness . . .'[30] Tommy he describes as reacting like a 'daisy flattening itself before the roller passes over it'.[31] Ruth was rich, a society hostess and a splendid and very greedy cook, author of *Lovely Food*, *More Lovely Food* and *Lovely Food in Wartime*. They bought the fine Queen Anne mansion in the middle of the village, seeing it as their cottage from London. Gerald foresaw the time when instead of saying 'I went to Eton' or 'I fought in the International Brigade', people would say 'I had a cottage at Aldbourne.' But, though Gerald and Gamel were quite often asked, VSP said Ruth didn't think Gerald totally presentable. 'He was asked to her Grade II parties.'

There were, more significantly, signs of something new stirring in his mind at the beginning of this year. He suddenly began to read a great deal of French medieval literature and Provençal poetry, and from there moved to Spanish medieval poetry and on to the poetry of sixteenth-century Spain. Then Russell sent him his *History of Western Philosophy*.* This excited Gerald so much he had to take sleeping pills as well as long notes.[32] The possibilities of Russell's

---

* The US edition. Presumably paper shortages delayed its publication here.

combination of brief biographies followed by and linked to clear exposition of the work particularly struck him.

He was still visiting the Foreign Office in March but the Spanish talks effectively ended this year.* They, too, along with *Segismundo*, had kept him welded to Spain and things Spanish. At their height, between one and two million people had listened to the talks and by the end the BBC was receiving more letters from Spain than were sent to all the other foreign sections combined.[33] Gerald found he was quite famous when he returned to Churriana.[34]

Early in 1946 Gamel was in bed for six weeks, possibly with suspected TB, and rather enjoyed it. Poffett sat on her bed, the fire crackled and she worked – correcting the proofs for a second edition of her fairy stories and at her novel, whose punctuation was giving difficulties (Gamel, like Byron, preferred the dash).

She also typed Part II of *Segismundo*, but in July Gerald put this aside, at Chapter 18. In *Personal Record* he says he burnt it, which he did but not for thirty years. It is clear that, like *South From Granada* and *St Teresa* and *Mr Fisher*, he merely meant to set it aside for a while. The following year he was talking about returning 'with new zest to my novel'.[35] Lynda Pranger, one of the few people to read it, says it was a picaresque novel of innumerable scenes – many of them lively and amusing but many more very boring. VSP said the same. Gerald told Lynda he often got extremely bored writing it. The reason for its failure was clear. 'Plot' and narrative are the humblest of the novelist's arts and Gerald, years before, had said he despised them, but this was partly because he could not master them. Even picaresque novels – his attempted solution – perhaps especially picaresque novels, require some form of onward-going drive, and this *Segismundo* apparently did not have at all.

There was another reason Gerald was bored by narrative. Writing

---

* In 1947 and 1948 Gerald gave one talk, and the last two in 1949. It is also just possible that he did some work on *A Life of One's Own* this year. A letter from Gamel to Bertie Russell, undated but before they fell out – probably late 1945 or early 1946 – says that he did. Gerald himself notes elsewhere (MSS, MF archive) that he showed part of *A Life . . .* to his father, who was 'non-committal'. To do this, he would have had to have written some of it about now. And it can only have been an early section. Anything later, and his father wouldn't have been non-committal at all. These indications are very slight and I have accordingly placed the start of *A Life . . .* where they become unmistakable. But if he did start now, it is an interesting re-inforcement of the argument set out under *South From Granada* (see pp. 436–7).

to VSP about the Spanish novelist Pío Baroja a little after this he noted that though Baroja's apparatus of character and plot was slipshod and improvised, Gerald found 'a sort of secret elation – a grey lyrical feeling that seems to whisper some consolation. It is not character or action that interest him, or the difference between characters – but that half-felt thing that lies underneath things and is present in everyone.' It was these things – intimations – 'the climate, the feel of living' that Gerald wanted to convey. He was, still, really yearning after poetry.

At all events, after five years' work, having created seventy-five characters and written 200,000 words, he simply could not bring himself to heave it all into action again.* But the reason he put it aside with so much ease was because something far more exciting now engaged him. Gerald had decided to write (or had been commissioned by Cyril Connolly – it is not clear which) two articles on St John of the Cross for *Horizon*.

This was familiar territory,† but he worked hard for six weeks, until September. Divided into an account of the life and an introduction to the work, the first article shows with what verve Gerald could write once provided with a narrative. The second was his first sustained work of literary criticism and for this reason deserves a brief look, while reserving closer attention for the book which eventually evolved from these articles.

One example can show the extraordinary clarity and creative energy he brought to critical writing – adding, in this case, to the close

---

* It is very difficult now to find out much about the contents of *Segismundo*, though fragments remain. Segismundo is the chief character in Calderón's *La vida es Sueño* (*Life is a Dream*). In the play, as well as humanity, he is, Gerald wrote in his book on Spanish literature, 'the classic example of the aggressive egoist who conquers his egoism', so some Gerald-identification may have gone on. Gerald's old desire to be a humble artisan found expression in Segismundo's becoming an apprentice cabinet-maker in Ciudad Real. The object of the book was to give flesh to the Civil War in the same way that Galdós' novels gave life to the Spain of 1860–90, and two of the main characters, brothers, fought on opposite sides, just as they lived on opposite sides of a river. Years later, Gerald kept one chapter from the flames, 'The Bustard Shoot'. It contains a marvellous description of the Sierra Morena in hot summer and a dramatic account of the shoot. Gerald told VSP he'd researched this to such a degree he felt he'd been shooting bustards all his life. Several times in the 1950s he tried to get this published in US magazines, but without success.

† A remark in a letter from Spain to Blair, 14 March 1949, that the manuscript of *St John of the Cross* was missing from Churriana makes it seem likely that he had written some sort of draft before 1936, though there is no other reference to it.

textual analysis his knowledge and feeling for Spain to bring the poetry alive for English readers. He had just explored* the fusion – or 'condensation' – of various personal elements, memories and so on in a single poetic symbol, phrase or passage, which is the method, Gerald suggested, by which poets obtain their force and richness. He now demonstrates this with the last lines of St John's *Cántico espiritual*:

> Y el cerco sosegaba
> y la caballería
> a vista de las aguas descendía.

> The siege was being raised
> And the horsemen,
> At the sight of the waters, were riding down.

These lines mean, St John tells us, that the passions of the soul have been assuaged, and the senses are descending to be purified in the waters. 'And yet,' writes Gerald, 'I do not think that in the whole of Spanish poetry there is a passage that calls up so vividly the Castilian-Andalusian scene before the incidence of motor transport: the string of horses or mules descending slowly to the river; the vague suggestion of frontier warfare, now over; that sense of endless repetition of something that has been done countless times before being done again, which is the gift of Spain to the restless and progressive nations. In these last two wonderful lines, with their gently reassuring fall, the horses descending within sight of the waters are lifted out of time and made the symbol of the peace of this land of eternal recurrence.'†

It is impossible to read those three lines again after that, even if you don't understand Spanish, without the scene Gerald has crystallised from them rising before your eyes.

> Y el cerco sosegaba
> y la caballería
> a vista de las aguas descendía.

* Something he developed, fully acknowledged, from Professor J. L. Lowes' study of Samuel Taylor Coleridge, *The Road to Xanadu*.

† I have in fact taken the quotation from Gerald's biography, *St John of the Cross*. It is virtually identical to that in the *Horizon* article, but he had improved it by one or two very small alterations.

8

It is likely Gerald had been revolving the idea of a new book since January. But it was the exhilaration he felt over St John, coupled with Russell's *History* suddenly showing him the way he could do it, and also another bad book by Allison Peers, that finally decided him to write a history of Spanish literature. He reviewed Peers' *St John of the Cross and Other Lectures* in the 27 July 1946 issue of the *New Statesman*, pointing out with force, concision and clarity its manifold superficialities. Then, as soon as he had finished his *Horizon* articles, he began his own research.

The decision to embark on such an immense undertaking so soon after getting bogged down in one almost equally large may have been helped by money, than which nothing is more stimulating to an impoverished writer.

Gerald had been getting increasingly worried about money all this year. Then suddenly in August his father's sister Maude died. It seems that she left all her money to Blair, but with extraordinary generosity his brother made half – £3284 (say £54,000) – over to Gerald.[36]

He paid Blair back many years later*, but he may have paid some back quite soon. At any rate an opportunity occurred within a year, as a result of a far more significant death – that of their father.

---

* He did this in 1962, during a complex manoeuvre avoiding death duties, by leaving £1000 each to Lydia and Ann, Blair's daughters. In fact by then, even taking into account a possible earlier repayment, he should have given them £3000 each. Gerald always ignored inflation when it suited him.

TWENTY-ONE

Spanish Literature and the visit to Spain

1

Nineteen forty-seven began with another seventeenth-century winter, the snow lying till 18 March. Gerald had shingles in February. 'It has a wonderful name', he told Ralph. 'Therpes Zesta', reminding him 'of oriental girls one used to meet at parties';* but a little later Gamel was telling Alyse how depressed it was making him. This was followed by a severe attack of Beethoven†[1] in March, and then in May he had to have his gums cut back. They were planning a holiday at Welcombe when they learnt his father was seriously ill.

But at some point before they left there was a revealing incident between Gerald and Miranda, now sixteen. She was drying herself while Gerald finished undressing, when she suddenly 'gave a shout of glee – "It's standing up! It's standing up!"'[2] Gerald saw to his intense embarrassment that this was true and quickly got into the bath. After this, he gave up having baths with her.

2

Hugh Brenan took three weeks to die of cancer of the prostate during June and July. Gerald and Gamel shuttled between Budleigh Salterton, Ronnie Duncan and Mrs Cottle. Gerald ordered the coffin well in advance (from now on his anxiety about death always manifested

---

  * Perhaps one of the girls was also called Therpes. The correct name for shingles is *Herpes Zoster*.
  † Gerald and Ralph's term for diarrhoea, which used to afflict Beethoven when composing. Gerald was now working very hard at *Spanish Literature*.

itself through coffins and money). The last three days he spent alone
with Mabel, taking copious and extraordinarily vivid notes.[3]

On the final night, he took the last watch, from twelve to six. His
father was in a deep morphia sleep. 'His face has become very severe,
the nose standing out below a marble forehead and his mouth open in
astonishment.' He imagined his father had looked like that when
Gerald was born and their long and stormy Oedipal conflict began.
'What a disgrace it would be to fall asleep on such an occasion.' He
didn't, but his mind wandered – and wandered across the pages on
his knee: a scene for *Segismundo* – father dying, son caught making
love next door to one of the maids; as his father's breathing altered,
how very odd that his next-door neighbour, Col Stokes, late RAMC,
was actually grandson of *the* Dr Stokes, 'inventor' of Cheyne-Stokes
breathing. At four o'clock, his breathing altered again. Gerald paused
in his notes. His father's eye was open. He was conscious. Gerald
called his stepmother and together they peered close. The good eye
was wide and solemn, the glass eye, crooked, stared at the ceiling.
Hugh died at 4.08 precisely.

The funeral lunch at the Rosemouth Hotel was jolly and
extremely noisy – Gerald, Mabel, Uncle Bertie, the nurse (somehow
appropriately deaf), and Blair. Hugh Brenan had left £62,000. Mabel
got the interest on £12,000, and £500 each from Blair and Gerald
which, to their extreme irritation, Hugh had made them promise to
give as he was dying. Gerald received £9500 (say £147,000); Blair
about £2000 more. These were the sums due to them under the terms
of their mother's marriage settlement.

Gerald did not mind his father's dying. He had spent his whole
life, as he noted while it took place, in longing for this moment that
would set him free. But he had admired Hugh's stoicism under
sometimes intense pain, and the death affected him. He rejoined
Gamel at Mrs Cottle's, but found that for three days he could hardly
walk.

3

Gerald's income was now about £1100 a year, say £17,000 at 1990
figures. A great deal better than before, but not what you'd call gross
wealth. And he had the inestimable boon of free capital, for emergen-

cies, for trips, for this and that (counterbalanced by Gerald's intense dislike of selling capital, which he only did when he absolutely had to).

It made not the slightest difference to his work. Like all writers, he sometimes had vague fantasies about bestsellers, but in fact all his life he only wrote exactly what he wanted with no serious regard for money at all. The two St John articles came out while his father was dying. VSP wrote and congratulated him. Now literary editor of the *New Statesman* (these are the years of his great 'Books in General' articles), he also offered Gerald reviewing. Gerald refused. He was working furiously at *Spanish Literature*.* By June he had reached halfway, by October he was condensing his chapter on Cervantes ('Hell!') for another article in *Horizon*.⁴

In fact, he enjoyed writing *Spanish Literature* more than almost all his other books. He kept on getting seduced into side-avenues of research – with *coplas* for example – and as he told VSP, 'I always like educating myself.'⁵ 'It was delightful,' Gamel wrote to Alyse, 'being with someone who was in such a full burst of creative energy.'⁶

A rather curious event took place between them in August. Gerald and Gamel borrowed VSP's flat near Regent's Park and from there, on 25 August, went to Hampstead Registry office and got (bigamously) married. It was so that Gamel could acquire British nationality, which in turn was probably to facilitate Miranda's naturalisation, which took place in July 1948. It gave Gamel a slightly bitter amusement that these aspects were the ones Gerald fussed over, not the marriage itself.⁷ Gamel's age on the certificate was given as forty-four, though she was in fact fifty-two.⁸

In October she learnt that *Patterns in the Sand*, her second novel about her childhood in the Deep South, had been rejected by Chatto and Windus.⁴ Ambitious as a writer (Desmond Hawkins noticed her 'intense' desire to be a poet), acutely, abnormally sensitive to criticism, she felt this as a grievous blow. Gerald longed for her to have

---

* Ever since he had read for eleven hours a day in the trenches, Gerald's concentration had remained formidable, with effects which were sometimes bizarre. He once, without noticing, ate an entire cake slice by slice while walking up and down thinking; and Frances can remember her son Burgo describing how he came upon Gerald at Ham Spray while he was reading for *Spanish Literature*. Gerald was holding his false teeth above his head in his left hand, clacking them absently together.

some literary success as an antidote to her melancholy. She eventually managed some translations, but the stricture she'd once applied to Gerald that he could never finish things he'd started, began to apply far more to her. Gerald also feared, now and at various times, that his success might upset her, but this was never so. She was always proud of his books, and generously delighted when he got good reviews. Since the age of twenty-three in New York, all her efforts had been bent on the literary life. When Gerald began, in Spain, to receive a measure of fame, she enjoyed being the eminent writer's wife – joining, as it were, Alyse and Phyllis Playter. She didn't even mind his colossal literary energy. When he was constructing the index for *Spanish Literature*, she told Alyse, he was 'indefatigable and would shame me if I could be shamed – but the battles I wage are fought elsewhere'.⁹

She was too proud to present her novel to another publisher for many years and, as Gerald had feared, her black moods of frozen indolence, of melancholy and guilt, increased steadily these latter years of the 1940s.*

4

Christmas lunch that year was at the Lowinskys, establishing as custom something begun the year before. It was followed by a party at the Bomfords. Gerald drank too much and played 'sandwich', where he was squashed into a passionate embrace with an unknown lady. Diana Dors came, aged sixteen – 'all smiles and lips and adolescent plumpness' – but Gerald thought that Miranda, 'without specs and wearing lots of rouge', the most beautiful girl in the room.¹⁰

---

* *Patterns in the Sand* still exists but I haven't been able to get hold of it. It was the story of her childhood, set deep in the 'Ole South' which, as she got older, glowed in her imagination with ever more roseate colours. Gerald wrote to VSP on 19 October 1947: 'Some chapters are good in a poetical way, but the general effect is too sweet and sugary. She will not write with the sharp malicious side of her mind because she is ashamed of it.'

This is probably accurate, but there is a patronising note. Gerald's attitude to Gamel's work, particularly the poetry, was complicated. He praised it, and to her face praised it carefully and fully. To others, there was frequently this patronising element, at times almost of dismissal. His saying that Gamel might be adversely affected by his good reviews or a new edition sometimes simply seemed a roundabout way of drawing attention to his success.

Parties continued into 1948. More given by Jimmy and Jane Bomford – on 31 January Tambimuttu came. 'He is a dark fawn-like creature who lives like a character in [Edward] Lear in a perpetual ecstasy brought on by beer and salad.'[11] Dylan Thomas and Caitlin arrived to stay with the art critic Mervin Levy. Gerald joined them in a pub crawl and once again drank too much. He tried to kiss Caitlin, whom he'd last seen in Churriana in 1935, but she gave him a frightful bite.[11] As Dylan left Bell Court late that night, the wine having run out, he raised the two dustbin lids under the moonlight – 'Ali Baba?'

All this highly unusual drinking caused chaos in Gerald's stomach – terrible Beethoven, then seven days of 'flu. But at last his father's money was beginning to flow. They decided to take a holiday in Ireland, but the money was used first to attack the kitchen. Out came the coal range and in went gas. The kitchen, Gerald told VSP, from a railway cab became a surgery; Gamel, in spotless apron, performed operations on eggs and bacon. Gerald also referred grandly to their central-heating installation – in fact a single electric radiator in one room. It was probably now they had the telephone installed.

As he liked to do before trips, Gerald cleared the decks in April, sending the bulk of *Spanish Literature* to Cambridge University Press and, possibly, to Penguin. Then in May they flew to Dublin. At once, both of them were in heaven. Travel was their element – and they hadn't been abroad since 1936. They read guide books, history books, books on archaeology, poetry; they 'visited the spot where Mr Bloom tossed himself off on the seashore'[12]; they explored Limerick, Tralee, Inch and Dingle for its Celtic antiquities; Gerald usually hated Guinness 'with its taste of boot polish and sulphuric acid' but here it tasted creamy and marvellous.[12] Ireland reminded Gamel of 'the Ole South' and she too became 'indefatigable', among other expeditions once walking twenty miles in six hours with him. Gerald returned to his youth (he hadn't been to Ireland since 1919). He botanised, climbed a mountain alone, observed, pondered, analysed. The moment he got back from the sixteen-day trip, he wrote VSP a letter which started to become, as he admitted, a lecture – but it was an inspired one. 'The Normans had a feudal conception of life, based on the idea of possession of land, whereas the Irish were organised in semi-nomadic tribes for whom kinship was the important thing. Feudal life implies roots in the soil, in material prosperity, in history, and expresses this conception in architecture and ambitious projects of all sorts. Tribal life means endless palaver, no fixed habits, a disposition to believe that things talked about are things done.'[13] And as he develops his theme, whether it is true or not, a resonance is set up, a sense of history, the exhilaration of expanding and revealing generalisations. Gerald would have illuminated wherever he had settled in exactly the same way as he illuminated Spain.

5

Miranda was now seventeen, and had left Beltane in July. She had a brief holiday with Gerald and Gamel, who were staying at Budleigh Salterton after three weeks at Welcombe, and then they sent her to the Truby King Mothercraft Institution, a nursery training school in Highgate. It was partly staffed by nuns, extremely strict, and by 16 August 'Nurse Brenan' was hating it. Gerald at first thought it was good for her – 'All Beltanians are soft'[14] – but as she grew more and more unhappy he became seriously concerned. He and Gamel went several times to London and on 16 September they took her away, having found her a position at Dartington as Student Matron, starting on 3 October.

They had acted with admirable promptness. Yet Gerald's attitude to Miranda was becoming increasingly split. It was as if there was a parallel Miranda somewhere deep in his head, different from his daughter – indeed not really his daughter at all. Now seeing Ralph and Frances all the time, VSP remained his chief correspondent, and he wrote to him in August about Miranda. He wanted her to have love affairs, but he wanted to arrange them himself. He wanted to watch Miranda have the love affairs he'd never had himself. 'Be disgusted if you like, but . . . such are the ogrish thoughts of a man of fifty-four who once had a daughter by a girl of fifteen!'[15] He wrote again five days later in a slight panic. His last letter may have given the wrong impression. His relations with Miranda were *perfectly* normal: 'between the private fantasy and the spoken word or act there is a gulf – in my case a very great one'.[16] Yes – in the bedrooms of the castle the most astonishing things went on; nothing very much happened on the surface.

None the less, other people noticed Gerald's growing attraction to Miranda. 'Julia and I would talk about incest,' said Lawrence. 'Bicycling made conversations very easy. Words like "incest" were continually floating over the hedges.'

Then Jimmy Bomford started to hang around Bell Court. 'Would Miranda like to ride his pony?' Instantly suspicious and jealous, Gerald questioned him. Bomford admitted at once he planned to seduce her – and was astonished Gerald should mind (no doubt Gerald had described his fantasies). Gerald now found he disliked Bomford intensely. Fortunately, Miranda went off to Dartington on 4 October. Gerald was left feeling guilt in several directions. 'When one turns against one's friends, one is really turning against something in oneself.'[17]

6

In December he finished *Spanish Literature*, all but the last chapter. He had learnt in August that CUP had accepted it, but couldn't publish it for two years. There is a suggestion in an earlier letter to Ralph that Penguin had agreed to do it provided it were sufficiently 'popular'.[18] Presumably Allen Lane thought it wasn't.

Gerald's achievement is astonishing, if for no other reason (and there are many other reasons) than the amount of work completed in so short a time. For a start, in two and a quarter years he'd read, digested and commented on, often at length, some 250 authors, many of them little known. It is true he had read a lot of them before, especially the early Spanish and Arabic poets (St John of the Cross was the first author he read on arriving in Spain in 1919). Nevertheless his system had been to read afresh selected texts from all his authors, and also all that the latest authorities had said about them. In addition he had searched everywhere to find every last biographical detail.* It is these, among other things, which give his book such vitality – as he had noticed they did to Russell's *History*.

Nor had Gerald written *Spanish Literature* only during these two years. Twice he'd broken off to write other things.† And he'd been

---

* This research involved a long correspondence, between 1 January 1947 to 1950, all preserved at Texas, with John L. Gili of the Dolphin Book Co. in Oxford.
† A long short story, *Philemo, the Railway Train*, etc., written in one of his bursts of inspiration, twelve hours a day and smoking like a chimney from 21–25

side-tracked into *coplas* to such an extent that, together with those collected at Yegen and at other times, he now had enough for a large anthology.* And he made notes of other things he'd discovered when 'seduced', as he put it, down the various byways of research. One of these concerned Borrow.

Gerald admired Borrow and was influenced by him. *Jack Robinson* is full of weird characters singing to themselves in dingles. There are passages in *South From Granada* that remind one of the Norfolk author. He now thought he had found out that Borrow had lifted Belle of the Dingle and the lovemaking scenes in *The Bible in Spain* from two obscure Spanish plays. Gerald was struck favourably by this and remembered it when he came to write *South From Granada*.†

Sometimes writing twelve hours a day, it is hardly surprising that Gerald began to flag during September, becoming affected by 'low cravings to weed the garden'.[19] Nevertheless he struggled on with the difficult last chapter through Christmas and into 1949.

Christmas itself was the usual Lowinsky lunch followed by a visit to the Bomfords. Gerald had now forced Jimmy Bomford to promise he wouldn't touch Miranda,[20] which seems to have made Bomford so depressed they only played cards.

Immersed in his work in things Spanish, Gerald increasingly longed to get out of England 'and its doll's house scenery'[21] and be

---

October 1947; and again a series of spoof utterances of great writers *Talking from Hades* (both in MF archive).

* Apart from Yegen, most of his sources were published. He used especially the collection by F. Rodríguez Marín, and the *Biblioteca de Tradiciones Populares Españolas*, in particular Vols. 1, 2, 4 and 8 (MSS, Texas).

† The plays in question are by Tirso de Molina (c. 1584–1648). From the first, *La Gallega Mari-Hernández*, Gerald thought Borrow may have been influenced to take the robust qualities of Isopel Berners. The tough Galician heroine of the play fights a duel with a Portuguese knight and wins, whereupon he marries her. From the second play, *Marta, La Piadosa*, Borrow could have got the idea of the Armenian lessons, since in the play a lover, Don Felipo, teaches his girl Latin. Sir Angus Fraser, the foremost Borrow scholar alive today, to whom I am much indebted over this matter, feels the links are tenuous, though not out of the question. The most one can say is that Borrow may have read Tirso – he certainly read Lope de Vega, Cervantes and other writers of the Siglo de Oro – and may have picked something up. Whether Gerald was right or not does not alter the effect this discovery had on him when he was writing *South From Granada*, where it was significant. (Gerald's position is set out in letters from Augustus John to the Gypsy Lore Society on 5 November 1948, and from Gerald to the Society on 6 September 1948; to John Davenport, undated, 1948; and to Sir Angus Fraser, 24 September 1977.)

back in Spain itself. By January 1949 he and Gamel were making plans to fly out in February. It seems likely that both Penguin and Kingsley Martin's Turnstile Press had expressed strong interest in a book on the country.

Gerald finished the last chapter of *Spanish Literature* and made his Will (since he envisaged both himself and Gamel being killed in an air crash, he left everything except his books to Miranda, on whom they'd be 'wasted', also leaving instructions to Blair to keep her from the clutches of Bomford).[22] There remained Poffett. After some thought, Gamel and he decided to ask Hope to look after both house and cat.

7

Gerald's last close contact with Hope had been in 1927, when his old mentor had returned from America with £1000, intent on engineering the financial killing of his life. He planned to raise still more money (Gerald gave £50), race round Europe buying paintings, then sell them in America at a huge profit.

Disaster struck from a totally unexpected quarter. A few years before, Hope had met a young Italian girl called Mireille. In those complicated days there existed something called a *'demi-vierge'* – a girl who allowed practically anything but remained 'intact'. Mireille, a cold beauty but with the pathos of poverty, was one such. Hope fell slightly in love, and she asked him to take her to New York. He agreed. A pretty girl would enhance his selling. He seems also to have entertained sudden hopes, which were encouraged, of at last overcoming the ghastly sexual inhibitions of his upbringing. But in New York, Mireille turned against him. She wouldn't let him in her bed. She wouldn't even go out with him. Then came the slump. Hope failed to sell a single picture. He had to sleep on the sofa and seems to have had some form of nervous breakdown. He returned to England penniless, knowing he would now never make the fortune he needed and craved.

Hope never recovered from this fiasco. Once again, he roamed the world – but now almost solely in search of the cheapest places to live. Letters came from exotic places asking for money. In one he told Gerald he suffered from 'a loneliness like a toothache'. In 1934 Gerald sent money to Hope in Bali on his way to Japan; he was in China in February 1935 (letters went quickest marked 'via Siberia'); Tibet and India in 1938 (Gerald sending £50); he finally returned to England in 1943.[23]

Gerald's comments on Hope in *Personal Record* from then on almost invariably express extreme irritation. But he never forgot that Hope had obtained the money from Tiz that enabled him to sustain his escape from his father, had perhaps ensured that escape in the first place – and he never let him down. Late in 1949 he gave Hope the tiny two-roomed annexe attached to Bell Court.

8

Gerald and Gamel landed in Madrid on 10 February, Gerald with 'flu (he was ill three times during the two-month visit). At once his letters became lyrical – 'Such girls, such girls! . . . they frown, pout, open their mouths like whales, squint yet remain adorable.' The pavements were like velvet, 'a little boy pees in the street . . . the nightingales start up while one sips one's Manzanilla'.[24] After eight days, they went by a train 'like a broken down donkey' to Cordoba. Smelling the sour smell of washed tile floors in their cheap hotel, 'I felt completely at home here. This was the Spain I knew.'[25] By Malaga, on 26 February, he not only felt he hadn't been really happy for thirteen years, 'It seems . . . I haven't lived at all.'

So much did they long to get to Churriana, yet dread what they might find, that they put it off till 2 March. The beauty, as they walked from the bus stop, was Vergilian, 'taken from a time when the world was young, poetical and cruel and when the word Mediterranean meant civilisation'. Then – their house, and Rosario opening the door! She collapsed in a heap on Gamel and had to be lifted onto a chair 'like a Dickens heroine'.

The house was full of tenants, but everything was safe, all their possessions piled neatly in the *mirador*. And the garden! The grove of Burmese canes, four foot in 1936, was now forty foot high, the beds full of arum lilies, cherries, roses, freesias, orange and lemon trees, '. . . and it was all mine!' Overwhelmed with gratitude, Gerald wrote to Blair that in the event of the crash he seems always to have expected '£500 at *least*' was to be sent to Rosario and Antonio, who were begging him to return. This was quite unnecessary. They had already decided to live there again as soon as Miranda was settled.*

They stayed on at Churriana for ten days, 'where every day gives the sensation of a week'. Rosario and Antonio gave them their own rooms and the villagers besieged them – partly because they were desperate for money, partly because Gerald was popular as a result of his broadcasts. And all the time he continued his ten-page-a-day diary from which he eventually constructed *The Face of Spain*.

They also saw Don Carlos, who'd caused them so much trouble in the Civil War. He held the same frightful right-wing fascist views and was not doing well, very poor and living in a dingy flat. He had a job Cervantes had once had: going into the Sierras – at this time as full of brigands as in the eighteenth century – to find corn hidden by landlords which they sold on the black market.

From Churriana they went to Granada for ten days. Here they managed to track down the lonely *barranca* where Lorca was buried; finally, heading home to Madrid on 1 April, Gerald's stomach was 'in convulsions'.

Only one thing marred their visit – but this to such a degree that Gerald found it almost unbearable. In Madrid, there were Civil War cripples every few yards. 'Some have no legs at all and creep along on all fours wearing a sort of boot on their hands.' The suffering, the poverty was appalling. People there and all over Spain were dying of starvation 'in a Belsen atmosphere'.

They flew back on 18 April, these scenes and others still violent in their heads, to an England about which, 'for all its meanness of mind and grey philistinism and its dread of reality', one could at least say, like Orwell, 'it was a country where people did not kill each other'.

It was also a country with rain. The agony of Spain had been partly caused, and much compounded, by several years of drought. Soon after they got back to the pudding-faced English – 'Rain – Rain – Rain. We have longed for it and now it is here, streaming through

* Gerald enjoyed toying with other possibilities, but he was probably really always determined to return to Spain when and if it was possible. One of the reasons he insisted to CUP (letter of 18 June 1943) that he must very carefully oversee any Spanish translation of *The Spanish Labyrinth* was that 'This is a political work on a contemporary theme and I am responsible for what is said in it. Since I shall return to Spain after the war this is important to me.'

the air, crawling like worms on the lawn, seeping into one's brain, making a noise like someone licking his lips.'[25]

Nevertheless, Gerald and Gamel had made the firm decision that they would live in Spain again. But before that point was reached they were to pass through a crisis as violent, as far as Gerald was concerned, as it was short, and as difficult to deal with as any in his life.

TWENTY-TWO

In Love with Miranda

*'Guilt? It's something I've not felt except over quite trifling things
– say, forgetting to answer a letter.'*

Tom Fisher in *A Holiday by the Sea*

1

During May, June and July 1949 Gerald corrected *Spanish Literature*, finishing during a week's duty-visit to Mabel. He then began to organise his notes for *The Face of Spain*. Gamel meanwhile typed *Spanish Literature** and gathered herself for work of her own. She had agreed to translate Galdós' *La de Bringas*, and began at the end of August when they were all holidaying at Welcombe. But by this time a rather peculiar situation had developed between Gerald and Miranda.

Whatever one may think of Gerald's behaviour with Miranda, either before or during this period, he had achieved one thing: she was completely open with him, trusted him and had, at eighteen and a half, none of his own crippling inhibitions about sex. Arriving at Budleigh Salterton she told Gerald she was very worried that she was physically abnormal. Three boys had clumsily tried to make love to her at Dartington. Each had been unable to, causing her acute physical pain. Gerald told Gamel to talk to her about virginity (passages in *One Way of Love* suggest that Gamel had had similar problems). He

---

* The procedure was that Gamel typed swiftly from Gerald's manuscript. He then made detailed corrections and alterations to this and it was sent away to be retyped by an agency. If Gamel didn't like something '½%' appeared in the text beside it. She typed on 'The Society' – the Facile model, which Gerald gave to Rosario's daughter María when Gamel died.

himself suddenly had a brilliant idea – a way in which he could both help Miranda and realise the fantasy he had outlined to VSP two years earlier. He decided to ask Jaime Gutiérrez, the handsome, gentle, sensual Spanish anarchist who was so successful with women, to come to Welcombe and seduce his daughter for him. Jaime duly arrived on 20 August.

'Gerald did not say it in so many words,' Jaime remembers, 'but he made it clear.' Gerald did, however, say it in so many words to Miranda. He tried, or so he told VSP, to leave the young couple alone, but Jaime insisted he accompany them, Gerald becoming increasingly excited by each expedition, on their picnics, their naked bathings and rock climbings and photography – 'the atmosphere of a youth hostel'.[1] Miranda was rapidly attracted to Jaime and therefore flirted with Gerald. At one point she made him pick some flowers and put them in her bush (Gerald had given her *Lady Chatterly's Lover*). 'I felt excited and disturbed and began to think my position a dubious one.'[1] But he was no longer in control of events; he could barely control himself. Not long after this Jaime successfully made love to Miranda.

They returned to Bell Court, Miranda soon leaving to stay with Jaime in London. It is clear that Gamel was getting extremely uneasy by this time. Gerald told VSP she had overheard some of his conversations with Miranda, was jealous and disapproved – Gerald sounds almost surprised – on 'what one might call moral grounds'.[2] Gamel wrote to Alyse Gregory and in October, when Miranda returned, she fled – staying away three weeks, first with Alyse, then Ronnie Duncan.

Something close to chaos now descended on Bell Court, made the more palpable because builders were getting Hope's annexe ready. Hope himself turned up for two days. Jaime came down for week-ends, and Miranda also had one of her Dartington boyfriends to stay and slept with him. Now in the grip of a devastating lust which he knew he could not possibly satisfy, or even express, Gerald found some relief in telling Miranda everything he could remember about his own lovemaking with Juliana. One day he arrived at Ham Spray 'in a perfect frenzy',[3] and poured out what he felt in graphic detail, 'speaking about Miranda as if she weren't his daughter at all'.[4] But his main relief, or release, was a series of extraordinary letters to VSP –

fifty-six pages in October alone*⁵ – 'In writing . . . I shall forgive myself', but they are less confessions than a substitute for what he could not do. Nor was it just lust. All his old Carrington symptoms returned: ungovernable excitement and agitation, jealousy, violent scenes followed by abject apology, lying weeping in his room, sleeplessness, racked by terrible feelings of emptiness and pain. He would 'of *course* go to bed with her if she would let me . . . For in "love-lust" one rises above even egoism and is ready to burn oneself and everyone else in a great bonfire.' Nevertheless, like some medieval monk beset by demons, he struggled furiously to subdue his feelings, first refusing to allow himself to fantasise about sleeping with Miranda and then, when that failed, 'a new system. Bromides, sleeping pills, moral discipline and a lot of masturbation (do I shock you?).'

Gradually, he gained control of himself. When Gamel returned at the end of October, he had pulled himself together – 'I can briefly describe it by saying I remembered Miranda was my daughter and very young and helpless'. He added he couldn't quite face seeing VSP at the moment after sending him such letters. He and Gamel were still getting on badly in December,⁶ but a job had been found for Miranda in Paris, starting in January; meanwhile she took a secretarial course in Swindon, going quite often to London.

What effects did this frantic upheaval have? On Miranda, perhaps not a great deal, except that she was through one important rite of passage. She was apparently an extrovert, lively, humorous, attractive girl – 'a little silly', said Jaime, 'but sweet. Actually, sweet was a

---

* All quotations here and in this section come from these letters, which also indicate the genesis of what was happening. When he had last made love to Juliana in 1934 Miranda, aged three and a half, had been watching. Juliana suddenly reached out and placed Miranda's little hand on Gerald's penis. '"*Agarrala bien, niña, que estas cosas van a ser tu delicia.*" "Hold it well, little girl, because that thing is going to give you delight." And to me she said, "I want her to grow up like me." I wanted it too.' Gerald's mistranslation of the Spanish (it should be 'these things are') is surely significant. But it is possible that none of this happened and Gerald just wrote it to VSP to both excuse and excite himself. At one point, describing with great vividness how he made love to Juliana this last time he writes, 'Picture the scene' in a slightly suspect way. But whether he did or not – and I choose to think he did – it clearly went on in his head, and what it suggests is that he had long nurtured a fantasy that Miranda would not just be a recreation of Juliana for other men, but for him too. He was the better able to do this, the taboo was less strong, both because she was nearly four before he had any real contact with her, and because it was some time before he was sure Miranda was, in fact, his daughter.

word she used a lot.' She was, of course, quite aware, as Frances put it when she met them both on the train, that 'something was *up*'.[7] She was in no danger from Gerald, who disguised all physical feelings and explained his scenes as the normal reaction of an overfond father to boyfriends. She teased him; she used him. Frances had met them on the way to London, where Gerald trailed after Miranda like some enslaved Humbert Humbert and spent £60 on dresses and 'French' underwear.

His own reactions were mixed. At last he was living intensely again. He looked and felt years younger; Frances recorded his voice ranging 'between low poetical, romantic tones and a husky, ironical shriek'.[8] He was partly proud of still being able to have such strong feelings (he re-read his Carrington journal); but he was also determined to find out why he had become so unbalanced. He now told VSP he had decided to write his autobiography, something he had mentioned once or twice before. Just as *The Spanish Labyrinth* had been written to explain the Spanish explosion, so his autobiography would discover, and tell the truth about, this personal one. He did not feel guilty – 'after all one has no control whatever over one's feelings'.

But he did mind hurting Gamel: 'I have injured her.' At one point she had said she would leave him and live in a caravan in Dorset. He told VSP that he would never be able to make love to her again.

'After making love to their wives,' Gerald was fond of saying now and later, 'most men think – thank God *that's* over for three weeks.'[9] And Gerald always felt he had to restrict himself when he was working and during these years he worked very hard indeed. Probably the comparative rarity of the event contributed to the violence of Gerald's reactions when his libido did occasionally surface in a direct way.

No doubt a good many couples cease to make love after nineteen years together. No blame attaches.* Nevertheless, as people get older lovemaking, however rare, is of far more profound importance psychologically than physically. There had been times before when Gamel felt she had had to restrict herself for Gerald. 'I chained the wilder part of my nature', she once told Alyse. The results were remorse and pain 'and certain wild unsettled impulses either chained

---

* Yet Gerald felt guilty. This guilt found typically oblique expression in his novel *A Holiday by The Sea*. Here it is by ceasing to sleep with her husband that Dora drives him mad.

or frozen or astray'.[10] From now on Gerald ceased to make love to her and she had to chain the most powerful impulse of all and she was, as Gerald wrote, 'of a more than usually sensual disposition'.* She minded, and a sad poem of her minding remains.

> Lying beside him in the night
> My thoughts go on, my thoughts go on . . .

The thoughts are of guilts, of fears; then

> My lips are weary for a kiss
> They have not found,
> They turn in the dark for what they miss,
> They shall not find it overground.
> My thoughts go on, my thoughts go on . . .

And from now on Gerald was surprised to find that this gentle woman, who agreed with people as a matter of principle, was legendary for doing so, in private often ceased to agree with him. She was also perfectly well able to exercise on him, again as yet in private, that sharp and malicious side of her mind of which he had said she was ashamed.

2

Gerald had a severe bout of 'flu at the beginning of 1950, reading Herodotus, Thucydides and Dante – 'that lean wolflike man, full of the spite of exile'.[11] His climatic descriptions of hell reminded Gerald of England in January. Then Jimmy Bomford gave two farewell parties for Miranda and on 27 January she left for Paris. She was to be an *au pair* with Catharine and Jean Gimpel, whose brother Charles Gerald had met through the Bomfords. (The Gimpel's father René was a picture dealer and collector, their mother a Devine. Jean's brothers ran the successful dealers in London.)

Gerald knew he really loved Gamel, but he would like 'an attachment' with a woman of thirty-seven to write letters to. 'I love

---

* This in the manuscript of *Personal Record* at Texas. In the book itself he toned it down to 'of a sensual disposition' – as he did several passages that could be used to imply his marriage was not happy. In a letter to Ralph of 12 April 1957 he said it was difficult for Gamel to share a bed with a man and not think of sex.

with a pen in my hand.' Instead, gloomily forced into 'viewing Venus through a telescope',[12] the pen sped across the pages of *The Face of Spain* – often from ten in the morning to one the following morning. Gamel – sometimes helped by Gerald or Hope (now a regular part of their life) – was nearing the end of *La de Bringas* (*The Spendthrifts*).

In March, the weather suddenly became deliciously un-Dante-like. 'It follows one about like a pleasant dream,' Gerald wrote to VSP. 'Our garden is full of large white and blue crocuses which open their petals in a vast yawn to take in a bee.'[13] He finished *The Face of Spain* (then called *A Spanish Diary*) on the 31st, when Gamel also finished *La de Bringas*.

Miranda had not been idle either. By 22 March she was already having an affair with Xavier Corre, the good-looking brother of Catharine Gimpel. He had just become a doctor and by April they were engaged. On the 22nd Gerald went out, shortly followed by Gamel, to meet Corres and Gimpels.

Paris was sustained euphoria. Sitting in cafés, especially Les Deux Magots, Gerald wrote poems in French, planned to start a new novel 'next week', saw Camus and Sartre come in ('I *think*') and 'I even dream . . . I can dance and will invent a ballet entirely made of hops and pirouettes.'[14] (One of the things that gave Gerald enormous pleasure was that, like her mother, Miranda was a marvellous dancer.) The Corres and Gimpels were all delightful and in a burst of francophilia he planned to sell the Churriana house and come and live half the year in Paris.

The three-week visit exhausted him (he had three bouts of 'flu in six weeks) but he immediately took up *Mr Fisher* again and in three months rewrote nineteen chapters.* Gamel also had a minor success when two of her poems were published in *Everybodys* by Kenneth Hopkins, a young Powys devotee.

It was to Powys' Dorset they went in July. Gamel swam and sunbathed, Gerald went on voyeur expeditions,[15] and they saw Alyse and Theodore Powys. Miranda's marriage was now looming (Gerald dreaded it. 'I shall refuse to wear a top hat'),[16] but they still managed some guests at Bell Court: Lawrence Gowing, Vero Richards, a

---

* The book finally contained eighteen chapters. It looks as if he had in fact finished the first draft during the 1930s and that all his subsequent work was rewriting. The complete sequence of manuscripts has not survived.

frequent visitor whose beautiful young wife Marie-Louise Berneri had recently died, Jaime Gutiérrez again and Julian Pitt-Rivers.

Miranda and Xavier arrived on 11 August, and on 15 September, after the usual convulsions of emotion and organisation a wedding entails, they were married from Blair's house in London.

In the event, Gerald loved the wedding. There was as much champagne as anyone wanted, caviar sandwiches, gladioli of a salmon-pink colour suggesting 'you could eat them too'. Beryl de Zoëte came first and left last. Arthur Waley told Dr Dent all his 'early Ping, Ming and Ting' were late Victorian. Gerald got rather drunk and fell for Alec Penrose's niece Ann Smyth, 'a girl of nineteen with a luscious, debauched or rather longing-to-be-debauched expression'.[17] He even loved his top hat and by the end said he wanted to give dozens of weddings.

Gerald promised Miranda an allowance of £60 (£830) a year. In his letters to her about money he frequently resembles his father (he wrote one now, for instance, explaining how expensive the wedding had been – adding her present into the total cost).[18] On the surface, his feelings appeared to be on an even keel, but it seems likely he continued to have discreet fantasies about her – his letters frequently contain salacious details or anecdotes.

But the most interesting effect of his brief and agonising passion for Miranda – and one which suggests it was in fact only part of a much more profound movement of his psyche – was an event which began on 27 November.

3

Gamel had left briefly for London, at once making Gerald uneasy. 'She is my oxygen tent.'[19] But while she was away and continuing after she got back, until 5 December, he was seized by one of his fits of inspiration, one of the most violent. Gamel describes him writing day and night, while they ate lunch at three and supper at ten. It was as though he had suddenly been allowed to descend deep into his subconscious, which was now revealed in the form of a castle.

The Lord of the Castle is a three-act poetic drama forty-seven small pages long.[20] (The form was no doubt to some extent due to the enormous vogue at the time for the verse plays of Christopher Fry,

Ronnie Duncan, Louis MacNeice and Eliot.) Emanation, who once ruled the kingdom, is the spirit of childhood and delight but above all of poetry. He has been locked away by his son Reason in a dank dungeon deep below the castle because of his anarchic inefficiency, and the play opens with Emanation's terrible and beautiful threnody: what he is now, what he was once, what he has seen – a threnody which leads him in a series of dazzling arabesques through the whole created universe. He has not only seen everything; woven in at length, but tautly, Emanation is also our *experience* of these things. And now there returns the key word in Gerald's youthful philosophy, not heard since his letters to Hope in 1916. 'Purity! That word once more! How it channels in my head, how it slides like silk along my inmost veins!'

But, though it has many fine lines and some marvellous and moving images, a close analysis need not really concern us. Emanation has followers, especially among the poor and the young. Reason, who is a combination of Gerald's father and Ralph, offers him his freedom: stay in the castle, don't invite insurrection, behave with dignity. Emanation refuses. '*Reason*: What further concessions can you ask? *Emanation*: Everything. *Reason*: That is not possible. *Emanation*: Then nothing. *Reason*: What do you mean by that? *Emanation*: I shall remain here.'

His function is to weep. This is not useless. His tears keep alive what Reason and the castle have rejected. Without Emanation, 'without the sudden flash of joy which is also like a memory, a stab of pain, your subjects would die of inanimation.' In Gerald's interior castle, where his youthful poetry has now been permanently imprisoned, Reason, the father in him, had been made to reign – the scholar had won over the poet.

But there is more to it than this. In January that year, he had written a letter to Frances lamenting the passing of youth, why had he not used it, not realised 'that soon all that sharpness and sweetness and poignancy would ebb away?'[21] The real destroyer of those flashes of joy was age, finally death, and it was his coming to terms with them that underlay this great upwelling, just as it had underlain the last one, in *The Clergyman and the Mouse* (which had, oddly enough, taken place nine months after Laura Rae, as this did nine months after his passion for Miranda).

No one likes growing old, but at one level Gerald accepted it with stoicism and, more or less, decorum. At another level he didn't accept it at all. To him, growing old was the destruction, *while he lived*, of what had been his essence – and he fought it furiously, just as he had fought furiously to attain it as an adolescent and a young man. Nor, one could argue, is *The Lord of the Castle* without optimism. That spirit of 'purity' he and Hope had raised up, with the peculiar, totally un-Christian, Rimbaudian sense of unsullied intensity they had given it, could not only be preserved; the tears of the imprisoned poet could revive it. At any rate, in a few years that spirit was to make gigantic struggles to escape again, nearly wrenching the bars from their sockets and causing great shudders to be felt throughout the castle. And, as for the battle against age and death which was the fundamental reality behind this struggle, Gerald, however ridiculous he may sometimes have appeared, very nearly won.

There is one last significant aspect to these incidents. On 23 October he had dropped *Mr Fisher* and for the first time taken up his autobiography. The writing of *A Life of One's Own* gave Gerald profound satisfaction – 'Like solving a long and difficult puzzle,'[22] he told Frances, when writing to ask her for a botanical guide to South Africa.

What is interesting is his way of writing it. He describes lying in bed or in a chair and letting his mind wander, noting down any memory that floats up.[23] This method of free association which, as tenuous memory jogged tenuous memory, is what it amounted to, is of course one of the classic ways therapists reach the unconscious. Gerald was, in effect, analysing himself and though he did not always make the connections, it also explains that phenomenon of juxtaposition which is sometimes so startling in *A Life* . . . , and which earlier proved so useful in suggesting clues to his complicated character.

4

Immediately after finishing *The Lord of the Castle* Gerald collapsed with a bout of 'flu. He also, Gamel told Alyse, suffered a severe reactive depression. He thought his play was like *Ossian* and quite worthless.[24] However, he pulled himself together and continued *A Life* . . . . He also braced himself for the publication of *The Face of Spain*, which came out in December.

The book, which was dedicated to Gamel, roughly follows their Spanish trip and this provides a narrative frame, while at the same time allowing ample room for those long, discursive detours he could make so fascinating into art and architecture, gossip, rumour, history, geology, archaeology, people and literature. While flying out, he imagines he can see from 20,000 feet the Black Lagoon where the body was buried in Antonio Machado's poem *La tierra de Alvargonzález*. He even included his dreams.*

Very noticeable among the detours is his fascination with the Spanish national character – something he shares with Spaniards. Sometimes it is simple observation. 'That is the Spaniard all over. He is a man without conflicts. He believes he is always in the right whatever he does and this conviction gives him more vitality.' Vitality which would be crude were it not imposed on a peculiar refinement and melancholy. 'All vital races feel keenly the existence of the anti-vital principle; it haunts them more persistently than it does the busy, phlegmatic, vaguely worrying English.' And as he spins his endlessly varying speculations, one feels him almost inventing the Spaniards – as he was to invent Hetty seven years ahead. Are the Spaniards a simple race in comparison to the English and French? 'As in their climate and scenery, the half-tones appear to be left out. Or is it that, like music written in an unfamiliar mode, we are unable to take in all the complexities? This seems to me the more probable hypothesis.' It is also the politer hypothesis, the more flattering to his hosts.

But what one enjoys most are the flow of ideas and the distinction of the writing: its humour, and imagery, the poetic flashes of joy, the sharpness, idiosyncrasy and delicacy of observation: a 'cantankerous-looking fig tree', the bevies of small brown hawks he saw at Ciudad Real 'with fan-like tails and wings, who catch insects and share the niches in the stonework with the pigeons', or, at a cemetery with its drawers and large marble tombs, where it was 'as though the spirits of the dead had been given their choice between country villas and city flats'. And, endlessly trundling in the little, slow, hot trains, coming out of a tunnel, say, and 'seeing on the left a slow muddy stream bordered with tamarisks and oleander', Gerald, like a painter

---

* 'Once, after reading Dante, I dreamed that I had joined an archaeological expedition for excavating the ruins of the Christian Hell which had just been discovered – its fires long extinct with the decay of the faith that had created them and its famous monuments covered over with ash and sand.'

with a range of colours special to him, sprinkles the book with the highly coloured flowers of his botanical knowledge: 'Periwinkles and yellow marigolds were in flower and the hedges and the farmhouses we passed looked white and clean with their pots of geraniums and iron *rejas.*'

The book is given weight by his account of the terrible poverty. This altered Gerald's view of Franco, whose supposed stability (along with the Marshall Aid he recommended) he now regarded as necessary for Spain's recovery. He continued to think that the ultimate solution was for a monarchy with a moderate left-wing government.

Weight, too, slightly too much, was added by his art criticism and descriptions which he had learnt from Roger Fry could be a form of literature.*

But *The Face of Spain* is really an extremely well-written travel book. If it is not the most profound of Gerald's books about Spain it is one of the most delightful. Friends praised it and so did reviewers, the two sometimes being the same. Desmond MacCarthy called it 'A remarkable book and a delightful one'; Rose Macaulay said it was 'A book of great balance and nearly as good in its way as his *Spanish Labyrinth*'. It consolidated his reputation as a writer on Spain.

It also made some money. The advance from the Turnstile Press was £200. It went through three impressions during 1952 and was reprinted by Hamish Hamilton in 1957. The most journalistically successful episode, his long search for and eventual discovery of the place where Lorca had been buried, was bought by the *New Yorker* for $1000, and also appeared in *Les Nouvelles Littéraires*.[25] It is exciting to read, full of Goyaesque detail like the open pit-of-the-dead in the Granada cemetery, crammed with 9000 skeletons, all with their heads smashed in and all fully clothed. The perfectly preserved body of a colonel in the Civil Guard, recently pulled from his drawer because his relatives had stopped paying his rent after fifty years, lay on top of the grisly heap. He was in full dress uniform, his sheeny flesh green and black.

---

* Too much for me. Not for Lawrence Gowing. 'Plainly,' he wrote to Gerald on 20 January 1951, 'you can be a critic of painting of the very first order any time you have to turn to it . . . On El Greco you are especially good – more to the point, as a matter of fact, than anyone since Max Dvorak. Then I found the view of Velazquez very stimulating – and I have embodied it whole into my own notions which are just forming.'

Ian Gibson says that everyone in Granada knew where Lorca was buried, but it may not have been so easy to pry the information out of them in 1949. In any event, as a result of his 7500-word *New Yorker* extract, Alfred Knopf asked Gerald to write Lorca's life. He refused, saying that, presumably because of the regime, 'it is a thing impossible to do',[26] thus leaving the way open for Gibson's own definitive and absorbing biography.

By June 1959, *The Face of Spain* had made him £1446.12s.od (£14,150), more than *The Spanish Labyrinth* had by that time.

5

Gerald's book was attacked in Spain,* and they therefore decided on the spur of the moment to go to Italy, where VSP had just been.[27]

Gerald sent a new Will to Ralph, with practically everything left to Miranda except that, if Bell Court were sold, Hope, as a reward for making Tiz leave him her money, was to have 'access to baths and use of the kitchen sink' in perpetuity and also to keep the annexe.[28] He sent *The Lord of the Castle* to Ronnie Duncan, suddenly and gaily added a last appendix to the half-finished proofs of *Spanish Literature* – 'Just a little pirouette of pure erudition'†[27] – and on 27 February 1951 they set off.

Gerald and Gamel followed the usual 'remorseless' schedule they both so much enjoyed: Paris to see Miranda and Xavier, Rome, Naples, then round Sicily and back round Magna Graecia, Naples, Rome and northern Italy – twenty-two towns and innumerable ruins, villages, galleries, churches, buses and squalid hotels in two months. And by the time they returned Gerald was proficient in Italian.

As well as loving travelling together (Gamel was as tireless as

* Gerald was sometimes nervous that as a result of *The Spanish Labyrinth* he would not be allowed to return and live in Spain – although Julian Pitt-Rivers had found out that this was very unlikely. However, in *The Face of Spain* he refrained from attacking Franco overtly and, though he did not mince his words about the appalling poverty, presumably the cause of the attacks in Spain, felt he had balanced this by recommending Marshall Aid. For the same reason he would not let VSP publish extracts, either of his letters at the time or from the book, in the *New Statesman* – 'far too left-wing' (letter to VSP, 4 March 1949).

† Probably the appendix on 'Socialist' tendencies in Spain in the seventeenth century'.

Gerald 'except up hill'), he was, as he says in *Personal Record*, filled with gratitude to her for seeming not to mind the cessation of their lovemaking. 'I love her every year, every month more and more,' he told Ralph on their return. 'Only I, who see under her defences, know what a rare character she is and how she deserves to be made happy.'[29] Now, as they whizzed about Italy, Gerald kept a diary in case anyone later wanted a book, meanwhile reading Thucydides, Herodotus, Vergil, Baedekers and grammars. Observations, ideas, generalisations bubbled out of him and streamed back in a series of delightful letters.[30] For the first time he loved Rome – 'This great museum inhabited by a few underpaid bank clerks, lawyers and professors'. Had VSP seen the vomitorium outside Caligula's dining room where he used to be sick? In Naples their *pensione* was eccentric, as was the *padrone*. He had no dining room ('I find them inartistic, I prefer pianos'). 'The Italians,' Gerald wrote, 'like brutal noises as the English like brutal foods.' In Taormina, Truman Capote, a reader of Gerald's books, gave a small party for them. Fortunately they were able to have their first bath in three weeks before meeting the fastidious little American. Easter was also in Sicily, at Enna, where the Sicilians stuffed themselves with iced cakes, sugar lambs, eggs, seals and fish: 'All representations of Christ! There is something to be said for eating one's God, when he is made of the finest sugar and cream.'[30]

The moment they got back to England, on 27 April, both of them took to proofs: Gamel correcting *La de Bringas*, and Gerald completing those of *Spanish Literature*. (Hope also read them for him.) He sent the index in June and then continued with *A Life of One's Own*.

Since the improvement in his fortunes, Gerald's *rentier* guilts seemed to have increased with the burdens of VSP's literary journalism (amongst other reviews, an article on a famous new author *every week*, he groaned this year).[31] This was now incessant, as his friend, living in London, in debt, struggled to educate his children and write his stories. On 12 June Gerald suddenly sent him £1000 (say £12,500), along with a letter of great charm and tact,[32] in which he emphasised that he did not expect VSP to pay him back unless he, Gerald, was in trouble, a reassurance he repeated.[33]

Shortly after this extremely generous gesture gracefully carried through, *A Life* . . . had reached Radley. The reliving of those terrible days plunged him into depression. He was swept by waves of Beethoven and smoked so much he made himself sick and had to give it up. 'I smell the disgusting smells, I suffer the ancient misery.'[34] Even a visit from Miranda couldn't cheer him. She made him trail round Cheltenham's shoe shops with her. 'Her object was to find a pair of shoes that will prevent her ever having to walk at all.'[34] Finally during July and August Beethoven got so bad the doctor thought he might have stomach cancer. Momentarily exhilarated, as always, by the threat of serious illness, Gerald had the usual tests. All were negative.

But there was another reason for all these nervous reactions. On 28 September *Spanish Literature*, dedicated to the memory of Roger Fry, was finally published. Gerald immediately began to smoke again.

6

The method followed in *The Literature of the Spanish People*, almost certainly taken from Russell, was a short biographical sketch, an account of the work, often with comparisons from writers or other figures an English reader might be familiar with (Chaplin, for instance), finally a 'placing' both in Spanish and usually Western literature, and in a social and historical context.

In the earlier part of the book, where biographical details were hard to come by, he relied to a greater degree on a more general biography of the period – that is, history. His interest in the metrical developments leading to and on from the *copla*, in which it seemed new discoveries had been made, provided another invigorating and unifying element.

First used by him in *The Spanish Labyrinth*, the sharpness and vividness of the biographical sketches show what Gerald could now do with this demanding form. Cervantes, 'Elderly, shabby, obscure, disreputable, pursued by debts, with only a noisy tenement room to work in . . . was still carrying on his inescapable vocation of literature. We are *Don Quixote* as we are Joyce's *Ulysses* . . .'

We are also quite often Gerald. The analyses are shot through with autobiographical echoes: Ibn Hazam laments 'the timidity produced by love – how for example some men have been known to kill themselves because they did not dare to declare their passion.'* (Ibn Hazam lived 994–1063 and is compared to Stendhal. Gerald's favourites – Proust, Stendhal, Joyce, Svevo, Rimbaud – dominate the comparisons.)

Cyril Connolly, just beginning his long reign at the *Sunday Times*, praised it almost unreservedly. He only lamented that there were not more translations because they were so good (they were by Gamel). He noted, among much else, that with Góngora 'Mr Brenan advances to the major act of criticism, the discovering, explaining and re-installing of a great writer who is nearly lost to us'.[35] Góngora lost to Spaniards? But surely the point here is that, for the vast majority of his readers, Gerald was doing this for an entire national literature.

In particular, he did it for the poets of the Arabic period and the early Middle Ages. And here he gives a sense, as all good histories of this sort should, of writers developing one out of another, of a literature unfolding, of something akin to a common purpose. And the purpose, or rather the literature that resulted, is above all Spanish. Here, as always, Gerald's insight was particularly acute. He noted – and the observation struck with added force at a moment it was so observably true – how many Spanish writers had either been in prison or exiled. From this derived the note of solitude and a special and stubborn realism. It was because it was riveted to this realism, the reality of Spain, and a certain 'dryness of imagination', that so little of Spanish literature had travelled. But, Gerald goes on, 'this pungent national flavour will be one of its chief charms. It takes us out of our Anglo-Saxon skins as neither Italian nor French literature do. Behind every book we read, we feel not so much a new author as the pulse of a strange and peculiar society. For of all European literatures Spanish is the most homogeneous. The popular poetry of the village, still being made and sung today, drifts like smoke into the brains of the cultured writers.'

The quality of *The Literature of the Spanish People* was instantly

---

* The echoes are particularly noticeable when the writer or the passage touches on love. So Auziàs March (1397–1459) – '. . . the pleasure he seeks in love is his pleasure in suffering . . . For since the human mind is endowed with a greater capacity for painful sensation than for agreeable ones, suffering offers a depth and richness of feeling that pleasure can never give.' Debatable – but it would be a stimulating debate. The feeling one has here and on many occasions, that Gerald was writing out of his own experience and from his own preferences, are what give the book its energy, its fascination – and what infuriated narrow scholars.

recognised by practically all who reviewed it – except one. Allison Peers had been smarting for decades under their exchanges. Now he pounced. It was Mr Eccleshare of CUP who warned Gerald[36] on 29 October that Peers, 'this elderly, spiteful pedant' as Gerald described him to VSP,[37] was writing unfavourable reviews in the *Times Educational Supplement* (unsigned), the *Manchester Guardian* (initials), and the *Spectator* (signed).

Gerald almost panicked. He rushed his 'spiteful pedant' letter to VSP on 30 October, now terrified lest Peers 'or his henchmen' might have captured the *Times Literary Supplement* itself. VSP at once got Geoffrey Brereton to review *Spanish Literature* in the *New Statesman*: 'Nothing else covers the ground in so persuasive and lucid a way.'[38] Alerted by Gerald, other people who admired him came to his defence.[39] Professor Edward Wilson promised to review it.* J. B. Trend reviewed it in the *Listener* – 'The best account of early lyric poetry in the Peninsula which has yet been written'[40] – and also routed Peers in a fiery note to the *Times Educational Supplement*, referring caustically to 'the vapourings which have so often passed for Spanish studies'.

But Peers had been routed by a tide of critical praise it would be boring to go on quoting† before Gerald's defence was even set in motion. By 6 November he was euphoric. Professors, he told VSP, were writing from Yale and Boston, Cambridge had invited him to lecture. The book would become a textbook and would make money like Macmillan's *Elementary Mathematics*. Had he written it when he was thirty-five it would have meant girls. Now at fifty-five it was too late.[41]

---

* Admirers did not mean dishers-out of slavish praise. Professor Wilson did indeed praise the book but he made a number of trenchant criticisms, particularly of Gerald's treatment of Calderón, which Gerald agreed were all well deserved. But differences of opinion over judgements in a book of this sort are to be expected. The livelier the book, the more expected. Gerald had been very nervous in case his book would not pass the scrutiny of professional Spanish scholars – 'It's most difficult test' – and this in general terms it more than did (see article by Wilson, 'Gerald Brenan's Calderón', *Bulletin of the Comediantes*, IV, no. 1, 1952; his review in *Modern Language Review*, no. 47, 1952 (pp. 595–6); Gerald to VSP, 6 November 1951 and Gerald to CUP, 31 October 1951).

† The only thing that may have faintly irked Gerald was that several reviewers compared it, by way of praise, to Strachey's *Landmarks in French Literature*. For most of his life Gerald despised this book. Only when he was very old and their ancient rivalry had vanished did he allow it some merit.

One can ask, as with *The Spanish Labyrinth*: Will his book last? Critical works practically never survive. Perhaps only Aristotle and Coleridge. Even writers all ages admire, as Gerald wrote, are admired for different reasons at different periods, so that great writers seem to be recreated by succeeding ages. Johnson's Shakespeare is not ours' and, when we read him, seems barely relevant. In English universities, his chief market, Gerald has to an extent been replaced by the seven-volume *Literary History of Spain* and P. E. Russell's *Spain: A Companion to Spanish Studies*. Cambridge University Press are allowing Gerald to go out of print for the first time in forty-one years as this is written. Not a bad innings.*

Marvellously written, lucid, showing critical perception and exposition of a high order, *The Literature of the Spanish People* consolidated Gerald's reputation as a writer. But it also finally established him as by far the most original and interesting of those, in whatever field, writing about Spain. This was shown when a year later, to anticipate slightly, he was asked to put his name forward for the Alfonso XIII Chair of Spanish at Oxford. He had powerful backers and it is likely he would have got it. Julian Pitt-Rivers and Raymond Carr went to ask him in October 1952. Gerald was appalled. He'd never been to university. He couldn't possibly do it.[42] (On several occasions he showed quite disproportunate humility in the face of universities.) Next, Hugh Trevor-Roper went in November. This time Gerald refused because he said Gamel couldn't live without servants.[43] His backers gave up.

Gerald would have enjoyed many things about university life: the level of talk, the gossip, the society of young people – he would have been a brilliant lecturer and extremely stimulating tutor. He would have been stimulated himself; with some of the girl undergraduates, no doubt, sometimes over-stimulated. But he would not have been

* Yet are they right? There is always an almost irresistible temptation to read the latest book published, when in fact it is often not as good as something that has gone before and says nothing particularly new. It is, of course, true that literary taste changes, but it does so slowly. All the books that have replaced Gerald were published in the early 1970s. There are some fine books in the *Literary History*. The volume on the eighteenth century is particularly good – stimulating and interesting on a century which, on the whole, bored Gerald. But both the *Literary History* and Russell's *Spain* are collaborative works and inevitably, therefore, lose Gerald's sense of a controlling taste and vision. In my view, for someone coming upon Spanish literature for the first time, nothing equals *The Literature of the Spanish People*; even for those who know the literature well, Gerald still has much that is original and stimulating. And, of course, he is delightful to read.

able to stand the snobbery of Oxford then, the overpowering sense of cliques and groups, the deadness of dons. However drunken, boring and often second-rate it was, he would always have preferred the rather ramshackle, mostly American expatriate society towards which Gamel and he were now rapidly heading.*

* For some additional comments on *The Literature of the Spanish People* see appendix D.

TWENTY-THREE

Last Days in England

> *¡Ay, mi niña! ¡Ay mis amores!*
> *¡Ay, mis ojos de terciopelo!*
>
> Poem by Gerald to Poffett the cat, 1950

> *You are the comfort purring in the house*
> *Softness of blankets,*
> *Warmth of fires and stoves . . .*
> *The tame: untamed, the house-bound: fierce and free,*
> *Treading a velvet path*
> *By moon star.*
>
> *To Poffett and All Cats* by Gamel

1

Gerald's plans, made at Miranda's wedding, were still Spain till the end of 1953, then to sell the Churriana house, perhaps to Janetta, and live half in France and half in England.¹ But late in November 1951 Gamel's mother died, and they learnt that Gamel's favourite brother Con was dying too. Everything else was abandoned and they made hasty preparations to fly to America, Gerald borrowing £200 from Ralph.

As so often with Gamel's books, this crisis somewhat shadowed the publication of *La de Bringas* on 8 December. This is the best of her translations and received good reviews, especially from VSP in the *New Statesman*. It is still the most enjoyable, the liveliest and most subtle version in English – despite occasional mistakes.*

---

* At one point, for example, she translates 'I shall choke her' (or 'drown' her – the Spanish is *'la ahogaré'*) as 'I will have a fit.' Verbs were never Gamel's strong

But to a woman of Gamel's ambition, it was still only a translation – and not even a translation of poetry. However, the events which caused them to fly to America on 18 December were eventually to bring forth her longest and one of her finest poems. This was because they tapped the deepest springs of her poetic gift; the springs, that is, of regret, nostalgia and above all guilt.

2

Gerald and Gamel spent five days in New York – seeing e. e. cummings and Horace Gregory – and then went south to Aiken, South Carolina. At first, as Gerald had feared, Gamel felt lost and disoriented – on top of her distress at finding that Con had died before they got there.

Gerald, however, was both stimulated and delighted. Letters flowed back:[2] the negroes with their delicacy and quality of 'rising fresh every morning' – whose problems were never mentioned; and the astonishing Spanish moss, trailing from the trees, so sad and beautiful, and not a moss at all, but an aerial plant 'related to the pineapple'. He noticed how totally unlike Gamel was to her big, tall,

---

point. When speaking she tended only to use the present tense. *La de Bringas*, set in 1868, is the tale of Rosalía, and how, after frustrating years under her husband's thrift, she suddenly goes on a maniacal orgy of spending helped by her extravagant and bankrupt friend the Marquise of Tellería. The drama lies in the agonies and terrors of trying to keep the evidence of her vice, in the apartment of the labyrinthine palace where they live, from her mean civil-servant spouse. He is busy creating an enormously detailed picture out of human hair. It is, according to Gerald, Galdós' comic masterpiece. He compares it to Dickens and Balzac at their best with the 'grave ironic tone of Cervantes'. I have not read Galdós' other novels (even Gerald hadn't read them all – he wrote at least forty-nine) but *La de Bringas*, at least, which is wholly delightful, is comic and astute about human nature in a way far more reminiscent of Trollope.

Gamel made a good number of minor, and usually judicious, cuts to the text – something usually frowned on today. In later years Frances Partridge remembers how Gamel developed a fantasy that it had sold 20,000 copies but that she had only been paid for 2000, a fantasy Gerald continued and embellished in *Personal Record*, giving sales of 70,000. In fact it sold 5000 copies, with a small paperback deal later. Gamel was paid a flat fee, as was customary then (letter from Lord Weidenfeld to author, 2 May 1991).

talkative, racist, kindly half-brother Bill Woolsey. She must have taken after her mother 'who lay in bed and read books all day . . . [and] died in a garret in Jacksonville because she couldn't be bothered to look after her affairs or eat'. (And who, when not drunk, was vivacious and very cultivated.) Gerald even managed at first to enjoy 'clanging, noisy' Jacksonville, when Bill drove them there. The oceanarium had an octopus 'six feet across [that] looked like Dali's dream of female sexual organs. It could even turn itself inside out.'

But at Jacksonville they had to sift through 'the rubbish of a lifetime'. Then the Will was contested and they had to be driven endlessly to and fro to see lawyers across the vast monotonous country, untouched and untouchable. 'Americans just perch on their unyielding continent.'

He was more and more swamped by it. It was the same 'stagnant society from which as a boy I revolted and escaped' – too rich, too comfortable, too materialistic, too moralistic, and 'I don't like hygiene'. Gamel, on the other hand, sank back into its melancholy, seedy beauty, its drifting, monotonous decay, as if returning to herself. When they left on 25 February, she wanted to stay, while Gerald couldn't wait to get back. He at once hurried round to Ham Spray and talked so much that Frances thought he looked like someone who'd just been shot off a machine at a funfair.[3]

3

In fact, shooting off again was what Gerald and Gamel had to do the moment they returned. Ruth Lowinsky wanted to drive to the south of Spain and had said she would give them a lift. They set off a week after getting back from America.

The journey was leisurely, from 5 to 24 March, and something of a disaster. Both complained bitterly when they got back; Ruth to Anthony Hobson that she'd been forced to stay in a succession of cheap hotels chosen solely for their sordidness and their revolting food. She remembered in particular a *gazpacho* which, to the eye of the authoress of *Lovely Food* and *More Lovely Food*, was clearly just oil poured on tepid water.[4] Gerald told Frances he was completely flattened by Ruth – not even being allowed to speak Spanish. When they broke down in Spain, Ruth waddled importantly forward, shoving him aside with the words '*Yo soy el capitán aquí.*' Gerald collapsed with 'flu on arrival and their friendship never really recovered.

The house at Churriana was full of tenants. The Spanish ones agreed to move for varying small sums. But their tenants the Gouldings, who had most of Gerald's furniture and the whole of the ground floor including the only bathroom for £11 p.a., refused. Gerald at once embarked on a lawsuit. He and Gamel camped in three rooms on the first floor. The paint was peeling, the windows were broken, tiles crashed from the ceiling and they had to share the waterless w.c. with three families of working-class Spaniards (one man repaired shoes and bicycles on the landing; another old man squatted in 'a stable we didn't even know we had'[5] and made coffee out of chick-peas for the black market).

But there was no more talk of living in England and France. In fact, Gerald was in bliss – no hygiene, space, a sense of time and abundance, and the garden! 'Such numbers of birds always singing, such water, and trees and flowers.'[6] Cigarettes at seven and a half pence for twenty meant he was smoking himself to death. And once again he was fascinated by village life and the interplay with it of Rosario and Antonio. By 20 May the Spaniards had left, and a gigantic *obra* began.

Both of them worked. Gamel was translating some Mexican poetry. Gerald finished the first draft of *A Life* . . . in April (at this point it ended with the Walk), looked briefly at *St Teresa* and then started revising *A Life* . . . , a task which, with one unpleasant hiccup, occupied him for the next eighteen months.

And he also discovered he was beginning to be famous. Spanish literary reviews were publishing rave notices of *Spanish Literature* and every two days someone called to see him, 'As if I were Ann Hathaway.'[7] The Gouldings, only visible by their eyes peering out, had just refused a bribe and Gerald decided his 'fame' would help with the lawsuit, now to be vigorously pressed. They set off home on 16 June via Madrid (for Gerald to do an article for the *New York Review of Books*) and then Roc'h Gwenn near Morlaix in Brittany, where they arrived on 27 June.

The visit to Roc'h Gwenn, the Corre family home, was to see his grandson Stéphane, born on 11 May.* It had been very hot in Spain and Gerald had longed for cool and rain. But it was hotter still – 97°: the hottest year since 1172, according to Gerald. At this time he got on well with all the Corres. In some respects Xavier was not unlike him. He had, as a GP, the same obsessional attitude to work. He would also look at you, saying nothing – then his eyes would suddenly twinkle and something slightly outrageous or surprising would come out, if to a girl flirtatious. The visit was a success, though short: they were back at Bell Court on 1 July.

4

The last six months at Bell Court were spent in farewell visits – from Miranda, Xavier and Stéphane in August, then to Cornwall, to London, frequently to Ham Spray. Also 'Packing, Packing, Packing, Packing, Packing. This sounds like the beginning of one of Bernard Shaw's love letters,' Gerald wrote to VSP, 'and in fact I have fallen in love with Packing.'[8] Gamel couldn't throw anything away. He'd given up smoking.

In October he finished revising the first 85,000 words of *A Life* . . . (the completed book was planned at 120,000) and in November he sent it to Harold Raymond at Chatto and Windus, who had apparently earlier expressed interest. At this stage, he told Raymond, he envisaged three volumes: one to 1914; the second from 1914 to 1952; the third of his literary life in Spain and London.[9] Gerald used to say in conversation and letters that Chatto turned the book down. This is not true. Raymond and Cecil Day Lewis read it and, while not accepting it, suggested considerable rewriting – less about school, cutting, making the stages of his life clearer. But they wanted to see it again after that.[10]

'Day Lewis is an unimaginative, rather priggish and conceited, but able man and I don't value his opinion on books of this sort,'[11] a disgruntled Gerald told Blair. Nevertheless, it was this advice he followed, and to good effect, over the next year. Raymond had also told

---

* Gerald was comforted to find, or think, that Stéphane looked like Hugh Brenan. The way he constantly looked for, and commented on, resemblances of this sort indicates how seriously he had doubted Miranda was his daughter (Gerald to Ralph and Frances, 30 June 1952).

him that *A Life of One's Own* was the title of a book by Joanne Field that Chatto had published that year.[12] Gerald sensibly ignored this.

In November, Gerald had been offered $7500 (£32,500 at 1990 prices) by an American publisher to write a short history of modern Spain. 'I refused immediately of course,'[13] he told VSP. One reason he refused was that, once in Spain, they would be quite well off. Gerald had so far been left a total of £19,354 (£358,117 at 1990 prices).* From this one must deduct capital spent on houses, cars, Gamel's operations, holidays, VSP's gift etc. (say £80,000). Also, Gerald could never be bothered to do anything with his investments and this, along with inflation, acts of generosity, and the selling of capital, steadily reduced it. When he died in 1987 there was £14,000 left. But onto this one should add Gerald's earnings. Between 1952 and 1962 *The Spanish Labyrinth* and *Spanish Literature* brought him on average an additional £2000 a year at 1990 prices, and there was more from other books, a few articles, and rent, then sale of Bell Court. In general terms, and very roughly, one can say that over this ten-year period Gerald's income averaged about £26,000 p.a. at 1990 prices.

Once again, a reasonable income, especially in the Spain of the 1950s, but not great wealth. It necessitated some care. And people's attitude to money is often only marginally connected to the amount they have. The anxiety generated by his poverty between 1919 and the end of the 1920s, and more particularly that inculcated since childhood by his father's highly neurotic reactions, remained with Gerald all his life. This anxiety was coupled with, or expressed by, alternating terror that he was bankrupt or exuberant discoveries that he was rich.

There was a second reason for refusing to write a history of modern Spain. After *Spanish Literature* Gerald told Blair he was never again going to write books that required years of research – 'above all, no *suite*, no spadework.'[14] Nor did he. He also began to lose his interest in Spanish politics. He felt that his time in England had been all work. 'I've been leading a dog's life for years,' he told Bunny. 'Now I want to be a human being again.'[15] This desire to make up for

---

* In addition, Gamel had been left $6000 or £2150 (£26,019 at 1990 prices). However, she kept the capital in America and Gerald seems to have allowed her to use the income for herself. The money was available for emergencies, and in one emergency – the final one – he used it.

lost time was to become marked over certain periods during the next twenty years.

One last terrible thing remained to be done. For months he and Gamel had been worrying about Poffett. In the end, riven by guilt, they decided the best thing was to kill him. 'The crime is accomplished,' he told Ralph on 29 December.[16] 'Poffett had convulsions which lasted five seconds, slid across the floor and fell dead.' As usual, pressure of feeling required more letters and the same day he wrote to Blair explaining that Poffett had been buried in a shroud of one of Gamel's silk shawls and his own best silk handkerchief.[17]

On 2 January 1953 they sailed in the *Orantes*. Gerald was nearly fifty-nine and was to live in Spain for the rest of his life.

PART IV

Wild Oats

1953–1968

'*April 1953: As dusk fell the hills beyond Malaga sank into folds of velvety darkness and lights shone from the town and the lighthouse. "I never get tired of watching the lighthouse," Gerald said. "It never says No; it can only say Yes."*'

Everything to Lose by Frances Partridge

TWENTY-FOUR

The Return to Spain

1

Gerald and Gamel arrived in Churriana on 7 January 1953 to find things much as when they'd left. Rosario's daughter María had been very ill and Rosario had had to spend all the money for the *obra* on medicine, and the tenants were not budging – still retaining most of Gerald's furniture, some books and half the house, including kitchen and bathroom.

In reality what was left suited Gerald far more than their former grandeur. A kitchen was built in an old woodshed fifty yards away. They had one downstairs room (the dining room), then up the back stairs a large library on the left looking over the garden through the bamboos, a little higher up on the right the lavatory and then a high, tiled corridor with two large bedrooms and two small; a corridor room was made by planking over the old staircase, and above everything was the *mirador*. The requisite degree of *posada* discomfort was provided by tepid food, the dishes scrubbed clean, or fairly clean, in cold water, cheap wine (poured by Gerald into smarter *Banda Azul* bottles for grand guests), no fireplaces (just two Aladdin oil stoves in winter), no bathroom (to install one might prejudice 'the case') or any running water in the house, continually multiplying cats, and a lavatory which was flushed by emptying in a jug of water – a fact particularly detectable during the hot summers.

Churriana was still fairly primitive then too. The background to the next twenty years is the tourist and expatriate invasion of the strip from Malaga to Algeciras, which brought badly needed money and eventually turned the road winding along that once lovely coast into a roaring, stinking, murderous race track and the little *pueblos* into imitations of Las Vegas. But in 1953 there was only one car in

Churriana and no motorbikes; the loudest noise 'the sound of horses trotting, a herd of goats pattering'[1] and from Gerald's garden the song of the nightingale and the golden oriole. All the water came from the Fuente del Rey up the road. Spain itself was still poor. If you dropped any bread in a restaurant, barefoot, ragged children rushed to grab it. Gerald and Gamel saved up their change and Gamel distributed it to *los pobres* every Saturday, along with clothes often sent to them by their friends.*[2]

Gamel loved doing this. In fact, at first Gerald's letters speak continually of her new happiness. She slept like a log 'without dope'.[3] She abandoned practically everything to do with the house more or less at once. And why not, with effectively four servants? Cooking, ordering, deciding – all were left to Rosario, in brief consultation with Gerald. Already by February he was having to cut the flowers for the table – 'her natural indolence has returned',[4] he told Ralph, rather irritably. She retained only feeding the cats (a stray settled in and rapidly multiplied) and making marmalade. Even here, Rosario cooked and cut up the cat food.[2] Gamel served it. And, according to Frances, she only *stirred* the marmalade. In the end, this lack of practical function was one of the things which undermined her. Now, it was wholly delightful.

Besides which, she was working. Somewhat to Gerald's surprise, she had suddenly taken to writing science-fiction. She was not remotely scientific, but she liked science-fiction as a metaphor of her life.† She was also translating Spanish poetry in a desultory way for a possible anthology.

Gerald had been asked by Knopf to write a life of St Teresa,[3]

* Alyse and Phyllis in particular. Gamel in her turn sent back what she could. A hangover from the war were 'suicide pills'. Spanish chemists rarely required prescriptions for drugs then and Gamel became an entrepot for killer potions. At this time she was recommending Alyse, appropriately enough, to take Dial. And in the late 1950s she sent both her friends sodium amytol (Gamel to Alyse, undated but January 1959). Gerald didn't want to be left out and got Xavier to give him Gardenal, a proprietary name for phenobarbitone. One would think Gerald the least likely person to commit suicide, but in fact these pills were used many years later in pathetic circumstances (as indeed were Gamel's).

† She could express her loneliness, her guilts, indirectly, without mentioning them. Her story, *The Star of Double Darkness*, for instance, was about the loneliness of living on one of the planets. Also 'It is like being a child again,' she told Alyse in December 1961. They were fairy stories. Alyse and Phyllis sent her paperbacks and she found sci-fi comics in Malaga.

probably in response to a suggestion from him. He glanced at his notes, but he was still engaged in the struggle to revise *A Life* . . . , finding at each point, as he told VSP, the question 'Is this worth mentioning? Can this interest anyone?' And at each point finding the same answer – 'Yes, if it can be made interesting.'[5] But in April he also mentions again an idea he'd first had at Yegen, and then revived briefly in the 1930s – a travel book about Andalusia.[6]

Gerald's pattern was breakfast at about 9.15, either outside at the glass table or, if cold, in the passage room. Work till lunch at two – sometimes with a glass of wine at the end.[2] Siesta, then a walk with Gamel. Gerald took up botany again to make these walks more interesting.* Then work from four till seven and reading in the evening. Gamel didn't really have a pattern. Sometimes she'd work in one of the little upstairs rooms. Often she would drift dreamily past the stocks, the orange blossom, the heavy-scented arum lilies of the garden, or sit there waiting for hours – or a day or weeks or months – for inspiration, when she would suddenly write rapidly.

Guests came: Michael Swann and Hugh Gibb in March; Hugh Trevor-Roper in April ('Quite delightful'),[3] followed by Ralph and Frances. Ralph was about to have his only book, *Broadmoor*, published – a fascinating account, much praised by Gerald. Shortly after this, it was discovered Ralph had diabetes, a first, but sinister crack in his robust good health. Gerald at fifty-nine wrote sympathetically about age. Honor Tracy dropped in briefly during May, having met Gerald once years before with Arthur Waley. This tough, kind, heavy-drinking, witty Irish writer, spiky red hair *en brosse*, was destined for a long, at first sunny, eventually extremely stormy relationship with the Brenans. They both, but Gamel in particular, made friends with Marjorie von Schlippenbach, who has already been mentioned with her father in the Civil War.† And Gerald met Don Modesto Laza

---

* In fact, Gerald had never given up botany, but he now continued it with renewed zest. Gerald, according to the Smythies (authors, with Oleg Polunin, of *Flowers of South-West Europe*, Oxford 1973) and to close friend Rosemary Strachey and Frances, both near-professional botanists, was not a *real* botanist. He often made elementary errors and his method of identifying a plant was to leaf through the illustrations. None the less, in general terms, he knew a good deal. As with any subject he touched, he always knew curious and unusual facts not found in books. He knew the mythological histories of plants; from Yegen, from people in Churriana, he knew which cured headaches or caused abortions.

† See note to p. 311.

Palacios, a Malaga chemist. Modesto, who had been an *alcalde* (mayor) of Malaga, was a polymath such as Gerald loved – ugly, lively, immensely energetic and curious, able to read French, English, German and Italian, Malaga's leading botanist, keen on archaeology, and a mine of information on Spanish life, especially sexual life. They went on expeditions together – botanising or looking for Pompey's cave or a Greek factory[7] – and he became virtually the only really intimate Spanish friend Gerald ever had.

But, if less than intimate, an American couple Cyril Connolly brought south in February, Bill and Annie Davis, were to play a much larger part in Gerald and Gamel's social life.

2

Cyril was involved with the Davises because Jean Bakewell, his first and now ex-wife, was Annie's sister. He introduced them to Gerald because they wanted to buy a house in the south.

Bill, in his early forties, was a big, balding, shambling man, with a deep, hoarse, mechanically indistinct voice, who walked with a slight slouch or list, as if holed below the water line. A New Yorker, Bill's father had been a prominent Chicago lawyer; what Bill did or had done no one really knew. He was an ex-alcoholic and there was a menacing air of controlled violence about him. Kind, unless crossed socially (when he could be fearsome – he once knocked someone out for arguing about his choice of restaurant), adroit, even cunning, coarse, a snob, quite well-read, a genuine lover of Spain, this complex, opaque man had very little money. This, and there was a lot, was all his wife's.

'Whereas one's heart slightly sank when Bill sat down next to one,' said Frances, 'it rose when Annie did.' Although anyone could see Bill depended on her emotionally as well as financially, she thought her life with him hung by a tenuous thread. Flustered, genuinely kind and gentle, she was not at all stupid, but she moved and spoke and even seemed to think very very slowly; then all at once her curiously slab-like Americo-Indian or Mexican face would come alight and she'd say something apposite.

Gerald was instrumental in the Davises' buying La Cónsula (for $50,000) just up the road from him. The house had been built in the nineteenth century by a Neapolitan and, with its long, elegantly balustraded balcony and slender marble pillars, it had an Italian feel. There was a huge garden with a small swimming pool, large *alberca*, little lawns, a tennis court and enormous trees, in particular the largest ungrafted avocado anyone had ever seen – a helicopter would have had to pick the fruit. Here, behind high walls and massive iron gates, the Davises entertained.

The pleasures of the host: reflected glory, grateful guests, power. Bill enjoyed all these, especially the last.* He was a perfectionist – adept and shameless flatterer of the famous, dragooning servants, choosing the best food himself, knowing the best flamenco, best bullfights, best restaurants. And he was ruthless. His children were sacrificed to his guests (the knobs on the doors that barred them off were set on purpose out of their reach); and when Hemingway installed himself at La Cónsula, everyone, his oldest friends, were dropped on the spot. Yet he could be kind and when people were in trouble, even those he stood nothing to gain from, generous in his support.

3

In May, summer arrived. 'Chorus of jubilant birds from dawn to dusk, brilliant light, a feeling that the day will go on forever.'[8] On the 30th Gamel and Gerald had to go to Madrid for him to write another 'literary letter' for the *New York Review of Books*.

Gerald was nervous and longed for something that would help, perhaps a title – he favoured 'Lord Pimpoon'. He dreaded 'the looks

---

* He enjoyed getting his guests drunk and seeing what happened. On one occasion he opened a letter and, without admitting what he'd done, taunted the sender with its contents. This was a mistake. His victim had influence where, as far as Bill was concerned, it mattered. Desperate to become a member of White's, he found himself inexplicably blackballed for eighteen years. Barbara Skelton observes in *Tears Before Bedtime*, how, as well as serving, he often manipulated and despised his guests.

of curiosity directed at me'.⁹ Then, on the way, a crash marooned them at Baeza for twelve hours.

Gerald was delighted. He collected every scrap of paper in the station and scribbled a joyous letter to VSP. 'This letter is authentic. This letter bears the stamp and smell of Spain – Anis, dried urine, frying oil, dust, dust, dust . . .' This, the acceptance of the boredom, the beggars, the heat, the flies, was 'the most important thing in the world . . . the answer to the ugly comfort of our English middle class'. Gerald never lost this feeling. To him, Spanish inefficiency, so exasperating to others, was part of the point. He wished that like Machado he had settled in 'this decrepit town where they kill the trees in the square by peeing against them'.¹⁰

Madrid was difficult at first (Walter Starkie of the British Institute thought Gerald was after his job and blocked every meeting), but Lord Pimpoon needn't have worried. He plucked up the courage to ring the novelist Carmen Laforet and soon saw everyone he wanted.

They arrived back on 10 June. Hope had come to stay for ten weeks and soon maddened them. Now seventy, he was critical, argumentative and had grown hugely greedy, his pants bulging disgustingly out of his unfastenable trousers. He'd come partly to get his books. Gerald had them crated and despatched, but he noticed Hope kept a large, locked canvas bag in the library. For several days Gerald eyed it suspiciously. Then Hope went into Malaga. Gerald managed to find the key. The bag was full of books, but Gerald's books! Furious, he swapped them all for mathematical books Hope had rejected.

Or thus in *Personal Record*. It is a mark of Gerald's gentleness towards Hope that in a letter at the time he says he only took back two books.¹¹ He also defended Hope against others. Ralph, who as usual handled all Gerald's affairs in England, had managed, despite the eccentric conditions, to let Bell Court to the painter Darsie Japp. The Japps complained about the depth of Hope's baths. Gerald explained to Ralph that it wasn't to get clean – Hope believed aristocratic skin was permanently clean – but to relieve his rheumatism.¹²

In August Xavier and Miranda came for three weeks, as they were to do until 1967. In later years, for a period, the unending blue skies extending on and on through June, July, August, September, the relentless heat, induced a sort of summer madness. But in 1953

'The days follow one another like the great empty rooms of a palace. We walk to the sea, bathe, talk to Rosario and Antonio, visit Malaga.'[13]

At last it began to get cooler. Work became easier. He had nearly finished revising *A Life* . . . – which seemed dated and appallingly old. 'Sometimes I think I remember Waterloo.'[13] At the end of September, though he had rejected Knopf's offer of $2000 as too small, he took up *St Teresa* in earnest again. Gamel heard him groaning.[14]

'The monotony of Spanish life is lit up by strange flashes,' he wrote to VSP just before Christmas.[15] There had been a drama in Churriana. Antonio's dog, a cringing, feeble mongrel, had suddenly gone mad with rabies. It tore four bantams to shreds. Five dogs had to be destroyed. The whole Brenan household had to have injections and, unnecessary injunction, were forbidden baths. Gerald found the injections 'delightful'.[15]

The year ended with Gerald missing England, especially London – 'nostalgie de la smog'.[16] Once again, as at Yegen only less so, letters became a lifeline. He would often find himself composing them in his head and, whereas before he felt guilty if he wrote them in 'working hours', now he sometimes actually called them work. At Ham Spray, their arrival was awaited eagerly – on a par with the *New Statesman* or the *Sunday Times*. Ralph, always at his best at breakfast, read them aloud. Gerald had numerous correspondents, but Ralph now replaced VSP as his most regular one. They wrote to each other once a fortnight, and much more often when love eventually turned up at Churriana.

4

1954, Gerald's sixtieth year, began with snow and frost – in the *pueblo*, they thought the North Pole had exploded and hid under their beds. He told Ralph the last snow was in 1884; frost not since 1492[17] (in fact Gerald had reported snow in 1935).

Weather was a leitmotif of his letters – an English habit. The tenants featured regularly; so did money. Expatriates were only allowed £300 p.a. from England. It was possible to cash cheques in Gibraltar but this was a bore. In March, Sir Walter Monckton, who had been staying at La Cónsula and clearly took to Gerald, persuaded the Treasury to let him have his 'full income'.*[18]

Ralph's health, since diabetes, was a central worry. Gerald frequently tried to cheer him up. Sweet letters, to one of which Ralph answered, 'It is now nearly forty years since our . . . lives became entangled and I wish to say now the attachment on my side has been one of the greatest pleasures in my life. Whenever I see your handwriting on an envelope . . . my spirits rise spontaneously – and I thank you for the long years of friendship.'[19] Gerald's reply did not quite match Ralph's instinctive warmth, though he no doubt felt it. 'You have always been for me in a class by yourself – you and Carrington. No one else near. Gamel – well, she is part of me, my climate, the air I breathe.'[20]

Friends, the news of them whether good or bad, guests – all grew in importance; and there was more than enough of both. He was extremely upset when Molly MacCarthy died at the end of 1953. 'Life as one grows older gets more and more sad until one becomes reconciled to leaving it.'[21] He worried about Helen Anrep, who'd had a stroke. But in February Alyse came for a successful two-and-a-half month visit. And in March Llewelyn's friend Louis Wilkinson took a house in Torremolinos with a new wife. 'He is seventy but looks eighty . . . He kept up his fucking too long,'[22] Gerald noted, showing how long his ancient fears lasted. There were expeditions – up a mountain with the Consul, to a horse-fair at Ronda. Gerald always grumbled there was too much social life and could never resist it – especially the frequent dinners at La Cónsula.†

But social life didn't stop work. Virginia Woolf's *A Writer's Diary*

---

* 'All I have to do now is to earn a full income,' added Gerald, ironic and lighthearted. In a later letter this year (18 September) he put his unearned income at £320. This was nonsense. Everyone above a certain income likes to be thought poorer than they are and Gerald was no exception. In particular, he liked people to think that he depended for at least half his income on his writing. Fortunately, this unhappy state of affairs did not arrive for many years.

† Cyril was there in February, also an ex-mistress of his, Peggy Bainbridge (later Strachey). 'I remember Gerald holding forth at length about the merits of incest, especially between father and daughter. "So much better for the poor girl to be initiated by a loving parent than by some clumsy impatient youth."'

had just come out and *Encounter* had asked him to review it. Gerald's admiration grew. 'How consistently alive and intelligent,' he observed to Ralph. 'There is something crystalline about her mind that makes her, like Keats, a sort of embodiment of genius. Had the reservoirs been greater, the reach deeper, she would have been a very great writer indeed.'[21]

But the main work, since September, had been *St Teresa*. It bored him stiff, 'But the subject is grand – austere, dramatic, monotonous – and no one can do it but I.'[21] Then, in April, he suddenly abandoned it. After working on it intermittently for thirty years all the research had been done and a third written.[23] No doubt, as with *Segismundo*, he thought he'd go on again sometime. He never did – finally sunk, he'd say later,[24] by the huge mass of his material.*

But the immediate reason was that *Der Monat*, a magazine edited by Mervyn Levy from Berlin, had asked for an article 'about Spain'. No sooner had he started than Gerald realised this was the book that had been at the back of his mind for so long. He had begun *South From Granada*.[25]

5

In July, Gerald and Gamel went to England to finish packing and to see friends. Staying the weekend at Ham Spray Frances noted that Gamel had taken to dyeing her hair jet-black.[26] It was also now that she began to look at herself continually in her little hand mirror and to apply more and more make-up.

Gamel had a certain vanity – she had after all been very beautiful

---

* Every biographer will feel a deep pang of sympathy. In 1965/6 he suggested that Honor Tracy should finish it. (Honor to Gerald, undated, MSS, MF). In 1965 he also offered all his material to VSP (Gerald to VSP, 17 March 1965). Gerald later destroyed this. The comments that slipped into letters are tantalising. Once more, restarting in 1953, he told Ralph in December 1954, the saint had reminded him of Carrington. Ralph would not find her '"mysticism" difficult. Imagine a poet like Mallarmé or Auden or a novelist like Flaubert, devoting their life to forcing out of themselves every scrap of deeper or finer feeling they possessed.' He felt drawn (no doubt by self-identification) to the intensity and drama of lives 'devoted to improving the quality and energy of life'. Also she was, like Carrington, complex and paradoxical – fascinated by self-analysis, yet still a woman of 'wit and charm and feminine appeal' (to Ralph, 7 May 1954). One cannot help regretting that he gave up.

– but the ageing of a beauty pretending to be younger is particularly trying. Gamel, about to be fifty-nine, was supposed to be fifty. There was more anxiety than vanity in her obsessive perusal. There was also despair – the terrible feeling that she had wasted her talent. In compensation she began to dwell increasingly on a time when none of this had happened – especially the past of the 'ole South', with decaying plantations, black mamas, Spanish moss.

By August they were back. Eleven cases of books arrived at Gibraltar – and were refused entry into Spain. Gerald pleaded, and at last the customs officer deigned to look into one box. On top, by chance, were Cervantes, Quevedo and volumes of Spanish poetry. 'He smiled,' said Gerald, and let the lot through free of charge. [27]

It grew hotter and hotter. Xavier and Miranda came – spending their time 'making love and going to the beach'. [27] Gerald moved into his hot weather mode. 'The long summer days pass, slow, interminable, beautiful, boring, like the trucks of a goods train when one is waiting at a level crossing. I work. I listen to the water falling. I watch the sunset. I walk in the garden by moonlight, but I do not seem to have much tension. Is this old age coming on? Does it matter if it is?' [28]

The weather at last grew cooler. Work picked up. In fact, for Gerald it had scarcely slackened. Unlike all his other books, the first draft of *South From Granada* seemed to pour out of him almost effortlessly. By September it was finished. But now, as always, he embarked on two years' slow, painful rewriting, cutting, revising and then rewriting every page again and again.

Julian Pitt-Rivers' *The People of the Sierra* had just come out. The anthropologist's work had a considerable effect on Gerald, but since all drafts were later destroyed it is difficult to say how. A letter written now, while he was reviewing the book, says he is making *South From Granada* more autobiographical[29] – perhaps in contrast to Pitt-Rivers, whose approach is entirely impersonal.* Or possibly, fascinated as he was by the younger man's anthropological detail, he strengthened this part of his own book. Rosario's daughter remembers him writing it. 'He'd forgotten everything. Luckily my mother had a good memory. He'd come into the kitchen. "Tell me about the witches", or "What did you do about so-and-so?" Four minutes later

* By design – to intrude himself would have been totally inappropriate. Gerald thought very highly of it and showed this by reviewing it favourably in three publications – the *Listener*, the *Manchester Guardian* and the *Times Literary Supplement*.

he'd be back. The food would burn. "What's that bit on the plough you pull up?" It was more my mother's book than his,' said María.

In November Gamel sold her science-fiction story 'The Star of Double Darkness' to the *Saturday Evening Post*. Gerald was pleased, but slightly irritated she got so much money; '$850 . . . It was only ten pages of typescript long.'[29] And it had taken two years to write. Gamel planned a book of them, but no more were published, though in all Gamel wrote twenty-four.[30]

Guests came: Hugh Trevor-Roper again, and Augustus John and Dorelia, for whom Gerald found a house in Torremolinos. About to offer the tenants a £200 bribe, he had a sudden brilliant new wheeze about them. It seemed the wife might have committed bigamy. He'd get them turfed out on grounds of immorality.[29]

Since classical times the role of the writer, the bard, has been that of entertainer at the great man's table. As with the Bomfords and the Lowinskys, so now with the Davises; Gerald and Gamel had Christmas lunch at La Cónsula.

6

The pattern established in these two years lasted, with significant disruptions, for the next thirteen: guests, local social life, expeditions, work, letters.

Richard Hughes and his wife stayed in mid-February; in April they were visited by Edmund Wilson and his mother (Wilson was later to say that Gerald had written the best articles the *New York Review of Books* ever published); there was also a 'mass' of professors and scholars, both English and Spanish. Expected but never coming were Julio Caro Baroja, the nephew of the great novelist and, awaited with some interest, Joanna Carrington, the beautiful young daughter of Catharine and Noel.

Cyril Connolly was at La Cónsula during February, being extremely demanding as usual; also Robin and Mary Campbell, of whom Gerald was to become fond. Cyril was back again in the summer and Bill sent him to vet Ethel de Croisset, who had taken the Fuente del Rey opposite La Cónsula. Young, American of impeccable New York background, wealthy, sophisticated, beautiful and recently divorced, her journalist husband had worked for Jean Ploureau, the great French newspaperman of his day. As a result she knew everyone: Sartre, Camus, Louis Aragon; André Malraux was a friend, Matisse an acquaintance. No wonder Cyril approved. As for Gerald and Gamel, from now on new friends tended increasingly to become polarised. Ethel – at first and for many years on her annual visits – fell into the Gamel camp.

There was an odd development with VSP. Over the years Gerald seemed to forget from time to time that he'd given him the £1000. He would suddenly become incensed because he wasn't being paid back. He would write angry letters about it to Ralph,[31] who would explain VSP's difficult circumstances. Gerald would subside. The Pritchetts came to stay, the friendship easily survived (for one thing Gerald never mentioned the matter to VSP, who was totally unaware of these perturbations), but the decline in their correspondence is noticeable.

Money anxiety was probably the cause, as with the first of these letters in February.[32] If so, it was alleviated in April, when his uncle Bertie died and Gerald inherited £1500 (£16,500) – the last of those fertilising trickles from the great millionaire's river of his Belfast grandfather.*

No doubt buoyed up by this, Gerald and Gamel made two expeditions this year. The first was to Yegen in May to take photographs for *South From Granada*. The camera broke, but once again the quietness, the sound of running water enchanted him. Yet he could not remember what he had felt long ago. 'As one grows older one becomes a different person, inheriting by some strange magic a young man's memories.'[33] Many of his old friends were now white-haired or, like Gerald, nearly bald; Paco had died just three months before in Argentina. Juliana was living in Granada.

The second visit was to Galicia, where Ralph, Frances and Janetta had taken a house at San Fiz, near Betanzos, La Coruña.† Miranda had had a daughter, Marina, in January, and after their annual holiday at Churriana the Corres drove Gerald and Gamel to Vitoria in the Basque Country. Then, laden with mackintoshes (Gerald like all Andalusians saw Galician weather in monsoon terms), they took a series of buses to Betanzos.

---

* In total Gerald inherited £20,854 during his lifetime, or £375,000 at 1990 prices.

† The house belonged to Natalia Jiménez, the daughter of Manuel B. Cossío, the great Spanish expert on El Greco.

Despite, as usual, several fierce arguments between Gerald and Ralph, noted Frances, the visit was a success.[26] But she also noted Gamel's sadness – sitting apart for hours on the beach with her mirror. Gerald complained he had nothing to say to her, simultaneously explaining he couldn't live without her. All they could talk about together was the cats. These complaints were now to become a leitmotif of his letters and conversation – Gamel drifting about the garden, doing nothing, not even putting the butter away,[34] descriptions elaborated in much the same ingenious way as the sea in *Mr Fisher* or the oceans of air in *South From Granada*. But there was a sharper edge. Those pointed and critical remarks, a 'volley of pinpricks',[35] that had begun after he had ceased to make love to her, were now made in public – and had become increasingly numerous and increasingly caustic.

And Gerald was also, in these complaints, expressing his own inner restlessness. 'I feel like a house that is wired all over for electricity,' he also said to Frances on this holiday, 'but the current has never been switched on.'*[26]

They left in September and weaved home by bus and finally plane via Madrid, where they had a long lunch with the novelist Pío Baroja.

Exhausted, Gerald collapsed with 'flu when they arrived. He also began to worry about his heart (there may have been talk about Ralph's heart at San Fiz), and gave up smoking. But this meant he could smell the cats, of which there were now six – a recurrent situation and, if rather less often than the sensitive guest would have liked, his letters to Miranda are a long chronicle of induced death. 'We had the vet in yesterday to put old Tortle out of the way.'[36]

---

* It was on this holiday that Gerald and I first met. Although I saw him regularly after this, and eventually got to know him well, I did not, as I explained in the introduction, play a significant role in his life till the end and therefore only enter the story then. But I remember the holiday vividly. Gerald had just got new false teeth and startled me slightly by saying it made no difference when you kissed girls. (He was sixty-one, I was twenty-two.) But we got on well immediately. I was fascinated by his conversation, his liveliness and his energy. I remember how charged the atmosphere became, almost frightening, when he and Ralph argued. One argument – almost a row – was about pacifism. I noticed Gamel alone with her mirror. She also used to make a curious mewing sound as she crawled out of the waves. She often did this when leaving or entering a room and I later realised it was a strategy to divert attention from herself. At the time I thought perhaps she imagined she was a cat, which she resembled – a very rare, very distinguished cat, from Tibet say. Perhaps this was true, too.

But there were more important matters concerning Miranda at this time. After the birth of Marina she suffered severe depression, with attacks of anxiety and claustrophobia. Gerald wrote to Xavier, '*Nous sommes vraiment très inquiets* . . . '[37] It is clear that this was more than just post-natal depression. She continued to have attacks in 1956 and 1957. She saw Dr Dent several times,* and in 1959 was seeing a psychoanalyst.[38]

Taken abruptly from her mother at three and a half, Miranda had not had a very secure childhood. Gerald recognised some elements; he put the attacks down to the disturbed months of the Civil War and uncertainty about her parentage (it seems possible he did not tell her about Juliana till 1949). But he and Gamel must carry considerable responsibility for this, which was no doubt exacerbated by their early habit of leaving her with odd, if carefully chosen, strangers. At the same time, far less was generally known about the effects of this kind of behaviour then. And, as parents, they can also take credit for Miranda's abundant confidence and competence. She was known, like her father, for her zest for life, her vitality and gaiety, and was an excellent, if rather over-strict, mother (her nickname in her family was 'La General').[39]

Just before Christmas Ralph sent Gerald a letter about Joanna Carrington: 'An absolute peach, making every mouth water,' and he added, a speculation which might have been designed (and probably was) to stir its highly susceptible recipient, that Noel identified her completely with Carrington. Ralph wondered if she had the same 'ruthlessness of character'.[40]

Christmas itself was at La Cónsula, with guests Barbara Skelton, the Campbells, Xan and Daphne Fielding. Once again, Gerald was the entertainer, but due, and awaited by both households with mixed feelings, was the Big Gun of English conversation at that period – Cyril Connolly.

---

* This intelligent, rather eccentric man was himself prone to depression. He had begun to lose patients again. He took to staying in bed till midday playing obsessive patience. If it came out – elation; if not – despair. Luckily it was about now he discovered his apomorphine treatment and, with Rhoda's help, made a success of it.

TWENTY-FIVE

A Great Hispanist

'I was with Garrow [Tomlin] looking at the girls in Oxford Street. I listened to myself talking and wondered where the words came from – surely not from out of my head.'

Gerald to Ralph Partridge, 25 April 1925

1

The best portrait of Cyril Connolly is contained in Barbara Skelton's *Tears Before Bedtime*.[1] She describes a figure endearing, funny, vulnerable – and a master of the sex-war quip in sudden flashes of phrase echoing those which peppered his reviews. Barbara, a heavy smoker, lit up during the cheese course. *Cyril*: 'I suppose you think the holes in the Gruyère are there for you to stub out your cigarettes.' *Barbara*: 'Have you seen my fucking gloves anywhere?' *Cyril*: 'Your fucking gloves are about as common out here as loving fucks.'

Records of his conversation are full of such quickness, but its distinction lay in those sudden sustained flights of fantasy which Gerald thought 'beat anything heard in England before'.[2] Flights which everyone who heard remembered – and which no one recorded. The closest Cyril came to them in writing was in *Bond Strikes Camp*, published in *Encounter*.*

* But I thought I had recorded one. I was staying in the house of a friend of Cyril's in the late 1950s. He arrived for lunch one Sunday, for some reason irritated by a long account by Arthur Koestler, covering several pages of the *Sunday Times* review section, of a trip he had made in a canoe down the Rhine. 'Have you seen that article of Koestler's?' Cyril said crossly. We agreed we had. There was a silence, Cyril staring glumly ahead. 'Imagine it,' he said in his flat voice with its slight edge, 'imagine having to go down the Rhine in a canoe with Arthur.' And

Cyril could be extremely charming and apparently engage in delightful conversation, particularly *à deux* with women. But it was these performances, of extraordinary brilliance, that were his *forte* – and they were not exactly conversation. After they had passed you were apt to find conversation had somehow been squeezed out of you. And there were his moods, his silences – the anti-matter of conversation, when he would sit 'brooding like a furious fallen Emperor'.¹ One had the feeling he was mined – a chance word, and the bomb would explode. Frances describes him at La Cónsula once after supper sitting stubbornly silent all evening flung back in what Janetta called 'the listening-to-music position . . . with his fat flat face parallel with the ceiling . . . Janetta . . . said afterwards that his excuse for this ostentatiously rude behaviour was that he was "desperately miserable".'³ But on these occasions, and they were not infrequent, he seemed to exude a sort of nerve gas, slowly paralysing drawing rooms and extinguishing entire dinner parties.

Gerald was far less of a prima donna than Cyril – though just as quick and prodigal of phrase. 'Wives are like air, you can't breathe without them.' 'Coughing is the artillery of the home.'⁴ It was a distilling quality, also evident in his letters, which grew as he became older.

He enjoyed talking and would therefore seize on anything that happened to be going. 'If his house had burnt down,' said VSP, 'he'd have been rather pleased from one angle at least, since now he'd have something to talk about.' And one reason for this was that, just as he had when a boy, he loved to live in his imagination. The Pritchetts remembered a time during the war during the Blitz when VSP had to go to London. Gerald said he'd go too. Dorothy was worried about how they'd get back. *Gerald*: 'No trouble at all. We'll come back by train. We'll come back with the evacuees.' *Dorothy or VSP*: 'There certainly won't be any trains running.' *Gerald*: 'We'll bicycle. We'll take our bicycles and ride back.' *Dorothy*: 'What will you eat?' *Gerald*:

---

then all at once a sudden glimmer of expression went across his large fat face, like someone blowing on a bowl of porridge. 'I'd be in the back,' he said, 'Arthur in front. After a while, Arthur would say, "Cyril, you're not pulling your vate" . . .' And for about fifteen minutes their trip got wilder and madder and funnier and funnier, until the conventional phrase 'helpless with laughter' was completely accurate. So vividly did I remember it, I thought I'd written it up in my journal. But when I went to look for the purposes of this book – nothing.

'We'll buy French loaves and cheese and some Chianti from King Bomba in Soho.'

'Such things,' remembered Dorothy drily, 'had for long been totally unobtainable.'

Gerald could be extremely perverse – out of boredom, to stimulate and challenge his listeners, to hide his real thoughts or feelings, to tease. He told Honor Tracy, a devout 'anti-Catholic Catholic',[5] that every large church and cathedral in Spain had an attached brothel for married women to obtain men. They went in through the church, so no one saw. 'He later topped this up,' snorted Honor, whose sense of humour deserted her with Gerald, 'with a friar sitting waiting to hear confession and give absolution.'

For obvious reasons, sex was a marked, even disproportionate topic in Gerald's conversation. Clare Sheppard remembered this in 1935. But, although it no doubt expressed the voyeur/vicarious-living element in his character, and the related love of gossip, it was not in the least offensive – though some people got bored. Jaime Parladé said, 'There was this extremely interesting man I wanted to talk to and he would tell me his theories about the girls of Malaga.' In fact, there was never any need to be bored by Gerald. He was – unless totally obsessed – the most accommodating of talkers. You only had to say, 'Yes, I see Gerald, but what exactly did you mean last night when you said Svevo was a more intelligent writer than Proust?' – and at once the wind of talk would change, the sails swing and fill, and away he'd go, small black eyes glittering.

But, to return to sex, Gerald was also discreet, in that there were a good many people he didn't talk to about it or talk in front of. Then, as with everything, what interested him was oddness, the unexpected, sex as exemplar of the surprising and the humorous in human nature.

VSP noticed this. 'It was always great comedy, which prevented him being shocking. One laughed. He never lowered his voice. My memory is often of trying to shut Gerald up while he talked loudly, one of those long sexual narratives, on a bus.'*

---

* By chance, I recorded one of these narratives in my journal. Gerald had become fascinated during the 1960s by a Swede called Sven who had a room above the Bar Central in Torremolinos. Sven's only aim was to have girls – hundreds, even thousands. 'He used to go to the beach, find an unattached girl, lie not far from her and stare at her. He would stare and stare with unwavering blue eyes from his

Stimulated, he would often astonish himself as much as those listening to him, 'moods of brilliance' as he made Tom Fisher say, 'when the words I'm using rise and float in the air above me without any connection with the person who is uttering them below.' Sometimes he reminded Frances of Virginia Woolf, both of them able to 'send up brilliant, fantastic and illuminating Roman candles of talk'.[4] He could easily become over-stimulated and begin 'literally to whirr like an alarm clock, a buzz of words'[6] issuing from his mouth – paradoxes, speculations, gossip, generalisations, often getting wilder and wilder and almost out of hand.

His voice on these occasions could become suddenly high. But when calm it was very pleasant, holding some distant echo of Ireland. It had what can only be described as a curious curl to it which made him very beguiling to listen to. And it was then, sitting calmly or walking with one or two or three friends, that he was at his best; alert, puffing amateurishly at his cigarette, able and indeed pleased to listen so that one exerted oneself, raised one's game, totally un-aggressive (rather rare in good talkers), indeed often diffident, amusing, instructive, original and in fact wholly delightful. A feeling of his vividness and precision of language can be got from his letters. His style was drifting and discursive, throwing out those fertile generalisations for which he had a gift, as it might be how important daydreams were and that this was a reason literature was the major art, 'talking his way up Spanish paths', as VSP remembered him, 'passing from village to village, switching, for example, from the idea that no village loves the next village, but only the next village but one, and this may have its roots in Arab habit, to expanding on the habits of birds, the problems of abstract art, T. S. Eliot's deficiency in historical sense, the nature of pretty girls, the ups and downs of sexual life, the moral and social influences of architecture . . . And this ends with an odd aside that gives sparkle to the learned phrases of his talk. The bishop who completed Salisbury Cathedral had been

---

brown face. Then he'd suddenly get up, go over to her and say, "Come." Mesmerised, she usually followed. When he'd fucked her he wrote her name in an enormous book. I occasionally called on him. Sometimes Sven would be lying on his bed too exhausted to move. He filled several books. Suddenly, quite recently, he gave the whole thing up. He became a homosexual and now lives with a boyfriend. He has become gentle, calm and happy.'

Queen Philippa's chaplain, a dwarf who was notoriously impotent. He built the finest spire in England.'[7]

Walking up the Spanish paths, or in the long warm nights in the garden at Churriana, the conversation lasting for two or three hours, Gerald suddenly taking wing and, as John Whitworth remembers, when the nightingales sang to interrupt him, clapping two books together to shut them up.

2

In fact Cyril's conversation, when he arrived in January, was entirely – and endlessly and to everyone – about his divorce from Barbara Skelton. Gerald was totally enthralled: 'Twelve men cited as well as Weidenfeld . . . Farouk . . . she and Cyril off to Tangier to make it up . . .' All this in a letter to Blair, who'd never even seen Cyril or heard of Weidenfeld.[8]

In January he reported to Ralph that the last of his teeth had gone. For all the old masochistic/reality reasons, Gerald always seemed almost to enjoy subjecting himself to the often very primitive doctoring and dentistry of rural Spain (Rosario had just had a hysterectomy in Torremolinos without anaesthetic),[9] but many of his letters now express a stifled loathing of and restlessness at the signs of ageing. Ralph and he also corresponded about Bell Court, which Vero Richards, who'd replaced the Japps, wanted to buy.

And the Churriana pattern continued as usual. Guests stayed: Carmen Laforet, Chapman Mortimer, e. e. cummings. The cats multiplied again (Yellow had six kittens). The case against the tenants crept forward. 'Spotty' John Strachey was in Torremolinos 'given his fare out by Daphne Fielding for old times' (in bed) sake – but who's to pay his return fare? Rosemary [his wife] has cut him adrift.'[10] The unfolding of the shifting, often seedy expatriate scene fascinated Gerald – but fascinated him, as had so many scenes in his life, as an observer on the fringes. He also enjoyed Strachey's '*louche*, sour conversation', whereas it bored Gamel.

On 11 September, after two and a half years, he finished *South From Granada* – and, almost as usual now, at once got 'flu. Cyril had introduced him and the book to his own publisher, Jamie Hamilton, the man who was to publish his next four books. Hamilton had, in fact, also at Cyril's suggestion, made an offer for the book unread in January (when it was called *That Corner of the World*).[11] Acceptance therefore came swiftly later in the month with, in Gerald's words, 'generous terms' – £350 (£3700), in fact not much more than he could have expected from CUP. As always, Gerald took trouble over the title. He changed it to *Andalusian Interlude*. Finally Cyril, who had a copywriter's genius for titles and headlines, came to tea in October, having thought of *South From Granada*.

South From Granada activity continued at a high pitch until January 1957 – borrowing photographs from Julio Caro Baroja, racing up to the Alpujarra again in December, telegrams and letters streaming out to Hamish Hamilton. Letters with corrections which often show an extraordinary memory for detail after thirty-five years. In one, for example, he alters the routes of two tiny streams in the Sierra.[12]

The reason, incidentally, Gerald was able to borrow photographs from Caro Baroja was that the novelist's nephew at last came to stay in November. 'More French than Spanish' was Gerald's initial verdict.[13] He found him a house which Baroja rapidly bought and to which he subsequently came every year, usually in spring and autumn.* Sympathetic, extremely intelligent, famed for his wit and discrimination, he was the only other close Spanish friend Gerald made. 'I thought him the most brilliant . . . [and] the most erudite of all Spaniards,' he told VSP years later.[14] Gamel, too, had a success now. In February 1955, thanks to Ronnie Duncan, the *avant-garde* literary magazine *Botteghe Oscure*, published from Rome in four languages and run, floating on an ocean of American money, by Princess Caetani, had accepted her longest and most ambitious poem, 'The Search for Demeter'. It came out in September this year. Gerald was able to praise it unreservedly, as did many people.

But the complexities of character which blocked Gamel were only partially susceptible to success and encouragement. In 1953, Gerald had obtained a contract from CUP for a volume of Spanish poetry to be translated by her and introduced by him.[15] She was still translating St John of the Cross and Góngora in 1955 – noting to Alyse how well

* And to which he was still coming when I talked to him in April 1990. He remembered Gerald, and especially Gamel, with great affection.

she and Gerald worked together. But she also says she seems to have a neurotic desire '*not* to finish anything',[16] and indeed her letters to Alyse are often started and then not finished for months. No more is heard of the CUP book after this. As a result of *Botteghe Oscure* – a name with a curiously apt ring – Gamel very slowly embarked on a series of sonnets, but 'The Search for Demeter' was the last of her work to be published.*

The Suez crisis in October saw Gerald at first angered – 'The sheer stupidity of it!' he wrote to Ralph.[17] Later, as the whole of Spain came to think it was right Nasser should be taken down, he saw some point in it. But, as he told VSP, his interest in politics had died away[18] though, always a devourer of newspapers, he continued to follow events closely. The *New Statesman*, the *Observer*, the *Sunday Times*, *The Times*, the *Manchester Guardian Weekly*, and the *New York Review of Books*, as well as several Spanish papers, all came regularly to Churriana.

And Gerald had taken up smoking (cigars) in October, after eleven months' abstinence – a record. He was putting on weight. But that month Ralph's health gave cause for anxiety again. It was found he had a tendency to thrombosis, and in December he had a slight thrombotic 'incident'. Gerald worried – and worried also about

---

* From 1929 until her alcoholic mother died, Gamel wrote to her every fortnight. But she could not bear to see her. Once, when her mother suggested coming to stay at Bell Court, Gamel was so horrified, she told Gerald they must flee to Italy at once (Gerald to Frances, 10 October 1967).
  'The Search for Demeter' is 342 lines long, and the only poem where Gamel did not use her very considerable skill with rhyme. In it, she is Persephone searching for her mother Demeter (Ceres) – who has in turn sought her: 'Now in the hollow shades/Demeter seeks her daughter,/and can not find her;/and I am seeking Demeter,/and can not find her.' In her search she travels, following the path Gamel and Gerald had taken down through Italy in 1951: 'Selinus, Himera, Segesta . . ./ Here are the temples/on the lovely coast/by the blue tideless sea.' It is regret and grief, and perhaps guilt, but guilt and grief restrained, mastered, and – as Persephone's call becomes that of a chorus – which also takes on the formal quality of a Sophoclean play: 'Can the heart return/down the long corridors/whose doors open on empty rooms?' The poem ends on a surge of optimism, knowing that spring will return: 'Summer will break/in great tides on the land . . .' We don't believe her. The grief that has gone before, however elegiac, has been too poignant. Nevertheless, though there are sometimes echoes of Eliot, there is no doubting that it is a distinguished and original work.

himself. Possessor, probably, of one of the strongest hearts in Europe, he hurried to his doctor with chest pains and was given pills. He told Ralph that Gamel, unlike Frances, was no help at all in dieting. She only wanted him to have what he liked. 'She would encourage me to eat arsenic "if I liked it".'[19] An odd example, somehow. It may, by a Geraldian twist of the subconscious, be connected with the next sentence, where he says ('and Gamel of course agrees') that he would really *love* to have Joanna Carrington to stay – say February? He wrote a similar letter to Catharine Carrington.[20]

Just so does the long quiescent volcano, many months in advance, give warning by tiny quivers and rumbles and sudden vents of hot steam that the magma is one more inexorably rising from its depths.

3

The Brenans do not seem to have spent Christmas 1956 at La Cónsula. Instead, they were asked to a big party the Davises threw for Laurence Olivier and Vivien Leigh on New Year's Eve. Gerald, their local celebrity, was put next to Vivien Leigh but found himself unable to remember a single film he'd seen her in. Later on, drinking water as everyone else got drunk (too much drink made him sick), an old inhibition revived. 'This awful inability to dance always discourages me,' he told Miranda, describing the party. Gamel, however, got off with Laurence Olivier and ended up passionately kissing him. When they left at three, Gerald deeply gloomy, she was so drunk she was staggering – 'The first time I've seen her in that state.'[21]

At the end of January he found a house just outside Churriana near La Cónsula – Buena Vista – which Ralph and Frances and Janetta took for six weeks. Ralph, on his diet, was better, and Gerald's heart symptoms suddenly vanished. In February, Honor Tracy took a house in Torremolinos for three months, visiting Churriana frequently. 'An old friend who I find splendid company,' Gerald told Blair.[22] Honor was in fact falling more and more in love with Gamel, which was eventually to lead to trouble. Even on that coast fuelled by alcohol, she was seen as a robust drinker. Three years later, when Gamel's own drinking was becoming noticeable,

Gerald used to say that when she stayed with Honor on Achill Island, Honor would thump a whisky bottle between them instead of a teapot.

Cyril arrived, Julio Caro Baroja stayed in his new house, Gerald took the whole Cónsula party out to Antonio Martín's – a fine fish restaurant in Malaga.* Plots against the tenants continued. The idea now was to prove that Miranda's children were so delicate they *had* to come out each summer. Dr Dent was roped in. Gerald and Gamel went on a brisk tour of Morocco with their friends the Murchies in March.

Gerald started the year by re-reading *Mr Fisher* and his notes. He also continued a long article on *Sybaris* he'd been doing intermittently since October 1954. And in March he began *Mr Fisher* in earnest again. But the whole year was dominated by a literary event of, to Gerald, crucial importance. On 28 March, Hamish Hamilton published *South From Granada*.

4

'The qualities I most appreciate in writers: the lyrical gift, the warmth in human matters, the sense of the beauty of the world, of the delight in being alive.'

Gerald to Ralph Partridge, 3 June 1954

South From Granada is the autobiographical account of Gerald's period in Yegen between 1919 and 1924 – though it is a chronological line he follows hardly at all.

A few of the incidents and portraits were drawn on for the account in this book: Strachey's and Virginia Woolf's visit, for instance, some details of his routine, one or two villagers. But it is rich in these: villagers like his own 'black' María, lithe, sexy, energetic, her skin shrivelled 'like the side of the Sierra' from being washed, not in water, but in strong aniseed spirit. Or the local gentry on whose faces 'boredom had settled . . . as dust settles in unoccupied rooms'. He is both detached, yet absorbs the village with an extraordinary delicacy of perception. The villagers don't shut poultry up to fatten. That would deprive the birds of their dignity. Depriving

---

* Still there, still good.

an animal of its dignity deprives you a little of your own. There was
an old woman whose pet hen had ceased to lay. She couldn't kill it
and excused herself by saying it was 'very noble'. 'No one thought
this absurd because nobility is the quality in a man that makes him
respected and birds may well have this quality too.'

Witches, murders, ghosts, sex, gossip, the whole anthropology
and calendar of the village is woven in with history, geology,
archaeology and literature in a way reminiscent of his conversation.
Indeed, in this aspect, it is the writing of a talker.*

But it is not in the least incoherent or wandering. For one thing,
it rests like a secure building on the granite foundations of his
knowledge. As Cyril observed, in a long and perceptive review,
Gerald was '. . . a poet and a romantic preserved by his irony and
scholarship from inflationary looseness'.[23] There is another reason. 'It
is a wonderful book,' Bunny wrote to him on re-reading it in 1972.
'In it every part is subordinated to the whole so that, though we are
led in one chapter into the brothels of Almería and in another are told
of successive waves of people colonising the south of Spain, everything is harmonious and inevitable – in fact a work of art, yet without
a rigid pattern imposed on it. This is partly because your character
emerges on every page to unify it.'[24]

This is true, and in this respect it resembles Turgenev's *A
Sportsman's Sketches*, another discursive book, filled with the spirit of
place and of a people, which is unified and given a distinctive
character by the way it is pervaded by Turgenev's great charm and
sweetness. Dr Theodore Redpath† noticed the resemblance as well,
but '*South From Granada*, a masterpiece of its kind, adds something to
Turgenev, since it embraces all classes, not just peasants'.

And Gerald's lyrical gift matches or surpasses Turgenev's,

---

* It is not, anywhere, the work of someone 'clearly influenced' by D. H.
Lawrence, as asserted by Jeffrey Meyers. There is not the remotest evidence of any
such influence either in Gerald's published work or in his letters. He shared some of
Lawrence's views – and disagreed with and was highly critical of most of them. But
writers can reach similar conclusions and feel similar things independently – just as
Lawrence's instinctive feelings about the unconscious were made at the same time
and often echo Jung's without owing anything to the work of the great
psychoanalyst. Something more than similarity has to be produced as evidence, and
such evidence as there is runs totally counter to Professor Meyers' unsupported idea
(see *The Legacy of D. H. Lawrence*, ed. Jeffrey Meyers, London 1987).

† For many years Professor of English at Trinity College, Cambridge.

whether building, by endless variations, the 'great oceans of air' in which Yegen seemed suspended or describing his enormous walks up into the high Sierra where the blue tit 'with its cheep-cheep-cheep seemed to be sewing together thin sheets of silence'.[25] Writing at the level Gerald constantly achieves here demonstrates that how you write is, in fact, often part of what you want to say, and it is at this point that prose and poetry join. It was in *South From Granada* that Gerald's poetic sensibility found its most complete expression.

His belief, whether true or not, that Borrow had lifted material from obscure Spanish plays released him in a different way. If Borrow could borrow, he would invent. In a sense, of course, in that it is a very careful work of art based on rigorous selection, the whole book is an invention. It does not describe the reality of his time at Yegen as revealed in his letters or accounts by other people at the time. The food is much pleasanter. He leaves out most of his loneliness and despair, and all of his struggles to write and his love for Carrington – say seventy per cent of his preoccupations.

Then there was his portrait of Ralph, to whom the book is dedicated. Frances records this conversation. *Gerald*: 'Oh, it wasn't unkind at all. I merely made you out a dashing philistine who slept with actresses – just what everyone would like to be.' (The rather malicious twinkle in his eyes belied his words.) 'Anyway, I sent it to you, and you passed it for publication.' *Ralph*: 'Yes, I did, though my solicitor thought there were grounds for libel. But what I really objected to was your picture of yourself as a selfless angelic character anxious to do everything for us, when really what you were after was seducing my wife.'[26]

This is typical of both of them. It is in the highest degree unlikely Ralph showed the passages to his solicitor, but he wanted to get his (quite justified) dig in. And Gerald's portrait of him is just the first of a series of slanted accounts he seemed, as old jealousies revived with writing, unable to resist.

But there are inventions pure and simple. It seems probable that his experiences as a *novio* are partly invented. In the book he woos Carmen of Almería through the iron *rejas* of her window for two weeks. Then she allows him to come and see her in the public gardens with her sister. Gerald comes, sees them – and his beautiful Carmen is almost a dwarf! He flees.

Gerald described this incident, which in fact took place in 1930, to Ralph at the time.[27] But there was no garden and Carmen (her name) wasn't a dwarf. It is inconceivable he would have left out two such delicious details. But three years later, describing it to Angela Culme-Seymour, Carmen has become 'stumpy'. *South From Granada* saw her final shrinkage.

The major invention, the long and extremely vivid chapter on the brothels of Almería, Gerald always freely, even proudly, admitted.[27] And, in a *tour de force*, he is guided round the brothels by Augustín, a man who adores the prostitutes and seems to be their passionate and eloquent lover – until at the end he is revealed to be completely impotent. A great lover who is impotent! And Gerald ends, Proust-like, how impossible to put such a character in a book, when he has already done so.

One Spanish reviewer, D. Esteban Salazar Chapela, head of the Spanish Republican Party abroad, writing in *El Nacional* of Mexico, realised the brothel chapter was an invention – and praised it as *saladísimo* (very witty) and 'profoundly true to Spanish life'. Most took it at its brilliant face value.

There were major reviews in the leading English papers, all favourable. VSP praised his novelist's eye and tireless curiosity 'which will even describe the sound of hundreds of silkworms munching in cottage rooms'.[29] Honor wrote in the *New Statesman*.

It is the book of Gerald's that is most likely to survive.* It also finally confirmed him as the finest English writer on Spain this century. This is therefore a good moment to look at him briefly in that context.

---

* It was already reprinting by May, and has been more or less continually in print ever since. A new Penguin edition is planned as I write. It also made Gerald money. The *Anchor Review* and *Atlantic* published extracts in America, where Farrar, Straus brought it out in October 1957. By 1959 it had made him £998.3s.1d (£9750). The regime always delayed Gerald's books in Spain, though they circulated secretly. *South From Granada* was published there, to similar praise, by Siglo XXI in May 1974.

5

'*He knows us better than we know ourselves.*'
Puig de la Bellacasa, Spanish Ambassador in London
1983–1990, to Frances Partridge

It is easier to speculate about a country not your own; you are not involved, you have an objective viewpoint. And no doubt there are characteristics in all nations which are more easily seen by outsiders. And this seems especially true of Spain, perhaps because of its complexity; or perhaps because of the strong regional feeling. Gerald himself once wrote it was the abundance of paradox that struck sparks from the English mind[30] – though Spain has struck sparks from writers and painters from many European countries and also America.

The major figures in England are Richard Ford and George Borrow, who both wrote about the Spain of the 1830s.* Ford is an extremely alive writer, who had a good grounding in Spanish history and, also like Gerald, a strong visual sense (he did many pencil and wash drawings as he perambulated Spain). His book is full of vivid incident, sharp observation, fine descriptions of place and scene, and a mass of historical and contemporary information. As for Borrow, no one can surpass him for adventures, the amount of fascinating factual detail, the number of extraordinary characters. Neither Ford nor Borrow spent anything like the time in Spain that Gerald did but both gain much in interest from their distance in time.

However Gerald is, as it were, catching them up here. And *South From Granada* and *The Face of Spain* have sufficient incident, characters and range of observations to stand the comparison, if not equal the quantity. Then, neither Ford nor Borrow are prolific in ideas, and they lack the depth of Gerald's historical sense; and, of course, they cannot begin, in the face of his studies of Spain's history, politics and literature, to equal Gerald's range.

* Richard Ford, *A Handbook for Travellers in Spain* (1845) (the best edition is the three-volume Centaur Press edition published in 1966 with an introduction by Ian Robertson); George Borrow, *The Bible in Spain* and *The Zincali, or the Gypsies of Spain* (numerous editions). For a brief but typically illuminating account of Richard Ford and other, particularly French, commentators on Spain see Gerald's article in the *New York Review of Books*, 26 January 1967.

But these comparisons are not what strike Spaniards. To them, Ford and Borrow, however interesting, are observers looking in from outside; and often observers, coming as they do from Britain's triumphant age, who are either patronising or arrogant. What fascinates Spaniards is how intuitively, almost instinctively, Gerald divines things they themselves either hadn't noticed, or else supposed only a Spaniard could notice. All other foreigners who write about Spain are outside; Gerald is inside. When Jaime Parladé, a neighbour who knew Gerald well, read *South From Granada* he wrote to Bill Davis: 'It's so terribly accurate down to the most insignificant things . . . I couldn't stop fits of laughter that anyone but a Spaniard should notice such things.'[31]

How does one explain this? Gerald was not remotely Spanish. He was extremely English, of his time, of his class. He never even considered being naturalised. His friends were English or American, his focus in Spain was almost entirely on them or the expatriate community among whom he lived.

As far as *South From Granada* goes, something of its vividness comes from Gerald's delight in living vicariously. No doubt many writers share this; but impelled by his impotence or fear of impotence – that pain-filled side of himself he transmuted in this book so lightly and humorously – the voyeur element in his character gave it a peculiar intensity. It is doubtful if he would have written the book as well without this.

Raymond Carr thought that Gerald's view of the Spanish – as being spontaneous, passionate, free, humorous, independent and so on – was essentially romantic. He was in the mainstream of the romantic tradition – of 'colourful' Spain, the Arcadian peasant, *cante jondo*, flamenco, etc. – as, indeed, were Ford, Borrow, Orwell and most other foreign writers about Spain.

But because a view is romantic it is not necessarily wrong. And a romantic feeling for another country is probably a necessary initial ingredient for a writer to become sufficiently involved to write well about it. A great many of Gerald's views weren't romantic at all. He remained, as he did about most things, detached and ironic and often critical: Spanish pride, Spanish impatience, their easy optimism, their inability to co-operate, the corruption of local government, their bureaucracy, their inefficiency, their anger if frustrated and sudden tantrum-like violence – all this he observed and, if politely, noted. *The Spanish Labyrinth* itself was to a considerable degree an indictment.

But there may be a more interesting explanation for the peculiarly intuitive nature of his deeper perceptions about Spain. If one abstracts from his various books the statements he makes, and analyses them, a rather curious picture begins to emerge. Let us start with something trivial. 'This country of newspaper readers.' Then, 'Women, whom most people would regard as the real backbone of Spain.' The long struggle of the peasantry against nature, the wealthy and injustice meant that for centuries they could only find satisfaction in their imagination. That is why *Don Quixote* was so relevant to them. Again and again Gerald comments on the vitality of Spaniards – excessive when young, vitality which would be crude 'were it not imposed on a peculiar refinement and melancholy', vitality which, starved of outlets, resigns the middle-aged Spaniard eventually 'like a lizard to hours and days of passivity'. Their strong senses, a certain 'dryness of imagination', kept Spaniards – especially the writers – riveted to reality, the harsh, monotonous, Spanish reality. The Spanish preoccupation with pain and death he traced partly to their religion, the almost loving detail with which, for hundreds of years, they followed the torture of Christ and the martyrs; he saw the same preoccupation in their art, the baroque art 'which suited their native craving . . . for exacting every drop of emotion out of a situation, for carrying every feeling, and especially every painful feeling, to the point of orgasm'. *Menosprecio de la vida* – disdain for life: 'That phrase is like a bell that tolls its way through Spanish history.' Their pride, the famous Spanish pride, meant almost nothing was good enough. So – it had to be everything or nothing. *Todo o nada*. 'It is that attitude that has made both Spanish fanaticism and Spanish mysticism.'

Where have we heard that phrase before? 'Anyone who sets before himself as a way of life the ideal of Everything or Nothing is following, whether he knows it or not, a path that lies parallel to that of the saints.' It was a quotation earlier from *A Life of One's Own* and Gerald wrote it describing the state of mind that led him, at eighteen, into his great Walk. (He repeated it in *The Lord of the Castle*.) And who else lived in his imagination and in his books (thanks in the main, he felt, to a woman – his mother), who had founded his life on a search for 'reality', the most direct form of which was pain? Who else, even, devoured newspapers? Who else but Gerald himself.

Just as the biographer sets the stamp of his own face on that of his subject, so did Gerald see himself in Spain. This does not mean that either is necessarily wrong. They may have similar faces, which was what drew them together. Or, as a result, they more swiftly notice where they are different. Dozens of his observations about Spain have nothing to do with Gerald; and here the very complexity, echoing his own, seems to fascinate him: the challenge of the labyrinth.

Where this self-identification was obvious, Gerald was no doubt roughly aware of what drew him. The generosity of the Spanish poor in Yegen (and their admiration of this quality), their dislike of the rich, indeed almost his whole portrait of the Andalusian anarchists, with their frugality, their independence, their egalitarianism, their mode of travel, all this could be a portrait of Gerald as a young man.

But in general the process was unconscious, and the most fascinating demonstration of this was the way in which he discovered that Spaniards and he shared the same soul. 'I believe that the awareness of this contrast [between the struggling individual and the hostile world] is one of the things most deeply ingrained in the Spanish character. The Spanish soul is a border castle, adapted for defence and offence in a hostile land: *soberbia*, or pride, and an eternal suspiciousness are its most ingrained qualities, together with a distrust of any but its own skill and weapons. But what the garrison feels all the time is loneliness.'

If something of this sort did occur, then a number of things fall into place. The process started early and explains the sense of returning home, indeed of rebirth, that was so striking when he arrived in the Alpujarra. It explains the extreme nature of his reaction to the Civil War – to embark on a massive five-year book on a subject neither he nor anyone else had studied; and explains why, almost unable to write a book before, he now succeeded.

It is the central thesis of this biography that, as a result of his childhood and school experiences, Gerald withdrew deeply into himself, into that 'interior castle'. But this created difficulties. He longed to write, yet shrank from revealing himself. That is why he could never get started, and when he did, either hid under mountains of similes and metaphors or wrote pastiche.

Spain released him. He was now able to write about himself at sufficient remove, sufficiently obliquely, to evade his own guard. It

25 Gamel acting in a play in New York State. Mid-1920s.

26 Llewelyn Powys (*L*) and J. C. Powys (*R*). East Chaldon, Dorset 1931.

27 Gamel at Sorrento on her honeymoon with Gerald, 1931.

28 Gamel, Gerald and Ralph in the Granero at Yegen, 1933. The red curtains at either side could be pulled round in winter.

29 Part of the garden and house at Churriana in 1936. The *alberca* is just visible in front of the house.

30 Gerald reading at Churriana in 1936.

31 Gamel dreaming at Churriana in 1936.

32 Rosario, Antonio, María, with Miranda (standing) and Isobel.
Churriana, 1936.

33 Gerald striding out of the
front door of Bell Court at
Aldbourne. Early 1940s.

34 Gerald in Home Guard
uniform, with medal
ribbons. 1942–43.

35 Gamel in the sitting-room at Bell Court. 1940.

36 VSP in the garden at Ham Spray.

37 Gamel at the outbreak of war at Bell Court.

39 Miranda and Xavier Corre at their wedding in September 1950.

38 Gamel's great friend Alyse Gregory.

40 La Cónsula picnic line-up. (*From L to R*) Tom Bakewell, Gerald,
Annie Davis, Carol Bakewell, Cyril Connolly, 'Swiss girl', Gamel,
Bill Davis. February 1956.

41 Joanna Carrington and Gerald. Churriana,
April 1957.

42 Honor Tracy. An early
photograph of this
formidable woman.

43 Hetty at Churriana, late 1950s.

44 Cyril Connolly in 'the
listening-to-music'
position.

45 Ralph in 1960.

46 Gerald, probably in 1968.

47 Gamel in the garden at
Churriana, 1962.

48 Rosario in February 1960, at the
entrance to her kitchen.

49 Lynda with Gerald just after arriving at Churriana.

50 Frances in 1962.

51 Lars, Lynda and Gerald at Alhaurín. Late 1970s.

52 Gerald and Bunny. Late 1970s.

53 Gerald at the opening of the street named after him at Alhaurín el Grande in 1982.

54 Gerald, in March 1984 just before he left for Pinner, signing *Personal Record*.

is, therefore, no accident that his writing on Spain was followed at once by, merged into, autobiography; and that his best book should be an intertwining of the two. (It is probably relevant to note here that – albeit her age was also significant – it was a Spanish girl who fully released his sexuality for the first and only time.) But the castle, his defences, still seemed to impose their block when he tried to write novels or poetry, perhaps because of their roots in the unconscious. But Spain dissolved this too, allowing his poetry in under the disguise of prose and his intuitive gift to function unimpeded. Spain seemed to flow into him, his responses flow back effortlessly and continually. And this unconscious identification helps to explain why so many of his insights are flattering (which does not mean wrong). 'At heart all Andalusians are town dwellers, quick, emotional, talkative, artistic.' True? Unprovable in fact (though certainly true of Gerald); but such *aperçus* give a feeling of space and exhilaration to his prose – and are pleasant to read if you come from Andalusia.

Even when criticising Spain, Gerald was never arrogant, never sarcastic in the way Ford is for instance. 'He would run Spain down,' said Jaime Parladé, 'and its language, but if anyone *else* attacked them he would defend it. Very much as Spaniards do. He seemed to have a knowledge of Spain, it came naturally, he acted as if he had been born here. That is why he was so critical; he was bored by things as if he had been here all his life.' This consideration – the same consideration, in fact, one shows oneself – was noticed and appreciated in a country whose intellectuals were extremely, even notoriously sensitive to criticism.

'What the garrison feels all the time is loneliness.' Are we not all alone – and all feel it at the crises of love and death? Some of the things Gerald said about Spain are true of humanity and this gives his prose a resonance. Still more, as Gerald knew perfectly well, if not universal are true of other Mediterranean countries. Had he settled elsewhere, would he have written as well? Certainly, his curiosity, his reading and his scholarship would have functioned – as they did whenever he went to France or Italy or Greece. Would Italy have been too bland? France too puritan and too planned? Greece – well, not a linguist like Borrow, he always had difficulty with the language. No doubt he would have mastered it. The question is academic. But in order to produce the same intuitive insights, something of the same process of unconscious identification would have had to take place as happened with Spain.

It is Gerald's intuitive gift that raises him above Ford and Borrow, and in fact all foreigners writing about Spain. Indeed, has anyone written so well or so widely about any country not their own? Doughty or T. E. Lawrence about Arabia? Not really. Dickens or de Tocqueville about America? Just sketches the first; social, political and historical analysis the second. D. H. Lawrence, especially in *Etruscan Places* and *Twilight in Italy*, has the same instinctive sense of place and people, but not the range. It seems impossible to think of anyone who knew so much and wrote so well about another country's literature, history and people. Not an enormously elevated ledge on Parnassus, perhaps, but an interesting one – and unique.

6

Gerald was of course delighted with the reception of *South From Granada*. But this was not his chief preoccupation. Throughout 1956 and early 1957 his letters to Miranda contain more and more, and longer and longer accounts of the sexual scandals up and down the coast. In February and March 1957 it is not his book that fills his letters to Ralph and Frances, but the imminent arrival, in April, of the Carringtons' beautiful young daughter Joanna. So noticeable was his agitation that he told Ralph Gamel was jealous.[32] Then came a familiar and tell-tale sign. Gamel, Gerald went on, had no need to be jealous, since he was beyond being attracted. 'For me the sixtieth year has been decisive.' Actually, Gerald had been sixty-three in April – so sixty-fourth year. Love was about to come to Churriana, and in its wake Emanation, Gerald's imprisoned soul in *The Lord of the Castle*, driven to a frenzy, was almost to wrench from their sockets the iron bars of his dungeon cell.

TWENTY-SIX

Another Carrington

'Yet I think that the hidden masochist in me really enjoyed being treated badly . . .'

Gerald to Joanna Carrington, 23 January 1973

1

The young girl who arrived on 2 April was just under twenty-five. 'It was after two and a half years of a disastrous marriage,' said Joanna Carrington. 'I was extremely neurotic, six stone not nine stone, extremely remote and I wanted peace.' She was also very beautiful. Long golden hair fell beside a slender neck round a delicate heart-shaped face, with very full lips and large dark eyes. She had a sulky expression until she smiled – when she looked enchanting. Her beauty, Frances wrote, 'filled the room like a glowing lamp'.[1]

For a fortnight Gerald was able to retain some semblance of control. Every night, when Gamel went to her room to read or write poetry, Joanna poured out the story of her marriage and of herself. 'It was like psychotherapy. He was an astonishing listener. He got me painting again. He also taught me to smoke.' They went for long walks up into the Sierra and she was fascinated – by his energy, his charm, his conversation and his sensitivity. 'He was intuitive about people, like a woman.' And fascinated by his love affair with Carrington, whose letters he gave her to read. 'And of course I led him on. What young neurotic wouldn't?'[2]

Led him on – and drew him out in her turn. Not just touching his infinitely tender heart and tapping his wisdom, but letting him talk about himself in a way he hadn't done with Gamel for twenty-five years. He suddenly began to feel alive again.

On 15 April Joanna and Gerald climbed a mountain and she let him kiss her. He came bounding down the steep slopes passionately and almost uncontrollably in love with her. Four nights later, instead of leaving them to talk and smoke and drink wine or brandy far into the night, Gamel sat up too. 'I felt like exploding,' wrote Gerald. When Gamel and he were in bed, he told her what had happened. They talked for three hours. 'It must be fifteen years since we had such a talk.'[3] It took three sodium amytol each to get them to sleep.

Gamel was extremely upset and wanted to leave at once.[4] Of all Gerald's escapades during the next few years, this was the only one that hurt her, because she could see his feelings were deeply involved.[5]

Indeed, everyone could see this. Gerald and Gamel had bought their grave plot in Malaga's Protestant cemetery just before Joanna's arrival, and he now hoped, not explaining how, that this would 'be a steadying influence'.[6] He told Ralph and promised Gamel that it would only be 'a father/daughter relationship'[3] – perhaps not the most reassuring metaphor in Gerald's case. But his feelings were volcanic. When, on an expedition to the Torcal, Kate Murchie took his place between Gamel and Joanna (at Joanna's instigation) he was so furious he refused to get into the car until Kate moved.[7]

He had previously always enjoyed telling Miranda how he was leaving her the Churriana house. Now he promised it to Joanna, if she came and lived with them, with a boyfriend or husband if she liked (he suggested Julio Caro Baroja thinking, one feels, more of himself than the brilliant Spanish *savant*). He also poured out his love to her – in notes, declarations, introducing long discussions about whether, had he been younger, she would have married him or slept with him. Joanna's mood rapidly began to change. For one thing, she was half in love with a young man in London, a man she called Turino. For another, she'd come to Churriana for peace, not for what she described as 'excessive outbursts'.[8] She discovered in herself a cold vein of cruelty – as many people do when pestered and maddened by someone who does not attract them. Feelings of violent hostility and irritation alternated with renewed affection and interest. To Gerald, the light-house had changed its message – 'Yes-No, Yes-No, Yes-No.' 'I was horrible to Gerald', she said later, 'though not intentionally.'

Cruelty and pain were of course the last thing to discourage Gerald's love – indeed, as they had long ago, they defined it. All the agonising agitations he'd suffered with Carrington returned with her niece. Once more – 'the stale bitter taste of rejected love'.[7] Yet this was also what he craved. By promising to control his expression of love totally, Gerald persuaded Joanna to promise that she would return in September. And early in the morning of 6 May, her last, she finally allowed him into her bed and let him make love to her.

Or so we are meant to infer from the journal Gerald kept at this time. But like all Gerald's journals this one was largely written up afterwards and was meant to be read. Joanna is quite clear that nothing happened between her and Gerald. And his account does indeed have, both in the journal and letters, all the vagueness and imprecision, if also the vividness, of similar accounts in the past. He imagined, wrote it down – and it was as if it had happened. The only difference is that, unlike most of the past accounts, he nowhere else leaves a plain statement of the truth. The episode marks, that is, the final stage in these sexual inventions, in which his aim was to leave behind an impression of greater success. Thereafter he was to say modestly, but not without cunning, that he and Joanna had only made love once and had agreed that both would deny it.[9]

2

It is easy to laugh at Gerald, now and at times during the next five years – and his contemporaries did. But his feelings were intense, and he dared to have them and describe them honestly and fully. (Whatever he pretended at the time, there is no definite statement in *Personal Record* that he ever made love to Joanna, though it is possible to infer that *perhaps* he did. This was more honest than Bunny. *Aspects of Love* had just come out two years before, in 1955. This, according to Gerald, transposed Bunny's affair with a rich, sixty-year-old American into one with a young girl.)

When Joanna left, Gerald was desolate. 'And now the house seems horribly empty and lifeless. It is as though I were living in a morgue.'[10] He had lost a stone, and shut himself up in his room smoking thirty cigarettes a day and several cigars. He lay one entire Sunday flat on his bed groaning. He wrote up the Joanna journal, waited frantically for the post, wrote letters to Ralph and tried to restrict himself to two sixteen-page letters a week in reply to Joanna's, which were torturingly intermittent. His hare fantasies returned, to flee to some distant land and become 'an empty sheet of paper again'.[8]

Then all at once he erupted into poetry. For two months he wrote nothing else, surge upon surge of love poems, portraits of Joanna, 'dirges'.[11] Once more, he realised he should have been a poet. He discussed them all at length with Gamel (Gamel had a lot to put up with).* It saved him and by the end of July he was calm again. 'I have built up inside me seven feet of lead against her radioactive rays.'[11] He stopped writing poetry and took up *Mr Fisher*.

Meanwhile, the world continued to revolve. La Cónsula, as can be imagined, had been riveted by the events in Churriana. Bill got them up for dinner and, as was his wont, made Gerald drunk in order to pump him about Joanna. Gerald, though he had to rush out and be sick, was his match. He gave him a long dissertation on a poem he was writing for his grave.[12] Then Kenneth Tynan and Cyril arrived at La Cónsula – Tynan immaculate, apparently allergic to sun, emerging only briefly to deliver a few self-possessed remarks on the breeding of bulls, 'then withdraws to the darkened house again'.[13] Ethel de Croisset gave a party. A little later Ronnie Duncan and the Harewoods came, Bill in a knot of anxiety on this social peak.†

Social life went on, but Gerald was really only interested in what was going on inside his head. Xavier remembers how irritated he was

---

* Gerald's Joanna poetry is a little better than his Carrington verse:

> Out in the street the lovers talk
> Exchanging bouquets of themselves.
> Among their shapes my sad thoughts walk,
> phoenixes looking for their doves.
>
> Phoenixes torn and scratched and grey,
> yet raging with an angry life.
> The fire that burns their veins all day
> leaves both new blood and ash at night.

† Xavier and Miranda were staying, and the Churriana group was usually forbidden at La Cónsula at those times, but this was an emergency. Gerald and Gamel were asked to dinner. One exchange gave Gerald considerable pleasure, as he told Ralph in a letter of 24 August 1957.

> *Comtesse de Sales*: And what are Benjamin Britten and Peter Pears doing now?
> *Countess of Harewood*: They're in Canada screwing.
> *Comtesse de Sales*: I beg your pardon . . .
> *Countess of Harewood*: They are in Canada *screwing*.
> *Comtesse de Sales*: I . . . don't quite understand.
> *Countess of Harewood*: Oh – ! I see . . .! I mean they're giving *The Turn of the Screw*.

by the way Gerald rushed for the post that summer. The letters to Ralph are endless variations on the theme of Joanna. He 'longs to see that silver fish in my river'.[14] He sent her money and needed excuses to sell out.[15] The selling of Bell Court was advancing and he planned to offer her anything she wanted (something he'd already done for Miranda).[16] Then suddenly, 'I have had moments when I wish I was dead in sheer rage that I cannot be thirty-five again and marry Joanna and sleep with her every every every night.'[17] And nearly always these passionate outbursts called up, like an echo, the fact that he really needed Gamel just as much, her 'presence in the house, gentle, peaceful, low-voiced, beautiful, a little remote, not suited for any intimate or dramatic relation, yet with roots that reach through the whole of my nature. Not a mother figure really – for I don't need mothering – but a sort of tender, aesthetic constant to my life.'[17]

There was a terrible moment in August when he heard Catharine Carrington was coming, and he leapt to the conclusion that Joanna wouldn't come as a result. He wrote a furious letter to Catharine saying that if she came alone, he and Gamel would go to Greece. Then it turned out to be a misunderstanding. 'In one half hour I changed from being a sort of caged lunatic to a normal, contented person.'[18] He wrote and apologised to Catharine, who must have been fairly astonished.

Joanna arrived for her second visit on 10 September.

3

The lead turned out to be ice; in the fire of his love it melted at once and within a few days he was in despair – and bliss. 'I have never known such force of feeling . . . This is a thing that will last my life.'[19] Joanna was now 'headlong in love' with Turino (named after the café they'd met in). Gerald's 'outbursts' therefore irritated her even more. Under the impact of afternoon indifference and cruelty, alternating like some fiendish brainwashing exercise with evening sweetness, as well as his own heroic efforts to curb too overt expressions of his passion, Gerald once again went through agitations and fluctuations of mood, of row and reconciliation, as tormenting as any with Carrington.

'His jealousy,' said Joanna, 'was a *nightmare*. He would accuse me of sleeping with taxi drivers. Once poor harmless old John Whitworth came to tea. Gerald went out to pee. When he came back he said furiously in front of Gamel, "*You flirted with him.*" He was beside himself.'

On another occasion Jaime Parladé had great difficulty preventing him fighting a duel with Juan Manuel Figueras, a notorious local womaniser. (One can see why Gerald wrote so well about *Don Quixote*.) But it was his scenes with Joanna that infuriated Gamel. She became jealous herself and began to drink heavily. At lunch she would bang the plates down belligerently and fire her 'volleys of pinpricks'.[20]

Yet in the four months' visit there were many peaceful and happy moments. 'We are all working hard,' Gerald told Ralph in mid-October. 'The miracle is coming true.'[21] The 'miracle' was that Joanna should live 'as a daughter' with him and Gamel. The work: Gerald's article on *City of the Sybarites*, which had been turned down by the *New Yorker* in July the year before, was accepted and published by *Encounter* in October, and he was now hard at *Mr Fisher*, into which Joanna was to be incorporated whole as Eleanor; Joanna painted; and Gamel was translating the works of Sister Juana Inés de la Cruz, a beautiful seventeenth-century Mexican nun, who was also a poet.* Gerald organised endless expeditions – to Antequera and Cabra, to Granada and Cordoba, to bullfights (Joanna refused to go). In November he and she had two blissful days alone in Seville where Joanna had to get divorce papers signed by the Consul – delicious meals, wandering from bar to bar, Gerald at his best, gay, informative, talking away but not about love or sex. But fluctuations began again on their return. Joanna painted a portrait of Gerald on the train, his 'head as red as a tomato and giving out a sort of purplish gas . . . it might have been done by Francis Bacon'.[22]

Then Joanna insisted that Turino came out. Gerald had to take another huge grip on himself. When Ralph and Frances arrived on 28 November, they went at once to see the Brenans. 'Gerald looks as if he had gone through a mangle and every drop of emotion squeezed out, his eyes unfocused. Joanna was pale, thin, and composed.'[23] It was Gamel who greeted them most warmly with her lipsticky kisses.

---

* Gamel and one of her best friends in Spain, Marjorie von Schlippenbach, were co-operating on the book. Marjorie wrote the introduction and critical notes; Gamel selected and translated the poetry. It was finished but never published.

The Partridges took Buena Vista again. Gerald called at once, and thereafter frequently, talking obsessively about Joanna for hours. But Ralph's arrival brought into prominence a layer of complication that had always been present. In no real way like Carrington, Gerald had at once identified Joanna with his old love, as everyone knew he would and as indeed did Noel her father. But this also raised up, at an unconscious level, his ancient rivalry with Ralph. Needing his friend as an outlet and *confidant* for his volcanic feelings (as he had in the 1920s), many of his letters now and for the next three years are also really saying – look how much more successful with girls I am now than you are. This was another reason for the contents of the Joanna journal, immediately given to Ralph and Frances to read.

Ralph was half aware of this (he called Gerald's ostentatious leaping up and down mountains 'competitive goatmanship') but only became fully so three months later. He and Gerald had a rather complicated row after Christmas which was really the result of Gerald's rage at Burgo Partridge, Ralph's son (with whom Joanna flirted mildly largely to irritate Gerald), taking her out to a Torremolinos nightclub till three in the morning. In April, at Ham Spray, Ralph suddenly said to Frances Gerald was involved 'with *Carrington's ghost!*' When he'd come to Buena Vista to say how well he was getting on with Joanna, the true message was, 'You see, I've got Carrington after all.'[23] (The insight was prompted by Gerald suddenly sending a stream of letters justifying his behaviour with the first Carrington.)

Although at one level it was this turbulence Gerald wanted, as he knew perfectly well, at another it was too much. A further scene, when Gerald threw all the presents he'd planned to give Joanna out of the window, seemed finally to drain him. Frances felt he'd 'worn himself out with emotions about her. He's like a piece of tattered stuff that's been washed and washed until hardly any colour remains.'[23] On her last day, on a picnic in the mountains of Mijas, he suddenly said bitterly about Torremolinos, 'Sex is distilled there – all the water of love boiled out of it.'[23] Her departure on 6 January was a relief.

4

They moved on into 1958. Cyril and later Xan and Daphne Fielding were at La Cónsula. Ruth Lowinsky suddenly died in January. Peter Feibleman, a rich American whose novel had just come out, appeared. Bell Court plus Hope was finally sold for £1750 to Miss Smyth, the niece of Alec Penrose's. Gerald gave £200 to Hope. In early April the Brenans went to Madrid so that Gerald could write an article for *Holiday* magazine.

He sent a few cheques to Joanna, and decided he had 'bowed out'.[24] But her influence had been considerable. It marked a further step in Gamel's retreat; from now on she and Gerald had separate bedrooms, to Gerald's relief. He himself always remained grateful to Joanna for showing him he could still feel intensely. Fuses had blown, but once more strong currents had coursed along the wires – and if once, why not again?

Gamel sensed this. Ronnie Duncan asked her if she would take in Tsai-chin – a twenty-four-year-old Chinese girl who had been having a nervous breakdown. Gamel, clearly apprehensive that every April was going to bring some Joanna-like bomb into the house, seems to have got out of it.[24] But in vain; danger was in fact approaching from another quarter. The marmalade-coloured figure of Hetty McGee already bulged upon the horizon.

TWENTY-SEVEN

Hetty

'*How much does she love me, how much is self-interest – questions I have been asking myself for five years now and 100 times a day.*'
Gerald to Frances Partridge, 7 August 1963

1

At the end of April 1958 John Whitworth* told Gerald that the secretary to Peter Feibleman had rescued a young woman from Gibraltar Hospital. His account intrigued Gerald. He went, saw Hetty – and on 26 April she and Jason, her eight-month-old son, moved into Churriana. He at once explained this, and much subsequent behaviour, by telling Rosario that Hetty was his niece.†

Hetty MacGee (in fact, Mary at first) was the daughter of an Anglo-Dutch stockbroker called Scholten, and a much younger Liverpudlian Irish nurse. Scholten had died when she was fourteen and 'Mother couldn't hold me'. Art school had been followed by Soho, jazz musicians, drugs and years of wild and often sordid adventure. Finally, she had washed up in southern Spain with her child and heroin addict husband Tom, a US war veteran – who had

---

* John Whitworth, now nearly forty, was an almost over-gentle, intelligent, kindly man with a long, rather goat-like face, and prominent pale blue eyes. One of the gunners at the battle of Monte Cassino, this once active man had had his life almost destroyed when he'd fallen from a tree taking a swarm of bees and broken his back. His fiancée had thrown him over and, with very little money, he'd come to Torremolinos in 1952 to recover.

† Niece also held a delicious hint of ambiguity, for Gerald at least. Up to the Civil War, but continuing afterwards, the liaisons of elderly men, and in particular of priests, were always with their 'niece'.

been given a small pension as a result of a wound and knew he could obtain his dope more easily there. Tom had recently taken all their money and vanished. Hetty, distraught, had left her child with some Spaniards and collapsed.

Gerald was moved by her predicament, but there was also, he confessed in his first letter to Ralph about her, 'some physical attraction too'[1] – an element that becomes increasingly noticeable as the letter proceeds. Hetty was about thirty-one, but her round child's face, her vitality, her tough, short, sun-browned body with the texture and resilience of a squash ball, made her seem younger. She was energetic, gullible, self-deceiving, loyal, an exhibitionist, talkative, a marvellously rhythmic dancer who was ready to dare anything and go anywhere – courage helped since she was often nerveless with marijuana. There was something peasant-like about her, which made her shifts oddly touching, naïve and transparent. One of her lovers once said, 'What if I tell Gerald you've just said, "If I play my cards right, I'll get left the house and most of his money"?' Hetty rushed and told Gerald. 'Imagine my saying that!' 'Of course she said it,' said Gerald later, 'or thought it. And quite right too.'[2] Yet, despite a curiously two-dimensional quality, she was not shallow. There was within her, or at least Gerald sensed in her, 'a strange, very sad imagination'.[1] This showed in her paintings, which were original and often moving. Cedric Morris had recognised her talent and enrolled her in his art school. Had her life been more mundane, she might well have become a painter of some distinction.

Although Hetty could be tiresome, she was not socially insensitive, except in one respect. Her chief defect – and it was grave – lay in her conversation. This was enlivened because she had had extraordinary adventures and because she was a fantasist. To instance one out of thousands of inspired inventions, she told John Whitworth that Edith Sitwell had personally instructed her how to recite *Façade*. But she had a psychological mechanism which meant she could only think and speak in blocks. Almost anything she spoke about came in a vast block of associated but irrelevant events. No account of a visit to shop or beach, of a party, lasted less than twenty minutes; Gerald described one, in a letter to Miranda, lasting four hours.*[3]

---

* There was a celebrated story of Hetty and Cyril at La Cónsula. Hetty was not often asked there and, excited, was soon in full flow. Cyril, having in vain flung

Yet the appalling boredom this sometimes engendered did not at first trouble Gerald in the slightest. He was intermittently obsessed with Hetty for two years and she played a considerable, often disruptive but stimulating role for three more. Gerald always insisted he was not in love with her – by which he meant he suffered little or none of the agitation and pain by which he defined the state. Hetty's relief, after years of wandering and poverty, to be looked after in that beautiful house with its high walls, its peace-filled garden, and its fountain, to have her son Jason off her hands (Rosario, María and Carmen took him over entirely), to be paid for, was immense. She didn't mind if, at rather rare intervals, Gerald got into her bed, provided he didn't touch her – which he never did. But he was often jealous, and he talked about her so incessantly and inventively that meeting Hetty for the first time people had the impression they were meeting a character in fiction.

Her moving-in required a small lorry: cotton bed covers, drapes, cushions, rugs, guitar, easel, canvases, conch shells, kif pipe, toys, records and player, crockery . . . The fragrant, heady scents of joss-sticks and marijuana drifted down from a transformed library, its lights dimmed by red tissue, accompanied by the sound of the blues, Ella Fitzgerald, Bach, Vivaldi.

At the end of May they all went to Seville *en route* for the Whitsun festival of the Virgin of the Dew, the Romería de la Virgen del Rocío which takes place between Jerez and Huelva on the western side of the Gaudalquivir. 'Imagine,' Gerald wrote to Ralph, leaping at once into top literary gear, 'a great sandy plain, partly wooded with umbrella pines and eucalyptus and giving onto the Marismas.'⁴ And then, over ten careering pages, he described it: the guitars, the flamenco, the galloping horses in clouds of dust (Hetty on one behind an Andalusian *caballero*), the drinking, the booths, the dancing (Hetty doing a *sevillana*), the processions, the fires, the smells, the 'rattle of castanets, the whirl of bodies . . .'⁴ Gamel was recovering from 'flu and saw it all through a haze of fever (appropriately, she thought). Gerald stayed

himself into the 'listening-to-music position' and exuded huge quantities of his conversational nerve gas, suddenly sat up and barked, 'Will you shut the fuck up!' Hetty stopped, looked at him with her kohl-rimmed eyes as if he'd suddenly sung a few notes of *Traviata* or let a frog out of his mouth, then continued her monologue. Cyril was compelled to stump from the room.

up till 5 a.m. for two nights, then slept for four hours wrapped in a rug next to Hetty in a cubbyhole in the Davises' camp. At the end, as they all wilted, 'my high spirits irritated everyone'.[4]

By 6 June he felt Hetty had brought him bliss. 'A thousand, thousand blessings on her head.'[5] Bliss augmented when, on the 15th, Gamel flew to England for six weeks. From now on she did this every year. She would stay at 1 Orme Lane, Ronnie Duncan's 'cottage' off the Harewoods' house in London, or with the Sheppards in Fulham. Then visit Ham Spray, Ronnie, sometimes Bertie Russell, later on Honor and, most important, Alyse and Phyllis Playter and J. C. Powys. Back in Spain, she would always miss England. 'There is no one very interesting . . . in this rather isolated place. It's only when I first come back when I've known, oh, something better that I feel it.'[6] One must always make allowances for Gamel's desire to please her correspondent (that 'oh' carries a hint of something studied) but the note is constant and consistent. It was now she began to idolise Llewelyn as the great and perfect love of her life, forgetting the pain he had caused her and how she had fled to Gerald from him. Alyse and Phyllis sent her parcels of books and magazines as if she were in prison.

The moment Gamel had gone, Gerald and Hetty began to collaborate on a pornographic book.[7] They went to Madrid for three days for Gerald to research an article for *Holiday* magazine; there were drunken parties; Tom, Hetty's husband, turned up and moved in. He had been eking out his veteran's pension doing abortions with rusty forceps. Gerald, initially appalled, decided to like Tom and foresaw a *ménage à quatre* when Gamel returned. Hetty took Gerald into Torremolinos and introduced him to her friends in their bars and pads, with their guitars and drugs and silences and endless jazz – to Chris, Joseph, Nini, Jimmy, Cathy, Del Negro, Jean and Frédérique.

Slightly incongruous, diffident, detached, often bored, Gerald more or less kept his dignity – and if he shocked his own generation, so much the better. On the track of that 'ghost of sex and youth we sexagenarians pursue',[8] he required someone to be shocked. He saw their coarse, hedonistic drug-taking as an echo of his own lonely idealistic experiments at seventeen, and their poverty moved him. He began to show off by sprinkling his letters with their jargon and was soon dropping it into conversation with Ralph and VSP, to ludicrous effect – 'The real reason to dig late Henry James . . .'

The life Hetty had led had scoured away all trace of middle-classness. Gerald was able to identify her with the working-class girls of his youth, and so to echo that rebellion too. And Hetty was a dominant character; in many ways, he realised, more masculine than him. With Gamel he became masculine, 'which I rather dislike'.⁹ He discovered with Hetty that he liked to give way, to agree, as if the strong masochistic/feminine element in his character sought, with age, a gentler expression. This was an interesting presage of the future.

And as the summer progressed another pattern emerged. Gerald became exhausted and began to long for Gamel's return. He became temporarily sick of the jargon – 'The language of rebellious children.'¹⁰ It was also extremely expensive. Tom vanished with a 'loan' of 1000 pesetas. Gerald paid for everything – bullfight tickets, bars, people to meals, and a huge party he and Hetty gave with gypsy dancing. The Bell Court money vanished; perhaps soon shares would have to be sold.

Gamel arrived with Xavier and Miranda on 31 July, and three days later Hetty moved out into Torremolinos. Normally, all this signalled a return to sanity. But this year the momentum of Hetty swept them on. Gerald gave a party at the Bar Mañana and drank too much. He kissed Carol Bakewell, Annie Davis's sister-in-law, the party degenerated into chaos and Xavier, Gamel and Miranda left. Bayard Osborn, a good-looking rich young American painter/sculptor newly arrived with his wife Anita, drove a group home, Gerald sitting up on the back of the open car. Bayard stopped suddenly and Gerald was thrown out – according to him – onto his head. 'While I was still unconscious, but somehow on my feet,' he told Ralph, 'someone said Xavier was a bourgeois bore.'¹¹ Gamel and Miranda were listening upstairs. Gerald regained consciousness to stagger upstairs and be accused by Hetty of forcing Tom out of the house.*

Relief only came when he left for Paris, then England, on 23 August, given a lift to Nantes by the Corres. 'What's wrong with Paris,' he wrote to Gamel, feeling sad and alone, 'is that you are not

---

* One would have thought Gerald would have learnt a lesson from this. But there was another incident when he was riding on the back of the Osborn car full of young people. Gerald suddenly sneezed and sneezed his false teeth into the ditch. The car had to stop and everyone got out to search. 'The humiliation!' Gerald said, describing it to Charles Sinnickson.

here.'[12] But he managed to fit in a striptease show, particularly liking a stupid girl in the front ('as Titian knew, intelligence is anti-erotic');[13] and he probably did the same in London.* He saw Arthur Waley, whose flat was completely full of beds. Beryl de Zoëte was half off her head after a stroke. Frenziedly restless, she changed beds a dozen or more times a night.[14] Gerald also had a furious quarrel with Joanna who, tactlessly in his view, had asked her sister to their only supper. Back in Churriana he burnt all her letters.

But he returned to autumn calm. He visited Hetty in Torremolinos and, unable to work all summer (except for some appalling verse about Hetty),† he now took up *Mr Fisher* again. There were tremendous storms before Christmas, blowing down the pecan tree. Christmas itself was at La Cónsula. 'Sometimes life seems just like a play that one has seen a hundred times before.'[15]

2

> '*One never exhausts the geography of love. I do everything I can to help her find a husband, yet I am mad with jealousy when she goes off to do so or becomes interested in a man. And I turn my jealousy into moral rage against her sponging on me, although that is just what I want her to do . . . [Yet] I repeat, I'm not exactly in love with her and I find in her absence – bored and angry though I am – a certain relief.*'
>
> Gerald to Ralph Partridge, 30 December 1959

Hetty leaving, Hetty returning, Hetty's lovers, rows, reconciliations, scandals, tears . . . it can all only be indicated – but every inlet, every hillock in the geography of that land remains, as does every reaction of the chief, indeed only, surveyor. Gerald wrote 426 dense pages to Ralph over these three years, not to mention long letters to Frances, Bunny, VSP, Miranda and others. But Gamel's reaction to all this must be examined more closely, and this can be

---

* Gerald, as he explained to Frances in a letter of 10 October 1967, used to go regularly to strip joints in Soho. In 1964/65 he gave his Raymond Revue Bar ticket to Blair's wife Rhoda, thinking, her daughter Lydia Piper remembers, that she might enjoy using it.

† Sample: 'She's the most amazing girl in all this town./As she goes walking by the men fall flat down./But she isn't my girl. No, boy, she isn't my girl.'

most easily done through Honor Tracy who came to stay at Churriana in February 1959.

As Gerald had once done, Honor supplied the current needed to spark Gamel's love of life. She remarked on her liveliness and humour, her zest and desire for adventure (now sixty-three, Gamel went surfboarding with Ronnie this summer,[16] and a little later descended 1000 feet into a Welsh slate mine wearing a miner's lamp).[17] It is a very different picture to the one Gerald paints.

But Gamel also elicited profound pity, from Honor as from many people. She was painfully aware of that vein of unhappiness, Gamel's melancholy – and entirely blamed Gerald's behaviour with Joanna and Hetty. Honor left, this time after only a week, when she and Gerald had their first row.

John Whitworth completely agreed with Honor. At first in Gerald's camp, he moved to Gamel's (a not uncommon transition). 'The nightmare period,' he called it. 'Me, Gerald and say X would be discussing the state of the economy in England. Gerald would say, quite seriously, "Hetty says . . ." But Gamel suffered, oh yes, *suffered*.'

And in a subtle way, Gamel encouraged this. She did not say anything;* she had no need to. She had run away from her alcoholic mother to become an actress. She enjoyed playing her roles (Gerald spoke once of her 'endless façades');[18] the dreamy poetess wandering past the arum lilies, the mysterious fated daughter of the 'ole South' – and now the wronged wife suffering with silent, aristocratic dignity.

There was some truth in this, but not much. For one thing, Gamel had her own admirers, and they were numerous – her 'po-its' as Frances phoneticised them. It was not necessary to write poetry (John was an honorary poet); sufficient to enjoy sitting at her feet (literally, often) and listening to her talking about it or reading it. (Jimmy Burns-Singer, a friend of Hetty's, and a shy, very clever man whom Gamel loved, was probably the only genuine poet.) And then

---

* All her close friends – Honor, Alyse, John Whitworth, Frances – comment on her reticence. Marjorie von Schlippenbach didn't know she had been married before, or know about Llewelyn, till *Personal Record* came out. 'You would think two women who were close and intimate friends for nearly thirty years would discuss such things. We talked about books, her writing, gossiped about friends. I think she liked me partly because she knew I wouldn't try and penetrate her feelings.' This reserve, by *itself*, contributed to the sense of mystery Gamel engendered.

Gamel was fond of Hetty, as she made clear quite often, even if she was frequently very bored and exasperated by most of her friends. Gamel's moods of melancholy and despair and inchoate guilt were real enough but they had been severe already in the Thirties, as Gamel was well aware, long before Honor and John knew her. She was now for long periods no longer the centre of Gerald's attention, and she minded him making a fool of himself because it undermined her role as wife of distinguished writer. Marriage can inflict worse than that.

3

Hope turned up at the end of March, thinner but so delightful they kept him for two weeks. Then in April, Ralph had another heart 'incident'. Gerald was extremely worried and wrote trying to comfort him. He promised to write a lot of letters to entertain him – which he did, and they did.

In May Hemingway arrived at La Cónsula with, later, Antonio Ordóñez and other figures of the bullring. Bill had been pestering Hemingway to come for a year and, after checking with Kenneth Tynan that the house was comfortable and exacting a promise of complete privacy, he arrived for five months of bullfighting. (This was the season of Ordóñez's great *mano a mano* contest with Luis Miguel Dominguín, which Hemingway chronicled first for *Life* magazine and then in *The Dangerous Summer*.) Bill, in an ecstasy of snobbish and sycophantic excitement, turned La Cónsula into a fortress, but Gerald and Gamel were asked to lunch. Gerald wrote enthusiastically to Ralph, but in *Personal Record* he was more guarded, as well as acute. He told Jeffrey Meyers he was intimidated by Hemingway's '*presence*. It was as if, when he was in the room, there wasn't enough air for the rest of us.'[19] The Hemingways also came to lunch at Churriana. Gamel was understandably worried about Hetty talking too much but, according to Gerald, she was 'a great success with her enthusiasm for bullfighters and gitanos and flamenco'.[20]

Gitanos were a new craze. Hetty had virtually joined a group of gypsies in Malaga, pretending her mother was a gypsy queen. She even – 'would you believe it'[21] – begged from tourists in the streets.

But money was a problem. She now started Zarabanda Fabrics, planning to sell tie-dyed sarongs and painted pebbles.*

On 19 May Gamel flew to England. Too nervous to tell her before what he had been secretly planning for several weeks, Gerald now wrote guiltily saying he and Hetty were going to Morocco. 'Darling,' Gamel replied, 'I don't know what to say about your journey. I only hope all goes well – no typhoid, 'flu or cutting of throats. But you don't have to give me *so many reasons* for going. If I had money and a suitable companion, I'd set off tomorrow for the sources of the Amazon . . .'[17]

4

Travelling light in approved hippy style, Gerald and Hetty arrived in Tangier on 30 May, where Hetty instantly discarded Europe (including her knickers) and donned red slippers, earrings, charms and a *djellaba* (by mistake, they learnt on their return, a male one, which explained some of the merriment they caused). Gerald, indulging his fantasies just as much, told Ralph he was dressed like Colonel Fawcett. Going by bus or hitching, sleeping in hideously uncomfortable Arab *fondaks*, this oddly assorted couple reached the Atlas on 9 June. Gerald was impervious to kif because of his puffing system of smoking, but not impervious to temperature. In the cool of the Atlas he caught a cold; by Ourzazate, where it was 110°, he had become half-deaf. They now shared a taxi with seven Berbers and a ram and drove 130 miles south, slept beside the road, then hitched to Zagora – where it was 112°. Faint with heat, they were nearly finished by the desert fifteen miles further on. Although ravenous, they took a bus 150 miles back to Ourzazate, arriving at midnight, Gerald with 'flu and running a high temperature. From

---

* Gerald was divided. Ever since Pepita and Lily and Winnie, he had enjoyed the complex relations of money and love. At the same time, he and Hetty kept on having fantasies that she would make money out of things like pebbles. They were on safer ground with her paintings and etchings, which always did well. Tie-dyeing had been taught to Hetty by Gamel. It is a system of tying off separate bunches of a piece of cloth and dipping into different dyes, so that the material slowly becomes covered in a series of vague different coloured blodges. Hetty used to do it in the *mirador*, making a good deal of mess.

now on, he poured with sweat each night. Everything was closed for a festival and, in the raging heat, they watched Berber dances. Finally, at night, they were offered the carcase of a sheep too revolting to touch. Back, starving, over the Atlas to Fez and the great 'feast of sheep', the gutters running with blood and entrails. His temperature still rising, Gerald was again too disgusted to eat. He collapsed in Tangier; staggered up and collapsed completely when they reached Churriana on 22 June.

Morocco was his Watendlath with Hetty. He often told Ralph he wanted to make love to her, but that was not really the point. On this trip (and thereafter), in the hot cubbyholes or squalid rooms they'd slept in, 'naked together . . . we shared the same toothbrush and snotty handkerchief. She changed her Tampax in front of me.'[22] At last he'd realised, even more completely than with Winny, that far-distant voyeur dream of the girl undressing and not minding if he watched.

5

With Xavier and Miranda came the summer madness – Gerald and Gamel gave a party, there were parties in Torremolinos, expeditions to Ronda, the usual fluctuations in Hetty's life. The theory was that she would be independent – but at each disaster of love or finance she returned to Gerald. She now took a house in Churriana (Gerald paying half the rent, since Zarabanda Fabrics was on the slide). David Tennant gave a party in Mijas, and Michael Wishart, a talented young painter who 'loved Baudelairean tarts' as well as men, thought, mistakenly, that Hetty 'fitted the bill'.

With autumn came calm. Hemingway at last left La Cónsula. Gerald took up *Mr Fisher* again. And at the end of November, Gamel, who had been writing sonnets for two years, took an immense step. She sent all her poetry – her life's work – to Ronnie to send on to T. S. Eliot for possible publication by Faber and Faber.

Charles Sinnickson remembers calling on her just after this. It was unusually cold and Gamel, a volume of Latin poetry open, was lying on a sofa 'stretched out and glamorous, a long scarf round her neck' in front of a charcoal-burner. She pointed to the distant snow on the Sierra: 'Whenever I see snow on mountains, I think of this passage in Virgil.' She read it out and translated it.* I was very touched. She had been waiting for me.'

On Christmas Eve Gerald, Gamel and Hetty went to midnight Mass in the Convent Church. Gerald felt a strange, almost religious emotion standing between them. 'The two women I care for in such different ways. Hetty in a big coat, puffed out like a robin, a handkerchief tied round her head, her big brown eyes staring in solemn boredom . . . now and then feeling for my hand. Gamel aloof and sensitive.'²³

On 30 December Hetty and Jason left for Ramatuelle near St Tropez to stay (perhaps to live) with Michael Wishart.

6

'It's the peculiarity of life out here that though everything is new, everything has happened before,'²⁴ Gerald wrote in a letter about now. It resembled, that is, a kaleidoscope.

Prominent in 1960, a single, stark, jagged black fragment, was Ralph's declining health. His heart was now so bad that any excessive exertion was dangerous. He and Frances wintered in Alicante and Gerald, although he had 'flu, took a taxi the considerable distance to see them. Through all the distractions of this year, his anxiety over Ralph, his long letters to console and distract, are a constant.

Chief of the distractions still, a kaleidoscope in herself, was of course Hetty. In April, her hair now henna'd red, she returned from Michael Wishart. It hadn't, as she put it, to Gerald's secret delight,

---

* Vides, ut alta stet nive candidum
Soracte, nec jam sustineant onus
Sylvae laborantes, geluque
Flumina constiterunt acuto?

('Look, now the snow sparkles up there on the peak of Soracte. See, in the woods, the branches let fall their heavy coverings of snow: and look at the river – solidly frozen over.')

Aged thirty-eight, thin and highly strung, somewhat deficient in chin but not at all a weak man, Charles Sinnickson was an American who professed a strict High Anglicanism and elaborate prejudices upon which he based a Firbankian wit – 'What America really needs is a Stuart monarchy.' Extremely kind, he had a car (still a unique asset in Churriana) and became very fond of Miranda – a fact later to prove of significance. His religious beliefs were sincere and he was eventually ordained.

'worked out'. She lived at Churriana for a while, maddening Gerald by coming back late so that he lay awake listening for her. He turned her out, took her back, gave her money and, when she returned from various escapades chastened or ebullient, loved to lie on her bed, watching her dress, undress, make up and listening while, above the ceaseless background jazz, her colossal, highly coloured monologues unrolled round the room. Gamel endured stoically. 'She has behaved over all this Hetty madness in the most wonderful way,' Gerald wrote to Ralph. 'She's a woman in ten million and I don't deserve her.'[25]

The case against the sitting tenants was shaken into prominence. Judgement finally came in April. They lost. Gerald was furious. He told Miranda he planned to build a huge pigsty under the tenants' bedroom, and stock it with 'several big pigs'.[26] He also planned to bribe the defence lawyer with £1000, but finally – racing back and forth in the summer heat – he fought an appeal, only on 2 August to lose this too. The law worked strongly in favour of sitting tenants and it seems Gerald would have done better to buy another house, which he could have afforded, and rent them that. Instead, he issued a new writ.

Despite all this, he worked. María remembers him, even at seventy-three, bounding up the stairs two at a time to get to his table. He finished the nth rewrite of *Tom Fisher* in May, and then revised it one last time, but it was accepted midway through this by Jamie Hamilton while he was staying at La Cónsula. First begun in 1925, he had worked at it a total of nearly six years – longer than *Segismundo*. He posted it in October and began to rewrite and cut *A Life of One's Own*. In October, too, he was asked by Michigan Press to write a 'popular' history of Spain from 1789, became excited, but finally couldn't face the work.[27] Gerald also began to plan his last novel.*

---

* In many ways the expatriate coast life suited Gerald. There was a great deal of event, but also longish periods of calm. It was largely American, and so not cliquish in the upper- and middle-class snobbish English way he loathed. If some of the figures were a bit second-rate, Gerald didn't mind. Just as he could make unread eleventh- and twelfth-century Arab poets real and vital again, so he could get the best out of the people he lived among. But the drunken excesses disgusted him almost as much as they fascinated his voyeur side. One justification for the latter would be a novel. He'd thought of a title – *The Lighthouse Always Says Yes*. He couldn't think of a theme. I played a small part here. I stayed four months with Gerald this year. One evening Gerald told me of this difficulty. *JGH*: 'You must

During the summer, and particularly when Gamel had gone in June, the house filled with young people. And now it was not just Hetty's friends: nineteen-year-old Georgia Tennant would come down from Mijas – delightfully cat-faced, charming, very intelligent with 'moments of brilliance'.[28] Suna Portman, a beautiful young heiress, came to stay and got off with Bill Barker, a bisexual ex-actor and 'poet' from America. Gerald got to know and like the talented and witty writer and later TV director, Julian Jebb, whom he considered 'both a man and a girl at once, with the advantages of both'.[29] For the rest of his life Gerald was to enjoy the company of the young and this was a decisive effect of Joanna and Hetty. The young stimulated him. Unthreatened, he showed none of the perverseness that sometimes made tricky his relations with contemporaries. He was fascinated by, and perhaps envied, the increasing sexual freedom – and the casualties of that freedom, particularly the girls, moved him. He observed their love-affairs closely, and to that extent and in his fashion, shared them.

As summer subsided into autumn, grim news arrived for Gamel. T. S. Eliot had turned down her poems. Gerald was certainly not pleased (he at once offered to pay for their publication, an idea Gamel impatiently rejected); but it confirmed his view of her poetry: too melancholy, too monotonous, too self-indulgent. In *Personal Record* he says she now abandoned all literary ambition. This is quite untrue. At her death two trunks full of unfinished fragments, most dating from the next five years, were found; unfinished stories, unfinished poems, sketches of her life in Spain. There is something frantic in such a mass and such a mess. The inability to finish had become chronic. Gradually the feeling of guilt and despair at not fulfilling herself as an artist, which Otto Rank regarded as a primary cause of neurosis, ate into her. She drank more. She told Ronnie Duncan this year that she now lived entirely in the past. Gerald no doubt felt

---

make the theme disintegration.' *Gerald*: 'You're quite right. You've given me something.' He then said, 'The only people who survive here are those who work, especially the artists.' *JGH*: 'Yes, and that's why their collapse is the worst. There is nothing more horrifying than a lapsed artist.' *Gerald*: 'You are speaking very much to the point.' It never occurred to me I might write Gerald's life until it was suggested by my publisher six months before Gerald died. Nevertheless, I can see that this exchange has a ring of Boswell and Johnson.

sorry for her, but what he often expressed to other people was irritation at this disengagement.

A far more severe blow, as far as Gerald was concerned, struck in December. Ralph died suddenly after a heart attack. 'I can't believe it – it doesn't seem possible – Ralph has been the only man I really loved since the early '20s – forty years nearly – and I've always felt he was there – to talk to, to write to – always there. Even during our periods of estrangement I have loved him as much as at other times – I simply didn't want to see him and quarrel with him . . . Now there is a great hole in my life, a great emptiness, and it will never close.'[30]

He was still missing Ralph acutely a year later, when he wrote to Frances on the anniversary of his death. But the need to write a running commentary on his life had long been imperative. He had just written a long letter to Ralph when he was told by Annie of his death. He seldom wrote to Bunny, and to VSP only once or twice a year. Starting with letters to console her in her desolation, he gradually replaced Ralph with Frances. Of these two very close correspondents, in the end the letters to Frances, unhampered by any rivalry, are the more revealing.

'When the tide recedes all the rocks and shoals of the mind stand out . . .'[31] Ralph was in fact four months younger than Gerald but, as with his father's death, he felt himself weakened, subject to some profound unconscious disturbance. With his friend dying, a part of him had died too.

Gerald's depression lasted four months and, as emotional anxieties often did, manifested itself financially. At the start of 1961 he thought he was ruined. On 11 January he said he only had £7 left.[32] He wrote a letter to VSP which was meant to elicit the return of the £1000, but in terms so shrouded and oblique VSP didn't notice.[33] He arranged to write an article on the Caliphate of Cordoba for *Horizon*, a lush US travel magazine, but then, again as usual, he discovered £600 (£5750) in a blocked account and various other small sums. Wealth! He at once decided to go to Greece in April and, meanwhile, installed a flush lavatory and electric shower downstairs behind the dining room, and also glassed in the *mirador*.*

* Gerald was very proud of these improvements. Since the jug lavatory upstairs remained, there was little diminution in that particular *posada* element. The shower was frankly a nightmare. Primitive to a degree, it would trickle tepid water or cold water or, most of the time, heated its small supply to a terrifying heat and then,

Hetty fell in love with an American called Mitch in January, and vanished into Torremolinos. Honor took rooms nearby and ate her meals with them. Now in the grip of 'a violent crush'[34] on Gamel, she refused to see the Osborns, was extremely rude about Hetty and the only time Gamel 'stood out was when Honor suggested hanging the cats'.[34] Gerald gritted his teeth, but said nothing.

They had decided to take John Whitworth to Greece, 'the perfect travelling companion', and the three of them set off on 26 March.

7

From the point of view of his youthful dreams, his circumstances and opportunities, Gerald in fact did relatively little travelling. His dreams of distant travel were, and had been, really the hare dreaming of escape. Once he had escaped, there was no real need to implement them. So these rare journeys are important in his life.

They arrived in Rome – 'the azaleas shimmering with an almost unearthly delicacy in the parks' – and at once hurried into all the galleries, museums and churches. At Brindisi, he and Gamel stood at the end of the Appian Way, moved to be 'within 100 yards of where Virgil died'. On to Corfu and the 'gay austerity of its cities, past olives going back to the Venetians'. Then on again – on and on and on: 'the demon of travel has taken hold of me . . . Gamel as eager as I am to see ALL Greece.' Gerald had been longing to see it for thirty years and, as he did with all new acquaintances and places at first, he fell in love. 'This is a *much* more interesting and beautiful country than Spain . . . alive . . . intelligent . . .'[35]

There was only one drawback. The perfect travelling companion liked to land, preferably from a car, at comfortable hotels and sleep late, to linger, to sit for hours at café tables idly absorbed in the flow of faces, that traveller's television. 'He has had to accept,' Gerald wrote grimly to Frances on 5 April, 'that he will be kept a good deal on the move.' The letter continued, 'Tomorrow six or seven hours by

juddering and hissing, every four minutes loose a few golf-ball-sized drops of what felt like molten lava. Gerald and Gamel scarcely ever used it. The glass windows for the *mirador* were designed and given to them by Bayard Osborn.

bus to Athens, past all the famous names.' Whitworth remembered the trip as a nightmare of being kept on the move.

They had hoped to see Paddy Leigh Fermor and Eddie Gathorne-Hardy* in Athens – but for Leigh Fermor's house they had only a number in Kallipois Street, which was on no street map. Gerald sensibly consulted Plato. He decided it must be Callirhoë's Fountain in the *Phaedrus*. So they went to an unnamed street below the historical site of the fountain – and there it was! Eddie, not Paddy, opened the door, having borrowed the house.[36]

On to the Peloponnese. 'We did every single classical site,' John Whitworth remembered. Not in comfort. Up at 7.30, then hours on buses, squalid hotels (in Athens also a homosexual pick-up),[37] frightful food, and on ships they travelled deck class.

But Gerald's historical eye was as sharp as ever. 'Under history there is always geography and one simply cannot understand Greek history unless one sees that round every city that does not depend on a maritime carrying trade there is a fertile plain and that the size of the plain determines the importance of that city. The Greek polis becomes intelligible when one sees their country.'[38]

After the Peloponnese – the islands. Mikonos, Samos, Chios . . . Gerald saw them all with the eye of an Andalusian – green and tree-filled. By Mytilene John had had enough, and they split, he to Constantinople, they on to Salonika and Thasos. 'Gerald was maddening on Mytilene. He kept trying to prove he was younger than Gamel. Twice in the hot sun, while I took the bus, he more or less challenged her to walk miles back to our horrid hotel. She walked – and each time Gerald collapsed next day into bed.'†

But Gamel's letters back to Alyse are blissful. She hardly drank while they journeyed. Their marriage had been cemented in travel and, when they returned to Churriana on 16 June exhausted after two days on the train from Barcelona, it was temporarily cemented again.

* Uncle of the author.
† Gamel, with her one lung, was indefatigable but slow. A common sight on their walks, Frances remembers, was Gamel 100 yards in the rear, Gerald jumping bushes and rocks to show his youthful strength.

8

Gerald arrived back already consumed with anxiety about the publication of his novel – recently renamed *A Holiday by the Sea*. It came out on 13 July.

The plot of *A Holiday by the Sea* didn't detain Gerald and needn't detain us. What interested Gerald was Tom Fisher – not so much as a character but as a sensibility, and it is the descriptive writing from the point of view of Tom by which he demonstrates this that gives the book much of its distinction. Particularly with the sea, weaving in and out, echoing or counterpointing mood and action, 'Thumping monotonously on the beach like a French laundry woman on her wooden plank', or at vulgar nearby Littlesand, looking 'as cheap and as manufactured as a linoleum tablecloth'. The sea, the weather, the landscape are all part actors, sometimes in extended metaphors of great skill and complexity, at others brief, vivid and humorous: 'On this occasion, as it happened, the sky was brownish-yellow and furry. To leave the house was like walking into a camel's stomach.'

It was this, along with the wit and precision with which Gerald described Tom's seduction of a shop girl and affair with Eleanor (Joanna Carrington), and the subtlety of Tom's 'sterility', that led Francis Wyndham, in the lead review of the *Observer*, to call the book 'really distinguished'.[39] He compared it to L. P. Hartley's *The Boat* and Julia Strachey's *The Man on the Pier* (a book Gerald himself regarded as far too 'slight').[40]

Raymond Mortimer, on the other hand, who devoted one of his long rambling reviews to it in the *Sunday Times*,[41] particularly admired Tom's aphoristic elegance of phrase: 'But all paradises are fools' paradises . . . I dressed Eleanor so well in my love that I forgot it was my clothes that she was wearing.' 'Our civilisation is a proof that people are not improved by getting what they want.'

Yet these favourable elements are rather heavily counterbalanced. None of the other characters, except perhaps Eleanor a little, is developed at all. The book is oddly static and, almost without narrative action, is frequently interrupted by long, formal expositions of Tom's ideas, his listeners woodenly asking Socratic questions like 'So you mean so-and-so, then?' 'Yes,' says Tom, ploughing on. It moves with arthritic clumsiness, characters always 'taking turns' outside to alter location or focus; Tom takes twenty-six such 'turns'. And Tom himself is not superficial exactly, but lives almost entirely on the surface and becomes increasingly tiresome. One finishes the book with a sense of admiration, and relief.

The book had been rewritten and altered many times (Frances felt the first version was better). The student of Gerald can detect Carrington, faint as a ghost, still moving in the novel's depths. Tiny fragments of Gerald's distant love appear in Tom's dreams, the love itself remains in the hints of Tom's incestuous affair with Dora. Hubert/Ralph is made schizophrenic (this is Geraldese for rival in love) and Gerald revenges himself by – a nice irony – Dora refusing to sleep with him and then by making him commit suicide. And there lingers in Tom the feeling of a character crushed and forced back into himself by someone who has rejected his love. Carrington's lesbianism brushes Dora, but is incongruously dumped finally on a Mrs Hambledon-Jones. Set in 1932, the novel's seascape is Warren End, and the book is dedicated to Helen Anrep.

A Holiday by the Sea was reviewed favourably by Burns-Singer in the *Listener* and chosen by both Cyril and Anthony Quentin as their *Sunday Times* 'Book of the Year'. It came out later in America, France and Italy.

This was enough for Gerald. For three months he worked as swiftly as he could, cutting and rewriting the war chapter in *A Life of One's Own*. He was now eager to get at *The Lighthouse* . . . At long last, at the age of sixty-seven, he was becoming the creative artist he'd always felt himself to be.

9

Gerald's letters to Miranda, to whom he wrote every three or four weeks, are always full of village and servant gossip. 'Carmen has a *novio* – the Churriana baker's son. She has had her eye on him since she was 14.'[42] Carmen married him on 23 July.* Gerald and Gamel gave them enough to buy all the bedroom furniture, plus 22,000

---

* Today María's husband, a López, has a baker's shop in Malaga selling the bread that Carmen's husband bakes.

pesetas.[43] The *pueblo* tap-root was also reinforced this year when little Teresita joined the staff. Aged fourteen and brought in to look after Hetty's son Jason, she moved Gerald because, like Juliana, she came from the poorest family in the village. She was also extremely pretty, with the sort of piquant cat-face he liked, and eyes of a startlingly deep blue with thick, short, black lashes. Wages – two hundred and fifty pesetas a month.

Xavier and Miranda came, Orson Welles stayed at La Cónsula and this year, when Gamel went to England, Rosario, inclined to be stout, took the waters at Lanjarón. Left alone, Gerald invited another 'flood'[44] of young people to the house. Freddy Wildman, a rich American newcomer to the coast who was to become a friend, took a house nearby. From Freddy's guests Gerald was 'obliged'[45] to take in a young 'poet' Patrick Hutchinson and his Bardot-like twenty-one-year-old girl Loïs Morgan. While Patrick wrote poetry, Loïs passed the long hot days lolling on Gerald's bed in her continually collapsing bikini while, according to Gerald, they talked entirely about sex. Loïs remembers that his extreme interest did surprise her; but what struck her was his kindness. 'He loved to have young people round him, but it had to be on his terms – in his house where he was in charge. He very seldom came into Torremolinos. He wouldn't come and dance.' (This is hardly surprising. It was the time of the Twist.) They sploshed about naked in the *alberca* and Gerald took and kept a great many photographs.

Autumn came. Gamel returned and so did Rosario. 'No one wears bikinis any more or walks about naked and the voices are dimmed on the patio.'[45] After living in a tent on the island of Formentera and planning to be a cook on a boat to Egypt, Hetty was in London.

'I think what you have written about the war is so good,' Gamel had said in a letter to him while in London. 'I often find myself remembering it.'[46] *A Life of One's Own* was finally despatched to Hamish Hamilton early in December. But, unable to wait, Gerald was already hard at work on his new novel, *The Lighthouse Always Says Yes*. He planned it to sell 20,000 copies, and saw it in the genre of *Tender is the Night*. The hero was to be 'a mixture of Robin Campbell and Robert Kee'.[47]

Christmas that year was once more at La Cónsula, which David Niven and John Mortimer had just left. After Christmas Frances was coming to stay, her first visit since Ralph's death.

10

Frances arrived on 27 December and stayed till 30 January 1962. The long battle through her terrible grief at Ralph's death, cruel penalty for their exceptionally close marriage and movingly described in *Hanging On*, was by no means over.

She noticed the cold, the discomfort, the dust and dirt every-where, the cats 'licking the butter and being sick on the beds'.[48] They all three read after supper. Gerald and Gamel would fall asleep and snore.

Frances' reading was Carrington's letters, which Gerald had also been reading, and his autobiography. She disliked his portrait of Ralph, 'accurate as far as it went', but she sensed an overpowering need to 'discharge' all that he had once felt about his friend. He'd actually done this one night 'in a torrent of words . . . – relieving himself as it were'.[48] She asked him to take out some of Ralph's youthfully facetious letters which, very reluctantly, he did. It was a minor skirmish in what, eventually, became a fierce battle.

Hugh Thomas, whom he'd met before, paid a visit in February ('very easy and pleasant');[49] then in March Honor stayed for a fortnight. She had clearly determined to make it up with Gerald, and succeeded. Despite the vast quantities of drink consumed (Honor always contributed generously) the visit was 'delightful . . . in her boisterous Johnsonian way she is good company'.[50] It also, as always, cheered Gamel.

There were more deaths, as the endless Somme of old age approached. Augustus John had died at Fordingbridge in October the year before. Dorelia told Gerald he'd read *A Holiday by the Sea* twice before he died. John Dent died in January, in the middle of a game of patience. Beryl de Zoëte died in March, freeing Arthur.

Spring came and Gerald, whose delight in his garden never waned, walked round it every morning after breakfast, the air cool and fresh before the sun began to strike home. The nightingales still sang in the bamboos, once more enormous. There were picnics. 'When they bring in the grass for the cows, I'm always moved to see the poppies and marigolds among it.'[51] Moved, because it reminded him of Yegen.

Just before summer, a young man called Peter Ryan, who'd admired *South From Granada*, spent the day at Churriana. It was a visit that was to have incalculable consequences.

Gamel flew to London on 19 June – two days later Hetty arrived from Madrid, her hair jet-black again. She now used Churriana as a springboard for adventures which invariably went wrong. Shortly afterwards, Joanna arrived with her little daughter. Then Loïs arrived back in Torremolinos with *two* poets. Every day young people dropped in 'in trouble over something or other, and I try and settle their lives for them'.⁵² Gerald was stimulated, excessively so (after Miranda and Xavier left he collapsed with exhaustion), but emotionally he seemed surprisingly calm; deceptively as it turned out.

Even though Gerald now abandoned all attempts at writing during the summer (except for letters, which burgeoned at this time), work was still dominant. *The Lighthouse . . .* had faltered in the spring when he read Saul Bellow's *Henderson the Rain King*. 'I may be crazy, but I think it's the greatest novel to have appeared in the last 40 years.'⁵³ (Part of it had been published in *Botteghe Oscure*.) He wanted to burn his own book. In July, he agreed to write a short history of Spain for Macmillan's school series. Then, in the autumn, Ruedo Ibérico, who had also bought the French rights, published *The Spanish Labyrinth* in Spanish.

The Société d'Éditions Ruedo Ibérico was a highly successful emigré anti-Franco publishing house set up by José Martínez at 27 Boulevard Malesherbes in Paris. It had an effective underground distribution system and its banned books sold fairly widely in Spain (by 1969, for example, *The Spanish Labyrinth* had sold 8404 copies in Spain).⁵⁴ During the sixties and seventies it became important for young *avant-garde* intellectuals and those against the régime, and so also among some of the men who would one day rule Spain, to be seen with *El Laberinto español* on their bookshelves. Gerald began to become famous and fashionable in a way which eventually stood him in good stead.*

Then, as the summer drew to a close, *A Life of One's Own* was published.

---

* José Martínez finally returned to Spain. But he was an archetypal exile publisher and lost a lot of money, at last dying of a broken heart. Someone in Spain should write an account of this courageous man and his publishing house.

11

Some time during the Twenties, Gerald had told Ralph that what a writer should aim for, what *he* aimed for, was to be a romantic in ideas and feeling and classical in form and style.[55] He had pinched the remark from Stendhal,[56] but it is something he achieved – first in *South From Granada* and, predominantly, in *A Life of One's Own*. It now seemed to be impossible for Gerald to use a dud word or write a clumsy sentence. His habit of returning to his books over years (ten in this case) no doubt helped, but writing of this distinction is not achieved without a great deal of work. Written in just under three years, *A Life* . . . had nevertheless been much time in the cutting and rewriting.

Although as far as possible sources other than Gerald's books were used at the start of this book, his autobiography was still the chief one; it gave the shape, the feeling and was sufficiently quoted to have given some idea of its quality. Where the portraits in his novels are just laboured or perfunctory, here they are, as in *South From Granada*, delightful – full of humour, sharp, alive, wise, unusual.* Tiz, in particular, is masterly, both moving and very funny. It is, as pure narrative, exciting to read; it is also profound. Dr Theodore Redpath, who read it by chance at the same time as 'Rab' Butler's autobiography, was amazed at the superiority of Gerald's sensibility and attitude.[57] And Gerald is almost totally honest. Where he is evasive, one can easily forgive – why should someone, after all, tell the world every last one of his sexual difficulties? Where he fails to explore, one can understand. Gerald didn't examine his voyeur side because he didn't think he had a particularly unusual voyeur side. He thought everyone was like him in this respect.

But there is one minor element we must look at, since it is revealing about Gerald. When Gerald didn't want to tell the truth, his method was subtle, even cunning. He would state the facts very briefly, but then surround them and overwhelm them in the much

---

* And they got Gerald into trouble. Almost the entire James family wrote in fury about his description of Mrs Chrissie James, in particular about 'the profusion of reddish-purplish veins that spread like a river system over her cheeks'. One suspects, however, that the adjective they really disliked was 'suburban'.

longer, more brilliantly written and enticing version which he wished to impress. Thus with Ralph he briefly indicated his academic career at Westminster, his scholarship to Oxford, and his cleverness, before describing his gusto, his love of food and wine, his pursuit of shopgirls and tarts in Amiens, his boisterous singing, rolling his eyes till the whites showed, of 'coon songs', stamping out the rhythm. What Gerald did not point out was that *everyone* was singing 'coon songs' at this time. (Katherine Mansfield was singing coon songs at Garsington in 1916).[58] Ralph certainly had this side then, but what was interesting about him as a young man was the intuitive, sensitive, highly intelligent side which responded so quickly to Carrington and Lytton Strachey and which made him Gerald's best friend for forty years. The portrait is not in the least an unpleasant one; it is of someone charming and independent and vital – but rather coarse. The impression left is of a stomping, eye-rolling womaniser, a 'white nigger' singing coon songs. Not, one will later feel, the right man for Carrington.

None the less, as far as the book is concerned, this remains a minor element. VSP told him that it was the best book he had written,[59] but despite its qualities it does not have the originality of *South From Granada*. It was recognised immediately. VSP himself, in the course of a long review in the *New Statesman*, said this 'superb autobiography . . . has flashes of the best war writing I have ever read'. Raymond Mortimer in the *Sunday Times* thought he had never read 'a more vivid account of what it was like to be young before the First World War'. Peter Fleming in the *Listener* considered it must be among the 'most truthful ever written by a man about his early life'. In fact, all the major papers praised it at length, and more or less unreservedly, except for Harold Nicolson in the *Observer*. Bunny (to whom the book was dedicated) and Cyril wrote to him praising it, and Jamie Hamilton told him Graham Greene admired it.[60]

Like all Gerald's books, except what he now disparagingly referred to as his 'textbooks', it didn't sell very well, though it more than made the advance.* But he took pleasure in thinking of Chatto

---

* As the period and pressures he wrote about became steadily more remote, so an historical interest is added to the book's value as literature. It should be reprinted, as Michael Holroyd saw and tried to bring about. It was published very recently in Spain, in an edition slightly marred by a misleading introduction and cover (*Una Vida Propia*, Ediciones Destino 1989).

and Windus reading the reviews, and no doubt it braced him for the extremely unpleasant seismic shocks which struck in the autumn.

12

The epicentre of the October earthquake was, unsurprisingly, Hetty.

In fact, a preliminary quiver had been felt before, but at another point. Gerald's anxiety over money was complicated by a further internal struggle between his considerable generosity, the desire to give that came from his mother, and a meanness, a desire to withhold that came from his father. It was this side that he quite often showed Miranda. In fact, it would be too much to call his attitude mean. If she asked for help, which she sometimes did, especially later on, he always responded. But he did so grudgingly. He gave her a small allowance, but she was to pay it all back if she came into his stepmother Mabel's money – which he'd made over to her before he died. And his letters to Miranda frequently include accounts of his poverty in order to make her feel guilty – like the letter he sent her in 1961 saying he only had £7 left in the bank.[32]

This situation was itself complicated by Miranda's feelings towards Hetty. Superficially they got on well, but Miranda was understandably also jealous. In July, Gerald had written and told her he planned to leave Hetty £500, well over £4000 at 1990 prices. Miranda, at once furious, wrote and said that if he did, she would renege on the arrangement whereby she had to pay back Gerald's allowance. Gerald now became angry with Miranda – 'who is very well off already'* – but both refused to budge.

The impasse was resolved in October, though not in a way Gerald would have chosen. It should perhaps be said that a major cause of Hetty separating from her lovers was the fact that she was, in effect, a feminist before her time. Hetty's American lover Mitch had proved

---

* Gerald always expected Miranda and Xavier to contribute towards their holidays. By the end of the sixties they were contributing 2000 pesetas a day, which Xavier considered ample and Gerald not enough. Gerald had an exaggerated idea of what Xavier earned as a Paris GP, which was all they had to live on. It was sufficient, but not wealth. In the way that small farmers depend on the occasional bumper harvest to carry them through the more frequent lean years, Xavier relied on 'flu epidemics.

unusually resilient. When he realised that Mitch had become a fixture, though partly relieved, Gerald, though he pretended not to be, was also jealous and saw little of her. But by July, Mitch had gone. It was now Hetty who became difficult. 'She loses her sunny disposition and becomes rather like an injured Madame de Staël, though without the brains that made that woman perhaps even more wearing.'[61]

But by September Gerald and Gamel and Hetty were all living peacefully together again. 'Gamel seems really to like her.'[62] Gerald worked at *The Lighthouse* . . . and read Greek literature. A minor irritation was Macmillan's deciding against his doing their history. According to Gerald, *The Face of Spain* had convinced them he could only write for adults[63] – a ludicrous conclusion, if true. Rosario went to Lanjarón and Hetty, who was a good cook, did the cooking.

Then in mid-October she was struck by an allergy. She swelled up like a balloon until her eyes closed. Her temperature rose to 104° and, anxiously solicitous, Gerald spent the night on the floor of her room. The next day she was covered in spots: chickenpox. Three days later, by a coincidence on the very same day that the codicil leaving her £500 arrived in the post, Hetty bounced up, still a mass of spots and, to Gerald's irritation, went up to Mijas for a party.

She returned the following afternoon having picked up a 'monstrous looking Canadian beat called Al – a giant who suffers from curvature of the spine and looks like a question mark – they call him "The Vulture"'.[62] They both vanished into Hetty's room. As evening turned to night, Gerald's heart sank. The one thing he refused to tolerate was Hetty making love in the house. Suddenly – a brainwave. He turned off all the electricity in the house and took Gamel out for a walk. They walked – some of the things Gamel put up with! – till 11.30. Then Gerald took his torch and crept up to Hetty's room. He opened the door, shone the torch, and there was the most frightful sight: Hetty in the convulsive grip of the huge misshapen creature being ravished before his eyes and apparently enjoying it. Gerald slammed the door and shouted hoarsely, shaking violently with fury, disgust and distress, that they must leave the house at once, Hetty never to return. Ten minutes later he 'heard them slink out'.[62] Gerald then went and got the horrible bed – which despite his chaste and rare occupancy he secretly regarded as 'their' bed – and hurled it with Hetty's clothes into the storeroom. To his absolute astonishment – and it seems to have been quite genuine – he found that Gamel greeted the news that Hetty was never going to return with 'huge relief'.[62]

Of course he forgave Hetty, and of course she returned. But it marked a turning point. Hetty was to play a part in their lives until the end of 1964. But it was a diminishing part. Gerald did not see her properly for eight months, and then only briefly. When he saw her again at the end of 1963, for the first time almost he was bored.

TWENTY-EIGHT

Novels and the Last Years with Gamel

'Vicky O'Rourke's parties. The boredom and misery of the well-to-do is more poignant than that of the poor because it is a sign of the poverty of their natures and so is incurable. The poor at least know what they want.'

Thoughts in a Dry Season

1

T he broad pattern of Gerald and Gamel's life continued, with endless variations, for the next four and a half years.* The diastole of each summer, with Gerald like all Andalusians each year freshly astonished at the final months of tremendous heat, followed by the cooling systole of autumn.

They continued to communicate via the cats – Gris Gris wakes Gamel 'shrieking at the window'¹ when Gerald is in England; they both worry because Baby Pussy is wounded in a fight (Baby Pussy is a yard long). La Cónsula supplied celebrities and from time to time,

---

* However, although his capital was still by far the largest source of Gerald's income, the financial pattern altered significantly in one respect. In 1962 Derek Patmore introduced him to what Gerald regarded, not without reason, as a goldmine – the Harry Ransom Humanities Research Center at the University of Texas at Austin. Selling through Hamill and Barker in Chicago and Bertram Rota in London, he made $13,574 (£42,000 at 1990 prices) from 1962 till the end of 1968. (He sold everything they would take – his Carrington correspondence, journals, manuscripts, notebooks, poems – and had fantasies about selling his socks and his toenails.) His total income from all sources for these years (1963–1968) was very roughly £27,000 p.a. at 1990 prices. It should be remembered that Spanish inflation was now a factor. 1000 pesetas in 1955 was worth 378 ptas in 1970. (See Texas archives, CUP archives, Hamish Hamilton archives, *Historia Económica de España en el Siglo XX* by Ramón Tamames, Alianza 1986.)

as when Anthony Powell and Violet came, making Gerald realise how he missed good conversation.[2] The slow melting of his library began – Bill Davis and Cyril buying his modern first editions.

As Hetty receded, Gerald's life became slightly less hectic, though the new novel of course required occasional bouts of Torremolinos research. Older rhythms came back. Gerald read and reread intensely all his life, but now his reading once again enters his letters. At the start of 1963, for instance, he interrupted his Greek reading and turned to Henry James and Leon Edel. James was not a favourite novelist but 'I admire greatly his power of expanding a simple observation into something richer and fuller. His intellectual range is prodigious – greater than any novelist except Proust . . .'[3] By the autumn he was reading Pope, planning to read Dryden and then back through the Jacobeans to Shakespeare, 'Unless I take a deep breath and embark on Richardson's *Clarissa*.'[4]

As a result Gamel was, for a while, much nicer to him. Gerald put up with her contradicting and sniping – out of pity, because of Hetty, out of guilt – but he minded. Now, he told Frances in April, she was being sweet to him 'and that's all I ask for'.[5]

In fact, it would be possible to follow every shake of the kaleidoscope. Not only had Frances completely replaced Ralph, receiving a regular fortnightly or three weekly bulletin but, as well as VSP and Bunny, Gerald had young women to write to. Joanna, Hetty, Suna Portman, Loïs Morgan, Georgia Tennant and others received light, amusing, gossipy letters and Gerald loved in return to hear confidences about their lives.*

It would be possible to follow each multi-coloured fragment, and it would not be boring – on the contrary; but, as once with Carrington, it would take many pages. None the less, each year there are things of significance to be noted.

---

* And perhaps that was all, or at least a very large part, of what he ever wanted. There was never any real likelihood that Joanna or Hetty would have slept with him. In the ten years from 1955 several girls, according to Gerald, offered to do so. It was probably true – morals were extremely easy among some of them. However, like the tarts of Regent Street before them, probably what they liked about Gerald, among much else, was that they felt safe with him and knew he would refuse. This, after reporting the offers excitedly to Ralph (and later Frances), he invariably did, always pleading that Gamel would mind.

2

Honor now came regularly every year and stayed longer – for two months early in 1963. Gerald and she got on well on the whole, and if she irritated him (he called her 'The Policewoman' to Frances) he remembered how she cheered Gamel and remained fairly calm. She tried to get Gamel to go on a tour of Catalonia with her this year, but Gamel (to Gerald's pleasure, one senses) refused.[6]

During March Gerald was having difficulty with *The Light-house* . . . . Gamel's analysis, made in a letter to Alyse at the time, is shrewd: 'I was depressed about his novel because he seemed to be writing it just because he felt he *should* write a novel, he owed it to himself to write one – there was no wind in the sails.'[7]

Hope, now aged eighty, came for four days in May, leaving his heavy luggage at Malaga station and bringing only a small valise and a tiny bag with 'books for the train'. He was white-haired, doddery and his memory had gone. Nevertheless, Gerald watched him like a hawk. His old mentor was too wily for him. He was planning a tour over the whole of middle and north Spain – 'both mad and heroic',[6] Gerald observed; but as the train thumped out of the station his face, looking completely disoriented, was suddenly thrust through the window. 'Where am I going?' he shouted. 'Cordoba,' Gerald shouted back, suddenly moved as his oldest friend slowly vanished. However, when he got back to Churriana he found the 'books for the train' in a heap and two valuable French first editions missing.[6]

They never saw Hope again. He died in 1970, aged eighty-seven. He came into the last of the tiny legacies which had kept him going and was able to rent another cottage in Aldbourne. He had had an enormous influence on Gerald's life and character and, not least, his financial circumstances, so great indeed that in his published autobiographies Gerald, perhaps to an extent unconsciously, diminished it. But he fully repaid his debt by endless and generous support and finally giving him somewhere to live. This Hope did not relinquish. To the considerable irritation of the new owners, he kept on the Bell Court annexe as his 'library'.

In September, just as she was slowly beginning to recover from Ralph's death, a second terrible blow struck Frances. Burgo, her only child, who had just married and had a baby with Bunny's daughter Henrietta, died suddenly from an obscure and rare heart condition. Gerald sent what comfort he could.

The year ended calmly, despite Hetty's coming to collect her 'things' – no light task. She also took Jason, who must have now regarded Churriana as his home. Gamel had rewritten *Patterns in the Sand* over the year, a novel first finished in 1944. Honor gave it (in vain) to her agent. But Gamel now decided to write a book about her life in Spain. Gerald gave up smoking cigarettes and allowed himself three cheroots a day. He wrote *The Lighthouse* . . . in the morning and, having limbered up on Donne and other seventeenth-century poets, plunged into Shakespeare.

3

1964 was Gerald's seventieth year, and his slightly precarious health – extremely unusual – may have reflected some buried anxiety. It started with leg ulcers, phlebitis. Gamel nursed him – 'To feel one is loved by her one has to be ill,' he wrote to Frances.[8]

The doctor in Malaga prescribed adrenalin for two months. Gerald, who already had an overabundance of adrenalin, began to smoke dozens of his cheroots and shot up the mountains every day. He also went to a nightclub in Torremolinos – 'Not for pleasure but to gather impressions for my novel.'[9] Of course.

But while Gerald sizzled with adrenalin, Gamel declined again. She gave up her book on Spain and abandoned some new attempts at science-fiction. It was during this year she began to take what Gerald described as 'drams' – big swigs of neat brandy or gin to muffle her despair, either when she got up or in her room at night; later, throughout the day. Gamel, as one would expect, was extremely secretive about her drinking, though it was sometimes noticeable after the wine at meals. Gerald talked about it 'discreetly' to practically everyone.

Two old friendships, languishing slightly in the absence of sufficiently frequent transfusions of correspondence, were revived this year – perhaps another effect of being seventy. Bunny came to stay for a month at the beginning of 1964 and VSP and Dorothy at the end. Gerald was rather jealous of Bunny still making love at seventy-two, but consoled himself that it made his view of women in his books so rosy as to be almost ridiculous. What he enjoyed particularly with all of them was the talk.

On 4 June, on an impulse – and the episode shows how Hetty brought colour and dash into his life – he flew to Tangier for three days. Hetty was having an exhibition. She was sharing a house in the *kasbah* and, in describing its hangings, bronze flowers and her hippie friends, Gerald still noted that 'two doors away is the house Pepys lived in when directing the evacuation and the fig tree under which he sat is still to be seen'.[10]

The exhibition was a success. Julian Jebb was there with Menchu Escobar.* Gerald met William Burroughs – 'correct and erect and formal in his manner' – and Alec Waugh, bought a picture for £30 'to start her off with a red label'[10], and flew home with little Jason, who had begged to come back.

Hetty stayed calmly at Churriana during July while Gamel was away and then left with Jason for Mexico. 'I don't suppose she will be back in Europe for years,'[11] said Gerald, with a note of sadness. She was, but neither Gerald nor Gamel ever saw her again. However, Gerald and Hetty wrote to each other, so news filtered back, rather as it had with Hope. In 1968 she needed money in Oklahoma; in 1970 she was living in a commune in a log cabin on a small island off British Columbia; in early 1971 she was *en route* for India.[12] Hetty, though naturally motivated to some extent by self-interest, had genuinely loved Gerald and Gamel, and her last postcard arrived for Gerald two days after he died. There is a noticeable increase in Gerald's grumbling about Gamel after Hetty had gone – of her 'passenger' attitude to their life, her failure to condense 'into a real positive person'.†[13]

---

* One of the most attractive, flamboyant and successful social figures on the coast. At first poor, she eventually made enormous sums of money. Gerald admired the way that, as a Spaniard, she defied convention and lived exactly the life she wanted.

† When I talked to Hetty in 1989 she was just back from Nepal. Her second husband had died in tragic circumstances but their son, while still a toddler, had been revealed as a Chosen One. The little boy, according to Hetty, had successfully picked the right stone, the correct tin mug and by these and similar signs shown he was destined to be the next Lama of the monastery where Hetty had found refuge. Unfortunately the divine protection this afforded him did not extend to his mother, and Hetty had endless trouble over residence permits.

During the month with Hetty, just before flying to London, Gerald corrected the Spanish translation of *South From Granada*, although the book did not come out until 1974. He took a great deal of trouble with his translations and this time made so many corrections to the Spanish that the whole thing had to be retyped.[14]

The letter to Gamel telling her this all at once veers from its easy track of gossip and information. It was just after a festival. 'I walked into Torremolinos [this evening] and on to La Carihuela to see the Procession of the Virgen del Mar. It was lovely – the beach crowded with Spaniards, no foreigners at all. She was a small poor virgin and as it was rough they did not take her out in a boat, but just waded a few yards into the sea. It was dusk, rockets and candles and the usual moment of emotion when she reached the water.'[14]

And suddenly one has a sharp image of the tall, seventy-year-old man in the late evening light, bald, hair long at the back (he hadn't been able to get it cut) rising as always above the crowd of Spaniards round him on the beach, not feeling he was a foreigner, watching and being moved.

In London Gerald saw Julian Jebb again. 'Seeing Julian is like drinking a bottle of champagne,' he told Frances. 'There is something about him which reminds me of Frankie Birrell.'[15]

He also saw Helen Anrep and Arthur Waley. Helen was in bed, in her beautiful, run-down, dirty house outside Ipswich, amidst fields of blazing stubble. Her mind wandered slightly but she talked animatedly about the past while Gerald, as he used to do forty years before, sat on her bed. It was now that she told him she had been a little in love with him at Warren End. Gerald told Frances that this had occurred to him at the time, but that he hadn't let himself believe it.[16]

Arthur had been released from Beryl when she died in 1962 (at the perfectly human age, John Morris would have been relieved to learn, of eighty-two). He directed Gerald to the house of his new companion in Highgate. Gerald was slightly startled to meet a New Zealander, Alison Grant Robinson: 'An uncouth shapeless woman in her early sixties with large, flopping breasts which disdained a bra. Her grey hair was piled on top of her head . . . One could imagine her thirty years before leading the revels in a suburban nudist camp.'[17]

Gerald's leg continued to give trouble. During the summer the doctor decided he hadn't got phlebitis but dermatitis caused by smoking. Gerald, rather unfairly, blamed Joanna. 'Smoking has taken the place of VD in modern life.'[18] Then, in July, he had some obscure disease of spots covering his hands, making writing difficult. Just before VSP came in October, Gerald warned him that he had now developed 'ernypelis. It may be some time before I can wear a shoe and it is annoying to have a complaint I can't spell'.*[19]

Sometime during 1964 the nightingales fled the garden. The roar of motorbike exhausts now drowned the patter of goat feet in Churriana. The noise was too much.

4

Gerald's Spain seemed to be vanishing. Butane-gas heaters arrived in 1965. He bought one for the *mirador*. But ovens, heat . . . 'Without bugs, fried food at every meal and icy houses Spain will be no longer Spain.'[20]

They lived very quietly, seeing only John Whitworth and Freddy Wildman, who had taken Buena Vista on a long let. The rich son of a richer New York wine merchant, Freddy was generous, hospitable, voluble and had only one drawback – arguing after too much drink, of which he consumed a good deal. Gerald compared him then to a machine-gun.[21] He was also conversationally competitive and, not really Gerald's match, used to arm himself with information from *Time* and then bring the topics up. But he had written an interesting book on the Armada, and later wrote a successful guide to wine. Over the years, Gerald grew very fond of him.

His and Gamel's slight irritation with John Whitworth had long since vanished. Gamel loved him (María and Carmen can remember hearing her laughter whenever he called), and Gerald always enjoyed seeing him. He had inherited some money, which he had considerably increased by shrewd investment, and bought a convertible Volkswagen. In April, just after Gerald's seventy-first birthday, they all three went on a tour from Ronda to Cadiz – the latter to see the temple of Hercules on a tiny island off the marshes. 'It was there that Julius Caesar saw a portrait of Alexander the Great and vowed to

---

* Spelt 'erysipelas' – inflammation and swelling of skin, usually in the elderly, and dangerous before penicillin. It is likely Gerald's mysterious spots were this as well.

imitate him – with results we all know.'²² As a consequence of this they planned an immense trip for the following year: to Persia via West Africa and then up through Italy to England. '10,000 miles at our age!'²³

Age was being dealt with by Gerication, a vitamin and hormone mixture designed for this purpose. It seems to have been a miraculous preparation. Gerald found he had so much energy he could write both mornings and evenings, take his usual walk and then read Virgil in Latin before going to bed. As a result, he told Frances, *The Lighthouse* . . . went 'bounding ahead with little snail bounds . . . To work is, I think, the greatest happiness open to man – on which elevating thought I stop.'²⁴

By 2 July the novel was finished. He revised it, Gamel typed it and in October it was sent to Hamish Hamilton. Gerald at once began to plan another novel – a comedy of the interior life, marriage and old and middle age.

Helen Anrep died in March. They had lost touch, but thinking about her and reading Carrington's letters to him in preparation for the second volume of his autobiography and before selling them to Texas, revived the past. He reworked *Poor Robinson*, the satirical novella about his great love affair that he had written in 1925. (It reminded Gerald of a Tintin cartoon – an odd comparison, presumably deriving from his grandchildren's reading.)

At the end of the year, when so much rain fell that matches wouldn't light and Christmas – 'that horrid and very expensive season'²⁵ – loomed up, Gerication induced another great surge in Gerald's veins and on 30 December he began his new novel. It was now set in Tunisia, the better to utilise their forthcoming trip.

5

Gerald had been dreaming of going to Persia ever since Hope had written to him from there in 1913. John, he and Gamel set off in John's Volkswagen on 1 March 1966. Helilla, Tlemcen, then on to Algiers – Tunis, Kairouan, Gafsa, Tozeur, Tripoli, Djerba, Sfax . . . but the letters are not nearly as enthusiastic as usual. There was some danger. The French had only just pulled out of Algeria and no one would insure them. But there were two other reasons. Gerald, once so fearless, rejoicing in discomfort, was now at seventy-two an extremely fussy and anxious traveller. He was in a continual state of irritation over John's 'extraordinary mismanagement',[26] which, to his terrified eyes, seemed to be constantly threatening them with nights in the fields. He admitted that he insisted on comfortable hotels far more than Gamel did. He panicked about money – 'Quite unnecessarily,' John Whitworth said, remembering Gerald's fussing with a sigh. 'I'd filled a sock with pound notes.' It was too cold for interesting botany.

Of course they saw all the classical sites. And of course Gerald explained and illuminated them with his usual fascination, and observed with his usual speculative sharpness. The ruined towns were far too big for the tiny areas of cultivatable ground around them. 'The Roman Empire would not have fallen to the Barbarians if it had been able to make machine-guns, but it would have crumbled from inside because it had not been taught by Marx that the basis of every civilisation is production.'[27]

But by 8 April, after Sfax, they were sick of it. All idea of Persia was abandoned. They drove back to Tunis and on 13 April sailed for Palermo.

The drive up through Italy was far more enjoyable, though Gerald was often saddened by the changes even since he and Gamel were there fifteen years before. At Agrigento, 'One stares at the theatre where Aeschylus produced his own plays and at the tomb of Archimedes and sees great blocks of flats towering up all round.'[28]

But what becomes increasingly clear in his letters (and what John Whitworth remembers) is Gerald's impatience to get north. The reason for this, and probably the real reason he wanted to leave Africa so early, was that *The Lighthouse Always Says Yes* had come out in April.

Gerald was absolutely confident it would be a success. He also expected it would make a lot of money. He was not alone. Jamie Hamilton had been thrilled by it and thought the same. It was, he said, *far* better than *A Holiday by the Sea*. His readers all agreed. Their reports were so good Hamilton sent them to Gerald.[29] Gerald, not unnaturally, was in a fever to read the reviews.

They managed to buy the Sunday papers when they reached Montreux around 11 May. Montagu Haltrecht in the *Sunday Times* of 8 May was brutal and short: 'Thumbs down, but down for *The Lighthouse Always Says Yes*. Phrases abound like "a woman of amorous proclivities" . . . Pushing through them one discovers a story about a played-out

novelist . . . [whose] feebleness seems to warrant his self-obsession . . .
The author disposes of him at last in a car accident when the book is
long enough.' John Coleman in the *Observer* of the same date was only
slightly better, choosing to bury the book – 'a curate's egg' – under a
sprinkling of faint praise and sad critical puzzlement.

John Whitworth remembers Gerald's silence in the back of the car
as they drove up through France, and Gamel's gentleness with him.

6

The Lighthouse Always Says Yes seems almost to presage itself in the
character of its hero, Dick Somers, a novelist who lives in Calahonda
(Torremolinos) and is sick of writing novels that are successful in
America but don't 'tap deeper levels in himself'. *The Lighthouse Always
Says Yes* . . . is the story of his semi-disintegration and final destruc-
tion set in the more general self-destruction of the coast.

It is a curious book to read carefully because, page by page, there
are often good things. In the endless trivial affairs, the ghastly parties,
the drink, the writing is never less than excellent and sometimes
reaches heights; as when he contrasts the coast life with the surrounding Sierra which 'with its bleached rock, green oak branches and deep
blue sky . . . conveyed only remoteness and austerity'. Or when he
describes the garden at Churriana, or again, in a long virtuoso passage
at the end, a flamenco performance in Seville. A *roman à clef*, it has
one or two characters who are well caught. In Adrian Porson he gets
Cyril's tone exactly. Someone says he finds a character Jim's jealousy
amusing. '"You say that," replied Adrian, "because you can't ever
imagine Minnie being unfaithful to you. Otherwise you'd see that
other people's jealousy is painful to look at because it reminds one of
one's own. And how can Jim help being jealous? He's married to a
lovely girl and he feels all the time that he's nothing. Nothing, that
is, but a big banking account."' And at the end of the book the reader
sees that Gerald has, to some extent, captured the futility, the waste
of these expatriate lives – and also their sadness.

Nevertheless, the book is undeniably a failure. One feels, after a
while, an immense fatigue reading it. And one reason is precisely that
roman à clef. Real people are used not just as jumping-off points; they
are painstakingly transferred. Bill and Annie Davis, Freddy Wild-

man, Hetty, the Osborns, Charles Sinnickson, John Whitworth –
everyone is here *en clair*. As a result, Gerald had to take care not to
offend, when what was required was acid. Virtually the only invented
character is Dick Somers. Gerald seemed incapable of creating an
attractive hero or even a sympathetic one. To the extent, usually
large, that the hero is the author, his modesty no doubt inhibited him
here. Somers – Robert Kee and Robin Campbell long forgotten – is
weak and tiresome. Then there are many incidental embarrassments.
It is technically clumsy: he can't get people in or out of rooms (though
Kingsley Amis says this is one of the hardest things to do); the
dialogue which (like all Gerald's dialogue, probably owing to that
deficiency of ear which stopped him enjoying music) is stilted
becomes in the hippie scenes excruciating. One sees why his contemporaries winced at the height of the Hetty period. But the chief defect
is a failure of narrative. Or not narrative quite, though this is very
limp, but a lack of that current, that tension between events, which
can be felt even in books which are not particularly good when they
have come alive, when the author is engaged.

Despite the qualities of *A Holiday by the Sea*, Gerald's novels must
all be considered failures. Yet he spent far more time struggling to
write them, and to write poetry, than on anything else. It is necessary
therefore – and it may be illuminating – very briefly to speculate why
he could not manage these forms.

The simple view would be that it was just a lack of creative
imagination. One can admire the stubbornness, even integrity, with
which he persisted ('owing' it to himself, as Gamel observed); and
also regret the histories, the studies of Spain, of place, of literature
and of himself which he did so much better. But the simple view, as
often, may be too simple.

As we have seen, although he never wrote even passable poetry,
he had the sensibility, the intuitive insights, the language of a poet;
he was a poet in the way Virginia Woolf and Genet are poets. Then,
take narrative. This, as a glance at airport bookstores shows, is not
the most difficult of the novelist's skills; nor is it the most important
element in novels or even necessary. But if you write novels, as
Gerald did, which require and depend on narrative and you fail, then
clearly it is a serious defect. His picaresque novels failed for an
analogous reason, a lack of anything sufficiently compelling to carry

one on. Yet even this failure is not simple. Given a theme – his own life or someone else's, a history, even an extended anecdote like Lytton Strachey's arrival at Yegen – it is exactly the narrative drive and skill one notices.

The portrayal of characters is another weakness in the novels. But the portraits in all his other writing, including his letters, are one of the chief delights: vivid, penetrating, moving, humorous, alive (and in *South From Granada* sometimes invented). Gerald had, that is, several of the most important literary skills which one would expect to be utilisable in novels.

Gerald himself put forward various explanations. For *The Lighthouse* . . . he thought the reason was that the dramas of the coast were essentially trivial. 'Nothing serious or deeply felt can happen. When people die their friends hardly notice it . . . If one girl refuses, there will always be another . . . So the book floated away, the author like the characters undermined by the climate.'[30]

But he probably came nearer the mark with his eventual conclusion, which was that he could not write novels because he could not use himself or his deep feelings in his writing. He also said once that he could 'only create solitary figures and cannot imagine anyone having real relations with anyone else'. Is this an echo from the interior castle again? That, having withdrawn his emotions, he was reluctant to face them or explore them by releasing them in fiction? If this is so, it is something he shares with numerous English writers of similar background. Evelyn Waugh and Anthony Powell, to instance two out of dozens of possible examples, are also deficient in this way. But emotional depths are not their concern. And when the emotions retreat, it seems as if the intellect, the fantasy and the sense of humour are liberated. These English writers often gain in brilliance what they lose in profundity.

But Gerald *could* write about his deepest feelings. In *A Life of One's Own*, *Personal Record* and *South From Granada* he wrote about sex, his impotence (at a remove), his marriage, his love for his mother and hatred of his father, his agony at school. And here perhaps is the clue. He could write about them when they were real but not use them as a basis for fiction.

The second major result of his childhood and youth, the one he analyses, was the need to escape from the conventionality, the hypocrisy, the wealth, the snobbery and boredom into a life that was more real – one of poverty, intensity, pain and poetry. In this context, the life his parents lived was the fiction. To use his own deep experiences for fiction, to make them less 'real', therefore went against an absolutely fundamental structure in his character. And this explains why his creative current switched off the moment he tried to write novels. And this deep, unconscious desire to stay as close as possible to reality was rendered complicated by something else. Poetry, over the last hundred years, has on the whole ceased to be a vehicle for narrative fiction. As a record of moments of intensity and enhanced reality it was a legitimate aim for Gerald's creative impulse. Paradoxically, however, it was succeeded by novels, which were not. Gerald's writing life was bedevilled by this contradiction for forty-five years.

Not after *The Lighthouse* . . . . He gave up his 'comedy of the interior life' on the spot and never attempted fiction again. The struggle to come to terms with this was painful and his letter to VSP, when he felt he had done so in July, is a courageous one. 'Morally speaking,' it ends, 'this shock of complete failure has been good for me and has cleared away a lot of nonsense.'[30] He says the thought of writing his life disgusts him, but in fact six days later he began *Personal Record*.

But before this, and before returning to Spain, Gerald spent a gloomy week in London. Jamie Hamilton was almost as disappointed as he was at the novel's reception – and in fact never accepted another book from him.

Gerald also saw Arthur Waley for the last time – a visit which saddened, but also fascinated and slightly disconcerted him. Waley's spine had suddenly snapped and it was found he had advanced cancer, from which he was now rapidly dying. He was in some pain but, with morphia, lucid. Gerald now learnt from Alison that he was not impotent after all. She had seduced him in 1929 on a visit from New Zealand, when he was forty and still a virgin. She had returned to England in 1942 and been his secret mistress ever since. Just after Gerald left, he told Bunny, Waley was carried into the Registrar's office in a sling and married her. He died a few weeks later 'radiantly happy' because he was in love. 'Love – love – what a moment to feel it almost for the first time!'[31]

7

One of the chance survivors from Gerald's many archival bonfires (he had already had one in 1964 and another in 1966) is a Churriana wage-book. Even at a cursory glance one is struck by Teresita's rapid rise up the salary scales in Gerald's little kingdom. In 1960 she is paid 250 pesetas a month, by 1963 she gets a quarter of Rosario and Antonio's salary, by 1966 – half, or 1000 pesetas. In 1964 Rosario and Antonio get 900 pesetas for Christmas; Teresita gets 1300.[32] Thus does the pasha reveal his heart.

He told Frances how fond he was of Teresita in the first of two marvellous letters, the equal of anything in *South From Granada*, in which he describes the machinations about to take place. 'Spanish village girls are like cats,' he ends, 'and will sit on one's lap and purr if one offers them a saucer of milk.'*[33]

The problem, as he found when he returned to Spain, was love. Teresita, now a diminutive beauty of eighteen, was in love with an airforce recruit from Pamplona. The obstacle to their marriage was Teresita's poverty-stricken background. But the Machiavelli of Yegen had not lost his touch. He offered to let the wedding take place from his house and hold the reception, which he would also pay for, there; he bought Teresita a wedding dress and then, the better to impress the young man and his parents, invited them all to stay with him for the celebrations. Finally, he gave Teresita a dowry of 14,000 pesetas. This was enough to swing the day; none the less, the wedding was not without drama. It was very hot and Rosario was evidently seething. Teresita was 'a regular Galdós character'[33]: curious, obsti-

---

* It is likely that this is a typically oblique Geraldian way of letting out the literal truth. Two years before he died, when my wife and I were helping to look after him, he suddenly said one evening, 'Gamel once found me making love to one of the servants.' I said, 'What did you do?' Gerald simply turned down his mouth in the hapless woe-is-me expression of the naughty boy caught out. But he often used the expression 'to make love', as I described earlier, in the Edwardian sense of overt flirtation. If Gamel did once find him with Teresita perched on his knee (the letter to Frances also refers to *momentos locos* – mad moments), then it would explain a certain irritability she evinced towards the girl. Gamel didn't, for instance, care a hoot if Rosario or Gerald or María did the flowers, but if Teresita did them she would angrily rearrange all the vases.

nate, competitive with other girls, hard and proud, but very honest and with great charm and gaiety. She also, like all her family, had a violent temper. The crisis came when Rosario accused Teresita's brother of stealing a rubber duck. Teresita then exploded and called Rosario a *guarra* (a sow) and 'goodness knows what else. Words only to be forgiven, said Rosario, upon her deathbed, so she and her family had not spoken to Teresita since, refused to attend the wedding and sat about ostentatiously in their working clothes.'³³ After the service Teresita kissed Gerald warmly in front of the whole village.

The degree to which his successful campaign on behalf of little Teresita had stimulated Gerald was strikingly demonstrated two days later. A friend of Hetty's, Susan Bell, came to supper and stayed the night in order temporarily to escape her husband and three young children. About thirty-four, she was very attractive and kept on looking at Gerald. On an impulse, when they all went to bed, he walked along to her room. She was expecting him. She had 'one of those large liquid mouths that are so exciting. So we heaved and rolled about on the bed for a couple of hours till I could stand no more . . .' The next morning Freddy drove them to Torremolinos and Gerald 'watched her skipping down the road like a roe deer delighted to explore the town by herself . . . [I will] certainly never see her again – it has been my last fuck.'³⁴

Although Gerald sent an identical account to Miranda,³⁵ one has to ask: did this happen? After considerable detective work, it proved possible to trace Susan Bell. Two letters to her went unanswered, then came a brief but emphatic, perhaps over-emphatic, reply: '. . . the incident you referred to never happened. I wish to underline, never happened.'³⁶ Gerald, as we know, frequently, indeed usually, exaggerated things of this sort; he very seldom invents on the basis of nothing.* Joanna Carrington remembers receiving a letter at this time in which Gerald said Susan Bell allowed him to kiss her and lie in bed naked with her.³⁷

By the end of the year Gerald was considerably run down. Much as he admired Bellow, he couldn't finish *Herzog*. 'Reading a novel is an experiment in being someone else, and after one is sixty, one draws in.'³⁸ He developed a huge carbuncle on his back, which got

* The only time I can think of was in 1926 when he pretended to Carrington that he'd seduced a widow in Toulon. He was inspired by *The Milesian Tales* (see p. 222).

steadily worse. Gerald refused to see anyone but the village GP. His friends became worried and Janetta, hearing about it, drove over. She found him with a high fever and in great pain and at once insisted on driving him into Malaga. The carbuncle was lanced, Gerald was given antibiotics and slowly began to recover. But it is another demonstration of that exaggerated respect for even humble medical authority combined with masochism which characterised his behaviour in these situations.

8

In February 1967 Gerald wrote to Blair saying how worried he was over Gamel's drinking. As well as most of the wine at meals she now secretly drank four bottles of gin and brandy a week.*[39] Honor, who arrived to stay at the end of January, told Mark Culme-Seymour that they kept finding little glasses of neat spirit all over the house.[40]

Honor really believed that all Gamel's troubles, including her drinking, stemmed from Gerald's treatment of her. She had developed a subtle way of baiting him, hiding her barbs thinly under humour – 'Just look at the man,' she'd say to Gamel, 'he imagines he understands what we women think about. The poor crayture.'[41] This now provoked a furious row.

The details are not particularly important.† One cause of Gerald's irritation was that Honor's solution to Gamel's drinking was huge walks; Gamel's subsequent exhaustion probably contributed to what happened. One evening, about 16 January, Honor as usual baited, Gamel as usual sided with Honor and Gerald suddenly exploded and then went furiously to his room. When Gamel came to

* There is something touching in her choice. Larios gin and Fundador brandy were the cheapest strong drinks you could buy and in *The Lighthouse* . . . Dick economises by giving up whisky and drinking them instead. Fundador is fairly disgusting.

† Gerald's and Honor's accounts of the events of 1967/8 are frequently at variance. But Honor's virulence against Gerald when I spoke to her and in our lengthy correspondence was so extreme it vitiated much of her evidence. On the whole, when I could corroborate them both, Gerald was nearly always the more accurate. I have tried to pick my way between them and the various other sources (Gerald to Frances, 11 and 17 January 1967; unpublished chapter, *Personal Record* (MSS, Texas); Mark Culme-Seymour's journal, 11 January 1967).

bed, he went in and told her he thought it would be better if he left the house while Honor was there. Gamel was greatly distressed, but Gerald walked angrily from the room without his usual goodnight kiss. The next morning, after a sleepless night, he was packing when he heard a knock. He ignored it. Twenty minutes later he found Gamel unconscious outside his door.

Told by Gerald that she was drinking a bottle of spirits a day, plus a bottle of wine at each meal and whisky before, the doctor Don José not unnaturally pinpointed alcohol – in any case the endemic weakness of the expatriate community – as the chief cause, giving her hepatitis and a stroke.

Put to bed, tended and visited, stopped from drinking, Gamel steadily recovered. There was one relapse, when Blacky, her favourite cat, died suddenly.* Gamel staggered up, found the brandy bottle, and took an enormous swig. Gerald threw the bottle away. Thereafter, everything went smoothly. Honor and Gerald were reconciled, and Honor nursed Gamel with great sweetness and good humour – 'When I hear them talk . . . I hear a perpetual tinkle of laughter.'[42] By 26 February Gamel was up and eating out in the sun. Gerald was at last able to have 'flu. Her illness had brought them together. She was grateful that he never mentioned its cause, and then 'Old age is a great cementer of marriages.'[43] But he decided not to have Honor to stay again. She made him too angry.

One more event of importance happened before the major crisis of that year finally broke. Peter Ryan, the young man who'd seen Gerald briefly in June 1962, shared his London flat with two girls, one of them an art student at Chelsea Art School, Lynda Price, then aged twenty-four. They were not lovers, but thought they would go abroad together in Peter's car. So vague were their plans that not till Bordeaux did they decide on Spain, a decision largely prompted because Lynda was immersed in John Frederick Nims' translation of *St John of the Cross*. As they drove south, Peter said he knew a man called Gerald Brenan near Malaga. Should they drop in? Lynda

---

* A death of the coast. Having been on Gamel's bed for three weeks she was seduced, despite her age (they'd had her twelve years), by a handsome young male who turned out to be 'a sex maniac of incredible prowess'. Blacky returned to her station exhausted but soon afterwards ran out, went into convulsions and died. 'A stroke, following too many orgasms,' diagnosed Gerald, writing to Frances on 6 Feb 1967.

thought not, but then she read in Nims' notes that a Gerald Brenan had written two good articles on the Saint.

The couple called in at Churriana on 30 May. Peter was pursuing a Swedish girl and left Lynda with the Brenans, not before noticing that Gerald was plainly attracted to the young art student. Lynda herself was particularly drawn to Gamel, whose calmness she found soothing. It is clear Gamel liked her too, because she joined Gerald in suggesting Lynda should come and stay with them. Lynda agreed, but said she wanted to see more of Spain first. Not long afterwards she went to work in a souvenir shop in Toledo.

Gerald did not forget the beautiful girl who loved St John of the Cross (he lent her the articles and gave her *A Life of One's Own*). He took her forwarding address and in July wrote confirming that Gamel and he would like her to come in the autumn. But whatever daydreams he was already indulging – no doubt considerable – were abruptly driven from his mind when Xavier and Miranda arrived at the end of the month.

Xavier was shown the record of Gamel's blood diagnosis. He said there was no trace of hepatitis and he doubted a stroke. But what alarmed him far more was Gamel's left arm, which was considerably swollen. He also found a lump in her left breast which Gamel said she had been trying to forget. He took her at once to a heart specialist and a surgeon in Malaga. The specialist said she had not had a stroke in January but a heart attack. The surgeon found that cancer had spread from the breast down the arm and was inoperable. She would have cobalt treatment but Xavier thought she would only live about six months. Gerald at first refused to believe him, but this prognosis proved to be almost exactly correct.[44]

TWENTY-NINE

Gamel's Death

'It is really I who have the cancer,' Gerald wrote to Frances, in one of the agonies of grief that were to sweep him continually during the next four months until all other things – and there were other things – were obliterated. 'I can't contemplate life without her – the awful loneliness, the longing, the guilt, for there is always guilt because one has not shown all the love that deep down one felt.' He cannot even show her what he is feeling (it had been decided not to tell her). And all the time 'this throb, throb, throb of sadness and pity'.[1]

His pity – the emotion she had overwhelmingly aroused when they first met thirty-seven years before – was compounded because he felt in a way her disease was self-induced. And certainly there is a sense of Gamel, under the pressure of her bitter disappointments and frustrations, turning increasingly and ever more deeply inwards until finally she began to consume herself.*

They postponed the cobalt treatment for a month (Gamel was told it was for a harmless ganglion), and flew to London, where they stayed first with Charles Sinnickson, then with Rhoda and Blair. Gerald was already in a highly tense state. Clare and Sydney Sheppard remember he kept crying and having to go and pretend to look at bookshelves so that Gamel would not see his tears. To Frances, on the other hand, he seemed to be gratuitously insulting about Ralph (there was, in fact, a perfectly sound reason for this in Gerald terms). He bought Gamel clothes, materials for dresses and an expensive transistor radio.

Gamel, meanwhile, went to Wales and saw Phyllis Playter. On

* There is a growing belief, backed by a good deal of anecdotal evidence, that there is a link between mental states and the onset of cancer. It is possible that prolonged mental stress weakens the immune system.

her return she telephoned Alyse Gregory. Alyse, who had only been waiting for that call, recorded it in her journal – '*27 August*. Perhaps my last night on this earth – a beautiful summer night . . . Heard Florida's voice* – a lovely farewell unknown to her – my dear, dear old friend.' It was indeed almost the last entry. Shortly afterwards she took a large quantity of long-stored barbiturates and lay down to die on Llewelyn's cloak, having protected it with a rubber sheet. It was a decision long taken and implemented now by an awareness of failing powers. She dreaded being a burden to anyone.[2]

'Of course Alyse took your [illegible] tablets,' Phyllis wrote to Gamel soon after this. 'What has been happening to you?' she went on. 'Have you begun the treatment? Did you survive the journey and time in England? Oh Gamel I shall never know now how you are – and what you are feeling.'[3]

As usual with Gamel, it is impossible to know how much she told Phyllis. Several people who saw her in London thought she suspected what was wrong, but preferred not to think about it.[4] What fairly soon became clear is that, as Gamel said later when asked, Gerald would have done much better to ask Phyllis to help him instead of remembering 'the perpetual tinkle of laughter' and asking Honor, which he did in London.

Honor's presence at Churriana from September onwards introduced the first of two complicating factors into an inherently difficult situation. Gerald had mobilised all his immense resources of energy to deal with this crisis. He then found that Honor took more or less complete charge of the sick-room.

The second complicating factor, emotionally, was Lynda. All his letters about her now bear the familiar marks of Gerald gearing himself up to fall in love, including intimations of poetry. He had written in August to put off her possible visit in September. Lynda had replied asking if he needed any help looking after Gamel. Gerald had refused but had already suggested instead that when Gamel died she come and live with him, platonically of course, to continue her studies. Lynda had agreed.[5] When Frances and Janetta drove over to see the Brenans on 5 September, they were greeted first by Rosario, almost in tears. '*La quiero mucho, la quiero como a una madre . . .*' Gerald himself seemed close to despair. Describing the progress of the cancer

---

* Before she fled to New York, Gamel had lived with her mother in Florida.

he quickly broke down and had to walk away 'leaving J and me tortured by sympathy'.[6] Three minutes later, to her astonishment, he was totally recovered and describing to Frances how he would soon be living happily with Lynda – 'a father and daughter relationship you see'.[6]

Increasingly torn between these alternating poles, more and more under strain as Gamel worsened and his desire to help and nurse remained dammed up, Gerald became subject to wild mood swings – manic cerebral excitement followed by despair and horror. His hare side surfaced and he longed to flee. Anxiety, as often, was expressed in acute financial terror. He had bursts of creativity. He felt he could write poetry again. It was now he conceived the first vague outlines of the book that was eventually to become *Thoughts in a Dry Season*: a collection of ideas and comments on the lines of Cyril's *Palinurus*. But his chief outlet (and escape) was in an explosion of letters; to Bunny, to VSP, Michael Holroyd and Lynda, but above all to Frances. Those to Frances, written in tiny, clear, unbroken handwriting, must be among the most extraordinary ever written. One, speeding over eighty-two pages, ranges across his entire life: sexual, voyeuristic, marital, literary, philosophical, spiritual, giving, on the way, his views on Lytton, Leonard Woolf, Llewelyn Powys, reading, the novel, Gibbon, Freud, old age and himself – among other things.[7]

His letters to Lynda were shorter, but in similar self-exposing vein. They often startled and embarrassed her, and she began to have serious doubts about joining him. But she threw the letters away. Feeling he was under terrible stress, she decided, with the instinctive astuteness she was often to show with Gerald, that they were schizophrenic. And indeed split is what he was.

By the end of September Gamel was becoming increasingly depressed as a result of the cobalt treatment which was, by today's standards, fairly savage. Honor took her into Malaga every afternoon after giving her a large whisky (all drink embargoes had been lifted). The swelling in her arm had spread and begun to go down the leg, so that she seemed to have dropsy. The rays not only depressed, they were painful. 'I used to go into her room and smell burning steak,' Honor said; by 10 October she was trying to persuade Gerald to stop them, but the specialist in Malaga would only reduce them to three a week.

Honor, concentrating 'an extraordinary beam of love'[8] on Gamel, was in complete charge. Gerald saw Gamel at meals and, longing to help but not allowed to, spent some of his energy cleaning all the windows in the house. He saw her once more when he kissed her goodnight. ('When I go into Gamel's room and see her mute, sweet, sad face on the pillow, Lynda does not exist for me.')[7] Honor was soon retiring at 9 or 9.30, usually rather drunk. Gerald then wrote letters deep into the night. He would watch Gamel's open door from his table. This was because he'd once seen her light go on and went in to find her examining her 'poor burnt breast'[7] to see if it had shrunk. He soothed her and gave her a sleeping pill. At two or three he'd take one himself.

Gerald, too, longed to stop the treatments which Don José (the GP) and his chemist friend both told him were useless for such advanced cancer. But he felt, he told Frances, in a 'moral dilemma'. Not until Xavier agreed was it stopped, on about 20 October. The dilemma Gerald referred to was complicated. The treatments were very expensive. Gerald would not stop them for that reason if they were going to do any good. But if they were only going to prolong life for a short while – that is, prolong the agony – would it not be better to stop them for that reason alone? Gerald longed for Gamel to recover. At the same time he knew she couldn't and he longed to see Lynda. He was for a while, until Gamel's suffering overwhelmed him, two people.

No sooner did the cobalt stop than he was gripped by the fear that he would lose Lynda to someone else. Janetta became his *confidante* and persuaded him not to invite her at once to Malaga. 'But how soon can I pin her down?'[9] Janetta told him to ask her to come six weeks after Gamel had died, and at the end of October Gerald did this.[10] From now on, as the terrible process of Gamel's death unfolded, Lynda recedes in his letters.

Gerald and Honor now began to have a series of scenes, each uneasily patched up. The first was over Gerald letting Gamel see visitors Honor had forbidden. Honor who, Gerald realised, secretly longed for Gamel to die in her arms, then tried to get Gamel to come to Achill Island in Ireland with her. 'I am just a third party in a love affair,' Gerald wrote bitterly, 'in which Gamel clings to Honor, as she once clung to the gin bottle . . . I have ceased to be her husband.'[10] Nevertheless, smoking continually, taking librium three times a day, he managed to control himself, making it 'an absolute principle of life never to disagree with Honor'.[11]

By 12 November the doctor said Gamel was too ill to leave her room. Honor, desperate to halt the swift spread of the disease, now tried to get Gamel, behind Gerald's back, to agree to come to Lourdes. When Gamel, who didn't want to go, told him, he told Honor coldly that the idea was quite ridiculous. Gamel was completely irreligious, and it would be a total waste of time. 'Honor's face changed at once and a look of hatred came into it.'[12] That night she tried to stop Gerald seeing Gamel, but he pushed firmly past her, and forbade her to try and stop him again.*

Gerald's reaction to all this, apart from still more letters, was to become totally obsessed with money. When the pound was devalued in November he thought he was ruined. He asked Jaime to sell some furniture. Frances and Ethel de Croisset sent cheques in response to his letters (they sent a total of £600 between them over the period).[13] By 19 November Gerald was wondering if, at long last, he could ask VSP for the £1000. He also worried incessantly about the cost of the funeral. Teddy and Sue Southby, two of their closest friends on the coast, were astonished and rather shocked when Gerald suddenly appeared and asked Teddy if he could find him a cheap coffin.[14] Finally, in a letter which clearly gave him satisfaction, and which is an absolute miasma of money anxieties – the cost of coffins, burials, cobalt treatment, drugs – he finally asked VSP 'very reluctantly' to return what he could of the £1000.[15] VSP replied with a cheque by return of post[16] and had repaid in full by the end of April.†

---

* Honor's version, when I interviewed her, was that she simply asked Gerald to be quick with Gamel since she was tired. Even if this were so, quite apart from implying that Gerald was insensitive to Gamel's needs, which he was not, it seems the grossest impertinence, at the least, for Honor to try and curtail virtually the only visit she allowed the husband to his dying wife each day.

† It is often as difficult to be precise about Gerald's financial situation during these years as it is to be clear about his sexual behaviour in earlier ones. By chance (or on purpose) a scrap of paper with his calculations of his income from July 1967 to July 1968 survives in the MF archive. This gives his total income as £1118.2s.6d. The total should in fact be £7253 (around £36,000). One gets a strong impression that Gerald felt more comfortable being poor. It fitted with his early ideals, which he never really abandoned. It also, as it were, gave his money anxieties something to bite on. This would explain why he frequently underestimated his income, panicked, and then discovered forgotten and often large sums which made everything all right. It would be too much to say Gerald made money from the

During November and early December Gamel's left leg grew monstrously swollen. They would help her to hobble to the fireside and eat supper. Although she pretended she would live for years, she really knew now she had cancer, Gerald told Frances, and knew it was incurable. 'Her sad anxious face, especially in the afternoon, is very distressing.'[17]

But this was a period of momentary calm – although Gerald felt 'there was a live bomb in the house which if I spoke too loudly would explode'.[12] As Honor tired, Gerald took over more and more of the nursing, which in turn calmed him. He told Frances he could scarcely have coped without Honor. She contributed generously. She bought and cooked special foods. Only she could make Gamel laugh.

Gamel grew steadily weaker and weaker, and on 7 December had not eaten for five days. It must have been about now that Gerald in an unguarded moment let slip his plans for Lynda. 'From then on,' said Honor, 'I loathed him.' Soon they were meeting only at supper. For the only time in his life, Gerald compared events to those he'd undergone winning his MC in the First World War.

On 8 December Xavier and Miranda arrived and Honor went to stay with the Southbys. Xavier examined Gamel and cancelled the cortisone, which was why her face had been swelling. Her increasing weight, despite very little food, he diagnosed as water retention and obtained diuretics. During their last night, Gamel had a terrible attack of diarrhoea. The only person she would allow to clean her was Miranda.

Honor returned rested, but almost at once had another row when, after she had asked Don José to 'cup' Gamel's swollen leg, Gerald furiously told her not to go behind his back. Honor said, 'May God strike you dead on the spot,'[12] before slamming into her room. But she now hurt her back trying to lift Gamel and had to wear a sort of straitjacket. In great pain, she had to take a lot of the opium suppositories Ethel de Croisset had sent from Paris.

So things continued till Christmas – with icy winds and grey

---

generosity of his friends during Gamel's illness, but I doubt if he was much out of pocket. (The Davises gave him money, and so did Jean Gimpel.) This does not, of course, mean that his terror over money was not genuine. But it shows the degree to which it was displacement for far deeper and more powerful anxieties and strains (something of which Gerald was intermittently aware).

skies. There was one light note. Malaga won the *gordo*, the top prize in the lottery – 400 million pesetas. Thirteen million came to Churriana, 60,000 to Rosario. 'One very poor woman, with eight children, won 200,000 pesetas and went dancing through the village with her skirts above her waist.'[18]

During the night of Christmas Eve, Gamel had another violent attack of diarrhoea. Everything was saturated, but she was too weak to clean. More ominously she had sudden agonising spasms of pain in her leg. It was impossible to insert one of the few remaining suppositories because of the diarrhoea. They gave Gamel eight aspirins.

By 6 January the pain was too intense for her to use the bedpan during the night, so the bed was soaked each morning. Gerald, who now sat up most of each night, and either Rosario or Catalina – a girl who came in to help – put on clean sheets inch by inch. Don José refused morphia on the grounds that the pain was not severe enough. Honor, who felt her role was really over and had ceased to get dressed, followed him furiously down the corridor (in her pyjamas and dressing gown) saying 'What bloody good are you?', fortunately in English.[19]

By 10 January Gamel could hardly speak, her face continually furrowed with spasms of pain. They saved the opium for real emergencies, and dosed her with aspirin and librium; but really Gerald only had his love to keep the cancer at bay. As he sat next to her through the night he noticed she was not 'sleeping in the usual way. Out of weakness she shuts her eyes and associates herself with the beating of her heart and the coming of her breath, which is now laboured and now very faint. Making a great effort, she took my hand. More spasms of pain pass now and then across her face. I asked her, were they from her leg, and she answered, from all over. By stroking her forehead, I can soothe and drive them away.'[20] He resolved to ask for stronger pills.

He had his last altercation with Honor on 13 January (she had tried to stop him being woken at three to sit with Gamel). Honor, who had had a good deal of rum, said, 'I came here only to help Gamel and I find your company utterly distasteful to me. I am no longer of any use to Gamel, so I will leave.'[21] Shortly afterwards, she took a taxi into Malaga.

The relief was enormous. 'This house is my own again and I can be alone with Gamel.' The dying, in their solitude, need to be accompanied by hand 'to the very edge of the river'.[22] So he had written when his mother was dying of cancer – but he could not stand staying too long at Edgeworth then. This time he did not flinch, but the only way he could endure it was by writing to Frances, often as it happened, his account of what took place. Frances says she trembled when she had to open another of Gerald's letters at this time. And even today the researcher feels uneasy lifting them one by one from the file.

The afternoon after Honor left, the doctor refused to give more pain-killing drugs. They had left only aspirins and librium.* Gerald wrote in despair to Xavier. But it was therefore impossible, because of her pain, to change the sheets. Gerald sat by the bed. 'The sick are shut up in the little world of their disordered bodies . . . but the sense of a loving presence makes them feel less alone and not entirely isolated.'²³ The following evening, the 14th, they thought she was dying. Antonio and Rosario sat with him, Antonio with tears streaming down his face. Gamel could hardly swallow; it was difficult to get the librium down with a teaspoon of water. Gerald sat all night, got three hours' sleep in the morning, and returned. When he kissed her 'she returns my kisses with her poor lacerated lips which are about the only parts of her body she can still move . . . The pity – the pity – but one gets beyond tears.'²³ He sat through the night of 15 January. Occasionally Gamel groaned with pain. Gerald longed for death – and dreaded it. 'The darkened room, the deep shadows, the hiss of the small gas stove, the figure on the bed. I have come closer to Gamel these last few days than I have ever before. I can see by the way she kisses me how much my love means to her.'²³ By 7 a.m. on 16 January, Gamel had been in intense pain for two hours. Her throat was closing, her neck and chest stiff as boards. Gerald sent a note to the doctor, begging for morphia. He was dropping with sleep. The doctor came at 9.30. He refused morphia. It would *cause* death. He agreed to opium suppositories. Honor had finished the French ones, so Gerald sent for Spanish suppositories, though they are supposed to be weaker.† He managed to get two and a half

---

* A mild tranquilliser.

† The doctor seems to have believed that the Catholic Church forbade the use of drugs which might cause death in such circumstances. In fact Pope Pius XII had recently issued an encyclical, as Gerald pointed out, allowing doctors to terminate life in such circumstances. Opium suppositories, French or Spanish, are extremely mild.

hours' sleep, and then at twelve o'clock he, Rosario and Catalina decided to insert the first suppository. 'Gamel screamed with pain as we lifted her body an inch or two, but she was so caked with urine and faeces that Rosario could not find the place . . . her whole body quivers with pain when one touches it. However, we persisted, drew out her filthy towels, double sheets and gave her a slight sponge and quickly inserted clean ones. Then Rosario put in the suppository. Her face was wrinkled and contorted with pain and it was dreadful to see her.'[23] Gerald could stand it no longer and had to go downstairs. When he came back, Gamel was asleep but her face was compressed as though she still felt pain. By 2 a.m. on Wednesday morning, the 17th, Gamel was awake and in pain, but Gerald felt, as he always felt, that he should obey the doctor, who had said to establish a rhythm – one at night, one in the morning. At 6.30 a.m. she was groaning in her sleep, hard as a board, her lips and gums raw, the throat infected. At 8 a.m. they gave another suppository. Again Gamel screamed with pain. But she was asleep in five minutes. Gerald prayed she'd sleep all day. Outside the weather was beautiful – the wind gone, the sky blue, the sun shining.

There are no more terrible descriptions. Gamel died at 10.40 the following morning – 18 January. She was seventy-one. An hour after she died the post arrived with a letter from Xavier, saying that he had rung the cancer specialist in Malaga who had promised to prescribe morphia if it was needed.[12]

Reading these tortured and sometimes horrifying pages Gerald wrote to Frances, one longs for Gerald to go out and somehow force morphia from someone. In the unpublished chapter on Gamel's death he says he was about to go to the Malaga specialist himself when she died and Xavier's letter arrived. But that it did not occur to him till the very end is the measure of his immersion. It was not just his usual deference to doctors, nor the fact that he expected Gamel to die at any moment. It was that, virtually without sleep for six days and nights, he forced his entire being into succouring her. He could see nothing else, no other possibility.

Nor was his agonising ordeal yet over. Spanish law says a dead body cannot be kept in a house overnight. Gamel was put in her coffin and they asked the doctor for a death certificate. This he refused. Honor had warned him, or got Rosario to warn him, that she was 'frightened Gerald might ask his louche chemist friend for something to kill Gamel with'.[24] The doctor insisted on breaking open the coffin and examining Gamel's body minutely for tell-tale signs. Eventually it was nailed shut and Gerald, with all the servants, accompanied it to the cemetery.

The actual funeral was the following day, but Gerald could not face any more. Later, he put a stone at the grave and had carved there the first two lines of the song from *Cymbeline*, which she had been particularly fond of:

> Fear no more the heat o' the sun
> Nor winter's furious rages.

But Gamel had written her own epitaph, a last wild defiant cry:

> When I am dead and laid at last to rest,
> Let them not bury me in holy ground –
> To lie the shipwrecked sailor cast ashore –
> But give the corpse to fire, to flood, to air,
> The elements that may the flesh transform
> To soar with birds, to float where fishes are,
> To rise in smoke, shine as a leaping flame –
> To be in freedom lost in nothingness.
> Not garnered in the grave, hoarded by death.
> What is remembrance that we crave for it?
> Let me be nothing then, not face nor name;
> As on the seagull wings where bright seas pour,
> As air that quickens at the opened door:
> When I am dead, let me be nothing more.

PART V

The Long Last Movement

1968–1984

'I must leave no trail of miserable old age. I love life too much to accept any rationing of it . . . I don't want to live to be a croaker.'

Gerald to Ralph Partridge, 29 May 1958

'Old age is a very ricketty, unbalanced, furious state until it sinks into senility. I fear my own helpless excitability and changes of mood more than my decaying faculties.'

Gerald to Frances Partridge, 10 February 1968

THIRTY

After Gamel

1

For several months after Gamel died, Gerald told Miranda, he found his memory for names had gone completely haywire. David Mitchell saw him queuing in Torremolinos post office 'desolate and shrunken in a shabby raincoat and ancient black beret'.[1] He commiserated with him over Gamel's death, and Gerald turned away with tears in his eyes. Shortly after this, having sent some of Gamel's jewellery to Miranda, he was prevented on some technicality from sending the rest to the Woolseys in America. Agitated and distracted, he hurried out leaving the parcel on the central table in Malaga post office (John Whitworth remembered a Peruvian bird with emerald eyes). When he rushed back, it had gone.

Yet John regarded this incident as symbolic. Gerald half-wanted to get rid of Gamel, and half-didn't. There is some truth in this. After giving away a lot of her clothes, he had a series of huge bonfires over two weeks. There were trunks and drawers of letters, manuscripts and typescripts, notebooks and poems, long fragments of novels, stories and autobiography from childhood, through Yegen to quite recently, almost nothing finished, all endlessly rewritten, all versions preserved – and all evidence of that tremendous literary ambition which had gone largely unfulfilled and which had made her death, for Gerald, particularly tragic. He kept important letters and completed or nearly completed work; the poetry he determined to get printed privately. Everything else he burnt, including many of her letters to him.*

---

* I assume. Quite a number of these survive, but a large envelope (in the MF archive) marked 'Letters from Gamel 1930–1967', which has clearly been distended, is empty.

He also executed Gamel's will. She left £1100 (£8500) – £400 in her Spanish account, £700 in America.[2] There were bequests of £300 to Miranda, £100 to Antonio and £50 to Mrs Palmer, who'd worked for them at Bell Court; the rest she left to Gerald. There is some doubt whether Gerald gave Miranda her £300, but all the others he paid.

And as usual letters continued to stream out from Churriana. He briefly continued a correspondence begun in July 1967 with Jean Rhys. Gerald had read *The Wide Sargasso Sea* as a result of the seminal recommendation by Francis Wyndham (whom he regarded, since his review of *A Holiday by the Sea*, as 'a very good judge').[3] This, and her other novels, bowled him over. The real point, he told Bunny in a long and penetrating letter about her, was that she had invented an entirely new way of novel-writing. 'Their elliptical style avoids all explanations and keeps one all the time at the central point of feeling.'[4] He wrote her numerous letters outlining, among other things, a somewhat idealised account of his youth and sent her *The Spanish Labyrinth* and *Spanish Literature*. His pressing invitations for her to come and stay – 'If she is at all like her heroines, as I'm sure she is, she must be pretty neurotic, but I'm prepared for anything'[5] – had had to be cancelled when Gamel fell ill. He wrote his last letter, praising *Tigers are Better Looking*, on 20 May.[6]

Many more letters went to Michael Holroyd. They had begun to correspond over Holroyd's biography of Lytton Strachey in 1962, and Gerald had at once responded to the charm that must have facilitated the often sensitive business of biographical research. Despite frequent plans and attempts, they only met once, in London in September 1968, but an epistolary friendship developed to the point where Gerald made Holroyd his literary executor in December 1967.*

The first volume of *Lytton Strachey* appeared in September 1967, the second in February 1968. Gerald wrote to Frances, striking a

---

* Thereby, without telling us, replacing Julian Jebb and myself. He then added Bill Davis. In February 1968, he added Lynda (Gerald to Frances, 9 February 1966). Then in November 1968, he planned to remove Davis and Holroyd, to reinstate Julian and myself and keep Lynda (all this without telling anyone involved except Lynda). In the end only Lynda remained as literary executor. Gerald liked redistributing his favours in this way and quite often made and then unmade or altered codicils to his Will, again usually without the people concerned knowing.

lofty, boastful note: 'This publicity is just one of the penalties of growing old and having known remarkable people. I don't like my own account either. All the real essence of those times, all its happiness and anguish, escape between the cold, unexpressive words. Only poetry can give immediacy – prose biography just satisfies curiosity.'[7]

Most of the time his feelings were the exact reverse of these. He told Holroyd he had 'produced an extraordinary biography – perhaps the most balanced and understanding of this century'.[8] He thought it superior to Painter's *Proust* and was amazed 'how successful you have been catching the atmosphere of those remote days'.[9] That this was not just the usual hyperbole to author is shown by his repeating all this elsewhere[10] and in other letters to Frances. 'In his descriptions of people I've known he never puts a foot wrong.'[11]

One reason he didn't, in Gerald's view, put a foot wrong was that Gerald had often placed his feet for him. In this, and in recapturing those remote times, Holroyd (as he fully acknowledged) often relied quite heavily on Gerald's account* – to the extent that when Frances arrived to stay at Churriana in March, she found that Gerald, as well as being delighted with his own portrait, was behaving as if he'd more or less written the book. So much so, that she ventured some questions. '"I wonder why Holroyd speaks of Valentine Dobrée as being deformed," I said vaguely. "I don't remember she was." He looked slightly cornered. "Oh yes, I told him that. I think one of her legs was longer than the other, or something. I'm not sure what."'[12] There were similar matters she pressed him on. She also blamed, but did not tax him, for the portrait of the young Ralph which, though accurate as far as it went, to her mind overemphasised his early 'philistinism'.

Gerald helped Holroyd; but Holroyd helped him – by reviving his time with Carrington, and by throwing new perspectives on it. This was the part of *Personal Record* he had been writing while Gamel was dying, and which he continued to write now. (This in turn revived his old jealousy of Ralph, which is the reason for his

---

* Gerald was slightly surprised – and expressed his surprise – to find that Holroyd's account of Carrington's death was taken verbatim from his journal. He had forgotten that he had in fact had all those pages copied out by Gamel and sent to Holroyd to use, while, in another letter, telling him to use any phrases of his, Gerald's, he liked (Gerald to Holroyd, 22 October 1963, 5 December 1967).

seemingly inexplicable outburst against him to Frances when Gerald and Gamel were in London.)

Gerald always reacted defensively against any suggestion that his marriage to Gamel had been anything but happy. Again and again, throughout all this activity, he returned to their life together. She had given him calm, and had enabled him to work, 'not so much a person I focused on but the one I breathed';[13] he had given her a life, protection, interesting people. He had never, he told Frances – forgetting as people do their early years, his letters longing for their lovemaking, his intense desire to keep her from Llewelyn – 'never felt passionately about her either physically or mentally. Love, yes, and great community of tastes – the perfect marriage, but for one thing. That thing was openness and intimacy.'[14]

Gerald attributed this considerable, even crucial lack largely, and correctly, to Gamel's temperament. He also thought the fact that she was American and he was English constituted a fundamental block.[15] Yet – did not he himself want this? His self-absorption left little time, until towards the end of his life, for that full-time absorption in someone else required in a deep marriage.

Then, as the elements of their life revolved and revolved in his mind, the remoteness from each other of their final years rolled uppermost and he remembered how they had hardly communicated at all except over the cats. He confessed to Holroyd he now felt 'full of remorse' because he had not tried to make those years happier for Gamel.[16]

They had come close, perhaps closer than ever before, at the very end as he nursed her in her long death agony. Later, it was almost as if the terrible fire of this experience, as well as that earlier remoteness, had somehow consumed Gamel in him. For fifteen years he was hardly to refer to her again. This was perhaps partly yet another manifestation of the elaborate defence mechanism he had evolved, the ability to lock things he didn't want to remember into some inner dungeon. The obvious and overt reason was, of course, Lynda.

2

Gerald seems to have written to Lynda about ten days after Gamel died, suggesting she come south at the beginning of March. The date fixed on was 6 March – five days more than the discretionary six weeks suggested earlier by Janetta.

During Gamel's illness a chunk of ceiling had crashed down beside her bed. The workman who repaired it said Gerald needed a new roof. There was not time to manage this, but Gerald had the whole house whitewashed in preparation for Lynda's arrival.

This clearly made him apprehensive, and he accordingly asked Frances to come for a few days at the beginning of March to help ease her in. (Joanna, however, who also asked to come then, he hurriedly put off, terrified she would 'queer my pitch'.)[17]

But the central problem was how to break the news that, seven weeks after the death of his wife of thirty-eight years, he was taking a beautiful girl of twenty-four to live with him. To Frances he was simply defiant. When warning her that Lynda would be there too, he ends, 'people will say "Gerald's already got a new girl."' It wasn't true. He was 'merely like other widowers taking in a niece'.[7] It might throw doubt on his love for Gamel 'but one has to accept one's nature'.[17] His nature was to live in the future.

Other people were more tricky. To Hetty he wrote a harrowing description of his time alone in the echoing house and how he had then gone into Torremolinos and, quite by chance, met this lovely girl. He soon developed this, in a letter to VSP, into a severe psychosomatic illness. The Malaga doctor said nothing would help him, but then out of the blue – Lynda![18] He could not screw up his courage to tell Miranda – perhaps the most difficult person – till the end of March. He now added suicide. The psychosomatic crisis, the loneliness and despair brought on acute suicidal thoughts. Suddenly, he remembered Lynda. He wrote to her and she agreed to come. The symptoms vanished![19]

In fact, Gerald spent the month before Lynda came in a state of increasing excitement and anticipation. By 19 February he had been 'for several days in the highest spirits'.[17] And there was no nonsense about suicide or psychosomatic crises with Michael Holroyd. 'I want drama and excitement and problems to solve, come what may.' He was busy planning how much money he would need to 'assist my new protégée'.[16]

On 6 March, with only the faintest idea what to expect, the new protégée duly arrived.

THIRTY-ONE

Lynda

'*A la tarde te examinaré en el amor.*'
(*'In the evening you will be examined in love'.*)
St John of the Cross

1

In many respects, until he was finally overwhelmed by age (he was about to be seventy-four), the sixteen years Gerald spent with Lynda from 1968 onwards were the happiest of his life. Much of the credit for this must go to the serious-minded, unusual and strikingly attractive girl whom chance and Peter Ryan had brought his way.

In appearance she was tall and slender with long, thick, brown hair falling to her shoulders and, as Frances noted, 'truthful brown eyes and a friendly, catlike smile, a soft voice'.[1] The soft voice frequently broke into a low, gurgling laugh. She had a quick and delightful sense of humour and of the ridiculous, and instinctively adopted the slightly ironic, humorous, teasing approach to Gerald which, as it had years before with Helen Anrep, instantly soothed him. Other aspects of her character fitted into his as well. She had great zest for life and though diffident, even shy at first, soon became very high-spirited in company – perhaps too much so, for she quickly tired. As a result, she didn't like too much social life. In the old, the erotic bond is often replaced by a bond of ill-health. Lynda had a chronically bad back and a tendency to bronchitis and headaches; at first this made Gerald feel young and gave him a function; later, as he began to crack up, mutual ill-health drew them together.

And where her character contrasted with his, Lynda seemed to suit him even more. She was totally honest and undevious. She also, despite great tact and a gentle, pleasing manner, had an extremely strong will. Gerald had, on the whole, always got his own way (on this account, Julian Jebb gave him the nickname Major Brenan); he now discovered, as he had begun to with Hetty, that he was able to give way and that he liked it.

Lynda probably owed her strength of will to her parents. Her own nickname in the family was 'Tiger', and it was accepted by her loving and permissive parents that she had to get her own way. Marion Price was a gentle motherly woman whose Cheshire family had once owned a dairy business. Lynda's father came from long-lived stock (his own father lived to be 104) and he had considerable gifts which could have made money in business – had they been allied to a business temperament. Instead they were allied to an artistic one. Things like the pursuing of bills, and the paying of them, bored him. An engineering business he started went bankrupt. He next joined an ice circus. Mr Price designed the machinery that froze the ice. This job ended in some obscure way and the family moved to a Welsh mining village. Here he worked in a 'secret' job designing machinery to make one of the first antibiotics.

The family was never indigent but these fluctuations meant that, compared to Gerald's background, there was never much money about. This fact drew Gerald to Lynda, as did her complete lack of snobbery. (Lynda remembers class as much less of an issue in Cheshire and the North generally. Gerald's invariable 'What class are they?' about new arrivals from England always struck her as excessive.)

If not wholly successful, Lynda's father's career shows a certain boldness. This was inherited by two of his children. Lynda's brother Keith suddenly decided to go to South America. Lynda's decision to live with Gerald was itself bold – but she had a simple and very definite aim in view. The clue to this lies partly in her education.

Lynda was not only intelligent but well suited to academic study, which she enjoyed. Her education, however, had been patchy. Peter Ryan said that when they came to Spain she had no idea Ireland was an island. She thought it was joined to Brittany. (Lynda denies this, though she agrees her geography had been neglected.) Her interests lay in painting, writing (particularly poetry) and the theatre. She had hoped to go to Bristol University and do their theatre course. But they were full up and her A-level results had not come through. When they came – A-level English, History and Art – she went to Chelsea Art School to do a year's theatre design. Now her interest in painting came uppermost and she decided to do this. She stayed the four-year course and got her degree.

But she soon bitterly regretted not going to a university. Her main object in coming to Gerald was to read and to learn. Spain and Gerald would be her university.

There was a related, but deeper reason. Sometimes, observing Gerald in the Fifties and Sixties, one has the impression of two worlds, two levels: the world of youth in London, with its affairs and stress; and Gerald's safe, calm house in Spain with its fountain, books and flowers. Every so often a girl would fall from the frieze above, down into Gerald's world – where he would rescue them and become obsessed with them.

There was something of this with Lynda, but in fact she had also been passing through a personal crisis of a much more profound and fundamental nature. One manifestation was that, after four years, she had decided that she was not talented enough to be a painter. This decision was very painful. It was also symptomatic of a split she had noticed when she was quite young. She used to produce books – drawing pictures on one side and words on the other, but not sure which she really wished to do. Now she moved towards writing. She was helped through the spiritual element in this crisis of direction by the discovery of a medieval mystic called Meister Eckhart. Then she read Simone Weil and Eliot's *Four Quartets*; later St John of the Cross, whom she had already begun to translate when she was alone in Toledo. St John of the Cross had made her feel that she must go to Spain, that some good would come of it. The crisis was resolved before Churriana; but the working-out still required peace and time.

It is hardly surprising that Gerald noticed the obvious parallels. 'Her passion for work is really amazing,' he wrote a year later to Frances. She was reading Wittgenstein's *Tractatus*, in a temporary move into metaphysics from literature and poetry. She took, as always, full notes but 'put serious literary production some way ahead. This is the course I followed when I first went to Yegen.'[2]

The revival of enthusiasm, the return, for a while, of youth – that is one gift the pupil can bring the teacher. Lynda loved discussing not just books but ideas – she, as he had years before, wanted to learn about philosophy, history, mythology, anthropology. And then Gerald was an inspired teacher. He woke each morning, he wrote at this time in the notebook he was keeping for his *Thoughts*, feeling he knew nothing.[3] Such was the long legacy of his own anxiety at not having been to a university. But this need to know meant that when he re-read or re-discussed a book or a writer it was always as if for the first time, always a process of discovery, of learning. Gerald was also one of those people in whom the act of talking generated thought; this is not uncommon, but the speed and completeness with which he did this was exceptional. These were both reasons he was so stimulating.

Not that things always went completely smoothly at Churriana university. The habits of a lifetime are not changed at once. To those who had known him before, Gerald's giving way to Lynda seemed astonishing. It did not always feel like that to Lynda. 'Gerald's theory was that at his age he should decentralise his ego. I should be the recipient of its decentralisation. But I often felt I was just an extension of his ego. It was often Lynda wants this, Lynda thinks that – when it was Gerald thinking and wanting. It was irritating.' His desire to control would surface. 'One of the biggest rows was over Plato. I wanted to read the whole of Plato. Gerald said it was impossible. I should get bored. The thing to do was to select the best, the most important. I insisted I would read it all and I did.'

But nearly all the time they got on very well. Gerald would say what had interested him – Lynda would agree to read it or not. She chose. And whatever she chose, Gerald could discuss. 'I soon became very, very fond of him. I loved him, but I loved him as one loves a great-uncle. I enjoyed the companionship, the shared interests and the learning of new ones like botany. And then I loved the way he talked about books and writers.'

Gerald was aware of this and would have agreed – but these things did not fully define his own feelings by any means.

2

As he had with both Carringtons, especially Joanna, Gerald had really begun to fall in love with Lynda before she came. From the moment she arrived, therefore, progress was extremely rapid. Within five days he was telling Frances: 'When she leaves me I shall want to die.'[4] And from then on his talk about her (to anyone who'd listen) and his letters (to Frances, VSP, Bunny, Miranda, Joanna) are increasingly ecstatic. By 1 May, while Lynda was reading Plutarch, *The Golden Bough*, and Plato's *Dialogues*, he told Bunny he just wanted to sit and look at her face. 'Her happiness spreads out of her like a sort of radiance. Oh my lovely Lynda!' Her vocation was to be a poet. 'But when I see her I want to crush her, to eat her, vocation and all. Or else jump over a cliff for her sake, leaving what she will need for her life behind in a drawer.'[5]

This drawer, too, increasingly preoccupied him. Already in March, he longed to leave her the house. 'But I must leave all I have to Miranda.'[4] However, by the end of May he had altered his will to include her.[6] *Personal Record* would now be published after all, for her benefit. By July he was wondering just how much he could leave her 'without offending Miranda'.[7] (One notes 'offend' rather than 'hurt'.)

The absolute impossibility of Lynda ever allowing him to make love to her, or of having any desire for him to do so, made Gerald at one level at last relax. That Lynda would of course have boyfriends is another leitmotif of his letters, of *course* she would and should. He was absolutely prepared for that. But probably not for two years. It is noticeable that this moment, as their years together went by, always remains two years ahead – as impossible to reach as the horizon.

At another level, he felt the terrible poignancy of loving without being able to make love – 'it eats into one like an acid', he told Bunny.[5] And, as so often before, what could not take place in reality took place in Gerald's head. Almost as soon as Lynda arrived, he was wondering to Joanna if she would ever let him kiss her.[8] After some months he would kiss her goodnight. This simple, dry, distant peck became, to Frances, first an airy 'we kiss a good deal', and finally 'long kissing sessions'.[9] When Lynda and Gerald went to stay in September this year with Rose-Marie Duncan at Welcombe, Lynda was still in the car when Gerald came to the door. 'I've got two spare rooms, do you want one or two?' 'No, no – we always sleep together,' said Gerald hurriedly. If this would never happen, at least he could have the satisfaction of making other people think that it did. And in this he was often successful. Theodore Redpath, who got to know them both later, was absolutely astonished to learn that nothing at all went on, that Gerald had never even once kissed Lynda passionately. David Machin, his editor at Cape, sent a note to his assistant. 'As I am sure you guessed by the end of the lunch, she is his girlfriend. Not bad for a man of seventy-nine, is it?'*[10]

All of this, of course, Gerald kept completely hidden from Lynda – more or less. But she understood fairly soon something of what she'd got herself into. When Frances arrived, Lynda took her aside and said she'd no idea of Gerald's feelings when she'd agreed to come to Churriana. 'And I remember thinking quite early on "What on earth would happen if I left?"' She understood. But her extreme youth, her vulnerability, the fact she had no money at all, the identification he made with himself at Yegen, all this invested Gerald's feelings with a particular tenderness. The most he would allow himself at first was to wonder to her whether, had he been thirty-five, she would have married him. In his letters to Bunny and Frances, she answers, 'Yes, of course.' In fact, Lynda invariably answered, 'No. I could not have stood his egotism then'.

One can for a moment imitate the cadence Gerald was to develop so brilliantly for *Thoughts in a Dry Season*: great loves contain the seeds of their end; it is this which intensifies them. The reason Gerald and Lynda finally had to part was the disaster of Gerald's extreme old age. But this fundamental difference in their feelings was not insignificant. For Lynda – enormous fondness, but as for a great-uncle or a marvellous teacher. For Gerald – much much more.

* For the first and only time in his life a rather vainglorious note sometimes enters Gerald's letters about Lynda. In *Personal Record* he manages to subdue this to a slightly smug self-satisfaction. Raymond Carr says that he noticed a diffidence, an almost excessive modesty, in Gerald's attitude to him. Gerald professed the inferiority of a self-taught historian to a professional, university-trained one. I have explored the reasons for Gerald's excessive modesty. I don't think he ever really felt inferior to anyone in his knowledge of Spanish history, though he certainly began to feel out of date. But at this time Carr received a letter which he took to be an even odder gesture of deference. Gerald wrote and said he was living with this very young girl. Did Carr think it was all right? Gerald was not deferring, of course; he was simply boasting.

3

Frances came to stay for five days at the beginning of March.

It was cold and wet, and the house smelt of tom cat. She found – it seemed a little insensitive – that she was to sleep in Gamel's room, in the bed 'where those ghastly scenes Gerald's letters described took place'.'' Lying awake during the night, she heard the long hollow corridors echoing to the sound of Gerald clearing his throat and realised suddenly that, though Gamel had only just died, he had 'really been solitary for many years'.'' Solitary – and perhaps in some ways lonely.

He was neither now. Arriving braced for grief, she was told at once by Gerald he had no desire to talk about Gamel at all. Indeed, she soon realised with some astonishment 'there is really nothing I can do for him, none of the services most of my friends seemed to think I could provide. He is *perfectly all right*. What an extraordinary being.''

Gerald was not just all right, he was in top form. He gave her *Personal Record* to read, but then stood over her talking so much about it she couldn't read it. He showed how young he felt, 'by running when other people would walk, even hopping and jumping'.'' He talked of learning to dance. Frances saw at once, of course, that the reason was Lynda – whom she liked immediately. 'She seems to me sweet-natured, serious, a reader, reserved, attractive rather than pretty, thoughtful, but does not give herself away completely.''' One morning just before Frances left to join Janetta at Tramores, her new house behind Benahavís, Gerald explained that Lynda would be reading in the *mirador*, but 'Actually she was talking hard to him in his bedsitting room as I went out.''' It was talk that was to continue with undiminished vigour for seven years.

One can get a rather pale indication of how Gerald talked about books and writers from his letters during those years as, under Lynda's stimulus, his reading once more spills into them. As usual, he reread and rejudged all his favourites: Racine, Montaigne, Svevo, Stendhal, Proust, Joyce, Eliot; he even looked at Virginia Woolf again. Her novels he could now hardly get through. 'The interior monologue seems to me a mistaken technique for it does not allow the drawing of character. To be readable a novel requires characters, i.e. people seen from outside, and involved with one another and people's dreamings about themselves and their lives are not enough to make them real. Yet this was Virginia's vision of life, introverted and poetical, and to carry it through she was obliged to forgo her great gift for writing flowing prose. So one gets these ivory tower productions, written some of them in the agitated thirties, out of their era.'[12]

Reading Conrad's *Under Western Eyes*, he became impatient with its perfection as a work of art, its deployment of all the novelist's 'tricks, introduced after Flaubert, by I think Henry James, on the need for having everything seen through an observer's eyes . . .' He prefers Dostoevsky, 'a much poorer artist as well as a less intelligent writer', but who gives one 'an injection that alters one's whole way of feeling'.[13]

But it was not just writers of the past. Gerald read everything that came out if there was a chance it would be worthwhile. He was therefore often disappointed. Reading *Jake's Thing*, he asked VSP, 'When does the reality plane fade out and the satirical plane fade in?'[14] – though the subject of Amis' book was unlikely to endear itself to him. Nor, try as he would, could he ever enjoy Sylvia Plath, one of Lynda's favourites. He saw it as 'dry biscuit' poetry. But he admired many modern writers as well as Jean Rhys and Saul Bellow. He was particularly fascinated by Ivy Compton Burnett, to whom he frequently returned: '. . . the flaws are enormous, such as no other novelist could commit, but there are passages that seem to me profounder and more subtle than one finds in any other novelist. For example the relations of Felix with his father in *More Women than Men*. She has it in her to be one of the greatest of novelists, and yet she isn't.'[15]

Reading, as he sometimes did, in order to discuss with Lynda, Gerald was able at last to overcome his old prejudice against English writers of the past, though even now he couldn't allow Jane Austen to be quite English. 'What an amazing genius she was, more French than English, I would say, in the tightness of her style and her analytical powers. Of all the English novelists it seems to me she has stood the passage of time best.'[12]

He became so interested in her that he reread all her books, her nephew's biography and all her letters. These, too, were enchanting, and gave 'a picture of what her conversation was like in a peculiar vein of irony and teasing which one does not meet with in her novels. I think she must have been delightful to know – warm, gay, controlled and with a great capacity for enjoying the small things of life – not at all the sharp-eyed spinster she is sometimes made out.'*[16]

4

Gerald and Lynda settled almost at once into a minor variant of his usual routine: work in the morning, Gerald a siesta while Lynda went on reading, a walk, further work and reading, then talking and reading aloud in the evening.

Personal Record proceeded rapidly, though he continued to veer between publishing and selling it to Texas. He had reached Tiz by March, Toulon by April, polished off Carrington, Lily and Juliana during spring and summer, met Gamel by October and by December started the Civil War.

As he wrote his life, he talked about it; he also, as far as was possible, wanted to display it to Lynda: trips were already being planned to Yegen, Morocco, Greece and Italy.

In this vein they went to the Rocío in June. Lynda danced and galloped pillion on horseback. The three hectic, dazed days were both enhanced (for Lynda) and rendered fraught (for Gerald) by their driver/companion, the extremely good-looking, intelligent Peter Townend – a lover of Menchu's, and many other women. Lynda, not yet totally at ease with Gerald, liked him. Gerald eyed them narrowly. One afternoon Rosario, passing the two young people chatting at the *fuente* in Churriana, told Gerald they were planning to run off. There was, in Lynda's words, a 'Hullaballoo'. She was astonished, and then angry. 'I told him I wanted a rest from that sort of chaos.' Peter left for Italy and Gerald calmed down.

They restricted their social life because it stopped work, Gerald using Lynda's 'tiredness' to get out of things often only he wanted to avoid. They saw the Davises; Janetta and Jaime Parladé at Tramores; Marjorie von Schlippenbach and the Southbys. Julian Jebb came to stay, and soon after this, on 14 August, Lynda flew to London for her sister's wedding.

* By Gerald among others (see p. 209).

The day after, Gerald went to a party at Nerja given by the painter José Guerrero. 'Lorca's brother and sister were there,' he told Frances, 'I had met them both many years ago – he is a rather emphatic type of literature don, overheated in the USA, and she delicate and wisp like.'¹⁶ He also had some meals at La Cónsula, where Kenneth Tynan and his new wife Katherine were staying.*

On 26 August he followed Lynda to England, and her twenty-fifth birthday took place on their visit to the Duncans. They were back in Spain in the middle of September.

In October, Freddy drove them to Yegen. 'The news of my arrival spread rapidly and countless grey and white-haired old women and men came up to shake me by the hand and reminisce over the past.' They gave a party for him and Gerald noticed the improvements – lavatories, water laid on, houses now whitewashed: 'it is no longer a black village'. Lynda loved it and, once again, so did Gerald: 'No other village in southern Spain compares to it.'¹⁷ They made vague plans to buy a house there one day.

The only pattern not followed with Lynda was the annual visit of Miranda and Xavier. They told Gerald they were short of money and also wanted to stay at their house in Brittany. Gerald insisted to Frances that Miranda was not jealous of Lynda, as he had feared, and indeed Miranda's letters to him at this period are warm and loving. But the grandchildren remember how the family, like practically everyone else, were startled at the rapidity with which Gerald had set up house with Lynda. There was also the question of money.

Whenever Gerald felt guilty over money with Miranda he sent her a letter about the money he had made over to her – his mother's settlement of about £20,000 still being enjoyed by a senile Mabel in her old people's home. He wrote one of these letters now,¹⁸ and that he did suggests he was already planning some larger settlement on Lynda. On the whole, the Corres became increasingly thankful for Lynda's existence the older Gerald became. None the less, money was at times to be an issue.

It was also one of the reasons why at the end of 1968 Gerald and Lynda began actively to plan moving. His income, while he was still

* Earlier, in March, Honor had been there. Her mere presence in the neighbourhood horrified Gerald. He also feared some 'campaign'. But all she did was suddenly to announce at dinner, out of the blue, 'Of course, you know Gerald's never had a woman in his life.' (Gerald to Frances, 31 March 1969).

not poor, was slowly shrinking.* He estimated that a smaller house, dispensing with servants and their expenses and lower tax bills would save £500 a year.

Churriana had itself suffered from the tourist/expatriate boom which since 1960 had become overwhelming. As the *pueblo* grew, water became scarce. In 1968 Gerald had had to bribe to get enough for the garden. New building in front of his house meant you could no longer see the sea. The departure of the nightingales and the golden oriole had been followed by that of the little owls that used to hoot continually, all driven away by the noise of motorbikes and the thunder of big jets landing at Malaga airport.

But the most important reason was that the house at Churriana was saturated with the past and with Gamel. He wanted Lynda and himself to start somewhere fresh.

5

There is a vivid and pleasing picture of them both at the beginning of 1969. 'Here I sit,' Gerald told Frances, 'facing Lynda by a big log fire coughing, sniffing, blowing my nose, eyes streaming, head aching, a pile of used handkerchiefs on the floor beside me. That is, I have a heavy cold, and Lynda has one too. Indeed, it is *her* cold I have' – making it, one thereby understands, almost a pleasure to have – 'Outside a violent *levante*† blows and whistles and presses against the windows so that, as I am reading *Jane Eyre* and Lynda *The Possessed* we imagine that the ground is frozen hard outside and that a snowstorm is blowing from the moors or the tundra. And it really is cold. I am wearing my striped *djellaba* and we have all our meals upstairs by the fire.'[19]

Despite many distractions, they both worked hard all year: Lynda chiefly at philosophy, reading Russell, William James, A. J. Ayer

* This was largely because his investments were not so much mismanaged as not managed – though this year brings the only recorded instance of re-investment by a stockbroker (reported to Frances in a letter of 27 May 1969). Nevertheless, his investment income still provided by far the largest proportion of the total – about £12,000 p.a. at 1990 prices. *The Spanish Labyrinth* and *Spanish Literature* continued to produce the equivalent of £4000 a year. His total income from all sources from the end of 1968 to the start of 1978 was about £19,000 p.a. at 1990 prices.
† East wind.

and on through the other philosophers in Gerald's library; Gerald at *Personal Record*: Bertie Russell from copious notes in February,* then Bell Court and the war, until by July he and Gamel had returned to Spain.

But the major business of 1969 was selling Churriana and then building their new house. By February an American sculptor in Torremolinos called Reed Armstrong had offered three million pesetas (£18,000) and said he would keep on Rosario and Antonio. Gerald accepted at once, but agonising delays and complications continued for many months. Chief of these was, of course, the tenants, still skulking invisibly with most of Gerald's old furniture. A final flurry of wild and belligerent schemes subsided in the face of lawyers; the tenant found he could deal with Reed Armstrong; in the end Gerald had to pay 500,000 pesetas ('Their rent for the next 700 years,'[20] he told Frances angrily). Two more huge chunks of plaster crashed down just missing Gerald's bed, but a local builder climbed into the roof and, though Gerald had not asked him, pronounced it sound, which it wasn't. Finally, a film company offered a million pesetas more than Reed Armstrong but Gerald felt he must respect his first deal. The sale was not completed until August.

In February they also found the one-acre site outside and a little above Alhaurín el Grande, about 23km up the Coín Valley, where they were to build. Cost – 500,000 pesetas (£3000). In the evenings, like a newly married couple, they excitedly and often argumentatively drew plans: a simple rectangular house, with downstairs a big sitting/ dining room (24' × 11'), small kitchen, lavatory (which would flush), library for some 5500 books; upstairs two big bedrooms and a spare room with outside balconies and, at long last, a bathroom. And so it eventually turned out.

Teresita and her husband turned up briefly in February. Then on 30 March, Xavier and Miranda came for ten days, staying for Gerald's seventy-fifth birthday. Lynda had 'flu for almost their entire visit, no doubt aware of Gerald's anxiety about it. He very much hoped they would like Lynda, he told Frances, especially 'as they must guess that she is a risk to their interests as I must leave her provided for.

---

* 'I used to enjoy his company very much,' he told Frances in a letter of 8 February 1970, 'but I never cared for him as a man. Like Milton he was unloveable because he had no warmth in his personal feelings and too much hatred and rancour.'

Miranda is naturally generous – but still.'[21] In fact, they were never to come to Spain again. But all parties are agreed this had nothing to do with Lynda who, as well as being grateful to her, both Xavier and Miranda liked.[22] Xavier was now finding the south too hot in August and the drive there too tiring. He and his family were also becoming increasingly fond of the family house in Brittany. And the Alhaurín house was in any case too small for all of them, though the grandchildren came independently.

Their 'interests', however, were less easy. Except when he was hinting he would leave it to Joanna or Hetty, Gerald had always enjoyed telling Miranda he would leave her the Churriana house. He had now decided to put the house at Alhaurín in Lynda's name. Lynda did not want this and for a long time resisted, but she found his stubbornness too much for her. 'Gerald talked nonstop, as he did when things obsessed him. Week after week until you were worn out. That is always how he got his way.' And he gave good reasons: the avoidance of death duties, Miranda and the grandchildren's lack of interest, the preservation of his library.*

Gerald's own motives were not simply his obvious desire to keep her. His lack of sexual confidence, his diffidence about his looks, had always meant flats or houses or money had been involved in his relations with women. And then he loved Lynda. He loved to give her things.

He could not bring himself to tell Miranda for a year[23] (although he had pretended to Lynda she was in full agreement), and when he at last wrote he also had to admit he was leaving Lynda his books and furniture as well. He then quickly sent one of his mother's settlement letters[24] – explaining once again how she would get this money when stepmother Mabel eventually died.† Miranda's replies do not survive

---

* This weighed strongly with Lynda, as later events proved, but I doubt Gerald's concern was very genuine. He had always bought books to read them, not, as I noted earlier, to make a 'library'. He had long since sold or given away or had pinched by Hope most of the more valuable books. Besides, the library could perfectly well have been preserved by less drastic means. But he knew Lynda loved his books and this was just another way of binding her to him by getting her to accept the house. But this Machiavellian move, as Ralph and Frances would have described it, was to have consequences.

† Almost every letter of Gerald's to Miranda for years now follows Mabel's unbelievably slow descent to the grave, through deeper and deeper states of ga-ga-dom.

but she would hardly have been human had she not been somewhat piqued. It is noticeable from now on that, when they were worried about money, Miranda would write to Gerald (probably without telling Xavier) and ask for help. Gerald grumbled furiously to Lynda about it but seemed to accept this was justified and grudgingly paid up.

At the end of April María got married and Gerald gave her enough land for a house and 15,000 pesetas. Immediately afterwards,Gerald and Lynda set off for Morocco.

This journey – the National Service of Gerald's girls – was strenuous. They travelled 1275 miles by bus and 400 by train. 'Lynda stood the journey well,'[25] the seasoned traveller wrote to Frances, omitting to tell her that he himself succumbed to prolonged attacks of Beethoven deep into the Spanish Sahara, dangerous because of lurking scorpions. On the way back an Arab offered to buy Lynda. Gerald explained in pigeon Arabic that he could, but that she was almost unbelievably expensive – as her name, Lynda Price, indicated.[26]

They had decided to get a car for the new house and as soon as they returned driving lessons began. 'You can't imagine how boring and nerve-racking they are, with the instructor correcting one irritably all the time.'[27]

Gerald made a considerable fuss over the test, despite much talk of 'driving for over fifty years' to Lynda. He was also extremely competitive. When they both failed, he the theoretical, she the practical, he was 'caught out by a tricky question', he told Frances, while 'Lynda passed more by luck than good judgement'. On the other hand, her failing the practical was not only justified but fortunate. 'I don't think she was anything like good enough to pass. The parking test is really difficult even for a good driver and few people get through first time'[27] – except that ex-ace G. Brenan. But, to his intense irritation, he failed the theoretical again. It was not really surprising, he explained to VSP. It was very tricky and 'One has to absorb two large books and the questions are absurdly pedantic,'[28] though these also gave him pleasure. Each question had five possible answers – one correct, two plausible, two absurd. The absurd for 'H' (Hospital) were 1) there is *no* hospital here; 2) this means there is a telephone here. A cow sign (meaning 'Look Out – Cattle'), had – 'Accelerate, there is a wild bull after you.'[28]

At length they both passed, and on 21 September a smart little new Seat 600 arrived. 'The car goes beautifully,' Gerald told Miranda. 'Lynda is becoming a very good and prudent driver and I am getting back into my old form.'[29] Information which no doubt made Miranda's heart sink. Lynda thought he was a menace on the road. 'He appeared confident, but he clearly terrified himself because he had nightmares about his driving and used to wake covered in sweat.' Events were to prove her right.

The August week of the test was one of intense excitement: 21st – Churriana finally sold; 22nd – Gerald's test; 25th – he bought the land at Alhaurín in Lynda's name. The gigantic *obra* of building the house began on 30 September and continued, with all the usual trying complications, until March the following year.

Meanwhile, work continued. *Personal Record* was finished to 1953, and Gerald was haggling with Texas over money, having once again decided not to publish. He revised *Spanish Literature* for the CUP's fourth edition, promising a new chapter on Lorca.* He was also looking forward to his book on *coplas*, for which he had a contract with them. He continued to make notes for his *Thoughts* . . . and in October, Lynda and he began work on their joint life of St John of the Cross.

His old idea of extending his *Horizon* articles had been revived by Lynda's already being engaged in translating the poetry. This was to be the division. By December, when the roof had just gone on at Alhaurín and the tiles about to go down, he was 'deep in that extraordinary world where one doesn't eat and whips oneself every week and prays for eight hours a day and has raptures and ecstasies'.[30]

The year ended with death. Leonard Woolf and Dorelia John died, so did Boris Anrep. Hope was to die in January. Gerald had never felt more alive.

6

One matter oppressed their final weeks at Churriana, and this was the row with Rosario. By law, Gerald had to give her and Antonio 70,000 pesetas, but the custom was one month's wages for each year's service, which would have been £500 or 85,000 pesetas. Gerald

* This chapter was promised for years, but never got written.

proposed £800 or 140,000 pesetas. Not over-generous perhaps, but certainly fair. Besides which, they kept their house and Antonio his job. And Rosario had been able to pay into a pension fund from her wage, while he had contributed handsomely to both daughters' marriages.

But Rosario was outraged. She demanded £1800 (300,000 pesetas). She and Antonio wanted to buy land for a chicken farm and this would cover it. Gerald may have felt slightly guilty, because he told Miranda he finally gave them 170,000 pesetas,[31] whereas the true figure was 150,000 pesetas (£900).[32]

Gerald saw Rosario's anger partly as the result of economic greed and partly expressing her fury over the tenant, whom she'd fought even more tenaciously than Gerald. Her old enemy had finally triumphed. Not only that, the 500,000 pesetas he'd taken – part of which might have been hers – mostly went on building him a house in the garden, right under her nose. But really, Gerald told Frances, 'Master and servant is a difficult relationship, for though there is real affection, I think, between us, peasants are like animals in that they only love in exchange for material benefits, except within the family.'[33]

The family – that was the real issue, and it is what makes this little incident significant. Gerald knew and loved Spain, but he did not feel as a Spaniard would. Years before, writing about Don Quixote and Sancho, he'd noted that in Spain, and only Spain, master-servant love had been so strong it had transcended class and fortune. 'Even today, in out of the way places, the servant who has eaten of his master's bread is a member of his family.' Yegen, and Cádiar from which he'd rescued them, are out of the way places, and Rosario and Antonio had eaten his bread. He had often said he would never go and they, in their turn, had always known they would look after him when he was old. They begged him to stay but he wouldn't. María was quite clear that the real betrayal was emotional.

As such, it could not be repaired or, really, faced. Rosario never spoke to him again, though she didn't mind María and Carmen going to see him at Alhaurín. And, rather than blame Gerald, they blamed Lynda. She'd stolen him away. Rosario wrote to Miranda and said, a pure invention, that Lynda was now decked out in all Gamel's jewellery.[34]

But this sad incident was soon obscured by the excitement, anxiety and exertion of moving house.

Gerald worried about bills. He arranged to sell some furniture to Jaime. Then Texas, who had offered $2500 for *Personal Record* when Gerald was expecting $25,000, upped their offer to $5500 if additional letters were thrown in.

The Alhaurín house had been delayed by continual rain (caused, said Churriana, by Americans landing on the moon). On 12 March it was finally ready. A lorry ferried to and fro – eighty flowerpots, crockery, furniture, 5000 books. Gerald worked in a frenzy; Lynda's back gave out.

The last lorryload was dumped on 25 March. They felt the Alhaurín rooms had looked better empty. The Churriana furniture was out of place, too grand. But, with Gerald now nearly seventy-six, they were about to begin their new life together.

THIRTY-TWO

Peace at Alhaurín

1

Gerald's, or rather, to speak legally, Lynda's house at Alhaurín el Grande took its name from the dried river bed/goat track which ran past it up into the Sierra – Cañada de las Palomas.*

At 1200 feet, it was very slightly above the *pueblo*, with a rather mild view over the clustered roofs and whitewashed houses to one side, with beyond the mountains of Ronda, and ahead over the flat fields of the Coín valley to a still more distant Sierra.

The house itself was more or less exactly as they'd drawn it at Churriana, with the addition of a verandah down one side where they often ate at the big glass table. A car could just bump the three-quarters of a mile from the road, and there were a few scattered houses hidden around, but the overwhelming impression was of peace and isolation. They had olives, and badgers burrowed at the Sierra end of the garden; once more, Gerald could compete with nightingales. Above them, the *cañada* became pure dried river bed, with huge boulders and shingle beds. Thirty years before, it must intermittently have become a torrent after bouts of rain. Now the pine forest covering the Sierra de Mijas, which rose abruptly behind the modest, box-like house, sucked away all moisture. If you picked your way 100 yards up the river bed, you came on several large caves. Sometimes the two foxes who lived there would leap out over your shoulder and vanish silently and with the invisible rapidity of lizards away over the rocks – the lizards which, in fact, formed their chief diet. It was 'the Garden of Eden, though with Adam much older than he ought to be'.[1]

---

* A *cañada* is a goat, sheep or cattle track, so literally – Track of the Pigeons. It can also mean a gully and, though not here, a dale or glen between mountains.

A woman, María, came once a week to help clean, otherwise they managed together. Gerald laid the table and cleared away, washed up, made his bed and for a while, when he learnt Bunny did it, washed his shirts. They lived very frugally. For three years Lynda, who was to become an excellent cook, gave them ham and eggs for supper. Gerald used to say it was astonishing how different ham and eggs could taste taken regularly. Mood, the eggs, the ham – all played a part. 'Every night it's a different meal.'[2]

Despite all the difficulties and tasks attendant on moving into a newly-built house, they were back at *St John* by May and worked hard at it all year. In July, Gerald agreed that Neville Armstrong, a small independent publisher whom they'd met in Churriana, could bring it out. Lynda had changed from poetry to plays and their vast reading programme now included many of these.

Far from the coast in social terms, they saw fewer people, and saw those they did see less often. The Davises, in fact, were trying to sell La Cónsula. But Gerald was always alert for someone who might not be aware of the two-year vanishing horizon as regards Lynda and young men. When Karl, their architect's son, turned up with, as Gerald instantly noticed, 'an athlete's body', and was then clearly attracted to Lynda, Gerald was in a fever. He couldn't sleep all night. 'It is terrible at seventy-six to love a girl of twenty-six so much.'[3] Terrible yes; but one hears unspoken the words – splendid and enviable too. In fact a little later Karl wrote and said he 'sought marriage' – in vain however.

Not surprisingly other people speculated about this aspect of their relationship, not, though, from Gerald's point of view. When Frances came to stay for four days in July, she once again took warmly to Lynda – 'Smiling, beautiful and serene.' But she could not help wondering, 'And can this beautiful girl continue to abjure sex?'[4] Lynda herself was not troubled. 'I had decided against trivial involvements. I would wait for a proper relationship.' And this, in fact, she did. Frances' main preoccupation on this visit was combatting Gerald; even Lynda noticed that he was excessively provocative. In making her his chief correspondent in place of Ralph, in any case closely associating her with him, Gerald had in several respects transferred onto Frances roles once played in his life by her husband: *confidant*, audience, confessor – and now sparring partner. Frances, though she endeavoured to restrain herself, was quite able to give as good as she got. Lynda remembers her saying sharply to him at one point, and with some truth, 'For an intelligent person you have absolutely no self-knowledge at all.' It was in fact an ominous presage of things to come.

In August Gerald and Lynda went to London: Gerald stayed first with Blair and Rhoda while Lynda saw her family; they then both used VSP's basement flat. To further Lynda's new direction, they went to several plays – *The Tempest*, *Hedda Gabler*, and, at the Royal Court, *The Philanthropist*.

Shortly after their return, on 6 September, Lynda had 'flu. That afternoon, Gerald was to drive into Alhaurín with some empty bottles and buy food. Shortly after he had left, Lynda heard footsteps on the stairs and suddenly Gerald appeared covered in blood. The bottles had begun rolling about and, forgetting he was driving, Gerald had bent to pick them up, crashing into a boulder as a result. Thereafter, despite considerable complaint, Lynda refused to let him drive.

He finished the biographical side to *St John* in October and at once began his exploration of the poetry. The theatrical slant to their reading had led to Chekhov,* but the main task of the autumn was the garden. A bulldozer flattened the slightly sloping hillside and then lorryloads of earth were dumped. Gerald worked every afternoon to spread it.

As a result he had developed a hernia by the end of October. The Torremolinos surgeon asked some surprising questions. '"Do you have a great many erections?" he asked me after an exchange of eye flashes with Lynda in the waiting room. "Alas," I mutter, "alas, alas . . ." To cheer me up he said, "Well, anyhow, you'll be able to play golf again within a few days of leaving the clinic."'[5] There was also a suspicion (unfounded) either of prostate trouble or of a varicose vein on a testicle.

Full details of all this at once went to Miranda (his prostate was

---

* And so once more, via his correspondence, we can eavesdrop on his conversations with Lynda, this time as they talk of the Russian writer. 'He was very gay and amusing in company, went to stupid parties and got drunk and probably dropped into bed with numerous women, yet at bottom, as he said of himself, he was severe and harsh. He had one important love affair with a married woman and his heroic trip to Sahalin was made to break it off. A very complex and sensitive man held together by his strong sense of responsibility. I find him deeper in feeling and understanding of people and life than the more artistic Turgeniev' (Gerald to Frances, 28 October 1970).

first the size of a tangerine, then later shrank to a plum).[6] These bulletins, often lurid, became a regular feature of Gerald's correspondence with his daughter as old age took increasing toll. It was his method of eliciting a second opinion from Xavier.

The operation took place on 18 November. 'The place selected for the surgeon's knife is between my legs – not my balls, which today have a princely symbolic value, like the bronze cannon set up at Dover Castle to fire at the Spaniards . . .'[5] Small operations always stimulated Gerald. After it he wrote, albeit shakily, to Michael Holroyd, describing how his sexual organs had swollen to a gigantic size, also turning purple from some medicinal fluid. When the surgeon examined them, 'the little nurse of 21 stood *bouche béante*,* staring and staring'.[7]

The operation was a temporary success, but Gerald began shovelling earth again too soon. He was to be plagued with hernia troubles intermittently until almost the end of his life.

They spent Christmas alone together. Christmas dinner was a chicken, a pineapple and a bottle of wine.

2

1971 began with snow. Gerald finished the first draft of the poetry side to *St John* and began revising. Lynda fought on with translating the poetry. The garden was planted: wild flowers, apricots, pears, persimmons, pomegranates, poppies and also – to the 'great horror'[8] of their neighbours, who had not been suckled by she-asses – thistles.

But his letters to Miranda remain full of testicle and hernia anxieties, all exacerbated by renewed struggles to give up smoking. And in March they are joined by numerous dates of constipation, in a letter which veers charmingly, as the comparison strikes him, into Voltaire's hypochondria (bed and tisane at the faintest symptom).[9] At last Xavier summoned him to Paris for a thorough French check-up and he flew there on 25 March.

Everything was fine – 'My heart like a clock . . . my prostate that of a young man.'[10] On his return a telephone was installed – Alhaurín el Grande 245.

* Mouth open.

On 7 April, Gerald's seventy-seventh birthday, *St John of the Cross* was finally finished. Gerald now took an important step. They had been seeing a certain amount of Ronald Fraser, a writer, left-wing editor of New Left Publications and 'the only person out here of any intelligence'.*¹¹ Fraser's girlfriend, Charlotte Wolfers, was a literary agent, and when she suggested handling Gerald's books, he agreed. Although she was with Ronnie, Charlotte was still married to Johnny Wolfers; she still lived in the top of his London house and they continued to run the agency together. Wolfers was a shrewd and complex man who took out on publishers the very considerable stresses of his private life. This meant he either got his authors excellent terms or none at all. The Bloomsbury boom was well under way by now and Gerald must have seemed a good catch.† But soon it was personal fondness as well as (not always necessary) anxiety about his poverty – encouraged by Gerald – which spurred them on. Johnny Wolfers later worked wonders with reclaiming rights, selling foreign, paperback and serial rights and bumping up advances, but the couple's first essay on Gerald's behalf was not a success. Neville Armstrong was turned down flat, and was naturally furious. Gerald's plea for CUP was also dismissed. By November *St John* had been turned down by six publishers, including John Murray and Macmillan.

In May, Gerald and Lynda made a week's trip round Andalusia, taking in the sites of St John. They stayed in *paradores*. The little Seat 600 made such journeys easy and they were already planning to take it to Greece. It could also have increased their social life, but they preferred to be alone, working. Visits and visitors were widely

---

* Gerald also admired his book *In Hiding: The Life of Manuel Cortés* (Pantheon 1972), which he reviewed in the *New York Review of Books* of 10 August that year.

† Gerald about a quarter enjoyed the *éclat* from his minor association with Bloomsbury and three-quarters disliked it. Apart from anything else, he didn't believe they were a group. He reviewed *Carrington: Letters and Extracts from her Diaries*, edited by Bunny, in the 1 July issue of the *New York Review of Books*. 'If I had put what I thought about "Bloomsbury",' he told Frances in a letter of 7 June 1971, 'I would have said that it didn't exist except in the minds of Virginia and Leonard. They were just a number of people, most of them talented, who had known each other since Cambridge days.' In the review, however, he fully subscribes to the group thesis. 'The Americans had to be given the full myth.' Perhaps he felt afterwards he should have said what he thought, and this is why he wrote to Frances. At any rate he indicated something of his feelings by managing to write the entire review without mentioning that he'd even met Carrington.

spaced. Janetta and Jaime had recently married and Gerald and Lynda had lunch at Tramores in May. In July the Davises brought Cyril to lunch. He was considerably excited by Lynda and took Gerald upstairs. 'You have found a wonderful girl. When you come to London you must both have dinner with me. She is quite outstanding.'[12] They made the first new local friends, some Americans called Byron. Bill, who was writing his biography of Cervantes,* and Betty Byron became their closest friends at Alhaurín. Their dinners together were, said Lynda, 'hilarious' and they all met together regularly. Ian Gibson, working on his life of Lorca, visited them. And every two or three months they drove down to Buena Vista to see Freddy and his Swedish wife Lilly-Mu.† Nearly always her brother, Lars Pranger, would be there, with his intense blue eyes and slightly enigmatic manner.

Longer visits were paid by Gerald's grand-daughter, Marina, now sixteen and by Lynda's mother Marion. Marina, according to Gerald, was obsessed with boys.[12] Lynda said this was nonsense. 'Gerald *wanted* her to be obsessed with boys.' But she was allowed greater freedom than with Miranda and, with her charm and vivacity, was a great success with the Grosses, a local family with lots of young people, prominent among them Cuca.

Marion's visit, about which Gerald had been apprehensive, was also a success. For some reason he decided she was a representative of the English *pueblo*, a repository of deep common-sense wisdom, and relayed all her views approvingly (or reprovingly) to Frances. He was astounded when he discovered this archetypal figure was enjoying Svevo and Scott Fitzgerald. From then on they always got on well.

August and September were too hot for work. 'The slow monotonous summer unwinds every day like a veil.'[13] In the afternoons, Gerald worked in the garden pouring with sweat. He was reading for their Greek trip and vaguely planning his *copla* book with its 'learned introduction'.[13] He was also selecting his poetry for publication, something that, had it come to it, would certainly have taxed his new agents. At the end of the year they finally agreed to send *St John* to CUP.

---

* *Cervantes: A Biography*, New York 1978.
† From the Swedish *Lillemor* – Little Mother.

The year also ended in mutual ill-health. Lynda's health was a perpetual worry to Gerald and a perpetual pleasure. Frances received every detail. In June he had explained to her that Lynda's teeth were not 'exactly bad but hardly robust'. Like him she was subject to colds. Her back, until cured by osteopaths, became painful, especially after driving, and gave her migraines. 'That is,' the letter ended with satisfaction, 'she needs someone like myself to look after her.'[14] To his delight, it helped her back if he held an electric massage machine against it. Gerald himself had to go to the Malaga urologist in December, with renewed prostate anxieties. By Christmas they were sharing one of their 'flus.

3

Bunny and his daughter Henrietta came to stay for ten days at the beginning of 1972. Although at eighty only two years older, Gerald always spoke of him as unbelievably ancient – 'like a great tree standing alone in the middle of the field when all the others had been cut down'.[15] This visit marked the start of a new, close phase in their friendship. Bunny now lived alone in a cottage at Montcuq in the Lot and Gerald enormously admired the tough and independent way he managed. They talked and talked about the past; and then there was the almost equal pleasure of the departing guest. 'After all the cooking and washing up and talking, we go back like a piece of stretched elastic to our own shape.'[16]

Once the £1000 'gift' had been paid back, the warmth and regularity of Gerald's letters to VSP, even if they had only been marginally diminished, returned in full. (Had he not paid, Gerald had written to Frances, 'I would have been left with a poor opinion of him.'[17]) In February, writing to VSP about Lynda, he said, of *course* in two years she would have to get married. 'Do you know of any suitable young men?' A question expecting the answer no.

To Lynda's intense embarrassment he asked the same thing of the Redpaths who had rented Cuca Gross' house above them. Theodore Redpath took four terms' sabbatical from Cambridge over four years from 1970/71 to 1974/75. Always curious about universities, Gerald enjoyed the whiff of the common room Redpath brought, and they talked vigorously about literature. Later, Theo helped him fine-tune his *Thoughts* and the book was dedicated to him.

Gerald gradually became famous in Spain over these years; and was eventually to be celebrated. Fans, dons, other writers came to see him in increasing numbers. Some (to Gerald's delight) had titles – like the Marquis of Puebla y Parga, Duke of Mardas, who arrived from staying at Tramores this month and, in impeccable English, asked Gerald to go partridge-shooting on his estates near Toledo. Gerald refused.

In February, too, Charlotte Wolfers sent Gerald a telegram that *St John* had at last been accepted – by CUP. As Gerald had expected, the manuscript had been read by Professor Edward Wilson and his report was glowing: 'I read the biographical account of *St John* with so much interest that I could scarcely break off for food.' He noted the sympathy and delicacy with which Gerald wrote about the spiritual experience. 'His tact here seems to me remarkable.' But what must have relieved and pleased him most was Wilson's praise of Lynda's translations of the poetry. Gerald had often worried, both to Frances and VSP, that she wouldn't be able to do it well enough. Professor Wilson had no doubts. Though of course 'versions are open to some criticisms . . . the task undertaken is abominably difficult. Her compromise seems to me acceptable . . .' Indeed, as cribs, they were the best he'd ever read.[18] Gerald had naturally discussed her work with her, but the translations were entirely Lynda's. It was a considerable achievement. These praises were later echoed, and added to, by all the major reviewers.

But the first three months of the year were to a considerable extent spent packing for Greece. With advancing age, the preparations for these journeys, the talking, the planning, the map-scrutinising and the booking of tickets were almost as much fun as the travelling itself.

Then came a hitch. One of Gerald's eyes seemed to be malfunctioning. The oculist in Malaga diagnosed a double cataract. An operation would be necessary on their return in June. As an admirer of Gerald's work, he would do it for half price (£120). But a prostate operation was now definitely not necessary though, Gerald ended his report to Frances, 'As you know, I rather enjoy small operations.'[19]

He and Lynda and the Seat 600 sailed for Piraeus on 2 April.

4

Whenever Gerald had a temperature, something he seemed able to develop almost instantaneously, he became delirious (in past years these hallucinatory states had produced the *Clergyman* story and *The Lord of the Castle*). As they arrived in Athens Lynda discovered him staggering about the huge ship in a state of high delirium.

His temperature was 103°. The ship's doctors were furious at first, suspecting cholera which he'd been concealing. Lynda frantically packed and as soon as they docked Gerald was hurried ashore. It was grey, cold and raining. He had to sit for two hours while Lynda got the car. 'I shivered and shivered and shivered.'[20] Everyone, even their shipboard friends, had fled the cholera suspect, all but an unknown Iraqi who covered him with his fur coat and hat and sat beside him.

Gerald then directed Lynda for two hours until, at a small junction in a remote slum suburb, he suddenly announced, 'This is Syntagma Square.' The cholera was just a particularly severe Geraldian 'flu, and after three days in a tiny hotel he was well enough for them to move to the centre of Athens, where they were both instantly floored again by smallpox inoculations.

A demanding journey followed: the Peloponnese, Sparta, Paddy Leigh Fermor – 'a man after my own heart, with similar tastes . . . i.e. an adventurous background, a love of travel and a great love for poetry and for odd sorts of erudition'.[21] Back to Athens via Olympia and then on to the islands.

By 4 May they were in Istanbul, the weather still grey and wet. Gerald hated the mosques with their 'elephantine exteriors'.[22] At last the weather lifted. They drove down through Asiatic Turkey to the south, then back up the coast seeing all the sites from Ephesus to Troy, and continued across northern Greece into Bulgaria.

On 17 May they set off from Skopje to cross the north Albanian Alps into Yugoslavia *en route* for Montenegro and Italy. The road became narrower and narrower and then ceased to be metalled at all; the scenery grew wilder, with huge precipices, dense oak forests, snow on the peaks towering above them. They passed a village and Gerald wanted to stop for the night but, with Lynda now excited by the adventure, they both decided to press on, twisting up and up into the mountains. Suddenly there were torrents of rain, lightning, thunder echoing in the wild gorges. Gerald's window had broken and icy rain poured in. The road seemed to be dissolving, and now a tyre burst. They managed to change the wheel. At last, after darkness had fallen, they reached another village.

They found later that there was a perfectly good road which Gerald's map was too old to show. But Lynda had enjoyed the drive; Gerald had been frightened. They were crossing the country of his great Walk, and the terrible fears he'd felt at eighteen had returned. Then he'd only had an umbrella to fight off the wolves; this time, Lynda remembered, he also clutched his umbrella ready to beat off their attack. And from then on, as he had fifty years before, 'he always got in a panic if we hadn't found somewhere to stay the night – and this continued afterwards, everywhere, even in London.'

They reached Venice on 25 May, did north Italy, then drove along southern France and down Spain, arriving back at Alhaurín on 5 June.

Gerald's letters to Frances are full of Lynda's 'frailty', but this frail creature had just driven 11,000 kilometres single-handed in a small Seat 600, meanwhile supporting a Gerald frequently subject to attacks of Beethoven. They were both exhausted, but despite everything he'd loved it. Indeed, almost at once he began to plan a journey to Italy the following year. As always, he enjoyed seeing the galleries, the ruined cities and temples; he even, in retrospect, came to enjoy their terrifying drive; but what he loved most was the intimacy. Not the Tampax-and-shared-snotty-handkerchief intimacy of Hetty; Lynda was delicate and discreet in a way that was the antithesis of that. But just being with her, being in the same room in the cheap hotels they once again used; waking in the night, lying listening to the faint sound of her breathing and being swept with feelings of tenderness and gratitude.[23]

5

It was decided to postpone the cataract operation till after the Italian trip, and in August they flew to London, once again staying in VSP's flat, and then calling in on Paris to see Miranda and Xavier on the way back.

In England it was the time of Heath's confrontation with the miners, and here one might note an odd facet of Gerald's thought. Though he never voted in an election, he retained an interest in English politics long after his interest in Spain and her politics had declined. All his life his letters are full of comments, often shrewd. On Heath, for instance, he wrote, 'He is too obstinate and unimaginative. The miners deserve some consideration and now they, being also very obstinate and emotional people, are going to ruin themselves and their industry.'[24] Gerald's views on politics were not really either left or right, but entirely pragmatic. He shocked Ronnie Fraser, a Marxist, by quoting approvingly Solon's answer when asked the ideal form of government: 'In what circumstances? In what age? For what people?'[25] On aberrant modern states he would say, 'One must learn to disapprove of bad regimes, like that of South Africa, without feeling superior to them – since in similar situations we might feel tempted to behave in the same way.'[26] And 'pragmatic' could include feelings. He once told Vero Richards that he had decided to vote for Christopher Hollis, although he was a Tory, because he was against capital punishment.

He disapproved of the Franco regime, but his disapproval seems to have been fairly mild. He appreciated the personal liberty he enjoyed – and which anyone could enjoy as long as they avoided politics. But he thought Franco had brought prosperity and peace – and prosperity at last to the poor – and for that, much could be allowed.* But in fact, during his last sixteen years, Gerald's interest in Spain, except for short-lived revivals, fell steadily away. This was in part because he had been cut off from the taproot of his servants, partly because of his absorption in his life with Lynda and his work, and partly it was the narrowing of horizons as old age slowly swallowed him up. And there was something else that has been touched on. Most writers lose interest in a subject they've written about. Gerald had felt so passionately about Spain and the Civil War and devoted such intense energy for so long to understanding both,

* In fact historians of the period now seem to think that the growing prosperity of Spain from 1955 on was really just part of the general Western prosperity which exploded during those years. In so far as they had any effect, the acts of Franco and his ministers interfered with and retarded this growth.

that his political interest seemed to have been consumed. After *St John*, it was as if Spain itself was a book which he had finally completed.

6

The remainder of 1972 was taken up with health, work and the pleasant minutiae of their life together.

Gerald's eyes steadily worsened, and by December he was reading with a magnifying glass. None the less, he determined to do Italy before the operation. He was also now having expensive injections to keep his prostate at bay. (The reason Gerald worried about this so much was no doubt because his father had died of cancer of the prostate at seventy-seven. Gerald was about to be seventy-nine.) Lynda, meanwhile, was going to Janetta's dentist to have her teeth 'built up again and bridged like restorations to ancient buildings'.[27]

Perhaps not ancient enough for Gerald. She was twenty-nine. As always nervous of possible boyfriends, he now suggested a further joint work – they could do the *copla* book together, Lynda translating. Lynda, busy writing a play, did not commit herself.

At the same time as other books, Gerald continually added to his *Thoughts*, and with increasing interest and pleasure. He was compiling one section called 'He' entirely about himself. In October he sent Frances a bunch of entries on 'Love'.

Then in November the proofs of *St John* arrived. Gerald was pleased with it, in particular with the way he'd managed to deal with mysticism when he hadn't the faintest leaning towards it.

But the main decision, taken at the urging of his agents and, in particular, Bunny,[28] was after all to publish *Personal Record*. One strong consideration was that by putting the proceeds from it into a fund for Lynda he could do something to provide for her if he died. Pausing only for the proofs, he worked hard revising it from October till March 1973. 'I only wish I could have your advice,'[29] he wrote to Frances in November. He was soon to get it.

7

On 30 January 1973 Gerald sent Frances what he had written about Ralph. He was clearly slightly uneasy, because in an earlier letter, on 11 January, he'd said, 'I have done something to correct Holroyd's false impression of Ralph.' Both letters, in an attempt to soften Frances up, painted a pathetic picture of his poverty – dentists' bills, plumbing bills, prostate bills. The sole reason for publishing was to get money from Hamish Hamilton.

About 18 February Gerald received Frances' reply – in her words, five pages of 'reasoned fury'.[30] She was desperately upset by several aspects of his portrait and she wanted it changed. 'I feel,' she wrote in her journal, 'it would have been a betrayal of my love for R and my knowledge of his character *not* to have written something of the sort.'[30]

The violence of Gerald's reaction astonished Lynda. He rapidly became almost hysterical – pacing up and down, coughing repeatedly (as his father had done when angry), rubbing his hands agitatedly together and talking about it incessantly. He finally wrote his own furious counter-attack on 20 February, ending that she had rendered him 'senile', caused him to fall into the *cañada* and was fairly sure she'd given him 'a small stroke'.

At one level it is possible to explain these outbursts quite simply. If Gerald was thwarted or criticised by someone close to him it could occasionally spark his remembered anger at his father's attacks and criticisms and provoke the same reaction – fight back. This was particularly so if, like Ralph (or now Frances), they embodied something of his father to him.

But at another level one has to look at the actual points at issue. To Lynda, he said Frances was accusing him of lying – next to being a bore, the cardinal Bloomsbury sin. But, to shift things to ground where he felt more secure, he said she was accusing him of lying about Ralph as he had been before he met Lytton – that is, a brave man of great life-loving charm and good looks, but essentially a non-reading, non-thinking, rollicking, extrovert womaniser.[31] Whereas what Frances objected to was the totality of his portrait – that, just as he had in *A Life of One's Own* and by the same method, he had concentrated on those aspects so that they obliterated the rest. And this is shown by the sort of changes and cuts Gerald was eventually, very reluctantly, forced to accept. For example: 'with many rolling movements of his eyes' (Ralph as negro again) was changed to a plain flirting with a village girl; 'his look of an Oxford hearty' to 'look of a Varsity rowing man'; 'his loud Rabelaisian laugh' cut.[32] Of Ralph's frequently supporting him with loans at Yegen and London when himself poor, of his endless careful advice and sometimes almost feminine comfort, of that intensely alert, powerful and curious mind, almost equal to Gerald's in range and interest, of the hours, years in fact, of delightful gossip and intimate confidences – of all this, the stuff of their forty-five-year friendship, Gerald said almost nothing, and this in a book noted for its detailed and lengthy portraits, and after he had catagorically told Frances, after their last row on the subject, that he *would* include a proper portrait of Ralph incorporating all these aspects.[33]

The explanation, as usual with Gerald, probably lies in those interior dungeons into which he so often locked his strong emotions. When he began to write, the dungeons opened: he felt again in comparison with Ralph the misery and humiliation of his frequent impotence, his furious jealousy that Ralph – so clearly unsuitable – should have won Carrington, and, once again, that he was fighting his father in Ralph's combativeness.

The degree to which the process was unconscious was shown when Janetta went to Alhaurín to remonstrate on Frances' behalf. Gerald was at first frenzied. 'I won't talk about it. It's killing me. I don't know why it is, but it is.' Janetta persisted and suddenly, induced to talk about Ralph and his feelings for him, Gerald began to say such 'nice things' that Janetta said, 'Why not write that?' 'I will, I will,' Gerald said.[34] As soon as he began to write, however, all his complex feelings and reactions surfaced again. He promised both Janetta and Frances he would alter a great deal. In fact, he did not change a word.

But this row – Frances and he did not communicate for six months – was soon eclipsed by a drama, as far as Gerald was concerned, of far greater moment.

He and Lynda were booked to leave for Italy on 3 May. During April Gerald's eyes suddenly deteriorated so dramatically it became clear he would have to have the cataract operation at once. They were both nervous, since there was a risk of blindness.

The operation took place on 23 April. Soon after it, during the night (though he was in fact blind for three days) Gerald was discovered staggering about his room. Unable to use the bottle provided, he was trying to find the basin in order to pee. Thoroughly alarmed, the Malaga clinic rang Lynda. Gerald was always difficult in such circumstances and for the next week she sat up with him day and night, hardly sleeping at all. Lynda hated operations; they frightened and unnerved her. In order to relax and also have a bath, she took to calling in at nearby Buena Vista for an hour or two every day. It so happened that at first Freddy and Lilly-Mu were away and only Lilly-Mu's brother Lars was there. Gerald thought Lars was completely silent, but Lynda had always got on well with him and not found him silent at all. Now not only was he very comforting and helpful, but she realised she also found him increasingly attractive.

Gerald was weak when he came out and totally dependent on Lynda. His strength slowly came back, though it was a year before he mastered his new, very thick lenses. A few weeks after his return they both went to supper at Buena Vista. After it, while they were all talking, Lars left the room, shortly followed by Lynda. A few days after this she told Gerald that she had fallen in love.

THIRTY-THREE

Storms

'In every old man there is a King Lear waiting to break out.'
Gerald to Frances Partridge, 20 July 1973

1

When Lars Pranger was fifteen he had been taken to Paris. The city had had an extraordinary impact. Since then everything French held a sort of glow for him and he longed to return.

He did so on numerous occasions. In 1956, just before returning to complete the education insisted on by his strict Swedish father, he was visiting the apartment of a friend. All at once he noticed three collages on the wall in the style of Max Ernst. For some reason they struck Lars with the force of a revelation. *This* was what he wanted to do. He was a painter.

Not daring to rebel, he returned to Sweden and spent four years at the Stockholm School of Economics. After his degree, aged twenty-seven, he went to Paris looking for a job. He finally found one selling cash registers. The crisis came after six months. Lars had sold one cash register. He fled to Spain to become a painter.

In 1973 he was thirty-seven, laconic, fairly tall, with fine, dark red hair, piercing blue eyes often half-closed, a strong sharp nose and pointed ears. There was something puckish about him, with his ironic sense of humour and quick intelligence. He was fluent in English, French, Spanish and German. He had separated from his American wife and for several years had been living in a shack next to Buena Vista with his son Johan – called Pupi – eating with Freddy and Lilly-Mu and, while Pupi was at school, painting all day in his nearby studio.

'He has,' Gerald wrote much later that year, when he was at last beginning to come to terms with Lars, 'a passion for his art and a sort of religious feeling about light which he tries to express in [his] paintings.'[1] And gradually he became successful. His first three Swedish shows had already sold out and soon he was to get a gallery in Paris, Le Soleil Bleu. While continuing to sell well every year in Sweden, he now showed regularly in Paris, eventually moving to the Galerie Quatre-Vingt-Seize. In 1978 he won the first prize at the Lyons International Painting Competition and in 1987 he was taken on by the Arcadia in the Faubourg St Honoré.

Lars, like Gerald and Lynda, was entirely self-taught. Though a man of great gentleness and kindness, easy and pleasant to be with, he was also, clearly, a man of considerable determination. It was a quality he was to need over the next few months.

The fundamental differences in Gerald and Lynda's feelings, of which he had always been aware, were now, for Gerald, cruelly laid bare. Lynda was enormously fond of him, but she saw no reason why she shouldn't have a lover. As for Gerald, 'I *feel* as if I was her husband, absurd though that may be,'[2] he told Janetta.

In fact, his feelings were almost uncontrollable. For one thing – how could it be *Lars*? It was incomprehensible. Gerald had known him for thirteen years and never heard him utter a word. He had never read a book. His paintings were terrible – and he executed them in an explosives dump. His studio was virtually a bomb: 'One can't even talk in it, or at least Lynda couldn't, as it is so full of explosives.'*[3]

With Lynda, Gerald was by turns bitterly, coldly withdrawn and openly furious. They had rows, then made it up. 'I couldn't possibly have left Gerald. For a long time after his cataract operation he could see very little. He was totally dependent on me. I didn't even *want* to leave him.' She was also passionately in love. 'I was not going to abandon Lars.'

When she went to see Lars, which to Gerald seemed practically every night, he roamed the house sleepless, beset with fantasies. He had had 'violent erotic desires' for Lynda, 'yet they had to stay in my imagination for not only was I impotent'[3] but Lynda would not have

---

* This fantasy of Gerald's had its origin in Lars' solvents, which required some care with matches.

stood for it. He had terrible visions of Lars: 'an obscene figure, suggesting a rat',[4] and also a giant – as everyone was through his new spectacles. Tormented, he poured out his feelings to Bunny, Janetta and now once again, at Janetta's suggestion, Frances.

By the end of July this had been going on ceaselessly for two and a half months. Although her brother Keith, who had arrived to help Lynda with Gerald after the operation, was still there, she felt on the point of collapse. Gerald was now threatening to throw himself off the bridge at Ronda. Suddenly, one evening driving to have supper with Ethel de Croisset, when he was once again saying she wanted to leave him, 'I completely lost control with Gerald.'

Lynda told Gerald that she didn't want to leave him but that he was driving her away. If he went on she would go. They then arranged a schedule. Lynda would stay with Lars on Wednesdays and Saturdays; Lars would come for Sunday supper, but not stay the night. 'From then on things went smoothly.'

Not quite. Gerald hated his jealousy, yet could not contain it. 'It's my father's temperament coming out in me,' he told Janetta. 'Hidden under my equable self there's a violent, passionate nature . . .'[5] It was to be several months before he began to accept Lars and his jealousy burst out occasionally long after that; but from now on he tried to hide what he felt from Lynda.

The stages of acceptance began at once, though stage one was fairly odd. In August, while Lynda flew to England, Gerald stayed for two weeks with Miranda and Xavier in Brittany. 'Miranda is now a handsome woman of forty who talks French like a machine-gun. She holds the floor at meals and all men over fifty profess to be in love with her.'[6] Like Boris Anrep with Roger Fry years before, Gerald suddenly realised Lars was completely mad. 'A text-book case of the pre-schizoid personality,' he told Frances, looking up from one of Xavier's textbooks. He now became very nervous that when Lynda dropped him – 'as she has dropped all her lovers'[7] – Lars would simply disintegrate.

The moment Lynda returned she and Lars hurried away to be alone for three days and look at the house of a friend in Capileira, a *pueblo* high in the Alpujarra. Gerald was irritated, but the worst was over. They went to the Byrons on 4 September for Lynda's thirtieth birthday and he got indigestion ('I always dread dining with people who pride themselves on their cooking').[8] Then on 6 September Lars flew to Sweden and on the 12th, Gerald and Lynda set out on their long-postponed Italian trip.

2

Gerald's cataract operation permanently altered his appearance. Before, his mandarin's face had been notable by its small black eyes, which narrowed and glittered with excitement and became fixed and blank in concentration; now the pupils were vastly magnified to look like something in an aquarium. This complicated their journey because, although strong again – they climbed Vesuvius together – he still often had to be led. Also, cholera in Naples meant painful injections on the boat from Algeciras to Messina which knocked them both out.

But Lynda found both him and the trip fascinating. She drove them across Sicily, then up Italy while Gerald discoursed on all the familiar sites: Sybaris, Paestum, Naples, Pompeii, Herculaneum and so to Rome and the north. Gerald had a feeling for painting, but her degree enabled Lynda to play a leading role here. Only at Florence did he let slip a few snide remarks about Lars. They were discussing literature and he asked how she could talk to Lars, who knew nothing about books, poetry or philosophy. In fact, as Lynda pointed out, though Lars was not as widely read as Gerald – no one was as widely read as Gerald – he had the reading of any well-educated man and was far more knowledgeable than Gerald about late-twentieth-century poets. Lars was also intensely musical. In June Lynda and he had gone to the Granada music festival, the first of numerous visits. It was incomprehensible to Lars how someone like Gerald seemed incapable of listening to a note.

In Pisa, Gerald got 'flu and they had to abandon plans to visit Bunny. They embarked at Genoa, Gerald now delirious, and were back in Malaga on 29 October. Lynda immediately went to Buena Vista to be with Lars for a night.

Nineteen seventy-three ended with Gerald struggling to cut, at Cape's request, 30,000 words from *Personal Record*. It was almost the only work he had been able to do during a turbulent year.

3

Though neither Gerald nor Lynda may have got much work done, there were significant developments here none the less. Johnny and Charlotte Wolfers had achieved their first *coup* on Gerald's behalf. Cape were persuaded to outbid Hamish Hamilton with an offer of £4000, topped up with a further £5000 from Knopf, to which the *Observer* later added £1000 for two extracts (using only one). Gerald had already formally made over the rights of *Personal Record* to Lynda by deed of gift, and the money was paid into a bank account in her name. (In fact, the interest on this account was always used to meet their joint expenses, and it later allowed Gerald to make mollifying statements to Miranda about Lynda's financial 'contributions'.)

The second event was the publication of *St John of the Cross* in May. It is a pleasure to look briefly at this book since it is among his best; it is also, perhaps, at this point, salutary.

As a writer very close to eighty, Gerald could have been forgiven for simply re-working his two *Horizon* articles. In fact, though repeating the form of these, so much new material was added that the *Life* section of the book covers ninety pages compared to twenty-five in *Horizon*.

To some extent, Gerald's energy and the vitality of his writing, like the choice of subject, probably derived once again from self-identification. St John, born in poverty, followed with his monks a life of austere frugality which enabled Gerald to compare them to the anarchists in the Civil War. Brother Alonso, the cook, picked for salads anything his mule stopped to eat. St John drew his monks to God by showing them the beauties of nature – to such a degree that Gerald could compare his mystic's life to that of an artist. His mystical union with Christ, obtained partly during intense states induced by privation and suffering, was expressed in love poems 'of the most passionate . . . the most enchanting sort'.[9] Frugality, poverty, nature, intense states, pain, the poetry of love – St John touched fundamental chords in Gerald. There were some closer to the surface – St John's pleasure in teaching his young nuns, for example, transmitting his knowledge in circumstances of 'tender and

delicate intimacy'.¹⁰ He even had brushes with 'flu – *catarro universal*
– like the great epidemic of 1580 which killed his mother.

And much of the story itself was intensely dramatic – in particular
the furious struggles between the various Carmelite factions leading
to St John, although St Teresa's friar, being abducted and flung into
Toledo prison. Here, scourged, starved, in near-darkness, listening
to the Tagus roaring in its 'deep trench' outside, he came near to
death. Suddenly – the virgin appears. She promises freedom (Gerald
shrewdly relates this to a childhood memory, when he was saved
from drowning by a woman who pulled him from a pond). He
decides to escape – and this the emaciated, diminutive, poet-saint
does. It is as exciting as anything from a Second World War escape
story, and Gerald's telling of it is masterly, his prose, under the
pressure of his immense reading for *St Teresa*, rendered, by a process
of extraordinary condensation, as crystalline and sharp as a diamond.

But he relaxes the rein where necessary, as with the amazing
scenes after St John's death. Crowds swarmed in. 'They cut off pieces
from his clothes and bandages and pulled out the swabs soaked in pus
that had been placed in his sores. One of them bit off his toe, others
took snippings from his hair, or tore off his nails and would have cut
pieces from his flesh had they not been prevented.' There was a
contest for his body – Segovia against Úbeda. Dug up at night, the
corpse was smuggled to Castile and not returned until various limbs
and fingers were scattered over Spain.

One of his most interesting insights refers to a discovery he almost
witnessed when travelling once with Gamel. There was a story that
St John always vanished into a little belfry room of a monastery near
Iznatoraf. No such room existed, so the prior assumed it was a
legend. Then in 1933, just before Gerald and Gamel arrived, repairs
revealed the room and they saw it – a two-foot square, dark cupboard,
with a slit just showing a view of hills and fields. Gerald does not
make much of it – a few lines – but we feel how apt an imitation it
was of the human condition, trapped in this world, *confined*, and then
just able to glimpse, like a vision, the paradise of another world
beyond. And one wonders: would Gerald have been so struck by this
had it not echoed his own visions as a child – the moonlit path at
Dinard, the glittering river beyond the bamboos in India?

As far as the poetry went, he extended his *Horizon* treatment by
only eight pages. What pleased him most here was the praise accorded

Lynda's translation. One reviewer preferred Roy Campbell's verse version, though this has serious defects.* In fact, when appropriate, Lynda's often rhymed too.

¿Por qué, pues has llagado	Why then did you assault
aqueste corazón, no le	And wound this heart, but not
sanaste?	appease it?
Y, pues me le has robado	You rob me of my heart
¿por qué así dejaste,	And yet you leave it;
y no tomas el robo que	The plunder you have stolen – why
robaste?	not seize it?

But most reviewers recognised how skilfully she echoed the clarity, suppleness, elegance and delicate strength of the Spanish; also how she managed to give a sense of the poetry by use of assonance, vowel sound and rhythm. Note, for example, how in this verse from *El Cántico Espiritual*, she follows the rushing esses:

Mi Amado, las montañas,	My Belovéd in the Mountains,
Los valles solitarios	The wooded valleys, lonely and
nemorosos	sequestered,
Las ínsulas extrañas,	The strange and distant islands,
Los ríos sonorosos,	The loud resounding rivers,
El silbo de los aires	The loving breezes with their gentle
amorosos.	whispers.

Gerald, who always followed such details closely, had told Cambridge University Press it might be worth sending a review copy to Auden – and indeed Auden praised it fulsomely in the *New York Review of Books*. It was almost the last thing he wrote. Hugh Trevor-Roper made it his Christmas book. In fact all the reviews were long and favourable. *St John* came out in America that year, Spain in 1974, as a paperback in 1975, and was still making modest

---

* It was, for example, in Gerald's view, often florid and rhetorical where St John is delicate, elliptical and strange. It is also in places slovenly and inaccurate. Thus St John uses *adamar*. Campbell translates this as Christ effeminising the Bride – from *a-damar*. But *adamar* is an archaic word which means 'to love passionately'. St John wrote commentaries on his poems where he expresses 'to love passionately' in various ways. It would seem, therefore, that Campbell either hadn't read St John's own commentaries or, if he had, hadn't taken them in (see Roy Campbell, *The Poems of St John of the Cross*, London 1952).

sums for Gerald and Lynda in 1986, the same year a Danish edition was promulgated.

There is one last aspect to the book, and that is Gerald's own religion. In no sense a Christian or a believer, he always retained a feeling for religion and this allowed him to write about it with sympathy. In *Thoughts* . . . only 'Literature' has more entries than 'Religion' (twenty-three to thirty-three) and he there expressed a good deal of what he felt and believed. But there is a moving letter he wrote to VSP in 1971 where, with a sudden access of inspiration, he struggles to express an aspect of this.[11]

He doesn't, it starts, particularly value his own books but he has had a full life and feels gratitude to – 'I don't quite know whom. Since God has abdicated, I feel rather out on a branch, for I have all the Christian sentiments without any of the belief. Literature is going to come to an end, we are all going to be destroyed by the scientific techniques we are so proud of and civilisation as we know it will vanish.'

Since schooldays, he goes on, he has been frightened of people (especially when they belonged either to an upper or a lower class), but he has always valued his *feelings*. So 'I have evolved a philosophy' – and one feels him evolve it as he writes – 'that one is the sum of what one loves – literature, art, nature, women, friends. *J'aime, alors je suis*.' It is a mystical feeling and is what has always given him sympathy with religion, 'which in another and now out-of-date way says the same thing – so, in the matter of literature, I feel myself rather as being the reader than the writer, the mirror on which the great poets and artists of the past have thrown their reflection and without which and others like me they would cease to exist. I pride myself much more on this than on any little fragments I have been able with their aid to write . . . [though] I have done better, I think, than my very small talent could have led me to expect . . . And I have glorified $\sqrt{2}$ – I won't call him God – for the good things of this world. So I come back to old Christian sentiment.'

The letter begins to fumble as Gerald's insight fades. We need a new language of symbolism, since the Christian one has gone. 'For humanism is too narrow. Only the tops of our brains are human, our roots lie with animals and plants and with the whole of nature. Thus when we set up animal farms and destroy the wild vegetation and beasts we are really destroying ourselves. The only poet who has ever understood this has been Blake . . .

> The wild deer wandering here and there
> keep the human soul from care.'

No doubt the gods, God too, were projections of our minds 'or else they wouldn't have been much use to us . . . But I feel that we do need to look beyond ourselves, beyond human nature, and draw the meaning of existence and if possible our values from some other source.'

4

'Girls are fonder of octogenarians than septuagenarians – they find they have more panache and think they need more protection. Give them a push and they fall over.'

Gerald to author, July 1974

In his eighty-first year, it would have required a fairly violent push. His 'prostate' was at last diagnosed as lumbago and vanished after pills. Otherwise he was fine, now nearly accustomed to his thick spectacles and only needing Lynda's restraining arm in Malaga's traffic.

Theo Redpath had been reading *Thoughts* . . . and they saw a lot of him. Bunny came to stay. Keith Price, whose visit had been punctuated by trips around Spain, flew back to England.

Gerald was now actively trying to get his poems published, with Cyril's help. He finished cutting *Personal Record* in January and sent it to Cape. In March, Johnny Wolfers reported that Rainbird would pay £5000 for a coffee-table book on Spain. They suggested bullfighting. Gerald countered with Philip IV ('pungent love affairs, one of them with a nun'). [12] His dithering over this project kept it alive till July, when Gerald said he only wanted to do his *Thoughts* . . . and then the *copla* book.

But late in February, corresponding with David Machin at Cape about the use of her photographs in *Personal Record*, Frances, who had just seen Gerald in Spain, said she understood everything about her and Ralph had been cut out. [13] Machin, misunderstanding her anxiety, replied, no, it was quite all right. Nothing had been cut. She shouldn't worry.

Gerald's subterfuge was about to be found out.

5

In November 1973 Gerald had told Frances that Cape had forbidden him to mention again anything about Ralph that Bunny or Holroyd or he himself had already tackled. They also wanted deep cuts. As a result, 'You are both to be left out.'[14] This was a complete invention. Cape did ask for cuts and Gerald made them (in particular he removed entirely a long and absolutely vitriolic chapter on Honor Tracy). The one person he refused to cut in any way was Ralph. 'Sorry, no.'[15]

The details of the row, with its attendant explosions, which broke soon after Frances discovered Gerald had changed nothing at all, are all preserved in the Cape archive, Wolfers files, Frances' journals and Gerald's letters. They make stirring reading, but lengthy. Briefly, thus: Machin informed Gerald that Frances wished to see his text. Gerald replied: *Don't* show the text, but also don't tell her he'd forbidden this. Shortly afterwards, Noel Carrington appeared in the Cape offices and 'gently reminded'[16] Machin that Frances owned the copyright to all the Carrington material, which included the jacket, and to most of the photographs. If she couldn't see the text she 'might feel obliged to withdraw' all her permissions. Gerald was now himself obliged to let Frances and Machin make what changes they, or rather she, wanted, and they removed from Ralph the phrases noted earlier and similar 'eye-rolling', 'rollicking' philistine epithets.

Meanwhile, other 'victims' of Gerald's pen (as they began to see themselves, each alerting the other)[17] contacted Cape. Cyril asked to see what had been written about him.* This was a lively and often appreciative description, especially of Cyril's wit and the brilliance of his conversation, but it also dwelt on Cyril's indolence, appearance, his overpowering silences and other faults. Gerald felt that since these were often the staple of Cyril's own humour, it must be safe to

---

* He was not sent the text by Gerald, as various notes and letters of Gerald's aver (see Cyril to Cape, 28 March 1974).

mention them.* But people who make jokes about their defects usually wish to prevent others doing so.

Thus it proved with Cyril. He was bitterly hurt – and with some reason. He had supported Gerald's writing from the beginning, and effectively. He had first published *St John*, and then republished it in *Golden Horizon* (and for this reason Gerald had dedicated the book to him); he had given Gerald the title of his best book and then reviewed it. He was at that very moment pressing Alan Ross to publish Gerald's poems.

He was hurt – he was also furious. He crossed out savagely several passages he found 'particularly offensive',[18] often writing angry comments in the margin. When Gerald referred to Cyril's dominating silences he scrawled – 'GB confuses the horror and embarrassment which he causes CC and others by his naïve sexual boasting, which leaves them speechless.' His anger is to some extent the measure of Gerald's comments, for the portrait, as far as it went, was accurate.

The third victim was Joanna Carrington. She had specifically asked Gerald to remove 'thick negroid lips'. She also resented the inference that their attraction had been mutual and was only not consummated out of consideration for Gamel. Gerald still changed nothing. Joanna refused to write to him for a year.

As for Cyril, Gerald was appalled, the more so when he learnt Cyril was dying. He accepted all his cuts at once and also wrote, deeply ashamed, to Machin: 'I come out of this episode badly.'[21] In the end, Cyril behaved with dignity and magnanimity – 'You have written about me without knowing me sufficiently.'[19] He also sent a message just before he died to say that all was forgiven and forgotten.[20]

There is no sign that Gerald ever felt remotely guilty about his portrait of Ralph – though he agreed that all Frances' changes were 'entirely justified'.[21] By sticking to his position that what Frances really objected to was his description of Ralph before he got to know Lytton he was able to continue thinking he was right. But his stand is really an indication of how deeply he felt the humiliation of his impotence compared to Ralph, how bitterly jealous he had been of

---

* See for example 'Covetousness', Cyril's contribution to the book *The Seven Deadly Sins*, Sunday Times Publications 1962.

him and Carrington and how he still had to stand up to his father when he felt him embodied in the persona (and this included Cyril) of dominant men.

Frances did not easily forgive him, and she and Gerald did not meet or communicate again for six years.*

6

In March a notice had appeared in the Spanish press that the censor had decided that the works of Marx, Lenin and Brenan could now be published in Spain along, Gerald was pleased to see, with the *Kama Sutra*.

Accordingly, *South From Granada* came out in Spanish in May and was at once a great success. Journalists from Madrid, students and admirers came to Alhaurín, sometimes as many as seven a day. And in June Gerald and Lynda went to Yegen for five days while Alfredo Amestoy made a television film about him. Gerald at first refused to go. He was nervous, since he'd heard that Yegen was furious about the book and wanted to stone him. He was persuaded, said Lynda, when Amestoy suddenly thumped a great wodge of banknotes down on the table – 45,000 pesetas, or £350 (say £1650). In the event his fears proved false, though two families barred their doors.† Lynda fell ill, but before she left, she told Bunny, she noticed how much Gerald enjoyed it. He developed a special walk for the cameras. 'A kind of cowboy roll, reminiscent of Gary Cooper or John Wayne.'[22]

During the summer, Lynda went to England for a month. But Lars came a little later *en route* for Sweden and broke his ankle so badly he could hardly walk. Lynda stayed to help him, and in the

---

* It should perhaps be emphasised that Gerald's portrait was not in the least malicious or even in any way unpleasant. On the contrary, it was of a delightful man of whom he had clearly been very fond and whom he admired. But he stressed, especially at the beginning, Ralph's extrovert side largely because he wanted to impress how unsuitable Ralph was for Carrington.

† Juliana's family, for instance, didn't mind. On the contrary, her son Angel said they were rather piqued to find she wasn't mentioned at all. But a good many people didn't like old scandals being repeated, nor did they like the world knowing how primitive they had been. In this respect, the important betrayal was revealing nicknames. When Gerald went to Yegen it was a family known as 'Las Ratas' – the Rats – who were particularly angry.

end had to be away two months. Gerald became incensed, writing caustically to all his correspondents. By 17 October he was so cross he changed his Will, cancelling £2000 he'd left her.[23] Cape wanted him to go to England in November to publicise *Personal Record*. When Lynda, during one of many calls from Sweden, urged him to go, Gerald said, 'Why should I work to make money for someone who doesn't care?' Their Alhaurín neighbours, Claude and Zalin Grant, helped to look after him, and Keith Price flew out to do the same.*

Lynda, in fact, arrived back two days after he'd changed his Will, just in time to be with him as *Personal Record* came out in England, something, in view of all the fuss earlier, he'd been waiting for with some anxiety.

7

Numerous aspects of *Personal Record* have been dealt with already and do not need repeating. The book followed a pattern which he had been evolving from *The Spanish Labyrinth* onwards – passages of exposition interspersed with portraits. Here the portraits are often of considerable length (Gerald thought that made the book Proust-like) and there are some remarkable ones: Hope, Arthur Waley, Beryl de Zoëte, James and Alix Strachey; that of Tiz is a small comic masterpiece. Gerald knew this made the form of the book somewhat clumsy, but felt it was worth it (it was his portrait of Russell and the account of the visit Gamel and he made that the *Observer* extracted). It does mean sometimes that the often dramatic or fascinating narratives – his love affair with Carrington, the trip to Toulon in 1926, Juliana, the Civil

---

* 'Look after' is a relative term. I spent three weeks doing this with Gerald this summer. He did most of the washing-up and clearing away; we shopped together; and he washed all his own clothes. Cooking was what it amounted to, on the battered old gas stove whose oven dial had to be wedged with a match. We got on well, as always, though we had one furious argument over one of his *Thoughts*. He also, I see from my journal of 27/28 August, had one of his 'flus, during which he called me in one morning. 'I've had the most extraordinary dream. I dreamt I was to umpire a world competition to find the world's worst smell. Then I smelt the most terrible appalling smell. I woke up to find I had smelt you burning the toast. Isn't it odd what one's dreams do with things sensed by the senses when asleep.' It is odd, and what made it odder here was that I hadn't made any toast.

War – are severely held up. But it is delightful to read, as well-written as any of his books.

It gives the impression of being an extremely honest book, and Gerald often tells the truth where it must have been painful – about his affair with Carrington, for example, about his marriage and his poetry (apart from *A Holiday by the Sea*, excessive modesty means his other books are barely mentioned). VSP, as we noted earlier, said it was as honest as one could or should expect an autobiography to be. Indeed, he really only fails, apart from what we've looked at, over those things most autobiographers fail over – or don't even attempt: sex, and money. Guilt over his inheritance made him, by ignoring inflation, able to reduce it to about one eighteenth of what it was in real terms. As for sex, he simply could not bring himself to give the whole complex picture. There is in fact a curious ambiguity about many of the descriptions which might have alerted an astute reader, but reviewers missed this. Alex Hamilton, in the three-column lead review in the *Guardian*, wrote, '. . . he records enough women to sate Ziegfeld . . . Sympathetic as one may be to his need for them, they are finally a drawback [since] they interfere with better portraits.' Other reviewers followed suit. J. W. Lambert, in the *Sunday Times*, seems to have heard something of Hetty, referring to a 'belated fling on the Costa del Sol . . . over which he draws a veil'. (Hetty's brief appearance, incidentally, is typical of the account from 1953 on, which is perfunctory in the extreme.) What he'd heard had clearly irritated Lambert and he wrote a long, unfair and unpleasant review going on about 'glum sexual sarabandes'.

But, readable and interesting as it is, *Personal Record* is not as good a book as *A Life of One's Own* and Gerald's reviews were more mixed than usual. Philip Toynbee, in the *Observer* lead review, while praising it, especially the freshness and vividness of the portraits, was sick of Bloomsbury. And a good many other hearts sank at the sight of Carrington and Lytton again. Only Hugh Thomas, in a generous and acute review in the *TLS*, gave unstinted praise and later chose it as his Christmas book.

Personal Record came out later in Spain, America and as a CUP paperback. It did not sell very well and Cape lost money. 'It was their own silly fault,' Gerald told Bunny, 'for giving me such a big advance,'[24] which seems a bit unfair.

With *Personal Record* Gerald had, as it were, put his past behind him. He was soon to be eighty-one. There is a sense, from now on, of him clearing the decks to meet the final opponent – an opponent who was in fact to prove maddeningly reluctant to engage. But the most obvious evidence of this clearing was his last book – *Thoughts in a Dry Season*.

THIRTY-FOUR

Last Active Years

'I want to empty my mind on paper before I die.'
Gerald to Bunny Garnett, 12 July 1971

1

Lynda was continually astonished at the energy and concentration Gerald brought to his *Thoughts* – would have been as astonished with anyone, all the more a man in his eighties.

Gerald's aim, as the epigraph above indicates, was to put down what he thought about everything he thought important, and the task fascinated him. What indeed did he now think of Henry James or Proust or communism or abstract art or the French Revolution or jealousy or marriage? It was an inspired idea for Gerald because it meant he could spend most of his time reading. And read he did – the whole of Henry James again, for instance, to produce two short, careful paragraphs.

His letters are full of the book. In June to VSP: 'I have nothing to tell you because nothing ever happens to me. I have just become a machine for producing pensées.'[1] The book is to be called *Kaleidoscope* (by July it was *Miscellanea*) and would be dedicated to the Spanish Tobacco Company 'for it has been written so much with the aid of their products'. Lynda remembers he actually made himself physically sick with the little black cheroots and once, so immersed was he, he set fire to his chair.

Prompted by Johnny Wolfers, Cape suggested in February a selected edition of his letters, offering £2000. 'Who has ever heard of a writer consenting to the publication of his letters during his lifetime?' Gerald wrote to his agent. 'Can anything more shameless be imagined? The mere thought of it brings a blush to my cheeks. It is true that Pope offers a precedent, but he has been much abused for it.'² None the less – £2000 (£7900)! Rather shame-faced, Gerald agreed, but in fact this particular selection, despite Herculean efforts on the part of Wolfers, was never made.*

As Frances receded (pursued by waspish comments in various of Gerald's letters) VSP and, still more, Bunny became chief correspondents. There is something very warming about the friendship of these two old men. Bunny had various troubles at eighty-three – one was pulling on his socks. Gerald worried about this and became inventive, visualising solutions: 'I think', he wrote in one of several letters on the problem, 'you could get a clever workman to devise something for pulling on your socks – a ring to fit into a long handle and three clothes pegs.'³ They remained close, Bunny visiting regularly until he died.

In May, Gerald paid the now usual visit to Paris to see Miranda and Xavier and his grandchildren. He returned, again as usual, a francophile – he wished to be re-incarnated as a Frenchman.

The heat that summer was terrible – 110° in the shade. Gerald could no longer really take it and in August they all (and 'they' now meant Lars, his son Pupi and Misa the cat) went to Freddy's house in Capileira returning, on 15 September, refreshed from the 1500 metre coolness. While there, as well as Jean-Jacques Sempé, the French cartoonist whose 'pretty American girl'⁴ attracted Gerald, he met Eduardo Castro, 'a poet from Granada who has written a good and honest book on the death of Lorca'.⁵ Castro, by then metamorphosed into an enterprising journalist, was much later to play a short but extremely decisive role in Gerald's life.

These years before the final débâcle of extreme old age were peaceful, productive and happy. He worked hard at his *Thoughts*, while Lynda continued her huge programme of reading.† The

---

* Part of these efforts were, over a generous dinner, trying to enlist me as editor, a move Gerald had apparently agreed. I have never met anyone as determined as Johnny Wolfers but, without knowing the opinion Gerald had expressed, I really agreed with it. Eventually, Johnny became so drunk – alcohol was one of the tools of his trade – that I had to carry him home to bed. Later he suggested he might edit them himself, but by then Gerald had gone off the idea.

† Lynda's aim had been to educate herself and this she succeeded in doing, becoming over the years both widely and deeply read. She also became familiar with philosophy, psychology, anthropology and indeed all the varied subjects in

routine of her spending two nights with Lars and Lars coming to Sunday supper was now completely established. Gerald grew increasingly fond of Lars and eventually came to rely on him as much or more than on Lynda, though he occasionally regressed. When the couple went to Granada to see Lars' parents at the end of September, Gerald said crossly, 'I don't see why you have to go and see his parents. You're not engaged to him.'[6]

In November, Franco died. Gerald agreed that the regime was corrupt, reactionary and stupid – despite its prosperity – and that it was time Spain 'came out of its "nursery"'. Nevertheless he, like all ordinary people – who 'are mostly sorry for Franco's death'[8] – was apprehensive since he, like them, had not yet discovered what an extraordinary man they had been given as king.

In December, a bookseller from Haslemere suddenly arrived. His father had sung ballads and Gerald had known him in Weld Arms Cottage days. He therefore let the young man ransack his library – accepting £300. He never knew if he'd been cheated or treated generously; in the end he decided he'd been robbed of thousands.

2

1976 continued the even tenor of 1975. There was mild social life – to Tramores, for instance, in January to meet the Spenders. A convivial Scotswoman called Shay Oag, a writer on bullfighting, came to cook for him when Lynda went to England in June.

But the main activities were *Thoughts* and the Alpujarra. *Thoughts* manifested itself in his drinking 'almost as many cups of coffee as Catherine the Great',[9] haystacks of cheroots and cigarettes, and his always small handwriting contracting, even in letters, to the concen-

---

Gerald's dwindling but still substantial library. It is clear, from *St John*, that she could have become a translator of distinction, but she wanted to do original work. It was always difficult for her to find a subject, as it had been for Gerald. She tried poetry and plays, but then wrote a number of short stories which VSP, among others, admired. These are, of all things, the most difficult to place from an unknown writer. She had embarked on a novel, but then her first child was born, followed soon by a second, and the household became very arduous. It seems possible that, after all, painting is her true direction. Her work is delicate and elusive – a little reminiscent of Giorgio Morandi; but the vision is her own.

trated diamond points to which it always sharpened when he was intellectually stimulated. By January he'd reached 'Politics'; 'Revolutions' in February (reading twenty books on the French Revolution, as many on Marx, Lenin and Stalin), 'Nature' in May and by July he was revising the whole book.

That summer, he and Lynda decided to buy a small house in the Alpujarra. Once again, Gerald wanted to buy it in Lynda's name. This time, determined not to be swamped by him, she suggested a deal: the house in her name, but in return she would type *Thoughts* . . .

This was no light task. For one thing, she had only had twelve typing lessons and so was very slow if for that reason 'rather perfect'. But the main reason was Gerald's own perfectionism. Rewriting had always been a major element in his prose construction. Now he excelled himself. Every *pensée* was written two or three times, quite often as much as six times. Each version had to be typed out afresh. The cost, had they paid a typist in England (Gerald's custom), continually sending out new versions and paying for these to be typed and sent back, would have been considerable. The work took Lynda two years.

It had become clear that a house in the Alpujarra would be sensible (though it had long been a vague plan) because Gerald found the summers increasingly unendurable. Freddy lent them his Capileira house in July and they had discovered what they wanted and paid for it by the end of the month. It cost 125,000 pesetas, £1000 (£3200) and a further thousand pounds-worth of *obra*.

Fondales is the lower *barrio* of Mecina-Fondales, itself a little *pueblo* far below Pitres. When they discovered it, the road was still not finished, and Lynda remembers Gerald leaping down the bulldozed track, though he fell once. He had, in fact, given up regular walking just before his cataract operation and not resumed it; this, at eighty-two, 'was his last *active* phase'. The land was terraced – planted with crops, fruit trees, large chestnuts, walnuts and tall, graceful poplars. The inhabitants were independent, self-sufficient farmers whose ancestors had come from Galicia when the Moriscos were expelled in 1610.

The houses of Mecina-Fondales were built and joined in typical Berber style. Their own house at the edge of the tiny *pueblo* eventually had three bedrooms, a store, a kitchen/living/eating space and a bathroom, with two good terraces of land. It looked across a deep ravine to the precipitous flat face of a mountain rising, as Gerald described, like a vast variegated tapestry. Below, crossed by an ancient Moorish bridge, rushed an icy torrent from the melting snows of the Sierra Nevada.* Gerald was soon recognised and revered there. People said, '*El toro vuelve al fin a su querencia*' ('The bull returns in the end to its shelter' – the place it means to die).

They returned to Alhaurín on 14 September and soon afterwards had several visits from VSP and Dorothy, who took a house in Churriana during October. Then in October and November Johnny Wolfers came to stay for two weeks.

Sometime towards the end of the year he received a letter from Kenneth Hopkins asking to see some of Gamel's poems. A Powys expert,† it was Hopkins who had published two of Gamel's poems in *Everybodys* in 1950. As well as admiring her writing, he seems to have fallen slightly in love with her – partly with the photographs of her as a beautiful young woman, partly fascinated by the erotic elements in her work and her life as he had gathered it from his researches into Llewelyn. Now in semi-retirement in Norfolk he spent much time running a small private press and writing letters. He was soon suggesting a possible private printing of Gamel's poetry. Gerald, suddenly seeing a way to lighten his definite, if slumbering guilt over this, responded delightedly.

On 3 January 1977 he sent the final version of *Thoughts* (still unnamed) to Johnny Wolfers. It had taken five years, though with considerable interruption for *Personal Record*; soon afterwards he had a series of small fevers, with delirium and falling over, eventually diagnosed as a kidney infection.

Lynda felt later that subconsciously Gerald had expected to lay down his pen and die after this last work, and die romantically – 'he laid down his pen and died'. He didn't die; but for the first time his

---

* And at 3500 feet the difference in temperature from Alhaurín was psychological more than actual – though Gerald's bedroom in the depths of the little house was always, as he said, 'mushroom' cool.

† He wrote *The Powys Brothers* (Phoenix House 1967), a competent if not exactly inspired multi-biographical 'appreciation'. Presumably because Gerald and Gamel were still alive, he did not mention Gamel's affair with Llewelyn, though had he asked they would not have objected. He also published numerous books on English poetry, poetry of his own, an autobiography and various 'Selections' from work by Llewelyn and John Cowper Powys and others.

handwriting occasionally goes awry. About now he told Hopkins he was eighty-four when he was still eighty-two and in March 1977 he was complaining to VSP: 'Stiffness, rheumatism and failing mental faculties.'[10]

In fact, and for long periods, his mental alertness, his energy, his gift of phrase were still astonishing. But he had begun his long, slow – almost infinitely slow – decline.

3

The first six weeks of the new year were spent at Capileira – except for a brief break of two days at Alhaurín when Freddy returned from America* – while Lynda and Gerald oversaw the *obra* at Mecina. By 20 February it was finished.

In February, too, *Personal Record* came out in Spain and was an instant success, reprinting within a few weeks. Spaniards are personally reserved and discreet in their memoirs; there is no tradition of frank and self-revelatory autobiography. Dalí, Juan Goytisolo and perhaps Arturo Barea† are virtually the only recent examples, and only Dalí and Barea had then written. *Personal Record* therefore seemed astonishing and was seized on, especially by the young. Gerald came to symbolise the revolution in manners that was sweeping Spain. He was besieged by requests for interviews on television and in the press (all of which he refused) and by May the book had become, in that elastic phrase, 'a bestseller'.‡

Thoughts must have seemed – it seems so still – a difficult book to place. Various publishers turned it down, including Cape. Once again, Wolfers was forced to turn to CUP. Perfectly aware of the situation – 'We are therefore . . . a kind of last resort' – M. H. Black's recommendation of acceptance is a model of the civilised, humane and, as it turned out, shrewd judgment typical of that excellent

* This generous man returned from the death of his father a millionaire, a fact from which Gerald was quite often to benefit.
† See Barea's *The Forging of a Rebel* (Viking 1975) and Gerald's review in the *New York Review of Books*, March 1975.
‡ The Spanish version differs from the English version in that the end is shorter. There is, for example, less about Lynda, who is described, presumably in the interests of respectability, as Gerald's niece (a mis-relating repeated by Hugh Thomas in his *Times* obituary).

publishing house. 'My own view is that Mr Brenan is a writer of some quality: not a great writer, but not negligible either. He has given us three very successful books. Publishers often accept a "difficult" or speculative first book for the sake of what may come after; one might invert the logic and accept a last book for the sake of what has gone before.'[11] CUP did, however, demand massive cuts. So carefully had it been written, the actual *pensées* could only be shaved of a word or two. The editor forced Gerald to jettison five complete sections: Philosophy, Politics, Society, Revolutions and History.

The book still had no title. CUP suggested *Gleanings*. Gerald was appalled. 'A Victorian Lady's last volume of verse,'[12] he cried to VSP, begging for help. Finally, in September, he struck on the lines in Eliot's *Gerontion*, which were also spoken by an old man:

> Tenants of the house,
> Thoughts of a dry brain in a dry season.

He spent three weeks in May and June in Paris and then Brittany. Xavier gave him a thorough going-over and said he would live to be ninety. (Slightly less accurate than usual.) Then in July they all went for two months to Mecina. Gerald enjoyed it; and enjoyed it the more for Lars being there: 'We form a very closely knit family . . . I have never had a house I felt more at home in or felt the charm of family life.'[13] In a way, it was for the first time.

Life was very quiet. Charlotte Wolfers came in October, followed by VSP and Dorothy for three days. Gerald spent hours reading, occasionally having bonfires of his papers. And as he read, he revised his judgements. Reading *The Quiet American* in 1956, for instance, he thought Graham Greene, with his 'strong but schoolboy imagination'[14] was really a glorified thriller writer. Now 'To me he is the greatest novelist of his century in the English language . . . *The Heart of the Matter* and *The Quiet American* . . . are haunting in a way in which Hemingway and Fitzgerald never are.'[15]

And that waterfall he had said he had heard after fifty and had not really heard at all now resounded more and more often in his ears. He felt he was going to die because his past hypochondria came, as it were, to represent a whole lifetime of fragility and ill-health; and his past behaviour meant he *should* be dead. 'My life,' wrote this smoker who had never, in the eyes of real smokers, ever really learnt to smoke, 'hangs by a thread because my heavy smoking is bound to have weakened my arteries.'[16]

4

In January 1978 Gerald was given a new prize, the 'Master Club', just instituted in Spain for autobiography. There was no money, but the prestigious award brought a metal cylinder. It was to be presented by Camilo José Cela, a Spanish writer he admired – 'their Graham Green spiced with Swift' – but he decided not to go to the ceremony. 'I just can't deal with situations of that sort or stand, longing to pee, while the epithets are piled on my head in a foreign tongue.'[17] Besides, it would have meant going to Barcelona and '. . . I can't travel. I am slowly turning into a fixed object like a tree.'[18] At the end of November *The Spanish Labyrinth* had at last been bought to come out in Spain legally (netting Gerald £4,000). In February he appeared on Spanish television again.

It was ten years since Gamel had died. 'I never forget her,'[19] he told VSP. In extreme old age he thought of her more and more, sometimes confusing Lynda with her in his letters. But the revival now was probably due to the private publication of her poetry, which had already begun and stretched over years, with Kenneth Hopkins writing to Gerald voluminously.* Although Gerald's initial impulse had been largely guilt, he now totally revised his opinion of her poetry. Passages, he told VSP when he sent him her sonnets, reminded him of late Auden. 'And now a great wave of guilt has

---

* All the poems were published in limited editions by the Warren House Press. *Twenty-Eight Sonnets* in 1977, *The Last Leaf Falls* in 1978, *Middle Earth* in 1979, *The Search for Demeter* and *The Weight of Human Hours* in 1980, and in 1984 *The Collected Poems of Gamel Woolsey* with an appealing frontispiece of Gamel and a perceptive introduction by Glen Cavaliero. Gerald sent frequent cheques to pay for all this (there are records in the MF archive of £710 in 1977 alone), but Hopkins told me it cost him about £3000, some of which he recouped on the advances for *Death's Other Kingdom* and *One Way of Love*, which he introduced to Virago. His 'rehabilitation' of Gamel, as he described it, was to be completed by an edition of her letters and also the biography of her he planned to write. He died before he could begin either, though he did manage to write and publish two short booklets: 'Passages in the Life of Reginald Hunter' and 'Bertrand Russell and Gamel Woolsey' (both Warren House Press 1985).

swept me because I didn't appreciate sufficiently that Gamel was a real poet, though an irregular one.'[19]

Hopkins also published Gerald. Despite his wounded feelings, Cyril seems to have continued trying to get Gerald's poems published (in *Encounter*) till he died[20] – if true, a gesture of considerable charity. Gerald then offered them to Julian Berney, another independent publisher, but he too turned them down. Finally, he paid to have them printed by Hopkins.

The Magnetic Moment contained seventeen poems, the distillation from many hundreds of poems written throughout his life (though the introduction maintains the old fiction that he had been forced to give up poetry to earn his living and only started again when much older). Gerald distributed them. 'I can't think of an ordeal more to be dreaded,' ran the letter accompanying VSP's copy, 'than the receipt by post of a volume of verse written by an old friend.'[21] But his poetry had meant a great deal to him, charting his life in the way the title indicates; so much so 'that I could not raise the courage to burn them'.[22] It was, apart from sporadic bonfires for which he had ample courage, the last major clearance.

It is difficult to be precise about what fuelled Gerald's bonfires. Some time now he burnt *Segismundo*, though Lynda tried to save it. On the whole, it seems to have been his early poems, stories and attempted novels, though a lot of poetry was left. *St Teresa* went. But his determination to survive equalled Boswell's: abstracts remain of his entire life taken from pocket diaries 1919 to 1980, as well as some of the diaries themselves.[23] He preserved dreams. There are short accounts of key incidents like the deaths of his parents. On what he regarded as crucial issues he was determined his view would prevail. Thus there are three copies of his furious chapter about Honor Tracy. When Frances' *A Pacifist's War* came out later this year, Gerald made three copies in note form of his view of Ralph and sent one to Texas. (He did not read the book and mistakenly believed he was attacked in it. 'I am the main villain.')[24] It is possible, though there is no evidence except by their absence, that he destroyed records of things he did not want people to discover, like his short-lived lust for Miranda or the truth about him and Joanna. If this is so, he forgot his letters. But certainly these bonfires gave him a pleasing sense of tidying-up, as similar bonfires had no doubt done for his father and other Brenans before him.

The Seat 600, nearly ten years old and battered by crashes and their two huge journeys, started to give up. Using the *Spanish Labyrinth* money they bought a new car, a Citroën *deux chevaux*.

But now a decisive change took place in Gerald and Lynda's life together, which had also lasted ten years. Lynda was about to be thirty-five and she and Lars decided to get married in Gibraltar and have children. By April she was pregnant. In sympathy, Gerald once again struggled to give up smoking. But the major element in the change was that Lars and Pupi moved into Alhaurín. The move was suggested by Gerald. He was now extremely fond of Lars but he was also very conscious that he was ageing. He was terrified of becoming a burden to Lynda, but in small ways he already was. He would sometimes stagger and nearly fall when he stood up, causing her to start forward. When he rolled out of bed, which he tended to do when delirious with one of his 'flus, she found it impossible to get him back. There were many ways Lars would be a help. He was installed by the end of May and had paid for a new studio to be built behind the house by early December.

In July they all went to Mecina for two months. As Gerald's fame grew in Spain, so more people came to see him, with books to sign and so on. 'I must say I enjoy it,'[25] he told VSP. Gerald had given Johnny Wolfers one of the portraits of him by Carrington, and in June Wolfers had presented it to the National Portrait Gallery. Lynda told Wolfers that, though self-deprecating, Gerald was secretly 'delighted with the deal'.*[26]

Among the people who visited them was Bruce Chatwin, at the instigation of Magouche Phillips, who had recently married Xan Fielding. Chatwin visited them again at Alhaurín in October. Gerald preferred his Indian boyfriend Sumil Sethe. 'I really loved him and longed to know him better.' His comments on Chatwin, though to an extent due to a sense of rivalry – Lars described their conversations as 'verbal ping-pong' – were acute. 'He is a man enclosed like an

---

* The 'deal' was that Wolfers should keep the portrait for his lifetime, but in fact it is already in the Gallery. Gerald used it for *Personal Record* and it has been used for this book. Gerald told Wolfers (letter, 10 June 1978) that Carrington hadn't finished it, 'Hence the wooden look', but it is difficult to detect this. The portrait is probably the one done at Larrau, since the visit was truncated. The other portrait of Gerald by Carrington belongs to Xavier Corre. In my view it is less alive than this one.

insect in a tight coating of chitin – totally insensitive, needs to talk all the time' – and pretends to know more than he does. Typically, Gerald knew things about Tierra del Fuego that Chatwin hadn't discovered, including its extraordinary language 'which has the largest vocabulary in the world'. Gerald noticed that the writer had little feeling for nature. Chatwin also complained that his wife didn't give him enough money. 'I can't say I really liked him – an egotistic little boy – yet his energy was impressive.'[27] He gave the over-voluble young man all his old Eastern travel books bought during the First War, most now unobtainable, which Chatwin later sold.

He complained to VSP that he couldn't write any more; but he could read: in November all of Conrad, also some French writers – Huysmans and the Goncourts, neither of whom he liked. And he could write letters, the handwriting sliding a bit, but always, still, the sudden poetic phrase: 'Now a glorious sun has come out and the sky is the colour of some young ladies' eyes.'[28]

But by November they were being deluged in tremendous rain. Malaga flooded to a depth of two feet and all the rats in the sewers drowned and could be seen floating in the streets or just offshore. Events at Alhaurín were also dramatic – two births following each other in quick succession. On the 27th, that of Carlos Gerald Pranger, arriving in twenty minutes. Lynda was back home two days later. Then on the 30th *Thoughts in a Dry Season* was published.

5

What impressed Theo Redpath, as he carefully read and commented on *Thoughts* . . . before publication, was the enormous range of interests and depth of knowledge revealed – history, botany, birds, philosopy . . . so much noticed, so vividly commented on. 'It could be his masterpiece.'*

---

* Five sections were jettisoned; fourteen remained. Here they are, arranged not as they appear in the book – something which was very carefully planned, as was the order of the *pensées* themselves within each section, so that each complimented and led on to what followed – but in order depending on the number of pages (in brackets) Gerald devoted to each: Literature (33), Religion (23), Art and Architecture (20), Nature (17), Love (14), Places and Peoples (13), Life (13), Dreams (9), Writing, Ying Chii, People (6 each), Introspection (5). Asked to guess, one would have expected more on love, which includes sex.

Quite often, where the *pensées* were revealing biographically, they have been used as epigraphs – so a feeling of the book has already been given. It contains many other entries similarly acute about himself: 'He was a man who liked his friends, yet whenever one of them was mentioned he said something disparaging about him.' What Gerald left out was often equally honest or relevant. Sex: 'No, he was not normal in these matters because when he was young the situation of men with girls had not been normal either.' And 'He could have walked through a mine field or detonated a bomb without his heart beating faster. It was the human face that most frightened him, the evil face he remembered from his school days . . .' (both of these from the 'He' notebook in the MF archive).

The minute essays on everything from different writers to abstract art or the whale or Christianity, some of the most interesting parts of the book, though condensed into two or three paragraphs so elegantly and lightly they don't seem condensed at all, are none the less too long to quote enough of them to give an idea of their quality. The sense of humour first revealed in *Dr Partridge's Almanack* was now refined into something wholly delightful, particularly in the person of Ying Chii, the 100-year-old sage who lived on rice and vegetables in a cave in the province of Shansi: 'Hitler sent a secret emissary to Ying Chii to ask whether or not he should invade Russia. Ying took a sip of tea before replying and then said – "Why not?"'

Few other writers have attempted a whole book in this way: Pascal, La Rochefoucauld, Georg Christoph Lichtenberg (1742–99) and perhaps Flaubert's dictionary of *idées reçues*; there are Goethe's aphorisms, and those of the Frenchman Cioran, Logan Pearsall-Smith's *Trivia* books, Cyril's *Palinurus* – though much of this is quotation. Gerald is better than the last two and, with his variety of length and style, mood and approach, his humour and range, much more interesting to read today than the first six. As profound? As sharp? Quite often.

Successful examples of such works are therefore very rare – the form is a demanding one – and Gerald does not always succeed. One danger, as Robin Smyth noted about Cioran the French aphorist, is that it 'carries a small charge of pride in craftmanship, a flourish of satisfaction at having got . . . the thought so neatly fitted into a tiny space'.[29] Gerald sometimes makes one feel this. Another danger, as Philip Toynbee noted, is cynicism.[30] 'Intellectuals are people who believe that ideas are more important than values. That is to say, their own ideas and other people's values'.

Sometimes there is simply a lapse of awareness. 'But women also have their problems.' (This *pensée* follows one about men being impotent.) 'Thus making love to a girl for the first time can be like going into a dark room and fumbling for the electric switch. Only when a man has found it will the light come full on.' This is worrying because, though meant to be of general import, it irresistibly suggests a clumsy man groping for the clitoris.

But on the whole Gerald was astonishingly successful, and reviewers acknowledged this. The whole *Times* group was on strike, but eventually, in March 1979, *The Times* gave him a belated but very good review. Philip Toynbee, despite reservations about cynicism, was also full of admiration – particularly about the little essays.[30] VSP reviewed the book glowingly in the *New York Review of Books* (the book reminded him of Gerald's conversation) and, at his urging, this paper printed extracts. *Thoughts* . . . sold surprisingly well, went into two editions and CUP, as it thoroughly deserved, made a modest profit.

One telling personal observation came from Bunny. After considerable praise, he adds, 'The most obvious omission is that you say nothing about children who rouse such profound instincts and tie lovers together. My deepest emotions have been for my children . . .'[31]

Gerald had enjoyed writing *Thoughts* . . . almost more than any of his other books, but it was not his favourite – this was *A Holiday by the Sea*, followed by *Spanish Literature*. On the whole, his view of his own work was remarkably objective and clear – though modesty and remembered ambition could still distort this. 'Only if I had written a few lines of good poetry would I wish to survive.'[32] He was aware he had written no indisputably great work, 'Yet I don't say that in disillusion or disappointment, for to have tried is something – indeed a great deal.'[33]

He recognised he was a competent historian – perhaps even more than competent. But he was quite clear that he was not a Hispanist, in the sense that that term is used today of someone, usually an academic, who has deliberately devoted themselves to a study of one or more aspects of Spain and her civilisation. As a writer, he felt that what distinguished him was the expression of a particular sensibility, with the insight and intuition and literary gift that grew out of it. 'I think my best literary qualities are a certain way of handling language and a certain sort of erratic imagination.'[34] To Miranda he said more simply, 'I know I am rather a good writer and leave it at that.'[35]

In a sense, Spain overwhelmed this. When an English television journalist came to interview him in July 1981 it was because he was celebrated in Spain. 'I have ceased to be an English writer and become a Spanish one.'[36] He was proud of his fame there, of the prizes and appreciation, and he thought that, were he indeed to survive, it would only after all be as someone of interest to a few future Hispanists.

Thoughts . . . was the last book he wrote, but not quite the end of his writing. He was to produce one more short story and one more review the following year. Then, apart from letters, silence. Except for love, reading and writing were the most important things in Gerald's long life, and the first had often been contingent on the second. With the end of writing, it gradually became clear that an essential spring had broken. In the end, love too became impossible.

THIRTY-FIVE

Old Age

'*It is no joke to be nearly eighty-six and feel senility stealing over one.*'

Gerald to Kenneth Hopkins, early 1979

'*When one ceases to be afraid of dying, one becomes afraid of not dying.*'

Gerald to VSP, 23 December 1982

1

The image of rocks emerging as the tide recedes was recurrent throughout Gerald's life and now, as with many old people, various elements constant in his character began to stand out with a certain starkness as his great energy ebbed away.

But in 1979, some of the constants were intermittently almost as before – there was still a depth of water in the bay, surges of energy still there. In February he suddenly wrote a short story, 'The Inner Life', about a shop worker who has a paralysed wife he doesn't love yet is perfectly happy. This has various resonances, obvious enough, with his past and with past work, but was eventually burnt.*

Later in the year he wrote his last review for the *New York Review of Books*.¹ In his discussion of *Spain: Dictatorship to Democracy* by Raymond Carr and Juan Pablo Fusi, in which he gave the book almost unreserved praise, he showed all his old seemingly effortless

---

* I assume. It doesn't survive. 'Farewell literature!' Gerald wrote gaily to VSP (26 February 1979), explaining he'd decided the story was no good. 'I have had some pleasant romps with you (for I love writing) but they have only been romps after all and therefore of no importance.'

grasp of things Spanish. The portraits, in a few concise, clear sentences, were as vivid as ever. Here is the beginning of his brief sketch of Franco:

> He was not a man whom many people could feel drawn to and he had a very limited mind, yet his strong rather negative charisma combined with his absolute confidence in himself and his instinct for keeping in power by playing off one group against another made him for forty years the undisputed master of his country. His slowness of mind turned out to be a merit: in a land where everyone talks fluently, he listened and said nothing. His caution too was proverbial, but when he decided he must act he did so at once. He could then be ruthless at getting rid of even his closest collaborators without softening their dismissal by an explanation.

A letter to Kenneth Hopkins at the end of the year is planning the *copla* book. He still followed Bunny's literary life. There was talk of *Lady Into Fox* being made into an Australian film, only there were no foxes in Australia. Gerald suggested 'Lady Into Kangaroo'.[2] Then he was delighted to be offered the Chair of Religion at Boston University on the strength of *St John*. He wrote and told Miranda – 'So ha, ha, ha!'[3]

Nevertheless, age advanced inexorably. His hernia seemed to be returning and in March he had two serious attacks of 'flu. Gerald's overriding fear, which was to grow into an obsession, was of being a burden to Lynda and Lars. In March he tried, as he often did, to defrost the fridge. His method was with hammer and screwdriver, but this time, he told Miranda, there was 'a violent *swish* and a rush of gas'.[4] They had to buy a new fridge for £140.

A child, and soon children, altered the whole focus of the house. At first Gerald was fascinated. His imitation of an owl provoked Carlos' first smile. He grew so swiftly 'that now the villagers say he weighs more than his mother. He has . . . a strong sense of humour, which he shows by imitating my smoker's cough and then collapsing in laughter. No one has ever laughed at my jokes so heartily before.'[5] He was fond of children in a rather abstract way, but Lynda and Lars were permissive, child-centred parents in the modern manner that Gerald's generation would have found almost impossible to imagine. On the surface, he was always patient and tolerant, but inwardly and therefore in his letters he was often exasperated. By September Carlos was 'a great lumpy boy who wriggles about on all fours . . . Nothing in the house is safe from him.'[6] By November he was walking and 'a great menace'.[7] In the end, Lynda's children often made Gerald feel overwhelmed.

In May he want to Paris to see Miranda and Xavier. It was only for five days because Miranda was to have a minor operation. Gerald was touched how concerned about him they were despite this.

July to early September were spent as usual in Mecina-Fondales. He missed Misa the cat, the only member of the household not to come. He had with her, he told VSP in a vein reminiscent of his cat exchanges with Gamel, 'a close but dignified relation, for she is a creature of unbending personality, rather like a maiden aunt'.[8] And here – as indeed he did all year – he read continually: Gibbon for the fourth or fifth time, all of Racine again, Doughty's *Arabia Deserta*, Chateaubriand's *Mémoires d'outre-tombe*. Fine passages, 'but I cannot like the author, a cold egotist, who is always trying to pretend he is neither conceited nor ambitious'.[9]

Gerald's need to control events had always been apparent, but usually disguised. Now Lynda noticed how frantic he became if he couldn't control something he minded about. In anything relating to Gerald alone she invariably deferred to him; and frequently in their joint life. But not always. For example, at the end of the year they planned a vegetable garden. Lynda said they should have a compost. Gerald didn't want one. They had several heated discussions. In the end there was a compost, but Lynda was astonished at his anger, even fury.

This was related to another trait. Severe anxiety, as we have seen, had sometimes expressed itself financially. But now Gerald more and more frequently thought he was ruined. They were converting one end of the living room at Alhaurín into a kitchen/dining room. Gerald imagined this would cost millions of pesetas. The vegetable garden was to save money.

For the same reason he decided they must sell some furniture, and this demonstrated a third old trait re-emerging in exaggerated form – the disdain for possessions. He told Miranda they would have to sell *all* the furniture.[10] He would particulary miss, he told Bunny a little later, a Baroque mirror dating from Molière and Calderón 'in which so many bewigged gentlemen must have examined their faces'.[11]

His letter to Miranda was in fact to usher in the next of the major crises by which, like so many stations of the cross, Gerald was driven into extreme old age.

2

It is at the start of 1980 that Gerald's letters begin to refer to his own imminent death. His only vague worry is the cost of the funeral. He has chosen an epitaph: 'GB, *escritor inglés, amigo de España.*'[12] Quite soon all this was to become an obsession.*

Miranda's reaction to the news that Gerald was selling all his furniture, much of it valuable, was, naturally enough, to ask if she could have some of it herself. Gerald agreed. Endless letters passed but, since he saw no great urgency, there were endless delays. He got an ulcer. Lynda had a thumb that needed lancing. Sending furniture to Paris was very expensive. It turned out they might need an export licence. The difficulties seemed 'insuperable', he told Blair.[12] Miranda's letters became more and more frantic. Finally, after Gerald had written saying it was almost impossible to get the furniture to her, she sent a furious and wounding denunciation of him as a father. Lynda guessed, though she was not sure, since

---

* Yet, when stimulated, he was as indomitable as ever. I stayed for a few days at the start of the year. Here are three short extracts from my journal. (A journal at last, many years too late, of some use.) 'January 6: Gerald leaning forward and shuffling, a frail but quite recognisable version of his old thrusting progress. His trousers are baggy and seem to be held, just, midway round his hips. I said last night, "Your trousers look as though they might fall down any second." Gerald said, "You can write a necrophiliac piece after I am dead about how I look"' . . . 'I went out this morning and saw puffs of smoke shooting out from behind an olive, like a small cannon firing or those toys of Winston Churchill with tiny cigars. Gerald appeared head up, cigarette in his mouth, looking up the garden, then at the sheep, the sun shining through the stiff grey fringe which is all that is left of his hair. He said, "You have to get over various obstacles on the way to old age, and the last is cancer." That is where he sees himself now' . . . 'Bunny, still writing and publishing at eighty-eight, is a challenge. "I admire Bunny far more than I ever did when I was young," said Gerald. "To live alone like that, cook for himself and so on, at that age, is an enormous achievement. The point is Bunny has a tremendous sense of his own presence. It's enough for him."'

Gerald, deeply hurt and also guilty, destroyed it without showing her, that it also referred to his 'girls' – Joanna, Hetty, and herself.

In fact, Miranda was dying of cancer. In later years, Xavier insisted Gerald '*must* have known'. It is abundantly clear from all the evidence that he did not. Xavier, who could hardly bear to face it himself, had told him the operation was to remove a harmless polyp. Miranda herself did not know till late, and when she learnt, wrote Gerald a letter of reconciliation, though without mentioning her illness. Even Stéphane and Marina didn't learn how serious their mother's illness was till December 1979, and then only through Clare Gimpel.[13] Gerald knew, of course, that she had continued to be unwell after the operation. He was told first she was ill from the anaesthetic; later that she'd picked up 'a rare bug'.[14] He wrote numerous anxious letters.

The news of her death, therefore, by telephone on 18 March, came as an appalling shock. For a moment, he was furious he hadn't been warned; then he realised Xavier had found it too much. He wrote a distraught letter the same day – why she and not me? And he wrote again on 19 March and 7 April. They were sweet letters; loving about Miranda, tender to Xavier. He sent £2500 (nearly £5000) at once to help with the funeral expenses; as soon as he could he arranged for Jaime to buy the furniture Miranda had wanted and sent the money to Stéphane and Marina.

Xavier, distracted by grief for many months, eventually partially resolved it, as people often do, by anger; in this case anger against Gerald. He said, among other things, that Gerald had never loved his daughter. But to say Gerald hadn't loved Miranda would be to give quite the wrong impression of his feelings about her. Once she left the magic zone of fifteen to twenty, she vanished almost entirely from his fantasies. In general, if quite often bored by her as a little girl and later disappointed she was not more intellectual, he was always fond of her. He was pleased at her generosity and warmth, proud of her vitality, delighted she could dance, proud (and relieved) at her eminently satisfactory marriage. None the less, there was an element of detachment in his relations with her; it was this that was noticed by Xavier, who was particularly warm and close to his children, especially when they were small. Lynda once heard Gerald telling someone after Miranda died, 'It's not that I loved her that much, but the way she died was particularly cruel' – and Bunny's observation about *Thoughts* . . . has force here. A central clue lies in Gerald's remark about Chekhov – a man held together by his strong sense of responsibility. It was an insight deriving from Gerald's own character. He was famous among the Brenans for his scrupulousness in family matters. As was noted earlier, nearly 1500 pages of letters to Miranda survive, from when she was eighteen to the day she died; many more have been lost. He was aware of all the major moves in her life; if she was in trouble he worried and tried to help. Over money, he became Hugh Brenan – but he always stumped up. He was not a marvellous father, but he was a kind, consistent and conscientious one.

Certainly, Miranda's death,* which was compounded as so often in his households by the death of Misa the cat at the same time, affected Gerald more than any previously. He took far longer than usual to recover from a minor and obscure illness at this time and indeed, as his physical and mental decline became ever more marked, Lynda felt he never fully recovered from Miranda's death. His handwriting deteriorated further and he became unable to tell the difference between the pound and the peseta. And from now on his letters not only say he is about to die, but that he wants to. Frances, knowing from experience the pain of such a terrible blow, was moved to contact him. Once more they met and wrote to each other. His first letter to her says he longs to die.[15]

3

However, now eighty-six, his life went resolutely on. Carrying stones in the garden brought on his hernia again. Once his need to live intensely, his humour, had been partly satisfied by the dramas of the coast. Now he had to make do with the fiendish complications of his truss. If you didn't order the belts properly, he told his friends the Southbys, you died a terrible death, your intestines in knots.

Bunny had Ménière's Syndrome. Gerald discovered it was a disease of middle age and that Luther, Caesar and Swift had had it.

* She was forty-nine. By coincidence her mother Juliana died about two months later, not knowing that her daughter had died first.

He sent congratulations. In May, Johnny Wolfers came to stay, giving them a washing machine.

During the two and a half months' stay at Mecina, despite many peaceful days and days when he was stimulated by visits, he remained haunted by death. He told VSP that, as a result of the First War, his parents and Gamel, the process 'frightens me'. He also became more and more worried at the cost of his funeral, which he saw as astronomical – 'here funerals are so expensive that parents start paying for their son's funeral when he is ten.'[16] He wished he was in a cannibal society and could be eaten. Failing that, he envied Frances' solution – the body left for medical research. It seemed impossible to organise in Spain. He also talked for almost the first time about suicide with Xavier's pills.

It is important, at this point, to keep Gerald's endless talk of death in proportion. The reason he wanted to die, he made plain, was not despair or depression but because he didn't want to be a burden to Lynda and Lars. But planning suicide in a letter to VSP in August, he says he can't quite do it now because he is too interested in the outcome of the strikes in Poland.*[17] To Frances he wrote that he knew he should die but really 'I feel like going on till 100. I still enjoy life, but against my will.'[18] Really, his letters now and for a while are typical announcements from inside the castle walls – Gerald expressing what he means by saying the opposite. To be excused for being a burden by acknowledging it, apologising for it, and pretending, indeed making conscious efforts to want death as a solution. But under his breath one hears him whisper: '*Life.*'

And once in the trenches of old age, life brings endless examples to follow. Charlotte Wolfers died that autumn. And on 15 September Gerald learnt that Blair, who had cancer of the colon, had died of a stroke.

Gerald's letters to Blair as a young man are fond, paternal, sometimes a bit impatient. The note is – worshipping younger brother, kind but slightly evasive elder. This had continued all their lives. His two nieces remember how their father adored Gerald, and how Gerald would come and stay, rush in, dump things and rush out

---

* He was also frighened that he would fail. 'I have a good poison,' he told Kenneth Hopkins (letter, 29 January 1977), 'but if I took it it might end me in a lunatic asylum . . . Spanish asylums are little changed since 1600'. This, as events were to show, was not entirely an idle fear.

to see obviously more interesting people. Gerald's letters to Rhoda, while saying how much he liked his gentle, intelligent, rather cynical younger brother, ends saying they could never quite be intimate. Talk always got round to their father, 'which made us both uncomfortable'[19] – that father whom Gerald had fought and defeated for both of them.

Nevertheless, these two deaths cast him down – especially since, again, both intimated: why not him? Lynda was pregnant again, and the household, with two men, one old, a small child and now no María to help, was demanding. In an attempt to rouse him they got out all his old *copla* book notes. Gerald spent a morning going through them and then said it was impossible.*

4

During 1981 Gerald's letters became more and more wild, with dates and names muddled as he dipped into confusion and then emerged.

On 20 February he heard that Bunny had died. He wrote to Frances, musing how fond he had become of him. One response was to leave his body to the medical school in Malaga. The Southbys had just done this and explained how to do it. 'So I'm saving £600.'[20]

As Lars and Lynda became less and less able to stimulate him, he took to spending hours on his bed, dreaming of the past.

On 6 April, the day before Gerald's eighty-seventh birthday, Lynda had a daughter, Emily, in the Limonar Clinic in Malaga. Marion Price came out by bus from England to help. Gerald, momentarily excited by the fact that it was a baby girl that had

---

* All the material, mostly collected in the late 1940s, was there, including notes for the 'learned introduction', a good deal of which was written. He had copied out thousands, indeed tens of thousands of *coplas*. He had read well over 100 books on folklore. (One list in the MF archive contains eighty-two books.) The point is that Gerald over-researched all his books to the extent he did because he enjoyed doing it. In this case, in typical Gerald fashion, he'd gathered so many examples from Italy, Sicily, Greece, Turkey, Malaya, China, Wales, Persia, Arabia, Syria, Palestine, Libya, Japan, Australia, Georgia, Lithuania, Latvia and Russia that a research student of Professor Juan Antonio Díaz López's at Granada University naturally supposed Gerald intended a world anthology. But a letter to Gerald Howson (undated, but July/August 1965) makes it clear the book was to be drawn from Spain only; though the introduction would deal with this little verse form worldwide.

arrived, took to reading Spock and became a vague expert; except
'. . . the art of rocking eludes me. Of the women here, only Lynda's
mother was good at it.'[21]

But by the time they went to Mecina, Lynda noticed how he
more and more seemed to reject the past, voicing guilt and regrets
about Miranda, Carrington, Gamel, even his books. He suddenly
wrote to John Whitworth and said he was destitute. Lars had to write
hurriedly himself and explain it was a fantasy (John Whitworth, with
characteristic generosity, wrote at once to say he would support him
if necessary). Just before this, Gerald had written to VSP telling him
they subsisted entirely on cold rice pudding for economy.[22] This was
nonsense. They ate well – but Gerald liked rice pudding and it suited
his always precarious stomach. Not surprisingly, however, this letter
worried VSP.*

Though fond of him and often fascinted, Gerald was increasingly
got down by Carlos; and soon Emily, to be a child of considerable
energy glorying in an increasingly chaotic house, joined forces with
her brother. Gerald's letters resound to the sound of Carlos screaming
'incessantly in his falsetto voice that gets on my nerves'.[23] He decides
that with his 'deep, loud, shrill voice' he is going to be an opera
singer.

But his continuing protestations that he wants to die are still
almost invariably accompanied by the caveat – in order not to burden
Lynda. And he remained maddeningly strong and healthy. He hoped
a stroke might carry him off. One morning Lynda and Lars were
startled by a knocking at their door. Then they heard Gerald's voice,
rather deep. 'I think the process has started now. I'm going back to
bed for it.' Nothing happened.

---

* Lynda was interesting about these 'I'm ruined' letters. She said Gerald
enjoyed the idea of being ruined, of being martyred. It was yet another evolution of
his masochistic side. But his financial anxieties had some basis in fact because he did
over these years get steadily poorer. His income for 1978 to the end of 1983 was
about £9500 p.a. at 1990 prices, for a growing household. But Lars contributed, and
so did Lynda with her small income from the *Personal Record* money. Aside from an
extraordinary windfall, Gerald's income from 1984 to 1987 would have been
£4–5000 p.a. at 1990 prices, but by then, as we'll see, money no longer mattered.

5

People had always been one of Gerald's chief stimulants, and the household now saw very few people. The tiny child-dramas of their peaceful life did not stimulate him; on the contrary, they got him down.

But an exciting event took place in January 1982. Alhaurín el Grande honoured Gerald by naming a street after him. Supported through a cheering crowd of a thousand, Gerald stood with the *alcalde*.* A string was pulled. A cloth fell. 'Camino Gerald Brenan. Huge Cheers!'[24] This was followed by a lunch on two floors for 200 people organised with typical Spanish gaiety and skill. 'Whenever I made a remark there were cheers. Everyone was smiling at me and I was very happy.'[24] Rosalía de Castro was read (one of Gerald's favourite Spanish poets) and a setting of St John's *Cántico* was sung by Amancio Prada, a Galician, a graceful tribute to Gerald who had contributed 'to revive and honour a very strange Spaniard of a past age'.[24]

He was deeply touched and proud, and particularly pleased because, apart from Rosario, some of the old Churriana servants were there (every surrounding *pueblo* had contributed to the event). The British Consul was going to send a report to the ambassador. 'Perhaps I shall help him give back Gibraltar by showing how popular I have made the English.'[24]

He spent a lot of time in bed in March, but cheerfully, studying the birds, 'My protegées'. A rare blue thrush landed on his window sill. 'It was a very elegant bird of a very dark blue shade and for a moment stood staring at me and then went off. It was as elegant as the Princess of Wales, but more interesting as it was a bird.'[25]

Gerald's moods ebbed and flowed with his energy but, determined not to be a burden, his energetic moods could now be as dangerous as the others were depressed.

Some time in April, Lars suddenly heard a tremendous thump while working in his studio. Gerald had come into the garden,

---

* The mayor. The street is the main one leading into the centre as you come from Alhaurín de la Torre.

forgetting his stick, to carry in firewood. He had slipped, fallen and broken his femur. There followed what Lynda remembered as a 'nightmare period': hospital, great pain, a hip-replacement operation, expense.* It was made harder by Gerald's memory. Lars and Lynda would manage to take the children and make the long journey into Malaga. Half an hour after they got back Gerald would be on the telephone, furious: 'Why do you never come and see me?' They only managed to survive because Bill and Betty Byron took half the burden of visiting and tending Gerald in hospital – 'heroic help', as Lynda put it.

Already, before this, Lynda had herself begun to be got down by the growing air of despair which now seemed to hang about him. Without the rigid scaffolding of work, which had so long sustained him, she felt he was increasingly disintegrating. Indeed his broken leg, with the need it brought of having to learn to walk again, for a while provided a goal which he pursued with tenacity. Despite this, the break depressed him a great deal, and in June he was particularly low. He was also more and more confused in what had become, in the natural course of events, a child-dominated house. One morning he wasn't awake at nine o'clock. He was still asleep at twelve. Lynda and Lars then found his 'suicide' pills open on his desk, with an old note of Xavier's – 'Take fifty.' Gerald had taken fifteen. The pathetic gesture of despair was probably numerically about accurate: 30% – I would die if I could to relieve you; 70% – I really want to live.

Nor had his fears about a Spanish lunatic asylum been totally unfounded. He was more or less off his head for a week and caused them much anxiety, as well as guilt and trouble. In these circumstances he became incontinent and often fell out of bed. It was as much as they could both do to haul him back again.

Once again it was an event that he found stimulating as much as their two and a half month stay in Mecina-Fondales (where he nearly set fire to himself smoking) which temporarily raised his spirits. Gerald had always been extremely scornful about awards for writers, especially, as with VSP's knighthood, when he knew the writer. But

---

* As so often, defrayed by one of the most generous of his friends, Ethel de Croisset. She sent, unasked, 30,000 pesetas. In fact, despite his regular moods of financial ruin, Gerald could afford the operation. Lynda and Lars put the money into an insurance against other, certain, disasters of a similar sort.

when he learnt he was to receive a CBE in November he was delighted.*

Although still hobbling on crutches, his letters at once became more cheerful. 'All sorts of things take up my time,' he wrote to Frances in September, 'washing, bathing, shaving and going to the loo. These are the occupations of invalids, as well as drinking tea. And then comes the question of stamps and envelopes and addresses.'[26] He was also doing his best to get on with Carlos. The reason for this was that the CBE would be presented by the ambassador and Gerald was very nervous the children would ruin it. 'They usually spend the lunch hour screaming in very high voices. They are quite undisciplined and like most children love noise.'[27]

In the event, the ceremony on 28 November was a success. Sir Richard Parsons and his first secretary arrived from Madrid in the ambassadorial Rolls-Royce (later axed). They took one look at the *cañada* and decided to walk, formally dressed, carrying two bottles of champagne in a cooler and Gerald's insignia. Lynda had cooked a delicious lunch, Gerald had carefully concealed 'my frayed shirt cuffs',[28] the children were fairly quiet. Then Parsons made a short speech about services to literature and Anglo-Spanish relations, draped Gerald with his order and they drank the champagne.

The ambassador found Gerald 'a man of great sweetness and charm' and they talked about literature. 'He couldn't keep talking all afternoon so I read to him from *The Oxford Book of Victorian Verse*. Browning, I expect.' Gerald, who couldn't see Parsons was reading from a book, was astonished an ambassador should have so phenomenal a memory. Indeed, he told Kenneth Hopkins, the range of culture in general and especially the knowledge of poetry now thought necessary for senior diplomatic posts was quite amazing.

6

At the end of December 1982 Gerald, almost as a matter of routine, dashed off another of his letters to VSP about how they could only afford to live on cold rice pudding.[29]

---

* So many people tell me that it was 'really' them who put Gerald forward for the CBE, that the simplest thing is to say the Foreign Office suggested his name.

This time his old friend, seriously worried, acted decisively and effectively. He first got in touch with the Royal Literary Fund and rapidly had £4500 sent to Gerald. Then, initially with Raymond Carr, who later left it to VSP, he arranged that Gerald be given a Civil List pension. By March 1983 he was in receipt of £800 a year. 'What do I owe this to – I simply don't know,' he wrote to Kenneth Hopkins.* The letter had come from the Queen's Secretary. 'Do I have members of the Royal Family who read my books and like them?'[30] But he felt that, on the eve of his eighty-ninth birthday, after a lifetime of financial anxiety, his money problems were over. 'Indeed the problem will be how to spend it.'

Not so easily solved, indeed insoluble, was Gerald's steady descent into extreme old age. Sometimes he could review the growing shambles with detachment and even humour. His hernia, he told VSP, was worrying, he had 'multiple diarrhoea',[31] and he hadn't signed a cheque for a year and a half (Lars dealt with all household bills). 'My clothes are losing their buttons and dropping off me . . . Dressing to receive the ambassador was a tremendous business.'[32]

But as the year wore on Gerald became more and more depressed. He gave up reading and could now hardly write letters. He spent most of his time in bed, or shuffling from bed to chair, from chair to bed. Lynda and Lars seemed to have lost all power to interest him or even stir him. Only certain visitors could stimulate him, and very few visitors called. By December 1983 he was going to bed at the same time as the children.

Despite the exasperation and exhaustion Gerald felt as a result of Lynda's children, they themselves loved him, their tottering substitute grandfather. John Green, who lived in the Alpujarra and who, with his Danish friend Per Larsen, was one of the few close neighbours there who *could* stimulate Gerald, recalls a poignant exchange at this time. Gerald as usual was talking about wanting to die.

Carlos: 'I hope you never die, Gerald.'
Gerald: 'What?'
Carlos: 'I hope you never die.'

* Gerald never met Kenneth Hopkins, and indeed lived in considerable dread that he might suddenly appear from England. But with the vast correspondence Hopkins managed to generate over the publication of Gamel's poetry still continuing, Gerald as was his custom often included odd items about his life.

Gerald: 'What?'

Carlos: 'I hope you never die.'

Gerald:'*What* did you say?'

Carlos (desperately):'DIE! DIE!'

Gerald: 'I don't think that's very nice Carlos.'

Some time later this year the idea was promulgated of a selection from Gerald's and Ralph's correspondence edited by Xan Fielding. As well as giving a portrait of a friendship, it was hoped that discussions with Xan, whom Gerald liked, would stimulate him. Unfortunately Ronda, where Xan lived, is a considerable and difficult distance from Alhaurín el Grande and this aspect of the scheme did not really work. By the time the book came out in 1986 Gerald's interest in everything was minimal.*

But in fact, despite Gerald's decline during 1983, it was Lynda, forty in September, who began to break. She had now been with Gerald fifteen years, the last five of them increasingly arduous, with Gerald declining, Lars having to work hard at his painting, her children growing. It was a child-dominated household, yet one in which in many ways a very old man dominated the most. She had nursed Gerald through operations, breakages, endless bouts of 'flu and fever. So strong, in fact, had the habit of looking after Gerald become that Lynda often felt it was her children she was neglecting. And Gerald's fame in Spain meant that journalists and admirers were continually trying to see him. He didn't want to see any of them and it always fell to Lynda to put them off and often receive, as a result,

---

* *Best of Friends* was published by Chatto and Windus in 1986. It is scrupulously if somewhat economically edited and demonstrates, if demonstration were necessary, how much of Ralph's character Gerald left out of his portrait. But despite many marvellous letters of Gerald's, it cannot really show his full range as a letter-writer. The decision to produce a short book (244 pages) in relation to the material available and the necessary inclusion of Ralph's letters meant that only about one-fifteenth of Gerald's letters to Ralph could be included. Gerald was fonder of Ralph than of any other man during his life, but the tensions in their friendship put certain constraints on the correspondence. Also, he didn't feel he had to try with Ralph. If I had to judge I would say Gerald's finest letters were written to Frances, VSP and perhaps Carrington. But in his colossal correspondence there are dozens, even hundreds of extraordinary letters, or extraordinary passages in fairly ordinary letters – not just to other old friends like Bunny or people he admired like Michael Holroyd, but to the BBC or his publisher or a girl who'd dropped in from Torremolinos – when Gerald's pen unexpectedly takes wing, as much to his surprise, one feels, as his correspondent's. And all this, obviously, Xan Fielding couldn't include.

a good deal of anger. To this one should add a further, quite understandable dimension. Lars and Lynda had been together eleven years now; for six of these married with a growing family. They had never been able to live alone.

When Lars went to Paris in March, Marion Price came to help her, since Lynda could no longer cope on her own. In fact, Gerald's hernia was so bad that month that he had to go into hospital again. Lynda grew alarmingly thin. 'She went through hell with them all in that little house,' Mary Kennedy, another close neighbour, said succinctly.

Though permanently exhausted and always extremely anxious that Gerald was going to set fire to himself or break another bone, what chiefly distressed her was his despair. She asked Ethel de Croisset what she thought she should do. 'Gerald has been in love with someone or other all his life. Have you tried employing a young, pretty Spanish girl?'

But at the end of the year it suddenly occurred to Lynda that really the only thing that stimulated him now was talking to his old friends. And most of his old friends lived in England. Any decision of this magnitude would have to be Gerald's. She decided to put off a full discussion until after Christmas.

The subject must have come up in some form before then, however, because in December Gerald wrote to VSP. He realised, he said, he was a very great burden on Lynda. Did VSP know of any homes for writers? 'I want to leave and settle in England for the rest of my life.'[33]

7

Lynda and Lars came in for a good deal of criticism for their eventual decision to put Gerald into a home, especially from those who did not know the circumstances. In Spain, this is not yet nearly as common a solution as it is in England, America or Sweden to this problem that grows steadily more and more appalling all over the Western world. There is a cultural difference here. And in the *pueblos*, however little they might like to do it, close neighbours, the family all help look after the very old. Lynda was alone.

The size of her burden can be gauged by the fact that in a few months, after only slight deterioration in his condition, it took a staff of three women to care for Gerald, with the addition of the police when he needed lifting. It was absolutely clear there would have to be some radical change. The question was, to what?

The first idea was to build onto the house at Alhaurín and employ someone to look after Gerald. This would require money. Lynda and Lars wrote to Xan and Magouche Fielding, Janetta and Ethel de Croisset. Xan replied with a short, rather vague letter; Janetta never received her letter; Ethel sent $1500.

But the most important reason that they did not pursue this solution was that it was vetoed point-blank by Gerald. Lynda was determined he must fully consent to anything that was done. He refused even to consider the idea of being looked after in some separate wing.

There remained, it seemed, only the solution of Gerald being looked after somewhere else. They first looked for a home in Spain. One was found in Malaga, but it was fifty-percent lunatics. There was another in Ronda, but it was reported to be freezing in winter. Besides, a home in Spain would have brought Gerald no closer to his old friends.

His close friends in Spain, those who did know the circumstances at Alhaurín, were in no doubt about what was best. The Southbys had noticed that the only time Gerald came alive now was when the talk was about London. They strongly urged Lynda and Lars to find somewhere there. 'We thought that's where he would be happiest,' Marjorie von Schlippenbach was also quite clear. 'She couldn't possibly cope. He was falling about.' She too pressed for London.

The decision was taken to follow two courses. The first was to let Gerald see for an experimental period – for the duration of the Andalusian summer which was now too much for him – whether or not he would like to live in London. If he didn't like it then he would come back and they would follow the second course – appeal to the Spanish authorities for help in looking after him.

There is no doubt that Gerald's main reason for agreeing to go to London so readily was because, as he had always said, he could no longer bear to be a burden to Lynda. He wrote one or two rather apprehensive letters to VSP. Nevertheless, as prospectuses poured in, he grew considerably stimulated. At one point he might have gone to a home for old officers, apparently run by Field-Marshal Auchinleck's daughter. Gerald fantasised about reminiscing over the First World War.

In the end Marion Price found Greenways in Pinner. It was close to her, and Gerald could afford it – something Lynda felt to be very important to his pride.

In some respects, Greenways was not entirely suitable. But better alternatives needed money. In fact, more money was in the process of being raised. Xan and Magouche's rather unhelpful response had not been due to indifference, but because they were about to go on holiday. On their return, and with a now alerted Janetta, they set about the problem in earnest. During March and April the Fieldings and Pritchetts, Janetta and Frances all conferred. On 28 April, Xan agreed with Dorothy Pritchett that he and Magouche would consult with their friend Jacob Rothschild and set about building a fund.[34] Unfortunately, none of this was communicated to Lynda or Lars. Chronic lack of communication was to characterise the next few months.

On 13 May, shortly after his ninetieth birthday, Gerald set off with Lars from Malaga Airport for Pinner. He was about to embark on the last, and not the least dramatic period of his long life.

PART VI

Alone

1984–1987

'*All deaths are sad except one's own.*'
Gerald to VSP, 14 August 1966

THIRTY-SIX

The Pinner Episode

'We in England measure out our egoism and altruism to suit the occasion. We have a measure appropriate to every situation, and if we haven't one we pretend to have. The Spanish nature is to move in one step from one extreme to another. When we are feeling horrified by Spanish insensitivity, Spanish negativeness, Spanish egoism, we come across some act of generosity and sheer goodness of heart such as one could scarcely find in any other nation.'

Notes for *Spanish Literature* at Texas

Greenways Residential Home, in the suburb of Pinner on the Uxbridge Road, run by the efficient Mrs Graham, was in many respects ideal. It was set in a pleasant leafy garden. Care was excellent. The inmates, though some were very rickety, were not gaga. There was not the usual faint odour of urine and Vitamin B. It was close to Marion Price.

But it was close to no one else. The journey out was a typical London nightmare – an hour or hour and a half however you did it. And most of Gerald's old friends were themselves old – VSP and Frances, for instance, in their eighties. Nevertheless, a good many people made the laborious trek, and many of them several times. Johnny Wolfers, Georgia Tennant, Charles Sinnickson, Gerald's nieces Lydia Piper and Ann Cary with her husband Roger, the Sheppards . . . Stéphane flew over from Paris, Janetta flew from Spain. When VSP went Gerald said how odd it was he should be near Harrow, the school he nearly went to in 1908. Even Peter Ryan, who had introduced Gerald to Lynda, journeyed out. Gerald said to him, 'I was too much for Lynda. I married her and wore her out.' True, in a way.

I drove up from Norfolk to see him on 19 May. Gerald was sitting in the hall (to avoid the television, I later realised) in a suit, a crutch across his knee. He was frail but perfectly clear. Old figures hobbled about us, whom he totally ignored. 'They speak extremely slowly.' But suddenly he was alert. 'Someone's coming.' In fact, an old lady passing him had farted. I explained and he laughed. Low in spirits at first, he cheered up after a while. We talked about Lowry. At seven o'clock I helped him up to his minute, bare room. Bedtime. He said, 'I don't read, don't talk, don't watch television. I wander in the past. I like the scenery. Sometimes I don't think at all.' Lars stayed in London two weeks to settle Gerald in and arrived just before I left.

The great problem for Gerald's friends was to discover whether or not he wanted to remain in London. He veered from moment to moment, usually agreeing with any strong opinion expressed by whoever he was talking to. The one constant was that, though he might want to be with Lynda, he didn't want this if the burden was too great for her. Much of his veering was to protect her and Lars.

It was also clear that if he remained in London it couldn't be at Greenways. It was too far away; he also needed more room – enough for some of his furniture and books. He had about £5000 p.a.; to find somewhere more suitable would require £10,000 p.a. On the other hand, if he returned to Spain, which seemed quite possible, considerable sums would be needed there too. Fund raising now continued in earnest. Frances and Janetta wrote to his friends: Xan and Magouche continued with Jacob Rothschild; I was asked to approach the Royal Literary Fund again and any other trusts and charitable foundations I could discover.

Meanwhile, the MP for Watford, Tristan Garel-Jones, who led the Spanish lobby in the House of Commons, had become active on Gerald's behalf. He had contacted Michael Heseltine, then Minister of Defence. The idea was that Gerald's distinguished military career would allow him into a more commodious, more central and subsidised ex-officer's residential home in London.

However, all these efforts to help Gerald, which would have eventually borne fruit, were abruptly rendered superfluous by dramatic events in Spain.

About a week after Gerald left, Shay Oag decided to speak to the press. The man she chose was Eduardo Castro. The young poet who admired Gerald and whom he had met a few times in the Alpujarra and at Alhaurín was now a responsible and successful journalist. What he heard led him to believe that Gerald had been turfed out of his house against his will and was now incarcerated in London. Not surprisingly, he was somewhat perturbed.

The swiftness and explosiveness with which his story was taken up requires some explanation. Gerald was both famous in Spain, and also much loved. But it was not only that he was fashionable in cultured circles, he also symbolised the experiments in freedom – intellectual, social and political – of post-Franco Spain. He symbolised the country's steady progress back into Europe. And the young radicals who had been proud to show *The Spanish Labyrinth* on their bookshelves during the Fifties, Sixties and early Seventies were now, numbers of them, in positions of power or influence. To which one must of course add that rapid self-fuelling process by which big media events generate their paper and celluloid fire-storms.

It was this that developed over the two weeks after Lars returned to Spain on 1 June. Soon Spanish journalists and TV reporters laden with equipment were besieging a bewildered Mrs Graham and then invading the doddery calm of Greenways. The Spanish ambassador, Puig de la Bellacasa, a sympathetic and cultivated man, now several times made the long journey to Pinner. He told Frances he was quite certain that something would be done – and done quickly.

I had been continuing to visit Gerald every five or six days, and when I drove up on 14 June it was clear that he did now want to return to Spain. It was also clear the endless reporters and stream of friends had exhausted him. He was lying on his bed with his spectacles off, looking drained (pleasing, I noted in my jounal, to see his small sharp eyes again instead of the usual hugely magnified orbs like big pebbles in a cloudy pool). We talked about what might happen, and about Greenways. 'You wouldn't believe this place at night – it's totally dead,' said Gerald, as though he was in some supposed-to-be-pleasure-loving city inexplicably silent after dark.

He wanted to return to Spain – but not if Lynda and Lars couldn't cope with him. He was also determined not to cause enmity between them and other people. It was this that underlay his reply now in one of the Spanish television reports. 'Why are you here?' 'I don't know.' 'It is quite clear,' said his interviewer to camera, 'that he is being held in this place against his will.'

The resulting uproar in Spain brought a rapid finalisation to the rescue plan. This was that the *Junta* of Andalusia, the regional government, would pay for a nurse and a maid to look after Gerald, while Alhaurín el Grande would pay his household expense and give him a pension. It was possible the pension would be met by the Spanish government.

One of the odder features, not only of the rescue planning but more particularly of the furore in the Spanish press and on TV, was that no one made any attempt to question or consult the Prangers. In the press they were the object of extremely wounding and totally untrue innuendo and, from a variety of often aggrieved sources some of the more irresponsible journalists did consult, straight lies.[1] Now however, Cristóbal González, an assistant to the mayor of Alhaurín, came to see them. He was to be almost their only contact with the Spaniards during these events. He asked them under what conditions they would have Gerald back. Lynda and Lars realised that, though the English experiment had not been remotely tried, it was impossible to continue with it. Since, under the plans which Cristóbal had outlined to them, the house at Alhaurín would be full of maids and nurses they said they would be willing to move to Mecina-Fondales. Knowing that what Gerald wanted was to return to Lynda, and what the Spaniards wanted was the *réclame* of Gerald returning to his 'family', Cristóbal asked if they would live close by if the *Junta* paid any rent. Lynda and Lars rather reluctantly agreed.

A deputation consisting of Lars, Javiér Torres Vela, the Andalusian Minister of Culture, the *alcalde* of Alhaurín Francisco Jiménez Díaz, Eduardo Castro and Cristóbal flew out to talk to Gerald. He agreed to the plan. Lars flew back to arrange the move. So did Javier Torres Vela and Eduardo Castro.

The two men from Alhaurín remained behind. It was clear Gerald couldn't be moved at once. On 17 June, completely exhausted, he had become delirious and during the night had wandered into several of the old ladies' rooms, causing chaos. When Marion Price, who came to see Gerald almost every day with washing, pullovers, rice pudding and the like, arrived Gerald said, 'You should have been here last night. There was a tremendous party. People throwing bottles about.'

To understand what followed it is necessary to know about another curious development in the press/TV uproar. Gerald's small, much depleted library was built up into something astounding. (This was part of the most scurrilous innuendo, which was that Lynda and Lars were an evil, grasping couple intent on getting Gerald's wealth by locking him away in distant London.)[1] Spanish papers talked of 40,000 or 50,000 precious volumes, reports taken up by the British press.[2] The library soon assumed the status of a major international collection – the Bodleian, say, or the Biblioteca Nacional in Madrid.

Alhaurín was not a rich *pueblo* and, after the excitement and prestige of Gerald's return had died away, the *alcalde* and his supporters knew quite well that they could expect difficult questions about the drain he was causing on the town's meagre resources. It is clear that early on they decided it would be easier to deal with these if they could get something as tangible for the town as a valuable library. It was surely reasonable, in view of what they were doing, to ask if it might be left to the *pueblo* after Gerald died (and so indeed it proved. It is likely they broached the matter when they first saw Gerald. But in the end it was not primarily Gerald but Lynda, to whom the books had been left, who agreed).

The second thing that happened was that Charles Sinnickson, now a priest, went by his own admission slightly off his head. In touch with Spain, he had decided that Lynda was indeed a grasping villainness. Seeing Gerald on Saturday 16 June just after Stéphane had called, Charles was deeply impressed when Gerald vaguely said he'd like to give his grandson something.

Charles, without asking anything further, decided Gerald wanted to alter his Will.* There was, however, very little time before Gerald, in Charles' words, went back 'into the clutches' of Lynda and

---

* Charles' kindly, well-meaning but ill-judged effort arose from the misapprehension that Miranda, of whom he had been very fond, had been unknowingly cheated out of her just inheritance – and so, therefore, had her children. Gerald had made it quite clear to Miranda in a letter of 29 May 1975 exactly what he was leaving Lynda and what Miranda (and see Miranda to Gerald, 8 June 1975). In this exchange what upset Miranda was not Lynda's share – which both she and Xavier agreed was a fair expression of his affection and return for many years' care – but that she learnt then for the first time that Lynda had gained £10,000 from *Personal Record*. Gerald later explained how this was used for joint household expenses. Ironically, in 1984 Plaza y Janés paid £24,000 for a new edition of *The Spanish Labyrinth*. With this, Mabel's money and the last of his capital, the grandchildren received a total, at 1990 prices, of around £76,000 when Gerald died. *The Spanish Labyrinth* and *South From Granada*, whose royalties they were also left, continue to bring in comfortable sums today. Gerald cannot be accused of leaving Miranda or her children too small a proportion of what he had.

Lars. He was to fly back on Thursday 21 June. Marion, who saw Wednesday as 'get ready day', was already busy ironing and packing. On Monday, again without consulting anyone, Charles rang Halsey Lightly and Hemsley and told Patricia Magrath that Gerald wanted, as a matter of urgency, to change his Will in favour of his grand-children. She was to prepare various codicils leaving increasing amounts (Charles dictated what amounts) and come at once to Greenways. First thing Wednesday morning was agreed.

On Tuesday, now in a state of high excitement, Charles decided to strengthen his campaign by enlisting the support of Spain. Taking an interpreter, he hurried round to the Spanish Club in Connaught Square, where Paco Jiménez and Cristóbal were staying. The two Spaniards listened with dawning comprehension and increasing horror at what he was planning to do. Did he mean that the contents of Don Geraldo's house were to be left to his grandchildren? Yes, said Charles, sweepingly. To two young children living in *Paris*? Yes, said Charles. But, said Paco and Cristóbal, Don Geraldo has left his exceedingly valuable library to the Comunidad of Alhaurín el Grande. Sensing a danger to his schemes, Charles improvised swiftly – quite all right, the grandchildren (who knew nothing of this proposed change in their fortunes) had signed a paper allowing all such bequests to stand.

When he had gone, the two stocky, dark, blue-chinned Andalu-sians, deeply suspicious of all the English and nervous and out of their depth in London, decided the only thing they could do was to kidnap Gerald and bring him as fast as they could onto Spanish soil – that is to say, the Spanish Club in Connaught Square.

Early on Wednesday morning, therefore, Paco Jiménez and Cristóbal arrived at Greenways. But they found that three Spanish TV journalists were already there talking to a Gerald nervous about his forthcoming journey. And shortly afterwards Charles hurried in propelling forward Miss Magrath with her codicils.

There ensued the most horrendous scene. Charles, employing the journalists as interpreters – interpreters who soon took sides – shouted, then shrieked at Paco Jiménez and Cristóbal, who them-selves shouted back. It was clear to them Charles was being paid by the grandchildren. 'How could a man of the cloth be so greedy for money?' The Grahams tried to turn everybody out. Miss Magrath became outraged and said she'd been Gerald's solicitor for forty years.

They all appealed to Gerald, and Gerald, exhausted, began to cry. Charles was forced to withdraw, saying that if Gerald died, which now seemed likely and imminent, the Spaniards would be entirely responsible. Gerald was bundled into a car and driven at high speed to the Spanish Club.

It was soon after this that Marion arrived with six shirts and two handkerchiefs, all freshly cleaned and ironed, along with various other items and a suitcase. She was told Gerald had vanished. 'His clothes weren't even in proper suitcases,' she afterwards lamented, 'just stuffed into Safeways plastic bags.'

I saw Gerald in the Spanish Club just before he was flown back to Spain next day. He was pretty mad with agitation and exhaustion and began to describe a terrible journey to Seville he'd made the night before. I thought then, as I was to often during the next three years, that as his tremendous will-power finally disintegrated, disparate elements of his life and character were able to escape for a while and assume control of events. This time farce and tragedy had each had a turn.

But the gesture made by Spain was of such marvellous and spontaneous generosity, the series of moves of such swiftness and practical kindness, that they warm the heart still today. As Gerald said at the start of the chapter, one can scarcely imagine it of any other country. Certainly not of England. Xan Fielding wrote, 'Just imagine the mayor and corporation of, say, Godalming doing the same for an aged foreign poet.'[3]

That it went wrong later cannot detract from it. Indeed, that it did is not really anyone's fault. The ideal solution would have been for Gerald and Lynda and Lars to have lived in a large Spanish house, with Gerald totally paid for and looked after by two or three servants and nurses. His old friends would then have been flown out in ordered waves and brought in throughout each week to see him.

Clearly impossible. The tragedy of Gerald's last years was a tragedy of old age.

THIRTY-SEVEN

The Endless End

'We sit all day waiting for something to happen – and nothing happens; we sit waiting for someone to come – and no one comes.'

Gerald to author, 13 August 1984

1

Most biographies of people who live a very long time pass over the last few years with decent swiftness. Is this really decent or even correct – or wise? When we reach it we will find our old age as important as what went before. More important, since we will be in the process of living it and more vulnerable. And extreme old age is now almost more likely to be our lot than not. Know thine enemy.

The vast parabola of Gerald's life encompasses this as it encompasses so much else in our century. Only at the end, when nothing happened but the slow, infinitely slow descent towards death, is decent swiftness possible.

It is not possible after Pinner. Already exhausted, Gerald arrived at Madrid airport in a plane besieged by cameras and reporters. The same thing took place at Malaga. Here, to his surprise, Shay Oag thrust herself forward and embraced him.

He reached Cañada de las Palomas in a state of exhaustion. Lynda and Lars, who had moved into the Huerta La Tena just down the road, were very worried indeed about his health.

Events continued to bombard him. One, if too confused to enjoy it, he much appreciated. On 2 July a vast and prestigious delegation toiled under the boiling sun up the rock-strewn *cañada*: the Spanish Minister of Culture Javier Slana, the President of the *Junta* of

Andalusia José Rodríguez de la Borbolla, the Andalusian Minister of Culture Javiér Torres Vela, the *alcalde* of Alhaurín el Grande, numerous other national and local dignitories, reporters and, hovering at the back, Cristóbal. They presented Gerald with the top award of the Spanish Socialist Party – the 'Pablo Iglesias'.

Soon after this, the obsession of the *ayuntamiento* of Alhaurín with Gerald's books became overwhelming. They formally asked Lynda and Lars if the Comunidad could have the library after Gerald's death. Lynda, aware that they were already having to justify what were clearly going to be considerable expenses, agreed – provided Gerald did too. An important document, replete with seals, was drawn up. Fortunately, Lars noticed it assigned a great many other things to the Comunidad besides books, including the copyrights to all Gerald's books. A second document was prepared. And soon a second distinguished delegation trudged up under the July sun: notaries, cultural delegates from Seville and Malaga, the *alcalde*, reporters, and hurrying to and fro – Cristóbal.

Gerald, slowly recovering and beginning to react against what he had been put through, refused to sign. The notary asked him some questions and decided he was not fit at that moment to make such a decision. The delegation withdrew in some confusion.

And confusion was increased by Gerald now saying that he wanted to return to England. 'I was taken prisoner by the Spanish press,' he told a journalist from the *Daily Telegraph*, who found him trying to write a letter on these lines to the British Consul in Malaga. 'I want to come back to Britain. I was born British and I always will be British.'[1] He told other people the same, including Ethel de Croisset, who thought it was because he felt guilty about Lynda.

It was also that, reduced by exhaustion and age, he now tended to agree with anyone who put their views with energy. Spanish and English reporters seemed to elicit different answers. When Cristóbal turned up alone one night after the library débâcle and dictated a short statement making over the books to Alhaurín, Gerald signed this. Since there were no witnesses, Cristóbal made him sign it twice. This pathetic document, of no legal value, was then carefully locked away.*

---

* I have it with me now, Gerald's once clear handwriting and the two wavering signatures almost illegible. This library obsession continued for the next two years.

2

In August my wife Nicky and I borrowed the Prangers' rented house for a month while they escaped for a while to Mecina-Fondales with the children.

A routine had already been established. Gerald and a staff of three; Carmen González Burgos who cooked, and two girls, Rosa and Milagros who, though often together, roughly took it in turns to look after him – both sleeping in the house. The excitement of all the publicity was still in the air and the police were much in evidence. A crackling walkie-talkie was used by the girls to order food and a motorbike would roar up with aubergines or eggs or chickens. But they roared up a lot anyway, to flirt with the girls or just for the sake of roaring. Sometimes the house looked as if it were being raided – the police lolling about, Gerald incongruous in the middle in a woollen skull-cap and his spectacles like two magnifying glasses. This pattern endured till he died, except that the police soon vanished.

We too established a routine. We had lunch with him at one-o'clock, arriving early to drink and talk before. Then Nicky would cook supper there and we spent the evening with him till he was tired. Later, we added tea, because Milagros said he woke from his siesta at five and then waited impatiently till we arrived at 7.30.

At first he became tired easily and early. One had the feeling of a love-affair that had ended. Gerald was depressed and often slightly mad – but mad with the poetic truthfulness of Lear. Almost the first thing he said to us was, 'I used to have a house called Cañada de las Palomas but apparently it's lost. No one can find it!' Or else, like his great-aunt Tiz long ago, he had two identical houses, the real one somewhere else. On one of these early afternoons he said, 'I was often impotent with women. Something timid in me made me fail at the last moment. Or I would think I was going to fail and wouldn't dare try.' My journal notes how sad he looked as he said this, and how I tried to comfort him, telling him it happened to many men.

At one point all the books suddenly vanished from the house. Lynda, furious, telephoned the *junta*, who knew nothing about it. The books were replaced the next day.

Gerald agreed. After a while he said, 'At other times I was all right.' It was a subject he returned to.

The bridge of his nose hurt, Beethoven returned and his nights were wild. He'd get up, pee, wander about, fall over. It was a trial for the girls. In the morning you'd ask how he'd slept. 'Very well.'

But gradually he grew stronger. The entries in my journal become lighter. On the afternoon of 19 August he was talking about Moroccan history. 'I used to know a good deal about Morocco. I've read everything there is to read. You should study it. It's very interesting. It would do you good.' Four days later I noted how important food was to him. He ate a lot and enjoyed it a lot. 'Today a wooden box arrived from a cardiologist. It contained very rich, solid, heavy, gooey cake-like cones coated in crystallised sugar flakes. Gerald ate two and said, "You can really only eat one of these." After a bit he said, "Odd present from a cardiologist."'

Food was in the capable, gnarled hands of Carmen. Dressed in black, sixty or perhaps sixty-five, she was a delight. She had a body like a barrel out of which stuck her thin, strong legs and her thin strong arms. She walked very upright in a stumpy, robot-like way, pigeon-toed, determined. 'She laughs and smiles and absolutely *loves* the amount Gerald eats. "He loves *everything* I cook," she says. Her other great talent is flamenco. She sits on the terrace, clapping her hands, singing about gypsy love. When she stops she cackles with pleasure. Gerald said the other day she was at the stove making up a song about her cooking. She swears she'll never leave him.'

Nor did she. But Milagros (who had begun to read Verlaine) and Rosa left. The financial arrangements were not yet running smoothly, and indeed never went exactly like clockwork, and the two girls kept not getting paid (just as we were continually rung up by the irate owner of the Huerta La Tena and asked for the rent).* But this was the only change. While we were still there María del Carmen García Aragón and Josefa Vera de la Rosa arrived. Vera was strong, competent, gentle and humorous. When she pulled him to his feet facing her (he now needed help standing or walking) she'd ask him if he'd like to dance. Vera, too, succumbed to the ethos of the house and one day when Mary Kennedy called she was reading *Thus Spake*

---

* It seems impossible to discover what the generosity of the Spaniards eventually cost them. It was probably in the region of six million pesetas a year (about £30,000).

Zarathustra to Gerald. María del Carmen was tiny, but also intelligent and highly competent, especially with the dozens of pills he now had to take.

One afternoon Carmen the cook and María del Carmen were talking behind him at tea. Gerald had been silent, apparently oblivious. All at once he said, 'How soft their voices are when they are not in action.' It was true. They were talking like two canaries, very gently up and down, quite different from the raucous Andaluz when shopping or in the street. I thought how easily and accurately, still, he absorbed the Spain of his youth, the way it flowed into him.

Lynda came five or six times. Gerald always perked up. When, as usual, he spilled a good deal of tea down his front he said, 'Lynda bought these mugs. They're no good. They leak.' Later, she was chatting to Nicky about cooking and said beans needed a thorough washing in running water. Gerald said suddenly, 'I get a thorough washing in running water every day.'

As he recovered from the battering of Pinner and reporters and publicity he began to read again. Our afternoons became very peaceful. Gerald read, flicking his ash vigorously and inaccurately. I read. Nicky drew and painted.* Just before we left he was halfway through a thick Spanish guide to the Alpujarra. Occasionally he would pause and comment: 'Extraordinary feeling it gives one to read that an elderly Roman woman of a certain weight was buried at so-and-so in AD 70.'

We had to go at the end of August. It was sad leaving. As I held him in my arms, so light, so very very fragile, I remembered his tough thick arms, his energy at Churriana, racing the wind, smelling of sweat.

3

The Spanish gift for the sudden, spontaneous and effective act – whether of generosity and kindness or something more violent – is perhaps almost matched by their lack of follow-through. Gerald often commented irritably on this. It irritated him about the anarchists – and elsewhere: '. . . it is a characteristic of Spaniards to be satisfied

---

* The watercolour portrait of Gerald on the back cover was done now.

with gestures . . . and to neglect the real heart of the matter. The Arabs conquered the whole of Spain in two years. It took the Spaniards eight centuries to get rid of them.'[2]

Gerald was costing a considerable amount of money. There was understandably some reluctance to add Lynda and Lars to the burden. Also it does not seem to have been properly appreciated that the most important reason, perhaps the only real reason, Gerald wanted to return to Spain was to be close to Lynda. At any rate, life for the Prangers was not easy. They were badgered for rent they were not expecting to pay and their irritated landlord eventually asked them to leave. They were told another house would be found for them. And after that, no doubt, a third. A succession of uneasy dwellings stretched ahead. Furthermore, they had discovered that the relief and pleasure of living alone together with their children – for the first time in eleven years of joint life – was considerable. A weight of depression and anxiety was lifted. In September they decided to live permanently in Mecina-Fondales.

Mecina-Fondales was then about five hours from Alhaurín el Grande, depending on traffic. Lynda came down as often as she could. The trouble was that Gerald forgot. Mary Kennedy remembered him saying, 'Lynda hasn't been to see me for two years,' when Mary Kennedy knew Lynda had been the week before. But rather few people came – Bayard Osborn, Mark Culme-Seymour and Janetta occasionally, Cuca Gross, the Kennedys, Ethel in the summer. One trouble was that reporters were discouraged, since they exhausted him; as a result the Southbys, for instance, to get to him had to force their way in. But Gerald forgot all these visits too.

Nor could he any longer write letters. He tried – his last papers contain pathetic efforts, fragments of sentences, scrawls of attempted beginnings – but some essential mechanism cementing idea and execution had deteriorated too far. Since he could not answer, people gradually ceased to write.

Extreme old age is perhaps to a certain extent deliberate – due to a *determination* to live which has often, in the end, become unconscious, a sort of momentum of past determination. But it is not the happiest period of a life. Certainly Gerald was well looked after – perhaps too well. It became a point of honour to keep him alive. Continually pumped full of antibiotics, whenever anything serious went wrong the full resources of Spanish medicine sprang into play.

For instance in April 1985 Gerald was rushed to Malaga hospital with pneumonia. Bulletins appeared on television. He recovered. He was rushed in again in January 1986 with a bladder complaint and internal haemorrhage. Three doctors attended him under Dr Guillermo Cóler Martín. He recovered. These emergencies happened numerous times, each time Lynda and Lars were summoned and hurried down, each time Gerald recovered.

There was a period at the end of 1984 when, out of boredom, desperate at his condition, he planned to escape. He told Cuca Gross to get him a key (nothing was locked.) He asked Janetta for £100 in pesetas. Then this last effort of resistance died away and he became resigned.

He spent hours dreaming about the past. And now at last, in his dreams, he went on the tremendous journeys he'd planned with Hope when he was eighteen. When he returned from Pinner he thought he'd been to China and come back speaking Chinese. He congratulated Lynda and Lars on the speed with which they'd picked up this difficult language. But when he was not dreaming, as day after day passed and no one called, he was often very lonely. Lynda has one of his last letters, a scrap where he says he has never been so lonely in his life before.

4

I saw Gerald four more times. Nicky and I went over for two days in April 1985, just before his ninety-first birthday. Like most old men he was troubled by incontinence. I had sent him a box of John Bell and Croyden contraptions involving an attachment and a long tube with a bag and this was working.* He seemed steeped in boredom, the girls chattering around him, the television permanently on, all ignored by Gerald. But beside him were the new Graham Greene novel and a book on Wittgenstein. 'Do you like it?' 'I don't know. I can't read it. My mind's gone.' However, I noticed he was halfway through. His long Svevo-like battle against smoking had finally ended, in the defeat of the cigarette. He'd become so dangerous (one

---

* I'd sent the contraption unnecessarily, as it turned out. It was already being supplied by his extremely competent GP, Dr Burgos.

cardigan was crocheted with burns) that Vera and María del Carmen had removed his cigarettes. He didn't seem to mind.

We saw him again in November of that year. There was a fire of big dry olive roots, sparking and giving out heat. Gerald was upright in front of it wearing his woollen skull cap. His voice was now rather difficult to hear. He had really stopped reading (I saw piles of the *Observer* I'd ordered in unopened rolls). He said he'd been having a series of terrible dream journeys recently. He spoke of Gamel. He said she felt very close to him. He often had the feeling she was standing there waiting and he would look round expecting to see her.

We stayed for lunch, for which we'd brought a chocolate cake. Vera fed him, rather quickly. Gerald was clearly tired. I felt he had finally glided down and was now at rest, waiting for death. 'Sad, very lonely, but completely resigned. He cannot walk. He cannot lift his arms higher than his spectacles. He doesn't smoke. But his head is clear. He observes. And for hours he dreams.'

I returned alone in July 1986. There was a Dutch contract for *St John* to sign. Also, it had been suggested I write his biography. I explained this, ending – 'What do you think?'

'I don't know. I haven't thought about it.'

'Would you mind if I wrote your life?'

'No,' said Gerald after a pause. 'I suppose if anyone, I'd rather you. But it's not up to me, it's up to you.' Another pause. 'Anyone can write my life.' Pause. I wished I hadn't bothered him. 'It would have to be someone who knew me.'

'I know you a bit.'

'Yes, you know me very well.'

We had lunch, Gerald being fed. I talked about this and that but it was difficult to rouse him. Then I got out the contracts and held them while, very slowly, like a dying spider just moving its ink-dipped legs, he tried to write Gerald Brenan. Only the 'Ger' was discernible.

He was tired and depressed. María del Carmen and Vera picked him up and half-carried, half-dragged him out like a bundle of old sticks. María del Carmen said he would sleep till seven o'clock. When I went in, he was lying with an oxygen mask on. He looked comically, tragically up at me, the oxygen bubbling in from a man-sized cylinder beside the bed.

The last time I saw him was on 2 October 1986. It seemed as if he had been finally broken on the wheel of old age. He had had numerous small strokes and was lying in bed almost unable to speak, his face still more shrunken and skull-like. He would try and say something and get stuck on the first word. I asked him if the doctor had come. 'Doctor doctor doctor doctor doctor,' Gerald mumbled.

He began keening to himself. I felt it was both too painful to stay long and also pointless, but I sat for a while stroking his bony shanks under the covers. He didn't seem to notice, but when I bent over him before going I heard him mumble, 'Thank you thank you thank you thank you . . .'

Looking back as I walked out, I saw the plastic bag of urine hanging from his bed, being patted to and fro by a new kitten – last of a long line.

5

Gerald recovered from this distressing state. When Lynda and Lars last saw him, on 23 December, he was very frail but clear and calm. After a while, Lars found his weakness and helplessness unbearably sad and had to leave the room, but Lynda sat talking to him for a long time.

1987 began with a succession of beautiful mild days. His ninety-third birthday would have been in April, but it was not one he would see. Brenans die in January – his mother died on 7 January, Gamel on 18 January.

Ethel saw him on Saturday 10 January. 'He was in bed. He was sleeping a lot, like a child. He could still speak, though I'm not sure he recognised me. He was not in pain, he was warm and clean and fed and well cared for. Think of the agony it can be. It was a gentle end – if a bit late.'

Gerald began to sink the following Saturday. Lynda and Lars were rung at midday on Monday the 19th. The doctor said he did not think he could last. Lynda decided to drive down, but both the children had chicken pox. They had gone so often before and Gerald had so often recovered that they decided to wait. When they rang later in the afternoon they were told he was slightly better. But his heart began to fail during the evening. He died at eleven o'clock that night.

Epilogue

'They made me feel that I was born to be a letter writer rather than a writer of books . . .'
Gerald to Frances Partridge, 17 October 1966, after she had sent
him typed copies of all his letters to Carrington

1

Flying in late that windy Tuesday night for Gerald's funeral on Wednesday 21 January, I saw the Malaga lighthouse flashing in the darkness below. The lighthouse which had always said yes had at last – and long after time – said no.

There was, I soon learnt, a furious row going on between Alhaurín el Grande on one side and Malaga and the British Consul on the other, as to where Gerald should be buried.

This was no doubt intensified by the explosion of publicity that burst the moment he died. In England, the obituaries – those last reviews a writer never sees – were certainly numerous and extensive: three columns by Xan Fielding in the *Independent*, two full-length and anonymous columns in the *Daily Telegraph* (Lynda described as Gerald's niece); Hugh Thomas had written three columns in *The Times* and Frances a page in the *Spectator*. There was a particularly good and full one over several pages by David Mitchell in *Lookout*, the English magazine of the Costa del Sol.

All this was nothing compared to what took place in Spain. For years respected on account of his work, the Spanish media also thought, with some justice, that he had come back from London solely as a result of their efforts. They therefore felt that in some way he belonged to them. Alerted by Dr Burgos the instant Gerald died, his death headed all television and radio bulletins for two days and remained a major item for five. All the major newspapers and magazines ran long articles on him and these too continued for several days.

Janetta and I drove out to Alhaurín early on Wednesday. The weather had broken. There was a grey sky and fierce grey seas rolling in along the coast, and a strong wind shook the orange trees with their thick glossy green leaves and bright orange oranges.

There was a scene of some confusion and consternation at Cañada de las Palomas. The dispute over Gerald's body had been settled by an appeal to Stéphane. Gerald's grandson had remembered what everyone seemed to have forgotten, that he had willed his body to the medical faculty in Malaga. Stéphane insisted his grandfather's wishes be respected. Everyone had come expecting a funeral. Ian Gibson had flown in from Madrid. The girls Vera and María del Carmen were naturally there. Wreaths littered the ground. Carmen the cook had appropriated the largest, from the Ministry of Culture. She pointed out with pleasure the opulence of the blossoms. There was even a delegation from Yegen: five men, stiff with well-dressedness, looking rather ill at ease. All these people and various others were standing about needing a funeral and there was to be no funeral. Gerald had already vanished to the dissecting table. It was an anticlimax. At the same time, there was a sense of release, of escape. For two years trapped by his infirmities, surrounded by helpers and occasional friends, by doctors and reporters and policemen, he had finally, at the end, succeeded in eluding us.*

2

I am back in the south of Spain now almost exactly five years later, checking some last details for this book. Lovely weather – the almond

---

* And yet he was pursued even now in a modern repetition of the scenes he had described so vividly in *St John*. Reporters somehow got into the medical faculty and a grisly photograph of Gerald naked on a slab appeared in *Sur*. I noticed with a pang that his left hand had assumed, in death, the oddly rigid position he had always adopted to hold a cigarette. Cultural circles in Malaga protested at this and no more such photographs appeared.

blossom out on the bare almond branches, the oranges like Christmas decorations among their dark green leaves.

Gerald's library is now housed in Alhaurín. He is not buried there – yet. The medical faculty did not dissect, they simply embalmed. One day, again like St John, I suspect Gerald will move – but where? Perhaps I could suggest a precedent from England. Thomas Hardy's body lies in Westminster Abbey, but his heart is buried in Dorchester.

Cañada de Las Palomas has been sold and now has a swimming pool and a tennis court. Lynda and Lars have continued to live in Mecina-Fondales; Carlos and Emily go to school in Pitres. The last time I saw La Cónsula while researching here three years ago it was empty, but I was told it was to become a waxworks. I shan't check that again in case it's no longer true; I prefer to think of them all frozen there. Particularly appropriate for Cyril somehow, lying back for ever in the 'listening-to-music' position, in wax.

Will Gerald last and be remembered, and if so for what? His books have already been fully discussed but there is one last aspect of his life and work that has not been looked at properly, except that it permeates this book throughout, its presence felt on almost every page. I mean, of course, his letters.

The fact that so many of Gerald's letters survive – at a rough estimate over three million words of them – has almost nothing to do with his fame. He eventually had a reputation both in England and America but he was never remotely famous. He did become famous in Spain – at moments even celebrated – but he had no Spanish correspondents.

But to those who kept the early letters – Ralph, Hope and Carrington – the promise, if not of fame then of something special may have played a very minor part alongside affection. Certainly at first it was not much to do with the letters. Gerald always said he could prove how unintellectual Ralph was at the time of the First World War by his facetious young man's letters – all jokes, food and women. But Gerald's letters at this time are equally facetious; they are also far more stilted and pompous.

Yet Hope, a highly intelligent man who had met many of the leading writers and painters of his day, thought the young Gerald had genius. And his early letters often impress with their intensity – intensity of idealism, of energy, of determination, of goal. As he increasingly learnt, writing to Hope over four years, how to describe more and more simply what he was thinking and feeling and reading, whom he saw, what he did, the people he met, so the letters became increasingly interesting and delightful. It was the enormous correspondence with Carrington which completed his training as a letter-writer. After about 1921 people who kept Gerald's letters did so because they realised they were receiving something out of the ordinary.

A selection will have to encompass all his letters, not just the main figures of Ralph, Frances, Carrington, VSP, Bunny. Almost all writers think and create with a pen in their hand, the writing engendering itself – but it was true of Gerald to an exceptional degree. With a complex and original mind, vastly stocked with knowledge, fertile with ideas and inventions, any letter could suddenly take wing. One to the BBC, for example, about one of his children's scripts, suddenly veers into a four-page disquisition on the Armada.

What else does one notice? He is often very amusing. He is virtually unable to resist any item of gossip. As I noted at the time, when Barbara Skelton was possibly leaving Cyril for George Weidenfeld, Gerald, in the course of a quite different family letter, gave a vivid résumé to Blair. Blair had never met Cyril. He had never even heard of Weidenfeld or Barbara Skelton. But Gerald is so interested he tells him everything, as though talking to himself, which in a way he was. Just as he imagined everyone would walk the cliffs of Lulworth with a telescope, so he imagined everyone would be as interested as he was in Cyril and Barbara's love-life – and as a result it *is* interesting. Yet it is an odd trait.

One notices what might be called his gift of the casual phrase – and here I think he is the equal of Coleridge who in his notebooks (though much less in his recorded talk) would throw off original images and arresting phrases in the same way. There are hundreds, even thousands of examples in his letters. I think of some I quoted earlier. At Brighton to VSP while recovering on the pier from his attack of trench mouth during the war – and no doubt practising for *A Holiday by the Sea* – with the sea 'slipping and slopping up and down, shuffling and shoffling about like some thyroidless creature'. Or the potatoes tasting 'of dead men's toes' at Aldbourne, because he'd cooked them and because he was missing Gamel away in

London. Or spring at Bell Court following him about like a pleasant dream: 'Our garden full of white and blue crocuses which open their petals in a vast yawn to take in a bee.' Or him and Lynda returning like pieces of stretched elastic when Bunny had gone back to France. At its best this gift gives his letters the vividness and spontaneity of marvellous talk from someone whom VSP thought one of the best talkers and letter-writers in England.

But the letters deserve attention for two further reasons. A disadvantage of letters is that the writer may tailor them to the recipient – showing off or writing especially brilliantly or disguising aspects of him or herself. This is often true of Virginia Woolf, for example. And Gerald was certainly sometimes extremely self-conscious and aware of the effect he wished to make (or to disguise). But his letters are more noticeable for their modesty and humanity and lack of affectation. They are quite often remarkable for their reckless honesty. When he wrote to VSP in the white heat of his feelings over Miranda, for example, or in the truly astonishing letters he wrote to Frances while Gamel was dying, he doesn't seem to be conscious that he is actually writing to someone else at all. They are the revelations of a self stripped of all artifice.

And so, to paraphrase Peter Quennell writing about another unusual writer, there slowly builds up as one reads the letters, with their accounts of writers and books, their humour, their complaints and desires, their sudden naked confessions, a portrait of an extraordinarily gifted and unusually complex personality. Gerald accepted the various sides of his nature and made little attempt to reconcile them and the various aspects appear in his letters in rapid succession, like the flickering images of a zoetrope. His inconsistency, his perversity, his excitability and emotional explosiveness, his indiscretion and gossip and voyeur sides were as much part of him as the poet, the scholar, the critic, the historian and the polymath, and they all co-existed with a freedom and even a sort of shamelessness not equalled, perhaps, since Byron, the poet about whom Quennell was writing.'

And writing letters was a necessity for him. There is sometimes almost a feeling that Gerald lived in order to write a letter to someone about it – just as Boswell seems to live in order to set down his life in his journal. This means that alongside the building-up and slow revelation of a character we get, often in minute and fascinating detail, the unrolling of a long and unusually varied life.

It is possible that this enormous correspondence will eventually prove Gerald's most lasting memorial. Certainly it will be possible to double or treble or quadruple the total of his work. And it will mean that he will be remembered, not just as England's greatest Hispanist but, as he would have liked and as he deserved, as a writer.

Appendix A
Comparative values of the pound

These figures, which have been compiled for me by Dolf Mootham from statistics provided by the Central Statistical Office, must be regarded as impressionistic. Nevertheless, they give some idea of changing money values during the period of Gerald's life. The base is 1990. In other words, a pound in 1894 was worth £50.47 at 1990 prices.

1894	£50.47	1917	£24.45	1946	£16.54	1969	£7.12
1895	£52.69	1918	£21.21	1947	£15.47	1970	£6.68
1896	£53.28	1919	£20.05	1948	£14.40	1971	£6.50
1897	£51.01	1920	£17.31	1949	£13.94	1972	£5.69
1898	£50.48	1921	£19.10	1950	£13.66	1973	£5.28
1899	£51.01	1922	£23.20	1951	£12.39	1974	£4.71
1900	£49.44	1923	£23.20	1952	£11.83	1975	£3.93
1901	£48.94	1924	£23.09	1953	£11.56	1976	£3.19
1902	£48.41	1925	£24.15	1954	£11.34	1977	£2.72
1903	£47.92	1926	£24.78	1955	£10.97	1978	£2.49
1904	£47.44	1927	£25.31	1956	£10.47	1979	£2.28
1905	£47.92	1928	£25.91	1957	£10.14	1980	£1.92
1906	£47.92	1929	£26.35	1958	£9.85	1981	£1.69
1907	£46.53	1930	£27.24	1959	£9.76	1982	£1.51
1908	£45.21	1931	£29.23	1960	£9.63	1983	£1.44
1909	£45.21	1932	£29.96	1961	£9.36	1984	£1.37
1910	£44.82	1933	£30.75	1962	£9.05	1985	£1.30
1911	£44.37	1934	£30.22	1963	£8.96	1986	£1.24
1912	£42.82	1935	£31.75	1964	£8.78	1987	£1.19
1913	£42.79	1936	£30.77	1965	£8.26	1988	£1.16
1914	£43.20	1937	£27.87	1966	£8.05	1989	£1.08
1915	£34.98	1938	£27.56	1967	£7.76	1990	£1.00
1916	£29.58	1939–45 WAR		1968	£7.56		

Appendix B

Gerald took to Spain all the books he'd bought up till 1919 – itself a considerable quantity, some of which have been mentioned. He also brought all of his beloved Elisée Reclus' *Universal Geography*. As for the rest, I said he packed Borrow and Ford, but it was a guess – though a considered one. Gerald was never a collector. What he required were good working copies and when he bought a book he bought the best serviceable modern edition. Quite often he bought a new edition of a book of which he already had an older one. Much of his original library has been lost, sold or pinched (often by Hope). Of the books that remain, now belonging to the Comunidad of Alhaurín el Grande, available on display there, any book in an edition prior to 1919 of which there have been subsequent editions was probably one he took to Spain. Borrow's *The Bible in Spain* and Ford's *Gatherings in Spain* (he did not take the *Handbook*) both came out in later editions to Gerald's pre-1919 ones. On this basis, and remembering we will be missing a good number, we can make the following rough approximation as to what he took in 1919: in English, French and German literatures he took all the major classics in history, biography, criticism, as well as plays, novels and poetry. He also took a good many lesser writers in English including, for example, Disraeli, Trelawney, Pater, William Morris, Peacock, Beckford etc. In German and Italian he took the obvious main writers. In Italian, for example, there remain Dante, Croce, Ariosto, Tasso, Cellini and a good many early poets. The library at first had rather few Spanish writers. Nevertheless he took Quevedo, Calderón, Lope de Vega, Cervantes, Molina, March, St John of the Cross, Gil Vicente, Menéndez y Pelayo. He took the main Scandinavian playwrights. He took the main classical authors, Greek and Latin (nearly all in translation), also studies on all of them. There were books on architecture (including early Christian and Byzantine), on art (including Cézanne, the Cubists, and Italian, French and Chinese art). He took all the major philosophers, both ancient and modern (including G. E. Moore, Santayana, Swedenborg, William James). There was a great deal of religion and comparative religion and theology, including the religions of the Near and Far East, Chinese mystics, with histories of the Popes and the early

Church. There were two or three volumes each on anthropology, mythology, psychology (including some Freud), mathematics, physics and chemistry, geology, astrology, botany, ornithology and entomology (eleven volumes of J. H. Fabre in French). As well as numerous general histories, there were histories of Persia, Africa, the Near East, the French Revolution. There were numerous grammars to study Italian, Spanish, Old French, Greek and Latin. In all, Gerald took 2000 volumes to Spain.

Appendix C

A thorough exegesis of *The Spanish Labyrinth* would require an essay of sixty or seventy pages. Nevertheless, I should like to add a number of comments to the rather brief treatment in the text.

Although it was true to say there were no English historians of Spain comparable to Gerald before him, there were what one might call useful histories: dates, details of the national debt, battles and revolutions, the important activities of kings and queens and their chief ministers. Martin Hume (twenty publications) was such an historian; so was H. Butler Clarke.

Some examples should be given of acknowledgement from Hispanists and historians at the time. Professor J. B. Trend, perhaps the only exception to the strictures above, wrote of this 'learned and penetrating book . . . scholarly . . . mastery of both subject and method'.[1] He noted, as Trevor-Roper* did later, Gerald's extraordinary sensitivity to the way the past moved in the present, and said the chapters on the agrarian problem and on the history and philosophy of political organisations were the best on the subject ever written.[2] On the bibliography, Professor M. S. Henderson of Oxford described it as 'a piece of serious scholarship'.[3]

In fact time has obscured the strength of his bibliography in 1943. Arthur Lehning had enabled him to see material on the anarchist movement in Spain no one else had got hold of. He had read Spanish historians and work hitherto unknown in England, for instance, Díaz del Moral's *Historia de las Aquitaciones Campesinas Andaluzas*, or Julián de Zugasti y Saenz' *El Bandolerismo: Estudio Social y Memorias Históricas* (10 vols). Many of the sources which were primary then have since been printed here – as a direct result of *The Spanish Labyrinth*. This is true of *Oligarquía Caciquismo* by Joaquín Costa and *El Espartaquísmo Andaluz* by Bernaldo de Quiros.

---

* Here is the full passage from which I quoted a phrase on page 340: 'Ever since I read *The Spanish Labyrinth*, I have looked upon you as my ideal historian – you see the past in the present, and the present in the past, imaginatively, and yet with corrective scholarship, and you express it in perfect prose – and I would rather write for you than for anyone.' (Hugh Trevor-Roper – Lord Dacre – to Gerald, 11 March 1968, MSS, Texas.)

Gerald's twenty-three pages of bibliography themselves, therefore, had a considerable effect on the historiography in England. In more general terms, Gerald acted rather in the same way that Björn Borg made tennis a national game in Sweden. He was responsible for Raymond Carr writing Spanish history (see pp. 350-1), and it was Carr who, with his one-time associate Joaquín Romero Maura, started the whole school of Oxford contemporary Spanish history – now being succeeded by that led from London University.

It is much harder to detect any direct influence Gerald had on Spanish historiography, except at a remove. For one thing, Spanish historians are much less impressed by narrative history than are English historians. Then, immediately after the Second World War, the Franco regime was desperate to expunge its fascist connections. Historians in Spain now took 'to portraying Franco as a clairvoyant pioneer in the war against communism'.[+] In this context, Gerald was clearly not acceptable. But it was partly inspired by *The Spanish Labyrinth* that Hugh Thomas wrote his enormous *The Spanish Civil War* (London 1961). This sometimes seems to be faintly scorned by scholars, jealous perhaps of its success. It is a narrative account of dazzling skill and had immense influence: translated and smuggled into Spain by Ruedo Ibérico from Paris, it started the next wave of Franco historiography.

A department of government was set up by the dynamic Minister of Information, Manuel Fraga Iribane, and put under the direction of Ricardo de la Cierva in order to combat historical criticism. Now much more sophisticated history was required, in contrast to the crude propaganda sponsored by the Franco regime before, to combat accounts like Thomas', but Gerald had to be considered directly here as well, since *The Spanish Labyrinth* was also published by Ruedo Ibérico and secretly distributed in Spain from 1962 onwards.

As the Franco regime crumbled, a flood of Spanish historians sprang up, some naturally impatient that so far their best history had been written, through force of circumstances, by Anglo-Saxons. Since then, there has been, in Paul Preston's words, 'Wave after wave of detailed local research', gradually reshaping one area after another.[+]

And here Gerald has been corrected, if only in detail. A current preoccupation is the economic failure of Spain in the nineteenth century, something Gerald only addressed cursorily. Then there was a problem accounting for Catalan anarchism in industry. Gerald explained it by the migration of anarchist workers from Andalusia. In fact, it now appears that rather few southern workers went to Barcelona. It was Catalan peasants who migrated. Catalan anarchism, that is, can be explained by Catalan events – a discovery, it will surprise no one to learn, made by Catalan historians.

A more general criticism, and one made at the time, was that he devoted more space to Andalusia and saw Spanish problems through Andalusian eyes. In treating Gerald as they treat themselves, Spanish historians flattered him. But Gerald was not Andalusian; he was English. He had no particular regional axe to grind. As Raymond Carr pointed out to me,[5] he read far more about Catalonia than Andalusia (at the time, and given the material available, his explanation of Catalan anarchism was perfectly sensible). He was certainly sound on the land problem in Andalusia but, as Carr also noted, he was just as good on Galicia. In fact, when he came to write about the agrarian problem he devoted about one third of his space to Andalusia, two-thirds to the rest of Spain. But the eleven pages on Andalusia include a general survey of industrial workers all over Spain, and an historical section which the other provinces had already received. Remove these, and Andalusia gets almost exactly the space proportional to her size and importance relative to the other agricultural regions.

But what is noticeable is that, since he knew it so well, his portrait of Andalusia is often more vivid, and no doubt this gave an impression of bias. This, too, is probably what prompted the protests of the Right. He is often exasperated by the Left; he reserves the sting of his sarcasm, his anger, for the Right. 'With consummate foresight he (Gil Robles) had provoked the Reds into a premature rising which had ruined them . . . It was the tactics of the bull-ring – to provoke the animal to charge and charge again until he was worn out, and then kill him. There was a long tradition among the Spanish ruling classes of how to break a revolution. Indeed such arts contained for them the whole of politics.'

Anti-clericalism was a major feature of the Civil War. (In Andalusia in particular the victims of the Left were often priests or those close to the Church.) When Gerald was writing this was one of the major conundrums of Spanish history. He explained it by pointing to the disestablishment of the Spanish Church and then the taking and selling of its lands by the Liberals in 1835. Financial exigencies and self-interest gradually made the clergy dependent on the propertied and wealthy classes. As a result, they abandoned the poor whom they had often supported and made alliance with the rich. These then used the Church for political ends. It was this that alienated and infuriated the bulk of the people, the '*pueblo*'. 'In so far as it is possible,' wrote Julian Pitt-Rivers, 'to abstract a sequence of cause and effect from the multiple conditions of social history, this explanation has not been bettered.'[6]

Gerald extended his analysis to explain by this Church/wealth alignment the hastening of the steady decline of religion in Spain. This in turn left a spiritual hunger which was finally filled by the political ideologies. In particular it explained the religious fervour and the anger of the anarchists. 'I would suggest that the anger of the Spanish Anarchists against the Church is the anger of an intensely religious people who feel they have been deserted and betrayed.' In fact, it is likely that all revolutionary movements (which anarchism in the Civil War certainly was), by reason of their fervour, by their tendency to expand, become religious in nature. De Tocqueville made exactly the same comment about the French Revolution, and he too pointed to the decline in popular support of religion as a factor.

In fact, Spanish historians today often feel that Gerald's emphasis on anarchists and the poverty of Spain in general was too romantic. Also – acutely sensitive to any hint of the patronising – they see it as somehow making Spain seem to have been an underdeveloped country, something from the third world.

Nevertheless, in broad terms Gerald set the fundamental picture of the hundred years up to the Civil War and, despite much tinkering, it has not been changed. But there is a final perspective into which he must be set and it involves what we have just been discussing. Some years ago, Juan Goytisolo, one of Spain's most interesting novelists, suggested that Gerald's admiration of poverty represented his desire to escape from the wealth and soullessness of industrial civilisation.[7] This is not wrong exactly, but it ignores how extraordinarily personal and particular were the roots of all Gerald's thought. His embracing of poverty, particularly when young, derived entirely from his desire to escape from his father and Edgeworth into a more intense life – just as his love of Shelley and Rimbaud and Stendhal was due to self-identification.

But Goytisolo's remarks do lead to the last and most fundamental question about *The Spanish Labyrinth*. The thing that underlies many of Gerald's insights and much of his analysis is indeed Spain's poverty. It was the poverty of Spain, as well as its vast distances, that kept the *pueblo* isolated and therefore dominant. Again and again Gerald refers to the disapproval of luxury in the *pueblo* (the four-fifths of Spain's population he felt he knew through living in Yegen and Churriana), the boasting of how little they lived on, just as Don Quixote in his account of the Golden Age said that men 'nourished themselves on acorns'. (And as in fact they were still being forced to nourish themselves in the 1930s.)[8] And this is a fundamental feeling. It is indeed an ascetic creed, which values the human qualities of life above the material and, translated into the industrial terms of today, does represent a resistance to the tyranny, the pollution, the soul-destruction of only seeking wealth.

But Spain is poor no longer. Nor is the *pueblo* isolated. The forests of television aerials quiver to the game show *Precio justo*. People are as eager for money as everyone else, particularly in the towns. One would suppose, therefore, that this particular structure of Gerald's analysis, and it is the most important, no longer applies. Accurate at the time, it is now out of date. Certainly Gerald himself was quite aware this might be so and, disliking poverty more than he loved the qualities it can throw up, was on the whole pleased.[9]

Yet national character is an odd thing. We are no longer remotely like the people who fought at Agincourt or against the Armada, nor are we the nation of shopkeepers who defeated Napoleon (even if we installed the daughter of one in a prominent position for a while). Our materialism is gross. Yet our ancient military prowess – deeply rooted in a class structure which has survived long after its economic and social determinants have vanished, and which is ultimately feudal and so military, and also in the native courage and independence of an island people – this old aptitude for fighting only requires a Blitz or a Falklands or a Gulf to bring it roaring out once more. That is to say, the mechanisms of cultural inheritance, which probably lie in patterns of upbringing, often seem to be independent of whatever circumstances originally gave rise to the national characteristic that is being passed on. Those qualities in the Spanish character which Gerald loved may only be sleeping. One day his analysis here may turn out to be as relevant again as it was when it was first made.

NOTES

1 *The Cambridge Review*, 8 May 1943.
2 *The Civilisation of Spain*, OUP 1943. A professor at Christ's College, Cambridge, Trend was one of the leading Hispanists and historians of Spain of his day. His other books include *A Picture of Modern Spain: Men and Music* (London 1921); *Manuel de Falla and Spanish Music* (Cambridge, 1934); and *The Origins of Modern Spain* (Cambridge 1934).
3 Quoted by Gerald in *The Spectator*, 23 April 1943.
4 In these notes on the bibliography of *The Spanish Labyrinth* and its influence on the historiography I largely rely on discussions with Professor Paul Preston and on the brilliant and exhaustive article by him in *Revolution and War in Spain 1931–39* (Methuen 1984), which he also edited. The quotation comes from that essay. I was also helped by a discussion with Juan Pablo Fusi, the distinguished Spanish historian.

5 Interview, Raymond Carr.
6 *The People of the Sierra* by Julian Pitt-Rivers (London 1954).
7 *El arte de narrar: Diálogos, Colección Prisma* by Emir Rodríguez Monegal (Monte Avila, Caracas 1968).
8 *The Coming of the Spanish Civil War* by Paul Preston (Methuen 1983).
9 'Hispanophilia' by G.B. (*New York Review of Books*, 26 January 1967).

Appendix D

As with *The Spanish Labyrinth*, I would like to add, not alas one of Gerald's erudite pirouettes, but a few random comments to the rather short remarks on *The Literature of the Spanish People* in the text.

As always, Gerald's strong sense of history is everywhere evident in the way he comments on literary developments or describes them via their historical and social roots, and this in a particularly clear, common-sense way. It is this underpinning which gives the book a firmness and solidarity which are very satisfying. No doubt other writers have done the same, but it is the concision with which Gerald does it that gives force and exhilaration and, by making clearer the various literary developments, makes them more interesting. It is his de Tocqueville side again.

But this is balanced – or not so much balanced but shot through, as by sudden flashes of fire – by Gerald's gifts as a poet. He had the sensibility of a poet, even if he expressed it in prose. And he expressed it in his reading of poetry. See him, for example, on Lope de Vega, the seventeenth-century prodigy. Or on the way he saw that Góngora's inversions and latinisations, hitherto much criticised in his *Soledades*, had freed him from the ordinary habits and rhythms of speech, allowing him the effects he sought. Here Gerald combined common sense with acute poetic insight. 'A flight of cranes,' he wrote, analysing Góngora's images, 'is described as an "arc waxing and waning like moons and writing winged characters on the diaphanous paper of the sky . . ." Images such as these . . . seek to present not so much familiar objects as the state, nameless and evanescent, in which they have their being when they make their first impact on the senses . . .' They allow Góngora, he goes on, to convey a particular mode of experiencing the world.

This gift for reading poetry is particularly noticeable when he writes about the poets of the Muslim period and the early Middle Ages. In a letter to Cambridge University Press (31 October 1951) Gerald says that it was one of his aims to make this early literature, usually left to scholars and research students, 'interesting and readable'. But one feels he did this as much or more because it was these poets he had discovered as a young man at Yegen. Poets like Juan Ruiz, the Archpriest of Hita, 'one of the greatest poets of the Middle Ages, the equal of Chaucer,' to whom he devotes an entire chapter, and to whom he gives the highest possible accolade by comparing him to Svevo; or Alfonso Alvarez de Villasandino (1345–1425), 'the ease and naturalness of [whose] verse and a certain buoyancy . . . often make triumph over the conventionality of his themes'.

Or is it Gerald who triumphs? Not only is his enthusiasm infectious, illuminating many authors now unread; it is an end itself. We can be fairly sure (and, questioned, Professor Juan Antonio Díaz López of Granada University *was* sure) that if we read these ancient writers they would bore us and reveal that their obscurity, if sad, was perfectly justified. Gerald's ability to appreciate their poetry (rare enough in itself), the way he tells their tales and recounts their lives, is enough.

And there is here, perhaps, a general comment about criticism. It is to some extent a creative art. The feelings and reactions of the critic are not so much, or not only, felt at the time, at the first time, but are worked on and worked up later. Like poets, critics do not recollect but create their emotions in tranquillity, and all great critical works – though of course they must remain plausible – are really constructs built on original imaginative works. This is what gives them their validity, their excitement – and what makes us, often, so disappointed when we return to the originals.

But if this idiosyncracy of emphasis, the clear way Gerald wrote more about what interested him, is the source of the book's vitality, it also gives rise to more important criticism. After 1500, *The Literature of the Spanish People* loses the dynamic of a literature unfolding and becomes a series of essays on great writers (a fault Gerald acknowledged in that same CUP letter). The eighteenth century bored Gerald, and this is evident; by the nineteenth century he was flagging. He had exhausted what energy was left on Rosalía de Castro, the Galician poet he loved ('all the words in her poems lean in one direction under the wind of lyric feeling') and he couldn't really be bothered to deal properly with García Lorca, though he admired him. He severely underestimated Leopoldo Alas' *La Regenta*. And some of his comparisons are either wild or superficial.

These sorts of criticisms were particularly advanced by the more pedantic scholars in Spain when the book came out there. It is not, incidentally, easy to pin the date of this down. But Gerald signed a contract for a Spanish edition with the Argentinian publisher Editorial Losada in 1952. This seems finally to have appeared in 1958 and to have circulated in Spain from then on.*

But if his judgements could be challenged, his scholarship was not at fault. As in England, most Spanish criticism was in fact extremely favour-

---

* The book came out simultaneously in America in 1952, and was also published in France (1963) and in Italy and Yugoslavia (1970).

able. And Spanish students, especially, were amazed, as one is still when reading the book today, that where most books of this sort are dull, scholarly, uninformative, unadventurous and exhausting to read, Gerald was able to be so wild, so extreme, so generous, so alive and so free.

Reference notes

ABBREVIATIONS

G = Gerald Brenan
Gamel = Gamel Brenan
R = Ralph Partridge
F = Frances Partridge
C = Dora Carrington
Blair = Blair Brenan
Hope = John Hope-
    Johnstone
LS = Lytton Strachey
VSP = V. S. Pritchett
B – David (Bunny)
    Garnett
M = Miranda Brenan
JC = Joanna Carrington
VW = Virginia Woolf
HA = Helen Anrep
LlP = Llewelyn Powys
Alyse = Alyse Gregory

Janetta = Janetta de
    Parladé (née Woolley)
Lynda = Lynda Pranger
n.d. = no date
Int = interview with
HH = Hamish Hamilton
CUP = Cambridge
    University Press
Tex = the Brenan archive
    at the Harry Ransome
    Research Center at the
    University of Texas at
    Austin
MF = the Brenan archive
    held at Mecina-
    Fondales
ALOOO = A Life of One's
    Own

PR = Personal Record
Holiday = A Holiday by the
    Sea
Lighthouse = The Lighthouse
    Always Says Yes
Thoughts = Thoughts in a
    Dry Season
Sp Lab = The Spanish
    Labyrinth
Sp Lit = The Literature of
    the Spanish People
St John = St John of the
    Cross
SFG = South From
    Granada
FOS = The Face of Spain
DOK – Death's Other
    Kingdom

All unacknowledged quotations from named individuals throughout the book are from interviews with the author. As far as possible the location of unpublished sources – letters, journals, unpublished MSS etc. – has been given; sometimes in these notes, but mostly in the select bibliography. Personal letters whose location is not indicated are in the possession of the recipients, their heirs or private collections.

PART ONE

All important facts or quotations in Part One whose source is not indicated are from *A Life of One's Own*.

Chapter One

1 Int Lady Cary.
2 Family papers.

3 *Midnight Oil* by VSP, London 1971.
4 Exchange G and VSP, Nov 1974.

5 See e.g. G to F, May 1983.
6 G to C (unsent), Aug 1923.
7 Correspondence of author with Mr Simon Spicer, June 1988.
8 Int Mr McGill.
9 Int Mrs Stevens, Edgeworth.

10 Haileybury school records; Harts Army List; Army Lists 1888–93.
11 MS, MF.
13 Family papers.
14 Family papers. Int Mr McGill.

Chapter Two

1 Family papers.
2 *Child Development and Personality* by P. H. Mussen, J. J. Conger, J. Kagan, New York 1990.
3 Author's journal, 2 Jan 1978.
4 Ints Lady Cary, Lydia Piper.
5 *ALOOO* unpub MS (Tex).
6 G to C, 8 July 1921; to F, Feb 1932.
7 Int Lady Cary.
8 Ints Lady Cary, Lydia Piper.
9 *History of the Irish Rifles* by Lt-Col Laurie, London 1914.
10 *ALOOO* unpub MS.
11 Harts Army List.
12 *London and Its Environs* by Karl Baedeker, London 1905.
13 G to VSP, 27 Dec 1956.
14 Int Lady Cary.
15 G to B, 10 Feb 1980.
16 Int May Holder, Miserden.
17 *PR*.

Chapter Three

1 *Public School Year Book 1935*.
2 G to VSP, April 1980.
3 Ibid., 18 Aug 1978.
4 See e.g. G to R, 22 July 1957.
5 Family papers.
6 Lady Cary to author, Jan/Feb 1988.
7 *Holiday*.
8 Int Lady Cary.
9 *Lark Rise to Candleford* by Flora Thompson, OUP World Classics 1971.
10 G to VSP, 23 July 1967.
11 *The Frontiers of Paradise: A Study of Monks and Monasteries* by Peter Levi, London 1987.
12 G in BBC broadcast, 3 Jan 1949.
13 *ALOOO* unpub MS

Chapter Four

1 *The History of Radley College 1847–1947* by A. K. Boyd, Oxford 1948.
2 *ALOOO* unpub MS.
3 G to R, April 1921.
4 *Thoughts*.
5 Radley College school records.
6 Family papers.
7 *Life of Shelley* by Edward Dowden, London 1909.
8 *Caspar John* by Rebecca John, London 1987; *The Seventh Child* by Romilly John, London 1932; Poppet Pol to author, 16 March 1988.
9 G to Michael Holroyd, 24 Dec 1970.
10 *FOS*.
11 Quoted in *The Other Victorians* by Steven Marcus, London 1966.
12 *Sexual Behaviour in the Human Male* by Alfred C. Kinsey, London 1948; *The Public School Phenomenon* by author, London 1979.
13 Int Loïs Bucher (née Morgan).
14 *Child Development*, op.cit.
15 G to B, n.d. but Jan/April 1929.
16 Author's journal.
17 Radley College school records.
18 G to VSP, 6 June 1946.
19 Hope to G, 1910 or 1911 (probably 1911).
20 *My Life and Times 1915–23, Octave 5* by Compton Mackenzie, London 1966.
21 Int Lady Cary.
22 Lydia Piper to author, 11 Oct 1988.
23 Int Lynda.
24 MF.

25 G to F, 13 Jan 1968.
26 G to C, 20 Sept 1920.
27 G to B, 19 Oct 1929.

28 Int VSP.
29 G to C, 14 June 1923 (unsent).
30 G to Gamel, n.d., MSS, Tex.

Chapter Five

1 Correspondence of author with Mrs Blosse-Lynch, Jan/Feb 1988.
2 *Caspar John*, op cit.
3 MF.
4 MSS, Tex.
5 Hope to G, 30 Sept 1913.
6 Int Lady Cary.
7 G to Hope, 9 June 1915.
8 G to C, 6 Nov 1923.
9 MSS, Tex.

10 G to Hope, 12 Jan 1918.
11 Mrs Blosse-Lynch, loc. cit.
12 G to R, June 1921.
13 G to C, Aug 1923.
14 *Austria-Hungary* etc. by Karl Baedeker, 11th ed., London 1911.
15 G to Hope, Dec 1916.
16 MSS, Tex.
17 Ibid.
18 MSS, MF.

Chapter Six

1 MSS, Tex.
2 Hope to G, June 1914.
3 MSS, MF.
4 See e.g. G to F, May 1983.
5 G to F, 1 June 1981.
6 G to VSP, 4 April 1979.
7 G to C, 7 May 1927.
8 Hope to G, 31 Dec 1913.
9 Ibid., 7 Feb 1913.
10 Ibid., 16 Nov 1913.
11 Ibid., 27 Dec 1913.
12 *The Magnetic Moment* by G.
13 G to Hope, 31 Dec 1913.
14 MSS, Tex.
15 G to Hope, 31 Dec 1913.

16 G's war journal.
17 *Thoughts*.
18 *Arthur Rimbaud* by Enid Starkie, London 1961.
19 Hope to G, 27 Dec 1913.
20 Ibid., May/June 1914.
21 Taylor to Hope, 16 Oct/Dec 1913, Tex.
22 Hope to G, 1913/14.
23 G to Hope, 24 April 1914.
24 Ibid., 29 May 1914.
25 Ibid., 6 July 1914.
26 Ibid., 21, 29 May 1915; and see Hope to G, 18 Dec 1917.

Chapter Seven

1 See e.g. G to Chatto and Windus, 18 Dec 1952, or G to F, May 1983.
2 Noel Carrington to author, 18 May, 15 June 1987.
3 Int F.
4 Taylor to Hope, 24 April 1915, Tex.
5 MSS, MF.
6 G to Hope, 11 April 1915.
7 Taylor to Hope, 24 April 1915, Tex.
8 G to Taylor, Oct 1914, Tex.
9 Hope to G, Oct (?) 1915.
10 Ibid., 3 March 1916.
11 See e.g. Taylor to Hope, 7 Sept, Oct 1914, 6 Jan 1915; G to Hope, 7 April 1915; and letters throughout the war, Tex.
12 G to Hope, 5 July 1915.

13 Ibid., 11 April 1914.
14 Hope to Taylor, 28 April 1915, Tex.
15 Taylor to Hope, 24 April 1915, Tex.
16 G to Hope, 21 May 1915.
17 Ibid., 9 June 1915.
18 Hope to G, July 1915.
19 G to Hope, 24 Aug 1915.
20 Ibid., 19 Oct 1915.
21 MSS, MF.
22 G to Hope, 25 Aug 1915.
23 Ibid., 15 Oct 1915.
24 Ibid., 19 Oct 1915.
25 *ALOOO* unpub MSS, Tex.
26 G to Hope, 13, 15 Nov 1915.
27 R to G, 23 Dec 1915.
28 Hope to G, 21 March 1916.
29 *ALOOO* unpub MSS, Tex.

30 G's war journal.
31 G to Hope, 12, 20 Jan 1916.
32 Hope to G, 31 March 1916.
33 G to Hope., Jan 1917.
34 G to father, 26 July 1916, Tex.
35 G to Hope, Dec 1916.
36 *My Life and Times 1915–23, Octive 5*, by Compton Mackenzie, London 1966.
37 *Jack Robinson* by G.
38 R to G, 19 Oct 1917.
39 MSS, Tex.
40 G to VSP, 31 May 1955.
41 G to Hope, 16 Jan, March 1917.
42 R to G, n.d. but March or April 1917, Tex.
43 Ibid., 19 Sept 1917, Tex.
44 G's war journal.

45 G to B, 24 Nov 1978.
46 Int F.
47 G to Kenneth Hopkins, 12 July 1971, Tex.
48 Hope to G, 18 Dec 1917.
49 G's war journal.
50 G to Hope, 12 Jan, 1 Feb 1918.
51 Ibid., 3 May 1918 (used, rewritten, in *ALOOO*).
52 Ibid., 19 May 1918.
53 Public Record Office (PRO), refs: WO 95/822, WO 35/828.
54 MSS, Tex.
55 PRO war diary, WO 95/816.
56 G to Hope, 18 June 1918.
57 18 Corps HQ to Helen Brenan, 5 Aug 1918, MF.

Chapter Eight

1 G to Hope, 22 June 1918.
2 Hope to G, 13 Aug, 10, 30 Oct 1918; G to Hope, 18 Aug 1918.
3 G to Hope, 18 Sept 1918.
4 R to G, 7 July 1918.
5 G to Hope, 17 July 1918.
6 Ibid., 14 Oct 1918.
7 Ibid., 12 March 1919.
8 G to C, 8 May 1921.
9 G to Hope, 9 Feb 1919.
10 G's journals.
11 C to G, 26 June 1924. Unless otherwise indicated, the information in this section comes from *Lytton Strachey* by Michael Holroyd, Penguin 1971; *A Life of Dora Carrington* by Gretchen Gerzina, London 1989; and *PR*.

12 G to VSP, n.d.
13 *The Flowers of the Forest*, Vol. 2 of *The Echoing Grove* by David Garnett, London 1955.
14 G to Michael Holroyd, 10 Oct 1962.
15 Int May Holder, Miserden.
16 C to LS, 29 Aug 1919 (quoted *Carrington: Letters and Extracts from her Diaries*, ed. David Garnett, London 1970).
17 C to LS, 4 July 1918 (quoted Holroyd).
18 G to C, n.d. (Dec 1919?) list written on back.
19 *Julia* by Frances Partridge, London 1983.
20 G to C, Nov 1919.
21 G's pocket diaries, MF.

PART TWO

Any important facts or quotations in Part Two whose source is not given come from *Personal Record*; in Chapters Nine and Ten also from *South From Granada*.

Chapter Nine

1 *PR*.
2 *FOS*.
3 *Homage to Catalonia* by George Orwell, Penguin 1962.

4 C to LS, 23 Dec 1923, Tex.
5 G to K. Hopkins, n.d. but 1978, Tex.
6 G to Hope, 5 Nov 1919.

7 G to C, 1 Feb 1920.
8 MSS, Tex.
9 *ALOOO.*
10 G to C, 29 Nov 1919.
11 MSS, Tex.
12 G to R, 28 May 1955.
13 G to C, 29 Nov 1919.
14 'An English Writer Discovers Malaga', talk by G, 1945, in BBC archives.
15 MSS, MF.
16 B to Blair, n.d. (Dec?) 1920, family papers.
17 G to C, 29 Nov 1919.
18 Mark Culme-Seymour to author, 4 Oct 1987.
19 G to Hope, 5 Nov 1919.
20 Ibid., 12 Feb. 1920.
21 G to C., 20 May 1920.
22 *Sp Lab*; also numerous letters 1920/1/2.
23 G to R, 20 Jan 1920.
24 G to Hope, 12 Feb 1920.
25 G to R, 28 May 1955.
26 Ibid., n.d. but March 1920.
27 In these four paras. quotes from C to G, 21 Nov, 15 Dec 1919; 2, 12 Jan, 1 Feb, 1 March 1920, draft letters and notes, MF and Tex.
28 G to R, 20 Feb 1920.
29 C to G, 5 Aug 1920
30 G to C, 20 May 1920.

31 Ibid., 1 Feb 1920.
32 Orwell, op. cit.
33 G to C, 25 Oct 1920; 20–28 Aug 1923.
34 G to Blair, 2 Sept (?) 1920, family papers.
35 B, op. cit.
36 G to Hope, 25 May 1921.
37 Ibid., 10 March 1920.
38 G to R, July 1920.
39 Ibid., 16 Jan 1954.
40 G to Blair, June 1920, family papers.
41 Ints Yegen 1987.
42 G to Blair, Dec (?) 1920.
43 G to C, 22 July 1923.
44 MSS, Tex.
45 G to Blair, 3 May 1920.
46 G to C, 20 Jan 1921.
47 Ibid., 25 Oct 1920.
48 G to F, 10 Oct 1967.
49 MSS, MF.
50 G to C, 2 April 1921.
51 C to G, Oct 1920.
52 G to C, 2 April 1921.
53 Ibid., 26 Feb 1921.
54 Ibid., 8 May 1921.
55 C to LS, 8 May 1921, British Library.
56 C to G, 20, 21 May 1921.
57 Ibid., 8 June 1921.
58 See e.g. G to Blair, 17 Jan, 20 Dec 1920; G to R June 1920.

Chapter Ten

1 C to G, 28 June, 5 July 1921.
2 Gerzina, op. cit.
3 Frances Partridge, op. cit.
4 C to G, 8 July 1921 (and see G to Holroyd, 10 Oct 1962).
5 G to C, 8, 13 July 1921.
6 Ibid., 29 Dec 1920.
7 Ibid., 28 July 1921.
8 MSS, Tex.
9 G to C, 6 Aug 1921.
10 G to R, 13 Aug 1921.
11 G to JC, 7 July 1971.
12 G to C, 5 (?) Sept 1921.
13 See esp. MS note 1958 or 59, Tex.
14 C to G, 8 Sept 1921.
15 G to R, Sept 1921.
16 Ibid., 11 Nov 1921.
17 G to C, 15 Oct 1921.

18 MSS, MF.
19 G to R, 18 Feb 1922.
20 Ibid., 11 Nov 1921, 12 March 1922; G to C, 9 Jan 1922.
21 C to G, 14 Jan 1922.
22 Ibid., 27 Nov 1921.
23 G to R, Feb 1922.
24 G to C, 24 Dec 1921.
25 Int Yegen, July 1987.
26 G to C, 27 Feb 1922.
27 MSS, Tex.
28 G to C, 27 Jan 1922.
29 G to F, 13 Feb; to JC, 24 Feb 1966.
30 MS dated 20 Oct 1923, MF,
31 G to C, 13, 23 Feb; C to G, 12, 14, 27 March 1922.
32 G to R, 9, 10 Sept 1921; to Hope, 15 April 1922.

33 C to G, Feb 1922.
34 G to Hope, 4 May 1922.
35 G to C, 6 May 1922.
36 Ibid., 6 June 1922.
37 G to Hope, 26 May 1922.
38 Diary abstract, MF.
39 C to G, 4 May 1922.
40 Ibid., n.d. but early June 1922.
41 G to JC, 24 Feb 1966.
42 G to C, dated 8 (in fact 9) June 1922.
43 C to LS, July 12, Tex.
44 C to G, 14, 29 Nov 1922.
45 R to G, 10 June 1922.
46 G to C, 11 June, 30 Aug 1922.
47 Ibid., 23, 28 Jan, 10 Feb, 22 July 1923.
48 C to G, 6 Feb 1923.
49 G to C, 10 Feb 1922.
50 VW to C, 22 May 1923.
51 C to G, 28, 31 May 1923.
52 G to Leonard Woolf, 10 April 1923.
53 G to R, Oct 4 1923.
54 G to Blair, 9 Oct 1923.
55 *FOS*.
56 G to C, 1 Nov 1923.
57 Ibid., 28 Oct 1923.
58 G to VSP, 8 Nov 1971.
59 C to G, 26 July 1923.
60 C to G, 27 Aug 1923.
61 Ibid., 1 March 1923.
62 MSS, Tex.
63 G to B, 10 May 1929.
64 G to C, 23 Jan 1923.
65 *Mrs Woolf 1912–41* (Vol. 2 of *Life* of Virginia Woolf) by Quentin Bell, London 1982.
66 G to Rosemary Dinnage, 4 Nov 1967 (in fact 1977).

67 VW to G, 1 Dec 1923.
68 G to VW, 1 June 1923.
69 VW to G, 12 May 1923.
70 G to Leonard Woolf, 10 April 1923 (more likely 10 May).
71 Int F, Int Lynda.
72 G to VW, 30 April 1923.
73 G to C, 23 June 1923.
74 Constance Ellis in conversation with author.
75 *Sp Lit*.
76 G to C, 5 June 1922.
77 Ibid., 20 Aug 1923.
78 Ibid., 15 Feb 1923.
79 G to F, 16 Jan 1930.
80 G to R, 3 Jan 1923; to C, n.d. but early 1923, 23 Jan 1923.
81 C to LS, 28 Feb 1922 (quoted Gerzina).
82 LS to G (quoted Holroyd).
83 G to C, 28 Nov 1923 and *PR*.
84 C to G, 15 Sept, to LS 27 Aug 1923.
85 *Memories* by Frances Partridge, London 1981.
86 MSS, Tex.
87 C to LS, 23 Dec 1923.
88 C to G, 13 Jan 1924.
89 G to R, n.d. but Feb 1924.
90 *Voor Arthur Lehning*, ed. Tóke Van Helmond, En J. J. Overstegen, Maastricht 1989; see also *Tranvia – Revue de Iberischen Halbinael* No. 7, Dec 1987 (reprint of review Lehning published in Holland in 1948).
91 C to G, 3 April 1924.

Chapter Eleven

1 C to G, 3 April 1924.
2 G's journals, August 1925–March 1932.
3 G to C, 15 July 1924.
4 Ibid., 6 May 1924.
5 Ibid., 21 Jan 1925.
6 G to B, 16 Dec 1953.
7 G to VSP, n.d. but late 30s.
8 Gerald's journals, Jan 1926.
9 G to C, 2, 7 May, 14 July 1926.
10 Ibid., n.d. but probably June/July 1924.

11 Ibid., 12 April, n.d. but June/July, 24 Oct 1924.
12 Ibid., 4 June 1924,
13 Julia Strachey (quoted Gerzina).
14 C to G, 6 Aug 1924.
15 Ibid., July 1924.
16 Ibid., 24, 25 April 1925.
17 C to Alix Strachey, June 1924.
18 C to G, n.d. but July/Aug 1924.
19 G to C, 18 March 1925 (and see 22 June 1924).
20 MSS, MF.

21 G to C, 3, 4 May 1925.
22 C to G, July 1924.
23 G to C, n.d. but July 1924.
24 G's journals (quoting unsent letter to HA).
25 G to C, n.d. but July 1924.
26 C to G, 7 Oct 1924.
27 G's journals, 1 Aug 1925.
28 G to C, 2 May 1924.
29 G's journals, 10 June 1925.
30 G to C, 12, 28 Aug 1924.
31 Ibid., 28 Aug 1924.
32 HA to G, 31 Jan 1950.
33 C to G, 7 Aug 1924.
34 MSS, MF.
35 G to F, 17 Dec 1928.
36 G to C, 22 June 1924.
37 Ibid., 1 Feb 1925.
38 C to G, 1 May 1927.
39 *Holiday* notes and MS., Tex.
40 G to C, 3 May 1926.
41 C to G, 28 April 1926.
42 VW to G, 3 Oct 1926.
43 G to R, 3 Feb 1930.
44 G to F, 26 oct 1967.
45 See eg. C to G, 21 June 1926, 1 May 1927.
46 *The Nation*, 2 May 1925.
47 Ibid., 30 April 1927.
48 G to C, 24 Oct 1925.
49 *Memories*, op. cit.
50 G to C, Easter 1926.
51 *The Familiar Faces*, Vol. 3 of *The Echoing Grove* by David Garnett, London 1962.
52 G's journals, Dec 1925.
53 List on envelope of C letter, postmarked 11 June 1927, Tex.
54 G to C, 27 Feb, 18 March, 29 June 1925.
55 Ibid., 24 April, 1 Oct 1924; to R, 10 Dec 1925.
56 *SFG*.
57 VSP, op. cit.
58 G to Leonard Woolf, 20 June 1964.
59 G to VW, 2 June 1925.
60 MSS, Tex.
61 G to F, 9 Aug 1965.
62 *Golden Echo*, op. cit.
63 G to C, 25 Sept 1924.
64 Ibid., 20 March 1925; to R, n.d. but March/April 1925.
65 Ibid., 15 Feb 1927; GJ, Jan 1926.
66 Barbara Kei-Seymour to author, 11 March 1987; int F.
67 *The Familiar Faces*, op. cit.
68 G to Jean Rhys, 23 July 1967.
69 MSS, Tex.
70 G to Susie Simon, 3, 24, 31 Nov 1924, 11, 27 Jan 1925, Tex.
71 G's journals, Jan 1926.
72 G to F, May 1983.
73 Holroyd, op. cit.
74 G to C, n.d. but April 1926.
75 G to R, 3, 4 June 1926; to Jean Rhys, 23 July 1967.
76 G to R, 3, 4 June 1926.
77 Ibid., 7 Oct 1926.
78 Conversation with author.
79 G to F, 10 Oct 1967.
80 G to C, 19 July 1926.
81 Ibid., 30 March 1927.
82 Ibid., 10 Dec 1926.
83 G to C, 8 Dec 1926.
84 Ibid., 27 Aug 1927.
85 C to G, 27 Feb 1927.
86 C to Julia Strachey, 27 March 1927.
87 G's journals, March/April 1928.
88 G to C, 9 April 1927.
89 G to Holroyd, 16 Dec 1967.
90 Int Alison Anrep.
91 G to C, 3 July 1927.
92 C to G, 27 May 1927.
93 Ibid., 30 May 1927.
94 Ibid., and G to C, 29 July 1927.
95 C to G, 13 Aug 1927.
96 G to C, 4 Nov 1926.
97 G to R, 12 Oct 1927.
98 G to C, 10 Dec 1926.
99 Ibid., 13 Dec 1926.
100 C to G, 15 July 1925.
101 Ibid., 10 May 1928.
102 G to Johnny Wolfers, 25 June 1979.
103 MSS, Tex and MF.
104 *PR* unpub MSS, Tex.
105 *Memories*, op. cit.
106 G's journals, March/April/May 1928.
107 C to G, 15, 26 March 1928.
108 G's journals, Aug/Sept 1928.
109 G to F, n.d. but June 1928.
110 Ibid., 23 Dec 1928.

111 C to G, 14–18 Nov 1928.
112 Int F.
113 *Memories*, op. cit.
114 MSS, Tex.

115 G to R, 23 Oct 1929.
116 G to F, 6 Dec 1968.
117 G's journals, Oct 1929.

Chapter Twelve

1 G to F, n.d. but 28 April 1929.
2 G to B, 10 May 1929.
3 G to F, 18 May 1929.
4 G to R, 27 June 1929.
5 Ibid.
6 R to G, 5 June 1929.
7 MSS, MF.
8 G to B, 10 Sept 1929.
9 G's journals, Aug/Sept 1929.
10 *Historia Económica de España en el Siglo XX* by Ramón Tamames, Madrid 1986.
11 G to R, 10, 17 Sept 1929.
12 R to G, 5 June 1929.
13 G to R, 10, 17 Sept 1929.
14 G to B, 2 Jan 1930.
15 *Memories*, op. cit.
16 G to R, 10 Dec; R to G, 22 July, 21 Nov 1929.
17 G to R, 23 Oct; to B, 6 Nov 1929; *PR* unpub MS, Tex.
18 G to R, 26, 27 Nov 1929.

19 G to B, 15 Aug, 14 Dec 1929; to F, 16 Jan; to Blair, 14 April 1930.
20 G to R, 3 Feb 1930.
21 G to Blair, 14 April 1930.
22 Int F.
23 G to F, 19 March 1930.
24 G to VSP, 19 Oct 1949.
25 G to R, 20 April 1930.
26 Ibid., 26 April 1930.
27 Author's journals.
28 G to R, 17 June; to Blair, 21 June 1930.
29 G to R, 17 June 1930.
30 Ibid., 7 June 1930.
31 Ints Lady Cary, Lydia Piper.
32 Int Lydia Piper.
33 G to Blair, 21 June 1930.
34 G to B, 14 June 1930.
35 G to Blair, 14 June 1930.
36 Poppet Pol (née John) to author, 16 March 1988.

PART THREE

Any important facts or quotations in Parts Three and Four whose sources are not given come from *Personal Record*.

Chapter Thirteen

1 *Memories*, op. cit.
2 G to R, 26 April 1930.
3 G's journals.
4 *The Cry of a Gull: Journals 1923–48* by Alyse Gregory, ed. Michael Adam, Out of the Ark Press, 1973.
5 Kenneth Hopkins notes, biog. Gamel.
6 Gamel to Ray Garnett, n.d. but July/Sept 1934, MF.
7 Gamel to Alyse, March 1964.
8 *Middle Earth* by Gamel.
9 LIP to Gamel (quoted *The Brothers Powys* by Richard Percival Graves, London 1983).

10 C to G, n.d. but 15/6 July, 27 July 1930.
11 G's journals.
12 MSS, MF.
13 Gamel to LIP, Jan 1931.
14 B to G, 14 Aug 1930, 13 March 1931.
15 G to Gamel, 8 Aug 1830, MF.
16 G to C, 13 Aug; C to G, 14 Aug 1930.
17 C to G, Oct 1930.
18 See e.g. G's JC journal, Tex, MF.
19 Int F.
20 Int Igor Anrep.
21 G to R, 2 Sept 1930.

22 *Everything to Lose: Diaries 1945–60* by Frances Partridge, London 1985.
23 G's journals.
24 Gamel to LIP, n.d. but Nov/Dec 1930.
25 See 'Pride' and numerous letters (quoted Graves).
26 Gamel to Alyse, n.d. but Feb/March 1931.
27 LIP to Gamel (quoted Graves).
28 C to G, 22 Nov 1930.
29 G to C, 5 Nov 1930.
30 Gamel to LIP, n.d. but about 5 Nov 1930.
31 G to R, 13 Nov 1930
32 Int Lady Cary.
33 G to R, 23 Nov 1930.

34 Ibid., 18 Dec 1930.
35 G to Gamel, Dec 1930, MF.
36 Gamel to G, 6 Dec 1930, MF.
37 Ibid., 10, 14, 16, 18 Dec 1930, MF.
38 G to C, 20 Jan 1931.
39 Gamel to LIP, n.d. but Jan 1931.
40 G to Blair, n.d. but Feb/March 1931.
41 G to F, 21 Oct 1963.
42 Trevor-Roper (Lord Dacre) to G, 11 March 1968, Tex.
43 G to R, 7 Feb 1931.
44 G to B, 21 Feb, 23 March; to Blair n.d. but March/April 1931; to R, 7 Feb 1931.
45 G to HA, 25 May 1931.

Chapter Fourteen

1 G's journals.
2 *Memories*, op. cit.
3 Int F.
4 C to G, 10 May 1927.
5 Gamel to LIP, 13 Aug 1931, MF.
6 Hopkins (quoted Graves).
7 Gregory, op. cit.
8 Gamel to LIP, 25 April, 7 June 1931, MF.
9 Ibid., 13 Aug 1931, MF.
10 Gregory, op. cit.
11 G to F, 10 Oct 1967.
12 Gamel to LIP, n.d. but 1938, MF.
13 Gamel to Alyse, n.d. but Feb 1931.
14 G to Rex Hunter, 12 Oct 1933, MF, Hopkins.
15 Gregory, op. cit.
16 G to R, 31 Dec 1931.
17 Ibid., 27 March, 4, 5, 11, 20 April 1932.
18 Ibid., 11 April 1932.
19 Ibid., 20–24, 29 Aug 1932.
20 G to B, 25 Sept 1932.
21 G to R, 16 Oct 1932.
22 Ibid., 12 Nov 1932.
23 G to B, 16 May 1933.
24 Int F.
25 G to M, 10 May 1978.
26 G to R, 11 Dec 1932.
27 Gamel to LIP, n.d. but Dec 1932, Jan 1933.
28 *Collected Poems* by Gamel Woolsey, Warren House Press 1984.

29 G to Roger Fry, 1 April 1933, MF.
30 G to B, 19 April 1933.
31 G to Blair, n.d. but May 1933.
32 G to B, 16 May 1933.
33 Int John Whitworth.
34 *Weekend Review*, 9 Sept 1933.
35 *Weekend Review*, 4 Nov 1933.
36 G to B, n.d. but Nov 1933.
37 VW's diary, 20 Oct 1933, from *Diary of Virginia Woolf: Vol. IV 1931–35*, ed. Oliver Bell, Andrew McNeillie, London 1982.
38 Roger Fry to G, 27 Oct 1933; *Letters of Roger Fry*, 2 Vols, ed. with intro. Denys Sutton, London 1972.
39 G to R, 22 Jan 1936.
40 *Diary of VW*, 8 July 1935, op. cit.
41 B to G, 27 Sept 1974.
42 G to R, 17 Oct 1933.
43 G to B, 19 Oct 1933.
44 Gamel to LIP, n.d. but Jan/Feb 1934.
45 G to R, n.d. but Feb 1934; also *PR*.
46 Ibid., 27 Feb, 3 March 1934.
47 Ibid., 7 April 1934.
48 G to F, 17 March 1934.
49 Angela Culme-Seymour to author, 8 Jan 1988.
50 Mark Culme-Seymour to Jan Woolley, 13 Dec 1933.
51 G to VSP, 19 Oct 1949.
52 G to R, 3 June 1934.
53 Ibid., 25 May 1934.

54 Gamel to LIP, 14 March 1934.
55 G to R, 28 May 1934.
56 Ibid., 4 May 1934.
57 G to Blair, June 1934.
58 G to R, n.d. but April/May 1934.
59 G to Blair, n.d. but June 1934.
60 Ibid., n.d. but Sept/Nov 1934.

61 G to B, 1 Oct 1934.
62 Roger Fry to G, 19 April 1934, in *Letters*, op. cit.
63 G to VSP, n.d. but Sept 1981.
64 G to HA, n.d. but Nov 1934.
65 G to R, 11 Oct 1934.

Chapter Fifteen

1 G to R, 12 June 1934.
2 Mark Culme-Seymour notes
3 G to R, n.d. but Dec 1934 or Jan 1935.
4 Gamel to LIP, 29 May 1934.
5 G to R, 23 Oct 1934, 4 Feb 1935.
6 G to F, 17 Oct 1935.
7 G to R, n.d. but March 1935.
8 G to F, n.d. but Jan 1935.
9 Ibid., 29 May 1935.
10 Ibid., 7 April 1935.
11 G to B, 30 May 1935.
12 G to R, 17, 27 Oct 1933; to Roger Fry, July/Aug 1934.
13 G to R, 11 Oct, n.d. but Nov 1934, 1 June 1935; to F, 2 May 1935.
14 G to F, 27 June 1935.
15 Ibid., 22 July 1935.
16 G to R, 4 Aug 1935.
17 Ibid., n.d. but Aug 1935.
18 G to B, 17 July 1935.
19 G to R, 13 Nov 1935.
20 Ibid., n.d. but 24–30 Aug 1935.

21 Ibid., 22 Sept 1935.
22 G to B, 22 Sept 1935.
23 *DOK*, London 1939.
24 G to R, 13 Nov 1935.
25 G to B, 22 Oct 1935.
26 Gamel to LIP, n.d. but 23 Feb 1934.
27 G to R, 5, 22 Jan 1936; to B, 17 July 1935.
28 G to HA, 11 Feb 1936.
29 G to R, 15, 20 March 1936.
30 G to F, 12 Feb 1936.
31 Ibid., 8 March 1936.
32 Gamel to LIP, n.d. but about 15 March 1936.
33 G to R, n.d. but May 1936.
34 G to F, 26 March 1936.
35 G to R, n.d. but 13 June 1935.
36 Ibid., 20 March 1936.
37 Ibid., n.d. but May 1936; to HA, 16 May 1936.
38 G to R, 12 June 1936; int Sheppards; Gamel to LIP, n.d. but May/June 1936.

Chapter Sixteen

1 *DOK*.
2 Jay Allen to G, 13 Aug 1936, Tex.
3 G to R, 28 July 1936.
4 Ibid., 8 Aug 1936.
5 Ibid., 19 Aug 1936.
6 Ibid., 22 Aug 1936.

7 *John O'London's Weekly*, 16 July 1943.
8 G to R, 15 Sept 1936.
9 Ibid., 14 Sept 1936.
10 Ibid., 17, 18, 30 Sept 1936.
11 Ibid., 17 Oct 1936.

Chapter Seventeen

1 G to R, 27 Nov 1936.
2 Gamel to Alyse, n.d. but Dec 1936, MF.
3 G to HA, n.d. but Jan 1937.
4 *Romantic Affinities* by Rupert Christiansen, London 1988.
5 Gamel to LIP, n.d. but about 7 Nov 1936.
6 G to R, 27 Nov 1936.

7 *A Pacifist's War* by Frances Partridge, London 1978.
8 G to F, 6 Nov 1936; to B, 18 Feb 1937.
9 Gamel to LIP, n.d. but early 1937.
10 *PR* unpub MS.
11 See e.g. G to B, 10 Jan 1937; to Chatto, 15 March 1937.
12 G to Chatto, 15 March 1937.

13 G to HA, 7 Dec 1935.
14 Gamel to LIP, 7 Nov 1936.
15 G to B, 17 Feb 1937.
16 *Neutralidad benévola: el gobierno británica y insurrección militar española 1936* by Enriques Moradiellos, Oviedo 1990.
17 G to VSP, 23 Dec 1979.
18 G to F, 24 Dec 1936.
19 G to R, n.d. but Christmas 1936.
20 Ibid., n.d. but summer 1937.
21 G to VSP, 1 May 1937.
22 G to B, 24 July 1937.
23 Gamel to LIP, n.d. but July 1937.
24 G to VSP, n.d.
25 Gamel to G, n.d. but Aug/Sept 1937, MF.
26 Gregory, op. cit.
27 G to R, 1 Sept 1937.
28 Gamel to LIP, n.d. but probably Sept 1937 or Jan 1938.
29 G to R, 2 Nov 1937.
30 Chatto to G, 29 Nov 1937.
31 G to F, 6 Jan 1938.
32 *Everything to Lose*, op. cit.
33 G to VSP, n.d. but July 1937.
34 G to HA, n.d. but Sept 1937.
36 Correspondence of G and Hugh Brenan, June/July 1940, Tex.

37 G to HA, n.d. but April 1938.
38 G's diary abstracts, MF; LIP to G, n.d. but Feb 1938.
39 G to R, n.d. but probably 17 or 24 Aug 1938.
40 G to F, 18 Nov 1936.
41 G to B, 27 Sept 1938.
42 G to HA, n.d. but Sept/Oct 1938.
43 G to R, n.d. but Oct 1938.
44 *Crockford's Clerical Directory*.
45 Int Lady Cary.
46 G to R, 6 Sept 1957; JC to author, Feb 1989; int Mrs Palmer.
47 Gamel to LIP, n.d. but Nov 1936 or Aug 1937 MF.
48 G to HA, 7 Dec 1935.
49 G in conversation with author; also *Thoughts*.
50 Gregory, op. cit.
51 Gamel to Alyse, n.d. but now.
52 Ibid. 7 Feb 1951.
53 G to F, n.d. but Feb 1939.
54 G to R, n.d. but 20 July 1939.
55 Ibid., 17 May 1939.
56 G to VSP, 23 Dec 1939.
57 Int Lynda.
58 G to VSP, 3 Dec 1939; MSS, Tex.
59 G to R, 4 April 1939.

Chapter Eighteen

1 G to R, 11 Sept 1939.
2 G to B, 11 June 1943.
3 Gamel to Alyse, n.d. but Oct 1939.
4 *A Pacifist's War*, op. cit.
5 G to VSP, 23 Dec 1939.
6 Gamel to Alyse, n.d. but March 1940.
7 G to F, 9 April 1940.
8 JC to author, Feb 1989.
9 G to VSP, 10 April 1940.
10 Gamel to Alyse, n.d. but April/May 1940.
11 Ibid., n.d. but April/May 1941.
12 *Invasion Scare 1940* by Michael Glover, London 1990.
13 G to F, 21 Oct 1940.
14 G to VSP, 29 Oct 1940.
15 Gamel to Alyse, n.d. but 1940.
16 MSS, MF.
17 G to VSP, 1 April 1940.

18 Ibid., 1, 6 June 1940.
19 G to F, n.d. but June 1940.
20 G to VSP, 23 Dec 1940.
21 Int Lawrence Gowing.
22 *A Pacifist's War*, op. cit.
23 G to HH, 31 Dec 1961.
24 G's journals, 29 May 1941, Tex.
25 G to R, 23 June 1941.
26 Ibid., 18 Sept 1941.
27 *A Pacifist's War*, op. cit.
28 Raymond Mortimer to G, Aug 1978, MF.
29 G to VSP, n.d. but Sept 1940.
30 G's journals.
31 Gamel to Alyse, n.d. but Aug 1942.
32 G to VSP, n.d., but Aug/Sept 1942.
33 G to Michael Holroyd, 16 Dec 1967.
34 Int Johnny Morris.
35 *Thoughts*.

Chapter Nineteen

1 *Manchester Guardian*, 7 May 1943; *Observer*, 18 April 1943.
2 *New York Times*, 15 Aug 1943.
3 *The Spectator*, 9, 23 April 1943.
4 *A Handbook for Travellers in Spain, 3 Vols*, ed. with intro. Ian Robertson, London 1966.
5 *Revolution and War in Spain 1931–39*, ed. Paul Preston, London 1984.
6 *Political Quarterly*, July 1943.
7 G to Leonard Woolf, 26 Oct 1943.
8 G to VSP, 31 Oct. 1979.
9 Gamel to Alyse, n.d. but mid-1943, CUP archive.
10 G to VSP, 10 June 1944.
11 *Spain 1808–1975* by Raymond Carr, Oxford 1982.
12 *The Coming of the Spanish Civil War* by Paul Preston, London 1983; *The Spanish Civil War*, by Paul Preston, London 1986.

Chapter Twenty

1 G to VSP, 14 April 1943.
2 MF.
3 G to VSP, 2 June 1943.
4 Ints Lady Cary, Lydia Piper.
5 CUP to G, 25 May 1943.
6 G to VSP, n.d. but 20–28 July 1943.
7 *A Pacifist's War*, op. cit.
8 G to CUP, 7 Feb 1943.
10 G to VSP, 3 Dec 1943; int Raymond Carr.
11 G to VSP, 20 Jan 1943.
12 CUP to G, 26 June 1944; G to CUP, n.d. but June 1944.
13 BBC memo, 21 Oct 1943 (Miss Manton to Casting).
14 Int Raphael Martínez Nadal.
15 Details, BBC archives.
16 *A Pacifist's War*, op. cit.
17 Gamel to Alyse, n.d. but either Jan 1941 or 1942.
18 G to VSP, 27 April 1944.
19 Ibid., 19 Oct 1949.
20 G to VSP, 3 Jan 1944.
21 Ibid., n.d. but summer 1943 or 1944.
22 Mr Guyatt to G, 10 Aug 1944, BBC archives.
23 G to VSP, 6 Nov 1944.
24 Ibid., 15 Feb 1945.
25 Ibid., 20 April 1945.
26 Ibid., 15 Feb 1945.
27 Int Janetta.
28 F's unpub. journal, 27 Aug 1945.
29 *Everything to Lose*, op. cit.
30 G to R, n.d. but probably end 1945.
31 G to VSP, 16 May 1946.
32 G to Bertrand Russell, n.d. but early 1946.
33 Int Nadal.
34 FOS.
35 G to VSP, UD but Dec 1947.
36 G to M, 6 Nov 1962.

Chapter Twenty-One

1 G to R, 4 Feb 1947.
2 G to VSP, 19 Oct 1949.
3 MF.
4 G to VSP, 19 Oct 1947.
5 Ibid., n.d. but Dec 1947.
6 Gamel to Alyse, n.d. but 1947/48.
7 Honor Tracy, correspondence with author, 23 Nov 1987–31 Jan 1989.
8 Certificate No. 88, 25 Aug 1947, Hampstead Registry Office.
9 Gamel to Alyse, n.d. but June/July 1949.
10 G to VSP, n.d. but late Dec 1947.
11 Ibid., 16 Feb 1948.
12 G to F, n.d. but May 1948.
13 G to VSP, n.d. but June 1948.
14 Ibid., n.d. but Aug/Sept 1948.
15 Ibid., 4 Aug 1948.
16 Ibid., 9 Aug 1948.
17 Ibid., 16 Sept 1948.
18 G to R, 26 June 1947.
19 G to VSP, 6 Sept 1948.
20 G to VSP, 3 Jan 1949.
21 Ibid., 20 Nov 1948.
22 G to Blair, 31 Jan 1949.
23 See letters Hope to G, MF, Tex.

24 Quotations this section from G to
   VSP, 21 Feb, 4, 29 March; to Blair,
   14 and n.d. March 1949; and from
   FOS.

25 G to VSP, 12 July 1949.

Chapter Twenty-Two

1 G to VSP, 9 Oct 1949.
2 Ibid., 19 Oct 1949.
3 F's unpub. journal, 19 Oct 1949.
4 Int F.
5 Sources G to VSP, 4, 9, 11, 15, 17,
   19, 25, 28 Oct, 11 Nov 1949; also 3
   above.
6 Gamel to Alyse, n.d. but Dec 1949.
7 F's unpub. journal, 11 Oct 1949.
8 *Everything to Lose*, op. cit.
9 G in conversation with author; int F.
10 Gamel to Alyse, n.d. but Feb 1940.
11 G to VSP, 29 Jan 1950.
12 Ibid., 15 Feb 1950.
13 Ibid., 9 March 1950.
14 Ibid., 27 April, 9 May 1950.
15 Ibid., 17 July 1950.
16 Ibid., 31 March 1950.
17 G to R, 16 Sept 1950.
18 G to M, n.d. but Oct 1950.
19 G to VSP, n.d. but 27 Nov, 1 Dec
   1950.
20 MSS and notes, MF and Tex.
21 G to F, 14 Jan 1950.
22 Ibid., 28 Nov 1950.

23 G to VSP, n.d. but mid-Nov 1950.
24 Gamel to Alyse, 14 Dec 1950.
25 *Les Nouvelles Littéraires*, 31 May 1951.
26 G to HH, 16 March 1956.
27 G to VSP, 24 Jan 1951.
28 G to R, 16 Feb 1951.
29 Ibid., 11 July 1951.
30 Quotations from G to R, 18, 27
   March, 7 April; to VSP, 6, 10, 13,
   14 March, 8 April 1951.
31 VSP to G, 5 Aug 1951.
32 G to VSP, n.d. but 12 June 1951.
33 Ibid., 3, 5 July 1951.
34 G to VSP, 27 June 1951.
35 *Sunday Times*, 4 Nov 1951.
36 CUP to G, 27 Oct 1951.
37 G to VSP, n.d. but 30 Oct 1951.
38 *New Statesman*, 10 Nov 1951.
39 Internal memo, 31 Oct 1951, CUP
   archives.
40 *Listener*, 1 Nov 1951.
41 G to VSP, 6 Nov 1951.
42 Int Julian Pitt-Rivers.
43 Trevor-Roper (Lord Dacre) to
   author, 28 April 1989.

Chapter Twenty-Three

1 G to R, 19 July, 4 Dec 1951.
2 All quotations this section from G to
   F, 27 Dec 1951; to VSP, 6, 17 Jan, 6
   Feb 1952; to R, n.d. but Dec 1951,
   16 Jan 1952.
3 *Everything to Lose*, op. cit.
4 Anthony Hobson in conversation
   with author.
5 G to R, 25 March 1952.
6 Ibid., 20 May 1952.
7 Ibid., 30 May 1952.

8 G to VSP, 17 Dec 1952.
9 G to Chatto, 21 Nov 1952.
10 Raymond (Chatto) to G, 3 Dec 1952.
11 G to Blair, n.d. but Dec 1952.
12 Raymond to G, 3 Dec 1952.
13 G to VSP, 12 Nov 1952.
14 G to Blair, n.d. but July 1949.
15 G to B, 29 Dec 1952.
16 G to R, 29 Dec 1952.
17 G to Blair, n.d. but 29 Dec 1952.

PART FOUR

Chapter Twenty-Four

1 Gamel to Alyse, n.d. but 1953.
2 Int María López.
3 G to Blair, 4 April 1953.
4 G to R, 16 Feb 1953.
5 G to VSP, 16 April 1953.
6 G to Blair, 25 April 1953.
7 G to VSP, 30 Nov 1954.
8 Ibid., 25 May 1953.
9 G to R, 7 May 1953.
10 G to VSP, 30 May 1953.
11 G to R, 6 Aug 1953.
12 Ibid., 15 Oct 1953.
13 Ibid., 18 Sept 1953.
14 Gamel to B, n.d. but Sept/Oct 1953.
15 G to VSP, 20 Nov 1953.
16 G to Blair, 6 Dec 1953.
17 G to R, 10 March 1954.
18 Ibid., 20 March 1954.
19 R to G, 4 Feb 1954.
20 G to R, 12 Feb 1954.
21 Ibid., 3 Jan 1954.
22 G to R, 5 April 1954.

23 G to VSP, 26-30 May 1955.
24 G in conversation with author; author's journals, 24 July 1986.
25 G to R, 21 Feb 1954.
26 *Everything to Lose*, op. cit.
27 G to R, 15 Aug 1954.
28 Ibid., 6 June 1954.
29 Ibid., 1 Nov 1954.
30 G to HA, 29 Oct 1954.
31 See e.g. G to R throughout 1955, and 18 Dec 1960.
32 G to R, 27 Feb 1955.
33 Ibid., 2, 15 May 1955.
34 G to VSP, 26, 31 May 1955.
35 G to R, 20 April 1957.
36 G to M, 30 Dec 1955, and see G to Blair, n.d. but May 1956.
37 G to Xavier Corre, Dec 1955.
38 G to M, n.d. but 23 April 1959.
39 G to VSP, 30 May 1979.
40 R to G, Dec 1955.

Chapter Twenty-Five

1 *Tears Before Bedtime* by Barbara Skelton, London 1987.
2 G to Michael Holroyd, 2 Dec 1974.
3 *Everything to Lose*, op. cit.
4 *The Spectator*, 31 Jan 1987, obit. by F.
5 G to R, 28 May 1955.
6 F's unpub. journal, 29 Aug 1968.
7 *New York Review of Books*, November 1978, VSP.
8 G to Blair, 8 Jan 1956.
9 G to M, n.d. but 1955/6.
10 G to R, 21 Jan 1956.
11 HH to G, 24 Jan
12 G to HH, 30 Nov 1956.
13 G to R, 2 Nov 1956.
14 G to VSP, n.d. but 1983/4.
15 CUP to G, 12 May 1953.
16 Gamel to Alyse, n.d. but March 1955.

17 G to R, 11 Oct 1956.
18 G to VSP, 8 Nov 1956.
19 G to R, 22 Dec 1956.
20 Ibid.
21 G to M, n.d. but Jan 1957.
22 G to Blair, n.d. but Feb/March 1957.
23 *Sunday Times*, 31 March 1957.
24 B to G, 21 Feb 1972, MF.
25 *PR*.
26 *Everything to Lose*, op. cit.
27 G to R, '3' in fact 23 Feb, 22 March 1930.
28 G to VSP, 26, 31 May 1955; to HH, 17 June 1975; int John Whitworth.
29 *The Bookman*, April 1957.
30 *New York Review of Books*, 26 Jan 1967.
31 Quoted letter HH to G, 6 June 1957.
32 G to R, 27 March 1957.

Chapter Twenty-Six

1 *Everything to Lose*, op. cit.
2 JC to author, Feb 1989.
3 G to R, 20 April 1957.
4 *PR* unpub. MS.
5 G to R, 20 April 1957; Int F.
6 G to VSP, 7 April 1957.
7 G's JC journal, Tex, MF.
8 G to R, n.d. but 8–10 May 1957.
9 Ints F, Janetta; author's recollection.
10 G to R, 6 May 1957.
11 Ibid., 13 June 1957.
12 Ibid., 30 June 1957.
13 Ibid., 30 July, 19 Aug 1957.

14 G to R, 28 June 1957.
15 Ibid., 30 July 1957.
16 G to M, n.d. but 1956.
17 G to R, 22 July 1957.
18 Ibid., 24 Aug, 6 Sept 1957.
19 Ibid., n.d. but May (?) 1957.
20 Int JC.
21 G to R, 11 Oct 1957.
22 G to Catharine Carrington, n.d. but late Nov 1957.
23 *Everything to Lose*, op. cit.
24 G to R, 21, 26 March 1958.

Chapter Twenty-Seven

1 G to R, 26 May 1958.
2 Author's journals, 28 July 1960.
3 G to M, 5 Jan 1962.
4 G to R, 29 May 1958.
5 G to JC, 6 June 1958.
6 Gamel to Alyse, 20 July 1960.
7 G to R, 10 June 1958.
8 Ibid., 15 Oct 1958.
9 Ibid., 23 June 1958.
10 Ibid., 12 July 1958.
11 Ibid., 8 July 1958.
12 G to Gamel, 27 Aug 1958, MF.
13 G to R, 26, 28 Aug 1958.
14 *PR* unpub. MS.
15 G to R, n.d. but Christmas 1958.
16 Gamel to G, n.d. but June 1959, MF.
17 Gamel to G, 7 June 1959, MF.
18 G to R, 30 April 1957.
19 Jeffrey Meyers to author, 23 April 1987; see 'A World Historical Moment' by Jeffrey Meyers, in *Arizona Quarterly* No. 42, Winter 1986.
20 G to R, 11 May 1959.
21 G to F, 17 March 1959.
22 G to R, 1 Dec 1959.
23 Ibid., 23 Dec 1959.
24 G to author, 21 Dec 1961.
25 G to R, 26 May 1960.
26 G to M, 9 March 1960.
27 G to R, 27 Oct, 22 Nov; to VSP, 18 Dec 1960.
28 G to F, 17 Oct 1966.
29 G to author, 1 June 1964.
30 G to F, n.d. but 2/3 Dec 1960.

31 Ibid., 8 March 1961.
32 Ibid., 14 Jan; to M, 14 Jan 1961.
33 G to VSP, 18 Dec 1960.
34 G to F, 10 Feb 1961.
35 Ibid., 30 March 1961.
36 Ibid., 14 April 1961.
37 Int Lynda.
38 G to F, n.d. but May (?) 1961.
39 *Observer*, 16 July 1961
40 G to Michael Holroyd, 16 Dec 1967.
41 *Sunday Times*, 16 July 1961.
42 G to M, n.d. but autumn 1960.
43 Ints María and Carmen López.
44 G to F, 11 April 1962.
45 Ibid., 7 Oct 1961.
46 Gamel to G, 30 Aug 1961, MF.
47 G to F, 16 Nov 1961.
48 F's unpub. journal, 9 Jan 1962.
49 G to F, 23 Feb 1962.
50 Ibid., n.d. but March 1962.
51 Ibid., 21 May 1962.
52 Ibid. 27 July, 1962
53 G to Blair, 7 April 1962.
54 CUP to G, 16 Aug 1972.
55 G to R, n.d. but about 1925.
56 See intro. by M.R.B. Shaw to Stendhal's *Le Rouge et Le Noir (Scarlet and Black)*, Penguin Classics 1953.
57 Int Dr Redpath.
58 C to Mark Gertler, Sept 1916, Tex.
59 G to F, 26 July 1962.
60 HH to G, 27 Sept 1962.
61 G to F, 26 July 1962.
62 Ibid., 22 Oct 1962.
63 Ibid., 21 Aug 1962.

Chapter Twenty-Eight

1 Gamel to G, n.d. but Aug 1963, MF.
2 G to F, 22 Oct 1962.
3 G to VSP, 19 Jan 1963.
4 G to F, 21 Oct 1963.
5 Ibid., 18 April 1963.
6 Ibid., 24 May 1963.
7 Gamel to Alyse, 12 March probably 1963.
8 G to F, 15 Jan 1964.
9 Ibid., 22 March 1964.
10 Ibid., 7 June 1964.
11 Ibid., 21 July 1964.
12 G to B, 20 April 1968, 12 July 1971; to M, 23 Sept 1970.
13 G to F, 22 oct 1962.
14 G to Gamel, 21 June, 17 July 1964, MF.
15 G to F, 27 Sept 1964.
16 Ibid., 13 March 1965.
17 *PR* unpub. MS.
18 G to F, 1 June 1964.
19 G to VSP, 4 Oct 1964.
20 G to F, 9 Jan 1965.
21 See Bernie in *Lighthouse*.
22 G to F, 17 March 1965.
23 Ibid., 11 May 1965.
24 G to F, 24 Feb 1965.
25 Ibid., 10 Dec 1965.
26 Ibid., 11 March 1965.
27 Ibid., 9 April 1965.
28 Ibid., 22 April 1965.
29 HH to G, 17 Aug 1965; and see MSS, Tex.
30 G to VSP, 10 July 1966.
31 G to B, 3 June 1966; also *PR* unpub. MS.
32 Wage book, MF.
33 G to F, 28 Aug and n.d. but Sept 1966.
34 Ibid., n.d. but early Sept 1966.
35 G to M, 3 Sept 1966.
36 Susan Bell to author, n.d. but Nov 1988.
37 JC to author, Feb 1989.
38 G to F, 14 Dec 1966.
39 G to Blair, 19 Feb 1967.
40 Mark Culme-Seymour's journal, Jan 1967.
41 *PR* unpub. chap., Tex, MF, and with author.
42 G to F, 22 Jan 1967.
43 Ibid, 26 Feb 1967.
44 Ints Xavier Corre, Lady Cary; G to F, 10 Aug 1967.

Chapter Twenty-Nine

1 G to F, 10 Aug 1967.
2 Gregory, op. cit., and *PR* unpub. chap.
3 Phyllis Playter to Gamel, 7 Sept 1967.
4 Int Lady Cary.
5 G to F, 17 Sept 1967.
6 F's unpub. journal, 5 Sept 1967.
7 G to F, 10 Oct 1967.
8 Ibid., 26 Oct 1967.
9 Int Janetta.
10 G to F, 2 Nov 1967.
11 Ibid., 12 Nov 1967.
12 *PR* unpub. chap.
13 Ibid.
14 Int Southbys.
15 G to VSP, 27 Nov 1967.
16 VSP to G, 29 Nov 1967.
17 G to F, 22 Nov 1967 (dated 1927).
18 Ibid., 25 Dec 1967.
19 Ibid., 6 Jan 1967.
20 Ibid., 11 Jan 1967.
21 Ibid., 13 Jan 1967.
22 Ibid., 6 Jan 1938.
23 Ibid.,13–17 Jan (incl.) 1967.
24 Int Honor Tracy.

PART FIVE

Chapter Thirty

1 *Lookout*, Feb 1987.
2 G to M, 1 Feb 1968, 5 Jan 1969.
3 G to Jean Rhys, 14 April (in fact May) 1967.

4 G to B, 27 July 1967.
5 G to F, 29 July 1967.
6 G to Jean Rhys, 20 May 1968.
7 G to F, 8 Feb 1968.
8 G to Michael Holroyd, 20 Nov 1967.
9 Ibid., 16 March 1968.
10 Conversation with author.
11 G to F, 6 Nov 1967.

12 F's unpub. journal, 9 March 1968.
13 G to F, 26 Jan 1968.
14 Ibid., 24 Sept 1967.
15 *PR* unpub. MS.
16 G to Holroyd, 1 March 1968.
17 G to F, 19 Feb 1968.
18 G to VSP, n.d. but March 1968.
19 G to M, 26 March 1968.

Chapter Thirty-One

1 F's unpub. journal, 7 March 1968.
2 G to F, 15 July 1968.
3 MSS, MF.
4 G to F, 11 March 1968.
5 G to B, 1 May 1968.
6 G to F, 20 April 1968.
7 Ibid., 23 July 1968.
8 G to JC, 12 March 1968.
9 G to F, 10 Jan 1972.
10 David Machin to Dickinson, 24 Aug 1973, Cape archives.
11 F's unpub. journal, 7, 8, 9 March 1968.
12 G to F, 15 July 1967.
13 Ibid., 9 Feb 1969.
14 G to VSP, 30 March 1979.
15 G to F, 23 April 1971.
16 G to F, 15 Aug 1968.
17 Ibid., 6 Oct 1968.

18 G to M, 6 Oct 1968.
19 G to F, 2 Jan 1969.
20 Ibid., 14 Feb 1969.
21 Ibid., 13 April 1969.
22 Ints Xavier Corre and G's grandchildren.
23 G to M, 8 Aug 1970.
24 Ibid. n.d. but Aug/Sep 1970.
25 G to F, 26 May 1969.
26 G to author, 10 May 1969.
27 G to F, 15 July 1969.
28 G to VSP, 8 Aug 1969.
29 G to M, n.d. but autumn 1969.
30 G to F, 18 Dec 1969.
31 G to M, 14 July 1970.
32 G to F, 7 April 1970; accounts, MF.
33 G to F, 20 June 1969.
34 Ints Stéphane and Marina Corre.

Chapter Thirty-Two

1 G to F, 2 May 1970.
2 Author's journals, 2, 3 April 1972.
3 G to F, 3 May 1970.
4 F's unpub. journal, 13 July 1970.
5 G to F, 28 Oct 1970.
6 G to M, 7 Nov 1970.
7 G to Michael Holroyd, 26 Nov 1970.
8 G to F, 10 Jan 1971.
9 G to M, 4 March 1971.
10 G to F, 26 March 1971.
11 Ibid., 23 April 1971.
12 Ibid., 12 July 1971.
13 Ibid., 29 July 1971.
14 Ibid., 20 June 1971.
15 Ibid., 12 Oct 1972.
16 Ibid., 30 Jan 1972.
17 Ibid., 20 April 1968.
18 Report, CUP archives.

19 G to F, 12 Feb 1972.
20 Ibid., n.d. but April 1972.
21 Ibid., 21 April 1972.
22 Ibid., 12 June 1972.
23 G to JC, 23 Jan 1973.
24 G to F, 12 Feb 1972.
25 Ibid., 8 Oct 1971.
26 Ibid., 10 Oct 1971.
27 Ibid., 21 Dec 1972.
28 B to G, 21 Nov 1969, MF.
29 G to F, 15 Nov 1972.
30 F's unpub. journal, 10, 15 Feb 1973.
31 G to David Machin, 31 May 1974, Cape archives.
32 *PR* unpub. MS (cf pub. version).
33 G to F, n.d. but May 1967 or 1968.
34 F's unpub. journal, 6 March 1973, quoting Janetta.

Chapter Thirty-Three

1 G to F, 8 Nov 1973.
2 G to Janetta, 25 June 1973.
3 Ibid., 20 June 1973.
4 G to F, 20 July 1973.
5 G to Janetta, 16 July 1973.
6 G to VSP, 1 Aug 1973.
7 G to F, 21 Aug 1973.
8 Ibid., 5, 10 Sept 1973.
9 *Sp Lit.*
10 *St John.*
11 G to VSP, 8 Nov 1971.
12 G to Johnny Wolfers, n.d. but March 1974.
13 F to David Machin, 28 Feb 1974, Cape archives.
14 G to F, 16 Nov 1973.
15 G to Charlotte Wolfers, 4 June 1973;

author to Machin, 23 Feb, Machin to author, 24 Feb 1989.
16 Machin to Johnny Wolfers, 1 July 1974.
17 F's unpub. journal, 20 March, 3, 6, 23 April 1974.
18 Cyril Connolly to Machin, 1 April 1974, Cape archives.
19 MSS, MF.
20 Machin to G, 22 July 1974, Cape archives.
21 G to Machin, 22 July 1974, Cape archives.
22 Lynda to B, 1 July 1974.
23 G to solicitors, 17 Oct 1974, MF.
24 G to B, 13 March 1977.

Chapter Thirty-Four

1 G to VSP, 17 June 1975.
2 G to Johnny Wolfers, 1 Feb 1975.
3 G to B, 12 Oct 1974.
4 G to Blair, 5 Oct 1975.
5 G to Johnny Wolfers, 25 Sept 1975.
6 Int Lynda.
7 G to VSP, 28 March 1976.
8 G to Blair, 15 Nov 1975.
9 G to VSP, 28 March 1976.
10 Ibid, 20 March 1977.
11 M. H. Black's report, CUP archives.
12 G to VSP, 9 Aug 1977.
13 G to B, 16 Sept 1977.
14 G to R, n.d. but 12 or 20 Jan 1956.
15 G to VSP, 23 March 1978.
16 G to Johnny Wolfers, 23 Sept 1977.
17 G to VSP, 19 Jan 1978.
18 G to B, 16 Jan 1978.
19 Ibid., 7 Feb 1978.
20 G to Kenneth Hopkins, n.d. but late 1977.

21 G to VSP, 23 March 1978.
22 G to B, 16 Jan 1978.
23 MF.
24 G to B, 18 Sept 1978.
25 G to VSP, 18 Aug 1978.
26 Lynda to Johnny Wolfers, 24 June 1978.
27 G to VSP, 24 Oct 1978.
28 Ibid., 12 Nov 1978.
29 *Sunday Times*, 17 Dec 1989.
30 *Observer*, 14 Jan 1979.
31 B to G, Nov 1978, MF.
32 G to F, 6 Nov 1967.
33 Ibid., 1 May 1968.
34 G to B, 17 Nov 1978.
35 G to M, n.d. but 27 Jan 1978 or 1979.
36 G to VSP, 27(?) July 1981.

Chapter Thirty-Five

1 *New York Review of Books*, 27 Sept 1979.
2 G to B, n.d. but about June 1979.
3 G to M, n.d. but early 1979.
4 Ibid., 31 March 1979.
5 G to VSP, 5 Aug 1979.
6 G to Kenneth Hopkins, n.d. but Sept 1979.
7 Ibid., 26 Nov 1979.

8 G to VSP, 6 Sept 1979.
9 G to Hopkins, n.d. but Oct 1979.
10 G to M, 26 Dec 1979 (and see 26 Oct 1978).
11 G to B, 10 Feb 1980.
12 G to Blair, 5 March 1980.
13 Ints Stéphane and Marina Corre.
14 G to Blair, 20 Jan 1980.
15 G to F, 1 April 1980.

16 G to VSP, 10 Oct 1980.
17 Ibid., 28 Aug 1980.
18 G to F, 22 Nov 1980.
19 G to Rhoda Brenan, 27 Oct 1980, family papers.
20 G to F, 20 Feb 1981.
21 Ibid., May 1981.
22 G to VSP, n.d. but winter 1981.
23 Ibid., n.d. but July/Sept 1981.
24 Ibid., '19 Nov', in fact about 6 Jan 1982.
25 Ibid., 2 March 1982.
26 G to F, 26 Sept 1982.
27 G to Hopkins, n.d. but Nov 1982.
28 G to VSP, 23 Dec 1982.
29 Int VSP.
30 G to Hopkins, 8 March 1984.
31 G to VSP, n.d. but 1983.
32 G to Hopkins, n.d. but 1983.
33 G to VSP, n.d. but Dec 1983.
34 See Xan Fielding to VSP, 12 April; Fielding to Dorothy Pritchett, 28 April 1984; and replies (author's files); ints Janetta, F.

Chapter Thirty-Six

Any important facts or any quotations whose source is not given come from author's journals.

1 David Mitchell's *Lookout* archive.
2 See e.g. *Observer* during June 1984.
3 *Independent*, 21 Jan 1987.

Chapter Thirty-Seven

1 *Daily Telegraph*, 7 July 1984.
2 *Sp Lab*.

Epilogue

1 *Byron – A Self-Portrait: Letters and Diaries 1798–1824*, 2 Vols, ed. Peter Quennell, John Murray, London 1950.

Select Bibliography

The object of this bibliography is to give information regarding the major sources of material relevant to Gerald and (less thoroughly) Gamel Brenan. These fall into three groups:

1. Their own published works. In these I include a short list, itself selected, of articles and reviews which I consider important.
2. Letters from or to them and unpublished MSS, notes, diaries, journals etc.
3. Published books in which they feature with some prominence or which have some striking importance to understanding them.

I have not thought it necessary to give a full list of all the books I read and used, though of course many of these can be found in the text or reference notes.

1. Gerald Brenan
Published works

(As George Beaton) *Jack Robinson: A Picaresque Novel*, Chatto and Windus, London 1933
(As George Beaton) *Doctor Partridge's Almanack for 1935 . . .* , Chatto and Windus, London 1934
The Spanish Labyrinth: An Account of the Social and Political Background of the Spanish Civil War, Cambridge University Press 1943; second edition 1943; first paperback edition 1950; reprinted ten times 1962–85; reprinted 1986, 1987, 1988; Canto edition 1990
   Foreign editions: all CUP editions came out more or less simultaneously in America; Israel – Am Oved Publishing Society, Tel-Aviv (contract 1944); Mexico – pirated edition 1946 (also circulated secretly in Spain); Holland – N.V. Uitgeversmaatschappy G.A., Amsterdam 1947; Spain – Ruedo Ibérico, Paris 1962 (numerous reprints, a pocket edition 1977), and Plaza y Janés, Barcelona 1985; France – Ruedo Ibérico, Paris, 1963, and Editions Champs Libres, Paris 1984; Yugoslavia – Nobit Publishing House, Belgrade 1970; Italy – Garzanti, Milan 1970; Denmark – 1987
The Face of Spain, Turnstile Press, London 1950; three impressions 1950; Turnstile Press remaining copies issued by Hamish Hamilton, London 1957; paperback Penguin and Hamish Hamilton, London 1965; new Penguin edition, London 1987
   Foreign editions: Spain/Argentina – Editorial Losada, Buenos Aires 1952

The Literature of the Spanish People: From Roman Times to the Present Day, Cambridge University Press 1951; second edition 1953, reprinted 1962, 1965, 1970; CUP paperback 1976; Penguin paperback 1963
  Foreign editions: America – CUP editions appeared more or less simultaneously in America, and Meridian Books, New York 1957; Spain/Argentina – Editorial Losada, Buenos Aires 1958; France – Paris 1963; Italy – Garzanti, Milan 1970; Yugoslavia – Belgrade 1970
South From Granada, Hamish Hamilton, London 1957; reprinted 1957; new edition Hamish Hamilton and Penguin 1963; new Hamish Hamilton edition 1974; CUP paperback edition 1981, reprinted three times 1980–1988; Folio Society edition 1988
  Foreign editions: America – Farrar Straus, New York 1957, and Grove Press, New York 1958, and Octagon Books, New York 1976; Spain – Siglo XXI Editores, Madrid 1974
A Holiday by the Sea, Hamish Hamilton, London 1961
  Foreign editions: America – Farrar Straus, New York 1962; France – Calman Levy Paris 1963
A Life of One's Own: Childhood and Youth, Hamish Hamilton, London 1962; new edition by Jonathan Cape, London 1975; CUP paperback edition 1979
  Foreign editions: America – Farrar Straus, New York 1962; Spain – Ediciones Destino SA, Barcelona 1989
The Lighthouse Always Says Yes, Hamish Hamilton, London 1966
Personal Record: 1920–1972, Jonathan Cape, London 1974; CUP paperback edition 1979
  Foreign editions: America – Knopf, New York 1975; Spain – Alianza Editorial, Madrid 1976
St John of the Cross: His Life and Poetry, with a translation of the poetry by Lynda Nicholson, Cambridge University Press 1973; reprinted 1975, paperback edition 1975
  Foreign editions: the CUP edition appeared in America; Spain – Editorial Laia, Madrid 1974; Denmark – 1987
The Magnetic Moment: Poems, privately printed Warren House Press, North Walsham, Norfolk 1977, in edition of 115 copies, 75 numbered copies for sale
Thoughts in a Dry Season: A Miscellany, Cambridge University Press, 1978; reprinted twice 1979
  Foreign editions: the CUP edition appeared in America; Spain – Plaza y Janés, Barcelona 1986
Best of Friends: The Brenan-Partridge Letters (selected and edited by Xan Fielding), Chatto & Windus, London 1986

Selected articles and reviews

Anonymous review of *St Jean de la Croix et le Problème de L'Expérience Mystique* by Jean Baruzi, *Nation*, 31 January 1925
Review of *Studies of the Spanish Mystics* Vol. I by Allison Peers, *Nation*, 30 April 1927
Article, 'Spanish Scene', *Current Affairs* No. 7, July 1946
'St John of the Cross, His Life and Poetry: 1. Life', *Horizon* No. 88, May 1947
'St John of the Cross, His Life and Poetry: 2. Poetry', *Horizon* No. 89, June 1947
'Cervantes', *Horizon* No. 103, July 1948
'City of Sybarites', *Encounter*, Oct 1957
'When Islam Ruled Iberia', *American Horizon*, pp. 72–93, Vol. V, Sept 1962
Prologue, *Babel in Spain* by John Haycraft, Hamish Hamilton, London 1958
'In the Labyrinth', review of *Spain 1808–1939* by Raymond Carr, *New York Review of Books*, Nov 1966

'Hispanophilia', review of *A Handbook for Spain 1845* by Richard Ford, *New York Review of Books*, Jan 1967

'Caudillo Country', review of *Politics and the Military in Modern Spain* by Stanley G. Payne, *New York Review of Books*, Sept 1967

'A Hidden Life', review of *Carrington: Letters and Extracts from her Diaries* ed. David Garnett, *New York Review of Books*, July 1971

'True Grit', review of *In Hiding: the Life of Manuel Cortes* by Ronald Fraser, New York Review of Books, August 1972

Prologue, *The Spanish Cockpit* by Franz Borkenau, University of Michigan Press, 1974

Prologue, *Las Cosas de España* by Richard Ford, Ediciones Turner, 1974

'An Honest Man', review of *The Forging of a Rebel* by Arturo Barea, *New York Review of Books*, March 1975

'La Guerra Civil en Málaga', *Historia y Vida* No. II, Año X, 19 June 1977

'Out of the Labyrinth', review of *Spain: Dictatorship to Democracy* by Raymond Carr and Juan Pablo Fusi, *New York Review of Books*, Sept 1979

1. Gamel Woolsey
Published works

Middle Earth: Thirty-Six Poems, Simon and Schuster, New York 1931
Death's Other Kingdom, Longman's, London 1939; new edition Virago, London 1988
One Way of Love, intro. Shena Mackay, Virago, London 1987

Translations

Spanish Fairy Stories, London 1944
The Spendthrifts (*La de Bringas* by Benito Pérez Galdós), Weidenfeld and Nicolson, London 1951

Privately printed editions

Twenty-Eight Sonnets, Warren House Press, North Walsham, Norfolk 1977
The Last Leaf Falls, Warren House Press 1978
Middle Earth, Warren House Press 1979
The Weight of Human Hours, Warren House Press 1980
The Search for Demeter, Warren House Press 1980
The Collected Poems, intro. Glen Cavaliero, Warren House Press 1980

Periodicals

'The Search for Demeter', *Botteghe Oscure*, Sept 1956

2. Unpublished Sources

The largest source of Brenan material is held by the Harry Ransom Research Center at the University of Texas at Austin. This contains all the correspondence between Gerald and Hope-Johnstone, Carrington and V. S. Pritchett; Gerald's journals, most of his surviving MSS and typescripts and a good deal of poetry. There is also a mass of miscellaneous material: a large number of letters from and to Gerald from people he knew at all stages of his life from 1914 to 1978, notes on love affairs, blurbs, and numerous letters of Carrington's to people in her circle. The second major source, only slightly smaller, is the archive held at Mecina-Fondales by Lynda and Lars Pranger. This contains many duplicate typescripts of things held at Texas, as well as other MSS and typescripts of stories, essays and poetry (a great deal) not held there. There is all the material for the *copla* book. There are all the surviving letters between him and Gamel, and in addition a large number of letters from friends and acquaintences throughout his life – Garnett, Waley, Russell, John etc. There are pocket diaries from 1917 onwards and abstracts from these up until the time he became unable to write. There are numerous account books and financial calculations, dreams, descriptions of major events like the deaths of his parents, details of Wills, fragments of *Segismundo*, and a considerable body of physical memorabilia like medals, sketches, and flowers and locks of hair he picked and cut just after Carrington died. Frances Partridge holds the correspondence between her and Gerald and between Gerald and Ralph, as well as the MSS of her complete diaries. This material will eventually go to King's College, Cambridge. The Brenan family papers, in the possession of his nieces Lady Cary and Lydia Piper, contain all the surviving letters of Gerald to Blair, the journal of Helen Brenan, and various miscellaneous documents and notes. Gamel's letters to Llewelyn Powys, Alyse Gregory, John Whitworth and Phyllis Playter are at present in private collections. Francis Wyndham has the letters to Jean Rhys. McMaster University, Ontario holds some of the Russell correspondence. The originals of the Brenan/Woolf correspondence are in the University of Sussex Library, MSS section. Letters to publishers and other institutions are on their files or in their archives; letters from publishers after 1971, unless otherwise stated, are on the files of Margaret Hanbury, the literary agent who took over John Wolfers' agency. For the rest, all personal letters, unless otherwise indicated, are in the possession of the recipients or their heirs.

3. Other published sources

It should be clear from the text or the reference notes which published books the interested reader would find most worthwhile referring to, but for convenience the most important are listed again here, along with others not noted elsewhere. In addition, it is interesting to read some of the key volumes in Gerald's early development in the editions he would have been most likely to have read. I have also listed these:

Baroja, Julio Caro, *Los Baroja (Memoria, Familiares)*, Madrid 1978
Berrichon, Paterne, *La Vie de J. A. Rimbaud*, Paris 1897
Borkenau, Franz, *The Spanish Cockpit*, London 1937
Borrow, George, *The Bible in Spain*, 2 Vols, London 1896
Gerald Brenan Al Sur del Laberinto by Juan Antonio Díaz López *et al*, Litoral Malaga (no date)
Homenaje a Gerald Brenan by A. González Troyano *et al* (subsidiary part of *La Imagen de Andalucía en los viajeros Románticos*), Ronda 1984, Malaga 1987
Carrington: Letters and Extracts from her Diaries, ed. David Garnett, London 1970
A Life of Dora Carrington by Gretchen Gerzina, London 1978
Castro, Eduardo, Diaz-Lopez, J. A., *Guia General de la Alpujarra*, Granada, 1992
Cyril Connolly: A Journal and a Memoir by David Pryce-Jones, London 1963
Davies, W. H., *The Autobiography of a Super-Tramp*, London 1908

Díaz López, Juan Antonio, *Gerald Brenan – Hispanista Angloandaluz*, Granada 1987

Dowden, Edward, *Life of Shelley*, London 1909

Letters of Roger Fry, 2 Vols, ed. with intro. Denys Sutton, London 1972

Garnett, David, *The Flowers of the Forest*, London 1955, and *The Familiar Faces*, London 1962, Vols II & III of *The Echoing Grove*

Gibson, Ian, *Un Irlande's en España*, Barcelona, 1981

Gregory, Alyse, *The Cry of a Gull: Journals 1923–48*, ed. Michael Adam, Out of the Ark Press 1973

Hopkins, Kenneth, *Bertrand Russell and Gamel Woolsey, Passages in the Life of Reginald Hunter*, Warren House Press 1985

Jefferies, Richard, *The Hills and the Vale*, London 1909; *Hodge and his Masters*, London 1880; *Field and Hedgerow*, London 1889

Augustus John by Michael Holroyd, London 1975

Monegal, E. Rodríguez, *El arte de narrar: Diálogos, Colección Prisma*, Monte Avila, Caracas 1968

Partridge, Frances, *A Pacifist's War*, London 1978; *Memories*, London 1981; *Julia*, London 1983; *Everything to Lose: Diaries 1960–63*, London 1985; *Hanging On: Diaries 1960–63*, London 1990

Pitt-Rivers, Julian, *The People of the Sierra*, London 1954

Powys, Llewelyn, *So Wild a Thing: Letters to Gamel Woolsey*, ed. Malcolm Elwin, Out of the Ark Press 1973

The Brothers Powys by Richard Percival Graves, London 1983

Pritchett, V. S., *Midnight Oil*, London 1971

Rámos, Antonio Espejo, *Ciega en Granada: Murío buscando a su hija la hija de Brenan*, Granada 1990

Reclus, Elisèe, *Universal Geography*, 17 vols. Hachette, 1895

Lytton Strachey by Michael Holroyd, Penguin 1971

Svevo, Italo, *Confessions of Zeno*, trans. Beryl de Zoëte, London 1930

Thoreau, Henry, *Walden*, Boston 1893

Tracy, Honor, *Spanish Leaves*, London 1964

Index

Note: Abbreviations used in this index are the same as those used in the reference notes, listed on page 623, with the addition of Chu for Churriana, Gerald's village in Andalusia. Illustrations are indicated by *il*.